Interactive Teaming

Enhancing Programs for Students with Special Needs

FOURTH EDITION

VIVIAN IVONNE CORREA
University of Florida

HAZEL A. JONES
University of Florida

CAROL CHASE THOMAS
University of North Carolina—Wilmington

CATHERINE VOELKER MORSINK
Slippery Rock University of Pennsylvania,
Dean Emerita

PEARSON

Merrill
Prentice Hall

Upper Saddle River, New Jersey
Columbus, Ohio

Library of Congress Cataloging-in-Publication Data

Interactive teaming : enhancing programs for students with special needs / Vivian Ivonne
Correa . . . [et al.]. —4th ed.
    p. cm.
  Rev. ed. of: Interactive teaming / Carol Chase Thomas, Vivian Ivonne Correa, Catherine
Voelker Morsink. c2001.
  Includes bibliographical references and index.
  ISBN 0-13-112592-3
  1. Children with disabilities — Education — United States. 2. Team learning approach in
education — United States. 3. Communication in education — United States. 4. Group
guidance in education — United States. I. Correa, Vivian Ivonne. II. Thomas, Carol Chase.
Interactive teaming.

LC4031.T46 2005
371.9–dc22

2004019253

Vice President and Executive Publisher: Jeffery W. Johnston
Acquisitions Editor: Allyson P. Sharp
Editorial Assistant: Kathleen S. Burk
Production Editor: Sheryl Glicker Langner
Production Coordinator: Carlisle Publishers Services
Design Coordinator: Diane C. Lorenzo
Photo Coordinator: Cynthia Cassidy
Cover Designer: Ali Mohrman
Cover image: Corbis
Production Manager: Laura Messerly
Director of Marketing: Ann Castel Davis
Marketing Manager: Autumn Purdy
Marketing Coordinator: Tyra Poole

This book was set in Palatino by Carlisle Communications, Ltd. It was printed and bound by Phoenix Color Book
Group. The cover was printed by Phoenix Color Corp.

Photo Credits: Patrick White/Merrill, pp. 2, 40; Anthony Magnacca/Merrill, pp. 92, 170, 280; Tim Cairns/Merrill,
p. 132; Tom Watson/Merrill, p. 202; Scott Cunningham/Merrill, pp. 244, 308, 364; Karen Mancinelli/Pearson Learning,
p. 334; David Mager/Pearson Learning, p. 398.

Pearson Prentice Hall™ is a trademark of Pearson Education, Inc.
Pearson® is a registered trademark of Pearson plc
Prentice Hall® is a registered trademark of Pearson Education, Inc.
Merrill® is a registered trademark of Pearson Education, Inc.

Pearson Education Ltd.
Pearson Education Singapore Pte. Ltd.
Pearson Education Canada, Ltd.
Pearson Education—Japan

Pearson Education Australia Pty. Limited
Pearson Education North Asia Ltd.
Pearson Educación de Mexico, S.A. de C.V.
Pearson Education Malaysia Pte. Ltd.

10 9 8 7 6 5 4 3 2 1
ISBN: 0-13-112592-3

Dedication

To my loving husband, John C. Ziegert, for his patience, encouragement, and support through the challenges of writing this fourth edition. The true accomplishment to celebrate is our love and devotion. To Hazel Jones, my colleague and friend, for agreeing to co-author the fourth edition with me. Her contributions to the new edition have been significant. I would not have been able to do this without her. To Joyce Tardaguila-Harth, one of the finest doctoral students, for her dedication, hard work, and support through the process. I could count on her without fail! Muchas gracias, amiga! Lastly, to my parents, Lilly and Arnaldo Correa, and Lilly Correa, Diana Bell, Arnie Correa, Sandy Correa, Nicholas Correa, Ellie Ziegert, and Abby Ziegert for their continued love and support throughout the years.

VIVIAN IVONNE CORREA

To my family, especially the children, Austin, Madison, and Noah Graham, Joe and Samantha Dillon, and Lauren and D. J. Hranicky, who remind me every day of the joys of life. To Vivian Correa, for providing me this opportunity to stretch and patiently supporting me through it. And a special thank you to my friends Mary Louise Hemmeter, Johnell Bentz, and Michaelene Ostrosky for their support and encouragement.

HAZEL JONES

Preface

Interactive teaming in special programs is a concept of service delivery for school-age students who are currently placed in special education programs or are at risk for referral to such programs. The model proposed in this book is based on several assumptions:

- An increasing number of students are failing in the traditional public school program, in both general and special education.
- The needs of individual students are too complex to be handled by a single professional working in isolation, and the needs of all groups of students are too diverse to be addressed by the knowledge base of a single profession.
- Increased diversity in cultural differences, both between professionals and families and among professionals from different cultures, further exacerbates the difficulty both have in providing effective instructional programs and of developing effective communication systems.
- The time of trained professionals and the scarce resources of public education systems are too valuable to be wasted on uncoordinated or duplicated efforts that produce marginal results for students with special needs.

The opening paragraph and previously listed items were the beginning ideas featured in the preface to the first edition of *Interactive Teaming,* published in 1991. As the fourth edition goes to press 14 years later, the same assumptions are still present and the need for effective teaming models is even greater. The number of students served in special education programs continues to grow, and the cultural diversity of the population continues to increase. Yet, the time professionals have for collaboration and the resources of school systems seem to diminish instead of increase.

During this same time span, much attention has been given to organizational models or school restructuring/reform efforts that call for skills in collaboration and teaming. Transformational leadership, school-based and site-based management, macro-system reform efforts, inclusion and transition models, and early childhood intervention programs all require collaboration and team decision making to be successful.

The interactive teaming model described in this text is based on transdisciplinary teaming and collaborative consultation models. The model focuses on two concepts:

1. *Consultation.* The sharing of knowledge by one professional with another.
2. *Collaboration.* Mutual efforts between professionals and parents to meet the special needs of children and young people.

The model includes key elements of school leadership efforts, adult learning theories, and recognition of the importance of sensitivity to cultural differences.

This text is divided into three parts, each with several supporting chapters. Part I provides a foundation and overview of the contextual framework within which current and future programs for serving students who have special needs and are at risk will need to be provided. The emergence of a new population of school-age students and the need for a new, coordinated model of implementing special services are highlighted. Part I provides an outline of this model along with comparisons with existing models. The historical development of the new model includes a brief discussion of the models that preceded it: the medical model, the triadic model of consultation, the refinement of the triadic model to collaborative consultation, and the further extension to variations of the school-based and teacher assistance teams. Each represents a step closer to the interactive teaming model proposed in this text; the strengths and documented factors in the effectiveness of previous models have been incorporated into the new proposal.

Part II outlines the facilitating factors that make the teaming model work and addresses the barriers to effective team functioning. The facilitating factors include understanding the roles and perspectives of team members, enhancing communication skills, developing leadership and service coordination skills, empowering team members through professional development, and supporting family involvement. Each factor is presented through a review of the relevant literature with descriptions and examples of applications.

Part III features implementation of interactive teaming in four contexts: programs for (1) students from culturally and linguistically diverse backgrounds, (2) infants and preschoolers with special needs, (3) students with mild disabilities, and (4) students with severe disabilities. The necessary knowledge and skills of team members are described in their roles as direct service providers and as consultants/collaborators who provide indirect services.

Although the intervention strategies, team members, and their specific interactive processes differ by settings, all teams operate within the framework of problem identification, intervention, and evaluation of effectiveness. The concluding chapter features an extended case study showing how the model is applied, and provides guidelines for implications of interactive teaming for the future.

The guidelines by which the interactive team operates are modifications of those used in school-based management teams. The culture of the school—its values and rules—provides the contextual framework for establishing its goals. Teachers, parents, and other team members—rather than administrators and specialists—are empowered to analyze problems, make decisions, and evaluate programs designed to attain common goals. These goals are related to the provision of effective educational service programs for the students on whom the team focuses its efforts.

This book was developed by an interactive team, with each member serving as consultant and collaborator to the three other members. Although Carol Chase Thomas and Catherine Morsink did not participate in this edition, their contributions continue in the spirit of each chapter.

ACKNOWLEDGMENTS

Revising a textbook invariably turns out to be much more of a challenge than anticipated, especially when the authors are located in different states and have many other roles and responsibilities. We are fortunate in that we shared a common commitment to the goal of advancing the interactive teaming model, and that we had excellent supporters in this endeavor. We appreciate the constructive suggestions provided by the reviewers of the revision plan: Randel D. Brown, Texas A&M University; Wendy W. Murawski, California State University, Northridge; and Miriam H. Porter, George Mason University. Our students in graduate courses provided invaluable insights on how the text could be improved. We also wish to thank Gladys Torres for her assistance in research, Arnie Correa for his assistance with the pharmaceutical content in Chapter 11, and Kristin Young for her summary and application of content in a medical setting. Special thanks go to Joyce Tardaguila-Harth for providing us the support we needed in conducting new research, managing the copyright permission systems, and being a great friend! We couldn't have done it without you! Allyson Sharp and Kathy Burk at Merrill were always helpful, patient, and encouraging persons with whom to work.

VIVIAN IVONNE CORREA
HAZEL A. JONES
CAROL CHASE THOMAS
CATHERINE VOELKER MORSINK

EDUCATOR LEARNING CENTER: AN INVALUABLE ONLINE RESOURCE

Merrill Education and the Association for Supervision and Curriculum Development (ASCD) invite you to take advantage of a new online resource, one that provides access to the top research and proven strategies associated with ASCD and Merrill— the Educator Learning Center. At **www.EducatorLearningCenter.com** you will find resources that will enhance your students' understanding of course topics and of current educational issues, in addition to being invaluable for further research.

How the Educator Learning Center Will Help Your Students Become Better Teachers

With the combined resources of Merrill Education and ASCD, you and your students will find a wealth of tools and materials to better prepare them for the classroom.

Research

- More than 600 articles from the ASCD journal *Educational Leadership* discuss everyday issues faced by practicing teachers.
- A direct link on the site to Research Navigator™ gives students access to many of the leading education journals, as well as extensive content detailing the research process.
- Excerpts from Merrill Education texts give your students insights on important topics of instructional methods, diverse populations, assessment, classroom management, technology, and refining classroom practice.

Classroom Practice

- Hundreds of lesson plans and teaching strategies are categorized by content area and age range.
- Case studies and classroom video footage provide virtual field experience for student reflection.
- Computer simulations and other electronic tools keep your students abreast of today's classrooms and current technologies.

Look into the Value of Educator Learning Center Yourself

A four-month subscription to Educator Learning Center is $25 but is **FREE** when ordered in conjunction with this text. To obtain free passcodes for your students, simply contact your local Merrill/Prentice Hall sales representative, who will give you a special ISBN to give your bookstore when ordering your textbooks. To preview the value of this website to you and your students, please go to **www.EducatorLearningCenter.com** and click on "Demo."

Discover the Companion Website Accompanying This Book

THE PRENTICE HALL COMPANION WEBSITE:
A VIRTUAL LEARNING ENVIRONMENT

Technology is a constantly growing and changing aspect of our field that is creating a need for content and resources. To address this emerging need, Prentice Hall has developed an online learning environment for students and professors alike—Companion Websites—to support our textbooks.

In creating a Companion Website, our goal is to build on and enhance what the textbook already offers. For this reason, the content for each user-friendly website is organized by topic and provides the professor and student with a variety of meaningful resources. Common features of a Companion Website include:

For the Professor—

Every Companion Website integrates **Syllabus Manager**™, an online syllabus creation and management utility.

- **Syllabus Manager**™ provides you, the instructor, with an easy, step-by-step process to create and revise syllabi, with direct links into Companion Website and other online content without having to learn HTML.
- Students may logon to your syllabus during any study session. All they need to know is the web address for the Companion Website and the password you've assigned to your syllabus.
- After you have created a syllabus using **Syllabus Manager**™, students may enter the syllabus for their course section from any point in the Companion Website.
- Clicking on a date, the student is shown the list of activities for the assignment. The activities for each assignment are linked directly to actual content, saving time for students.
- Adding assignments consists of clicking on the desired due date, then filling in the details of the assignment—name of the assignment, instructions, and whether or not it is a one-time or repeating assignment.

- In addition, links to other activities can be created easily. If the activity is online, a URL can be entered in the space provided, and it will be linked automatically in the final syllabus.
- Your completed syllabus is hosted on our servers, allowing convenient updates from any computer on the Internet. Changes you make to your syllabus are immediately available to your students at their next logon.

For the Student—

- **Overview** and **General Information**—General information about the topic and how it will be covered in the website.
- **Web Links**—A variety of websites related to topic areas.
- **Content Methods and Strategies**—Resources that help to put theories into practice in the special education classroom.
- **Reflective Questions** and **Case-Based Activities**—Put concepts into action, participate in activities, examine strategies, and more.
- **National and State Laws**—An online guide to how federal and state laws affect your special education classroom.
- **Behavior Management**—An online guide to help you manage behaviors in the special education classroom.
- **Message Board**—Virtual bulletin board to post and respond to questions and comments from a national audience.

To take advantage of these and other resources, please visit the *Interactive Teaming: Enhancing Programs for Students with Special Needs,* Fourth Edition, Companion Website at

www.prenhall.com/correa

Brief Contents

Contents

Note: Every effort has been made to provide accurate and current Internet information in this book. However, the Internet and information posted on it are constantly changing, so it is inevitable that some of the Internet addresses listed in this textbook will change.

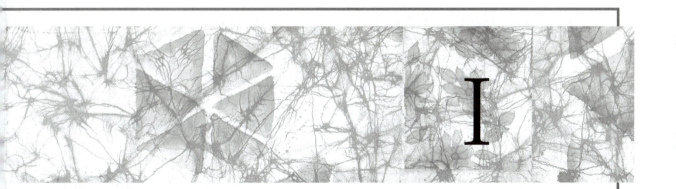

Context and Foundations

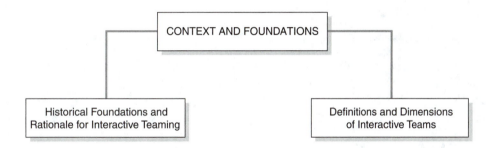

OVERVIEW

The first part of this text provides a summary of the historical and legal foundations that have contributed to the development of consultation, collaboration, and teaming models, as well as perspectives on current and future service delivery systems for students who have special needs. Chapter 1 describes the population for whom people on an interactive team will need to be concerned. The chapter also includes a review of past and current service delivery approaches and some of the problems inherent in implementing those approaches. The chapter concludes with a summary of the research on effective schools, a description of models that emphasize collegial problem solving among professionals, and an application showing the factors that set the tone for effective interactive teaming.

In Chapter 2, consultation, collaboration, and teaming are defined; selected models are described, along with barriers to their implementation and positive features; and the dimensions of the interactive team are identified and explained. In addition, the interactive teaming model is presented.

Historical Foundations and Rationale for Interactive Teaming

Topics in this chapter include:

- ◆ Definition of interactive teaming.
- ◆ Why interactive teaming is needed now.
- ◆ Legal basis for special education services.
- ◆ Historical and legal foundations for collaboration and teaming.
- ◆ Common elements contributing to interactive teaming.
- ◆ An application that sets the tone for success of an interactive team.

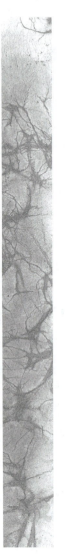

Janice, a classroom teacher in a middle school, became a teacher because she wanted to make a difference in the world—to excite students about social issues and creative writing—to help young people learn, discover, and grow. She is the kind of person who should be a teacher. She is bright, knowledgeable, enthusiastic, empathic, and optimistic about the future.

Yet, 2 years ago, Janice was on the verge of dropping out of the profession. She had been given more students than she thought she could handle, and when she tried to refer those with learning and behavior problems to the school's special programs, she was told these students would be placed on the "waiting list." The principal explained that the special programs were overloaded because there were too many students with special needs in her suburban school: students whose parents had divorced, students addicted to drugs and stealing to support their habits, and students—barely more than children themselves—who were pregnant.

Janice felt discouraged and isolated. She and the other teachers in her building went into their classrooms and closed their doors, trying to cope single-handedly with their students' bored expressions, lack of ambition, and belligerence. Worst of all, Janice thought nobody else cared. Parents didn't come to PTA meetings; they didn't seem to care. The other teachers gathered in the faculty lounge only to gossip and collapse between classes; they didn't seem to care. But that was 2 years ago.

Today we see a new Janice. As a member of an interactive team, she is consulting and collaborating with other professionals and with parents to design and carry out plans that make her programs for students with special needs more effective. Sometimes the team is just two people—Janice and the special education teacher, for example. Sometimes, if a student has severe or multiple disabilities, a larger group is gathered to work as a team. Sometimes Janice is the consultant, the expert who knows more than the others about the specific subject area with which a student is having difficulty. At other times, Janice is a collaborator, working with others to carry out the decisions made on the student's behalf by those who make up the team. She now considers her job more challenging and more rewarding because she thinks the team makes better decisions than each person could make alone. She also feels that she is part of a dynamic learning community.

Janice, the teacher described in the vignette, has developed a new enthusiasm for teaching as a result of being part of a professional group—an interactive team—that shares responsibility for students with special needs. In this chapter, *interactive teaming* is defined, and a rationale is presented for why interactive teaming is needed in today's schools and in the schools of the future. The times when interactive teaming is most appropriately used—when decisions need to be made about the program for students with special needs—are described. The limitations of current approaches are discussed, and the components of promising new practices from which the new interactive teaming model is derived are described.

DEFINITION OF INTERACTIVE TEAMING

The word *teaming* is used here to mean professional and parental sharing of information and expertise, in which two or more persons work together to meet a common goal. In this case, the goal is to provide the best possible educational program for a given student with special needs. The *interactive team* is one in which there is mutual or reciprocal effort among and between team members to meet this goal.

Note that interactive teams do not operate in isolation to serve students with special needs. Instead, they operate within the context of other macro-level teams. These include strategic planning teams, which guide decisions in partnerships across the boundaries of schools, businesses, and community agencies. Macro-level teams also encompass district-wide teams focused on extended school service or quality improvement, and the university/school district teams that monitor professional development schools with student teachers. The interactive teams described in this text are micro-level versions of these larger teams, illustrative of school and business trends in collaboration.

Each team member may engage in *consultation,* any activity in which he or she is the expert who possesses more knowledge or skill than other team members about the issue being discussed. When the team member consults, she does this by sharing knowledge or skills, or by explaining or carrying out actions that demonstrate this knowledge. As a member of the interactive team, however, she shares knowledge in a reciprocal rather than an authoritarian manner. In an interactive team, the consultant is not always the same person; the person who consults possesses the necessary knowledge and expertise on a given topic at a particular time. The team member, such as Janice, may be a consultant on the academic subject of teaching creative writing; at the same time, Janice may also be the recipient of consultation from the school psychologist, who has more knowledge about behavior management. Similarly, the parent might be the consultant on the home behavior and history of the student, while being the recipient of the speech-language therapist's recommendations on language development.

The team member also engages in *collaboration,* a mutual effort to plan, implement, and evaluate the educational program for a given student. Collaboration is cooperative rather than competitive. It consists of joint or coordinated actions by team members to reach their common goal. For example, if Janice is a member of a team working with a gifted student who has cerebral palsy and requires an adapted computer for creative writing, she would collaborate with the special education teacher, the occupational therapist, the adaptive technology specialist, and the student's parents to plan, implement, and evaluate the student's special program. Although most team discussions are held face to face, it is also possible for a team to communicate through e-mail or interactive video technology as a way to save time and reduce distance.

The application of a committee designing a camel (Figure 1.1) illustrates the spirit and process that an interactive team displays as members shift between consultative and collaborative roles. Just as these specialists with diverse backgrounds and

The Camel: A Horse Designed by a Committee

No doubt you have heard that a camel is a horse designed by a committee. Well, it's true. I know, because I was there. I'll tell you what took place. It was mid-morning on the 30th; the entire committee assembled and seated themselves.

"Acme Caravans Incorporated is opening a new market. They have the exclusive franchise for a trans-Sahara trade route and have invited our company to submit a proposal on an order for twenty horses to carry the trade goods, and forty more to carry the caravan's supplies and the pack horses' food and water. This committee is to develop our company's response."

"So they want sixty horses. Model 701B I suppose?"

"Maybe we should think about that. Remember, we used the 701B horse for that high-mountain job last winter, and it floundered when the snow was loose packed and powdery. The sand may be just as bad."

"You have a point there. The 701's small feet sank too deep. Maybe we need a model with a larger foot size."

"Yeah, make it about twice the diameter—maybe padded somewhat on the bottom so it will really spread out."

"Hey, that sounds good. Just like snow shoes—I mean, sand shoes."

"Anything else?"

"Well, yes. Two front toes would give a better grip than just one."

"OK. Let's make it two front toes on each foot. Got that?"

"I've read in the North Africa tour book about the extreme temperatures—135 degrees in the daytime and 40 degrees at night."

"What are you saying? Do you think we should increase the R rating of the exterior covering of the 701B?"

"Insulation pays off in the long run. And besides, don't you still get a tax break on weatherproofing?"

"How about an extra six inches of thick hair and fur on the back and head, and a couple of inches all around?"

"Not a bad idea. As for colors, mauve and taupe are really in this year."

"I don't know. I'm more inclined to the earth tones."

"Why don't we give some choices? Perhaps from a light sand beige to dark chocolate?"

"Is something bothering you?"

"Well, yes. The insulation is OK, but it may cause a real buildup of internal heat at maximum RPMs."

"I don't know. I thought we might gear it down to about 2 $\frac{1}{2}$ MPH as the cruising speed. At that rate we can keep the heat-loss/heat-gain pretty well balanced."

"We can still have a passing gear that can get its speed up to Mach point-oh-five when necessary."

Figure 1.1

Decision making by the interactive process.

Source: From "The Camel: A Horse Designed by a Committee," by Noojin Walker (March, 1988). *The Clearing House, 61*(7), pp. 329–330, 1988. Reprinted with permission of the Helen Dwight Reid Educational Foundation. Published by Heldref Publications, 4000 Albemarle St., N.W., Washington, DC 20016. Copyright © 1988.

"Sounds good. This fur will also protect the skin from the abrasion of the hard-blowing sand."

"Speaking of sand, do you remember the attempted helicopter rescue in Iran? That sand and dust really clogged up the choppers' air intake."

"Played heck with their vision, too."

"What we need is a way to keep the sand out of the system. Can we change the nostril of the 701B from an open hole to perhaps a slit that can open and close on demand?"

"Sure."

"And while we're at it, we can modify the eyelids and brow so that they are somewhat over-hanging."

"And increase the number and length of the eyelashes?"

"Definitely! You can't overestimate the value of keeping the vision protected."

"Neat! And these sand and wind protection features can also double as glare reducers. Man! That sun is bright!"

"Excuse me, but I have recalculated the heat-loss/heat-gain and the two-point-five MPH."

"So?"

"Well, we're going to have to lengthen the stride and cut down on the leg action if we are going to keep the heat from building up."

"OK, so what do you figure?"

"It needs a stride that will require legs that are eight meters tall."

"Wow! That would be one tall 701B! How would you ever get it loaded—with a crane?"

"Can't you adjust its thermostat? What's its operating temperature range anyhow?"

"Well, it's the usual plus-or-minus one degree tolerance."

"Let me figure—yeah, that's much better. If the internal temperature could vary 10 or 12 degrees with no burnout, it would let us shorten the stride some, and shorten the legs without increasing the leg action and RPMs."

"It would still be taller than the 701B, but we can program it so that it kneels down to be loaded or mounted."

"If it's going to kneel, do you think we should extend the insulation to the knees—maybe some fur pads there? That sand gets fiercely hot."

"Good idea."

"I don't know whether to mention this or not, but if we increase the operating temperature range to 12 degrees, this modified 701B won't need to sweat as much."

"What does this mean?"

"Sweating and its evaporation is a cooling mechanism. It's not going to need it."

"Well, what does that mean?"

"It's not going to lose as much water—not nearly as much."

"You know, if it doesn't lose much water by sweating, and if we were able to add the right kind of reserve water tank, it might be able to go a week or more without having to be refilled."

"These legs are long enough to let us hang a belly tank underneath just like the jet fighters."

Continued

"No good! No good! It would not leave enough height underneath to give good clearance over those rough bushes."

"And besides, when it knelt down to be loaded, it would be awfully uncomfortable—mashing all of that water."

"OK, then, let's put it on top."

"Hey, what's that going to look like—a big hump sitting up there?"

"Sure, but that's not all bad. It will be a good base to secure the loads to."

"Right. And the rider will have a much better field of vision."

"Should it have one hump or two?"

"Good question. Why don't we configure two models and let the buyer decide which one he wants?"

"Hmmm. A one-hump and a two-hump model. Marketing will like that."

"I don't know. How are we going to keep all of that water from sloshing around inside that hump as it gets empty? Do you plan to use tubes and baffles?"

"My suggestion is to make it somewhat collapsible. Fill the hump with fibrous connective tissues, sort of like your tubes and baffles. And pack the whole thing with fat. You know fat allows for a lot of water absorption. I figure it can carry 10 percent of the total body weight right there in that hump—or humps."

"I get it. As the fat and water are used the hump gets smaller. Sort of a built-in gauge to tell you how much is still left."

"Super plan! We could also modify the metabolic processes so that the water metabolized from the fat stays right inside the system."

"Sure. Any water that can be saved or recycled is just that much less that it will have to drink en route."

"Will that be a problem—I mean modifying the metabolism?"

"Not really. Our subcommittee has planned a truly rugged digestive system. So far, we can fuel this baby with any kind of desert vegetation—cactus, brush, and even those bitter thorny-bushes. And if necessary, it can digest dried fish, bones, leather, even a blanket."

"That's enough; we get your drift. So actually it can carry enough food and water in that hump to last for a week or more, and also eat almost anything along the way."

"Where are we with the payload?"

"Our calculations show that it will be able to carry about a half-ton, for a week or more, at a steady pace of $2\frac{1}{2}$ miles an hour."

"Is there any danger of overloading it?"

"Not much. We can build in a warning mechanism—groaning, followed by bellowing, and that sort of thing."

"Right on! And as the critical weight is approached, it can be programmed to spit at the loader to get his attention."

"Excellent proposals! With all of these warnings I figure we can load it to within one straw of breaking its back."

"Gee! This modification is really an improvement over the original 701B, at least in this terrain."

"But what is the cost?"

Figure 1.1
Continued.

> "Well, our cost subcommittee projects that if we use all natural materials and no plastics, the unit cost will be just a little more than the cost of the standard 701B horse. But because it doesn't require the exotic fuel, the extra water, and the support units to carry it all, we calculate that the total job will be about a 50 percent savings to Acme Caravan."
>
> "Great!"
>
> "OK, what about a name?"
>
> "What do you think of CARAVAN MODEL ECONOMY LANDCRUISER?"
>
> "Not bad. It's a little long, but. . . ."
>
> "Group?"
>
> "Sure. That's good. We can market it as CAMEL. It's easier to say. The ad group will love it."
>
> "Good work. I guess that takes care of this business. Unless there is anything else, the committee is adjourned."

disparate vocabularies have functioned together to design a product for the desert that is superior to that which any one of them could have designed alone, so too can members of the interactive team respond to the demanding environment facing educators in the coming years. As we shall see, tomorrow's education and health-related professionals will not be facing stable, happy, eager students from the "grassy meadows" of affluent suburban schools. They will be largely placed in desolate rural areas or in urban blackboard deserts, where the majority of their students live in poverty, come from single-parent homes, speak another language or represent another culture, and have largely abandoned their hope that education is the key to a better future.

WHY INTERACTIVE TEAMING IS NEEDED NOW

This model of consistent consultation, collaboration, and team-based decision making is especially vital now because of the increase in the number of school-age students who are disabled or at risk for school failure. Because there are so many students who experience difficulties, and because their difficulties are so complex, education, social services, and medical professionals working in isolation are unable to provide these students with appropriate educational programs. Although we stress the importance of interactive teaming with at-risk and special needs populations, in the current climate of accountability, the ability to work collaboratively with other professionals and parents is critical to promoting the success of all students.

Target Population

The target population served through interactive teaming practices is the group of school-age students who are currently identified as having special needs and who have been placed in special education programs or included in the regular classroom with related special services. It also includes students who are at risk for being placed in such programs and students experiencing school failure without placement.

Students in Special Education Programs.   Those students classified as having a disability are defined by Public Law 94-142, the Education of All Handicapped Children Act, passed by the U.S. Congress in 1975, amended in 1990 (P.L. 101-476) and again in 1997 (P.L. 105-17) as the Individuals with Disabilities Education Act (IDEA). These are students with specific learning disabilities, mental retardation, hearing impairments, visual impairments, speech or language impairments, emotional disturbance, orthopedic impairments, autism, traumatic brain injury, and other health impairments. Because of these conditions, the law permits these students to receive special education and related services. A total of 6,606,253 children and youth at risk or with disabilities, ages 0–21, were served in special programs during the 2000–2001 school year. The number of children and youth with disabilities has grown at a steady rate, with a 28.4% increase since the 1991–1992 school year (U.S. Department of Education, 2002). Four disability categories account for the majority of students ages 6–21, including specific learning disabilities, speech or language impairments, mental retardation, and emotional disturbance.

There has been an increase in the number of children who meet the criteria for services specified in IDEA, and who are being identified and served according to the requirements of the law. The number of these students who are currently being educated, at least part time, in the general education classroom has also increased. McLeskey, Henry, and Hodges (1998) indicated that there was an increase of 12.8% in the number of students identified as having a disability in the 6 years between 1988–1989 and 1994–1995. Basing their findings on data from the annual reports to Congress, McLeskey et al. determined that the total number of students with disabilities served in resource rooms and separate school settings declined (by 16% and 20%, respectively), and those served in separate classes increased slightly (by 5%), while those served in general education classrooms increased significantly (by 60%) within the 6-year period. Data from the 24th Annual Report to Congress (U.S. Department of Education, 2002) show that nearly 50% of all children with disabilities were being served in the regular classroom at least 80% of the time in the 1999–2000 school year.

The most rapidly growing and most controversial category of exceptionality is that of learning disabilities. The number of students identified in the learning disabilities category grew by 70% between 1988–1989 and 1994–1995 (McLeskey et al. 1998). Spear-Swerling and Sternberg (1998) refer to the increase in the number of students with learning disabilities as an "epidemic." There has been long-standing concern about how learning disabilities are defined and much discussion about alternative methods of identification (Fuchs, Mock, Morgan, & Young, 2003). The journal *Learning Disabilities Research and Practice* recently devoted a 2003 issue to this topic. Spear-Swerling and Sternberg recommend that special educators serve as learning specialists who work with low-achieving students in addition to those who are identified as having a disability. Although issues of identification and placement remain controversial, one thing is clear: With millions of children entering school each year, ever-increasing numbers of them will need special assistance.

Students at Risk for School Failure.   While only those students who have been formally identified according to the procedures specified in IDEA are classified as having a disability, they are not the only students in need of the services of the interactive team. The term *at risk* was originally defined by Reynolds (1989) as follows: "The term at risk . . . refers to children who fall into various categories for which the base rate (or group frequency) for experiencing educational difficulties is relatively high" (p. 129). Reynolds further specified that children who either have a disability or are at risk are classified together as students with special needs.

> Special needs children show one or more of the following characteristics which have significance for educational planning: (a) they are not responding positively to the instruction offered to them in basic academic skills (usually reading); (b) their social behavior in school is unacceptable; (c) they are falling badly behind classmates in learning in academic subjects; (d) they have significant physical limitations or major health problems; (e) English is not their primary language (often associated with important cultural differences as well); or (f) they are extremely limited in experiences which provide background for formal education. (p. 130)

The 1997 reauthorization of IDEA included an option for states to provide special services for students who are at risk but have not yet been identified. This is essentially an option to extend the "developmental disabilities" classification to students through the age of 9. Twenty states have adopted this category (U.S. Department of Education, 2002). Some special educators see this as an attempt to prevent students from needing placement (Turnbull & Cilley, 1999), while others believe that service to students at risk constitutes a diversion of funds from those within the protected class specified by law.

Increase in Students at Risk

A number of demographic variables and related social problems have combined to create a large number of students who are identified as having a disability or are at risk for educational problems in the school population. One key influence on academic failure is poverty. While the U.S. Census Bureau (2002) reports overall declines in poverty, the child poverty rate still surpasses the adult age groups. Estimates for children under age 18 are at 16.9% and even higher for children under 6 (19%). Families with children are estimated to make up 40% of the homeless population, and children are the fastest growing segment of the homeless (Smith & Smith, 2001). Some are concerned that this group is among those at greatest risk for school failure (Rafferty, 1997–1998).

In 2001, an estimated 903,000 children were found to be victims of child abuse or neglect (U.S. Department of Health and Human Services, 2003b). More than half of these children were removed from their homes. As a result, current statistics indicate that the population of children in foster care has risen to about 600,000, of which 70% are school age (Lovitt, 2003).

Another group of children considered at risk for school failure are recent immigrant children and those with racial, cultural, and linguistic differences. Since 1979, the number of school-age children whose primary language is not English has increased by 6% (Snyder & Freeman, 2003a). The Urban Institute's study of immigrant populations reported that many children of immigrants live in poverty, attend schools where they are segregated linguistically, and have a high rate of high school dropouts (Fix, Zimmerman, & Passel, 2001).

One particularly troubling statistic recently reported by the U.S. Department of Health and Human Services (2003a) determined that at least 1 in 10, or as many as 6 million, youths may have emotional problems severe enough to disrupt their ability to interact effectively. This report warns that school failure is often associated with untreated mental health disorders, in addition to other problems including suicide.

Certain environmental factors also contribute to the numbers of children at risk. For example, the effect of lead poisoning, largely from ingestion of paint, can place a child at risk for failure. While lead poisoning in the United States is on the decline, a 1999–2000 report from the Centers for Disease Control (CDC; 2003) indicated that the lead exposure reduction goal for the year 2000 was not achieved and that tens of thousands of young children are exposed. An estimated 2.2% of children ages 1 to 5 years were reported to have had elevated lead blood levels during 2001. Lead poisoning is particularly harmful to children as it may cause a number of health, behavioral, and intellectual problems.

One environmental factor that often creates a situation where children are exposed to multiple risk factors is living with a parent who abuses alcohol or drugs. Data from the Substance Abuse and Mental Health Services Administration's (SAMHSA; 2003a) National Survey on Drug Use and Health (NSDUH) estimates that 22 million Americans ages 12 or older were considered drug and/or alcohol dependent. In another report, more than 6 million children were estimated to live with at least one parent who abused or was dependent on alcohol or an illicit drug (SAMHSA, 2003a). A recent study of mothers with substance abuse problems found that their children were more likely to be exposed to multiple risk factors associated with poor physical, academic, or socioemotional outcomes (Conners et al., 2003). It is the cumulative effect of these factors that poses the greatest threat to the child's development and learning. In addition, Conners and her colleagues found that the instability of their lives made it difficult for these children to develop the social and emotional skills needed to form stable and supportive relationships with adults.

Finally, while researchers have found that environmental factors outweigh the consequences of prenatal substance exposure, a child born with fetal alcohol syndrome (FAS) is another matter. FAS is one of the leading causes of mental retardation. Current estimates of the prevalence of fetal alcohol syndrome are between .5 and 2 cases per 1,000 live births (Hankin, 2002). Some children may have only some of the criteria for an FAS diagnosis, resulting in a diagnosis of fetal alcohol effect (FAE). This condition has been associated with hyperactivity and learning problems (Heward, 2003).

The implications of these conditions clearly call for increases in special programs. In addition, the needs and severity of the problems these children may encounter will require a variety of professional expertise. Effective intervention strategies will begin with these professionals working together in collaborative teams.

Demographic Changes.   Demographic changes that have taken place during the past 40 years have implications for the education system that will impact the learning of school-age children. Many of these changes were projected by Hodgkinson (1988). Other demographic changes, as they relate to the education of students with special needs, are summarized in Chapter 7. Among the most significant generic changes are the aging of the population and the increased proportion of young persons who are at risk for school failure. Changes in family structure have also caused fewer children to have the emotional advantages of two-parent families and after-school care.

Related Social Problems in Secondary Students.   In addition to the dramatic changes in demography, school-age students face a number of social problems that increase the likelihood they will have school-related difficulties. These social problems have led to an increase in the number of secondary-level students with special needs, which place them at risk for school failure. One problem that adolescents continue to face is the rate of teenage pregnancy. While the rates of teenage pregnancy have begun to decline, it is still a significant health issue for adolescents. Approximately one-half of teenage mothers are on welfare within 1 year (Monahan, 2002). In addition, babies born to teenage mothers tend to have lower birth weights than the babies of older mothers, which makes them at higher risk of neurological problems (Monahan, 2002).

Another problem that today's teens face is the high number of violent incidences in which they either participate or are victims, or to which they are exposed. In a recent report by the CDC (2002), homicides were the second leading cause of death for youth between 10 and 19 years of age in the United States and the number one cause of death for African Americans ages 15–24. Adolescents in this country are at much higher risk of death than in other industrialized countries (Children's Defense Fund, 2002; Hechinger, 1992). Results of the 2001 Youth Risk Behavior Survey conducted by the CDC (2002) found that during the 30 days preceding the survey 17.4% of high school students had carried a weapon.

The issue of high school dropouts remains a major concern in schools. The dropout rate has decreased and was at 9% nationally for the year 2000. Great variability exists across individual states ranging from a low of 4% to a high of 17% (Kids Count Online Data, 2003). However, approximately 3.2 million young adults ages 16 through 24 were not enrolled in school nor had they completed a high school program (National Center for Education Statistics [NCES], 2001). This report indicates that high school dropouts are more likely to be unemployed, earn less money, and apply for public assistance than high school graduates. In addition, high school dropouts represent a disproportionate number of prisoners and death row inmates.

In-depth interviews with 100 school-leavers over an 8-year period indicate that, although some step out and drop back in, those who leave do so because they find little support at school (Altenbaugh, Engel, & Martin, 1995). These students, unless provided with assistance, are in danger of becoming a new "underclass." The real-life students behind these data are at risk for school failure; if they become parents, they are in danger of perpetuating the same conditions that will place their own children at risk.

LEGAL BASIS FOR SPECIAL EDUCATION SERVICES

The interactive team operates in response to a 1975 federal law, the Education of All Handicapped Children Act (P.L. 94-142), amended in 1990 and again in 1997 as the Individuals with Disabilities Education Act. A detailed explanation of the 1997 amendments is provided by Turnbull and Cilley (1999), using the six principles that form a framework for the law: (1) zero reject, (2) nondiscriminatory evaluation, (3) appropriate education, (4) least restrictive educational placement, (5) procedural due process, and (6) parent and student participation. The implications most relevant for the interactive team are summarized here.

The intent of the law is to provide persons with special needs an equal opportunity to participate in and contribute to society. Funding flows from the federal level through the states to the local education agencies to assist them in implementing the law, providing special education and related services for students identified as having a disability or at risk for school failure, and in need of services. Provisions of the 1997 reauthorization also allow some of the costs of special services to be shared by other public agencies in addition to schools. Emphasis also is placed on comprehensive planning to provide a sufficient supply of appropriately trained teachers and other personnel. Restrictions are placed on suspension of services for students whose behavior results from their disability, a team decision is required for any change in placement, and an appeal process is specified. Regulations make an effort to balance the rights of the IDEA student with those of others to ensure school safety. Regulations also specify that the same persons serve on the student's evaluation/placement team and on the team that develops the individual educational plan. Nondiscriminatory evaluation procedures and parental participation/consent are strengthened, while requirements for participation in the general curriculum and in the postschool transition services and development of the preschool individualized family services plan are clarified. Bilingual education and behavioral interventions are encouraged when deemed necessary by the team, and mediation of differences is encouraged prior to requests for due process hearings.

Section 504 of the Rehabilitation Act of 1973 is a civil-rights law that prohibits discrimination on the basis of disability. Section 504 complements the special education mandates of IDEA with procedural requirements that often parallel IDEA. The Americans with Disabilities Act of 1990 also provides strong legal and civil-rights support for equality of opportunity and the value of individuality. Discrimination on the basis of disability is forbidden, and the barriers that prohibit people with special needs from participating in activities in public locations must be removed. As businesses, public service agencies, and educational institutions have begun the process of implementing these laws, consultation and teaming approaches among employees and employers have been used.

FOUNDATIONS FOR COLLABORATION AND TEAMING

In the early 1970s, professionals in special education and school psychology began to comment on the changes needed in their fields to improve services to students with special needs and the professionals who were working with or teaching those students. Deno's (1970) model of service delivery for special education students included consultation services as the first level above total regular classroom integration. Lilly (1971) stated that professionals needed to change how they viewed children with mild learning and behavioral problems, and how they behaved toward those students. He suggested that rather than labeling the *students* as exceptional, the *situation* should be considered exceptional. Instead of functioning in a direct service role with students with mild disabilities, Lilly proposed that special educators serve in a support and training role for the regular classroom teachers who would have primary responsibility for educating the children. During that same time frame, professionals called for psychologists to move away from the limited test-and-report approach to one that focused more on teacher consultation and the development of interpersonal functioning and helping relationships (Fine & Tyler, 1971).

Legal Influences for Collaboration and Teaming: 1970s, 1980s, and 1990s

A legal impetus for teachers, psychologists, and others to work together on concerns about students with special needs appeared in 1975 in Public Law 94-142, the Education for All Handicapped Children Act. Although child-study teams existed in some systems before this, the law and its accompanying regulations served as a catalyst for professionals working together. P.L. 94-142 ensured that a multidisciplinary team that includes at least one person, either a teacher or other specialist with knowledge related to the suspected disability, made evaluations. The law also specified that placement decisions be made by a team that includes members with knowledge of the child, the meaning of the evaluation data, and the placement options. The primary decision-making role is with a team of people including parents, teachers, related service providers, administrators, nurses, physicians, social workers, and counselors.

The passage of Public Law 99-457, Education of the Handicapped Act Amendments of 1986, further strengthened the idea of professional collaboration or teaming, in this case to meet the needs of young children. Part H of this law requires states to "develop and implement a statewide comprehensive, coordinated, multidisciplinary, interagency program" for early intervention services. This legislation includes children from birth through age 2 who have been diagnosed as having a mental or physical condition that is likely to result in a disability. At the discretion of a state agency, it can also include children who are considered at risk for developmental problems.

Public Law 94-142 was amended again in 1990 by Public Law 101-476, the Individuals with Disabilities Education Act (IDEA). In this legislation the exceptionalities of autism and traumatic brain injury were added, and references to "handicapped children" were changed to "children with disabilities." The law stipulated increased collaboration among special educators, classroom teachers, and related services personnel, and placed more emphasis on transition services for students age 16 or older. The latest amendments to the Individuals with Disabilities Education Act were passed in 1997, and the regulatory provisions were issued in March 1999. In general, the three themes in the 1997 IDEA amendments are (1) increased emphasis on parental participation in decision making, (2) participation of children with disabilities in the general curriculum, and (3) development of behavioral intervention/management plans. As Coben, Thomas, Sattler, and Morsink (1997) noted, each version of the law addressed issues that called for increased collaboration and involvement of families and a range of professionals in program design and implementation for students with disabilities.

Most important for operation of the interactive team is the amended law's clarification of requirements for serving students in the "least restrictive appropriate educational placement." According to Turnbull and Cilley (1999), it is presumed that the general education program is appropriate unless shown to be inappropriate. Case law requires collection of evidence on attempted modifications (supplemental aids and services) prior to the team's decision for placement in a more restrictive environment. Turnbull and Cilley summarize the rules for decision making on placement in the appropriate educational environment, now included in the law:

1. educational benefit to student
2. nonacademic benefit to student
3. possible negative effects of general class placement
4. costs involved in accommodating placement (p. 44)

Yell (1998) further specifies that, in assuring placement in the least restrictive environment, school districts are required to have access to the entire range of placements, from which they may choose the best match for the individual student's needs. This range extends from the regular classroom through special schools. Neither *inclusion* nor *mainstreaming* (the older term) are required in this effort to balance both the educational and social benefits to the child with a disability and the effect of placement on others, including classmates and the teacher.

Expanding Applications: Late 1970s, 1980s, and 1990s

Starting in the late 1970s, consultation and teaming approaches began to receive attention beyond the original proposals for support and helping relationships and the legal requirements for identification and placement. Special issues on consultation and collaboration appeared in such professional journals as *Behavioral Disorders* (1981), *Teacher Education and Special Education* (1985), *Remedial and Special Education* (1988), *Preventing School Failure* (1991), *Journal of Teacher Education* (1992), *Remedial and Special Education* (1996), and *Journal of Learning Disabilities* (1997). A new journal, the *Journal of Educational and Psychological Consultation,* focusing entirely on consultation was initiated in 1990. A number of textbooks targeted for special educators, psychologists, and other related professions were published on the topics of consultation, collaboration, and teaming in the late 1980s and early 1990s. In the late 1990s the number of texts available on collaboration and teaming increased dramatically.

Consultation and collaboration received much support as:

◆ An effective way to reduce regular educators' referrals for special education services (Adelman & Taylor, 1998; Sindelar, Griffin, Smith, & Watanabe, 1992).

◆ A skill all teachers need to respond to for changing school practices (e.g., Denemark, Morsink, & Thomas, 1980; President's Commission on Teacher Education, 1992; Pugach & Johnson, 2002).

◆ A requirement for the success of students in mainstreamed classrooms (Friend, 1984; Salend, 1994; Wood, 2002).

◆ An approach to dealing with the unique needs of secondary-level pupils (Huefner, 1988; Patriarca & Lamb, 1990; Stowitschek, Lovitt, & Rodriguez 2001; Tindal, Shinn, Walz, & Germann, 1987).

◆ An important element in infant and preschool programs (Hanline & Knowlton, 1988; Lowenthal, 1992; Summers et al., 2001).

◆ A model for transition planning (Kohler & Field, 2003; Sileo, Rude, & Luckner, 1988).

◆ A strategy to reduce teacher burnout (Cooley & Yovanoff, 1996; Fore, Martin, & Bender, 2002).

Consultation, collaboration, and teaming have been recognized and supported by professionals inside and outside special education settings, as well as in various other types of service delivery programs. Related services such as those provided by school counselors, speech-language pathologists, and physical therapists are finding an increasing amount of their role descriptions to be consulting with teachers and serving on multidisciplinary teams (ASHA, 2000; Lindsey, 1985; Sandler, 1997; Umansky & Holloway, 1984). Pediatricians have supported the concept of consultation and collaboration, and their input is critical in supporting a child's development (Committee on Children with Disabilities, 2001). Child-care and home-based programs are utilizing consultation as a way to meet professional-development needs

(Jones & Meisels, 1987; Klein & Sheehan, 1987; Palsha & Wesley, 1998) and pediatric nurses are serving as consultants to these programs to promote health and prevent illness and injury (Evers, 2002). Community-based programs for people with developmental delays have implemented consultative services (e.g., Como & Hagner, 1986; Powers, 1986). In addition, consultation has been used to address the needs of individuals with special needs who live in rural settings (Obi & Obiakor, 2000).

Other settings utilizing collaborative approaches include rehabilitation centers and mental health clinics (Kaiser & Woodman, 1985), transitional programs for adults with special needs (Hasazi, Furney, & DeStefano, 1999), and vocational and industrial education programs (Feichtner & Sarkees, 1987; Spencer-Dobson & Schultz, 1987). Community colleges are developing partnerships with members of the localities in which they serve to create vocational opportunities (Orr, 2000). Recent research has also investigated the use of interdisciplinary problem-solving teams (IPSTs) to meet instructional, behavioral, and motivational needs of high school students (Rubinson, 2002). Person-centered planning teams are being used on a voluntary basis to help families and individuals with special needs plan for the future (Callicott, 2003).

Collaboration and teaming models received extensive support in three educational arenas in the late 1990s: middle schools, inclusion settings, and school reform initiatives. Teachers and administrators in middle schools have implemented collaboration and teaming models in their efforts to reconfigure their schools from a junior high approach. As Gable, Hendrickson, and Rogan (1996) noted, "Collaboration holds special promise at middle school where the organizational structure is well suited to interdisciplinary teamwork" (p. 235). They described collaborative teams comprised of teachers from various content areas along with one or more specialists that engaged in structured problem-solving processes to examine curricular goals and needs of individual students. Implementation of teaming in middle schools has resulted in improved connection of general and special education services with the student's educational objectives and cooperative lesson planning (Ryan & Paterna, 1997); better use of faculty skills and improved strategies for dealing with diverse populations (Clark & Clark, 1997); and higher student achievement in math, reading, and language arts (Erb, 1997). As part of the Beacons of Excellence research priority from the Office of Special Education Programs, U.S. Department of Education, Caron and McLaughlin (2002) reported that collaboration and a sense of shared responsibility for all students were key elements for overall school success in the two middle schools represented in their study.

The ability of schools to serve children with special needs in inclusive general education classrooms depends largely on faculty and administration sharing the responsibility of educating all children (Hunt, Soto, Maier, & Doering, 2002). The best configuration for providing inclusive programs is the use of teams of professionals and parents (Idol, 2002). In fact, Stanovich (1996) referred to collaboration as "the key to successful instruction" in schools where inclusion is being implemented. Changes in demographics, school standards and student performance expectations, instructional practices, and service delivery models necessitated the use of collaborative and teaming approaches (O'Shea, O'Shea, & Algozzine, 1998). Hobbs and Westling (1998) observed that the "degree of success of inclusion can be related to several factors, perhaps the most important being teachers' preparation, attitudes, and opportunity for collaboration" (p. 13).

The school reform movement is the third arena where collaboration and teaming models have received much attention and endorsement by researchers. Many have suggested that schools for the 21st century will encourage teaming among teachers, and ideal schools will be characterized as collegial and collaborative (Fulton, 2003). The National Commission on Teaching and America's Future (1996) noted that teachers currently do not have enough time with their colleagues, and that one of the turning points that will indicate progress is when all teachers have access to high-quality professional development and regular time for collegial work and planning. Teaming models have been described as ways to support curriculum alignment and professional development (Danielson, 1996; Darling-Hammond, 1997) and as an essential component of teacher effectiveness (O'Shea, Williams, & Sattler, 1999). Pugach and Johnson (2002) commented:

> Many developments in the reform-minded educational scene, which has existed since the early 1980's, have converged to encourage educators to rethink the role of adult-adult relationships in schools and to realize the value of professional collaboration and the need to establish it soundly as an expectation for teachers. (p. 6)

Teacher Preparation and Professional Development

The Council for Exceptional Children supports the importance of consultation, collaboration, and teaming by inclusion of this area as one of the 10 domains in the *CEC Performance-Based Standards for All Beginning Special Education Teachers (2003)*. (See the CEC Website for all 10 standards and knowledge and skills competencies http://www.cec.sped.org/ps/.) The content for each standard includes a common set of knowledge and skill competencies that all beginning special education teachers are expected to demonstrate. Accordingly, CEC sees collaboration as a necessary means for assuring that individuals with exceptional learning needs have those needs addressed. Beginning teachers are expected to demonstrate mastery of this standard through the mastery of their chosen specialty area as well. The CEC knowledge and skill base for all entry-level special education teachers for Standard 10 on collaboration is listed below.

Special Education Standard #10: Collaboration
Common Core Knowledge of:

CC10K1.   Models and strategies of consultation and collaboration.

CC10K2.   Roles of individuals with exceptional learning needs, families, and school and community personnel in planning of an individualized program.

CC10K3.   Concerns of families of individuals with exceptional learning needs and strategies to help address these concerns.

CC10K4.   Culturally responsive factors that promote effective communication and collaboration with individuals with exceptional learning needs, families, school personnel, and community members.

Skills:

CC10S1.   Maintain confidential communication about individuals with exceptional learning needs.

CC10S2.   Collaborate with families and others in assessment of individuals with exceptional learning needs.

CC10S3.   Foster respectful and beneficial relationships between families and professionals.

CC10S4.   Assist individuals with exceptional learning needs and their families in becoming active participants in the educational team.

CC10S5.   Plan and conduct collaborative conferences with individuals with exceptional learning needs and their families.

CC10S6.   Collaborate with school personnel and community members in integrating individuals with exceptional learning needs into various settings.

CC10S7.   Use group problem-solving skills to develop, implement, and evaluate collaborative activities.

CC10S8.   Model techniques and coach others in the use of instructional methods and accommodations.

CC10S9.   Communicate with school personnel about the characteristics and needs of individuals with exceptional learning needs.

CC10S10.   Communicate effectively with families of individuals with exceptional learning needs from diverse backgrounds.

CC10S11.   Observe, evaluate, and provide feedback to paraeducators. (pp. 59–60)

The Interstate New Teacher Assessment and Support Consortium (INTASC) (2001) has also developed standards for general education teachers who will work with students with special needs. These standards were developed in response to IDEA amendments mandating an increased role for general educators in inclusive settings and place an emphasis on the collaborative relationship between general and special educators. The standards also address more traditional forms of special education collaboration and teaming such as working with related service professionals, families, and other agencies. Principle 10 states: "The teacher fosters relationships with school colleagues, families, and agencies in the larger community to support students' learning and well being" (INTASC, 2001, p. 37). Teacher certification in a number of states requires passing the PRAXIS II tests. Core principles of the specialty area test on special education also include content on collaboration in the section on professional roles (cited in Heward, 2003).

Increasing numbers of teacher-preparation programs are beginning to incorporate instruction on collaboration into their curriculum, both through modeling by university faculty (e.g., Hohenbrind, Johnston, & Westhoven, 1997; Welch, 1998) and through design of field-based experiences (Hobbs & Westling, 1998; Morsink, 1999).

Limitations of Traditional Approaches

Limited effectiveness of traditional approaches to service delivery have contributed to the increased use of collaboration and interactive teaming for serving students with special needs or who are at risk for school failure. Frequently, services are delivered primarily through the individual efforts of regular and special education teachers who staff "lower tracks" or special pull-out programs, and through social services personnel who provide a variety of related services that may be uncoordinated. "Top-down" bureaucratic fixes often are offered when looking for improved educational outcomes. These approaches are limited in their effectiveness, and none has typically incorporated interactive teaming. The inability of special education teachers to provide consistently high-quality instruction and the presence of marginal professional and parent interactions and follow-up are among the major limitations in these current approaches.

"Top-Down" Bureaucratic Solutions

One of the most common responses to poor performance on the part of students is to "raise the standards." Barth (1998) has discussed the relative merits of the most widely recognized state standards for student achievement. The Virginia standards, for example, are praised because they state clearly what students should learn in academic subjects at each grade level. At the same time, they are flawed because they are rigid in specifying grade-level mastery without regard for individual learning-time requirements. In addition, competition may exist among states to see which can set the highest standards, an action that can result in standards that are unreasonably high (Cross, 1998).

Existing state standards have much in common. Accountability ensures that the achievement of students with special needs is of concern to school districts as the 1997 IDEA reauthorization includes language that requires participation in testing by students with special needs. It also presents a dilemma for students who do not meet standards; neither retention in grade nor social promotion are particularly good options. Retention has, in fact, risen nationally to an average as high as 32%; it is a practice shown to have negative long-term effects on student achievement and contributes to students' disengagement from school (Owings & Magliaro, 1998). Social promotion has also been widely criticized. Passage of the No Child Left Behind Act of 2001 (NCLB) continues this practice by requiring states to set standards in the core subjects of reading, math, and science. NCLB requires accountability for achievement based on these standards through annual statewide assessment. This practice is controversial because the consequences of failure are high; students will not be promoted, schools will be sanctioned, teachers and administrators may be replaced, and many believe that the focus of instruction will narrow to the content and skills emphasized on the test (Linn, 2003).

Some reformers have the opinion that public schools have been unable to respond effectively to the needs of students who are increasingly diverse and have proposed alternative private or charter schools, often with vouchers for students. Vouchers and charter schools were developed to give parents a choice and new options. Charter schools have been opening nationwide since 1992 and currently serve more than 500,000 students in 2,348 charter schools nationwide (Bulkley & Fisler, 2002; NCES, 2003). Since that time many studies have been conducted on the effectiveness of charter schools relative to a number of concerns including student academic improvement, the results of which are inconclusive (see Bulkley & Fisler, 2002, for a review). In a recent study of charter schools and students with special needs, researchers found that the percentage of students with special needs enrolled in charter schools is less than that in public schools (RPP International, 2000). Reasons given for the difference include a reluctance of some parents to enroll their children as well as that of school personnel who felt they could not meet the students' needs (Fiore, Harwell, Blackorby, & Finnigan, 2000). Others cite the regulations involved in serving students with special needs as limiting the autonomy of the charter school (Rhim & McLaughlin, 2001). Although some reports suggest that charter schools look like their public school counterparts in terms of race and ethnicity, others have found that charter schools enroll disproportionately higher numbers of minority students (Frankenberg & Lee, 2003) and that these charter schools tend to have fewer resources and less academic curricula than those serving mainly white students (Fuller, Gawlik, Gonzales, Park, & Gibbings, 2003). French (1998), in his case study of state-mandated reform, issued this alert:

> In the end, while this narrow, authoritarian approach to standards and assessment may result in overall increases in student achievement and pockets of significant achievement in some districts, the achievement gap between low-income students, students of color, and more affluent white students will most likely continue to remain large and may possibly even widen. (p. 190)

While this achievement gap is what proponents of school choice, either through vouchers or charter schools, want to overcome, it remains to be seen if they will succed.

Marginal Professional and Parent Interactions

One of the major limitations of special programming is that it has not led to an increase in either professional or parent/professional interactions. Although intended to provide coordinated programs for students with special needs, many efforts have resulted in further fragmentation of special services. Johnston, Allington, and Afflerbach (1985) found that students who are taught in separate settings (general and special education classes) often receive entirely different, conflicting approaches to reading instruction. They found the majority of specialists did not know what kind of instruction the child was receiving in the general education classroom, and only 8% of the classroom teachers could identify the materials used in the special class. More recent research reports general education teachers' dissatisfaction with the IEP process (Menlove, Hudson, & Suter, 2001). These teachers reported feeling as if their concerns were not valued; they also felt disconnected from the process.

Traditional programs are also limited by a lack of meaningful parental participation in decision making. Minimal parental involvement in the team decision-making process, particularly as it relates to the IEP conference, is one of the major problems in traditional special education programs. In their study of 73 parents of children with special needs, Garriott, Wandry, and Snyder (2000) found that while 89% always attended IEP meetings, more than half attended to be informed rather than be equal participants in the process. Minimal parent participation has been found in meetings planning adolescent transitions from school to the adult world as well (Boone, 1990). A low rate of participation is characteristic of parents who represent cultural and linguistic minorities (Kalyanpur & Harry, 1999).

The 1997 regulations in IDEA strengthen the role of parents, require participation by general education personnel, and improve decision making by keeping the team membership constant across placement and program-planning functions (Turnbull & Cilley, 1999). All of these changes support the rationale for teachers and parents to work collaboratively in interactive teams. The importance of parents' contributions to the education of their children has been increasingly recognized as essential for school reform (Fullan & Watson, 1997; Toch, 1999). Similarly, it is widely recognized that successful schools, both for the majority of students (McLaughlin & Schwartz, 1998) and for students with special needs (Hobbs & Westling, 1998; Hunt et al., 2003) are those that have a common focus on student learning, with goals that are collaboratively determined.

Effective Schools Research

Some new practices, based on the concepts that underlie the model of interactive teaming, offer promise for program improvement. These practices are derived from the summary of research on effective schools, which focuses on teams that have been able to facilitate academic achievement and social adjustment in students who are at risk for school failure. These practices also appear to enhance the effectiveness and morale of the professionals who implement them.

A summary of the research on effective schools determined that schools in which there is a central mission, on which the school works as a team, are more effective than those in which there are individual teacher goals. In schools with a central mission, productivity, morale, and effectiveness increase (McLaughlin & Schwartz, 1998), and the teacher's sense of isolation is lessened (Wadsworth, 1997). Effective schools research also stresses the importance of strong school leadership, collaboration, high student expectations, and an ability to respond to individual students' needs (Guthrie, 1998; Wang, Haertel, & Walberg, 1997; Young, 1999). Adding to these, Reynolds and Teddlie (2000) include a focus on learning and monitoring student progress, school-based staff development, and parental involvement as generally accepted characteristics of effective schools.

In an extensive study of a teacher's sense of efficacy, Ashton and Webb (1986) found that feeling a lack of efficacy is often related to the teacher's belief that he or she is isolated in the futile attempt to solve complex problems. The most effective schools are those in which the staff members are able to collaborate to improve the quality of their services to students. The challenges faced by today's students and the climate created by concerns for accountability will not allow for teachers to continue the practice of teaching in isolation. Effective practice of quality teachers follows from a supportive collaborative environment (Fulton, 2003; Holm & Horn, 2003).

A recent study of five high-performing, high-poverty elementary schools in Texas conducted by the Council of Chief State School Officers and the Charles A. Dana Center at the University of Texas at Austin (2002) found similar key strategies. These five schools set high goals for all students in the belief that they would be accomplished. To achieve these goals the leadership and faculty worked collaboratively on several concerns, including designing strategies for instruction, overcoming academic barriers to learning, and brainstorming interventions for students with special needs before referral. In addition, faculty view parents as "critical partners" in their child's education.

THE COMMON ELEMENTS CONTRIBUTING TO INTERACTIVE TEAMING

The most promising proposals for improving schools' responsiveness to the increased number of students with special needs are those that include the features of teacher empowerment, shared "ownership" of problems, and the common goal of providing each student with the best possible program. These same features are incorporated into interactive teaming. Friend and Cook (2003) emphasized the importance of voluntary participation among equals to establish mutual goals through shared responsibility as essential in successful collaboration. Several factors involving collaboration account for the successes in the effective schools research, such as the emphasis on community participation and ownership, shared leadership by teachers, and the emphasis on student learning (DuFour, 2003). Examples of ways in which innovative leaders can work around the bureaucratic structures in schools to facilitate collaboration include helping teachers network their skills, encouraging a buddy system for parents, and enhancing communication among constituents (Wilson & Firestone, 1987).

Among the successful attempts to encourage collaboration and teaming in new teachers are those that provide mentors or coaches (Stansbury, 2001). The practices that facilitate teacher collaboration include opportunities to develop lesson plans and units, to talk together about new ideas, and to observe each other in classrooms (Flowers, Mertens, & Mulhall, 2000; Reese, 1995). In her study of beginning teachers, Angelle (2002) found that mentors in effective middle schools took on the role of coach, model, and professional-development specialist. All of these approaches involve some form of interactive teaming, although the implementers have not used that label.

History of Success

The most encouraging thing about the use of interactive teaming is that it has been successful even in schools with the most difficult students. These schools have a large number of students who have special needs or are at risk, particularly minority students who do not believe that school achievement is related to economic gain (Olson & Rodman, 1988). They are schools with the worst combination of poverty, low parental achievement, and racial and cultural isolation. The staff members are the newest and least prepared teachers—those trained to work with an average and ideal student population that no longer exists.

These old excuses for school failure—the poor home environments of a few students—are no longer valid when these limitations are representative of the majority of the student population (Olson & Rodman, 1988). One of the successful team responses to school failure has been implemented in New Haven, Connecticut, by a team of Yale University, public school, mental health, and community personnel (Comer, 1989; O'Neil, 1997), and extended throughout the nation to several other school districts (Schmoker & Wilson, 1993). In this program, success has been attributed to the collaborative contributions of people with diverse areas of expertise. Comer has also been able to document improvement in the educational achievement of parents as well as their children.

Maeroff (1993) describes some effective teams used to facilitate school change. First offered through leadership academies, such as those sponsored by the Rockefeller Foundation at the University of New Mexico and Michigan State University, these teams grew in strength as they developed the support of colleagues, learned new process skills, facilitated an academic excellence atmosphere, and forged new links with business and the community. According to Maeroff, some of the factors that increased the team's ability to succeed in making changes are as follows:

- Set important priorities for school.
- Model appropriate skills and interactions.
- Anticipate resistance and provide responses.
- Interact with peers in school and help the community become involved.
- Keep sense of humor and positiveness.
- Find time to work together.
- Maintain communication.

Maeroff indicates that teams may initially believe that their school's problems (lack of budget, time, clear mission, knowledge; temporary staff; unions) are so severe that the team cannot be of much help. It is important for the team to focus on the major problems of students, rather than dealing with superficial issues.

More recently, Meyers, Meyers, and Gelzheser (2001) present a comparative case study of three teams in a small, rural school district where the state legislature had required every district to implement shared decision-making teams. These researchers found that successful teams used a positive group process and active involvement of all team members. The teams were able to function more effectively when administrators used shared leadership strategies and roles, and the power of the teams was clarified. The teams who felt that their decisions were taken seriously were more successful than those who were skeptical of top-down administration. Finally, a key factor appears to be a common vision, without which team members felt frustrated and stifled.

Smith (1992) describes the common strengths of teams in which university and school partners have come together to agree on common goals for professional practice. A survey of the 38 programs that won the Association of Teacher Educators (ATE) Distinguished Program in Teacher Education awards, 1977–1989, found that award-winning programs had common factors. These factors included practical or clinical collaboration, which featured both learning how to teach and acquisition of interpersonal relationship skills for the participants. Most had a governance team with representatives from both partners, and a structure that allowed for the relationship of theory to practice. Characteristics that seemed to enable partnerships to survive over time included equality between partners, emphasis on significant school-based programs with collaboration in the settings where education occurs, and the assignment of responsibility based on participants' skills. Collaboration continues to be a key element of successful university-school partnerships (see Epanchin & Colucci, 2002; Heimbecker, Medina, Peterson, Redsteer, & Prater, 2002; Jenkins, Pateman, & Black, 2002, for model examples of partnerships).

These successful teams—both micro teams that function within a school, and macro teams that extend to include school partnerships—have a common element: They are planned and implemented by representative, interactive participants, as opposed to being mandated by legislatures or district administrators. They follow the recommendations of the Carnegie report for new governance structures, and they respond to the concerns of the chief state school officers that schools cannot help the most difficult students without providing a whole range of special services (Olson & Rodman, 1988). Teacher and related professional competence, combined with the belief that even the most difficult students can learn, are viewed as essential elements in the success of these teams.

Technology and Collaboration

The demographic and social changes in today's classrooms represent a new population of students and a new set of circumstances that cannot be addressed by old mandates. Successful reform needs to include provisions for collaborative activity at a collegial level. Technology applications provide expanded opportunities for collaboration. Higher education and K–12 faculty are able to collaborate across time and space, "visit" each other, participate in conferences with distant experts, and create shared simulations and products (Baston & Bass, 1996). Increasingly, studies and reports of successful telecommunications networks for collaboration are appearing in the literature. These systems are being developed to foster collaborative activities in a number of different ways. For example, the Lighthouse Project was designed to provide beginning teachers the opportunity to dialogue with more experienced teachers and higher-education faculty to problem solve and reduce isolation (Babinski, Jones, & DeWert, 2001). Hobbs, Day, and Russo (2002) describe the Virtual Conference Room site they established as a way for small groups of special educators to collaborate on problem situations. The Bloorview MacMillan Children's Centre in Canada describes a project in which online support is provided to support the reintegration of students with traumatic brain injury into their local schools and communities after treatment (Verburg, Borthwick, Bennett, & Rumney, 2003). The project included Internet-based courses about reintegrating students, videoconferencing-based and e-mail-based support, and an online question and answer support process. These are but a few of the examples of using technology to facilitate collaboration among education professionals. As computer and communication technology continues to advance, the potential for increased collaboration appears limitless.

Decision Points in Teaming

Figure 1.2 illustrates the differences between a traditional system of serving students with special needs and the proposed system called *interactive teaming*. It follows the five decision points modified from the work of Salvia and Ysseldyke (1988), initially identified as referral, screening, classification, instructional planning, and evaluation of pupil progress.

As decision point 1 in a traditional system, referral is costly and time-consuming; there is often a backlog of referrals, and students may have to wait a long time before services can begin. In the interactive teaming model, a prereferral team meets to discuss the educational needs of a student even before a referral is made. At this stage, the team members might be able to resolve the problem and eliminate the need for a costly referral.

Decision point 2 involves screening. In a traditional system, this means the student is tested by several isolated specialists and that the data from testing may not be well integrated. Screening is most often followed by classification—the identification of the student as having a disability. Interactive teaming proposes joint problem solving by members of the team to ensure that multiple inputs are received before making the decision about classification.

Decision point 3, services, is most often characterized in a current system by the delivery of expert advice by consultants who tell the practitioner what to do with

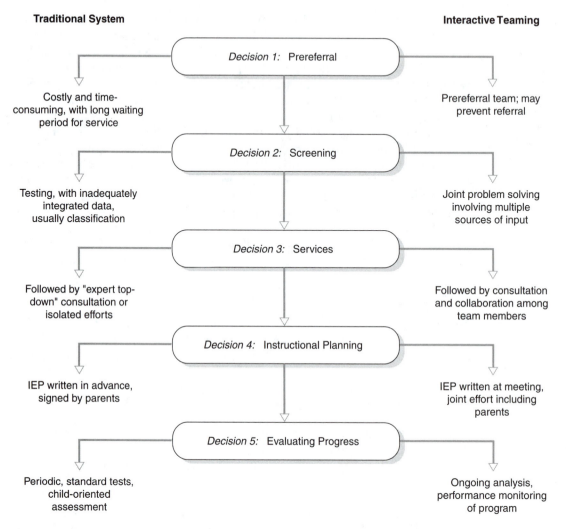

Figure 1.2
Contrasts between the traditional system and the proposed model for interactive teaming.

the student, and by the individual efforts of teachers to provide remedial instruction. In interactive teaming, "services" are characterized by coordinated consultation and collaboration among the team members.

Decision point 4 involves the development of an instructional plan. In a traditional system, the IEP is often written before the meeting and presented to parents for their signature. In interactive teaming, the IEP is written during the meeting, and represents the joint efforts of team members, including parents.

At decision point 5, evaluation, the child is traditionally given periodic tests focused on standardized measures of achievement to determine whether he or she has mastered the prescribed program content. In interactive teaming, the focus of evaluation is on the program; measurement is ongoing and the analysis is focused on ways in which the team can change the program to increase its effectiveness.

Application of Interactive Teaming

Working as an effective team member is much more challenging than working alone. The team members have differing perspectives, speak varying "languages," and demonstrate a range of behaviors that results in both effective and ineffective resolution of problems. Figure 1.3 gives an example of effective interactive teaming in action.

Dan Hayes, a school psychologist, is responsible for the assessment of students in three schools in the district. The district also expects its psychologists to serve as consultants and team members in their assigned schools. Dan has commented often on the variance in how well he believes he is able to meet that expectation in his three assigned schools.

At the meetings at Maxway Elementary, Dan feels primarily like a reporter. The assistant principal, Mrs. Payton, is in charge of all meetings to discuss students, and she prides herself on running brief and efficient meetings. The usual format is to have Dan and his colleagues present their assessment data and recommendations in round-robin fashion. However, questions and discussion are not encouraged because of the extra time involved, and Mrs. Payton says such talk among professionals usually only confuses the parents. After the professionals make their reports, Mrs. Payton provides a summary and a list of options to the parents. The parents usually are silent listeners until this point, and Dan thinks they often are intimidated by the number of professionals present and Mrs. Payton's business-like approach. He has commented to his colleagues that more often than not, the parents select the first option presented and rarely ask questions. He has tried to talk to Mrs. Payton about various ways to enhance the input of the professionals, but the response always has been "Why make things more complicated than they are? We've always done it this way, and I don't want to change now. Our meetings go quickly, so let's not do anything that might prolong them."

At Zion Primary School, Dan believes his role is more like that of a consultant, but he is uncomfortable with being introduced to the parents as the "expert" and being viewed as the one whose recommendations should carry the most weight. Because the principal at Zion does not like to ask his staff to attend meetings regularly, Dan finds that he frequently has to attend several meetings to discuss the

---

Continued

Figure 1.3
Setting the tone for effective interactive teaming.

same issues on a single child because not all the personnel are willing or able to meet at the same time. In addition to the strains this places on his schedule, Dan is aware that trying to attend several meetings is a hardship for some parents.

In contrast to these two schools, when Dan attends meetings at Anderson Middle School, he feels like more of a team member. The principal, Mr. Gutierrez, has identified one day per week as a meeting day, and he encourages his staff to be available for meetings on students or curriculum matters. Mr. Gutierrez posts the schedule for the meetings on students and lists which teachers and professionals need to attend. Although he attends the meetings, he contributes as a team member rather than as team leader. The leadership role is rotated among Dan, a special educator, a regular classroom teacher, and the counselor, based on a schedule they designed at the beginning of the year.

Input from the parents is encouraged, and all the professionals value the exchanges and ideas among the team members. Team members frequently consult and collaborate with others outside of the group meetings, and any additional information or strategies obtained in those sessions are shared at the beginning of each team meeting. Dan thinks the situation at Anderson is advantageous to all of the people involved, and that the quality of the decisions made is much higher than at his other two schools.

This vignette illustrates various processes professionals and parents can engage in to share information on students. It also describes the effects the setting and attitudes can have on what actually occurs and how well people are able to fulfill their roles. In this example, Dan was able to complete the assessment tasks expected of him in a similar way at all three schools. However, implementation of the aspects of his role that involved consulting and serving as a team member varied markedly among the three schools. This variance was due to the attitudes of the team members on what should be done by whom, who is considered the "expert," the leadership style implemented, the value placed on input from others, and a lack of willingness to change. However, at Anderson Middle, Dan was able to be a consultant, collaborator, and team member—and his colleagues also were able to serve in those roles.

The interactive teaming model proposed in this text has been developed as an attempt to take into account the myriad factors affecting the provision of educational and other types of program services for students with special learning and behavioral needs. In addition, appropriate implementation of the model should reduce the discrepancies in how services are delivered and how professionals and parents interact.

The model is built on components of various approaches and service delivery alternatives that have been presented and researched primarily in the fields of special education and school psychology. However, it is important to note at the outset that interactive teaming includes not only psychologists and special educators, but also parents and other professionals who are concerned with the welfare and education of children. These professionals include regular classroom teachers, physicians, social workers, counselors, physical and occupational therapists, adapted physical educators, assistive technology specialists, speech-language clinicians, and other related services personnel.

Figure 1.3
Continued.

SUMMARY

Educators and related professionals now experience intensified pressures to collaborate in the solution of increasing education-related problems for these reasons:

◆ The majority of our students have complex special needs.
◆ Traditional programs are ineffective in serving the increasing numbers of students with complex special needs.
◆ Proposed solutions that do not take into account the body of knowledge about the process of change will not be any more effective.

Those who have summarized the research on effective schools suggest the following:

◆ Teachers in these schools are committed to a central mission.
◆ This mission is focused on maximizing the educational opportunities for students.
◆ Teachers in effective schools work together as a team to achieve this goal.

An examination of consultation, collaboration, and teaming reveals that:

◆ These approaches have been advocated by professionals from various disciplines for at least the past 25 years.
◆ A legal basis for the approaches exists in federal laws such as P.L. 94-142 and amendments to it, as well as in state and local education agency service delivery alternatives.

The model proposed in this book—interactive teaming—is a response to the nation's increasingly complex problems in special needs programs because it incorporates the features of teacher empowerment, community responsiveness, and professional collaboration, all of which characterize effective schools for students who have special needs or are at risk.

The interactive team is a group that functions at the highest level of professionalism because it involves both consultation and collaboration. The interactive teaming model includes components that have been used previously to provide services to students with mild disabilities and in programs that provide educational, medical, and social services to students with severe disabilities. The historical foundations and specific dimensions of interactive teaming will be described in detail in the following two chapters.

ACTIVITIES

1. Observe interactive teaming in your own classroom or program, or interview a person who teaches in such a program. How do the students in this program differ from those in your classes when you attended school? In what ways are the professionals in this program collaborating (or failing to collaborate) to provide effective educational and medical services for students with complex needs?

2. Describe your attitudes about or past experiences with activities in which you were asked to interact with others (classmates, other professionals) to develop a product (e.g., group product for a course, selection of a curriculum, etc.) or an educational program. Did you feel that the effort was collaborative? In what ways did your experiences lead you to be optimistic about the benefits of interactive teaming? Pessimistic? What, in your opinion, has to happen if collaboration is to succeed?

3. Interview an administrator and a parent about their preferences for consultation, collaboration, or teaming. List reasons they prefer one over the other or a combination of the two approaches. How were their preferences affected by previous experiences?

4. Construct a table listing the benefits and disadvantages of consultation and teaming. Compare your list with those of your classmates or colleagues. What similarities or differences were noted? Were any of the differences due to professional training or role (e.g., special educator, psychologist, social worker)?

REFERENCES

Adelman, H. S., & Taylor, L. (1998). Involving teachers in collaborative efforts to better address the barriers to student learning. *Preventing School Failure, 42*(2), 55–60.

Altenbaugh, R., Engel, D., & Martin, D. (1995). *Caring for kids: A critical study of urban school leavers.* London: Falmer Press.

Angelle, P. S. (2002). Mentoring the beginning teacher: Providing assistance in differentially middle effective schools. *High School Journal, 86*(1), 15–28.

ASHA. (2000). Guidelines on the role and responsibilities of the school-based speech-language pathologist—executive summary, *ASHA Leader, 5*(8), p. S28.

Ashton, P., & Webb, R. (1986). *Making a difference: Teachers' sense of efficacy and student achievement.* New York: Longman.

Babinski, L. M., Jones, B. D., & DeWert, M. H. (2001). The roles of facilitators and peers in an online support community for first-year teachers. *Journal of Educational and Psychological Consultation, 12*(2), 151–169.

Barth, P. (1998, March). Virginia's version of excellence. *The American School Board Journal,* 41–43.

Baston, T., & Bass, R. (1996). Teaching and learning in a computer age. *Change, 28*(2), 42–47.

Boone, R. (1990). The development, implementation, and evaluation of a preconference training strategy for enhancing parental participation in and satisfaction with the individual transition conference (Doctoral dissertation, University of Florida, 1989). *Dissertation Abstracts International, 51*(3), 618A.

Bulkley, K., & Fisler, J. (2002). A decade of charter schools: From theory to practice. *CPRE Policy Briefs.* Retrieved from Consortium for Policy Research in Education Website February 2, 2004, at http://www.cpre.org

Callicott, K. J. (2003). Culturally sensitive collaboration within person-centered planning. *Focus on Autism and Other Developmental Disabilities, 18*(1), 60–69.

Caron, E. A., & McLaughlin, M. J. (2002). Indicators of Beacons of Excellence schools: What do they tell us about collaborative practices? *Journal of Educational and Psychological Consultation, 13*(4), 285–313.

Centers for Disease Control and Prevention. (2002). Youth risk behavior surveillance—United States, 2001. *Surveillance Summaries,* MMWR 2002:51 (SS–04).

Centers for Disease Control and Prevention. (2003). *Surveillance Summaries,* MMWR 2003:52 (No. SS–10).

Children's Defense Fund. (2002). Facts on youths, violence, and crime. Retrieved December, 2003, from Children's Defense Fund Website at http://www.childrensdefense.org/education/prevention/factsheets/youth.asp

Clark, S. N., & Clark, D. C. (1997). Exploring the possibilities of interdisciplinary teaming. *Childhood Education, 73*(5), 267–271.

Coben, S. S., Thomas, C. C., Sattler, R. O., & Morsink, C. V. (1997). Meeting the challenge of consultation and collaboration: Developing interactive teams. *Journal of Learning Disabilities, 30*(4), 427–432.

Comer, J. (1989). Children can: An address on school improvement. In R. Webb & F. Parkay (Eds.), *Children can: An address on school improvement by Dr. James Comer with responses from Florida's Educational Community* (pp. 4–17). Gainesville, FL: University of Florida, College of Education Research & Development Center in collaboration with the Alachua County Mental Health Association.

Committee on Children with Disabilities. (2001). Role of the pediatrician in family-centered early intervention services. *Pediatrics, 107*(5), 1155–1158.

Como, P., & Hagner, D. (1986). *Community work development: A marketing model.* Stout, WI: Stout Vocational.

Conners, N. A., Bradley, R. H., Mansell, L. W., Liu, J. Y., Roberts, T. J., Burgdorf, K., & Herrell, J. M. (2003). Children of mothers with serious substance abuse problems: An accumulation of risks. *American Journal of Drug and Alcohol Abuse, 29*(4) 743–759.

Cooley, E., & Yovanoff, P. (1996). Supporting professionals at-risk: Evaluating interventions to reduce burnout and improve retention of special educators. *Exceptional Children, 62*(4), 336–355.

Council for Exceptional Children. (2003). *What every special educator must know: Ethics, standards, and guidelines for special educators* (5th ed.). Arlington, VA: Author.

Council of Chief State School Officers and the Charles A. Dana Center at the University of Texas at Austin. (2002). *Expecting success: A study of five high performing, high poverty elementary schools.* Washington, DC: Author.

Cross, C. (1998, October 21). The standards wars: Some lessons learned. *Education Week, XVIII,* 32, 35.

Danielson, C. (1996). *Enhancing professional practice: A framework for teaching.* Alexandria, VA: Association for Supervision and Curriculum Development.

Darling-Hammond, L. (1997). *The right to learn: A blueprint for creating schools that work.* San Francisco: Jossey-Bass.

Denemark, G., Morsink, C. V., & Thomas, C. C. (1980). Accepting the challenge for change in teacher education. In M. C. Reynolds (Ed.), *A common body of practice for teachers: The challenge of Public Law 94–142 to teacher education.* Washington, DC: The American Association of Colleges of Teacher Education.

Deno, E. (1970). Special education as developmental capital. *Exceptional Children, 37,* 229–237.

DuFour, R. (2003). Building a professional learning community: For system leaders, it means allowing autonomy within defined parameters. *School Administrator, 60*(5), 13–19.

Epanchin, B. C., & Colucci, K. (2002). The professional development school without walls: A partnership between a university and two school districts. *Remedial and Special Education, 23*(6), 349–359.

Erb, T. O. (1997). Meeting the needs of young adolescents on interdisciplinary teams. Reviews of research. *Childhood Education, 73*(5), 309–311.

Evers, D. B. (2002). The pediatric nurse's role as health consultant to a child care center. *Pediatric Nursing, 28*(3), 231–238.

Feichtner, S., & Sarkees, M. (1987). Working together: The special needs team. *Vocational Education Journal, 62*, 22–24.

Fine, M. J., & Tyler, M. M. (1971). Concerns and directions in teacher consultation. *Journal of School Psychology, 9*, 436–444.

Fiore, T., Harwell, L. M., Blackorby, J., & Finnigan, K. S. (2000). *Charter schools and students with disabilities: A national study.* Washington, DC: Office of Educational Research and Improvement, U.S. Department of Education.

Fix, M., Zimmermann, W., & Passel, J. S. (2001). *The integration of immigrant families in the United States.* Washington, DC: The Urban Institute, 2001. Retrieved January 31, 2004, from the National Institute for Literacy Website at http://www.nifl.gov/

Flowers, N., Mertens, S. B., & Mulhall, P. F. (2000). How teaming influences classroom practices. *Middle School Journal, 32*(2), 52–59.

Fore III, C., Martin, C., & Bender, W. N. (2002). Teacher burnout in special education: The causes and the recommended solutions. *High School Journal, 86*(1), 36–45.

Frankenberg, E., & Lee, C. (2003). *Charter schools and race: A lost opportunity for integrated education.* Cambridge, MA: The Civil Rights Project at Harvard University.

French, D. (1998). The state's role in shaping a progressive vision of public education. *Phi Delta Kappan, 80*, 185–194.

Friend, M. (1984). Consultation skills for resource teachers. *Learning Disability Quarterly, 7*, 246–250.

Friend, M., & Cook, L. (2003). *Interactions: Collaborative skills for school professionals* (4th ed.). New York: Longman.

Fuchs, D., Mock, D., Morgan, P. L., & Young, C. L. (2003). Responsiveness-to-intervention: Definitions, evidence, and implications for the learning disabilities construct. *Learning Disabilities Research and Practice, 18*(3), 157–171.

Fullan, M., & Watson, N. (1997). *Building infrastructures for professional development: An assessment of early progress.* New York: Rockefeller Foundation.

Fuller, B., Gawlik, M., Gonzales, E. K., Park, S., & Gibbings, G. (2003). *Charter schools and inequality: National disparities in funding, teacher quality, and student support.* Policy analysis for California education, Working paper series 03-2, April, 2003. Retrieved January 2004, from http://pace.berkeley.edu/pace_publications.html

Fulton, K. P. (2003). Redesigning schools to meet 21st century learning needs. *THE Journal, 30*(9), 30–35.

Gable, R. A., Hendrickson, J. M., & Rogan, J. P. (1996). TEAMS supporting students at risk in the regular classroom. *The Clearing House, 69*(4), 235–238.

Garriott, P. P., Wandry, D., & Snyder, L. (2000). Teachers as parents, parents as children: What's wrong with this picture? *Preventing School Failure, 45*(1), 37–44.

Guthrie, J. (1998, November 21). 20/20 vision: A strategy for doubling academic achievement in America by the year 2020. *Education Week, XVIII*, 24–25.

Hankin, J. R. (2002). Fetal alcohol syndrome prevention research. *Alcohol Research and Health, 26*(1), 58–65.

Hanline, M. F., & Knowlton, A. (1988). A collaborative model for providing support to parents during their child's transition from infant intervention to preschool special education public school programs. *Journal of the Division for Early Childhood, 12*, 116–125.

Hasazi, S. B., Furney, K. S., & DeStefano, L. (1999). Implementing the IDEA transition mandates. *Exceptional Children, 65*(4), 555–566.

Hechinger, F. (1992). *Fateful choices: Healthy youth for the 21st century.* New York: Carnegie Corporation.

Heimbecker, C., Medina, C., Peterson, P., Redsteer, D., & Prater, G. (2002). Reaching American Indian special/elementary educators through a partnership with a Navajo Nation school district. *Remedial and Special Education, 23*(6), 372–379.

Heward, W. L. (2003). *Exceptional children: An introduction to special education* (7th ed.). Upper Saddle River, NJ: Merrill/Prentice Hall.

Hobbs, T., Day, S. L., & Russo, A. C. (2002). The virtual conference room: Online problem solving for first year special educators. *Teacher Education and Special Education, 25*(4), 352–361.

Hobbs, T., & Westling, D. (1998). Promoting successful inclusion through collaborative problemsolving. *TEACHING Exceptional Children, 31*(1), 12–19.

Hodgkinson, H. (1988). The right schools for the right kids. *Educational Leadership, 45*, 10–15.

Hohenbrind, J., Johnston, M., & Westhoven, L. (1997). Collaborative teaching of a social studies methods course: Intimidation and change. *Journal of Teacher Education, 48*, 293–300.

Holm, L., & Horn, C. (2003). Bridging the gap between schools of education and the needs of 21st-century teachers. *Phi Delta Kappan, 84*(5), 376–380.

Huefner, D. S. (1988). The consulting teacher model: Risks and opportunities. *Exceptional Children, 54*, 403–414.

Hunt, P., Soto, G., Maier, J., & Doering, K. (2003). Collaborative teaming to support students at risk and students with severe disabilities. *Exceptional Children, 69*(3), 315–332.

Idol, L. (2002). *Creating collaborative and inclusive schools.* Austin, TX: Pro-Ed.

Interstate New Teacher Assessment and Support Consortium. (2001, May). *Model standards for licensing general and special education teachers of students with disabilities: A resource for state dialogue.* Washington, DC: Council of Chief State School Officers.

Jenkins, A. A., Pateman, B., & Black, R. S. (2002). Partnerships for dual preparation in elementary, secondary, and special education programs. *Remedial and Special Education, 23*(6), 359–372.

Johnston, P., Allington, R., & Afflerbach, P. (1985). The congruence of classroom and remedial reading instruction. *Elementary School Journal, 85*, 465–477.

Jones, S. N., & Meisels, S. J. (1987). Training family day care providers to work with special needs children. *Topics in Early Childhood Special Education, 7*, 1–12.

Kaiser, S. M., & Woodman, R. W. (1985). Multidisciplinary teams and group decision-making techniques: Possible solutions to decision-making problems. *School Psychology Review, 14*, 457–470.

Kalyanpur, M., & Harry, B. (1999). *Culture in special education: Building reciprocal family-professional relationship.* Baltimore: Brookes.

Kids Count Online Data. (2003). Retrieved from the Annie E. Casey Foundation Website at http://www.aecf.org/kidscount

Klein, N., & Sheehan, R. (1987). Staff development: A key issue in meeting the needs of young handicapped children in day care settings. *Topics in Early Childhood Special Education, 7*, 13–27.

Kohler, P. D., & Field, S. (2003). Transition-focused education: Foundation for the future. *Journal of Special Education, 37*(3), 174–184.

Lilly, M. S. (1971). A training based model for special education. *Exceptional Children, 37*, 745–749.

Lindsey, D. (1985). A model performance appraisal instrument for school physical therapists. *Clinical Management, 6*(5), 20–26.

Linn, R. L. (2003). Accountability: Responsibility and reasonable expectations [2003 Presidential address]. *Educational Researcher, 32*(7), 3–13.

Lovitt, T. (2003). The educational plight of foster children in schools and what can be done. *Remedial and Special Education, 24*(4), 199–203.

Lowenthal, B. (1992). Collaborative training in the education of early childhood educators. *Teaching Exceptional Children, 24*(4), 25–29.

Maeroff, G. (1993). Building teams to rebuild schools. *Phi Delta Kappan, 74*, 512–519.

McLaughlin, M., & Schwartz, R. (1998). *Strategies for fixing public schools.* Cambridge, MA: Pew Forum, Harvard Graduate School of Education.

McLeskey, J., Henry, D., & Hodges, D. (1998). Inclusion: Where is it happening? *Teaching Exceptional Children, 31*(1), 4–10.

Menlove, R. R., Hudson, P. J., & Suter, D. (2001). A field of IEP dreams. *Teaching Exceptional Children, 33*(5), 28–33.

Meyers, B., Meyers, J., & Gelzheiser, L. (2001). Observing leadership roles in shared decision making: A preliminary analysis of three teams. *Journal of Educational and Psychological Consultation, 12*(4), 277–312.

Monahan, D. J. (2002). Teen pregnancy prevention outcomes: Implications for social work practice. *Families in Society, 83*(4), 431–439.

Morsink, C. (1999). *21st century teachers for a better future* (Final Report to Howard Heinz Endowment). Slippery Rock, PA: SRU College of Education, unpublished manuscript.

National Center for Education Statistics. (2001). *Dropout rates in the United States: 2000 executive summary.* Retrieved January 2004, from http://nces.ed.gov/pubs2002/droppub_2001/

National Center for Education Statistics (NCES), U.S. Department of Education. (2003). Common core of data (CCD), "Public Elementary/Secondary School Universe Survey." Retrieved February 2004, from NCES Website at http://nces.ed.gov/pubs2003/overview03/table_09.asp

National Commission on Teaching and America's Future. (1996). *What matters most: Teaching for America's future.* New York: National Commission on Teaching and America's Future.

Obi, S. O., & Obiakor, F. E. (2000). Rural students with exceptionalities: Refocusing in the new millennium. (ERIC Document Reproduction Service No. ED452629)

Olson, L., & Rodman, B. (1988, June 22). The unfinished agenda, part II. *Education Week,* 17–33.

O'Neil, J. (1997). Building schools as communities: A conversation with James Comer. *Educational Leadership, 54*(8), 6–10.

Orr, M. T. (2000). Community colleges and their communities: Collaboration for workforce development. *New Directions for Community Colleges, 115,* 39–50.

O'Shea, D. J., Williams, A. L., & Sattler, R. O. (1999). Collaboration across special education and general education: Preservice teachers' views. *Journal of Teacher Education, 50*(2), 147–157.

O'Shea, L. J., O'Shea, D. J., & Algozzine, R. (1998). *Learning disabilities: From theory toward practice.* Upper Saddle River, NJ: Merrill/Prentice Hall.

Owings, W., & Magliaro, S. (1998). Grade retention: A history of failure. *Educational Leadership, 56*(1), 86–88.

Palsha, S. A., & Wesley, P. W. (1998). Improving quality in early childhood environments through on-site consultation. *Topics in Early Childhood Special Education, 18*(4), 243–257.

Patriarca, L. A., & Lamb, M. A. (1990). Preparing secondary special education teachers to be collaborative decision makers and reflective practitioners: A promising practicum model. *Teacher Education and Special Education, 13,* 228–232.

Powers, M. D. (1986). Promoting community-based services: Implications for program design, implementation, and public policy. *Journal of the Association for Persons with Severe Handicaps, 11,* 309–315.

President's Commission on Teacher Education. (1992). American Association of State Colleges and Universities.

Pugach, M. C., & Johnson, L. J. (2002). *Collaborative practitioners, collaborative schools* (2nd ed.). Denver, CO: Love Publishing Co.

Rafferty, Y. (1997–1998). Meeting the educational needs of homeless children. *Educational Leadership, 55*(4), 48–52.

Reese, J. (1995). Investing in the profession: Four recommendations. *English Journal, 84*(2), 66–67.

Reynolds, D., & Teddlie, C. (2000). An introduction to school effectiveness. In C. Teddlie & D. Reynolds (Eds.), *The international handbook of school effectiveness* (pp. 3–25). New York: Falmer Press.

Reynolds, M. (1989). Students with special needs. In M. C. Reynolds (Ed.), *Knowledge base for the beginning teacher* (pp. 129–142). Oxford, England: Pergamon Press.

Rhim, L., & McLaughlin, M. (2001). Special education in American charter schools: State level policy, practices, and tensions. *Cambridge Journal of Education, 31*(3), 373–383.

RPP International. (2000). *The state of charter schools: 2000.* Washington, DC: Office of Educational Research and Improvement, U.S. Department of Education.

Rubinson, F. (2002). Lessons learned from implementing problem-solving teams in urban high schools. *Journal of Educational and Psychological Consultation, 13*(3), 185–217.

Ryan, S., & Paterna, L. (1997). Junior high can be inclusive: Using natural supports and cooperative learning. *Teaching Exceptional Children, 30*(2), 36–41.

Salend, S. J. (1994). *Effective mainstreaming: Creating inclusive classrooms* (2nd ed.). Upper Saddle River, NJ: Merrill/Prentice Hall.

Salvia, J., & Ysseldyke, J. (1988). *Assessment in special and remedial education* (4th ed.). Boston: Houghton Mifflin.

Sandler, A. G. (1997). Physical and occupational therapy services: Use of a consultative therapy. Model in the schools. *Preventing School Failure, 41,* 164–167.

Schmoker, M., & Wilson, R. (1993). Transforming schools through total quality education. *Phi Delta Kappan, 74,* 389–395.

Sileo, T. W., Rude, H. A., & Luckner, J. L. (1988). Collaborative consultation: A model for transition planning for handicapped youth. *Education and Training in Mental Retardation, 23,* 333–339.

Sindelar, P. T., Griffin, C. C., Smith, S. W., & Watanabe, A. K. (1992). Prereferral intervention: Encouraging notes on preliminary findings. *The Elementary School Journal, 92,* 245–259.

Smith, A. C., & Smith, D. J. (2001). *Emergency and Transitional Shelter Population: 2000.* U.S. Census Bureau, Census Special Reports Series CENSR/01-2, U.S. Government Printing Office, Washington, DC.

Smith, S. (1992). Professional partnerships and educational change: Effective collaboration over time. *Journal of Teacher Education, 43*(4), 243–256.

Snyder, T. D., & Freeman, C. E. (2003). Trends in education. *Principal, 83*(1), 50–52.

Spear-Swerling, L., & Sternberg, R. (1998). Curing our "epidemic" of learning disabilities. *Phi Delta Kappan, 79,* 397–401.

Spencer-Dobson, C. A., & Schultz, J. B. (1987). Utilization of multidisciplinary teams in educating special needs students. *Journal of Industrial Teacher Education, 25,* 68–78.

Stanovich, P. J. (1996). Collaboration—The key to successful instruction in today's inclusive schools. *Intervention in School and Clinic, 32*(1), 39–42.

Stansbury, K. (2001). What new teachers need. *Leadership, 30*(3) 18–21.

Stowitschek, J. J., Lovitt, T. C., & Rodriquez, J. A. (2001). Patterns of collaboration in secondary education for youth with special needs: Profiles of three high schools. *Urban Education, 36*(1), 93–128.

Substance Abuse and Mental Health Services Administration (SAMHSA). (2003a). *Children living with substance-abusing or substance-dependent parents.* The NHSDA Report (Office of Applied Studies). Retrieved December 2003, from http://www.samhsa.gov/oas/nhsda.htm

Substance Abuse and Mental Health Services Administration (SAMHSA). (2003b). *Results from the 2002 national survey on drug use and health: National findings* (Office of Applied Studies, NHSDA Series H-22, DHHS Publication No. SMA 03-3836). Rockville, MD. Retrieved December 2003, from http://www.DrugAbuseStatistics.SAMHSA.gov

Summers, J. A., Steeples, T., Peterson, C., Naig, L., McBride, S., Wall, S., Liebow, H., Swanson, M., & Stowitschek, J. (2001). Policy and management supports for effective service integration in early head start and part c programs. *Topics in Early Childhood Special Education, 21*(1), 16–31.

Tindal, G., Shinn, M., Walz, L., & Germann, G. (1987). Mainstream consultation in secondary settings: The Pine County model. *Journal of Special Education, 21,* 94–106.

Toch, T. (1999, January 18). Outstanding schools. *US News and World Report,* 48–51.

Turnbull, R., & Cilley, M. (1999). *Explanations and implications of the 1997 amendments to IDEA.* Upper Saddle River, NJ: Merrill/Prentice Hall.

Umansky, D. L., & Holloway, E. L. (1984). The counselor as consultant: From model to practice. *School Counselor, 31,* 329–338.

U.S. Census Bureau. (2002). *Population profile of the United States: 2000 (Internet Release).* Retrieved December 22, 2003, from the U.S. Census Bureau Website at http://www.census.gov/population/pop-profile/2000/

U.S. Department of Education. (2002). *24th annual report to Congress on the implementation of the Individuals with Disabilities Education Act.* Retrieved November 2003, from strategic and annual reports at http://www.ed.gov/about/reports/annual/osep/2002/index.html

U.S. Department of Health and Human Services. (2003a). *Child and adolescent mental health.* Retrieved December 2003, from http://www.mentalhealth.samhsa.gov/publications

U.S. Department of Health and Human Services. (2003b). *Child maltreatment 2001.* Retrieved December 2003, from the Administration for Children and Families Website at http://nccanch.acf.hhs.gov/topics/overview/facts.cfm

Verburg, G., Borthwick, B., Bennett, B., & Rumney, P. (2003). Online support to facilitate the reintegration of students with brain injury: Trials and errors. *NeuroRehabilitation, 18,* 113–123.

Wadsworth, D. (1997). *Different drummers: How teachers of teachers view public education. A report from Public Agenda.* New York: Public Agenda.

Wang, M., Haertel, G., & Walberg, H. (1997). *What do we know: Widely implemented school improvement programs.* Philadelphia, PA: Mid-Atlantic Educational Lab, Temple University.

Welch, M. (1998). Collaboration: Staying on the bandwagon. *Journal of Teacher Education, 49,* 26–34.

Wilson, B., & Firestone, W. (1987). The principal and instruction: Combining bureaucratic and cultural linkages. *Educational Leadership, 45,* 18–23.

Wood, J. W. (2002). *Adapting instruction for mainstreamed and at-risk students* (4th ed.). Upper Saddle River, NJ: Merrill/Prentice Hall.

Yell, M. (1998). The legal basis of inclusion. *Educational Leadership, 56*(2), 70–73.

Young, D. J. (1999). The usefulness of value-added research in identifying effective schools. Paper presented at the Joint Conference of the Australian Association for Research in Education and the New Zealand Association for Research in Education. (ERIC Document Reproduction Service No. ED440810)

Definitions and Dimensions of the Interactive Team

Topics in this chapter include:

◆ Definitions of consultation, collaboration, and teaming.

◆ Models of consultation, collaboration, and teaming.

◆ Dimensions and goals of consultation, collaboration, and teaming.

◆ Impediments to and positive features of consultation, collaboration, and teaming.

◆ Discussion of the bases for the team's work.

◆ A model of an interactive team.

◆ Descriptions of the aspects of team membership and leadership.

◆ Procedures for implementing the interactive teaming process.

◆ An application illustrating the contrast between a successful and unsuccessful team meeting.

When the Jordans' son, Dontaye, was 4 years old, he became seriously ill in the middle of the night. Hearing her son crying, Mrs. Jordan checked on Dontaye and found him to have a very high fever. She awakened her husband, and they took the boy to the emergency room. On the way to the hospital, Dontaye had a seizure.

The pediatrician at the hospital diagnosed the problem as a respiratory infection and said the seizure was caused by the high fever. He prescribed a baby-aspirin substitute and an antibiotic and assured them that Dontaye would be much improved in 48 hours when the medication began to take effect. The Jordans took Dontaye home feeling optimistic that their son would soon be back to his energetic, talkative, happy-go-lucky self.

Two days later, however, Dontaye was still listless and unresponsive. His mother called their family pediatrician, who said to give the medication one more day, and if he still was not improved to bring him in for an appointment. The next day Dontaye did not talk at all when his mother awakened him. She immediately dressed him and took him to the pediatrician. Dr. Corley examined Dontaye and noted that the infection had caused respiratory distress and an asthma-like condition. She prescribed another medication and suggested that he not return to his preschool program for at least another week.

After a week, Dontaye seemed better, so his parents sent him back to his preschool program. At the end of the first day, his teacher called. She said Dontaye was withdrawn and that during playtime the recreation specialist had commented that he displayed autistic-like behaviors, such as twirling and flapping his hands. The next day the director of the preschool called. He said that Dontaye seemed to have lost some of his language skills and that he was striking out at peers when they approached him. He inquired whether Dontaye could have suffered brain damage or emotional trauma from the infection and suggested that his parents might want to consider moving him to a preschool for children with special needs.

Now extremely concerned and confused, Mrs. Jordan called Dr. Corley again and suggested that she talk with the people at the preschool about how the respiratory infection could be affecting Dontaye's behavior. Mrs. Jordan said she was feeling like a "go-between," trying to relay all the messages from one person to the next, and she stated that she would like everyone involved to meet to share their observations, discuss possible causes, and suggest what needed to be done. Dr. Corley agreed to come to a meeting the following week.

The Jordans contacted the preschool personnel, who also agreed to attend a meeting. At the meeting, all the professionals shared their observations about Dontaye, and his parents commented on his behavior at home. Although at first they were quite defensive, eventually the educators agreed they might have been hasty in labeling some of Dontaye's behaviors as autistic or brain damaged. The educators and parents discussed some strategies for interacting with Dontaye. Everyone agreed to meet again in 3 weeks to discuss any changes or improvements that might occur after all of the medication had been taken.

The effects of professionals and parents operating in "separate worlds" are illustrated at the beginning of this vignette. When no one is in charge, everyone functions as a separate entity, even though each individual is concerned with the same child. Consequently, communication does not occur and the results often are fragmented services for a child and confusion for adults. After the Jordans were able to get the professionals to communicate, the situation improved, but much time and energy could have been saved if the people involved had been able to operate within a team framework from the beginning.

In Chapter 1, *interactive teaming* was defined as a mutual or reciprocal effort among and between members of a team to provide the best possible educational student program. The strength of this approach is the potential for effective, comprehensive, and cohesive services when all the people involved work together instead of functioning as separate individuals or disciplines. Interactive teaming includes features from the collaborative consultation and transdisciplinary teaming models used primarily in special education and school psychology. Interactive teaming incorporates components identified in research on effective schools, decision-making processes, and adult learning, recognizing that all the components and factors must be implemented within the context of a school or institutional program for at-risk students or those with identified special needs.

This chapter provides in-depth definitions for collaboration and teaming while examining the dimensions of interactive teaming. Incorporated in the dimensions are the purposes and objectives of the model, descriptions of the competencies of team members, and processes and procedures for implementation. Part II of the text, Facilitating Factors, provides additional information on how to address potential barriers to interactive teaming, such as a lack of understanding of roles, the process of change, miscommunication, ineffective leadership, insensitivity to cultural diversity, and limited family involvement.

The complex challenges facing today's schools demand that educators and other school personnel work together to facilitate student learning. As discussed in Chapter 1, these demands come from a variety of sources. The demographic characteristics that place children at risk are many (e.g., poverty, abuse, violence, drug and alcohol abuse, dropout rates, teen pregnancy, mental health problems) and require a wide range of expertise. In addition, increased numbers of children with special needs are being served in general education classrooms for most or all of the day. These issues, added to the fact that both federal and state policies are mandating greater accountability for student outcomes through standards-based reform and high-stakes testing, are compelling educators to use a more collaborative approach to teaching.

Schools succeeding at facilitating students' academic and social learning and growth develop a collaborative culture that some are calling "professional learning communities" (DuFour, 2003; Fullan, 2000). General educators are working together in grade-level and interdisciplinary teams with special educators, speech-language pathologists, Title 1 teachers, reading specialists, and others to improve student outcomes. They are also building strong partnerships with parents (Turnbull & Turnbull, 2001) and communities (Sanders & Harvey, 2002).

The extensive support for consultation, collaboration, and teaming from a variety of viewpoints and service delivery options, along with legal mandates and support from key professional organizations, makes further exploration of these approaches vital. The next sections will define consultation, collaboration, and teaming; discuss characteristics and processes; and delineate how aspects of these approaches are part of the foundation for interactive teaming.

CONSULTATION AND COLLABORATION

Definitions

The variety of consultation definitions primarily is due to the differences in the philosophical views and professional roles of the authors that began in the early 1970s. Tharp (1975) described consultation as a triadic process in which the consultant attempts to bring about changes in a target person through a consultee or mediator. Bergan's (1977) definition included two forms of consultation, depending on whether the goals were considered to be long range (*developmental* consultation) or designed to remediate an immediate problem (*problem-centered* consultation). Brown, Wyne, Blackburn, and Powell (1979) noted that consultation is a process involving the establishment of trust and communication and "joint approaches to problem identification, the pooling of personal resources, to identify and select strategies that will have some probability of solving the problem that has been identified, and shared responsibility in the implementation and evaluation of the program or strategy that has been initiated" (p. 8).

Based on their extensive review of the literature, West and Idol (1987) concluded that consultation has at least three general meanings: *medical,* in which a doctor calls on the expertise of another physician for counsel; *organizational,* which involves change in a system; and *mental health,* in which a consultant provides assistance to another professional on problems the latter may be experiencing with a client. Idol-Maestas (1983) focused on the support regular classroom teachers can gain from consultants that will help them cope with students' academic and social behavior problems. Friend and Cook (2003) summarized the many definitions of school consultation as "a voluntary process in which one professional assists another to address a problem concerning a third party" (p. 151).

The collaborative nature of consultation has received much attention in the literature for school psychologists (cf. Gutkin, 1999, Gutkin & Curtis, 1982; Piersel, 1985). Gutkin reviewed the literature, challenging whether consultation is truly collaborative, and concluded that consultants tend to be "both directive and collaborative at the same time" (p. 180) and function in two dimensions of collaborative-noncollaborative and directive-nondirective. Collaborative consultation in special education has tended to stress that the approach is a voluntary, nonsupervisory sharing of resources and expertise where the participants work together as equals on a mutual goal (cf. Conoley & Conoley, 1992; Friend & Cook, 2003; Idol,

Paolucci-Whitcomb, & Nevin, 2000; Pugach & Johnson, 2002). Sugai and Tindal (1993) emphasized a behavior-analytic approach to consultation in which solutions are developed based on gathering information that is then analyzed within the context of the problem situation.

Special educators have advocated collaborative forms of consultation used for collaborative *problem solving* (Medway, 1979; Salisbury & Evans, 1997). Collaborative problem solving is effective in solving school-wide problems and issues (e.g., implementing a school-wide positive behavioral support program) or working on a challenging problem within a particular teacher's classroom (Pugach & Johnson, 2002). Collaborative consultation and collaborative problem solving offer a method for professionals to interact and produce creative solutions to problems that are comprehensive, dynamic, and more likely to facilitate positive outcomes for students than if addressed independently (Heron & Harris, 2001; Idol et al., 2000). In addition, the context of collaborative endeavors that are goal oriented can strengthen professional relationships when situations are accurately assessed and expectations are appropriate for the interaction (Cramer, 1998).

In distinguishing consultation from collaboration, Friend and Cook (2003) define collaboration as "A style for direct interaction between at least two coequal parties voluntarily engaged in shared decision-making as they work toward a common goal" (p. 5). Furthermore, defining collaboration as a "style" implies that it occurs in combination with a task or activity, determining how the activity is occurring.

Models

From their examination of the literature in special education and school psychology, West and Idol (1987) identified 10 models of consultation. Three models are discussed here because they are essential to an understanding of interactive teaming. Those models are *triadic* (and its relationship to collaborative), *organizational*, and *behavioral* consultation.

As previously indicated, *triadic consultation* (Tharp, 1975; Tharp & Wetzel, 1969) involves three people: consultant, mediator, and target. Tharp (1975) describes the roles of each person as follows:

1. The *target* is the person with the problematic behavior, the change of which is the primary goal of the directed influence.

2. The *mediator* is the person with the available means of social influence for effecting that goal.

3. The *consultant* is the person with the knowledge to mobilize the mediator's influence. (p. 138)

In the triadic model, the target may be a student or an adult in whom others believe a behavior change is desirable. The mediator is a parent, teacher, or other professional who will be attempting to bring about a behavior change in the target.

The consultant can be a parent, teacher, administrator, or other professional who has expertise to share regarding strategies to change the behavior.

In the illustration of the triadic model in Figure 2.1, the existence of two dyads within the model is also shown in the bottom part of the box. The dyads are consultant-mediator and mediator-target. Each influences the other, and there is an indirect influence of the consultant on the target, as shown by the dotted line in the top diagram.

Collaborative consultation is essentially an extension of the triadic model. The target typically is a student with some type of problem, the mediator usually is a regular classroom teacher, and the consultant can be a special educator, speech therapist, principal, or the like (Idol, Paolucci-Whitcomb, & Nevin, 1986). In most cases, the consultant in a collaborative consultation does not interact with the target. As such it is considered an indirect support (Walther-Thomas, Korinek, McLaughlin, & Williams, 2000). Although this model can result in collaboration and sharing among professionals with various types of expertise, implementation has primarily focused on a triadic relationship among regular and special educators attempting to meet the needs of students with special characteristics.

Organizational consultation (e.g., Ikeda, Tilly, Stumme, Volmer, & Allison, 1996; Sugai & Horner, 1999) focuses on the process of change in the systems of an organization or group of people. The interactions among group members, interrelationships among subsystems, shared decision making, and communication skills are highlighted in this model. The consultant can be anyone within the system and

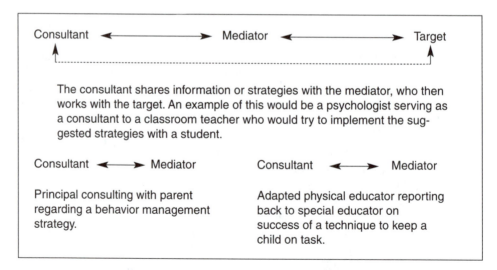

Figure 2.1
The triadic model.

Source: From "The Triadic Model of Consultation: Current Considerations," by R. G. Tharp, 1975, p. 137. In C. Parker (Ed.), *Psychological Consultation: Helping Teachers Meet Special Needs,* Reston, VA: The Council for Exceptional Children. Copyright 1975 by Council for Exceptional Children. Reprinted with permission.

is viewed primarily as a facilitator of the group process. Organizational consultation has primarily occurred for school reform and restructuring efforts. However, Senge et al. (2000) proposed shifting attention away from restructuring schools to creating the "learning community" based on relationships between students, families, teachers, and their school.

Behavioral consultation (Bergan, 1977) is based on social learning theory and the application of the principles of applied behavior analysis. The primary emphasis is on student behavior change, so it can be considered a client-centered and problem-solving approach (Piersel, 1985). Proponents of behavioral consultation, especially in recent years, also have indicated the importance of considering a child's interactions within a total environmental system to understand influences on behavior (Cipani, 1985; Friend, 1988; Hawryluk & Smallwood, 1986; Illsley & Sladeczek, 2001), and they have noted that some degree of change will occur in the consultee's behavior as a result of involvement in the consultative process (Sheridan, Welch, & Orme, 1996).

The defining features of the behavioral consultation model are the use of direct observation methods resulting in problem definitions in observable and measurable terms, identification of target behaviors for change, and the use of data-based intervention and assessment methods (Gable, Korinek, & McLaughlin, 1997; Hawryluk & Smallwood, 1986). Sugai and Tindal (1993) focus their behavior-analytic and best practices approach to consultation on the learned nature and lawfulness of behavior and the potential for change by manipulating aspects of the environment. Currently IDEA requires that schools conduct functional behavioral assessment (FBA) for children with special needs if an alternate placement is being considered. Proponents of behavioral consultation see this as an appropriate service delivery method, particularly for school psychologists who increasingly are called upon to conduct the FBA, given the common theoretical foundations of the model and FBA (O'Neill et al., 1997; Wilczynski, Mandal, & Fusilier, 2000).

Dimensions

The dimensions or characteristics of consultation can be affected by the consultant's emphasis or focus. However, Gutkin and Curtis (1982) identified a set of core characteristics they believe are present in almost all the models they reviewed:

1. *Indirect service delivery.* Working on a child's behavior through another professional rather than directly with the child.
2. *Consultant-consultee relationship.* Establishment of an open and trusting relationship.
3. *Coordinate status.* Viewing the consultee as an equal, rather than operating in a hierarchical power structure.
4. *Involvement of the consultee in the consultation process.* Active participation of the consultee throughout the process.

5. *Consultee's right to reject consultant suggestions.* The freedom to select among the options presented instead of being pressured to follow along with every recommendation.

6. *Voluntary nature of consultation.* Participants are involved because they recognize a need and want some assistance, not because they are being forced to attend.

7. *Confidentiality.* The information provided is not shared with others who are not involved in the consultation process.

The dimensions or elements of collaboration are similar to those previously listed for consultation. Friend and Cook (2003) suggest several defining characteristics of collaborative interactions. These authors note that collaboration is a voluntary endeavor based on a mutual goal. In addition, participants share resources as well as responsibility for participation, decision making, and accountability for outcomes. Finally, all participants are equally valued; that is, each participant has something valuable to contribute and values the contributions of others. Mostert (1998) cited the same dimensions as those previously listed and added *communal trust, collective involvement, action for problem solving, collaborative resources, confidentiality,* and *focus on the student as priority.* Another element mentioned by Villa, Thousand, Paolucci-Whitecomb, and Nevin (1990) is the importance of participants *monitoring and adjusting their emphasis on task and relationship behaviors.*

Goals

Some authors stress the *helping relationship* goals of consultation and collaboration (e.g., Fine & Tyler, 1971), whereas others focus more on *training* or *teaching* another professional such skills as assessment, programming, management, and monitoring (e.g., Idol-Maestas, 1983). In their review of six consultation service delivery models, Idol and West (1987) noted that they focused on three types of outcomes: changes in students, changes in teachers, and changes in systems. Collaborative relationships between general educators and content area specialists may be formed in response to the teacher's need for assistance to develop effective instruction for her work with a struggling student. However, they also may result in a professional development activity as the teacher works to improve his or her own practice (Fishbaugh, 1997; Pugach & Johnson, 2002).

Idol, Nevin, and Paolucci-Whitcomb (1994) described other possible positive outcomes of collaborative consultation: changes in the collaborators and changes in the organization. They stated that as a result of engaging in the collaborative process, the collaborators are expected to:

1. Increase their individual knowledge bases by learning from each other.
2. Improve their interpersonal skills (communication, group interaction, and problem solving).

3. Make cognitive and emotional shifts in their own intrapersonal attitudes toward how to be more effective team members and toward what the learning possibilities might be for learners who have special needs or who are currently experiencing school failure. (p. xii)

Competencies

Studies in the area of competencies considered necessary for effective consultation have focused on those needed by consultants as well as by consultees. The interactive and confidential nature of consultation makes empirical measures difficult to obtain, so the research has tended to take the form of recommendations, consensus ratings among professionals, or self-reports.

Special educators who serve as consultants typically are in the role of resource teacher (Voltz, Elliott, & Harris, 1995). In a survey of resource teachers, regular classroom teachers, and principals regarding their views on the skills needed for consultation, all three groups indicated that resource teachers should possess the skills usually considered integral to a consultative role (Friend, 1988). However, the consultant aspect of this role has been the topic of considerable debate since the mid-1980s in terms of whether (1) this is an appropriate expectation (Brown, Kiraly, & McKinnon, 1979); (2) it is an important element for the success of mainstreaming (Speece & Mandell, 1980); (3) principals and regular classroom teachers see it as a vital part of the resource role (Evans, 1981); (4) special educators feel confident in the role (Aloia, 1983); and (5) it is an expectation or policy by the state departments of education (West & Brown, 1987).

Recommendations regarding competencies generally are similar to those presented by Haight (1984), who suggested that the consultant role requires specific knowledge in a variety of areas; skills in analysis, problem solving, and synthesis; and the ability to promote human relations, communication, and skill development in others. In a survey of 100 interdisciplinary experts, West and Cannon (1988) found that the competencies receiving the highest ratings by both regular and special educators working in a collaborative consultation model were the areas of personal characteristics, collaborative problem solving, and interactive communication. Meyers (2002) adds that consultants should be familiar with theory and research, including skill in applied research, and aware of how contextual factors influence behavior.

In their review of the literature, Brown, Pryzwansky, and Schulte (1998) identified five primary characteristics needed by consultants: (1) a high level of awareness of his/her values, which is especially important in cross-cultural consultation; (2) the ability to solve problems; (3) high levels of ego development including increased self-awareness and reliance on self-generated standards; (4) the ability to establish working alliances including empathy, genuineness, and positive regard; and (5) a willingness to take interpersonal risks. These characteristics support the notion that effective consultation centers on interpersonal processes and problem solving and that consultants must possess the skills necessary for building relationships in addition to the knowledge they will need to provide assistance (Gutkin, 2002).

The training to develop consultation competencies typically is included in programs for health and medical practitioners (Courtnage & Healy, 1984) and school psychologists and counselors, but such training is less often a part of the course of study for special educators (Salend & Salend, 1984) and even more limited—if present at all—for regular educators. However, training in consultation competencies is still limited in most programs; it is usually available at the graduate instead of the undergraduate level (Gable, Young, & Hendrickson, 1987), and only during one semester of coursework (Gravois, Knotek, & Babinski, 2002). Gutkin (2002) also noted in the introduction of a recent special issue of the *Journal of Education and Psychological Consultation* that there is a lack of research available to answer some of the basic questions on training school-based consultants related to theory and practice.

As collaboration-based service delivery models in educational settings have increased, the roles and activities of educators have been impacted accordingly (Foley & Mundschenk, 1997). A survey of elementary and special educators serving students with behavior disorders identified collaboration competencies similar to those previously described for consultants but also included recognition of the importance of the roles of fellow collaborators, knowledge, and skill in effective communication; knowledge and skill in the use of a variety of assessment and instructional approaches; knowledge of general education curricula; and knowledge and skill in modifying and adapting methods, materials, and evaluation systems to meet students' needs (Foley, 1994). Pugach and Johnson (2002) proposed that collaborative professionals recognize the complexity of collaboration, acknowledge the creativity of working with others, enjoy the social nature of joint problem solving, appreciate their own growth during the process, and reflect on professional practice.

A collection of collaborative teacher education programs that are designed to prepare both general and special educators have been gathered in a volume edited by Blanton, Griffin, Winn, and Pugach (1997). Hudson and Glomb (1997) also outlined programs at several universities that focus on collaboration instruction for all educators.

Process

The process implemented in consultation is based on the focus, type of problem, and the people involved. Although described in a variety of terms by different authors, the process generally includes the steps listed in Figure 2.2 (compiled from Aldinger, Warger, & Eavy, 1991; Brown et al., 1998; Cipani, 1985; Dettmer, Thurston, & Dyck, 1993; Gutkin, 1993; Heron & Harris, 2001; Idol et al., 1986; Kampwirth, 1987; Kurpius, 1978; Sugai & Tindal, 1993).

TEAMING

Definitions

A team has been described as an organized group of professionals from different disciplines who have unique skills and a common goal of *cooperative problem solving*

> 1. *Establishing the relationship.* Meeting and establishing trust with the consultee.
> 2. *Gathering information.* Checking a variety of sources to get background on the problem.
> 3. *Identifying the problem.* Determining the history and frequency of the problem, defining it in measurable terms.
> 4. *Stating the target behavior.* Considering whether the behavior needs to be increased or decreased, and by what criteria the behavior is to be judged.
> 5. *Generating interventions.* Discussing options to consider, selecting ones to try.
> 6. *Implementing the interventions.* Putting the interventions into effect and collecting data on their success or failure.
> 7. *Evaluating the interventions.* Determining whether the desired outcomes have been reached and modifying them as necessary.
> 8. *Withdrawing from the consultative relationship.* Ending the process when the goal has been reached or an agreement is made not to continue.

Figure 2.2
The process of consultation.

(Pfeiffer, 1980); where positive interdependence exists among members who pool their resources as they work together (Snell & Janney, 2000); and learning, growth, and change occurs as they attempt to collaborate (Bailey, 1984). Dettmer et al. (1993) stated that consultation, collaboration, and teaming share two characteristics: "engaging in interactive processes and using specialized content to achieve shared goals" (p. 16). They also noted that collaboration and teamwork allow participants the opportunity to build on the strengths of their colleagues. Katzenbach and Smith (1999) distinguished a team from a group of people who have been given a common assignment in the following definition:

> A team is a small number of people with complementary skills who are committed to a common purpose, performance goals, and approach for which they hold themselves mutually accountable. (p. 45)

Models

Three models of teams, as well as three types of committee approaches, have been identified. The teaming models are described first: multidisciplinary, interdisciplinary, and transdisciplinary. These three models are illustrated in Figure 2.3.

The *multidisciplinary team* developed from the medical model as people with expertise in various fields shared their observations about a patient, and frequently those findings were reported to one person (Hart, 1977). A multidisciplinary team will have a common purpose and engage in problem solving around that purpose (Pfeiffer, 1981). However, the members of the team contribute information and understanding but are not coordinated or integrated in the process.

Figure 2.3
Model of teams.

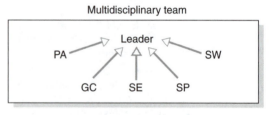

Multidisciplinary team

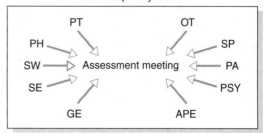

Interdisciplinary team

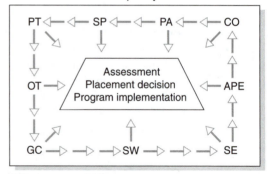

Transdisciplinary team

Key:
PA = Parent
GC = General education classroom teacher
SE = Special educator
SP = Speech-language clinician
SW = Social worker
PH = Physician
PT = Physical therapist
OT = Occupational therapist
APE = Adapted physical educator
PSY = Psychologist
CO = Counselor

An *interdisciplinary team* may include the same members as the multidisciplinary team, but in this model the team is more focused on coordination of information and services (Carpenter, King-Sears, & Keys, 1998). Team members from different disciplines perform their specialized functions independently but will share information more often as they assess, plan, and implement programs for students. The results of the team should provide more complementary services and reduce duplication and gaps.

The *transdisciplinary team* is the most recently conceptualized as well as the most collaborative approach among the three. Philosophically, transdisciplinary team members assume the interrelatedness of a student with disabilities' multiple needs (Rainforth & York-Barr, 1997). As professionals and family members work together to integrate goals and objectives from each discipline, skills are shared, roles are exchanged, and mutual training of expertise occurs (Friend & Cook, 2003). For example, the classroom teacher may use strategies she has learned from the occupational therapist to facilitate a child's handwriting goals. This model, used most frequently with students with severe disabilities and in early intervention and preschool programs, could be implemented with children having a variety of disabilities in other settings.

Dimensions

The characteristics of the transdisciplinary approach apply most directly to the interactive teaming model, so they will be summarized here and examined in more detail later in the chapter. The literature offers a number of team features. The first is that the team members have a shared focus, and their goals are aimed toward service delivery. Although it seems simplistic, awareness of team membership also is essential; that is, individuals should perceive themselves and be perceived by others as forming a team (Feldman, 1985). Also, changes in membership can influence effectiveness and should be explained when they occur. Teams function most effectively when operating according to a designated set of norms or values. A key operating norm is maintaining regular meetings and multiple lines of communication for sharing information, knowledge, and skills (Orelove & Sobsey, 1991). Interdependence among team members occurs when members share resources and talents, learn from each other, give and receive help, and divide the work (Snell & Janney, 2000). Friend and Cook (2003) include the team members' unique skills and perspectives in their list of team characteristics as they offer a rich context for creating programs and services. Characteristics specific to transdisciplinary teams include role-release implementation and a professional-development approach where information and skills as well as roles and responsibilities are shared among members (Lyon & Lyon, 1980) and therapy services are integrated instead of delivered in isolation (Orelove & Sobsey, 1991).

Goals

The two obvious goals for teaming approaches are similar to the ones described for consultation: *improvement in treatment or education for a child with special needs,* and the *training of professionals in skills beyond their own areas of expertise.* Other benefits espoused for teaming approaches include improved accuracy for assessment and placement decisions, reduction in referrals to special education (Korinek & McLaughlin, 1996), a forum for sharing a variety of perspectives, the development and evaluation of programs, providing consultative services to parents and community members, and an extension of psychoeducational services into schools (cf. Kaiser & Woodman, 1985; Orelove & Sobsey, 1991; Pfeiffer, 1980, 1981; Reynolds, Gutkin, Elliott, & Witt, 1984). Outcomes for teams also can include technical assistance, role enhancement, and professional development opportunities (Pryzwansky & Rzepski, 1983). Others have suggested that the transdisciplinary team model facilitates viewing the child and family as part of an ecological system of which both family and school are a part (Siders, Riall, Bennett, & Judd, 1987; Stanwood, 1988). Thomas (1986) suggested implementation of a team approach as a strategy to reduce the high school dropout rate.

Competencies

Foley and Mundschenk (1997) noted that the current emphasis on teaming results in at least three implications for preservice and inservice teacher preparation: (1) need for reciprocal cross-disciplinary training, (2) knowledge of the professional perspectives of others, and (3) inclusion of joint instructional and behavior management methods courses, collaboration seminars, and practicum experiences. Katzenbach and Smith (1999) stated that team members need to have technical or functional expertise, problem-solving and decision-making skills, and interpersonal skills such as risk-taking, active listening, and objectivity. Although special educators and psychologists, as well as those from other disciplines, have been expected through role descriptions and legal mandates such as PL 94-142 to participate as team members, the number of training programs designed to improve competencies in this area remains limited. A number of universities have developed programs designed to improve various teaming skills at both preservice and inservice levels (e.g., Courtnage & Healy, 1984; Hudson, Correa, Morsink, & Dykes, 1987; Siders et al., 1987; West, Idol, & Cannon, 1989). These programs are described as competency based and include both coursework and field-based experiences. Competency areas developed in these programs vary and may include consultation theory and models; research on theory, training, and practice; interpersonal communication; collaborative and consultation problem solving; equity issues and values/belief systems; evaluation of consultation effectiveness; systems change; and school politics and power. Other programs are based on an interdisciplinary orientation including general and special educators (e.g., Duchardt, Marlow, Inman, Christensen, & Reeves, 1999; Hudson & Glomb, 1997; Lesar, Benner, Habel, & Colemen, 1997; O'Shea, Williams, & Sattler, 1999; Rosenberg & Rock, 1994). Training skills include some of those previously mentioned as well as collaborative programming; perspectives and attitudes; nonverbal communication skills; verbal and listening skills; and strategies for problem solving, cooperative planning, and managing conflict.

Process

The process or sequence of steps in teaming is determined by the type of need presented and the purpose (e.g., identification, IEP development, change in placement) of the meeting(s). Thus, if the purpose of a meeting is to develop an IEP, the sequence of steps might include the sharing of progress data and the establishment of annual goals by the parents and professionals. If the purpose is a change in placement, team members will need to present their data and justification for the change. An example of a detailed sequence of the major steps for a referral process outlined by Courtnage and Healy (1984) is displayed in Figure 2.4.

Fishbaugh (1997) noted that the "use of teaming requires shared leadership, goal setting, and decision making" (p. 114). She listed four steps in the implementation of the teaming process:

1. *Team focus.* Team members should identify a team vision, goal, or purpose.
2. *Role sharing.* Team roles include a team leader or facilitator, team recorder, team reporter, and team observer.
3. *Individual accountability.* Each team member has to share responsibility for achieving team goals.
4. *Team processing.* Group processing serves as the team critique in order to monitor team effectiveness. (p. 114)

Considering the possible ramifications of forming teams, Mostert (1998) recommended that the reasons for forming a team should be clear to all members. In addition, team members should consider how their other work responsibilities might be affected, the types and amount of resources available, and the procedures under which the team will operate. Finally, the team plan should be discussed with administrators.

Committee Approaches

Four additional examples of professional groups collaborating to provide services to children and adolescents are *teacher assistance teams* (Chalfant, Pysh, & Moultrie, 1979), *school consultation committees* (McGlothlin, 1981), *prereferral intervention models* (Graden, Casey, & Christenson, 1985), and *collaborative inclusion teams* (Gibb et al., 1998). These approaches use many of the consultation strategies previously described, and often are referred to as collaborative consultation models because the educators involved provide indirect services to students. They are designed to assist teachers in making appropriate referrals, as well as to support teachers who are providing services in inclusive settings or working with students who do not qualify for special services. The committees could be considered interdisciplinary in composition, although they often are composed primarily of regular and special educators with occasional involvement from administrators and parents. As typically implemented, they would not be viewed as transdisciplinary because they are

Major flow steps of the referral and interdisciplinary meeting process
1. Gather the initial student information.
2. Complete the initial checklist for identifying behaviors of concern.
3. Designate concerned behaviors and determine the need for data collection.
4. Determine the procedures to collect additional data.
5. Collect additional data, analyze the data, and formulate a referral decision.
6. Complete the referral form.
7. Prepare the pupil for referral.
8. Describe the need for an evaluation meeting and give the roles of participants.
9. Determine relevant student information needed for presentation at the evaluation meeting.
10. Prepare for the evaluation meeting.
11. Evaluate the evaluation meeting—procedures and affective domain.
12. Describe the need for an IEP meeting and give the roles of participants.
13. Determine relevant student information needed for presentation at the IEP meeting.
14. Prepare for the IEP meeting.
15. Evaluate the IEP meeting—procedures and affective domain.
16. Describe the need for the reevaluation meeting and give the roles of participants.
17. Determine the relevant student information needed for presentation at the reevaluation meeting.
18. Prepare for the reevaluation meeting.
19. Evaluate the reevaluation meeting—procedures and affective domain.
20. Describe the need for referring special education students after placement.
21. Activate referral and staffing follow-up activities for those special education students who indicate: (a) unusual progress, (b) significant academic behavior problems, (c) a need for outside resources.

Figure 2.4
The process of teaming.
Source: From "Interdisciplinary Team Training: A Competency- and Procedure-Based Approach", by L. Courtnage and H. Healy, 1984, *Teacher Education and Special Education, 7*, 3–11. Copyright © 1984 by Special Press. Reprinted with permission of Special Press and the Teacher Education Division of the Council for Exceptional Children.

not involved in all of the procedures for a child from assessment to implementation; rather, they are designed to address day-to-day problems that may arise in a particular school or to serve as prereferral screening committees to determine if a student needs to be continued in the referral process and considered for placement in a special program.

Of the approaches, the prereferral intervention model has been implemented most often by state and local school systems and has received increased attention from researchers. It is designed to provide immediate assistance to a teacher seeking help for a child. By its nature, it promotes interactions between general or regular educators and special educators, and results in sharing of problem-solving strategies for students who do not qualify for special services (Pugach & Johnson, 1989a).

Several reviews of research have delineated the positive outcomes of prereferral intervention, including increases in teachers' abilities to meet a variety of needs, improvements in teachers' attitudes toward students with learning and behavior problems, decreases in overidentification of students as having disabilities, and positive changes in student achievement and behavior (cf. Bahr, Whitten, Dieker, Kocarek, & Manson, 1999; Morsink & Lenk, 1992; Nelson, Smith, Taylor, Dodd, & Reavis, 1991; Sindelar, Griffin, Smith, & Watanabe, 1992). However, several authors have also pointed out the problems with quality and validity of research on prereferral (Safran & Safran, 1996; Sindelar et al., 1992), the need for additional training on interventions and formative and summative evaluation procedures (Nelson et al., 1991), the importance of striving to achieve parity between classroom teachers and specialists (Pugach & Johnson, 1989b), and the significance of administrator support on consumers' satisfaction (Kruger, Struzziero, Watts, & Vacca, 1995).

IMPEDIMENTS AND BARRIERS

Consultation

The factors that can hinder the implementation of consultation result from a number of causes. The general structure of schools hinders consultation efforts. The fact that professionals have existed as separate entities for such a long time—and frequently have established their own "language" and "turf"—often makes communication difficult (cf. Reppucci & Saunders, 1974). Not having the time to work together and talk is likely the biggest barrier to implementing consultation (Brownell & Walther-Thomas, 2002). Consultants may find that even when the time is available, the consultees are resistant to their suggestions (Gonzalez, Nelson, Gutkin, & Shwery, 2004). Differences in levels of skill and expertise, as well as the number and type of responsibilities, flexibility in working environment, and differing views of the status of one's position, can present problems (Parker, 1975). Witt (1990) questioned whether a collaborative relationship could be established given the typical hierarchical nature of consultation being provided by "experts" in school settings.

Other impediments include lack of the following: role definition (Haight, 1984), standardization of consultation (Kratochwill & Van Someren, 1985), training for consultants and consultees and inservice programs (Idol & West, 1987; Johnston, 1990; Wilczynski et al., 2000), and policies and leadership at the state level (West & Brown, 1987). Kampwirth (1987) cited two more barriers: the consultant attempting to be all things to all people, and those involved in the process becoming discouraged when change is not immediately evident. Underfunding and faulty assumptions about program effectiveness have been mentioned as well (Huefner, 1988).

Lack of consistent implementation of consultation also has been problematic. As Lilly (1987) noted in an article 16 years after his original description of the concept, "[C]onsultation has been written about more than it has been practiced in special education" (p. 494). This may in fact be due to the lack of conceptual clarity, professional preparation, and mature discussions of the aspects of various models (Friend, 1988). Pragmatic barriers (e.g., insufficient time, overwhelming caseloads); conceptual barriers (e.g., differences in the thinking of special educators and classroom teachers, problems with hierarchies among education professionals); attitudinal barriers, especially the belief that change should be immediate; and professional barriers due to a lack of training or differences in training have been described by a number of authors (e.g., Johnson, Pugach, & Hammitte, 1988; Welch, 1998). In a description of a collaboration project designed to prepare elementary teachers to work in urban settings, Morsink (1999) noted barriers such as confusion about responsibilities, lack of time for collaboration, and the challenges of creating a common mission among different educational entities.

Teaming

Many of the barriers to teaming are similar to those described for consultation, such as the problems associated with a lack of time, the need for appropriate resources (personnel and material), lack of collaborative skills and varying levels of experience of team members, and lack of administrative support (see Karge & McClure, 1995; Mostert, 1998; Walther-Thomas, Bryant, & Land, 1996; Walther-Thomas et al., 2000).

In their discussion of transdisciplinary teams, Orelove and Sobsey (1991) grouped factors that hinder teams into three categories: (1) philosophical and professional challenges (differences in philosophy and orientation of team members, diminishment of professional status, and isolation of parents); (2) interpersonal challenges (threat of training others and threat of being trained, role conflict, or ambiguity); and (3) administrative challenges (failure to understand the approach, resistance to change, concern about professional ethics and liability). Problems identified in the literature continue to support this grouping.

Team operation may pose a barrier if the team does not operate as a participatory group, but rather as a forum for powerful people to develop support for their opinions (Yoshida, 1983). When the process is not going well, members may blame problems on the perceived weaknesses of other members rather than taking responsibility for the team's effective operation (Fleming & Fleming, 1983). Bailey (1984) attributed team dysfunctions to a lack of consideration of teams as developing and changing units composed of subsystems that need to function in a cohesive manner. Karge and McClure (1995) identified negative attitudes as a key barrier to the team process.

Positive Features

Although the barriers described in the preceding section have resulted in some implementation problems for consultation, collaboration, and teaming models, the approaches have several positive features that remain important for consideration.

The first positive feature is of primary importance: the potential for improved services for students with special needs and at risk for school failure. Professionals meeting to share perspectives and knowledge and striving to provide a cohesive and comprehensive array of services will be much better able to address the variety of needs presented by such children than educators, health professionals, or social services operating independently. The results of several studies on consultation and teaming show positive gains for students, as well as improvements in the skills and attitudes of teachers (cf. Adamson, Cox, & Schuller, 1989; Givens-Ogle, Christ, Colman, King-Streit, & Wilson, 1989; Idol-Maestas, 1983; Nelson & Stevens, 1981; Polsgrove & McNeil, 1989).

The second positive feature is the opportunity for the development of professional skills. Although consultation approaches often are viewed as one "expert" providing information to another, in the collaborative consultation models it is recognized that *all* parties have knowledge to share with others. In teaming approaches the range of possible interactions and knowledge exchange becomes even greater because of the number of people from various fields who are involved. In the transdisciplinary teaming model in particular, the opportunities are enhanced because the team operates on a basis of professional sharing from the time of the initial assessment through the implementation phase. An additional benefit that should result from such professional interactions is an increase of collegiality among the people involved, which fosters the development of a professional learning community.

An added positive feature is the role that developing collaborative cultures or a professional learning community can play in teacher retention. In a review of the literature on teacher retention and attrition, Billingsley (2003) found that many of the reasons teachers give for leaving or staying in teaching are related to the work environment. Quality teachers stay in teaching when the climate is positive and collegial, the administration is supportive, and opportunities for professional development are provided. Teachers also want time for reflection and opportunities to have input and feel valued (Langley, Seo, Brownell, Bishop, & Sindelar, 2003). Helping to support beginning teachers through organized and systematic induction programs also facilitates teacher retention. Several key elements of an effective induction program identified by Griffin, Winn, Otis-Wilborn, and Kilgore (2003) are provided in a collaborative environment including a supportive culture that provides opportunities for new as well as experienced teachers to interact, mentor, and offer explicit goals for induction.

ELEMENTS OF SUCCESSFUL COLLABORATIONS

Creating collaborative schools is a developmental process that takes time and nurturing (Pugach & Johnson, 2002). Key requirements have been identified that may facilitate the development and implementation of school-based collaborative approaches. An early review on successful collaborations by Wangemann (cited in

Wangemann, Ingram, & Muse, 1989) noted the following "ingredients" that remain essential today:

1. Clarity of purpose.
2. Complementary dissimilarity between the partners.
3. Overlapping self-interests.
4. Sufficient time to build bridges of communication and trust.
5. Clarification and coordination of roles and responsibilities within the partnership.
6. Shared ownership.
7. Emphasis on action rather than structure building.
8. Adequate resources.
9. Leadership from key administrators.
10. Institutional commitment to the satisfying of mutual self-interests.
11. An ongoing system for research and evaluation.
12. An understanding of each institution's culture.

Effective school leadership is an important variable for developing a collaborative culture. Covey (1991) emphasized the significance of shared values or governing principles, and said strategies, structures, systems, skills, and styles will flow from these values. The philosophy of Deming (1986), which endorses the idea that the role of management or leadership is to improve the system or organization so that individuals can work together, is relevant in education as well as business (Blankstein, 1992). Several of Deming's (1986) principles are especially relevant to teaming models: (1) Create constancy of purpose for improvement of products and services, (2) adopt and institute leadership, (3) break down barriers between staff areas, (4) institute a vigorous program of education and self-improvement for everyone, and (5) put everybody in the organization to work to accomplish the transformation. Trimble and Miller (1996) described ways administrators could maximize team functioning in secondary schools by sharing authority, cultivating teacher leadership, training all team members, using situational leadership, modeling effective team-leadership behaviors, providing incentives, supporting the teams, and moving teams beyond managerial functions.

An array of collaborative structures is available to schools and teachers. Careful consideration of philosophy, school and teacher history, and school goals should be made before adopting any structure. In addition, choosing compatible collaborative structures, combining alternatives, adapting models to fit your needs, and making adjustments based on evaluation data are helpful considerations (Laycock, Gable, & Korinek, 1991). As Pugach and Johnson (2002) remind us, change is slow and not easily achieved. Collaboration will look different from program to program and school to school, with multiple efforts occurring simultaneously.

Certain characteristics can maximize the effectiveness of teams. O'Shea, O'Shea, and Algozzine (1998) identified eight characteristics of effective teams. They stated that effective teams share common goals, are results driven, have competent members, have a unified commitment to their work together, work in a collaborative climate, hold high standards of excellence, have principled leadership, and receive external support and recognition. Other hallmarks of effective teams include face-to-face interactions, positive interdependence, trust, assessment of team functioning, and individual accountability (Fishbaugh, 1997).

Katzenbach and Smith (1999) focused on what they considered team basics: skills, accountability, and commitment. Figure 2.5 illustrates the various components of each area. Based on the research of these authors and others who have been involved in the study or implementation of models that contain components similar to interactive teaming, 10 dimensions have been identified that are considered essential:

1. Legitimacy and autonomy.
2. Purpose and objectives.

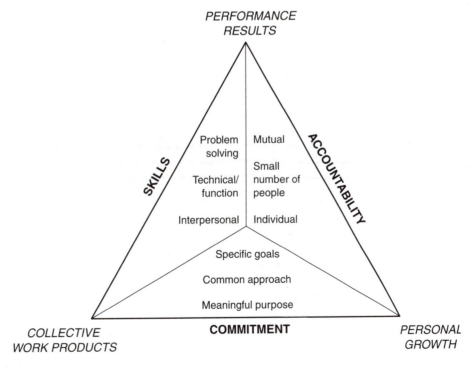

Figure 2.5
Team basics.
Source: Reprinted by permission of Harvard Business School Press. From *The Wisdom of Teams: Creating the High-Performance Organization*, by J. R. Katzenbach and D. K. Smith, Boston, MA, 1999. Copyright © 1999 by McKinsey & Co., all rights reserved.

3. Competencies of team members and clarity of their roles.

4. Role release and role transitions.

5. Awareness of the individuality of team members.

6. Process of team building.

7. Attention to factors that affect team functioning.

8. Leadership styles.

9. Implementation procedures.

10. Commitment to common goals.

Each of these dimensions is examined in more detail in the remainder of this chapter.

Legitimacy and Autonomy

To be successful, any group must have a reason to exist and the freedom to operate. Team decision making and consultation with families are stipulated by Public Laws 94-142, 99-457, 101-476, and amendments to the Individuals with Disabilities Education Act (IDEA); therefore, the legitimacy of a framework such as interactive teaming is supported by law, as well as by a recognition of the need to collaborate by professionals in various fields (cf. Turnbull & Cilley, 1999, or the IDEA Website at http://www.ideapractices.org). However, even if a legal basis exists and individuals endorse teaming, the team and its decisions must be valued by organizations, administrators, and staff to be effective (Phillips & McCullough, 1990).

A second consideration is the necessity of autonomy and the support for this concept. Time and support personnel must be provided for team members so they are able to plan and reflect together, and to be responsive to the accountability measures that often accompany increased autonomy (Friend & Cook, 2003; Pugach, 1988; Snell & Janney, 2000). When collaborative efforts are authorized by the administration, the stage is set for developing a more collaborative environment (Johnson, Pugach, & Devlin, 1990). Collaborative efforts are supported by administrative authorization through organized meeting times for teachers to engage in mutual problem solving, assistance for teachers with clerical work and other noninstructional tasks, and times for collaboration provided in faculty or inservice meetings.

Part of team autonomy is realizing that the "constellation" of people involved may change over time, depending on the purpose of the information sharing (e.g., assessment results) or decision making (e.g., placement, intervention design) about a student or client. As a result, all members of a team may not be involved in every interaction. Consultation and collaboration between individuals or among subgroups should be viewed as enhancing the overall effectiveness of a team and contributing to team consistency and cohesiveness. The interactive teaming model and illustrations of how consultation and collaboration can occur among members are shown in Figure 2.6.

Figure 2.6
The interactive teaming model.

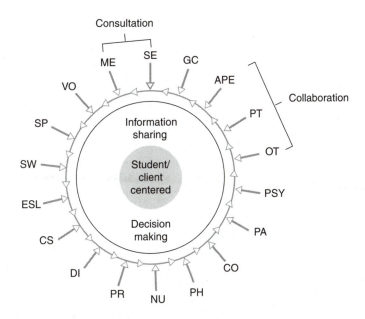

Note: Not all of these persons will need to be present at every meeting.

Key:

PA = Parent
GC = General education classroom teacher
SE = Special educator
SP = Speech-language clinician
SW = Social worker
PH = Physician
PT = Physical therapist
OT = Occupational therapist
APE = Adapted physical educator

PSY = Psychologist
NU = Nurse
CO = Counselor
PR = Principal
DI = Dietician
CS = Computer specialist
ESL = English as a second language
VO = Vocational specialist
ME = Migrant educator

Purpose and Objectives

A team needs an identified purpose, objectives, and performance goals to guide its actions (Katzenbach & Smith, 1999). The major purpose of interactive teaming is to share information and expertise to ensure that the best possible decisions are made and effective programs are implemented. The types of decisions an interactive team can be involved in include those identified by Salvia and Ysseldyke (1988): referral, screening, classification, instructional planning, and evaluation of pupil progress. Specific objectives will be derived from the decisions made and the roles people will play in implementing those decisions (cf. Gutkin, 1996). For example, a social worker may participate in an interactive team meeting at which the decision is made to place a child in a special education program. She is aware of a community program that offers free tutoring for economically disadvantaged students, and she thinks this child would qualify. Her objectives are to determine eligibility, make the necessary contacts if the child is eligible, and then assist with communication with the child's grandmother, who is acting as guardian.

ASPECTS OF TEAM FUNCTIONING

Competencies of Team Members and Clarity of Their Roles

Team members should first be able to demonstrate competencies in their own disciplines before they are expected to acquire knowledge in other areas (Siders et al., 1987). In addition to the discipline-specific competencies, they will need to be competent in the areas previously described as essential for consultants and team members (e.g., collaborative problem solving, interactive communication, leadership, awareness of cultural diversity, referral, and evaluation). Maher and Hawryluk (1983) cited several other considerations for selection of team members: (1) a willingness to receive training in other areas, (2) the ability to participate in a problem-solving situation, (3) possession of enough time to contribute to team processes, and (4) the potential for implementing their own tasks as identified by the team.

Along with attainment of individual competencies, team members must be accurate in their perceptions of the competencies and roles of others (Orelove & Sobsey, 1991). At times members may be unclear about the expertise of people from different disciplines or the roles those people should play in a team situation. Clarity of roles and expertise is essential and will be explored further in Chapter 3.

Role Release and Role Transitions

In addition to understanding the roles and recognizing the competencies of others, team members must be able to "release" their own knowledge and share it with others. *Role release* has been defined by Lyon and Lyon (1980) as referring "to three levels of sharing between two or more members of an educational team: general information, informational skills, and performance competencies" (pp. 253–254). They described the first level as sharing knowledge about basic procedures or practices, for example, a special educator explaining to the principal the behavior management system he or she is using in the classroom. Informational skills include teaching others to make judgments, for example, an adaptive physical educator teaching a regular classroom teacher how to determine if a child is using a correct skipping motion in a game. The third level, performance competencies, includes training another person to perform specified skills, such as an occupational therapist teaching a parent how to use an adaptive feeding device with a child who has a severe disability.

A similar conception of sharing roles and expertise was presented in a publication by the United Cerebral Palsy Association and cited by Golightly (1987). She described the six "role transitions" as follows:

> First, role extension entails designing and implementing instructional objectives within one's own discipline. Second, role enrichment involves designing instructional objectives to include strategies from other disciplines. Third, role expansion involves deriving information from the deliberate pooling of knowledge and skills among team members. Fourth, role exchange permits carrying out the intervention strategies learned from other team members. Fifth, role release involves effectively imparting disciplinary skills to others and providing follow through to ensure appropriate application. Sixth, role support, used in complex interventions, entails using consultative back-up when extensive disciplinary expertise is needed. (p. 128)

Role sharing is most likely to occur in teams where mutual trust is established and professionals are committed to designing the best program for the students, instead of being concerned with protecting their own "turf" (Mather & Weinstein, 1988; Snell & Janney, 2000). Role release is especially important when teachers are working with the inclusion of students with special needs in general education settings (cf. Salend, 1998; Smith, 1998; Tiegerman-Farber & Radziewicz, 1998; Wood, 1998).

Awareness of the Individuality of Team Members

Team members must be aware of each other's individuality. Persons on interactive teams must be cognizant of and sensitive to factors such as cultural differences, variety of backgrounds and educational experiences, and stages of professional development.

Team members must seek to understand their own cultural values and racial identity, as well as the value systems of the racial and ethnic individuals with whom they will be collaborating (Brown et al., 1998). Helms (1992) advocated the development of an "autonomous racial identity." This approach incorporates a "positive view of one's own race, an integration of information about the characteristics of other racial groups—including their similarities and dissimilarities to one's own race, and a dedication to the abandonment of racism" (Brown et al., 1998, p. 162).

Sue, Arredondo, and McDavis (1995) described several multicultural competencies that are applicable to interactive teaming situations: awareness of one's own assumptions, values, and biases and how they affect culturally diverse clients; understanding the worldview of the culturally different client; and developing appropriate intervention strategies. Building on the work of Sue and others, Ramirez, Lepage, Kratchowill, and Duffy (1998) outlined the following competencies: (1) understanding the impact of one's race/ethnicity and culture, (2) valuing and understanding the impact of other races/ethnicities and cultures, (3) adapting a culturally responsive consultation style, and (4) adapting culturally responsive strategies during the problem-solving stages.

Brown and his colleagues (1998) noted that race and ethnicity are variables that influence problem solving and decision making and suggested consultants should be able to "match their worldviews with those of their consultees" (p. 164) and will be able to do so through immersion in the cultural literature. However, Harris (1996) cautions that this method may lead to stereotypes and that it is better to learn about the cultures of those with whom you work (i.e., other team members or consultees) individually instead of as members of a particular group.

In addition to cultural issues, differences in training and approaches to educational services will affect the success of teaming, and such differences need to be explored and addressed. Teachers should explore personality factors, teaching philosophy, and classroom management style before they embark on any collaborative venture, especially an inclusion model (Bruneau-Balderrama, 1997). (See Chapter 3 on roles of team members for additional information.)

Research in the areas of adult learning and professional growth also has implications for interactive teaming. As Fishbaugh (1997) commented, often individuals fail to consider adult stages of development in interactions with coworkers. She stated: "Adults are not finished products. On the contrary, individuals continue to develop throughout their life stages" (p. 133).

Three models useful for understanding adult development are Professional Stages, Career Cycles, and Conceptual Stages. Awareness of these potential differences may enhance a team member's ability to understand another individual's responses and behaviors in certain situations.

Peryon (1982) paralleled the Professional Stages of teachers with the phases of adulthood described by Sheehy (1977). Peryon identified these stages as:

1. *New teachers.* They strive to become the ideal and use what they have been taught; they need support, encouragement, and recognition as professionals.

2. *Teachers with 5 to 10 years of experience.* They have confidence and know what works for them; they need to be recognized as competent.

3. *Middle period of teaching.* They often are rethinking old ideas and analyzing their professional goals for the future; they need to be given a chance to grow and be reinforced for new achievements.

4. *Mature period of teaching.* They have reached self-actualization in terms of their careers; they need to be recognized as top professionals and be needed by others.

Burke, Christensen, and Fessler (1984) presented the concept of Career Cycles. Their model is similar in some ways to the stages described by Peryon; however, it includes induction and both career wind-down and exit. It also incorporates more of a systems view because factors in the personal and organizational environments are included. The Career Cycles are illustrated in Figure 2.7. It is important to note that teachers or other professionals do not necessarily proceed through these cycles sequentially according to years of experience, and in fact they may be in two cycles at the same time. Examples of the latter point are beginning professionals (induction)

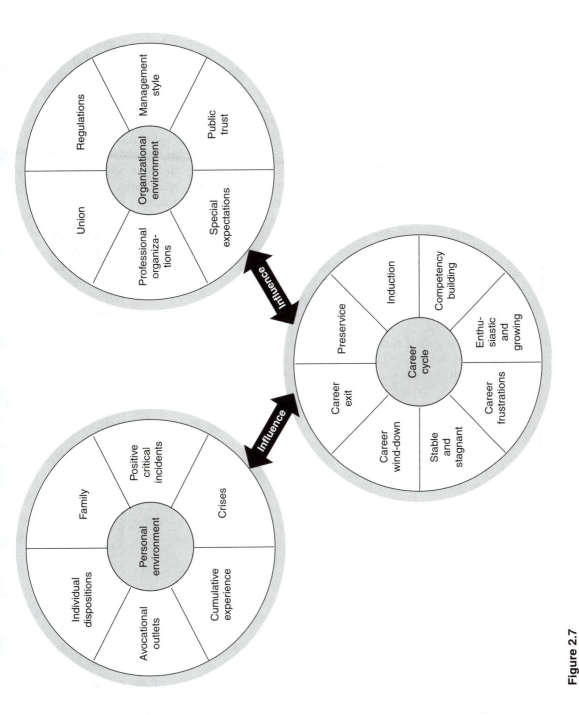

Figure 2.7

A model of the stages of the teacher Career Cycle and the environmental factors that affect it.

Source: From *Teacher Career Stages: Implications for Staff Development*, by P. S. Burke, J. C. Christensen, and R. Fessler, 1984, Bloomington, IN: Phi Delta Kappa Foundation. Reprinted by permission.

who are competent and growing, or beginners who are experiencing career frustration. (For additional information on adult life stages, see Glickman, 1995.)

The third approach to be discussed is the Conceptual Stages of adults identified by Hunt (1981) and further developed by Sprinthall and Thies-Sprinthall (1983). These researchers contend that adults develop a mode of responding to complex situations such as teaching. Their behaviors and verbal comments may be affected by the conceptual stage at which they are functioning. These stages are not necessarily correlated to years of experience or intelligence; rather, they illustrate how a person may respond in a given situation. The three stages of this model (A, B, and C) are described in terms of teacher traits and practices. Stage A is characterized by concrete thinking and highly structured methods of teaching (e.g., reliance on curriculum guide, detailed instructions, sticking to the facts, and Bloom's Level One or Two). In Stage B the teacher moves into more abstract thinking, using some different teaching methods to address student differences, and is more self-directed and autonomous. The Stage 3 teacher's instruction applies all six levels of Bloom's taxonomy, shows evidence of originality in adaptations, and is delivered using appropriate teacher models. The teacher also becomes more reflective of her own practice and its relationship to student learning.

The Process of Team Building

One frustration often voiced by members on a newly formed team is "Things aren't happening quickly enough." Two important considerations interactive team members should recognize are that teams are comprised of individuals, and those individuals must have time to develop as a unit (cf. Bailey, 1984). To do so, teams progress through developmental stages in their formation and operation (Friend & Cook, 1997). Tuckman and Jensen's (1977) five-stage model of team building is probably the most well known:

1. *Forming.* Individuals become oriented to the team; communication networks are started; purpose is discussed.
2. *Storming.* Conflict may occur as members question roles, procedures; polarization may occur; leadership may be tested.
3. *Norming.* Role relationships are redefined; team goals are established; leadership is defined and accepted; trust is built.
4. *Performing.* Members work to accomplish the task.
5. *Adjourning.* Members deal with changes in relationships and feelings about self-esteem, depending on whether the task was satisfactorily completed.

Considering that teams need time to build and for individuals to adjust, team members can understand that immediate efficiency is not always possible. Teams may also move back and forth between stages as they encounter new issues or membership changes. In addition, those who have served on teams before will usually adapt much more quickly than those who are new to this process.

Attention to Factors That Affect Team Functioning

Three areas frequently mentioned as problematic to team functioning are a lack of involvement of all team members, an increase in interprofessional rivalry instead of collaboration or "boundary crossing," and a lack of structure in decision making (cf. Epstein, 1988; Kabler & Genshaft, 1983; Kaiser & Woodman, 1985; Yoshida, 1983). The implications of those areas for interactive teams will be considered in terms of the factors of goal structures, communication climates, roles in meetings, and consensus-building strategies.

Goal Structures.   Three types of goal structures may be held by participants in a group situation (Johnson, Johnson, & Holubec, 1986). The structures are *cooperative,* in which group members seek outcomes that are beneficial for all members of the group; *competitive,* in which the goals of the participants are linked so that each can win only if the others fail; and *individualistic,* in which no correlation exists between the goals of the group and the individuals. In the cooperative goal structure, the one most advantageous to interactive teams, all members of the group contribute to the design of a common solution to a problem. In the competitive structure, each member strives to win independently. In the individual goal structure, members may work side-by-side but alone, because they are working to accomplish their own goals. In their review of the effect of the three types of goal structures on the professional self-esteem, achievement, positive interpersonal relationships, and social support of adults, Johnson and Johnson (1987) found the cooperative structure to be superior in all areas.

Communication Climates.   Two distinctly different climates of teams can be readily identified by the behaviors of the participants (Gibb, 1961). In a *defensive climate,* participants may attempt to evaluate another's ideas in a judgmental manner. In a *supportive climate,* participants encourage others to describe events and situations, and they in turn attempt to describe what other speakers have said. In the defensive mode, the participant attempts to control the discussion by dominating or lecturing; in the supportive mode, the person asks others to assist in identifying the problem and possible solutions.

In a defensive climate, team members may enter a meeting with a predetermined strategy designed to manipulate the others into a decision. In a supportive climate, team members have engaged in planning, but their reactions are more spontaneous, depending on the needs of other group members and the situation. They allow others to express concerns and ideas that may not be on "their lists."

In a defensive mode, participants may be neutral, stating, "It doesn't matter to me" or "I don't care—whatever you want is fine." The neutrality of suggesting that anything others want is acceptable indicates this person is defensive by virtue of being uninvolved and unconcerned. In contrast, the supportive team member expresses empathy by restating and attempting to clarify feelings and ideas that may affect the problem.

Superiority is descriptive of the defensive climate, and equality is representative of supportive interactions. The school psychologist who acts as if she knows more than the others in the group, or the special educator who behaves as if general educators are "unspecial" and have nothing to contribute, is expressing superiority. In contrast, the principal who tells a parent that her observations of the child at home are important is emphasizing equality. Each participant is acknowledged as having a contribution to make to understand the problem; in this case, the mother's expertise in the child's developmental history and home behaviors is given recognition.

Considering the various types of goal structures and communication climates is important for interactive team members who wish to interact effectively with others on the team. The individual who is cooperative—who wants the group goals to be facilitated, as opposed to having his or her own agenda—is more successful in working with others. The individual who is supportive rather than defensive is better able to assist the group in achieving and maintaining a problem-solving focus.

Roles in Team Meetings.   In a classic study on the roles members can play in team meetings, Benne and Sheats (1948) noted that group participation can be divided into three categories of roles: *task, maintenance,* and *negative.* Both leaders and group members can play these roles, and all can play several roles during the course of a meeting. Task and maintenance roles are the ones most facilitating to the process of interactive teaming. A summary of the roles adapted from the work by Hybels and Weaver (1997) is included in Figure 2.8.

Consensus Building.   In addition to the goal structures, communication climates, and roles that members can play during meetings, the *decision-making processes* used to reach consensus will affect the team's functioning. If a process is not used, members tend to become frustrated and believe the team is not accomplishing anything, or that other team members do not value their thoughts and ideas.

In interactive teaming, participants should strive to work as a team and reach consensus decisions whenever possible. For consensus to be reached, team members must be aware of the needs of all involved and agree on a process for determining team decisions.

A number of decision-making processes have been identified in the literature. The challenge for team members is selecting the most appropriate one for their situation. Most are similar to the sequence suggested by Doyle and Strauss (1976) and further developed by Margolis and Brannigan (1987). These authors recommended the following steps: (1) define the problem, (2) analyze the problem and any factors that could be contributing to it, (3) generate possible alternatives, (4) establish and agree on criteria for selecting solutions, and (5) select and evaluate possible solutions.

Two examples of decision-making processes are Problem Resolution Through Communication by Fine, Grantham, and Wright (1979), and the Nominal Group

Task Roles

These people help get the task done, assist in coming up with new ideas, and aid in collecting and organizing information:
- *Initiators-expediters* suggest ideas and help keep the group on task.
- *Information givers and seekers* will track down information and enhance the quality of the discussion.
- *Critics-analyzers* look at the good and the bad in the data, detect points that need additional elaboration, discover information that has been left out, and model organized behavior.

Maintenance Roles

The people fulfilling these roles focus on the emotional tone of the meeting and also help keep the meeting going:
- *Encouragers* praise others for their contributions and the group's progress, are active listeners, and help others feel good about what is happening.
- *Harmonizers-compromisers* help resolve conflicts and determine solutions that are acceptable to everyone. They also remind others that group goals are more important than individual agendas.
- *Observers* help further group cohesiveness, and are sensitive and aware of the needs of each person.

Negative Roles

The individuals who are playing these roles slow the group down and interfere with progress:
- *Aggressors-resistors* attack others to make themselves look superior.
- *Recognition-seekers* and *self-confessors* call attention to themselves and make contributions that are off-task or lengthy.
- *Help seekers* join groups to meet their own needs and use the group to further their own agendas.
- *Withdrawers* make no contributions and may appear bored or shy.

Figure 2.8
Roles in team meetings.
Source: From *Communicating Effectively* (pp. 240–244), by S. Hybels and R. L. Weaver, 1997, New York: McGraw-Hill. Adapted by permission of McGraw-Hill, Inc.

Technique developed by Delbecq, Van de Ven, and Gustafson (1975) and summarized by Kaiser and Woodman (1985). Problem Resolution Through Communication stresses listening and communication skills, and it includes considerations of feelings and taking another's point of view (Figure 2.9). Nominal Group Technique is especially useful in ensuring that all team members participate in the decision-making process and that the decision reflects a consensus of the group. The steps in the Nominal Group Technique are listed in Figure 2.10.

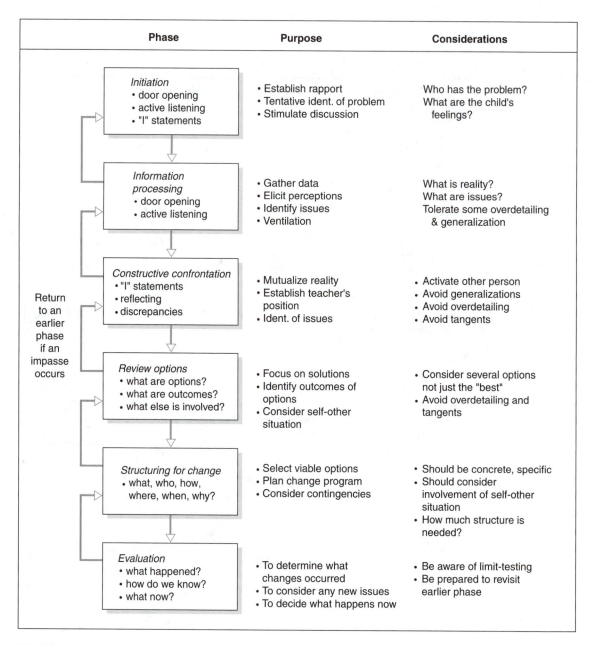

Phase	Purpose	Considerations

Initiation
• door opening
• active listening
• "I" statements

• Establish rapport
• Tentative ident. of problem
• Stimulate discussion

Who has the problem?
What are the child's
  feelings?

Information processing
• door opening
• active listening

• Gather data
• Elicit perceptions
• Identify issues
• Ventilation

What is reality?
What are issues?
Tolerate some overdetailing
  & generalization

Constructive confrontation
• "I" statements
• reflecting
• discrepancies

• Mutualize reality
• Establish teacher's
  position
• Ident. of issues

• Activate other person
• Avoid generalizations
• Avoid overdetailing
• Avoid tangents

Review options
• what are options?
• what are outcomes?
• what else is involved?

• Focus on solutions
• Identify outcomes of
  options
• Consider self-other
  situation

• Consider several options
  not just the "best"
• Avoid overdetailing and
  tangents

Structuring for change
• what, who, how,
  where, when, why?

• Select viable options
• Plan change program
• Consider contingencies

• Should be concrete, specific
• Should consider
  involvement of self-other
  situation
• How much structure is
  needed?

Evaluation
• what happened?
• how do we know?
• what now?

• To determine what
  changes occurred
• To consider any new issues
• To decide what happens now

• Be aware of limit-testing
• Be prepared to revisit
  earlier phase

Return to an earlier phase if an impasse occurs

Figure 2.9
Problem resolution through communication.

Source: From "Personal Variables That Facilitate or Impede Consultation", by M. J. Fine, V. L. Grantham, and J. G. Wright, 1979, *Psychology in the Schools, 16,* p. 537. Reprinted by permission of John Wiley & Sons, Inc.

Step 1—Silent generation of ideas in writing. Each member is asked to write down key ideas related to the issue under consideration silently and independently. The benefits of this step are that members can think/reflect freely; interruptions are avoided; undue focusing on a particular idea or content area is minimized; competition, status pressure, and conformity are avoided; the group remains problem-centered; and the group avoids selecting a choice prematurely.

Step 2—Round-robin recording of ideas. Each member is asked sequentially to provide one idea until all ideas are processed. The group leader records each item on a blackboard or flip chart. Benefits include: equal participation, increase in problem-mindedness, depersonalization—the separation of ideas from personalities, an increase in the ability to deal with a larger number of ideas, tolerance for conflicting ideas, encouragement of hitchhiking (generating new ideas from presented ideas), and the development of a written record.

Step 3—Serial discussion for clarification. Each idea is discussed in turn. During this process, each item can potentially receive adequate discussion/clarification, logic can be provided behind arguments and disagreements, and differences of opinion can be recorded without undue argumentation. It is important to stress here that steps 2 and 3 are solely for idea generation and clarification and not evaluation.

Step 4—Preliminary vote on item importance. Each member independently rank orders, in his or her opinion, the most salient items. Typically, a limit is placed (e.g., each member's top five). Independent listing minimizes status, personality characteristics, and conformity pressures. From the total list, the most salient items emerge, ranked in order, based on the total frequency of each item.

Step 5—Discussion of the preliminary vote—(optional). Each member is allowed a brief period to comment on the selected items. This allows the group to examine inconsistent voting patterns and also allows for discussion of items that received unusually high or low rankings.

Step 6—Final vote. The group combines individual judgment into a group decision using a mathematical procedure. This allows for a sense of closure, accomplishment, and documentation. It is important to note that the mathematical resolution may take the form of a rank ordering, a system of rating each item, or the selection of a single best item based on the frequency of votes for each item. The procedure should fit the group's needs.

Figure 2.10

Nominal group technique.

Source: From "Multidisciplinary Teams and Group Decision-Making Techniques: Possible Solutions to Decision-Making Problems", by S. M. Kaiser and R. W. Woodman, 1985, *School Psychology Review, 14,* pp. 464–465. Copyright 1985 by The National Association of School Psychologists, Bethesda, MD. Reprinted by permission of the publisher.

Leadership Styles

Leadership behaviors, styles, and beliefs are integral to the success of an interactive team. As will be explained in Chapter 5, any member of the team can serve as the leader, but someone must assume that role for the team's work to be completed. An individual may or may not assume the role of leader for the team based on his or her level of expertise in a given situation (Fishbaugh, 1997). The leader's role is to build commitment, fill gaps, and shift the leadership role as appropriate (Katzenbach & Smith, 1999).

Administrators such as principals, directors, or division heads do not have to function as team leaders in interactive teaming situations, but they can assist the team's work in other ways. Administrators need to provide program advocacy and promote the goals of collaborative efforts (Gerber, 1991). In addition, Gerber points out that the administrator's visible participation enhances credibility. Support for maintenance and durability of collaboration must be ongoing. An administrator in a team model works to create an environment in which team members feel empowered; such a leader has self-confidence and trust in others (Garner, 1995). Fuller (1998) had similar observations, noting that the leader must be someone who can provide guidance but who will let the team operate without undue interference.

Salisbury and McGregor (2002) studied five building principals known for their exemplary work. They found these principals to be self-directed risk takers, invested in relationships, accessible, reflective, collaborative, and intentional. These characteristics are similar to those described by advocates of schools becoming professional learning communities. Administrators working to facilitate professional learning communities engage in building shared knowledge for shared decision making, forming collaborative teams arriving at consensus, and having a focus on learning (DuFour, 2003).

Leadership styles affect how team meetings are conducted, the views others may have toward the person in the role of leader, and the opinions of the success of a model or system being implemented. The beliefs leaders have about what they consider to be the "rules of the game" also will affect the functioning of the team.

Hybels and Weaver (1997) identified three leadership styles in conducting team meetings: authoritarian, democratic, and laissez-faire. The *authoritarian* leader is definitely in charge and controls who talks and what they discuss. Under this type of leadership, individuals may not feel free to contribute or to share their honest opinions. The *democratic* leader ensures that all points of view are recognized and that all members are involved in contributing to a decision. This type of leadership generally results in increased motivation for team members and more creativity in decisions generated. The *laissez-faire* leader does not require or actually assume a responsibility for leading the group. As a result, typically very little is accomplished. The type of leadership style most appropriate for interactive teaming is the democratic style; however, if time for decision making is limited, the authoritarian style may have to be implemented on a short-term basis, but contributions from all members should still be encouraged. The laissez-faire style would not be suitable unless the purpose of the meeting is simply interaction without the necessity of accomplishing a task or making a decision.

Beliefs about the "rules of the game" when serving as a team leader will affect how one fulfills the role. The rules listed in Figure 2.11 are derived from literature, interviews with leaders, and personal experiences. Some are stated humorously, not because they should be taken lightly, but rather because "many a truth is stated in jest."

1. **Always do right. This will gratify some people and astonish the rest.** This rule can seldom be violated, even by those with established power. *Right* is defined in different ways by various societies and cultures, so it is essential that the leader learn the values of the culture or society. An entry-level leader must project and possess absolute integrity in the conduct of all affairs, and must understand that the standards are applied more rigorously to his or her conduct than to the conduct of others.

2. **Rose-colored glasses never come in bifocals.** This is another way of saying that there are no knights in shining armor who go around righting all wrongs with a stroke of the sword. The behaviors of a leader are often less than "perfect" in the judgment of others who do not have the total perspective that would enable them to understand the rationale for decision making. Sometimes a leader may have to struggle with what is "right" and balance it with what is essential to help someone save face or to comply with political realities that will allow a different "right" to occur in the future.

3. **If you mess up, 'fess up!** Everyone makes errors. Experienced leaders who don't admit and learn from their mistakes are bound to repeat them. Potential leaders who don't admit and learn from their mistakes will not be given an opportunity to repeat them. Successful leaders try to anticipate and prevent errors; when they have erred, they make sure they don't repeat them. They do this by rehearsing and planning, so that possible events are anticipated whenever possible.

4. **Criticism is a compliment.** The inability to accept and to profit from constructive criticism often prevents people from becoming successful leaders. Using the comments of others to one's own benefit can help a person grow in a role and be able to fulfill self- and others' expectations.

5. **If you yell at the umpire, you get thrown out of the game.** Experienced leaders know that you should not confront authority figures in public or cause them to lose face in front of others, even if they are wrong. They know that when you have an honest disagreement with the authority person, you should go to that person's office and close the door for your discussion. When you emerge, you should support the commonly agreed-upon position.

6. **Don't go off half-cocked until you have all the facts.** Overreaction is a common error, particularly among first-time leaders who might think they need to assert their authority. It can be costly, particularly if an action is taken before the whole picture is assessed.

7. **If I didn't laugh, my heart would break.** If the role of leader is taken seriously all the time, it is easy to become tense and discouraged, and eventually ineffective. Sometimes the best way to deal with a situation is to laugh and relieve some of the tension.

8. **Follow the invisible leader—the common purpose.** The most effective leaders have learned how to generate group support for their ideas by instilling within the group a sense of "ownership" for the ideas. They begin by listening carefully to what others have to say and by analyzing the effect of a particular plan on other team members.

Continued

Figure 2.11
Rules of the game.

9. **Speak softly but carry a big stick.** Some people who aspire to become leaders or who find themselves in leadership roles think they have to prove they are powerful by being pushy. This behavior usually has the opposite effect of turning people away from their leadership. Those who are successful have learned the value of using a soft, polite tone rather than acting every role as if they were starring in a tough-guy movie.

10. **It ain't over 'til it's over.** Going back into the game to try again, even in the face of an apparent defeat, is the mark of a champion. All experienced leaders know that you win some and you lose some. It isn't important, or possible, to win them all. Keeping your perspective is a matter of understanding that the score at the end of the game is more important than the score at the half, and that the win/loss record at the end of the season is the record that counts. Effective leaders are persistent in the face of obstacles. When they fail to win their points, they come back to pursue the issue in a different way or at another time.

Figure 2.11
Continued.

IMPLEMENTATION OF INTERACTIVE TEAMING

Implementation Procedures

The actual procedures involved in implementing the interactive teaming process should and will vary depending on such factors as the age of the child, the severity of the problem, and the types of professionals available. The steps presented in Figure 2.12 are generic ones that will need to be adapted to specific situations (cf. Aldinger et al., 1991; Fishbaugh, 1997; Gutkin & Curtis, 1990; Jayanthi & Friend, 1992; Mostert, 1998; Voltz et al., 1995). Additional information on implementing these procedures for different types of students is provided in Chapters 8 through 12.

Guidelines to remember when implementing the steps are (1) encourage everyone to contribute during the discussion, including the person presenting the situation; (2) reach consensus on the definition of the problem before discussing possible interventions; and (3) consider all factors that could be relevant to the problem or possible interventions. These factors could include materials, teaching techniques, antecedents and consequences of behaviors, criterion level of performance expected, classroom and home environments, and mastery of prerequisite skills.

Interactive team members also need to remain focused on the mutual and reciprocal sharing of ideas throughout the process, and guard against the team becoming dominated by one individual. O'Shea et al. (1998) noted:

Collaborative approaches can easily become expert systems unless participants consciously work to prevent this from happening. Because of professional role designations

The following steps need to be adapted to specific situations, including whether this is a first meeting, a follow-up meeting, or a meeting to make a specific decision such as determination of placement.

1. The person designated as leader or chairperson should *notify the other members* of a meeting time and place, and distribute any available background information to be read before the discussion.

2. At the beginning of the meeting, the leader should make sure everyone has met the others and *state the purpose* and agenda items.

3. The person who requested the meeting should *describe the problem(s)*. Other group members should ask questions for clarification, if necessary, and also contribute their own observations to corroborate or contrast with the problem being described.

4. The group should reach consensus on a specific, measureable, and observable *definition of the problem*. (For example, if the problem presented is "Gerry has a bad attitude about school," group members should ask questions and discuss the situation to determine if this means she does not start assignments when directions are given, is not making passing grades on tests, is not submitting her homework, or has been truant.)

5. If more than one problem is identified, each should be discussed, and then all should be *prioritized in terms of importance* to the child's and adult's well-being, *and in terms of severity levels*. The desired level of performance (e.g., 75% or better on tests, no more than two absences per month) also should be determined.

6. The *history and frequency* of the problem should be determined (e.g., the problem has occurred 17 times in the last 4 weeks).

7. Any *previous interventions attempted* should be discussed, and their success or lack of success should be presented. This is an important step to keep from continually suggesting ideas that have been attempted, and it is also an opportunity to build on strategies that have proved effective.

8. All team members should *brainstorm possible interventions*. Consensus should be reached on which interventions should be attempted in which order and by whom. Consistency in applying reinforcers and consequences should be a primary consideration. If consensus is not readily obtainable, one of the strategies described in this chapter on communication skills, such as the Nominal Group Technique, should be used.

9. Procedures for *collecting data* should be established. It is important to have a data collection system and to implement it to decide on the effectiveness or failure of an intervention. The major criteria for the data collection system are that it measures the target behavior accurately, is easy to implement, and does not interfere with teaching (cf. Tawney & Gast, 1984).

10. The *data decision rules* should be determined (i.e., how long an intervention will be attempted before switching to another one). An important consideration is that the intervention needs to be applied consistently and on consecutive days for at least 3 to 5 days before a decision can be made on whether it is having the desired

Continued

Figure 2.12
Implementation procedures.

effect. An additional consideration is that for some behaviors such as talk-outs, an intervention that involves removal of attention (e.g., ignoring) may result in the behavior getting worse before it gets better.

11. The *responsibilities* for each team member should be clarified. If one or more members are going to provide information or materials, conduct additional observations, consult with others, or serve as reinforcers or people who will deliver negative consequences, these expectations should be clear to everyone.

12. A *timeline for activities* and a follow-up meeting to assess progress should be scheduled.

13. The team should meet regularly to *evaluate the interventions* to determine if changes or modifications need to be made.

14. Members of the team should meet as needed to provide *consultative and collaborative* assistance to each other.

15. Team members should *evaluate team effectiveness* periodically and determine if any changes need to be made in operating procedures, team composition, or other areas.

Figure 2.12
Continued.

(e.g., administrator, school psychologist, special educator), specialty skills certain members may possess, and/or past experiences working together, "experts" within problem-solving groups may emerge. Teams committed to professional collaboration need to remember to: (a) establish a reliable, problem-solving format, (b) utilize effective communication skills, (c) periodically discuss their fundamental assumptions of effective collaboration, and (d) monitor their team's interactions on an ongoing basis to ensure the process is working effectively. (p. 339)

Commitment to Common Goals

The final dimension necessary for an interactive team to be a successful and effective operating unit is shared commitment to common goals. The primary goal is to meet the needs of students. To accomplish this within an interactive teaming framework, team members must believe that collaboration, teaming, and integrating services are viable and vital ways to meet students' needs. As Mostert (1998) commented:

Most societies and organizations operate on the understanding that, at least for part of the time, it is necessary for members to collaborate for the good of a common goal—a goal that most or all members agree is worth attaining. The necessity of collaboration should not eliminate the need for competition or individualism, but should rather be viewed as one tool for achieving certain goals that may be untenable in any other way. For example, collaborative efforts in certain circumstances may often achieve much more than any individual effort: many positive benefits are derived from working with others, and collective ownership and responsibility in professional work are often seen as preferable to individual risk-taking. (p. 15)

Consistent with this belief, those involved in interactive teaming must recognize that the "whole is greater than the sum of the parts"; that is, professionals and parents can achieve better results working together than when they operate as individuals or separate disciplines (Dunn, 1989; Garner, 1995; Gutkin, 1996; Pugach, 1988). The services provided will be more comprehensive and less fragmented, multiple interventions can be implemented simultaneously, and the chances of behaviors being learned and generalized are greatly increased (Adamson et al., 1989; Golightly, 1987; Idol et al., 1994).

A secondary goal, which follows from the first, is the support of the concepts of professional development and role release. Professionals and parents must be willing to share ideas and techniques with others, and support their fellow team members in implementing what has been learned. Such sharing may require "paradigm shifts" to better understand one another (Lopez, Dalal, & Yoshida, 1993), and taking responsibility for one's own learning as well as the learning of others (Skrtic, 1991).

If the commitment to students rather than "turf" or the commitment to assist fellow team members is missing, the team concept will not succeed. If the commitment and the other dimensions are present, the interactive team can be effective. As illustrated in Figure 2.13, the effective team is unified in working toward a shared goal, and the ineffective team is bogged down.

We next examine two descriptions of a team meeting, one unsuccessful and the other successful. In the first example, the leader does not seem aware of the necessary dimensions of teaming. He is not aware of the individuality of team members, does not attend to the process of team building, uses an inappropriate sequence of procedures, and exhibits an ineffective leadership style. Note how these factors interplay to produce an unsuccessful, dysfunctional teaming session.

APPLICATION: Unsuccessful Teaming

At the beginning of the first meeting of the team, the leader stated that this session needed to be "short and sweet" because he had a more important meeting to attend in 30 minutes. The foster mother for Angelina was immediately angered by the comment. She emphatically stated that she was not interested in participating in a meeting that people did not consider important. The social worker tried to calm her down, and suggested that the meeting proceed but that they could schedule additional time if needed. The leader then said, "Well, we all know that Angelina has been abused, and her biological mother is a crack cocaine addict. Now who has some ideas on what can be done?" The psychologist said he would like to share test results, but the special educator broke in and said she needed to know how to handle this child in her classroom tomorrow, because she had displayed very aggressive behaviors for the past 2 days. The foster mother began to describe how she used time-out at home, but the leader said, "I'm sorry to interrupt, but I really must leave for my next meeting. When would you like to meet again?"

In the second example, the leader ensures that the competencies of team members are recognized and their roles are clear. He allows time for the team to build and follows a sequence of steps to lead the group through the meeting. He also promotes the concept of role release. Notice how these factors promote successful teaming.

AN EFFECTIVE TEAM

A team is a unified group of people who join in a cooperative problem-solving process to reach a shared goal.

AN INEFFECTIVE TEAM

- Goals are unclear.
- Members are unprepared.
- Leadership is poor.
- Commitment to task is lacking.

EFFECTIVE

Participation and leadership are distributed among all members.

Goals are cooperatively formed to meet individual and group needs.

Ability and information determine influence and power.

Two-way communication occurs.

Decision-making steps are matched with situation; consensus is sought for important decisions.

Conflict is brought out and resolved.

INEFFECTIVE

Participation is unequal, leadership is delegated and based on authority.

Members accept imposed goals.

Position determines influence; obedience to authority is stressed.

Communication about ideas is one-way; feelings are ignored.

Decisions are made by the highest authority with minimal member involvement.

Conflict is ignored, avoided, or denied.

Figure 2.13

Characteristics of effective and ineffective teams.

Source: From "An Inservice Program for Improving Team Participation in Educational Decision-Making", by L. S. Anderlini, 1983, *School Psychology Review, 12,* p. 163. Copyright 1983 by the National Association of School Psychologists, Bethesda, MD. Reprinted by permission of the publisher.

APPLICATION: Successful Teaming

At the beginning of the first team meeting, the leader asked all the members to introduce themselves and describe their roles and relationships to Angelina. After this was accomplished, the leader suggested that each person share any observations or assessment data that had been completed at the time. He also encouraged team members to ask questions as each individual gave his or her report. Next, he asked everyone to identify what he or she considered to be the primary problems in this case.

After a discussion that included the history and frequency of the problems, the group was able to reach consensus that the two top-priority problems were Angelina's kicking others and hitting herself on the head. The leader asked if anyone had identified interventions that were successful for either of these behaviors. The foster mother described how she had used time-out, and the special educator discussed how she had used selective attention and praised Angelina when she interacted appropriately. The counselor suggested including Angelina in a peer group that she conducted for abused and acting-out students. The adapted physical educator discussed games he could share with the special educator that developed cooperation skills.

The leader recommended closing the meeting and scheduling the next meeting in 2 weeks to discuss Angelina's progress and how the interventions of time-out and selective attention were working in the other settings. He also recommended that individual group members continue their discussions in the intervening time so information on particular strategies could be shared. The counselor agreed to contact the foster mother about the groups, and the special educator and adapted physical educator agreed to meet the next day to continue their discussion on cooperative games.

SUMMARY

An examination of consultation, collaboration, and teaming reveals that:

◆ A variety of models have been reviewed in the literature.

◆ Dimensions, goals, competencies, and processes are similar in many instances.

◆ The approaches have barriers that can interfere with successful implementation.

◆ Among the positive features for consultation, collaboration, and teaming are the documented gains for students and professionals.

◆ Several components of consultation and teaming approaches that have been described in this chapter are incorporated into the interactive teaming model proposed in this text. Consideration of the research of models and programs with components of interactive teaming suggests that 10 dimensions must be present for the model to be effective:
  ◆ Legitimacy and autonomy.
  ◆ Purpose and objectives.

- Competencies of team members and clarity of their roles.
- Role release and role transitions.
- Awareness of the individuality of team members.
- Process of team building.
- Attention to factors that affect team functioning.
- Leadership styles.
- Implementation procedures.
- Commitment to common goals.

Factors considered to be possible barriers to interactive teaming—such as a lack of role understanding and communication skills, leadership problems, and a lack of awareness of cultural and family considerations—are addressed in the next section of this text.

ACTIVITIES

1. Interview a professional involved in service delivery to at-risk children or students with special needs. Ask how role release is accomplished in his or her job. Also ask which aspects of the role are difficult to release, and which aspects someone who does not have professional training in that area should not attempt.

2. Describe the professional growth opportunities you believe you would gain from being involved in consultation, collaboration, and/or teaming approaches. Would you need additional training to feel that you could be an effective consultant, collaborator, or team member?

3. Observe a team meeting and analyze the *goal structures, communication climates,* and *roles* that occur. What contributed to each? Were people consistent or did they change during the course of the meeting?

4. Interview four professionals who have been on teams. Ask them how the team was established and maintained. Also ask them to identify the decision-making processes and implementation procedures used by their teams. Finally, ask them to classify the leadership style of the person in charge of the team as authoritarian, democratic, or laissez-faire.

REFERENCES

Adamson, D. R., Cox, J., & Schuller, J. (1989). Collaboration/consultation: Bridging the gap from resource room to regular classroom. *Teacher Education and Special Education, 12,* 46–51.

Aldinger, L. E., Warger, C. L., & Eavy, P. W. (1991). *Strategies for teacher collaboration.* Ann Arbor, MI: Exceptional Innovations, Inc.

Aloia, G. F. (1983). Special educators' perceptions of their roles as consultants. *Teacher Education and Special Education, 6,* 83–87.

Bahr, M. W., Whitten, E., Dieker, L., Kocarek, C. E., & Manson, D. (1999). A comparison of school-based intervention teams: Implications for educational and legal reform. *Exceptional Children, 66*(1), 67–83.

Bailey, D. B. (1984). A triaxial model of the interdisciplinary team and group process. *Exceptional Children, 51,* 17–25.

Benne, K. D., & Sheats, P. (1948). Functional roles of group members. *Journal of Social Issues, 4,* 41–49.

Bergan, J. R. (1977). *Behavioral consultation.* Columbus, OH: Merrill.

Billingsley, B. S. (2003). *Special education teacher retention and attrition: A critical analysis of the literature* (COPSSE Document No. RS-2). Gainesville, FL: University of Florida, Center on Personnel Studies in Special Education. Retrieved January 2004, from COPPSE Website at http://www.coe.ufl.edu/copsse/main.php?page=019

Blankstein, A. M. (1992). Lessons from enlightened corporations, *Educational Leadership, 49,* 71–75.

Blanton, L. P., Griffin, C. C., Winn, J. A., & Pugach, M. C. (Eds.). (1997). *Teacher education in transition: Collaborative programs to prepare general and special educators.* Denver, CO: Love Publishing Co.

Brown, B., Pryzwansky, W. B., & Schulte, A. C. (1998). *Psychological consultation: Introduction to theory and practice.* Needham Heights, MA: Allyn & Bacon.

Brown, D., Wyne, M. D., Blackburn, J. E., & Powell, W. C. (1979). *Consultation: Strategy for improving education.* Boston: Allyn & Bacon.

Brown, L. F., Kiraly, J., & McKinnon, A. (1979). Resource rooms: Some aspects for special educators to ponder. *Journal of Learning Disabilities, 12,* 56–58.

Brownell, M. T., & Walther-Thomas, C. (2002). An interview with Dr. Marilyn Friend. *Intervention in School and Clinic, 37*(4), 223–228.

Bruneau-Balderrama, O. (1997). Inclusion: Making it work for teachers, too. *The Clearing House, 70*(6), 328–330.

Burke, P. S., Christensen, J. C., & Fessler, R. (1984). *Teacher career stages: Implications for staff development.* Bloomington, IN: Phi Delta Kappa Foundation.

Carpenter, S. L., King-Sears, M. E., & Keys, S. G. (1998). Counselors + educators + families as a transdisciplinary team = More effective inclusion for students with disabilities. *Professional School Counseling, 2*(1), 9.

Chalfant, J. C., Pysh, M. V., & Moultrie, R. (1979). Teacher assistance teams: A model for within-building problem solving. *Learning Disability Quarterly, 2,* 85–96.

Cipani, E. (1985). The three phases of behavioral consultation: Objectives, intervention, and quality assurance. *Teacher Education and Special Education, 8,* 144–152.

Conoley, J. C., & Conoley, C. W. (1992). *School consultation: A guide to practice and training* (2nd ed.). Boston: Allyn & Bacon.

Courtnage, L., & Healy, H. (1984). Interdisciplinary team training: A competency- and procedure-based approach. *Teacher Education and Special Education, 7,* 3–11.

Covey, S. R. (1991). *Principle-centered leadership.* New York: Simon & Schuster.

Cramer, S. F. (1998). *Collaboration: A success strategy for special educators.* Needham Heights, MA: Allyn & Bacon.

Delbecq, A. L., Van de Ven, A. H., & Gustafson, D. H. (1975). *Group techniques for program planning: A guide to Nominal Group and Delphi processes.* Glenview, IL: Scott, Foresman.

Deming, W. E. (1986). *Out of the crisis.* Boston: MIT Center for Advanced Engineering Studies.

Dettmer, P., Thurston, L. P., & Dyck, N. (1993). *Consultation, collaboration, and teamwork for students with special needs.* Boston: Allyn & Bacon.

Doyle, M., & Strauss, D. (1976). *How to make meetings work: The new interaction method.* Chicago: Playboy Press.

Duchardt, B., Marlow, L., Inman, D., Christensen, P., & Reeves, M. (1999). Collaboration and co-teaching: General and special education faculty. *The Clearing House, 72*(3), 186–193.

DuFour, R. (2003). Building a professional learning community: For system leaders, it means allowing autonomy within defined parameters. *School Administrator, 60*(5), 13–19.

Dunn, W. (1989). Integrated related services for preschoolers with neurological impairments: Issues and strategies. *Remedial and Special Education, 10*(3), 31–39.

Epstein, L. (1988). *Helping people: The task centered approach.* New York: Merrill/Macmillan.

Evans, S. (1981). Perceptions of classroom teachers, principals, and resource room teachers of actual and desired roles of the resource teacher. *Journal of Learning Disabilities, 14,* 600–603.

Feldman, R. S. (1985). *Social psychology: Theories, research, and applications.* New York: McGraw-Hill.

Fine, M. J., Grantham, V. L., & Wright, J. G. (1979). Personal variables that facilitate or impede consultation. *Psychology in the Schools, 16,* 533–539.

Fine, M. J., & Tyler, M. M. (1971). Concerns and directions in teacher consultation. *Journal of School Psychology, 9,* 436–444.

Fishbaugh, M. S. E. (1997). *Models of collaboration.* Needham Heights, MA: Allyn & Bacon.

Fleming, D. C., & Fleming, E. R. (1983). Problems in implementation of the team approach: A practitioner's perspective. *School Psychology Review, 12,* 144–149.

Foley, R. M. (1994). Collaboration activities and competencies of special educators serving students with behavior disorders. *Special Services in the Schools, 8*(2), 69–90.

Foley, R. M., & Mundschenk, N. A. (1997). Collaboration activities and competencies of secondary school special educators: A national survey. *Teacher Education and Special Education, 20*(1), 47–60.

Friend, M. (1988). Putting consultation into context: Historical and contemporary perspectives. *Remedial and Special Education, 9*(6), 7–13.

Friend, M., & Cook, L. (1997). Student centered teams in schools: Still in search of an identity. *Journal of Educational and Psychological Consultation, 8*(1), 3–20.

Friend, M., & Cook, L. (2003). *Interactions: Collaboration skills for school professionals* (4th ed.). Boston: Allyn & Bacon.

Fullan, M. (2000). The three stories of education reform. *Phi Delta Kappan, 81*(8), 581–584.

Fuller, G. (1998). *Win/win management: Leading people in the new workplace.* Paramus, NJ: Prentice Hall Press.

Gable, R. A., Korinek, L., & McLaughlin, V. I. (1997). Collaboration on the schools: Ensuring success. In J. S. Choate (Ed.), *Successful inclusive teaching, proven ways to detect and correct special needs* (2nd ed, pp. 450–471). Boston: Allyn & Bacon.

Gable, R. A., Young, C. C., & Hendrickson, J. M. (1987). Content of special education teacher preparation. Are we headed in the right direction? *Teacher Education and Special Education, 10,* 135–139.

Garner, H. G. (1995). *Teamwork models and experience in education.* Boston: Allyn & Bacon.

Gerber, S. (1991). Supporting the collaborative process. *Preventing School Failure, 35*(4), 48–52.

Gibb, G. S., Ingram, C. F., Duches, T. T., Allred, K. W., Egan, M. W., & Young, J. R. (1998). Developing and evaluating an inclusion program for junior high students with disabilities: A collaborative team approach. *B. C. Journal of Special Education, 21*(3), 33–44.

Gibb, J. R. (1961). Defensive communication. *Journal of Communication, 11,* 141–148.

Givens-Ogle, L., Christ, B. A., Colman, M., King-Streit, S., & Wilson, L. (1989). Data-based consultation case study: Adaptations of researched best practices. *Teacher Education and Special Education, 12,* 46–51.

Glickman, C. D. (1995). *Supervision of instruction* (4th ed.). Boston: Allyn & Bacon.

Golightly, C. J. (1987). Transdisciplinary training: A step forward in special education teacher preparation. *Teacher Education and Special Education, 10,* 126–130.

Gonzalez, J. E., Nelson, J. R. Gutkin, T. B., & Shwery, C. S. (2004). Teacher resistance to school-based consultation with school psychologists: A survey of teacher perceptions. *Journal of Emotional and Behavioral Disorders, 12*(1), 30–37.

Graden, J. L., Casey, A., & Christenson, S. L. (1985). Implementing a prereferral intervention system:

Part I. The model. *Exceptional Children, 51,* 377–384.

Gravois, T. A., Knotek, S., & Babinski, L. M. (2002). Educating practitioners as consultants: Development and implementation of the instructional consultation team consortium. *Journal of Educational and Psychological Consultation, 13*(1 & 2), 113–132.

Griffin, C. C., Winn, J. A., Otis-Wilborn, A., & Kilgore, K. L. (2003). *New teacher induction in special education* (COPSSE Document Number RS-5E). Gainesville, FL: University of Florida, Center on Personnel Studies in Special Education. Retrieved January 2003, from COPPSE Website at http://www.coe.ufl.edu/copsse/main.php?page=014

Gutkin, T. B. (1993). Cognitive modeling: A means for achieving prevention in school-based consultation. *Journal of Educational and Psychological Consultation, 4,* 179–183.

Gutkin, T. B. (1996). Core elements of consultation service delivery for special service personnel: Rationale, practice, and some directions for the future. *Remedial and Special Education, 17*(6), 333–340.

Gutkin, T. B. (1999). Collaborative versus directive/prescriptive/expert school-based consultation: Reviewing and resolving a false dichotomy. *Journal of School Psychology, 37*(2), 161–190.

Gutkin, T. B. (2002). Training school-based consultants: Some thoughts on grains of sand and building anthills. *Journal of Educational and Psychological Consultation, 13*(1 & 2), 133–146.

Gutkin, T. B., & Curtis, M. J. (1982). School-based consultation. In C. R. Reynolds & T. B. Gutkin (Eds.), *The handbook of school psychology.* New York: Wiley.

Gutkin, T. B., & Curtis, M. J. (1990). School-based consultation: Theory, techniques, and research. In T. B. Gutkin and C. R. Reynolds (Eds.), *The handbook of school psychology* (2nd ed., pp. 577–611). New York: Wiley.

Haight, S. L. (1984). Special education teacher consultant: Idealism versus realism. *Exceptional Children, 50,* 507–515.

Harris, K. C. (1996). Collaboration within a multicultural society: Issues for consideration. *Remedial and Special Education, 17*(6), 355–362, 376.

Hart, V. (1977). The use of many disciplines with the severely and profoundly handicapped. In E. Sontag, J. Smith, & N. Certo (Eds.), *Educational programming for the severely and profoundly handicapped.* Reston, VA: The Council for Exceptional Children, Division on Mental Retardation.

Hawryluk, M. K., & Smallwood, D. L. (1986). Assessing and addressing consultee variables in school-based behavioral consultation. *School Psychology Review, 15,* 519–528.

Helms, J. (1992). *A race is a nice thing to have.* Topeka, KS: Content Communications.

Heron, T. E., & Harris, K. C. (2001). *The educational consultant: Helping professionals, parents, and students in inclusive classrooms* (4th ed.). Austin, TX: Pro-Ed.

Hudson, P. J., Correa, V. I., Morsink, C. V., & Dykes, M. K. (1987). A new model for preservice training: Teacher as collaborator. *Teacher Education and Special Education, 10,* 191–193.

Hudson, P., & Glomb, N. (1997). If it takes two to tango, then why not teach both partners to dance? Collaboration instruction for all educators. *Journal of Learning Disabilities, 30*(4), 442–448.

Huefner, D. S. (1988). The consulting teacher model: Risks and opportunities. *Exceptional Children, 54,* 403–414.

Hunt, D. E. (1981). Teachers' adaptation: "Reading" and "flexing" to students. In B. Joyce, C. Brown, & L. Peck (Eds.), *Flexibility in teaching.* New York: Longman Publishers.

Hybels, S., & Weaver, R. L. (1997). *Communicating effectively* (5th ed.). New York: McGraw-Hill.

Idol, L., Nevin, A., & Paolucci-Whitcomb, P. (1994). *Collaborative consultation* (2nd ed.). Austin, TX: Pro-Ed.

Idol, L., Paolucci-Whitcomb, P., & Nevin, A. (1986). *Collaborative consultation.* Rockville, MD: Aspen Systems Corporation.

Idol, L., Paolucci-Whitcomb, P., & Nevin, A. (2000). *Collaborative consultation* (3rd ed.). Austin, TX: Pro-Ed.

Idol, L., & West, J. F. (1987). Consultation in special education (Part II): Training and practice. *Journal of Learning Disabilities, 20,* 474–494.

Idol-Maestas, L. (1983). *Special educator's consultation handbook,* Rockville, MD: Aspen Systems Corporation.

Ikeda, M. J., Tilly, W. D., Stumme, J., Volmer, L., & Allison, R. (1996). Agency-wide implementation of problem solving consultation: Foundation and current implementation, and future directions. *School Psychology Quarterly, 11,* 228–243.

Illsley, S. D., & Sladeczek, I. E. (2001). Conjoint behavioral consultation: Outcome measures beyond the client level. *Journal of Educational and Psychological Consultation, 12*(4), 397–404.

Jayanthi, M., & Friend, M. (1992). Interpersonal problem solving: A selective literature review to guide practice. *Journal of Educational and Psychological Consultation, 3*(1), 39–53.

Johnson, D. W., & Johnson, R. T. (1987). Research shows the benefits of adult cooperation. *Educational Leadership, 45*(3), 27–30.

Johnson, D. W., Johnson, R. T., & Holubec, E. (1986). *Circles of learning: Cooperation in the classroom* (rev. ed.). Edina, MN: Interaction Book Company.

Johnson, L. J., Pugach, M. C., & Devlin, S. (1990). Professional collaboration. *Teaching Exceptional Children, 22*(2), 4–4.

Johnson, L. J., Pugach, M. C., & Hammitte, D. J. (1988). Barriers to effective special education consultation. *Remedial and Special Education, 9*(6), 41–47.

Johnston, N. S. (1990). School consultation: The training needs of teachers and school psychologists. *Psychology in the Schools, 27,* 51–56.

Kabler, M. L., & Genshaft, J. L. (1983). Structuring decision-making in multidisciplinary teams. *School Psychology Review, 12,* 150–159.

Kaiser, S. M., & Woodman, R. W. (1985). Multidisciplinary teams and group decision-making techniques: Possible solutions to decision-making problems. *School Psychology Review, 14,* 457–470.

Kampwirth, T. J. (1987). Consultation: Strategy for dealing with children's behavior problems. *Techniques: A Journal for Remedial Education and Counseling, 3,* 117–120.

Karge, B. D., & McClure, M. (1995). The success of collaboration in resource programs for students with disabilities in grades 6 through 8. *Remedial and Special Education, 16,* 79–89.

Katzenbach, J. R., & Smith, D. K. (1999). *The wisdom of teams: Creating the high-performance organization.* New York: HarperCollins Publishers.

Korinek, L., & McLaughlin, V. (1996). Preservice preparation for interdisciplinary collaboration: The intervention assistance teaming project. *Contemporary Education, 68*(1), 41–44.

Kratochwill, T. R., & Van Someren, K. R. (1985). Barriers to treatment success in behavioral consultation: Current limitations and future directions. *Journal of School Psychology, 23,* 225–239.

Kruger, L. J., Struzziero, J., Watts, R., & Vacca, D. (1995). The relationship between organizational support and satisfaction with teacher assistance teams. *Remedial and Special Education, 16*(4), 203–211.

Kurpius, D. J. (1978). Consultation theory and process: An integrated model. *Personnel and Guidance Journal, 56,* 335–339.

Langley, L., Seo, S., Brownell, M., Bishop, A., & Sindelar, P. (2003). *COPSSE VI: Teacher Supply and Teacher Quality: Effective Policies and Strategies.* Teacher Education Division (TED), November 11–14, Biloxi, Mississippi. Retrieved January 2003, from COPSSE Website at http://www.coe.ufl.edu/copsse/main.php?page=014

Laycock, V. K., Gable, R. A., & Korinek, L. A. (1991). Alternative structures for collaboration in the delivery of special services. *Preventing School Failure, 35*(4), 15–18.

Lesar, S., Benner, S. M., Habel, J., & Coleman, L. (1997). Preparing general education teachers for inclusive settings: A constructivist teacher education program. *Teacher Education and Special Education, 20*(3), 204–220.

Lilly, M. S. (1987). Response to "Consultation in Special Education" by Idol and West. *Journal of Learning Disabilities, 20,* 494–495.

Lopez, E. C., Dalal, S. M., & Yoshida, R. K. (1993). An examination of professional cultures: Implications for the collaborative consultation model. *Journal of Educational and Psychological Consultation, 4,* 197–213.

Lyon, S., & Lyon, G. (1980). Team functioning and staff development: A role release approach to providing integrated educational services for severely handicapped students. *Journal of the Association for the Severely Handicapped, 5,* 250–263.

Maher, C. A., & Hawryluk, M. K. (1983). Framework and guidelines for utilization of teams in schools. *School Psychology Review, 12,* 180–185.

Margolis, H., & Brannigan, G. G. (1987). Problem solving with parents. *Academic Therapy, 22,* 423–425.

Mather, J., & Weinstein, E. (1988). Teachers and therapists: Evolution of a partnership in early intervention. *Topics in Early Childhood Special Education, 7*(4), 1–9.

McGlothlin, J. E. (1981). The school consultation committee: An approach to implementing a teacher consultation model. *Behavioral Disorders, 6,* 101–107.

Medway, F. J. (1979). How effective is school consultation? A review of recent research. *Journal of School Psychology, 17,* 275–282.

Meyers, A. B. (2002). Developing nonthreatening expertise: Thoughts on consultation training from the perspective of a new faculty member. *Journal of Educational and Psychological Consultation, 13*(1 & 2), 55–67.

Morsink, C. (1999). *21st century teachers for a better future* (Final Report to Howard Heinz Endowment). Slippery Rock, PA: Slippery Rock University College of Education.

Morsink, C. V., & Lenk, L. L. (1992). The delivery of special education programs and services. *Remedial and Special Education, 13*(6), 33–43.

Mostert, M. P. (1998). *Interprofessional collaboration in schools.* Needham Heights, MA: Allyn & Bacon.

Nelson, C. M., & Stevens, K. B. (1981). An accountable model for mainstreaming behaviorally disordered children. *Behavioral Disorders, 6,* 82–91.

Nelson, J. R., Smith, D. J., Taylor, L., Dodd, J. M., & Reavis, K. (1991). Prereferral intervention: A review of the research. *Education and Treatment of Children, 14,* 243–253.

O'Neill, R. E., Horner, R. H., Albin, R. W., Sprague, J. R., Storey, K., & Newton, J. S. (1997). *Functional assessment and program development for problem*

behavior. (2nd ed.). Pacific Grove, CA: Brooks/Cole Publishing Co.

Orelove, F. P., & Sobsey, D. (1991). *Educating children with multiple disabilities: A transdisciplinary approach* (2nd ed.). Baltimore: Paul H. Brookes Publishing Co.

O'Shea, D. J., Williams, A. L., & Sattler, R. O. (1999). Collaboration across special education and general education: Preservice teachers' views. *Journal of Teacher Education, 50*(2), 147–157.

O'Shea, L. J., O'Shea, D. J., & Algozzine, R. (1998). *Learning disabilities: From theory toward practice.* Upper Saddle River, NJ: Merrill/Prentice Hall.

Parker, C. A. (1975). *Psychological consultation: Helping teachers meet special needs.* Reston, VA: The Council for Exceptional Children.

Peryon, C. D. (1982). Systematic development of special educators as facilitators of mainstreaming. *Journal of Special Education Technology, 5*(3), 31–36.

Pfeiffer, S. I. (1980). The school-based interprofessional team: Recurring problems and some possible solutions. *Journal of School Psychology, 18,* 388–394.

Pfeiffer, S. I. (1981). The problems facing multidisciplinary teams: As perceived by team members. *Psychology in the Schools, 18,* 330–333.

Phillips, V., & McCullough, L. (1990). Consultation-based programming: Instituting the collaborative ethic in schools. *Exceptional Children, 56,* 291–304.

Piersel, W. C. (1985). Behavioral consultation: An approach to problem solving in educational settings. In J. R. Bergan (Ed.), *School psychology in contemporary society: An introduction.* New York: Merrill/Macmillan.

Polsgrove, L., & McNeil, M. (1989). The consultation process: Research and practice. *Remedial and Special Education, 10*(1), 6–13, 20.

Pryzwansky, W. B., & Rzepski, B. (1983). School-based teams: An untapped resource for consultation and technical assistance. *School Psychology Review, 12,* 174–179.

Pugach, M. C. (1988). Restructuring teaching. *Teaching Exceptional Children, 21,* 47–50.

Pugach, M. C., & Johnson, L. J. (1989a). Prereferral intervention: Progress, problems, and challenges. *Exceptional Children, 56,* 217–226.

Pugach, M. C., & Johnson, L. J. (1989b). The challenge of implementing collaboration between general and special education. *Exceptional Children, 56,* 232–235.

Pugach, M. C., & Johnson, L. J. (2002). *Collaborative practitioners, collaborative schools* (2nd ed.). Denver, CO: Love Publishing Co.

Rainforth, B., & York-Barr, J. (1997). *Collaborative teams for students with severe disabilities: Integrating therapy and educational services* (2nd ed.). Baltimore: Paul H. Brookes.

Ramirez, S. A., Lepage, K. M., Kratchowill, T. R., & Duffy, J. L. (1998). Multicultural issues in school-based consultation: Conceptual and research considerations. *Journal of School Psychology, 36*(4), 479–509.

Reppucci, N. D., & Saunders, J. T. (1974). Social psychology of behavior modification: Problems of implementation in natural settings. *American Psychologist, 29,* 649–660.

Reynolds, C. R., Gutkin, T. B., Elliott, S. N., & Witt, J. C. (1984). *School psychology: Essentials of theory and practice.* New York: Wiley.

Rosenberg, M. S., & Rock, E. E. (1994). Alternative certification in special education: Efficacy of a collaborative, field-based teacher preparation program. *Teacher Education and Special Education, 17*(3), 141–153.

Safran, S. P., & Safran, J. S. (1996). Intervention assistance programs and prereferral teams: Directions for the twenty-first century. *Remedial and Special Education, 17*(6), 363–369.

Salend, S. J. (1998). *Effective mainstreaming: Creating inclusive classrooms* (3rd ed.). Upper Saddle River, NJ: Merrill/Prentice Hall.

Salend, S. J., & Salend, S. (1984). Consulting with the regular teacher: Guidelines for special educators. *The Pointer, 28,* 25–28.

Salisbury, C. L., & Evans, I. M. (1997). Collaborative problem-solving to promote the inclusion of young children with significant disabilities. *Exceptional Children, 63*(2), 195–209.

Salisbury, C. L., & McGregor, G. (2002). The administrative climate and context of inclusive elementary schools. *Exceptional Children, 68*(2), 259–274.

Salvia, J., & Ysseldyke, J. E. (1988). *Assessment in special and remedial education* (4th ed.). Boston: Houghton Mifflin.

Sanders, M., & Harvey, A. (2002). Beyond school walls: A case study of principal leadership for school community collaboration. *Teachers College Record, 104*(7), 1345–1368. Retrieved February 2004, from http://www.tcrecord.org

Senge, P., Cambron-McCabe, N., Lucas, T., Smith, B., Dutton, J., & Kleiner, A. (2000). *Schools that learn.* New York: Doubleday.

Sheehy, G. (1977). *Passages–Predictable crises in adult life.* New York: Bantam Books.

Sheridan, S. M., Welch, M., & Orme, S. F. (1996). Is consultation effective? A review of outcome research. *Remedial and Special Education, 17,* 341–354.

Siders, J. Z., Riall, A., Bennett, T. C., & Judd, D. (1987). Training of leadership personnel in early intervention: A transdisciplinary approach. *Teacher Education and Special Education, 10,* 161–170.

Sindelar, P. T., Griffin, C. C., Smith, S. W., & Watanabe, A. K. (1992). Prereferral intervention: Encouraging notes on preliminary findings. *The Elementary School Journal, 92,* 245–259.

Skrtic, T. M. (1991). The special education paradox: Equity as the way to excellence. *Harvard Educational Review, 61,* 148–191.

Smith, J. D. (1998). *Inclusion: Schools for all students.* Belmont, CA: Wadsworth Publishing Company.

Snell, M. E., & Janney, R. (2000). *Teachers' guides to inclusive practices: Collaborative teaming.* Baltimore: Paul H. Brookes.

Speece, D. L., & Mandell, C. J. (1980). Resource room support services for regular teachers. *Learning Disability Quarterly, 3,* 49–53.

Sprinthall, N. A., & Thies-Sprinthall, L. (1983). The teacher as an adult learner: A cognitive-developmental view. *National Society for the Study of Education, 82nd Yearbook.* Chicago: The University of Chicago Press.

Stanwood, B. (1988). *Effective utilization of multi-disciplinary teams.* Unpublished manuscript. Wilmington: University of North Carolina–Wilmington, School of Education.

Sue, D. W., Arredondo, P., & McDavis, J. R. (1995). Multicultural counseling competencies and standards: A call to the profession. In J. G. Ponterotto, J. M. Casas, L. A. Suzuki, & C. M. Alexander (Eds), *Handbook of multicultural counseling* (pp. 624–644). Thousand Oaks, CA: Sage.

Sugai, G., & Horner, R. (1999). Discipline and behavioral support: Practices, pitfalls, and promises. *Effective School Practices, 17,* 10–17.

Sugai, G. M., & Tindal, G. A. (1993). *Effective school consultation: An interactive approach.* Pacific Grove, CA: Brooks/Cole.

Tawney, J. W. & Gast, D. L. (1984). Single subject research in special education. New York: Merrill/Macmillan.

Tharp, R. G. (1975). The triadic model of consultation: Current considerations. In C. A. Parker (Ed.), *Psychological consultation: Helping teachers meet special needs.* Reston, VA: The Council for Exceptional Children.

Tharp, R. G., & Wetzel, R. J. (1969). *Behavior modification in the natural environment.* New York: Academic Press.

Thomas, C. C. (1986, March). *Problem-solving strategies for school assistance teams.* Paper presented at the Region II Exceptional Children Administrators Staff Development Conference, Atlantic Beach, NC.

Tiegerman-Farber, E., & Radziewicz, C. (1998). *Collaborative decision making: The pathway to inclusion.* Upper Saddle River, NJ: Merrill/Prentice Hall.

Trimble, S., & Miller, J. W. (1996). Creating, invigorating, and sustaining effective teams. *NASSP Bulletin, 80*(584), 35–40.

Tuckman, B. W., & Jensen, M. A. C. (1977). Stages of small group development revisited. *Group and Organization Studies, 2,* 419–427.

Turnbull, A., & Turnbull, H. R. (2001). *Families, Professionals, and Exceptionality: Collaborating for Empowerment* (4th ed.). Upper Saddle River, NJ: Prentice Hall.

Turnbull, R., & Cilley, M. (1999). *Explanations and implications of the 1997 amendments to IDEA.* Upper Saddle River, NJ: Merrill/Prentice Hall.

Villa, R., Thousand, J., Paolucci-Whitcomb, P., & Nevin, A. (1990). In search of new paradigms for collaborative consultation. *Journal of Educational and Psychological Consultation, 1,* 279–292.

Voltz, D. L., Elliott, Jr., R. N., & Harris, W. B. (1995). Promising practices in facilitating collaboration between resource room teachers and general education teachers. *Learning Disabilities Research and Practice, 10*(2), 129–136.

Walther-Thomas, C., Bryant, M., & Land, S. (1996). Planning for effective co-teaching: The key to successful inclusion. *Remedial and Special Education, 17*(4), 255–264, Cover 3.

Walther-Thomas, C., Korinek, L., McLaughlin, V. L., & Williams, B. T. (2000). *Collaboration for inclusive education: Developing successful programs.* Boston: Allyn & Bacon.

Wangemann, P., Ingram, C. F., & Muse, I. D. (1989). A successful university-public school collaboration: The union of theory and practice. *Teacher Education and Special Education, 12,* 61–64.

Welch, M. (1998). Collaboration: Staying on the bandwagon. *Journal of Teacher Education, 49*(1), 26–37.

West, J. F., & Brown, P. A. (1987). State departments of education policies on consultation in special education: The state of the states. *Remedial and Special Education, 8*(3), 45–51.

West, J. F., & Cannon, G. S. (1988). Essential collaborative consultation competencies for regular and special educators. *Journal of Learning Disabilities, 21*(28), 56–63.

West, J. F., & Idol, L. (1987). School consultation (Part I): An interdisciplinary perspective on theory, models, and research. *Journal of Learning Disabilities, 20,* 388–408.

West, J. F., Idol, L., & Cannon, G. (1989). *Collaboration in the schools: An inservice and preservice curriculum for teachers, support staff, and administrators.* Austin, TX: Pro-Ed.

Wilczynski, S. M., Mandal, R. L., & Fusilier, I. (2000). Bridges and barriers in behavioral consultation. *Psychology in the Schools, 37*(6), 495–504.

Witt, J. (1990). Collaboration in school-based consultation: Myth in need of data. *Journal of Educational and Psychological Consultation, 11,* 367–370.

Wood, J. W. (1998). *Adapting instruction to accommodate students in inclusive settings* (3rd ed.). Upper Saddle River, NJ: Merrill/Prentice Hall.

Yoshida, R. K. (1983). Are multidisciplinary teams worth the investment? *School Psychology Review, 12,* 137–143.

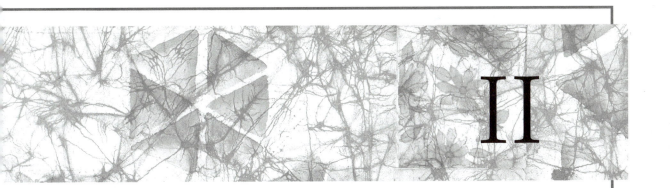

Facilitating Factors

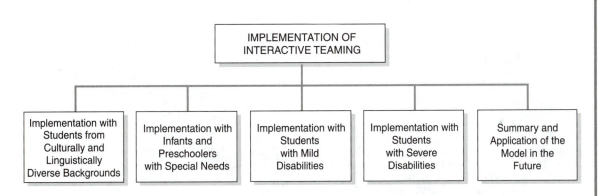

```
            ┌─────────────────────────┐
            │  IMPLEMENTATION OF      │
            │  INTERACTIVE TEAMING    │
            └─────────────────────────┘
```

| Implementation with Students from Culturally and Linguistically Diverse Backgrounds | Implementation with Infants and Preschoolers with Special Needs | Implementation with Students with Mild Disabilities | Implementation with Students with Severe Disabilities | Summary and Application of the Model in the Future |

OVERVIEW

The chapters in this part describe the facilitating factors that contribute to effective team functioning. Chapter 3, focusing on the roles of team members, provides descriptions of the roles of special educators, related professionals, and paraprofessionals. The chapter also illustrates how team members can provide direct services and serve as collaborators. In Chapter 4 communication is defined, and factors to consider in communication are explained. The verbal and nonverbal forms of communication are described, and strategies for managing conflict and resistance are presented.

Chapter 5 includes a definition of service coordination skills; in this chapter, essential parameters for the leadership of professionals are identified and guidelines for the procedures that team leaders should implement are explained. Chapter 6 includes a description of power and empowerment, and illustrates three types of professional development. The final chapter in this part, Chapter 7, contains descriptions of factors that have influenced changes in attitudes about family involvement and outlines how family members can assist in providing services to their children as they fulfill vital roles as interactive team members.

Understanding Roles and Perspectives of Team Members

Topics in this chapter include:

◆ Roles and perspectives of team members.

◆ Changes in the composition and functions of the team.

◆ Roles of team members, as direct service providers and as collaborators or consultants.

◆ Application of the interactive teaming model to a case in which the special education teacher and speech-language pathologist collaborate to help a special student with language development, and application of the model in a hospital setting, in which the pediatric nurse serves as team leader.

Darrell, a 12-year-old middle school student with a moderate cognitive disability, was the subject of a team meeting to plan his instructional program. Darrell went to live with his maternal grandmother after his mother died in childbirth. He was placed in a compensatory education program when he entered school as a 6-year-old, then placed in a part-time special education resource room a year later. In the current meeting to plan his instructional program, the team was to focus on moving Darrell into the regular education classroom part time, while continuing the support he and his family were receiving in the form of remedial reading, speech-language therapy, behavior modification, and nutritional counseling. His grandmother, who was elderly and unemployed, was receiving public assistance for herself and for Darrell.

The school psychologist said, "Darrell is functioning within the range of mild to moderate cognitive disability. His academic achievement scores, according to the WRAT, are significantly below his grade level but consistent with expectations given his mental age. He exhibits passive-aggressive behavior with adults, while becoming more openly hostile with his peers."

The speech-language pathologist said, "His primary disability is a moderate developmental delay in language acquisition, which impedes his social and academic functioning. I need to conduct a current language assessment, with particular emphasis on his MLU."

The dietitian said, "His nutritional intake may be a contributing factor to his attention deficit disorder. I suggest that he receive a more balanced diet, emphasizing complex carbohydrates, while limiting the number of exchanges in saturated fats and synthetic sugars."

The social worker said, "He is eligible for related special services such as speech therapy and nutritional counseling, which could be supported by third-party payments."

Darrell's grandmother, who was totally confused, simply nodded her head and smiled.

Darrell's case dramatically illustrates the differences in the roles, perspectives, and vocabularies of professionals on the interactive team. Because each person is a highly trained professional, he or she has specialized knowledge to contribute to the solution of problems. This professional training can be a major asset to the functioning of the team when the professional's knowledge is recognized and translated in a meaningful way. Or it can become a barrier leading to misunderstanding, territoriality, and conflict.

In this chapter, the differences in the roles and perspectives of team members are described. The changes in the composition and functions of the team are explained according to the context in which it operates—the program for students who are culturally different, who have mild disabilities, or who have severe disabilities. The contributions of each team member, both as a service provider and as a collaborator, are defined. The interactive teaming model is applied to Darrell's case, previously described, in an example showing consultation and collaboration between two members of the team, the special education teacher and the speech-language pathologist. The model is also applied to cases involving short-term hospital-related programs coordinated by the pediatric nurse.

ROLES AND PERSPECTIVES OF TEAM MEMBERS

The first major task in establishing interactions among team members is recognizing that these individuals have widely disparate roles, vocabularies, and perspectives as a result of their highly specialized professional training. These differences can lead to misunderstanding and bickering among participants (Pipho, 1997). These differences, however, can also be viewed as potential strengths if they are respected by all members of the team and used appropriately by the leader.

Collaboration among professionals is particularly difficult when it involves members of the education and the allied health professions. Eggers (1983) described their difficulties as follows:

> Imagine a sporting event with doctors, nurses, therapists and other health professionals competing against educators and developmental psychologists. Each team insists that the game be played on their field by their rules—impossible conditions for productive, organized competition. . . . The silliness of the image fades and is replaced by an image of a child being pulled in multiple directions by different types of professionals while bewildered, frustrated parents pace the sidelines. (p. 2)

The differences among members of the health-related and education professions are real. In health-related professions, specialists call the people they serve "patients" or "clients"; they provide "treatment" as short-term health care, usually in response to a crisis. Education-related professionals call the people they serve "students" and they provide "treatment" as long-term instruction from a developmental perspective.

In addition, the range and nature of the advocacy groups, organizations, and regulations with which each group must deal are different. While educators function within organizations dependent on public funds and regulated by legislative mandates, health professionals often receive reimbursement from third parties such as insurance companies, Medicaid, and the Social Security system, each having its own set of forms and payment schedules. Each group of professionals has its own perspective, as well as multiple layers of subspecialties. Collaboration becomes increasingly difficult as the layers of subspecialties increase.

Team Composition and Functions

The team's composition and functions are affected by new trends in service delivery which have increased the number of programs available at the preschool and postschool level, the presence of larger numbers of students with special needs in regular classrooms, and the expansion of health-related and justice system services for students with severe disabilities. Changes in the composition and functions of the team are also resulting from the fact that the number of persons on the team is variable, depending on the nature of the problems it addresses.

Trends in Service Delivery

Two trends in service delivery for students with special needs have implications for team composition and functions. One of these trends is the expansion of educational programs into preschool, postschool, and regular classroom settings. The other involves changes in the health care system.

Expansion into New Settings

The expansion of educational programs increases the need for professionals to interact with others outside of their traditional groups. For example, McLeskey, Henry, and Hodges (1998) documented a 60% increase in the number of students with special needs placed in general education classrooms from 1988–1989 to 1994–1995. Interactions frequently extend into the related professions of human and social services, including the juvenile justice system, making coordination both more important and more complicated. Professionals across agencies are required to advocate for children and help the families of these children negotiate the multiple bureaucracies that provide service delivery (Davenport, 1990).

Although it is difficult to work across these boundaries, preliminary data indicate that such efforts can be productive (National Center for Schools and Communities, 1998; O'Neil, 1997). Many of these programs extend school services into communities, providing after-school activities, legal and health assistance (Frischkorn, 1997), social services through family centers (Bush & Wilson, 1997), and comprehensive shelters for homeless families (Nunez & Collignon, 1997). The National Center for Family and Community Connections with Schools is assisting schools, families, and communities in making connections to improve student learning (SEDL Newsletter, 2002). Yale researchers, summarizing the results of 72 collaborative programs for children and their families, have concluded that interagency links have provided both program quality and cost effectiveness (Kagan & Rivera, 1990). They cited (1) training for caregivers and teachers, (2) consistent regulations based on joint planning, and (3) parental involvement among the practices they identified as promising.

New preschool programs reflect the growing emphasis on early intervention for children who have special needs or are at risk (Magna Awards, 1998). IDEA establishes that early intervention services be provided in the natural environments. The range of service delivery options for young children (e.g., home, Head Start, child care) broadens the type of professionals who may be participants in the team makeup for these children.

Recommended practices in early intervention establish the notion that programs serving young children be family-centered (Sandall, McLean, & Smith [Eds.], 2000). Successful service delivery will be based on understanding new family styles, diversity, and their adverse conditions (Vincent & Salisbury, 1988). Team members will need to include parents as full partners in decision making, de-emphasizing traditional views of "dominant and submissive" roles (Darling, 1989; Wells, 1997). They will also need to remain sensitive to the family's needs for privacy.

Preschool services also extend to the provision of services for infants as required by Public Law 99–457. At a state's discretion, services are offered for infants and toddlers who have been identified as having a developmental delay (as defined by the state), an established risk (i.e., Down syndrome), or a biological risk (i.e., premature, low birth weight), as well as those experiencing environmental risk conditions such as poverty or abuse. Decision makers will also need to consider the new research findings, which indicate that with intensive, high-quality instruction, a low student-teacher ratio, and establishment of a predictable environment, early intervention is effective in improving outcomes for young children at risk for or with developmental delay (Guralnick, 1998). Effective programs, however, will require collaborative planning among agencies.

Team members also need to design programs for postschool students who are transitioning between traditional schooling and employment. Among the issues these teams will confront are the following:

♦ Regulations in the Americans with Disabilities Act (ADA) require employers to analyze the essential functions of jobs and to make necessary modifications for workers with disabilities. While the ADA has helped to increase employer awareness of the dependability of workers with disabilities (Chamberlain, 1988), a 2000 survey by Lou Harris and Associates indicates that approximately two-thirds of adults with special needs are unemployed (cited in Heward, 2003).

♦ Transition teams will design and coordinate training that enables students to succeed in the workforce. Planning includes consideration of effective curriculum, placement in community-based programs, and supported employment to facilitate transition to adult life for individuals with severe disabilities.

♦ Interagency collaboration is a key ingredient to successful transition (Malloy, Cheney, & Cormier, 1998).

CHANGES IN THE HEALTH CARE SYSTEM

The context for changes in the health care system are summarized by Kristin J. Young, R.N., and reprinted with her permission, as follows:

As recently as 20 years ago, people were hospitalized for what would now be considered minor illnesses. Children, in particular, would stay for many days in a hospital ward, frightened by the equipment and the strangers around them. Their parents would not be permitted to stay at their bedsides except during visiting hours, and they would be required to leave the room any time a procedure was to be done, forcing children to endure it alone. This emotional stress could interfere with the healing process and prolong the child's stay. The nurses assigned to these wards were expected to care for as many as 22 patients. After dispensing medications, changing dressings, emptying bedpans, and administering other treatments, the nurse had little time to address comfort concerns or see to the special needs of those who were physically, mentally, or behaviorally challenged. When children were released from the hospital, their parents were expected to care for them, without receiving much training from the hospital staff. If parents had difficulty providing care, the children were sent to extended care facilities, often located far from their homes, to be cared for by strangers in stark white uniforms.

A number of factors, however, have had an impact on the way health care is delivered in the United States today. Giant steps have been made in the treatment of diseases and in the development of drugs. New requirements for insurance payments have resulted in diagnostic tests being conducted on an outpatient basis, with many illnesses now treated at home. State-of-the-art scanners and imagers can help physicians identify problems that previously required exploratory surgery. Television and the Internet have affected health care by providing ways to communicate and educate the public about health issues. Patient awareness and early detection are the surest ways of maintaining health and preventing complications. Consequently, our overall population is stronger, healthier, and living longer, including our children with special needs.

Children with special needs who must be admitted to the hospital are usually very ill, cannot be treated at home, and must stay for a long time. Their acuity level is high, requiring more skilled care. Doctors give less direct patient care; they oversee their patients' welfare with daily exams and change or write new orders to promote a good outcome, which the nurses carry out. Nurses have fewer patients, but they must now give a greater amount of care. Usually intravenous drug therapy is involved, which means the nurse is responsible for starting and maintaining the IV, something only doctors did in the past. Nurses are also responsible for coordinating the care a patient needs. That is where collaboration comes in.

Education professionals who work with P–12 students have become increasingly aware of and more involved in health-related issues in their classrooms. Demographic changes cited in Chapter 1 have led to increases in the numbers and complexity of health-related problems in school-age students. Teachers are encouraged, for example, to become more aware of and more responsive to health problems such as asthma (Anderson & Luong, 1997). At the same time, schools with limited budgets are hiring health aides rather than registered nurses as school nurses, in an effort to save money (Cowell, 1998).

A number of health care issues related to the education of students with special needs made national news in early 1999.

◆ On February 9, NBC-TV Nightly News reported that school nurses, now required in 17 states, were becoming primary care providers for many children with working parents. Now expected to do more than test vision and dispense bandages, the nurses are administering ritalin, teaching dental care, and helping to identify the victims of child abuse (NBC, 1999).

◆ On March 3, the Associated Press reported nationwide on the Supreme Court decision for Cedar Rapids, Iowa, finding that the daily health care by a registered nurse, for a high school sophomore who was quadriplegic and ventilator dependent, was essential for his access to integrated education, and should be financed by the school district under the IDEA (Associated Press, 1999).

◆ On August 3, *USA Today* reported on the recommendations from the American Academy of Pediatrics that physicians use a "media history" quiz with parents during their children's medical exams. The quiz would focus on children's television, movie and video viewing, video/computer games, Internet use, and radio/CD/tape listening habits, as well as child-parent interactions with books; it would also identify parental concerns about their children's use of tobacco, alcohol and drugs, sexuality, and aggressive behavior (Elias, 1999).

These examples are but a few of the many related to the scope and magnitude of changes in health care systems, which continue to impact methods of service delivery for students with special needs.

CHANGES IN TEAM COMPOSITION AND FUNCTIONS

As indicated in Chapter 1, an interactive team can consist of as few as two members or as many as are required to provide the specialized knowledge and skills for the student in question. The number of people on the team increases with the complexity and nature of the problem. Not all members are present at every meeting, and not every meeting of the team is formal. Professionals may interact informally as required to maintain communication and provide follow-up for the decisions made by the larger group.

It is also important to note that each team member has two functions: to provide direct services and to serve as a collaborator. *Direct services* are offered as individual "hands-on" activities with the special needs student and family. *Collaboration* falls under *indirect services,* that is, consultation on subjects in which he or she has expert knowledge, or team efforts to plan, implement, and evaluate the student's program.

Effective use of the specialized knowledge and skills of each member of the team requires an understanding of the knowledge and skills that other individuals have acquired through their professional training. It also requires appropriate application of these skills to the tasks for which the team has responsibility: planning, implementation, and evaluation of the special needs student's program.

The knowledge and skills of persons most often found on interactive teams are highlighted briefly in this chapter. In addition to the special educator, these teams can include family members, an administrator, classroom teacher, school psychologist, counselor, social worker, speech-language pathologist, English as a second language (ESL) or bilingual education specialist, migrant or compensatory education teacher, school nurse, physical therapist, occupational therapist, and other health-related professionals.

Team members may also interact with specialists in adaptive technology, adaptive physical education, behavior analysis, juvenile justice, and vocational or transition education, and they may be responsible for the supervision of para-professionals. As indicated earlier, the number of people on a given team is dependent on the nature and complexity of the student's problems. In addition, the number of people available and the degree to which they serve as specialists or as generalists depends on factors such as the size of the school district or clinical facility and whether it is in a rural, suburban, or urban area. These factors can affect a district's or facility's financial resources and availability of specialized personnel.

ROLES OF GENERAL AND SPECIAL EDUCATORS

One of the major goals of special education is to ensure that students with special needs progress in the general curriculum (Turnbull, Turnbull, Shank, & Smith, 2004). The special and general education teachers play a key role in achieving this goal. The role of the special educator changes according to the context in which service is offered. While the continuum of services is still available for students with special needs, the majority spend most of their time in general education classrooms (McLeskey et al., 1998; U.S. Department of Education, 2002). As a result, the work of special education teachers is shifting from that of providing isolated services for students with special needs to working in collaboration with other professionals, mostly general education teachers. In fact, in a recent CEC report, Kozleski, Mainzer, and Deshler (2003) found that 68% of special educators spent less than 2 hours per week in individual instruction with their students. As we have learned, these collaborative efforts can take a number of forms. Three common forms of collaboration seen in schools today are consultation, teaming, and co-teaching.

Chapter 2 presented two of these collaborative efforts in detail, consultation and teaming. This section provides information on the roles of special educators and general educators in providing services, collaboration, and team membership, followed by a more detailed description of co-teaching. Chapters 8 through 11 provide more detail on the context of teaching students who are culturally different or who have mild or severe disabilities.

The Special Educator

The students served by the special educator have a range of disabilities and are served in a number of settings. In school-based programs one method of direct service delivery is through small group or individual instruction in a resource setting or within the general education classroom. Students may also receive most of their instruction in a self-contained classroom with specific time periods in the general education classroom.

Students with Mild Disabilities.   Students with mild disabilities (i.e., those who are classified as having a learning disability, behavior disorder, or some mild cognitive, physical, or sensory disability) are most likely to receive services from the special educator in the small group setting previously mentioned. The primary functions of the special educator in this role are student assessment, program evaluation, and the provision of instruction.

For the student who has had difficulties, the special educator may conduct an educational assessment, administering a series of tests to determine the student's current levels of functioning and specific deficits in academic areas such as reading, math, and study skills. The special educator may also observe the student in the regular classroom or evaluate the student's behavioral characteristics, using checklists and interviews with parents and teachers to collect data related to program eligibility and placement.

When the team plans the student's educational program, the special educator presents the data that were obtained. The special educator may also discuss the difficulties that typically characterize students in the specific category for which this student is being considered and present program placement options that seem most appropriate. This may happen less formally during prereferral discussions.

When the instructional program has been implemented, the special educator measures the effectiveness of the program that has been designed, using continuous measurement techniques. These procedures enable the specialist to chart the student's performance on specific academic and behavioral objectives, and to obtain data that are useful both in making appropriate modifications and in communicating with other members of the team.

The special educator's primary responsibility is to provide explicit instruction in a structured environment (one-to-one or small group) short-term program. She will have knowledge of specific evidence-based procedures particularly suited to the learning needs of students with mild disabilities (e.g., learning strategies developed at the University of Kansas by Deshler, 1998, or Direct Instruction [Engelmann, Carnine, & Steely, 1991]). The competencies needed by special educators of students with mild disabilities have been studied in depth and will be summarized in Chapter 10.

Students with Severe Disabilities.   The student with severe disabilities often has multiple disabling conditions, which may include physical and sensory disabilities and/or some degree of cognitive or neurological impairment, as well as manifestations of behavior disorders. In addition, these students may take medications, suffer from seizures, or have special needs for medical equipment such as tracheotomy tubes or catheters. Special educators working with children with severe disabilities will have specialized skills allowing them to position, lift, and transport students; monitor use of medications and prosthetic devices; manage seizures; and modify aberrant behaviors. More complete information on the competencies needed have been studied in depth and will be summarized in Chapter 11.

The major function of the special educator who serves students with severe disabilities is to teach them and to synthesize their special related services. Because of the multiple disabilities involving related services of a medical nature, however, the teaching function may appear to be of secondary importance. The special educator plans, implements, and monitors an instructional program based on the student's current educational-developmental level. This program is most often based on the student's development of functional skills such as self-care, daily living, communications, and vocational skills that maximize the student's opportunities for full participation in society, with consideration for the quality of life. A few programs that serve students with severe disabilities are in special classrooms or center schools; for students who require a continuous level of special instruction and an integrated educational/medical program, this type of placement may be appropriate. For most others, however, placement in regular schools may be workable and beneficial (Biklen, 1988).

The special educator's role in providing access to general education and other inclusive activities will be through implementation of specialized instructional methods such as assistive technology and partial participation (Snell & Brown, 2000). Partial participation allows flexibility in what constitutes participation in the activity (i.e., the student approaches and participates in a task in a way and to the degree that is appropriate for her or him).

General Educator

As previously mentioned, students with special needs spend the majority of their time in the general education classroom. While this is more often the case for students with mild disabilities, the student with severe or multiple disabilities may also be served at least part time in the regular school program. Therefore, it is important to understand the unique skills and knowledge of the general education teacher as they may be applied to the development, evaluation, and implementation of the special student's instructional program.

The general education teacher brings to the team content knowledge of the discipline taught as well as the scope and sequence of the curriculum for particular grade levels or subjects. This general educator's primary responsibility is to implement the academic curriculum in the classroom. Peterson (1988) has pointed out that the role of the teacher is now viewed primarily as that of a "thoughtful professional," one who understands the relationship between teaching and learning and is able to enhance the student's cognitive functioning in a specific academic area. Effective teachers are those who use "reflective teaching," describing what they do and its effect on learners, and use this information to improve their instruction (Williams, 1996).

The general education teacher also has been trained as a specialist in human growth and development and is, therefore, in an excellent position to observe the student with disabilities' interactions with peers who demonstrate age- and grade-appropriate behaviors. Such observations are not possible in the special classroom, where this student is separated from peers who set the *norms* for age-appropriate learning and behavior. The general education teacher who observes a first grader reversing letters knows that other 6-year-olds sometimes do the same thing. The general education teacher who observes a moody, hostile adolescent recognizes that all adolescents are moody and may occasionally appear to be hostile or withdrawn. The general education teacher, by comparing the individual's behavior with the group norms, is also able to determine that a 9-year-old who frequently reverses letters or an adolescent who is consistently hostile or withdrawn may have special needs. When teachers make data-based observations of these behaviors, comparing the target student's performance with that of others in the group, they are able to determine the nature and severity of the problem. In making such observations, the teacher should take care to define the behavior precisely, specify the conditions for observation, and ensure that the observations are made under consistent environmental conditions (Haring & Phillips, 1972; Morsink, 1984). General education teachers who make such observations will be able to communicate the precise nature of the student's problems in coping with the school curriculum and the classroom environment. Some schools will have specialists in behavior analysis and/or adaptive technology to make or assist with these observations.

The general education teacher's most important role with the student who has special needs, both before and after referral, focuses on the provision of appropriate learning experiences. Wang, Haertel, and Walberg (1997), Nevin and Thousand (1986), and Villa and Thousand (1988) have summarized a number of strategies that have been found effective in accommodating the special student in the classroom environment. These include outcomes-based strategies such as peer tutoring, cooperative learning, mastery learning, and applied behavior analysis. In addition, it is important for the general education teacher to establish an effective environment in which all students can learn: one that has a positive classroom climate and that includes adapted teacher-directed instruction, followed by opportunities for students to practice their skills under supervision with teacher feedback (Morsink, Thomas, & Smith-Davis, 1987; Wang et al., 1997).

Finally, it is important to realize that general education teachers are trained to accommodate students in groups, rather than to tutor them individually. It is the general education teacher's primary responsibility to provide academic instruction for all members of the group and, as such, he/she is in the best position to assist the student with special needs in working with the group, learning to follow routines, and complying with accepted standards of group behavior. The general education teacher, however, may not be as effective as the special educator in providing intensive one-on-one or small group instruction on specific academic skills or behavior management. The same characteristics that enhance the teacher's effectiveness in whole-group instruction may limit the ability to deal with individuals who have diverse needs, particularly when teachers lack the technological and human support to simultaneously implement a variety of diverse teaching strategies (Gerber, 1988). It is possible, however, for a general education teacher, in a school with a principal who supports full inclusion, to accommodate the special needs of diverse students.

Collaboration

Collaboration with Students with Mild Disabilities.   One role that the special educator assumes when working with students with mild disabilities is as consultant. As such, the special educator provides information about the student's learning needs and characteristics, as well as special strategies and materials that have been found to be effective for students with certain difficulties.

The special educator also often functions collaboratively with others to collect additional data on the child's needs during prereferral or before placement in a special program. Following the guidelines in the IDEA, the team that conducts the assessment is the same one that designs the student's IEP (Turnbull & Cilley, 1999). Sometimes a behavior specialist and/or adaptive technology specialist is included on the team. This group might be called the *teacher assistance team*, which functions to identify educational problems and develop interventions to be implemented by the referring classroom teacher. Teacher assistance teams have worked effectively to help teachers implement interventions for students with academic or behavior problems (Chalfant, 1989; Chalfant, Pysh, & Moultrie, 1979), and they have been discussed in Chapter 2.

Similarly, a prereferral intervention model based on an indirect, consultative model of service delivery has been successful in preventing future student problems. In the prereferral intervention model, the regular classroom teacher and special education consultant work together to increase the teacher's ability to individualize instruction for heterogeneous groups of students (Graden, Casey, & Christenson, 1985).

Collaboration with Students with Severe Disabilities.   The multiple disabling conditions experienced by students with severe disabilities requires that the special educator coordinate the activities of related services professionals who design assessment and instructional procedures to accommodate the student's movement, vision, hearing, and postural limitations. The team leader coordinates the educational program through group meetings and review of the student's performance data, collected by the professionals who implement various aspects of the program. After reviewing these data, the coordinator determines whether the student is acquiring targeted skills and then communicates these findings to various team members, who subsequently make appropriate adjustments in the program.

Co-Teaching

Co-teaching is a collaborative service delivery option that is receiving increased attention and use as special and general educators work to successfully include students with special needs. Bauwens, Hourcade, and Friend (1989) first described cooperative teaching as "an educational approach in which general and special educators work in a coactive and coordinated fashion to jointly teach academically and behaviorally heterogeneous groups of students in educationally integrated settings" (p. 18). Later, Cook and Friend (1995) shortened the term to co-teaching, clarifying that its characteristics defined co-teaching as "two or more professionals delivering substantive instruction to a diverse or blended group of students in a single physical space" (p. 2). This definition first implies that the two co-teachers are equal and that delivering content is a coordinated effort where both have a role in teaching (Friend & Cook, 2003). Co-teaching has the potential to make the best use of the knowledge and skills of both teachers in the classroom.

A number of variations for co-teaching have been described. (See Friend & Cook, 2003; Hourcade & Bauwens, 2003; Walther-Thomas, Korinek, McLaughlin, & Williams, 2000 for more detailed information.) The *one teach–one assist* model involves the presence of both teachers in the classroom. One teacher is primarily responsible for the instruction while the second observes and moves about the room to assist students when needed. The advantage of this model is that it allows time for student observation, which is often difficult for teachers to do. The disadvantage is that, if used exclusively, it can relegate one teacher, most often the special education teacher, to the role of assistant. In *station teaching,* the teachers divide the content and take responsibility for planning and delivery. The students move between the stations in small groups. One drawback of this model is that it may be noisy and distracting to the students and teachers. *Parallel teaching* occurs when the two teachers split the class and deliver the same content to their own group. *Alternative teaching* is used when it is necessary for a small group of students to receive more intensive instruction. It might also be used to ensure that every student spends time with the teacher in a small group. The main drawback to this approach is that the students with special needs or those at risk may become stigmatized if they are primarily placed in the small group. Finally, the most collaborative co-teaching model is *team teaching.* When using this approach, both teachers are responsible for delivering instruction. For example, this might occur when one teacher talks while the other demonstrates, one talks while the other charts or makes notes on an overhead, or one talks while the other adds information. This method requires the most preparation and planning as well as a high level of trust and comfort with the teaching partner.

Co-teaching has many benefits for both students and teachers but requires extra time and effort to work effectively. Pugach and Johnson (2002) offer six principles for implementing co-teaching: challenge yourself to improve your teaching; share responsibility for all students; share responsibility for instruction; communicate regularly; support your teaching partner; and actively work to include all students.

APPLICATION: Informational Interview

This application is based on the original work of Beach (1985) and is used here with her permission. Jean Beach is the special educator (SE) who works with Darrell, the student presented in the vignette at the beginning of this chapter, in the middle school special education resource room. Jean has made some observations of Darrell's language functioning in the resource room, and she is concerned that he has speech and language difficulties that are out of her area of expertise. She arranges for an *informational interview* with a team member, the speech-language pathologist (SLP) who assists other students at the middle school. Jean is interested in observing the speech and language development program, in obtaining information about the referral process and screening/testing procedures, and in learning how to help Darrell and other students in her classroom who exhibit problems in language development.

Jean arranges to observe the SLP's language development group, which includes three other students from the special education resource room, during her planning period. Jean observes as the SLP directs activities in which the students learn analogies (e.g., "Pine trees have pine cones; apple trees have. . . . Trucks have wheels, dogs have. . . ."). Then she watches the SLP work with the group on articulating sounds in the initial, middle, and ending positions, using visual images presented as picture cards. Finally, she observes as the SLP administers a language test to another student to determine his difficulties in phonology, syntax, semantics, memory, word finding, and retrieval. Jean makes notes on her observations, organizes the data she has collected on her observations of Darrell in the special education resource room, and arranges to meet with the SLP the next day to discuss what she has seen and request assistance with Darrell.

The conference begins with small talk about the school and their common training at the university where they both obtained their degrees, and it continues with Jean thanking the SLP for letting her observe the language development group and testing session the previous day. Then Jean addresses her concerns about Darrell's language difficulties.

SE: I have a student named Darrell in my resource room, who seems to have a lot of difficulties in language development. According to his cumulative folder, he was in the speech program once before—he has a structural deficit (some sort of hole in the speech mechanism itself)—but he received help in articulation and then was dismissed. He isn't having articulation problems like those of the other students I observed yesterday, but he certainly would have trouble with the analogies. I believe he has a more general language deficit, and I'm interested in referral to you for further testing. How do I proceed?

SLP: Here is a simple form. You just put the student's name and the date on the top line; then add a one-line description of your reason for the referral. I do testing one day a week. I would start with a screening test to determine if there is a need for further testing, and then—if more testing is necessary—we would get parent permission for a complete evaluation, including articulation, language development, voice, and fluency. After testing, I would meet with you and the parents to give you the results of what has been done and to make suggestions for future programming.

SE: I wasn't sure about the district's policy on testing. Do we need parent permission for routine screening?

SLP: No, but we would need permission for a complete evaluation and, of course, for placement if that is needed.

SE: When I observed your group yesterday, I saw that another student in my resource room, who is paired with Darrell for some language activities, was having a lot of trouble with the analogies. Both of these students read at the preprimer level, although they're in sixth grade. I find that a tape recorder is quite helpful in work-ing with them on their reading vocabulary words. If you think the recorder would help you put words on tape, and then both of these students could listen to them to get a little more practice.

SLP: That's a really good idea. It is much more meaningful to students receiving spe-cial help if they can do some of the same language development activities in their own classroom. The coordination and repetition makes the special program more effective.

SE: When I work with both of these students in reading, I use a language experience approach that includes modified phonetics. Right now they are practicing the *sh* digraph in the initial position of words, such as ship, show, shine, and so on. Their words are pronounced on tape, while the student circles the picture show-ing the correct sound, given a choice of two pictures. I've been correcting their papers for the past 2 weeks and I've picked up certain consistent errors, which I've charted on graph paper. Would you be interested in seeing the graph?

SLP: Oh, yes! That would be very helpful. If we're both picking up the same error pat-terns, then we can work together more effectively to help the students.

SE: I also work with Darrell in a general language arts class, and I notice that it is re-ally difficult for him to respond appropriately during group activities. I know what he is trying to say, but it comes out wrong. He'll say "ain't got no" or something, and then the group laughs. How can I help him?

SLP: When you ask him to make a verbal response, do you use picture cards or some other kind of visual cues? Or do you just use words?

SE: I would be using a verbal format, with questions and answers.

SLP: It may be that he needs some additional visual cues to get the answers right. I have some syntax programs on picture cards; I'd be happy to let you borrow them to see if they might help.

SE: That would be great! I'll try that for a week or so and let you know how it works out. Listen, I know your planning period is over, and so is mine. But thanks again for letting me watch your groups yesterday and letting me watch you give the clinical evaluation of the language functions test that you might use with Darrell if needed. You've been really helpful in assisting me in working with him.

SLP: Thank you for giving me such precise data and descriptions of his problems. It will really help me in determining whether or not he needs additional testing and assistance. Since the copy machine is right next to my office and you use it a lot, maybe we can catch each other for a few minutes at a time to share information about Darrell and other students.

This conference between team members was highly productive for several rea-sons. Each acknowledged and respected the specialized training of the other. Both came together with the attitude that they shared a common goal of providing a bet-ter program for a student. Both shared and respected each other's expertise, showed a genuine interest in the other's program, and both expressed a willingness to continue the dialogue. Although the initial meetings were time-consuming—the meetings lasted between 20 and 30 minutes—subsequent meetings could be brief, and each team member could make the other's job easier by sharing materials and expertise focused on their common goal.

ROLE DESCRIPTIONS OF OTHER TEAM MEMBERS

As indicated earlier, the number of people on a team will vary, as determined both by the nature and severity of the student's problem, and by the size and resources available in the school district or clinical program. The roles of other team members are described in clusters, which include those with related or overlapping functions. These include the following: the program administrator; the behavior specialist, school psychologist, counselor, or social worker; the speech-language pathologist, the teacher of bilingual education or ESL; the physical therapist, occupational therapist, adaptive physical educator, and adaptive technology specialist; the vocational or transition specialist; the teacher of migrant or Title 1 programs; and the school nurse and other health-related professionals. The roles of family members and paraprofessionals are presented separately, in Chapter 7.

Program Administrator

The contributions and specialized knowledge of the administrator are considered first because it is important to emphasize that the person with this title is not ordinarily the team leader. The organization's administrator delegates responsibility for its coordination to a team leader. The role of the leader will be described in more detail in Chapter 5, but it should be noted that, although the administrator is not ordinarily the team's leader, the administrator sets the tone to establish a collaborative culture for the program, which supports the concept of teaming. In addition, a team functioning in a supportive collaborative culture will see its role in the organization's overall mission as important.

For the team to function effectively, it is particularly important for the administrator to understand and convey to the public that he or she values this team and has delegated to it decision-making authority for the programs of students with special needs. It is equally important for the administrator to provide the team members with information about the legal policies and procedures within which they are authorized to operate, and to provide them with information about the fiscal and instructional resources available to them in program implementation. After having established the team, however, the administrator steps down from the direct leadership role and delegates responsibility for the team's functioning to the team itself.

Those who have implemented school-based teacher assistance teams have learned that the administrator, who is typically responsible for teacher evaluation, often is not the best person to serve as the team leader because team members may be reluctant to share concerns about their effectiveness with the person who will evaluate them. The role of the administrator, therefore, is proposed as that of over-all management of the school or clinic and its programs, but not necessarily as a leader of the interactive team.

The specialized areas of administrator or director knowledge include but are not limited to the following: leadership and change; professional development and re-lations; planning and evaluation; public and community relations; personnel man-agement; and knowledge about budgets, law, educational and medical programs, resources, and facilities. In some cases, the school administrator is the instructional leader for the unit, although observations of what elementary and secondary prin-cipals actually do seem to suggest that this activity represents less than 20% to 30% of their time (Howell, 1981; Morsink, 1999). And, in clinical settings, it is unlikely that the director is trained in both education and the allied health professions in addition to having expertise in administration.

The administrator is charged with overall fiscal, legal, and programmatic re-sponsibility for the unit in which the team functions. This unit is usually a school, and its administrator is a principal when the team serves students from culturally diverse backgrounds or those with mild disabilities. It may be a clinic or special-ized organization with a director when the team serves students with severe dis-abilities. Because the administrator has overall responsibility for the unit, she must give permission for the team to function as a decision-making body, as well as pro-vide it with the necessary information and support to implement its decisions. Also, because the administrator has overall responsibility for the unit, he or she must balance the budget and see that all legal mandates and protections are ob-served while attending to the needs of all constituencies. The administrator's pri-ority is the welfare of the entire unit, rather than personal advocacy for the special needs of any one student or program.

Behavior Specialist, School Psychologist, Counselor, or Social Worker

Because the roles of these four professionals often overlap, we describe their roles in tandem. Large, affluent school districts may have all four of these individuals in every school, but those that are smaller or sparsely populated may have only one per school or per district.

Behavior Specialist.   The behavior specialist is a possible member of IEP teams that are considering the special needs of students whose behavior interferes with their own learning or with the learning of others in the classroom. A be-havioral assessment and intervention plan are required for any student who has been removed from any placement for 10 or more school days. The behavior spe-cialist, trained in applied behavior analysis, gathers information by making data-based observations of the student in the classroom environment; conduct-ing interviews with the student, teachers, and others; generating behavior sup-port plans; and assisting in the implementation and monitoring of the plan's outcomes.

This team member needs skill in the identification of problem behaviors and the ability to define them in concrete ways that lead to the development of plans. Successful behavior intervention plans include positive strategies, curricular modifications, and the use of supplementary supports to enable students to use appropriate behaviors. Therefore, it is essential for this team member to have in-depth knowledge of the possible causes and functions of behavior problems, as well as an understanding of the curriculum; the selection and use of assessment instruments; and the ability to develop, implement, and monitor objective interventions based on direct measurement techniques. While some preparation programs for school psychologists and counselors may include at least some of these skills, many special education programs offer degrees in applied behavior analysis and behavior intervention strategies. School districts might also contract with external public or private agencies to provide these services.

Psychologist.   A school psychologist is a psychoeducational specialist certified to administer formal tests of intellectual and interpersonal functioning. The school psychologist is also trained in the selection, administration, and interpretation of certain standardized and informal tests used to determine the student's eligibility for special programs and assists in planning those programs (Frisbee, 1988; Larsen, 1984). In small districts, the psychologist may conduct the entire assessment, whereas in larger districts, other specialists may be part of the assessment team as necessary for individual cases—physicians or audiologists for evaluating hearing, physicians or vision specialists for conducting an assessment of visual functioning, and so on. Because assessment is of such importance in the referral and placement of the special student, it is particularly important that the school psychologist select instruments that are free from bias and are administered in the student's own language, with adaptations for physical and sensory disabilities, and according to legally approved procedures (Larsen, 1984; Reid, 1987; Turnbull & Cilley, 1999).

Counselor.   The school counselor may also conduct observations or collect assessment data during the referral stage of program decision making, although this professional is more highly trained in the assessment of social and emotional skills than in the measurement of cognitive functioning. The counselor frequently consults with teachers and parents to design individual and group programs that assist students in developing their interpersonal skills and in coping with their emotions (Tobias, 1988). Frequently in secondary and middle schools, the counselor is also responsible for designing and coordinating the student's class schedule, and assisting students with making decisions about their future plans for higher education or vocational careers. Often, especially in small districts that do not have a social worker, the counselor also functions as a liaison with personnel from a variety of community agencies.

Social Worker.   The social worker is the professional who collects information about the student's home background and history. This person is familiar with the variety of community resources and related services that may be used to help the special needs student and the family, and serves as the liaison with professionals in these agencies. A school social worker may be involved as a person who can interface with the public assistance and justice systems for students in foster homes or who may be the recipients of Social Security or welfare funds. The social worker may also conduct observations of the student in the home or classroom, and may administer assessment instruments or implement programs to assist the teacher, the student, and the family in coping with the behavior of difficult students (Ryberg & Sebastian, 1981).

Overlapping Functions.   The psychologist, counselor, or social worker may collect information from the student's home, locate resources, or serve as a liaison with community agencies (Ryberg & Sebastian, 1981). The behavior specialist, psychologist, social worker, and counselor are all trained to observe the student in the classroom and then consult with teachers, parents, and other personnel in the design of programs to manage the student's behavior or to enhance his or her learning ability. This team member is often trained in child advocacy, counseling, group process skills, and consultation. The professional organizations for school psychologists and counselors have urged that their members expand their roles beyond the assessment of problems to their prevention (American Association for Counseling and Development, 1984; National Association of School Psychologists, 1974). For example, these professionals are frequently called on to provide schools with assistance in dealing with or preventing school violence, as shown in the following application.

The following application is reprinted with permission from its developers, Anne Kemmerer, Amanda Szurek, and Diane Carion (1999). It illustrates another way in which university faculty members and students in preparation for careers in education and related professions can and should be part of interactive teams.

APPLICATION: A Timely Workshop

Only hours after the tragic incident in Littleton, Colorado, a very timely program was initiated here at Slippery Rock University. Wednesday, April 21, was the culmination of a year's worth of planning. The School Collaboration Center, in conjunction with the Counseling Educational Psychology Department, College of Education, hosted 200 seventh-grade students from the Grove City Middle School. The topic: "Bullying and Teasing: Laying the Groundwork for Conflict Resolution." The goal: Making Grove City Middle School a bully-free zone. The principal, Ms. Kelly, and the guidance counselor, Mr. Wise, welcomed the program with open arms.

Twenty SRU graduate students, most of them future guidance counselors, facilitated a hands-on workshop for the 200 students. The workshop, planned by Dr. Anne Kemmerer, Dr. Pamela Soeder, and graduate student Amanda Szurek, gave the students an intense 3.5 hours of training including examples that defined "bullying," explaining what makes a victim, recognizing the difference between "tattling" and "reporting," and

teaching the skills to identify an adult in the school system that they can trust for reporting incidents.

The general program was a huge success. The real success will be determined
when one of these students takes on an assertive and active role when faced with this
issue because of the information shared at this workshop.

In larger districts, the behavior specialist, psychologist, social worker, or counselor may be able to provide follow-up consultation, conduct group or individual
counseling sessions, or work with parents. Some larger districts have been able, for
example, to offer group counseling sessions in areas such as substance abuse, divorce, and test anxiety, which help prevent the increase in referrals for special programs (Bernstein & Simon, 1988). In small districts this team member may be
serving several schools; fragmentation in job location may limit the position's functions to the administration and interpretation of psychological tests. In some instances, small districts are not able to employ a behavior specialist, psychologist,
counselor, or social worker. The person who serves in this capacity may be employed by a social services agency, or as a private consultant, working under contract with the school district.

The behavior specialist, psychologist, social worker, and counselor are heavily
involved in the delivery of sensitive information, and they are often required to
explain technical terms or to make suggestions for changes in the status quo. In
this role, it is particularly important that they use terminology that is clear, understandable, and inoffensive (Courtnage & Healy, 1984; Larsen, 1984; Tobias,
1988). These professionals' explanations should include information about the
limitations of test data and of classification procedures. These explanations
should also emphasize findings derived from multiple sources of information, as
opposed to conclusions based on a single data point, such as the numerical score
on a particular test.

The professional in this role frequently has the perspective of *child advocacy* as
a first priority (Sigmon, 1987). The perspective of child advocate may appear, at
times, to conflict with the perspective of the administrator or classroom teacher,
and it may not seem to be compatible with the overall goals of the organization or
the particular needs of the child's family. Team members need to remain sensitive
to this possibility of conflict in perspective.

Speech-Language Pathologist and ESL or Bilingual Specialist

The people who assume these roles have some functions and characteristics in
common, yet their training is also highly specialized. Both their specializations and
their common functions are presented.

Speech-Language Pathologist.   The person trained as a speech-language pathologist is an educational-medical professional certified by the American Speech-
Language and Hearing Association (ASHA). For the student whose difficulties

include speech or language development, the speech-language pathologist (SLP) is an essential member of the professional team. The SLP is responsible for the identification, evaluation, and intervention of communication disorders (ASHA, 2001), which may manifest as speech disorders (i.e., articulation problems, apraxia, voice, and fluency disorders) and language disorders (difficulty with one of the five dimensions of language: phonology, morphology, syntax, pragmatics, semantics).

One of the most important functions of the SLP is to administer a series of formal and informal tests to determine the nature and extent of the language difficulty. Serious language disorders are likely to influence a student's social communication (Westby & Clauser, 1999) and/or reading skill (Catts & Kamhi, 1999; Spracher, 1999). For a student with a mild disability, the SLP may be particularly interested in obtaining a language sample to determine the way this student uses language in everyday situations. For a student with a severe disability, the language assessment may focus on the student's ability to use and interpret gestures and to make basic needs understood, which may include intervention for augmentative/alternative communication use.

When the student is from a culturally different background, it is particularly important for the SLP to determine whether the student's language is simply different as a result of culturally determined patterns or whether it is deficient (Battle, 1998; Westby, 1985). The SLP may be asked to assist when the student's oral reading performance is characterized by numerous dialect differences, which are indicative of common language patterns that occur in black English or in students for whom another language (e.g., Spanish) is the first language. It is important for all who work with the student to recognize these patterns and distinguish them from language deficits (Battle, 1998; Roseberry-McKibbin & Brice, n.d.; Spache & Spache, 1986).

The collaborative role that the SLP takes is broad in that approximately 19% of students identified with disability fall under the speech-language impairments category (U.S. Department of Education, 2002). In addition, speech and language disorders are often associated with other disability categories (Turnbull et al., 2004). Speech and language services are provided through a variety of methods and settings. ASHA (2001) reports that the primary mode of service delivery for the 1999–2000 school year met individually or in small groups in a 20- to 30-minute session approximately twice per week. However, there has been an increase of services provided in the classroom. The SLP works collaboratively with the general education teacher to integrate the classroom curriculum in the intervention process (Ehren, 2000). The SLP may also provide consultation and training for the general educator and other staff members to enhance their understanding of strategies to facilitate communication across the day (Giangreco, 2000).

ESL or Bilingual Specialist.   The student with performance deficits caused solely by the fact that English is the second language should *not* be classified as eligible for special education, according to the 1997 IDEA amendments, although this student may be eligible for assistance in ESL or bilingual education. Conversely, the ESL student may not be denied special education services on the basis of his or her home language. When English is the second language for the student, the SLP should collaborate with a specialist in that language. Large districts may have specialists in ESL or in bilingual education. In small districts, it may be necessary to seek assistance from a community volunteer or a professional at a nearby university who is a native speaker of the language. It is also important for school districts to provide information to parents in a language they can understand, to assess students using instruments in their own language, and to provide uniform procedures for students to register for school, regardless of the country of their birth.

The ESL or bilingual specialist is aware of the problems inherent in teaching culturally different students, demonstrates knowledge about cultural differences, and applies this knowledge in the instructional setting (Fox, Kuhlman, & Sales, 1988; Wlodkowski & Ginsberg, 1995). He or she will also have knowledge about language development, language assessment, and multicultural education systems (Fradd, Weismantel, Correa, & Algozzine, 1988).

The team member who works with culturally different students also needs to be an effective collaborator. The understanding of one's own culture and cultural biases is an important step in the development of the flexibility and open-mindedness that characterize effective collaborators. Specific guidelines for these skills are presented in greater detail in Chapter 8 on cultural diversity.

Overlapping Functions.   There are five areas in which it is particularly important for the SLP and bilingual teacher or foreign language specialist to collaborate; these have been summarized by Fradd and Weismantel (1988):

1. *Student identification.* Data combined from both specialists can be used to confirm or refute a label, such as "learning disability," as determined by the language assessment.

2. *Assessment and diagnosis.* Language dominance needs to be established, and the label "disabled" is applied only when the student is deficient in measures of intelligence, academics, or social behavior, as measured in the dominant language.

3. *Placement.* It is desirable to place the student in an integrated group, including both bilingual and general education students when possible.

4. *Instructional planning.* For the bilingual student, this includes a dual language plan for instruction in the academic and social skills, as well as a model for providing these services.

5. *Achievement review.* The annual review should include new language samples and work samples from the academic areas being remediated, as well as progress in the direction of mainstreaming.

To avoid conflicts, gaps, or overlapping functions, it may be useful to further delineate the specific training and roles of the ESL and bilingual education resource teachers. These have been specified in detail by Fradd and Weismantel (1988). The ESL teacher provides instruction focused on whole language and cognition including grammar and linguistics. The bilingual teacher provides instruction first in the non-English language and culture; the sequence of this instruction begins with affective skills, then progresses to cognition and finally to academics. In large districts, there may be specialists in both ESL and SLP, whereas in smaller districts these functions may be filled by the same individual or contracted by the school to an external specialist.

When the student's major difficulty is language development and use, it is of greatest importance for all adults to provide consistent models and to have common expectations. For the learner who is culturally different and also has a severe disability, it may be more important to communicate in the student's native language and in gestures or universal signs when it is not feasible to provide instruction in the use of English as a second language. The SLP and the ESL or bilingual specialist are the people on the team who can best provide information on the type of program that is most appropriate for a given student.

Physical Therapist, Adaptive Physical Educator, Occupational Therapist, and Adaptive Technology Specialist

There are some commonalities and some differences between and among the functions and training of these professionals. Their roles are presented separately, and the overlapping functions are then discussed.

Physical Therapist.   The physical therapist (PT) is a link between medicine and education, because the PT understands students' medical problems as well as the importance of movement in learning (Morsink, 1983). This specialist intervenes when the student's needs are such that his or her physical limitations interfere with the ability to benefit from special education. Rapport (2003) defines PT services as those addressing posture, mobility, and organization of movement, focusing on skills that will increase the student's independence.

The physical therapist works to develop a program of assessment and intervention after the physician has referred the client for these services. Assessment of the disability includes a determination of the strength and range of movement, and the relationship between the movement and the individual's ability to learn or to perform learning-related functions. Services may be delivered directly (i.e., hands-on contact) or indirectly through interactions with adults in contact with the student.

Because it is important to continue the physical therapy program on a regular basis in everyday routines and activities, the PT works collaboratively with the special educator, classroom teacher, paraeducators, and parents. This collaboration involves training these adults and monitoring their efforts to meet the student's objectives (Rapport, 2003). The nature and type of program designed for the student with severe disabilities may include assistance with basic functional skills, such as feeding, self-care, and walking.

Adaptive Physical Educator.   This professional is trained in physical education, exercise physiology, and in the special needs of students with mild or severe disabilities.

Those providing adapted physical education are trained to provide remediation in the areas of physical and motor fitness, psychomotor skills, leisure and recreation skills, and affective development. In addition, the adaptive physical educator can collaborate with other team members in designing cooperative games and motor development activities that enhance the child's physical skills, self-concept, and interactions with peers. Sometimes this professional works with community agencies to design special physical education programs, such as horseback riding or swimming, for students with physical, emotional, or sensory limitations.

Occupational Therapist.   The school-based occupational therapist (OT) works with students who have physical, behavioral, or cognitive delays or disabilities. Swinth, Chandler, Hanft, Jackson, and Shepherd (2003) describe the focus of occupational therapy as "helping students engage in meaningful and purposeful daily school occupations" (p. 3). Similarly to physical therapy, occupational therapy in schools is designed to ensure that the student benefits from special education. For example, the OT creates or modifies special devices to assist the student with physical or sensory disabilities in sitting, walking, eating, writing, reading, and so on. The OT delivers services through direct services (i.e., working with small groups or individual students) or consulting with and providing training for other adults working with the students (e.g., special and general educators, paraeducators, parents).

Adaptive Technology Specialist.   In the computer-based society, the adaptations required for full functioning may be those that enable the person with physical limitations to use new technology, such as computers. Some adaptive technology specialists are trained to develop computer hardware and software that can be used by individuals with special needs. Computers may be modified so they can be operated by an individual using a stick attached to the forehead or foot; they may also be programmed to synthesize speech or to translate speech into print or Braille. Adaptive technology specialists are also highly trained in the selection and design of software, which emphasizes programmed or errorless learning, to enable the student with learning difficulties to practice and master complex skills. Their skills are valuable to the team that serves students with mild disabilities, as well as those with severe disabilities.

The adaptive technology specialist is a new potential team member. This person may be trained in instructional technology; computer science, with specialization in the adaptation of technology for students with special needs; or may be a special educator with advanced training in instructional technology. Adaptations are essential when their use will enable the student with special needs to learn and/or function in the least restrictive environment. The adaptive technology specialist may, upon receiving a referral on a student, observe or evaluate that student either in school, the home, or in a specialized technology lab. This team member may also read student records; interview the student, teachers, and parents; and complete a community-based assessment. The technology specialist allows for input from these persons before making a recommendation on the use of specific equipment, and then reports recommendations back to the IEP team for decision making.

The adaptive technologist relies on classroom teachers to provide input on the student's skills and specific needs in reading, writing, and language, listening and problem-solving skills, his or her work habits, and needs to produce printed output. Teachers and related services personnel also provide the adaptive technologist with information about concerns related to mobility, vision, hearing, speech-language, cognitive, or behavioral performance with which the student might receive assistance from adaptive technology. The technology specialist acquires information about the availability of existing hardware and software used and needed in the classroom or community environment. It is important for the adaptive technology specialist to have knowledge about exceptionalities and about the use and availability of the newest hardware, software, and special devices for augmentative communication and mobility, as well as the technical skills required to adapt existing devices to special needs. This specialist makes an effort to find the simplest—often lowest "tech"—solution, since adaptations do not necessarily improve in value just because they increase in cost.

Overlapping Functions.   Although the physical therapist, occupational therapist, and adaptive physical educator may all provide assistance with the development and use of motor skills, the PT is the only one whose assistance requires referral from a physician. The PT is more concerned with the development of basic motor skills, whereas the OT is more often concerned with the use of these skills in classroom and vocational settings. Both the PT and the adaptive physical educator are concerned with motor development; however, the PT works with clients individually and the adaptive physical educator also works with students in groups.

Both the OT and the adaptive technology specialist may have the training to design adaptive equipment for use with computers; the OT, however, usually does not have training in the development of programmed software for use with computer-assisted instruction or the selection of software appropriate for specific areas of the curriculum. These individuals may work together in large districts; in smaller, remote areas, one of these individuals may perform several functions if the team does not have access to all types of specialists.

Vocational or Transition Specialist

A vocational educator is specially trained in preparing students for specific types of vocations, including a variety of careers related to service industries in agriculture, food services, manufacturing, installation, and repair. Each vocational specialist is a professional trained in a highly specific area, who teaches this specialty in high schools or vocational schools. Although the vocational educator is knowledgeable in his or her area of training, this person does not always have training in adapting the vocational training program to the special needs of students with disabilities.

The transition specialist is more often an individual with generic training in vocational education and specialized knowledge in the training needs of adolescents and adults with special needs. This professional assists the student, the family, and the school personnel in making the transition from the world of school to work. The transition specialist helps the team plan for the student's continuing vocational/educational training, home and community participation (e.g., where to live, how to obtain transportation), family relationships, financial support, and recreation and leisure, as well as physical and emotional health (Boone, 1990). Planning for transition into the adult world is more difficult than planning for school-related programs, because there is no single agency to coordinate all aspects of the student's services.

Either the vocational educator or the transition specialist, or both, may work with the school and related community agencies to assess the skills of the student and match them with the requirements of a particular job. These professionals may be responsible for providing the student with special needs with prevocational training and for conducting on-the-job support services such as job coaching, which ensure that the student will have the communications and interpersonal abilities, as well as the vocational skills, to succeed in the world of work (Bell, 1989).

Realizing the key role that self-determination plays in the student's ability to clarify his or her own goals, transition teams must include this in all facets of planning (Steere & Cavaiuolo, 2002). Self-determination has been defined as a combination of skills, knowledge, and attitudes including such behaviors as making choices, problem solving, goal setting, risk taking and safety, and self-regulation and advocacy (Field, Martin, Miller, Ward, & Wehmeyer, 1998; Wehmeyer & Schwartz, 1998). Self-determination skills will need to be included on the IEP goals and objectives and in curriculum activities. The student's teachers and family members will play a key role in helping him or her to develop these skills.

Research on effective transition practices has highlighted the complexity of the transition process and placed an emphasis on transition-focused education (Kohler & Field, 2003). Furthermore, the perspective of transition-focused education views transition planning as "a fundamental basis of education that guides the development of all educational programs" (Kohler & Field, p. 176). These authors propose a framework for effective transition practices that is more student-focused in that the student participates more actively in the planning process and an emphasis is placed on student development (e.g., activities such as developing and applying self-determination, work-based learning experiences, and social skills development). Family involvement and interagency collaboration are still critical aspects of the approach. The transition team composition will include the school professionals working with the student to meet the educational plan goals (e.g., general and special educators, related services providers). Additional team members will vary depending on the student's goals and expected outcomes (e.g., higher education counselors, adult developmental disabilities service agents, employers, community-based adult services). Finally, the student himself or herself is a principal member of this team.

Migrant Education or Title I Teacher

School districts and communities that have a large number of people classified as migrant workers or as having incomes below the poverty level may have one or more specialists in migrant or remedial education. The specialist in migrant education has acquired knowledge about the particular problems of the migrant worker's family, including residential instability and educational discontinuity.

The teacher in a Title I program serves the children of families whose incomes are below the poverty level. These are the children whose caregivers are eligible for aid to dependent children. Often, they are from single-parent families. The Title I specialist is trained to provide enrichment activities and remedial training to students who are not achieving well in school and who have low levels of motivation or a low expectation for success. Federal programs now provide additional funding for whole schools with a high percentage of students who qualify for Title I funding. This Fund for the Improvement and Reform of Schools and Teaching (FIRST) Program (1989) enables the entire school to engage in collaborative efforts to effect school improvement.

School Nurse and Other Health-Related Professionals

In larger school systems, or in cases that involve clients with severe or multiple disabilities, a school nurse or other health-related professionals may be members of the team. When there is a medical problem, a physician will be involved in the diagnosis and in consultation or making recommendations for treatment, although the physician ordinarily interacts with the student's parents or other health-related professionals, rather than serving as a regular team member at school-based meetings.

School Nurse.   The school nurse may assist others in planning for educational programs that involve wellness, substance abuse, and prevention of disease. The specialized knowledge, skills, and judgment are especially needed for children with special health care needs and those with disabilities. As a member of a school team for students with the disabilities, the school nurse will be instrumental in addressing health-related issues including (but not limited to) planning for emergencies, identifying and removing health-related barriers to learning, and providing training to teachers and parents (National Association of School Nurses [NASN], 2002a). The school nurse may also serve as a liaison between school and family and between school and health care providers (NASN, 2002b). In some districts, school policies or bargaining agreements require that the nurse oversee particular health-related procedures, such as dispensing of medications. Each member of the team should request information regarding these policies. Some schools do not have school nurses, although services have to be provided for students with special needs somewhere in the district.

Pediatric Nurse.   Many children are hospitalized at some time, either for a short-term stay or for prolonged time periods, with more of their care delegated to the pediatric nurse. This health care provider can be viewed as a potential team member, particularly in the role of consultant to the school and parents, but also as a team leader within the hospital setting. The role of this team member is presented in greater depth in the section later in this chapter on interactive teaming in hospital settings.

Dietitian.   A dietitian or nutritional specialist may function as a consultant for students who, because of diabetes or other metabolic disorders, need assistance in planning and monitoring their diets. This specialist evaluates the individual's diet and nutritional status to determine the overall nutritional intake, as well as special needs such as those related to lower caloric intake or the reduction of sugar or sodium. The dietitian may work with the student's family, in addition to consulting with school and related services personnel, and may advise the team about special devices to assist with feeding or to monitor the intake of particular elements.

Other health-related professionals may serve as consultants or collaborators on the team as needed. In every case, each of these specialists has particular knowledge in an area that may be of primary importance to the student's treatment.

Physician's Role as Consultant

The physician contributes to the interactive team largely as a consultant. It is unlikely that, unless the student has severe and multiple disabilities, the physician will be directly involved in the educational program. The role of the physician has been addressed in detail by Ross (1984), who outlines the procedures for conducting an evaluation of the student. This evaluation focuses on a case history, including a description of the current illness, past history, review of systems, and family or social history. When appropriate, the physician may also conduct a neurological or sensory examination.

Students are most often referred to the physician because of symptoms such as hyperactivity, hearing loss, or seizures. When the physician's diagnosis is a condition such as epilepsy, cerebral palsy, muscular dystrophy, or developmental disability, the team will need to develop a complete plan that extends over a lifetime and allows such individuals to develop to their fullest potential.

Input from the physician is provided most often in the form of a written report, detailing the medical findings of an examination and making recommendations that may be implemented by others on the team. As noted earlier, recent recommendations from professional associations may lead to an expanded role in violence prevention for the physician (Elias, 1999).

The role of physicians in early intervention has been viewed as important to providing a seamless system of supports and services (Buck, Cox, Shannon, & Hash, 2001). Although that role was clearly articulated in the Part C legislation of IDEA, it has not been fully realized. Utilizing information gathered from a survey of physicians and Part C coordinators in their state, Buck et al. suggest some strategies for enhancing communication between early intervention providers and physicians, such as providing written information on early intervention, using technology to communicate with physicians, offering training, and providing regular updates regarding the progress of their patients.

Roles of Family Members and Paraprofessionals

Research is clearly supportive of family-school collaborations, indicating that they result in improved academic performance, reduced absenteeism, and improved discipline (Henderson & Berla, 1994; U.S. Department of Education, 1995). Epstein and her colleagues have developed a widely recognized model for family partnerships stressing the benefits to students and suggesting six areas for collaboration: parenting, communicating, volunteering, learning in home, decision making, and community (Epstein, 1995, Epstein & Sanders, 2000). In thinking about family collaboration for students with special needs, Turnbull and Turnbull (2001) built on Epstein's model by infusing community in all areas and adding relevant special education concerns (meeting family basic needs, referral and evaluation, individualizing education) as opportunities for partnerships. Establishing these types of collaborative partnerships, families and educators discover new sources of support for one another (Walther-Thomas et al., 2000). Family members often have perspectives that differ from those of the other team members, particularly when they represent different cultural backgrounds. Their role, knowledge, and perspectives are discussed in Chapters 7 and 8. Chapter 8 also presents the new emphasis on family systems and on the role of the parent or other family member as an equal member of the team.

The roles of paraprofessionals will be presented in Chapter 5; these individuals provide support to teachers and other professionals who assign, supervise, and delegate their duties.

INTERACTIVE TEAMING IN HOSPITAL SETTINGS

This section was adapted from the work of Kristin J. Young, R. N., with her permission. The section is focused on the role of the pediatric nurse as a member of the hospital-based care team. It includes information about children and young adults who are eligible for services under IDEA and those who are sick but do not necessarily have disabilities. Special educators should be aware that the "rules" are different for each of these groups. Also, if a child who is eligible for special education is hospitalized long term, the district may provide a teacher or use district funds to help support the hospital-paid teacher to continue this child's education.

The role of the pediatric nurse, who spends more time with the patient than does any other health care provider in the hospital, is presented here in greater depth. The nurse will witness changes in condition and report these changes to the physician so the care plan can be altered, if necessary. The nurse is the patient's advocate, and must be diligent in her efforts to obtain the most appropriate treatment. Patient care conferences are held informally throughout the day, during which the nurse, patient, family, and physician discuss options and give feedback regarding the viability of each option. Conferences also include pharmacists, respiratory therapists, physical therapists, X-ray technicians, recreational therapists, and teachers.

The nurse may work extensively with parents and other family members. Parents now are encouraged to stay with their children for the duration of their illness in many hospitals, and in some cases siblings and grandparents are also allowed to stay. This allows the family to continue to function as a unit; stress is reduced because the patient is not made to stay alone and the parents do not feel so helpless. As family members observe the nursing care their children are receiving, they become familiar with the procedures and learn to perform the simpler tasks themselves. Family members also provide insight into the child's character and response to certain treatments so that the staff can approach them in a way that is the least threatening to them.

The nurse also stays in touch with other hospital caregivers. Some hospitals employ teachers and child development specialists to provide learning, recreation, and stress management for their pediatric patients. The teacher often confers with the child's regular teacher to get assignments and identify learning needs. The teacher then works with children in a one-to-one situation during a time of treatment when they are most able to concentrate on schoolwork. If a child becomes too tired or too ill to continue working, the teacher may leave homework for the child to do later or make arrangements to come back at another time, thereby promoting the child's overall learning experience by responding positively to the child's needs.

The child development specialists provide informal teaching, recreation, and stress management. They are often referred to as "play ladies" because they have a storeroom full of toys, games, and crafting supplies. For example, a premature infant, who requires stimuli to keep his mind active, may respond to cassette tapes, crib mobiles, and infant exercisers brought in by the play ladies when the nurse cannot take time to play with them. Older children are encouraged to express themselves through artwork. The play ladies commission young artists to design Christmas cards which are sold to the public; the profits enable the hospital to purchase supplies, equipment, and more toys. One year a young cancer patient designed a card with a menagerie of elves, all of whom were bald to resemble herself in chemotherapy. Later, she gave them wigs so they wouldn't feel so out of place in the world. The play ladies also encourage the use of games to occupy time and provide diversion from the reality of hospitalization. The game "Chutes and Ladders" is very popular among chronically ill children because it demonstrates the ups and downs of their diseases and treatments.

The pediatric nurse also collaborates with social service and home care agencies when patients need assistance obtaining services. The family of a child diagnosed with leukemia, for example, will feel overwhelmed by the seriousness of the illness, not to mention the enormous bills and time lost at work when they choose to spend precious time with their child. Social workers, who interact closely with families, help them obtain medical benefits, clothes, transportation, and even living quarters when necessary. In other cases, there may be a suspicion of child abuse or neglect. At those times, the social worker investigates the situation and helps to determine whether the child's best interest is served by remaining in the current household or by being removed. When families need assistance performing specific health-oriented tasks, the social worker may arrange for the families to attend special classes or arrange for a home health care agent to visit the family for home visits.

In all of these situations, the nurse caring for the patient coordinates the different services. In many hospitals the "primary nursing model" is followed, which means one nurse is primarily responsible for seeing that all needed tests, care, and services are given before the patient is discharged. She is assigned to that patient every day and is involved in every aspect of his or her care. If she is not working on the day of discharge, she will often make preparations for home care or follow-ups prior to that day. In a managed care setting, however, every nurse is expected to give total care to every patient on any given day. In this way all nurses become more experienced in a wider variety of ailments, rather than focusing on one or two "primaries." They become more adept at problem solving and no longer rely on the "primary nurse" to do all the work. In this model, the primary nurse may delegate duties to other staff, but overall care is enhanced because more than one person is familiar with the patient's special needs.

An example of the work of a pediatric nurse is given in the following application.

APPLICATION: Caring for James
A Day in the Life of a Pediatric Nurse

6:45 p.m. I arrive on my nursing unit to take my assignment for the next 12 hours. It is Thursday evening and I am expecting to have mostly patients who are postoperative or who are receiving chemotherapy or IV antibiotics. I am not disappointed. My assignment consists of two children who had appendectomies that day, a young cancer patient just finishing her current round of chemo, and James, a 15-year-old with failing kidneys who is being admitted after an attempt to place an arteriovenous fistula for dialysis has failed. Ordinarily this would not require admission, but the doctors wish to try again tomorrow, and James lives several hours away from the hospital. As I sit at the table to take report on these patients, I am thinking the assignment is rather light, and I should have plenty of time to catch up on some paperwork tonight.

8:00 p.m. I have checked on all of my patients, given their scheduled medications, and seen to their comfort for the evening. I am now waiting for James to arrive on the floor from the recovery room. The recovery room nurse has told me that the procedure itself went fine, but that the dialysis catheter they tried to place in his forearm does not work properly. This is a problem occasionally, because many of these patients have scar tissue along their veins and arteries from multiple needlesticks occurring when blood samples are drawn or IVs placed. James's kidneys are still functioning enough that his life is not in peril, but he will need dialysis very soon. He has a history of noncompliance with his recommended treatment program, so he is losing his kidneys faster than he should lose them. He is awake from the anesthesia, and appears to be in an irritable mood. The recovery room orderly will find his family in the waiting area before they bring him up to the unit.

8:20 p.m.   James arrives on the floor on a stretcher. He is complaining loudly about being in the hospital and is already threatening to leave. After an orderly gets him situated in his room, I check his vital signs and do a quick physical assessment to ascertain that he is in no distress. Then I must ask him and his family members about his medical history and personal routines so that we may make his stay as comfortable and problem-free as possible. I learn that he is from a remote rural area of our state and lives with his grandparents, who have had legal custody since he was a toddler. His mother is minimally involved in his care and sees him only a few times a year. She is reported to be a drug and alcohol abuser, and is believed to have indulged heavily during her pregnancy with James. I notice that he has some mild characteristics of fetal alcohol syndrome, including a flat upper lip and wide-set eyes. His family tells me he has had trouble in school all his life, does not learn well, and acts out frequently. His aunt fears for his grandmother, saying she is not able to control his behavior, and he is sometimes violent. I also learn that he smokes cigarettes, and he is now quite verbose in his annoyance that he has been prevented from smoking since early that morning. Again he threatens to leave the hospital. I tell him that since he is a minor, he cannot leave without his grandmother's permission. If he escapes, police will be sent to bring him back. He says he doesn't care, and he doesn't believe me. I tell him it is the truth, but if he is desperate to get out of his bed and go for a walk, I will allow it as long as a family member or staff member is with him at all times. He is agreeable to these terms, and his aunt and uncle agree to go with him for a stroll outside.

9:00 p.m.   James is back in his room and is in a more pleasant mood. I have completed admission paperwork and am ready to proceed with his care for the remainder of my shift. As I change the dressing on his arm, he begins to talk to me about his personal life. As he talks, he seems to look through me in his conversation, as if he were talking to an imaginary person behind me, rather than to me. His voice is calm as he tells me about the many people he hates and how he would shoot them in the head if his grandfather would give him the right kind of gun. Then he decides he doesn't need a gun; he can cut their heads off with a long knife instead. His aunt, the only family member left in the room now, tells him not to say things like that. He rolls his eyes and shrugs. His aunt may not have custody of him, but she seems intelligent and obviously cares about him. I am glad she is there. I leave the room to check on my other patients and call his doctor to notify him of this behavior.

9:30 p.m.   I have called the physician to tell him the situation and convey my concerns about James's emotional well-being. He is also concerned, but does not know James personally, because he is covering for his regular doctor for the night. He tells me to keep things low-key for the night and let him know if the behavior gets any worse. I agree. I spend as little time in his room as possible, but keep observing him even though it makes me nervous. I ask my charge nurse and hospital security to listen for trouble, in case he is truly unstable. I can't stop the images of newspaper headlines from flashing through my mind.

12:00 a.m.   James has been watching TV in his room for a couple of hours. His aunt remains at his bedside. She suggests he should try to sleep now but he says he can't sleep. His aunt and I agree that he should not be given any narcotics to help him sleep. I call the pharmacy, asking them to recommend a non-narcotic sleep aid for a teenager. She suggests Benadryl, which will cause drowsiness without any adverse side effects. I phone the doctor to get an order for the Benadryl.

12:30 a.m.   When I get to James's room with the Benadryl, he appears to be dozing. His aunt is dozing in the cot beside him. I leave the room again, taking the Benadryl with me. I can give it to him later if he awakens and becomes restless.

3:00 a.m.   James is awake and wants to talk again. This time he has questions about his own mortality. He asks if I think he will go to hell if he dies. I ask him if he wants to speak to the chaplain. No, he'll try to go back to sleep. He doesn't want the Benadryl.

4:30 a.m.   James has been restless in his bed. Now he wants to speak to the chaplain. He is very demanding in his request. He seems totally unconcerned that most people are asleep at this hour. I promise to call the chaplain closer to daybreak. He is unhappy and grumbles "Okay." He curses that he doesn't want the Benadryl—it doesn't work.

6:00 a.m.   I call the chaplain and explain James's disturbing behavior and his request. The chaplain, who also has a degree in psychology, states he will come in as soon as he can.

7:00 a.m.   The chaplain is in James's room now, discussing James's beliefs and assessing his behavior. By this time, his doctor is there also, as well as the pediatric social worker, the hospital dietitian, the nurse for the upcoming shift, and some other family members. After the chaplain and I fill them in on the events of the night, the team recommends that permission be obtained for James to be evaluated by a psychologist. They feel that his condition should be closely monitored, since he may need to receive emotional, as well as medical, support and that special education may be needed. They express hope that various caregivers will collaborate to support his family members, to give him the care he needs in and near his home, where he feels comfortable, rather than in a distant residential environment. They discuss the possibility that a social worker might make arrangements for James to be home schooled. A home health nurse will monitor his physical condition and report any changes to his doctor. Ideally, she and a psychologist might introduce him and his family to behavior modification techniques to make him more compliant with his medications and diet. A dietitian will help create a menu he can follow with special attention focused on his kidneys' ability to process foods, fluids, and electrolytes. The chaplain says he wants to call James from time to time to check on his spiritual well-being. The team believes that James will benefit from this collaborative effort. If James can learn that he must follow guidelines to maintain his health, he can be put on a list for a kidney transplant. With appropriate help, the team believes that James should have a good chance of living a long, happy life as a normal, functioning member of society.

7:30 a.m.   I leave the hospital for the day, feeling that I have played a significant part in making a young man's life better than it was yesterday.

SUMMARY

Members of the interactive team are highly trained professionals, each with specialized knowledge and skills that may contribute to the joint solution of problems. The team may consist of as few as two persons or it may be much larger; the team's size depends on the nature and complexity of the student's problems and the size and resources of the facility.

New trends in service delivery and changes in the health care system have been summarized.

The roles of team members have been described; for the special educator, the roles differ somewhat, according to:

◆ The type of student: one who is culturally different, one who has a mild disability, or one who has severe, multiple disabilities.

◆ The SE's function as service provider or as collaborator.

The roles of other team members have been described, clustered by common and sometimes overlapping functions:

◆ The program administrator.

◆ The classroom teacher.

◆ The behavior specialist, school psychologist, counselor, or social worker.

◆ The speech-language pathologist and the English as a second language or bilingual specialist.

◆ The physical therapist, adaptive physical educator, occupational therapist, and adaptive technology specialist.

◆ The vocational or transition specialist.

◆ The migrant education or Title 1 teacher.

◆ The school nurse and other health-related professionals.

◆ The physician, as a consultant to the team.

The interactive team functions most effectively when each member understands and respects the expertise of others, and when all work together to accomplish their common goal: provision of the best possible program for a given student with special needs. The communication skills needed by diverse professionals in reaching their common goal are presented in the next chapter.

ACTIVITIES

1. Imagine you are a member of a team. Conduct an informational interview with one of the professionals on the special education team, using the guidelines presented here:
   a. Plan for the meeting by collecting data and writing down the questions you want to ask the other team member.
   b. Start the meeting by establishing rapport and finding areas of common interest or understanding.

    c. State the purpose of your meeting.

    d. Share the information you have collected for the other team member.

    e. Ask the questions you have prepared to elicit specific information.

    f. Summarize what you have accomplished and make plans for follow-up meetings in the future.

2. Write a series of questions to present to members of a panel who represent the professionals identified in this chapter. You might, for example, want to ask about their specialized training, previous experiences with other professionals, or suggestions for working together more effectively.

3. Construct a table summarizing the major role each direct service provider plays and describing the collaborative contributions that could be made by each professional on the team.

REFERENCES

American Association for Counseling and Development. (1984). Primary prevention in schools [Special issue]. *The Personnel and Guidance Journal, 62,* 443–495.

American Speech-Language-Hearing Association (ASHA). (2001). *School survey.* Retrieved from http:// www.asha.org.

Anderson, A., & Luong, C. (1997). Health: Facing down asthma. *NEA Today, 15*(7), 23.

Associated Press. (1999, March 3). *Court ruling extends rights of disabled.*

Battle, D. E. (1998). *Communication disorders in multicultural populations* (2nd ed.). Boston: Butterworth-Heinemann.

Bauwens, J., Hourcade, J. J., & Friend, M. (1989). Cooperative teaching: A model for general and special education integration. *Remedial and Special Education, 10,* 17–22.

Beach, J. (1985). *Interaction with speech-language therapist.* Unpublished paper, University of Florida, Department of Special Education, Gainesville.

Bell, F. (1989). *Potential training sites for severely handicapped persons in Alachua County.* Unpublished master's thesis, University of Florida, Gainesville.

Bernstein, R., & Simon, D. (1988). A stitch in time: The role of the school psychologist. *Counterpoint, 8*(4), 6–7.

Biklen, D. (1988). *Regular lives.* Washington, DC: WETA-TV Department of Educational Activities.

Boone, R. (1990). The development, implementation, and evaluation of a preconference training strategy for enhancing parental participation in and satisfaction with the individual transition conference (Doctoral dissertation, University of Florida, 1989). *Dissertation Abstracts International, 51*(3), 618-A.

Buck, D. M., Cox, A. W., Shannon, P., & Hash, K. (2001). Building collaboration among physicians and other early intervention providers: Practices that work. *Infants and Young Children, 13*(4), 11–20.

Bush, M., & Wilson, C. (1997). Linking schools with youth and family centers. *Educational Leadership, 55*(2), 38–41.

Catts, H. W., & Kamhi, A. G. (Eds.). (1999). *Language and reading disabilities.* Boston: Allyn & Bacon.

Chalfant, J. (1989). Learning disability policy issues and promising approaches. *American Psychologist, 44*(2), 392–398.

Chalfant, J., Pysh, M., & Moultrie, R. (1979). Teacher assistance teams: A model for within-building problem solving. *Learning Disabilities Quarterly, 2*(3), 85–97.

Chamberlain, M. (1988). Employer's ranking of factors judged critical to job success for individuals with severe disabilities. *Career Development for Exceptional Individuals, 11*(2), 141–147.

Cook, L., & Friend, M. (1995). Co-teaching guidelines for creating effective practices. *Focus on Exceptional Children, 28*(2), 1–12.

Courtnage, L., & Healy, H. (1984). *A model in team building.* Cedar Falls, IA: University of Northern Iowa College of Education.

Cowell, J. (1998). Health: Is the school nurse a nurse? *The American School Board Journal, 185*(2), 45–46.

Darling, R. (1989). Using the social system perspective in early intervention: The value of a sociological approach. *Journal of Early Intervention, 13*(91), 24–35.

Davenport, S. (1990). The child with multiple congenital anomalies. *Pediatric Annals, 19*(1), 23–33.

Deshler, D. D. (1998). Grounding interventions for students with learning disabilities in powerful ideas. *Learning Disabilities, 24*(5), 292–303.

Eggers, N. (1983, November). In C. V. Morsink (Ed.), *Context for generic guidelines for allied health and education professionals who serve persons with disabilities.* Synthesis of proceedings for Training Alliances in Health and Education meeting of the American Society of Allied Health Professionals (USDOE, OSERS, Grant G008301774). Philadelphia: American Society of Allied Health Professionals.

Ehren, B. J. (2000). Maintaining a therapeutic focus and sharing responsibility for student success: Keys to in-classroom speech-language services. *Language, Speech, and Hearing Services in Schools, 31*(3), 219–229.

Elias, M. (1999, August 3). Pediatricians defend media exam. *USA Today,* p. 10D.

Engelmann, S., Carnine, D., & Steely, D. G. (1991). Making connections in mathematics. *Journal of Learning Disabilities, 24*(5), 292–303.

Epstein, J. L. (1995, May). School/family/community partnerships: Caring for the children we share. *Phi Delta Kappan,* 701–702.

Epstein, J. L., & Sanders, M. G. (2000). Connecting home, school, and community: New directions for social research. In M. Hallinan (Ed.), *Handbook of the Sociology of Education* (pp. 285–306). New York: Kluwer Academic Publishers.

Esposito, B., & Koorland, M. (1989). Play behavior of hearing impaired children: Integrated and segregated settings. *Exceptional Children, 55,* 412–419.

Field, S., Martin, J., Miller, R., Ward, M., & Wehmeyer, M. (1998). Self determination for persons with disabilities: A position statement of the Division on Career Development and Transition. *Career Development for Exceptional Individuals, 21*(2), 113–128.

Fox, C., Kuhlman, N., & Sales, T. (1988). Cross-cultural concerns: What's missing from special education training programs? *Teacher Education and Special Education, 11,* 155–161.

Fradd, S., & Weismantel, J. (1988). Developing and evaluating the program. In S. Fradd & J. Weismantel (Eds.), *Meeting the needs of linguistically and culturally different students: A handbook for educational leaders.* Boston: Little, Brown and Company.

Fradd, S., Weismantel, J., Correa, V., & Algozzine, B. (1988). Developing a personnel training model for meeting the needs of handicapped and at-risk language-minority students. *Teacher Education and Special Education, 11,* 30–38.

Friend, M., & Cook, L. (2003). *Interactions: Collaboration skills for school professionals.* Boston: Allyn & Bacon.

Frisbee, C. (1988). *The role of the school psychologist with handicapped and at-risk students.* Unpublished manuscript, University of Florida, College of Education, Gainesville.

Frischkorn, D. (1997). Families and communities: You know you've been successful when. . . . *NEA Today, 15*(7), 21.

Fund for the Improvement and Reform of Schools and Teaching (FIRST). (1989, May 2). *Federal Register, 54*(83). (CFDA No. 84. 211A)

Gerber, M. (1988). Tolerance and technology of instruction: Implications for special education reform. *Exceptional Children, 54,* 309–314.

Giangreco, M. (2000). Related services research for students with low-incidence disabilities: Implications for speech-language pathologists in inclusive classrooms. *Language, Speech, and Hearing Services in Schools, 31*(3), 230–239.

Graden, J., Casey, A., & Christenson, J. (1985). Implementing a prereferral intervention system: Part I, the model. *Exceptional Children, 51,* 377–384.

Guralnick, M. J. (1998). Effectiveness of early intervention for vulnerable children: A developmental perspective. *American Journal of Mental Retardation, 102*(4), 319–345.

Haring, N., & Phillips, E. (1972). *Analysis and modification of classroom behavior.* Englewood Cliffs, NJ: Prentice Hall.

Henderson, A. T., & Berla, N. (Eds.). (1994). *A new generation of evidence: The family is critical to student achievement.* Washington, DC: National Committee for Citizens in Education.

Heward, W. L. (2003). *Exceptional children: An introduction to special education.* Upper Saddle River, NJ: Merrill/Prentice Hall.

Hourcade, J. J., & Bauwens, J. (2003). *Cooperative teaching: Rebuilding and sharing the schoolhouse* (2nd ed.). Austin, TX: Pro-Ed.

Howell, B. (1981). Profile of the principalship. *Educational Leadership, 39,* 333–336.

Kagan, S., & Rivera, M. (1990). *Collaborations in action: Reshaping services for young children and their families.* New Haven, CT: Yale University, Bush Center in Child Development and Social Policy.

Kemmerer, A., Soeder, P., Szurek, A., & Carion, D. (1999). *A timely workshop.* Slippery Rock, PA: SRU College of Education School Collaboration Center.

Kohler, P. D., & Field, S. (2003). Transition-focused education: Foundation for the future. *Journal of Special Education, 37*(3), 174–183.

Kozleski, E., Mainzer, R., & Deshler, D. D. (2001). *Bright futures: An agenda for action for changing the conditions of teaching in special education.* Reston, VA: Council for Exceptional Children.

Larsen, J. (1984). The school psychologist and the teacher. In C. V. Morsink (Ed.), *Teaching special needs students in regular classrooms* (pp. 72–74). Boston: Little, Brown and Company.

Magna Awards (1998). A jump start for at-risk kids. *The American School Board Journal, 185*(4), A26.

Malloy, J. M., Cheney, D., & Cormier, G. M. (1998). Interagency collaboration and the transition to adulthood for students with emotional and behavioral disorders. *Education and Treatment of Children, 21*(3), 302–320.

McLeskey, J., Henry, D., & Hodges, D. (1998). Inclusion: Where is it happening? *Teaching Exceptional Children, 31*(1), 4–10.

Morsink, C. V. (Ed.). (1983, November). (With contributors E. Ellis, N. Eggers, J. Wittenmyer, G. Meyer, T. Barker, H. Johnson, J. Anderson, B. Stone, H. Garner, B. Gellman, B. Simon, & C. Del Polito). *Context for generic guidelines for allied health and education professionals who serve persons with disabilities.* Synthesis of proceedings for Training Alliances in Health and Education meeting of the American Society of Allied Health Professionals (USDOE, OSERS, Grant G008301774). Philadelphia, PA: American Society of Allied Health Professionals.

Morsink, C. V. (1984). *Teaching special needs students in regular classrooms.* Boston: Little, Brown and Company.

Morsink, C. V. (1999). *21st century teachers for a better future* (Final Report to Howard Heinz Endowment). Slippery Rock, PA: SRU College of Education.

Morsink, C. V., Thomas, C., & Smith-Davis, J. (1987). Noncategorical special education programs: Process and outcomes. In M. Wang, M. Reynolds, & H. Walberg (Eds.), *Handbook of special education: Research and practice* (Vol. 1, pp. 287–312). Oxford, England: Pergamon.

National Association of School Nurses. (2002a). Asthma management in the school setting (Issue Brief). Retrieved from http://www.nasn.org/briefs/asthma.htm

National Association of School Nurses. (2002b). School nurses and the Individuals with Disabilities Education Act (IDEA) (Issue Brief. Retrieved from http://www.nasn.org/briefs/idea.htm

National Association of School Psychologists. (1974). The changing role of the school psychologist: Primary prevention. *School Psychology Digest, 3*(4), 4–25.

National Center for Schools and Communities. (1998). Community schools in the making. In *Conversations: Supporting children and families in the public schools.* New York: Fordham University Center.

NBC. (1999). School nurses. *Nightly News,* February 9, 1999.

Nevin, A., & Thousand, J. (1986). What the research says about limiting or avoiding referrals to special education. *Teacher Education and Special Education, 9,* 149–161.

Nunez, R., & Collignon, K. (1997). Creating a community of learning for homeless children. *Educational Leadership, 55*(2), 56–60.

O'Neil, J. (1997). Building schools as communities: A conversation with James Comer. *Educational Leadership, 54*(8), 6–10.

Peterson, P. (1988). Teachers' and students' cognitional knowledge for classroom teaching and learning. *Educational Researcher, 17*(5), 5–14.

Pipho, C. (1997). The possibilities and problems of collaboration. *Phi Delta Kappan, 78,* 261–262.

Pugach, M. C., & Johnson, L. J. (2002). *Collaborative practices: Collaborative schools.* Denver: Love Publishing.

Rapport, M. J. K. (2003). *Personnel issues in school-based physical therapy: Supply and demand, professional preparation, certification and licensure.* (COPSSE Document No. IB-2E.) Gainesville, FL: University of Florida, Center on Personnel Studies in Special Education.

Reid, W. (1987). *Assessment and the Hispanic American.* Gainesville: University of Florida Project on Bilingual Special Education.

Roseberry-McKibbin, C., & Brice, A. (n.d.). Acquiring English as a second language. Retrieved from the ASHA Public Website at http://www.asha.org/public/English+as+a+Second+language.htm

Ross, J. (1984). The physician and the teacher. In C. V. Morsink (Ed.), *Teaching special needs students in regular classrooms* (pp. 77–83). Boston: Little, Brown and Company.

Ryberg, S., & Sebastian, J. (1981). The multidisciplinary team. In M. Hardman, M. Egan, & E. Landau (Eds.), *What will we do in the morning?* (pp. 12–29). Dubuque, IA: William C. Brown.

Sandall, S., McLean, M., & Smith, B. (Eds.). (2000). *DEC recommended practices in early intervention/early childhood special education.* Sopris West.

SEDL Newsletter. (2002, February). SEDL's new center makes family-community connections to improve learning, Vol 14. Retrieved from http://www.sedl.org/pubs/sedletter/v14n01/

Sigmon, S. (1987). Present roles and future objectives for school psychology. *Journal of Social Behavior and Personality, 2,* 379–382.

Snell, M., & Brown, F. (2000). Development and implementation of educational programs. In M. Snell & F. Brown (Eds.), *Instruction of students with severe disabilities* (5th ed., pp. 115–171). Upper Saddle River, NJ: Merrill/Prentice Hall.

Spache, G., & Spache, E. (1986). *Reading in the elementary school* (5th ed.). Boston: Allyn & Bacon.

Spracher, M. M. (1999). Learning about literacy: SLPs play key role in reading, writing the ASHA leader online. Retrieved from http://www.asha.org/about/publications/leader-online/archives/99-00/literacy.htm

Steere, D. E., & Cavaiuolo, D. (2002). Connecting outcomes, goals, and objectives in transition planning. *Teaching Exceptional Children, 34*(6), 54–59.

Swinth, Y., Chandler, B., Hanft, B., Jackson, L., & Shepherd, J. (2003). *Personnel issues in school-based occupational therapy: Supply and demand, preparation, and certification and licensure.* (COPSSE Document No. IB-1E.) Gainesville, FL: University of Florida, Center on Personnel Studies in Special Education.

Tobias, A. (1988). *The role of the school counselor with handicapped and at-risk students.* Unpublished paper, University of Florida, College of Education, Gainesville.

Turnbull, R., & Cilley, M. (1999). *Explanations and implications of the 1997 amendments to IDEA.* Upper Saddle River, NJ: Merrill/Prentice Hall.

Turnbull, R., & Turnbull, A. (2001). *Families, professionals, and exceptionality: Collaborating for empowerment* (4th ed.). Upper Saddle River, NJ: Merrill/Prentice Hall.

Turnbull, R., Turnbull, A., Shank, M., & Smith, S. (2004). *Exceptional lives: Special education in today's schools* (4th ed.). Upper Saddle River, NJ: Merrill/Prentice Hall.

U.S. Department of Education. (1995). *School linked comprehensive services for children and families—What we need to know.* Washington DC: Author.

U.S. Department of Education. (2002). *24th annual report to Congress on the implementation of the Individuals with Disabilities Education Act.* Retrieved November 2003, from Strategic and Annual Reports at http://www.ed.gov/about/reports/annual/osep/2002/index.html

Villa, R., & Thousand, J. (1988). Enhancing success in heterogeneous classrooms and schools: The powers of partnership. *Teacher Education and Special Education, 11,* 144–154.

Vincent, L., & Salisbury, C. (1988). Changing economic and social influences on family involvement. *Topics in Early Childhood Special Education, 8*(1), 48–59.

Walther-Thomas, C., Korinek, L., McLaughlin, V. L., & Williams, B. T. (2000). *Collaboration for inclusive education: Developing successful programs.* Boston: Allyn & Bacon.

Wang, M., Haertel, G., & Walberg, H. (1997). *What do we know: Widely implemented school improvement programs.* Philadelphia: Mid-Atlantic Educational Lab at Temple University.

Wehmeyer, M., & Schwartz, M. (1998). The self-determination focus of transition goals for students with mental retardation. *Career Development for Exceptional Individuals, 21*(1), 75–86.

Wells, K. (1997). Professional development for parents. *The American School Board Journal, 184*(1), 38–39.

Westby, C. (1985). Learning to talk—talking to learn: Oral-literature language differences. In *Communication skills and classroom success* (Vol. 1, pp. 181–213). San Diego: College Hill Press.

Westby, C., & Clauser, P. S. (1999). The right stuff for writing: Assessing and facilitating written language. In H. W. Catts & A. G. Kamhi (Eds.), *Language and reading disabilities* (pp. 259–324). Boston: Allyn & Bacon.

Williams, A. L. (1996). Enacting constructivist transactions. In J. Henderson (Ed.), *Reflective teaching: A study of your constructivist practices* (2nd ed., pp. 105–120). Englewood Cliffs, NJ: Merrill/Prentice Hall.

Wlodkowski, R., & Ginsberg, M. (1995). A framework for culturally responsive teaching. *Educational Leadership, 53*(1), 17–21.

Enhancing Communication Skills

Topics in this chapter include:

♦ Description of a communication model.

♦ Characteristics of communication in interactive teaming.

♦ Factors to consider in communication.

♦ Forms of communication.

♦ Strategies for managing conflict.

♦ An application illustrating effective and ineffective communication.

Principals and central office personnel have circulated the following example of what can happen as people try to communicate with each other. The original source of this communiqué is not known.

Halley's Comet

A school superintendent told the assistant superintendent the following: "Next Thursday at 10:30 A.M. Halley's Comet will appear over this area. This is an event that occurs only once every 75 years. Call the school principals and have them assemble their teachers and classes on their athletic fields and explain this phenomenon to them. If it rains, cancel the day's observation and have the classes meet in the auditorium to see a film about the comet."

The memo from the assistant superintendent to the principals stated: "By order of the superintendent of schools, next Thursday at 10:30 Halley's Comet will appear over your athletic field. If it rains, then cancel the day's classes and report to the auditorium with your teachers and students. You will be shown films, a phenomenal event which occurs only once every 75 years."

The principals announced to the teachers: "By order of the phenomenal superintendent of schools, at 10:30 next Thursday Halley's Comet will appear in the auditorium. In case of rain over the athletic field, the superintendent will give another order—something which occurs once every 75 years."

Teachers told their students: "Next Thursday at 10:30 the superintendent of schools will appear in our auditorium with Halley's Comet, something which occurs every 75 years. If it rains, the superintendent will cancel the comet and order us all out to our phenomenal athletic field."

Students reported to their parents: "When it rains next Thursday at 10:30 over the school athletic field, the phenomenal 75-year-old superintendent will cancel all classes and appear before the whole school in the auditorium accompanied by Bill Halley and the Comets."

Chapter 3 described the roles of parents and various professionals. Interactions among people who may have different perspectives in a team or consultative setting are affected by how well those involved are able to use a variety of communication skills to share and receive information and to resolve conflicts. The humorous Halley's Comet example illustrates how important accuracy and clarity are in preventing misunderstandings that may result when people in different roles attempt to communicate with one another.

The importance of communication skills for consultants and team members has been strongly supported in the literature. In fact, many people believe expertise in communication may be the most vital skill the individual can possess. Gutkin and Curtis (1982) stated:

> At the heart of all consultation methodology is the consultant's ability to establish a helping relationship and communicate effectively with the consultee. At its most basic level, consultation is an interpersonal exchange. As such, the consultant's success is going to hinge largely on his or her communication and relationship skills. (p. 822)

Pugach and Johnson (2002) commented:

> Perhaps the most important skill of effective collaborators is the ability to communicate ideas effectively. Communication is the foundation of all interactions between humans. Without the ability to communicate, our lives would be barren. (p. 47)

Communication skills also have been identified, through research studies and inclusion in training programs, as required areas for development and expertise. In her study on the consultation skills needed by resource teachers, Friend (1984) surveyed principals, regular classroom teachers, and resource teachers. The educators said they placed much importance on such skills as establishing a climate of trust, explaining perceptions of a problem, defining problems, interviewing, resolving conflicts by using strategies to minimize hard feelings, and using specific strategies to facilitate interpersonal communication.

West and Cannon (1988) obtained similar results in their study of collaborative consultation strategies needed by regular and special educators. Their results included the description of competency statements in the areas of personal characteristics, interactive communication, and collaborative problem solving—all of which relate to communication as a facilitating factor in interactive teaming. Dieker and Barnett (1996) observed, "The overall success of co-teaching hinges on one major factor: communication between teachers" (p. 7). Bruneau-Balderrama (1997) described important elements in implementing inclusion, noting, "Probably the most important factor in the success of any collaborative endeavor is open and frequent communication" (p. 329).

This chapter includes a description of a communication model and a discussion of vital characteristics of communication involved in interactive teaming. Factors to consider in communication are explained. The nonverbal, listening, and verbal forms of communication are described, along with skills to be developed and barriers that can be present. The final section of the chapter deals with procedures for managing conflict and resistance.

COMPONENTS OF THE PROCESS OF COMMUNICATION

Definition of Communication

Communication can be defined as a dynamic and ongoing process in which people share ideas, information, and feelings. The skills involved in communication are considered the means through which this sharing becomes meaningful (Egan, 2001). Communication also has been defined as a "symbolic process whereby reality is produced, maintained, repaired, and transformed" (Martin & Nakayama, 2000, p. 78), and occurs when another person's words or actions are given meaning.

These authors also delineated the complexity of intercultural communication by describing it as "both cultural and individual, personal and contextual, characterized by differences and similarities, static and dynamic, oriented to the present and the past, and characterized by both privilege and disadvantage" (p. 49).

ELEMENTS OF THE COMMUNICATION PROCESS

The communication process comprises several elements, as shown in Figure 4.1. Hybels and Weaver (1997) described these elements as follows. *Senders-receivers* are the people who are sending and receiving the messages. Typically, people are senders and receivers at the same time because they are simultaneously initiating communication and receiving another's responses. The *message* is composed of the ideas and thoughts being transmitted through verbal and nonverbal forms of communication. The *channel* is the route traveled by the message, which typically involves multiple senses. We not only hear the message but we use a person's facial

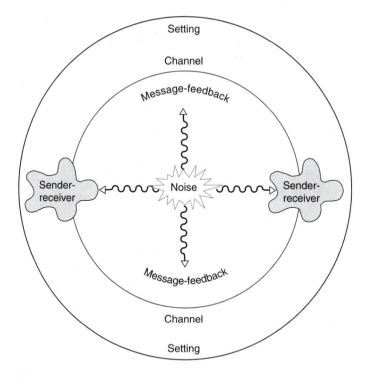

Figure 4.1
Elements of the communication process.

Source: From *Communicating Effectively,* 5th ed. (p. 13), by S. Hybels and R. L. Weaver, 1997, New York: McGraw-Hill. Reprinted by permission of The McGraw-Hill Companies, Inc.

expressions or the feel of a handshake to interpret it. *Feedback* is the response of the senders-receivers to each other; as in the message, feedback can be both verbal and nonverbal. Feedback enables the sender to gauge whether or not the receiver understood the message as it was intended. *Noise* is the physical (e.g., loud voices, truck passing) or psychological (e.g., daydreaming, planning a trip) interference that prevents the message from being accurately comprehended. The *setting* is the location where the communication is taking place. Because settings can be formal (e.g., office or auditorium) or informal (e.g., comfortable room, restaurant), they can affect the feelings people have while they are communicating. Another variable to consider is whether the location represents someone's "territory," such as the director or principal's office, and whether that location intentionally or unintentionally intimidates the others involved in the communication (cf. Dettmer, Dyck, & Thurston, 2002; Idol, Paolucci-Whitcomb, & Nevin, 2000; Martin & Nakayama, 2000).

When considering human communication, two other concepts are important: *continuous feedback* and *multichannel messages* (Friend & Cook, 2003). Continuous feedback refers to the simultaneous aspects of communication; that is, while sending a message, the sender receives information about the message or the environment and makes adjustments. For example, as the sender hears the message, he or she may decide that it isn't clear or that his or her choice of words was inappropriate and revise the message. Messages are multichannel in that more than one message is being transmitted simultaneously through different channels. Sometimes the messages are in agreement; that is, they are congruent (e.g., smiling or nodding while saying something positive). At other times the messages may be discrepant or incongruent (e.g., frowning while telling someone you are glad to see him or her).

CHARACTERISTICS OF EFFECTIVE COMMUNICATION IN INTERACTIVE TEAMING

In addition to being cognizant of the various elements of communication, team members need to be sensitive to the characteristics of effective interactions. Good communication is *purposeful*, with an intent clear to all parties; *planned*, in terms of thinking through what should be transmitted; *personalized*, according to the receiver's background; *open*, in terms of being able to express feelings; and *clear*, in that the words used are part of the other's language (Lang, Quick, & Johnson, 1981). On the latter point of clarity, Ehly and Eliason (1983) cautioned professionals in the fields of education and psychology to be aware of their use of jargon and "psychobabble" (e.g., IEP, EBD, CAT testing), which can interfere with understanding.

Personal characteristics such as *open-mindedness*, *acceptance*, and *flexibility* help to ensure positive individual interactions (Fishbaugh, 1997). Other significant interpersonal skills have been identified and include *risk taking, helpful criticism, objectivity, active listening, giving the benefit of the doubt, support*, and *recognizing the interests and achievements of others* (Katzenbach & Smith, 1999).

It takes time, and if it doesn't happen a team doesn't work.

Turnbull and Turnbull (2001) identified two prerequisites to effective communication that are vital to the teaming process: *knowing ourselves* and *developing respect and trust.* Gaining and maintaining the respect of others is obviously vital to the success of interactive team members. Establishing rapport can be accomplished by being willing to share information and learn from others (i.e., role release), treating others with respect, sharing credit for ideas, participating in activities beyond the scope of one's job (e.g., extracurricular and social functions), and demonstrating credibility by being aware of the domains of team members, such as showing an understanding of the dynamics of a regular classroom (Fishbaugh, 1997; Heron & Harris, 2001; Idol et al., 2000; Lopez, Dalal, & Yoshida, 1993; Spodek, 1982; Vargo, 1998).

Two final characteristics of communication required in teaming have previously been described in this text, but they merit repetition because of their importance: *confidentiality* and *sensitivity to cultural differences.* The willingness to protect the confidentiality of information shared in the collaboration and consultation of teaming interactions is vital (Gutkin, 1996). A person involved in such situations has only to be let down once by a consultant's or team member's breaking a confidence for him or her to be reluctant to participate again. Similarly, people from various cultures who receive adverse feedback on their communication skills or who are rebuffed by people who are unaware or uncaring about communication norms in their culture may learn to be defensive or unresponsive as a coping strategy.

FACTORS TO CONSIDER IN COMMUNICATION

Several factors affect the communication process as it occurs in the consultation and collaboration of teaming. These factors are related to personal characteristics; cultural differences; attitudes and experiences; the existence of backup support, such as data; and contextual and situational variables. Each of these factors is described in the following sections.

Personal Factors

The qualities identified by Rogers (1961) as most important for people in helping roles were empathy, genuineness, and unconditional positive regard. *Empathy* is the ability to understand the world of others by "walking a mile in their shoes." Empathy is not the same as sympathy, which involves feeling sorry for someone; rather, it is placing oneself in the situation to examine how that person feels (Brown, Pryzwansky, & Schulte, 1998; Egan, 2001). Two forms of empathy have been described: emotional empathy, or the ability to be affected by someone else's emotional feelings; and role-taking empathy, which involves the ability to understand another's frame of reference or point of view (Gladstein, 1983). Both require setting aside your own perspective or frame of reference in order to be open to another.

Genuineness is the ability to be "real" in caring for others, instead of dealing with them in a superficial manner. Gutkin and Curtis (1982) referred to genuineness as the "cardinal rule" of effective communication, though as Turnbull and Turnbull (1990) recognized, this level of caring is not always as easy as it may appear: "On the contrary, many go through life seeking to develop this quality in themselves. It requires hard work to awaken this quality in ourselves and inspire it in others" (p. 114). *Unconditional positive regard* is the ability to accept others without prejudice or bias, and to realize that they are entitled to their opinions.

Two other qualities Hybels and Weaver (1997) named as contributing to or detracting from communication are initiative and assertiveness. *Initiative* involves taking the lead, as appropriate, to facilitate the process. *Assertiveness* is the ability to stand up confidently for what one thinks or feels. Assertive communicators use language that portrays confidence and self-assurance without arrogance or aggression. These include using "I" messages instead of "you" messages, describing behavior objectively, stating what they want to happen, naming their own feelings, and expressing concern for others (Dettmer et al., 2002). Assertiveness is often confused with aggressiveness, but the latter refers to an attempt to establish power and control even at the expense of the feelings of others. An aggressive team member may speak and act as though he is not concerned with the emotions or positions of other members, and this may set up a confrontational relationship. In her study of the contrasting behaviors of assertiveness, nonassertiveness, and aggressiveness, Arab (1985) noted that those who are assertive are effective collaborators, whereas those who exhibit characteristics of the other two behaviors are not.

Another set of personal factors can play a role in the effectiveness of people in collaborative or consultative roles. These factors are predominantly concerned with how the person in a helping role attends to his or her own needs and how that process facilitates or impedes consultation. Fine, Grantham, and Wright (1979) cited the following considerations:

1. The consultant's identity remains the same; that is, his or her own orientation and feelings about life and self cannot be separated from the consultation process. In fact, Turnbull and Turnbull (2001) suggest that knowing yourself opens the door to better understanding of and appreciation for others.

2. The consultant needs to adhere to his or her own needs to be able to help others; that is, stress management and rejuvenation are vital in order to continue giving to others.

3. The problem belongs to the consultee, not to the consultant; that is, consultants should be facilitators and assist in problem solving, but they should not "own" the problem.

4. The consultant must be willing to let go of feelings about "the way it is supposed to be"; that is, remember the purpose is to help another person grow and develop skills, rather than force him or her to follow a certain program or become a "clone."

5. Lack of closure in this process is acceptable; the problems to be resolved will take time and cannot be forced or accelerated.

6. The consultant should not try to carry the burden alone; others in the system should be called on to share their expertise.

7. The perceptions and expectations of all concerned should be made explicit; that is, people in helping positions should clarify roles and responsibilities.

8. Alternatives should be offered to the consultee; that is, when a person is willing to try different interventions that have been suggested, the consultant should permit the person to select the one that seems most viable, and then support him or her in attempts to implement it.

9. People involved should view this as a problem-solving process; the solutions will take time, rather than being immediate answers. Also, a number of problem-solving approaches can be used.

10. A broad skill repertoire is essential; that is, people in helping roles must be familiar with a variety of strategies and techniques.

11. Success must be considered as a value judgment; that is, all possible outcomes of the helping process—such as changes in the child, system, parents, and other professionals—must be considered, rather than determining success or failure based on one indicator.

Cultural Differences

The changing demographics of today's schools makes it inevitable that school-based consultation will include providing services to individuals from a range of cultural backgrounds (Ramirez, Lepage, Kratchowill, & Duffy, 1998). Because teams and families will include members with diverse cultural norms and different interaction skills, it is important for interactive team members to develop expertise in *cross-cultural* or *intercultural communication skills* (Martin & Nakayama, 2000). The ability to acknowledge cultural differences in communication and relationships enhances the potential for success in interactions (cf. Jackson & Hughley-Hayes, 1993; Martin & Nakayama, 2000).

Differences in cultural norms among diverse ethnic groups have been identified related to how individuals perceive self, family, religion, sex roles, society, human nature, nature, and the supernatural (Hallman, Bryant, Campbell, McGuire, & Bowman, 1983). These differences and others, including race, religion, economics, and many forms of social behaviors, may be barriers between home and school (Belton-Owens, 1999). Lynch and Hanson (1992) stress the importance of open and respectful cross-cultural interactions to facilitate understanding. Harris (1996) commented: "People who are effective cross-cultural communicators tend to respect individuals; make continued and sincere attempts to take others' points of view, be open to learn, and be flexible; have a sense of humor; and tolerate ambiguity well" (p. 357). Harris identified four general skills that will lead to successful collaboration: (1) understanding one's perspective; (2) using effective interpersonal, communication, and problem-solving skills; (3) understanding the role(s) of collaborators; and (4) using appropriate assessment and instructional strategies. Generic and specific interpersonal and communication skills for a multicultural society are included in Table 4.1.

Table 4.1
Generic and Specific Interpersonal and Communication Skills for a Multicultural Society

Generic	Specific
Exhibit the following **interpersonal** skills:	
Be caring	Make continued and sincere attempts to understand the world from others' points of view
Be respectful	Respect individuals from other cultures
Be empathetic	Have a sense of humor
Be congruent	Tolerate ambiguity
Be open	Approach others with a desire to learn
Show positive self-concept	Be prepared and willing to share information about yourself
Show enthusiastic attitude	Identify the needed multicultural knowledge base
Show willingness to learn from others	Move fluidly between the roles of giver and taker of information
Be calm	
Try to live stress-free	
Be a risk taker	
Be flexible	
Be resilient	
Manage conflict and confrontation	
Manage time	
Exhibit the following **communication** skills:	
Listening	Work effectively with an interpreter or translator
Acknowledging	Use nontechnical language as an aid in equalizing differences between collaborators
Paraphrasing	Acknowledge cultural differences in communication- and relationship-building
Reflecting	
Clarifying	Use communication to create systems of meaning among collaborators
Elaborating	
Summarizing	Identify language practices that are disabling and change them
Grasping overt meaning	Ensure that problem identification does not conflict with cultural beliefs
Grasping covert meaning	
Interpreting nonverbal communication	Use information regarding socially hidden aspects of power that privilege or silence culturally diverse groups in problem solving
Interviewing effectively	
Providing feedback	
Brainstorming	
Responding nonjudgmentally	

Source: From "Collaboration Within a Multicultural Society: Issues for Consideration," by K. C. Harris, 1996, *Remedial and Special Education, 17*(6), 355–362, 376. Copyright 1996 by PRO-ED, Inc. Reprinted by permission.

Individuals from the nondominant culture who aspire to become professionals in special services programs and serve on interactive teams will confront some conflicts as they encounter the differences between what they value and the behaviors expected of "good" students and families in traditional schools. It may take more time, energy, and commitment on the part of professionals from different cultural backgrounds to develop a level of shared understanding, common knowledge, and communication skills that will provide them with a basis for collaboration. However, intercultural communication and collaboration of professionals with families allows all members of the team to contribute to the development of effective instructional programs for students from diverse backgrounds.

Attitudinal and Experiential Factors

Closely linked with personal qualities and cultural differences are attitudinal and experiential factors resulting from how team members feel about themselves, others, and the consultation or teaming process based on the experiences they have had. While the factors can be examined individually from every team member's perspective, for brevity's sake they are described in this chapter from the viewpoints of the consultant, consultee, and parents, because team members tend to fit into one of these three categories.

Weissenburger, Fine, and Poggio (1982) conducted a study on consultant and teacher characteristics as they related to consultation outcomes. They cited six teacher attitudes that may interfere with interventions suggested by a consultant (based on the work of Grieger, 1972): "(a) the child needs fixing, (b) it is wrong to express negative feelings, (c) children must not be frustrated, (d) children 'should-ought' to behave in certain ways, (e) children are blameworthy for their misdeeds, and (f) the child 'makes me' feel that way" (p. 263).

The study by Weissenburger et al. (1982) yielded several other attitudes that can affect communication and the teaming process. They found that consultant facilitativeness as perceived by teachers was positively related to problem resolution, as well as teacher attitudes of "I'm OK—you're OK." Teacher dogmatism, or holding tightly to one's own beliefs rather than trying to learn from others, was found to hinder the desired outcomes of consultation.

Parents' attitudes also are affected by their previous experiences. Parents' past experiences in dealing with professionals, personalities and values, and expectations and stereotypes can positively or negatively affect communication (Turnbull & Turnbull, 2001). In addition, Bailey (1987) noted that parents' and professionals' priorities for education or treatment are often different. He commented that parents may appear to lack motivation if they do not understand the relevance of requests, or they may lack the time, skill, energy, or resources to follow-up on recommendations. Professionals may not understand the needs of the family or may be unable to motivate family members, all of which contribute to the attitudes of both sides regarding future communication (Bailey).

Pruitt, Wandry, and Hollums (1998) studied 73 families that included children or adolescents who were receiving special education services. They found that the overwhelming majority of parents recommended that educators should realize that parents know and understand their children, and recognize that the contributions and suggestions of parents are valuable and should be respected. The parents also urged educators to use a more humane demeanor when discussing their children, listen more, interact in an honest manner, and treat individuals with dignity and respect.

Additional attitudinal considerations related to how perceptions can "color one's vision" are concerned with how parents may be categorized by professionals. Professionals may view parents in negative ways and thereby diminish effective communication. Professionals can consider parents as vulnerable clients, patients, the cause of the problem, adversaries, less observant, hostile, less intelligent, resistant, denying, or anxious (Sonnenschien, 1984). Any of these views may have a negative effect on expectations for success or the development of a productive relationship with parents.

Two final considerations are the use of emotion-laden words and the lack of common experiences. On the former point, it is important to realize that parents will be particularly sensitive to words that describe their child in terms such as *retarded, handicapped,* or *disturbed.* Although it may be necessary to use these labels in program placement, professionals should take care to explain their meanings, as well as their tentative status and limitations. Also, the negative effect may be softened if professionals introduce such terms to parents in a private setting, rather than using them first in a team meeting (Losen & Losen, 1985).

The lack of common experiences is particularly evident in cases such as a childless professional who cannot understand the fatigue experienced by a working single parent who is asked to implement speech and physical therapy follow-up every night with a child who has multiple disabilities. The parent may lack the professional's understanding of the importance of this follow-up in successful therapy. Open communication on the part of both parties can help bridge this gap. Interactive team members should remember to treat each situation individually and, as much as possible, avoid stereotyping parents and other professionals based on previous experiences.

Backup Support Factors

A source of backup support for communication interactions is the existence of data. Each team member will be able to provide different types of data depending on the area of expertise. For example:

◆ Parents will be able to describe developmental milestones and home behaviors.

◆ General education teachers can contribute data on curriculum, achievement tests, and group teaching strategies.

◆ Psychologists can delineate the interpretation of intelligence tests.

◆ Special educators can outline teaching techniques and strategies for individualizing.

- ◆ Adaptive physical educators and physical therapists can demonstrate movement limitations and modifications.
- ◆ Counselors and social workers can share perspectives on emotional factors.
- ◆ Assistive technology specialists can provide options for adapted microcomputers or other communication devices.

To provide these different types of data, team members will use observation as well as appropriate data-collection strategies unique to their professional fields, such as behavioral observations (Tawney & Gast, 1984; Zirpoli & Melloy, 2000), achievement and intelligence tests (Overton, 2000; Venn, 2000), or statistical interpretations of other types of tests (Kerlinger, 1986; Sax, 1997).

One strategy for collecting and sharing data that is useful at the beginning of a team or consultative process is the *informational interview* (Hudson, 1987), which was illustrated in the Application section in Chapter 3 on page 105. Any team member can use this strategy to establish rapport and share information with another. The six steps in the informational interview are these: (1) preplanning, (2) establishing rapport, (3) stating the purpose, (4) providing information, (5) using specific questions to obtain information, and (6) summarizing and planning a follow-up. These steps are illustrated in Figure 4.2.

Data collection is particularly important for the team as members attempt to identify problems, determine appropriate interventions, and evaluate the effectiveness of strategies that have been implemented. Team members will need to take the initiative in gathering appropriate data, organizing the data, and then sharing the results with others in an understandable manner.

Context or Situational Factors

The final factors that can affect communication are those related to the context or situation in which the interactions will occur. Hudson (1987) described two types of situations: proactive and reactive. In a *proactive* situation, parents and professionals meet to establish a positive relationship and share information. In this context they can be more relaxed, because they are meeting to anticipate and prevent problems. In a *reactive* situation, the team is meeting as a result of a problem being manifested, and therefore members may be more emotional. In a reactive context, the emphasis in communication must shift from information sharing to listening, supporting, and discussing possible interventions.

FORMS OF COMMUNICATION

All the factors previously described can affect both forms of communication—nonverbal and verbal—and listening, which is a "bridge" between the two forms. *Nonverbal* behaviors include attending to what is being said and encompass what

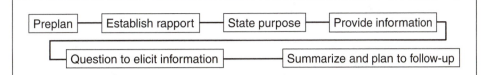

Steps:

1. *Preplan.* Formalize an appointment, review any background material, and decide on questions to be asked.

2. *Establish rapport.* At the beginning of the meeting, talk briefly about nonprofessional interests that people may have in common. In Hawaii, this is called "talk story." On the mainland, it is often called "small talk."

3. *State purpose.* Clarify the purpose of the meeting by stating that you are attempting to establish some common ground and to get to know each other in ways that will enable you to work together more productively.

4. *Provide information.* Discuss yourself as a professional. Talk about your "philosophy" of education if you are talking with another educator. You may have a diagnostic-prescriptive philosophy that emphasizes the importance of individual differences, which may be in contrast with the mainstream teacher's focus on group learning approaches. Or you may have an educational, as contrasted to a medical, orientation to treatment, which differs from that of some health-related professionals. Share your ideas in a way that suggests you are trying to identify areas of commonality. Share samples of the child's work or some supportive data if you are talking with a parent.

5. *Use specific questions to elicit information.* Ask questions about the other person's role, background, and philosophy. The focus here should be on ways in which you can work together. Search for commonalities in comparing what this person tells you and the information you provided to them.

6. *Summarize and plan to follow-up.* Stress the idea that this is the first step in what you hope will be a long and productive relationship. Thank the other person for his or her time and effort and indicate that you will be in contact again. If you have a specific time or purpose, state it and try to arrange a common meeting time.

Figure 4.2
Informational interview.

Source: From *Proactive and Reactive Consultation: A Model for Preservice Training,* by P. Hudson, 1987, unpublished manuscript, University of Florida, Department of Special Education, Gainesville. Adapted by permission.

is commonly referred to as "body language." *Listening* involves understanding the message and indicating that understanding to the sender. *Verbal* behaviors include such strategies as descriptive statements, paraphrasing, and questioning. Each set of skills is now described in more detail.

Nonverbal Behaviors

Most communication messages are transmitted in ways other than the use of words alone. In fact, it has been suggested that up to 90% of a message's content may be transmitted through nonverbal behaviors and vocal inflections. Pugach and Johnson (2002) commented that nonverbal communication is very powerful, and often the nonverbal messages are a more accurate representation of the actual intent of the communication than what is verbally transmitted.

Body Language and Attending Skills.   Body language often is the transmitter of silent messages, communicating a range of attitudes and feelings. Cramer (1998) noted that learning to "read" body language can help assess one's effectiveness as a speaker. She commented that the body language of the listener can signal the acceptance or understanding of what is being said, or it can indicate lack of comprehension or rejection of the speaker's message.

Closely related to body language are *attending skills.* These behaviors indicate that the listener or receiver is psychologically and emotionally present and listening. Egan (1998) suggested the acronym SOLER (straight, open, lean, eye contact, relaxed), summarizing five attending behaviors that indicate attention to the speaker: (1) *straight* refers to facing the person squarely or turning toward the person with whom you are communicating, (2) an *open* posture is with arms and legs relaxed instead of crossed, (3) *leaning* toward the other person at times indicates attentiveness, (4) maintaining *eye contact,* and (5) appearing *relaxed* and interested, not stiff or artificial in your attention. Effective use of these behaviors lets people know you are "with them" instead of thinking about or responding to other things in the environment, assists in establishing and maintaining good rapport, and puts the person in the position of being an effective listener.

Interpreting Nonverbal Messages.   Nonverbal messages can modify a verbal message in the following ways: confirm, deny, confuse, emphasize, or control (Egan, 2001). In certain situations, however, "negative" nonverbal signals can be sent to understanding or familiar listeners without penalty. If certain team members appear to be bored, when in reality they are simply tired, it is probable that the understanding listener will forgive them. In contrast, if they send the same signal to a team leader who is sensitive to the need for respect, inattentiveness may be interpreted as rudeness or hostility. It is permissible for the team member to assume a relaxed posture—leaning back, with hands clasped behind the neck—with an old friend, but the team member who portrays this nonverbal image to a parent or a newly introduced professional peer risks being thought of as uninterested and unwilling to modify professional beliefs. Obviously, the danger of misinterpretating nonverbal signals is more acute at the beginning of a relationship than after it has been established and people know how to "read" others' signals.

Being able to pick up on nonverbal signals is important for two reasons. First, team members can avoid sending messages that may hinder communication in the sense that the receiver perceives them negatively. Second, people who are able to accurately "read" their listeners' nonverbal behaviors can use this feedback to enhance their communications. When receivers send negative signals, the perceptive sender changes the verbal or nonverbal message being sent. Ignoring the signals can have disastrous consequences, whereas reading them and responding accordingly can have great benefits (Losen & Losen, 1985).

Considerations.   As Martin and Nakayama (2000) observed, nonverbal communication is symbolic, governed by rules that are contextually determined and developed through cultural experiences. Interactive team members must be cognizant of the fact that nonverbal communication behaviors differ among cultural groups. For example, in the mainstream culture of the United States, it is considered important for the sender and receiver to receive feedback by looking at each other's eyes. However, this may not be true in every culture; in many Asian cultures, too much direct eye contact is a signal of disrespect, particularly when given by a person in a position of lower status. The appropriateness of touch and physical proximity also varies according to cultural standards, with people in Hispanic cultures tending to touch more and stand closer than those in Asian cultures. Smiling, which usually signals happiness and acceptance in the dominant cultural groups in the United States, may reflect embarrassment or even anger in some Asian cultures. In high-context cultures, such as African American, there is less reliance on verbal communication, so nonverbal communication and interpretation are very important (Miranda, 1993). While these behaviors may serve as examples for this discussion, it is important to remember that a number of factors other than race will mitigate the influence of cultural identity, including socioeconomic status, age, gender, education, and geography. Overgeneralizations of cultural groups should be avoided.

For the successful team member, it is also important to remember that the word *culture* can have a very general meaning. In the broadest sense, a culture is any group that has a history and comes together around a set of common goals, standards, and language. The teaching profession is a culture, and it is different from the cultures of physical therapy and social work. Each school or agency often has its own culture, just as each family has its own set of standards and customs. The team member who is not aware of those nonverbal behaviors that are expected in a particular professional culture is well advised to behave conservatively; for example, be careful about invading another's personal space or using extended direct eye contact. This sensitivity to nonverbal communication differences is especially important for all team members in a new group at the early stages of their interactions.

Listening

Listening can be considered a "bridge" between the nonverbal and verbal forms of communication because it incorporates elements of both, and also affects both. Listening also is a way to understand thoughts and needs as well as to demonstrate empathy. As Covey (1989) stated: "Seek first to understand, then to be understood" (p. 235). Listening and understanding has three parts: the nonverbal behavior, the verbal message, and the person (Egan, 2001).

Importance of Listening.   According to Hybels and Weaver (1997), listening makes up more than half of the time devoted to the various communication skills (see Figure 4.3). Despite its importance, however, very few people are truly good listeners (Boyd, 2001). In fact, even at the purely informational level it is estimated that 75% of what is heard is ignored, misunderstood, or quickly forgotten. McKenna's (1998) estimate of the amount of time spent listening was much higher than Hybels and Weaver indicated. She stated that people spend up to 80% of each day listening. She also commented: "Listening is our most frequently used communication skill, yet we often feel that it requires no effort on our part" (p. 30).

Styles of Listening.   Gordon (1970) described two styles of listeners: active and passive. While most people tend to prefer one style or another, effective listeners use both styles depending on the situation. *Passive listeners* often are silent, but they remain involved in the interaction by demonstrating attending behaviors and giving words of encouragement. This style of listening is particularly appropriate when a team member needs to "vent" and share emotions.

In *active listening* the receiver is much more involved and animated. The listener frequently makes comments, asks questions, and shares his or her own experiences. Gordon (1970) believed this style of listening encourages people to express thoughts, assists in building relationships, and helps in finding solutions to problems. McKenna (1998) described this type of listening as *reflective listening*. She noted that reflective listening allows the listener to focus on the central points of the issue, and encourages the speaker to describe his or her feelings and position on the topic.

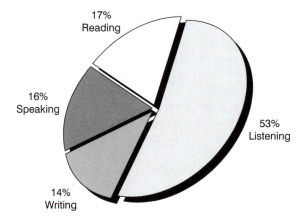

Figure 4.3
Percentage of time devoted to various communication skills.

Source: From *Communicating Effectively,* 5th ed. (p. 13), by S. Hybels and R. L. Weaver, 1997, New York: McGraw-Hill. Reprinted by permission of The McGraw-Hill Companies, Inc.

Active or reflective listening also communicates to other team members basic attitudes about how a receiver or listener feels toward and may react to another person. Gordon (1970) delineated these attitudes as follows:

1. You must *want* to hear what the other person has to say.
2. You must sincerely want to help the person with his or her problem.
3. You must genuinely be able to accept the other person's feelings, no matter how different they are from your own.
4. You must trust the other person's capacity to handle, work through, and find solutions to his or her own problems.
5. You must realize and appreciate that feelings are transitory in nature; consequently, you need not fear them.
6. You must view the other person as separate from yourself with alternative ways of perceiving the world. (summarized in Turnbull & Turnbull, 1990, p. 131)

Listening Skills.   In implementing active listening, Gordon (1974) recommended the following three steps:

1. The receiver should listen carefully to what is being said.
2. After hearing the expression of strong feelings, the receiver should restate the feelings.
3. After restating those feelings, the receiver should infer the reason for the feelings. The statement is "You feel . . . (angry) because. . . ."

This strategy can be used effectively in conversations among good friends as well as between a therapist and a client in a private meeting. There is, however, a certain amount of risk involved with using the "you" message in a team meeting, because the statement that one individual knows how and why another feels a certain way may be considered arrogant or rude. The suggested modification for use by team members is to soften the inference about feelings and to eliminate the use of the word *because.* This type of feedback is more appropriately used in a group discussion, particularly one in which the participants are relatively unknown to each other. The empathy statement in this case would be "It sounds as if you are angry about this. . . ."

Brammer (1988) described other skills to indicate a person is listening and to clarify what has been heard. *Paraphrasing* involves responding to basic messages being sent by another person. In doing so, the listener uses language similar to the speaker's to express understanding of the content. *Clarifying* includes restating points or requesting restatements to ensure understanding. *Perception checking* is a strategy to determine the accuracy of the feelings or emotions detected. These skills, along with examples to illustrate how they can be used, are summarized along with verbal skills in Figure 4.4.

1. **Listening Skills**

   Paraphrasing. Responding to basic messages—"You are feeling positive about this intervention, but you are confused as to the best way to implement it."

   Clarifying. Restating a point or requesting restatement to ensure understanding—"I'm confused about this. Let me try to state what I think you have said."

   Perception checking. Determining accuracy of feeling or emotion detected—"I was wondering if the plan you chose is really the one you want. It seems to me that you expressed some doubt; did I hear correctly?"

2. **Leading Skills**

   Indirect leading. Getting a conversation started—"Let's start with you describing how things are going with the first strategy."

   Direct leading. Encouraging and elaborating discussion—"What do you mean when you say there is no improvement? Give me a recent example of an incident in class."

   Focusing. Controlling confusion, diffusion, and vagueness—"You have been discussing several problems with Tommy's behavior in class. Which of these is most important to you? To Tommy?"

   Questioning. Inquiring about specific procedures in an open-ended way—"Please explain the behavior management system you are currently using," not "Do you have any type of management system?"

3. **Reflecting Skills**

   Reflecting feelings. Responding to the emotions expressed—"It sounds as if you are feeling very frustrated with this situation."

   Reflecting content. Repeating ideas in new words for emphasis—"His behavior is making you wonder about your effectiveness as a teacher."

4. **Summarizing Skills**

   Summarizing. Pulling themes together—"Let's take a look at what we have decided thus far. We have agreed to try peer tutoring and a different reinforcement system."

5. **Informing Skills**

   Advising. Giving suggestions and opinions based on experience—"Based on my 14 years as a teacher, I can tell you that idea will not work!"

   Informing. Giving information based on expertise, research, and training—"I attended a workshop on the jigsaw technique. Perhaps that strategy would help make the groups in your room more effective."

Figure 4.4
Communication skills.

Source: From *The Helping Relationship: Process and Skills,* 4th ed. (pp. 66–67), by L. M. Brammer, 1988, Upper Saddle River, NJ: Prentice Hall. Adapted by permission of Prentice-Hall, Inc.

Verbal Behaviors

Like nonverbal and listening skills, verbal signals are critical for team members who wish to send and receive messages accurately. The elements of verbal skills to be discussed are paralanguage, content-level sequences, verbal skills, and roadblocks.

Paralanguage.   Paralanguage refers to the way people say things or the vocal components of speech. The components of paralanguage are rate of speed, pitch, volume, vocal quality, rhythm, pacing or tempo, and the use of timing. Each of these components can affect the meaning and interpretation of what is being said.

Another important component of paralanguage is *intonation*. Often intonation (i.e., *how* it is said rather than *what* is said) is a more powerful and more primitive conveyor of meaning than simply words. The intonations in language convey warmth or disapproval to an infant, even before there is an understanding of words. When used by speakers of a foreign language, intonation also is effective in communicating meanings in the absence of specific word comprehension. The effective receiver or listener uses verbal intonation in a way similar to a handwriting analysis—to determine deeper meanings. Eisenhardt (1972) developed a series of examples that illustrate the point. She asked how many different ways the word *please* can be said and have it mean something different each time. A teacher might say "Please!" to a child tapping his pencil annoyingly, while a friend might say "Please" to another friend when begging for a favor. In each example the word remains the same, but the elements of intonation—*stress, pitch,* and *juncture* (pause)—convey different meanings.

The three elements of intonation can be used effectively by team members to communicate assertiveness, neutrality, or empathy, depending on the situation and the previous responses of others in the group. For example, suppose the team member assuming the role of leader needs to communicate emphatically that the group will not make a decision on the basis of a single, biased test. The intonation of the message would communicate assertively, "We will not violate this child's right to a multidimensional assessment, nor to the parent's right to due process!" The words *not* and *right* would receive stress; a pause for emphasis would be placed between the words *assessment* and *nor,* and the pitch would be lowered decisively at the end of the sentence.

Conversely, the team member who had just been told by a divorced mother that her ex-husband had refused to pay child support would use a different intonation to convey empathy. The response, "Things must be really tough for you right now" would be characterized by softer inflections: a wavy pitch without distinct juncture, and stress on either the word *tough* or *you,* depending on the focus of the conversation. (For additional information on these constructs, see McKenna, 1998, or Martin & Nakayama, 2000.)

Content-Level Sequence.   Different levels in the emotional content of verbal messages, each of which is appropriate at a different point in the sequence of developing a relationship with another person, have been identified (Fong, 1986). It is possible to share feelings with a close associate, but not with a stranger; it is easier to criticize a friend than an enemy. Each of these situations illustrates the importance of using the appropriate level of emotional content in communication. According to Fong, there are four levels: (1) small talk, (2) communicating an interest in common work or other experiences, (3) sharing some information about self, and (4) intimacy, the "you and I" relationship and feelings.

The first level, *small talk*, is characterized by impersonal contact, such as might be used with a total stranger in the supermarket. Appropriate topics of conversation to use with a person standing in the checkout line include the weather, prices, and headlines. All of these are impersonal topics that can be shared superficially with someone sharing a temporary environment. If the comments are too lengthy or personal, the listener likely will turn away in discomfort. On first meeting, to tell another person about a death in the family is the verbal counterpart of throwing one's arms around a total stranger. This may seem an extreme and unlikely example, but consider an IEP conference at which a school psychologist begins the meeting by telling a father—who is a total stranger—that his third-grade son cannot read and is being considered for placement in a class called "learning disabilities." In the absence of prior conversations in which these two people have built some type of relationship, this statement would be totally out of context and could have long-term effects on future interactions.

At the second level, the two communicators *discuss common interests* that have to do with their work environments or past experiences. The communication begins with some impersonal questioning, in which one or both people try to find out something that is shared. One person may say, "Where did you go to school?" The other answers, "I went to the University of Kentucky." The first rejoins, "No kidding, my brother went there, too. Are you as big of a basketball fan as he is?" If it turns out that there is a link, the communication will continue, and a higher level of communication can be established.

In level three, *sharing information about self*, the communicators attempt to exchange some thoughts, but not feelings. The initiator of the conversation would share his or her thoughts first, and solicit feedback on similar thoughts from the receiver. For example, suppose a special education teacher and a regular classroom teacher are conversing in the lounge. The classroom teacher says, "Jose seems to be having some trouble hearing in my class. Does he have that same problem when he works with you?" The response would remain on the informational/thought level, with the objective of common problem solving. There are no feelings expressed, but there is a sharing of a high level of thought. A conversation at this level would be much more difficult and less productive, however, for two individuals who had not shared the first two levels: "Isn't this weather great?" and "I enjoy camping, too."

At the highest level, *intimacy*, team members find it possible to share feelings that have to do with the "I" and "you" relationship. Conversations at this level are concerned with impressions, the way people feel about one another, and their reactions. At this level it is advisable to be cautious, even when people think they know each other well. Feeling-level conversations between people of the opposite sex or from different cultural backgrounds are particularly difficult, because they can be easily misunderstood or misinterpreted.

In any event, conversations at this level should not be attempted prematurely. After their relationship was well established through the three previous levels, two team members who were having difficulty might approach each other at this level. For example, a speech therapist had designed an outstanding program in language development for a child, but the program was not succeeding because the special education teacher was not providing follow-up in the resource room. The speech therapist could say, "I feel so discouraged by my efforts to teach Charles to speak in complete sentences. I'm getting the impression that this is an intervention program you do not support. Since I only have Charles for 30 minutes a week, the follow-up in your room is very important." Notice the use of "I" messages rather than "you" messages as an attempt to keep the other person from becoming immediately defensive and to better the chances for an open discussion.

Verbal Skills. Brammer (1988) described four sets of verbal communication skills, in addition to the listening skills that have been discussed. Those sets of skills are leading, reflecting, summarizing, and informing. *Leading skills* include direct and indirect leads, focusing, and questioning. The purposes of leading skills are to encourage the persons involved to get a conversation going, keep it on track, and encourage elaboration. *Reflecting skills* involve "mirroring" back feelings and content to the sender to communicate an understanding of one's frame of reference and feelings. *Summarizing skills* are designed to pull ideas together and ensure a common understanding of items that have been discussed and agreed on. *Informing skills* provide information based on experience, knowledge, and background. The two types of informing skills are advising and informing. The latter is preferable in most instances, because some people are insulted when they are given "advice" by another. These skills and corresponding examples are described in more detail in Figure 4.4.

One other important set of verbal skills relates to statements designed to provide feedback, which can be phrased as descriptive or judgmental. *Descriptive* statements are based on data. Whenever possible, the descriptive statement should indicate a measured quantity and time frame, as well as the source of the data. For example, after observing in a teacher's classroom, the counselor might say, "I noticed that John and Jennifer responded to five out of the eight questions you asked during the 20 minutes I was in your room yesterday." This type of statement described exactly what was seen, when, for how long, and where the observation took place. *Judgmental* statements are based on feelings, which can come across positively or negatively. The same situation could be described in a judgmental way as "It seemed to me that John and Jennifer answered most of the questions yesterday." This statement could be interpreted positively that John and Jennifer are doing well in class, but it also could be interpreted negatively if the implication was that the teacher primarily called on John and Jennifer because they knew the answers and that the teacher ignored the other students. As a rule, team members should use descriptive statements to avoid the chance that the message will be interpreted in a negative way.

Barriers. Gordon (1974) identified a number of "roadblocks" to effective verbal communication. These *roadblocks* are barriers to interactions among individuals or those in team situations. Examples of roadblocks are provided in Figure 4.5.

1. **Ordering, Commanding**
   Can produce fear or active resistance.
   Invites "testing."
   Promotes rebellious behavior, retaliation.
   "You must . . . "; "You have to . . . "; "You will. . . ."

2. **Warning, Threatening**
   Can produce fear, submissiveness.
   Invites "testing" of threatened consequences.
   Can cause resentment, anger, rebellion.
   "If you don't, then . . . "; "You'd better, or. . . ."

3. **Moralizing, Preaching**
   Creates "obligation" or guilt feelings.
   Can cause others to "dig in" and defend their positions even more ("Who says?").
   Communicates lack of trust in other's sense of responsibility.
   "You should . . . "; "You ought to . . . "; "It is your responsibility. . . ."

4. **Advising, Giving Solutions**
   Can imply other is not able to solve own problems.
   Prevents other from thinking through a problem, considering alternative solutions, and trying them out for reality.
   Can cause dependency or resistance.
   "What I would do is . . . "; "Why don't you . . . "; "Let me suggest. . . ."

5. **Persuading with Logic, Arguing**
   Provokes defensive position and counterarguments.
   Often causes other to "turn off," to quit listening.
   Can cause other to feel inferior, inadequate.
   "Here is why you are wrong . . . "; "The facts are . . . "; "Yes, but. . . ."

6. **Judging, Criticizing, Blaming**
   Implies incompetency, stupidity, poor judgment.
   Cuts off communication over fear of negative judgment or "bawling out."
   Child often accepts judgments as true ("I am bad"); or retaliates ("You're not so great yourself!").
   "You are not thinking maturely . . . "; "You are lazy. . . ."

7. **Name-Calling, Ridiculing**
   Can cause other to feel unworthy, unloved.
   Can have devastating effect on self-image of other.
   Often provokes verbal retaliation.
   "Crybaby"; "Okay, Mr. Smarty. . . ."

8. **Analyzing, Diagnosing**
   Can be threatening and frustrating.
   Other can feel trapped, exposed, or not believed.

Figure 4.5
Roadblocks to communication.

Source: From *Teacher Effectiveness Training,* by T. Gordon, 1974, New York: David McKay Co. Adapted by permission.

Stops other from communicating for fear of distortion or exposure.
"What's wrong with you is . . . "; "You're just tired"; "You don't really mean that."

9. **Reassuring, Sympathizing**
Causes other to feel misunderstood.
Evokes strong feelings of hostility ("That's easy for you to say!").
Other often picks up messages such as "It's not all right for you to feel bad."

10. **Praising, Agreeing**
Implies high expectations as well as surveillance of other's "toeing the mark."
Can be seen as patronizing or as a manipulative effort to encourage desired behavior.
Can cause anxiety when other's perception of self doesn't match praise. "Well, I think you're doing a great job!"; "You're right—that teacher sounds awful!"

11. **Probing, Questioning**
Because answering questions often results in getting subsequent criticisms or solutions, others often learn to reply with nonanswers, avoidance, half-truths, or lies.
Because questions often are unclear as to what the questioner is driving at, the other may become anxious and fearful.
The other can lose sight of his or her problem while answering questions spawned by concerns.
"Why . . . "; "Who . . . "; "What did you . . . "; "How. . . ."

12. **Diverting, Sarcasm, Withdrawal**
Implies that life's difficulties are to be avoided rather than dealt with. Can imply other's problems are unimportant, petty, or invalid. Stops openness when a person is experiencing a difficulty.
"Let's talk about pleasant things . . . "; "Why don't you try running the world!"
Remaining silent; turning away.

USING AND MISUSING FORMS OF COMMUNICATION

As team members use nonverbal, listening, and verbal skills, there are several considerations to keep in mind.

1. Match your verbal and nonverbal signals to reduce the likelihood of the message being misinterpreted. Usually the nonverbal message will be interpreted more strongly and will have the greater impact. For example, the team member who says to another, "Tell me how that intervention is going" and then looks at her watch is adding the message, "I am interested if you can give me your answer very quickly, because I have somewhere else to go."

2. Respond to the signals and paralanguage of others and modify behaviors as necessary. This includes being sensitive to cultural differences (e.g., Martin & Nakayama, 2000; Miranda, 1993) and gender differences (cf. Gray, 1992; Tannen, 1990).

3. Be sensitive to the context of the interaction and change roles accordingly (e.g., from leader to listener).

4. Implement the verbal levels of communication in the proper sequence to give respect to the extent or depth of the relationship, and so familiarity is not rushed or assumed.

5. Use the appropriate verbal skills without injecting roadblocks, employing stereotyped responses (e.g., using paraphrasing repeatedly), or jumping in with too many strategies too soon.

6. Be sensitive to the real intent of a message (i.e., hearing what is really meant). Several tongue-in-cheek examples of metatalk statements and their "real" meanings are contained in Figure 4.6.

Technology offers new avenues for communication among interactive team members. The Internet and World Wide Web offer rapid communication possibilities and accessibility to a variety of resources that can contribute to teaming and collaboration efforts. Communication via electronic mail can reduce time and scheduling difficulties since individuals do not have to be in the same place at the same time (Cramer, 1998). Chat rooms and videoconferencing offer real-time, text-based interactions, and allow team members including parents to communicate simultaneously without being assembled in the same location (cf. Grabe & Grabe, 2000). Examples of effective use of technology in collaborative contexts were provided in Chapter 1. Interactive team members are encouraged to use technology-based communication tools as one of the avenues of communication; however, they also need to recognize that many persons still prefer face-to-face meetings.

MANAGING CONFLICT

Even when decision-making processes are being implemented, factors are being considered, and appropriate communication behaviors are being used, conflicts may still arise. Two important considerations regarding conflict are that it is a naturally occurring phenomenon in groups or organizations, and that it may actually result in improved functioning in the system. Conflict resolution is an ongoing process, and supporting meaningful conflict resolution can result in implementation of creative practices. Owens (1987) noted that if a positive response is made to the conflict, people may be encouraged to search out effective ways of dealing with it, and improved organizational functioning (e.g., clarified relationships and clearer problem solving) may result. This cycle is illustrated in Figure 4.7.

Judith Martin, who writes about manners, points out some of the meanings behind metatalk:

How do you do? How are you? Both of these mean *Hello.* The correct question, when you want to know how someone's digestion or divorce is getting along, is *Tell me, how have you really been?*

Call me. This can mean *Don't bother me now—let's discuss it on office time,* or *I would accept if you asked me out* or *I can't discuss this here* or *Don't go so fast.*

I'll call you. This has opposite meanings, and you have to judge by the delivery. One is *Let's start something* and the other is *Don't call me.*

Let's have lunch. Among social acquaintances, this means *If you ever have nothing to do on a day I have nothing to do, let's get together.* Among business acquaintances, it means *If you have something useful to say to me I'll listen.*

Let's have dinner. Among social acquaintances, it means *Let's advance this friendship.* Among business acquaintances, it means *Let's turn this into a friendship.*

Please stop by some time and see me. Said to someone who lives in the same area, it means *Call me if you'd like to visit me.* Genuine dropping in disappeared with the telephone, so if you want to encourage that, you have to say *I'm always home in the mornings. Don't bother to call; just drop by.*

Please come and stay with me. Said to someone from another area, this means *I would consider extending an invitation at your convenience if it coincides with my convenience.*

We must get together. Watch out here, because there are several similar expressions. This one means *I like you but I'm too busy now to take on more friendships.*

We really must see more of each other. One of the tricky ones, this actually means *I can't make the time to see you.*

We must do this more often. Another variation. This one is really *This was surprisingly enjoyable, but it's still going to happen infrequently.*

Yours truly, Yours sincerely. The first is business, the second distant social. Both mean *Well I guess that's all I've got to say so I'll close now.*

Is all that clear? Oh, one last thing. People who say *I only say what I really mean,* really mean *I am about to insult you.*

Figure 4.6
Metatalk.
Source: From *Miss Manners' Guide to Excruciatingly Correct Behavior,* by J. Martin, 1982, New York: Atheneum Publishers, an imprint of Macmillan Publishing Company. Copyright © 1979, 1980, 1981, 1982 by United Features Syndicate, Inc. Reprinted by permission.

Friend and Cook (2003) suggest a number of positive outcomes that may result from conflict. For example, the quality of the decisions resulting from resolved conflict are often higher and include a wider range of ideas and options. This is because the discussions taking place are likely to be more reasoned and more thorough in terms of perspectives and options. Also, the team participants are invested in implementing these decisions and tend to have a stronger sense of ownership. These

Figure 4.7
Benefits of conflict.

Source: From Owens *Organizational Behavior in Education,* 3rd ed. (p. 249), by R. G. Owens, 1987. Published by Allyn & Bacon, Boston, MA. Copyright © 2001 by Pearson Education. Reprinted by permission of the publisher.

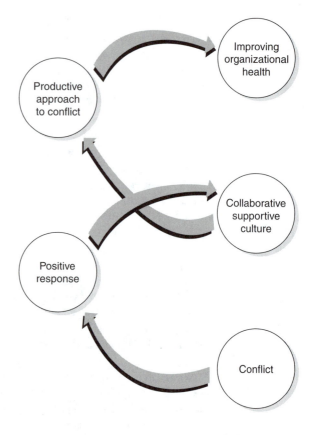

authors also suggest that successfully managing conflict fosters trust and open relationships while making future conflicts easier to address.

Conflict also may result in negative consequences, such as hostility and destructiveness on the part of group members (Owens, 1987). In such cases, team members may have to deal with a subset of the group or single individuals who are being resistant or defensive. Strategies follow for each of these types of situations.

CONFLICTS WITHIN THE GROUP

When conflicts occur within a team or group, the people involved need to remind themselves to consider problems from a systems perspective (i.e., the whole child or organization) and not to focus on or attempt to change individual members (Turnbull & Turnbull, 2001).

Weider-Hatfield (1981) suggested a process that may be useful.

1. Examine the problem intrapersonally and ask, "Why am I feeling this way? Why are the others feeling differently?"

2. Try to get an interpersonal and common definition of the problem and differences other group members perceive.

3. Discuss the goals everyone shares.

4. Generate possible resolutions collaboratively.

5. Weigh goals against resolutions.

6. Evaluate the resolutions after time has passed.

Walther-Thomas, Korinek, and McLaughlin (1992) developed a process for conflict resolution using the acronym RESOLVE. Their model is outlined in Table 4.2.

Many recommend that the first goal in resolving conflict should be dealing with emotions. McKenna (1998) stressed the importance of treating the other person with respect; listening until you experience the other side; and stating your views, needs, and feelings. Martin and Nakayama (2000) offered similar suggestions for dealing with conflict.

> (1) stay centered and do not polarize; (2) maintain contact; (3) recognize the existence of different styles; (4) identify your preferred style; (5) be creative and expand your conflict style repertoire; (6) recognize the importance of conflict context; and (7) be willing to forgive. (p. 308)

Negotiation is a conflict management strategy that has been used successfully in business and may be applied to education settings as well. When viewed as a technique for problem solving, Walker and Harris (1995) recommend answering three questions in planning for negotiation: (1) What do we want to achieve? (2) What is the context within which we operate? and (3) What problems are likely to be encountered? By answering these questions as well as the additional questions that will arise in doing so, team members are better prepared to face issues that may come up without being surprised by them. The team also will have collected data relevant to the issues, which are then used to form stronger position statements in order to persuade others. Crucial to the negotiation process is the ability to listen to the response of the other party and define the points of agreement and disagreement that might be conceded. Negotiation does require concessions but also enhances the possibility that an agreement can be reached. (See Walther-Thomas, Korinek, McLaughlin, & Williams, 2000, for an in-depth discussion of negotiation and persuasion.)

Another strategy for negotiating agreement was described by Fisher, Ury, and Patton (1991). They listed the following considerations: (1) separate the people from the problem; (2) focus on interests, not positions; (3) invent options for mutual gain; and (4) insist on using objective criteria.

The outcomes of conflicts within a group can be classified in three ways, depending on the results (Filley, 1975).

1. *Win/lose.* Some group members win, while others believe they have lost.

2. *Lose/lose.* Both groups are disappointed in the outcomes.

3. *Win/win.* All members are satisfied with the outcomes.

Table 4.2
RESOLVE: Managing Conflict in Team Situations

Before conflicts develop:

- Cultivate mutual trust, respect, and role parity among team members.
- Use effective problem-solving and communication skills.
- Anticipate others' needs, interests, and positions.
- Develop effective conflict management skills.

When conflicts occur:

- Stay calm, breathe deeply, and listen with an open mind.
- Separate the problem from the person presenting it.
- If the problem cannot be adequately discussed at the present time, schedule a convenient time within the next 24 hours to do so.
- Schedule an appropriate location and sufficient time to discuss the issue fully.

In conflict situations use RESOLVE:

Respond verbally and nonverbally to the other person's feelings and ideas. Use body basics of good communication (e.g., eye contact, body language, attending behaviors, breathing, facial expressions, vocal tone).

Encourage the other person to share his or her perceptions and feelings, and propose solutions that will be good for all parties.

Stay focused on finding an appropriate solution—don't get sidetracked by other issues.

Organize your thoughts carefully before the meeting. Be prepared.

Listen responsively (e.g., reflecting, clarifying, paraphrasing) to try to understand the other person's position and try to think of the other person's position.

Voice your belief that conflicts are opportunities to increase understanding and improve relationships. Thank the person(s) for his or her willingness to work with you to resolve this conflict.

End on a positive note with a written plan for implementation, monitoring, and follow-up.

After a conflict has been RESOLVEd:

- Follow through on commitments that you make during the conflict resolution session.
- Self-evaluate your own behaviors in handling the conflict, and
- Make changes to increase personal and professional effectiveness.

Source: From *Managing Conflict in Team Situations: RESOLVE,* by C. S. Walther-Thomas, L. Korinek, and V. K. McLaughlin, 1992, unpublished training materials, Williamsburg, VA: College of William and Mary. Reprinted by permission.

The process of negotiation researches mutual interests and aims to result in decisions and solutions that are satisfying for all. Filley (1975) identified another process through which win/win outcomes can be achieved. This process, known as *integrative decision making (IDM),* works from the perspective that conflicts are problems to be solved (Walther-Thomas et al., 2000). In IDM, participants consider relationships, perceptions, and attitudes that may be affecting the situation. They discuss and agree on a definition of the problem, and then generate possible solutions. The final step is reaching consensus, or at least majority agreement, on the best alternative(s) to resolve the problem.

DEALING WITH RESISTANCE

Karp (1984) defined *resistance* as "the ability to avoid what is not wanted from the environment" (p. 69). Friend and Cook (2003) point out that resistance is not always negative in that it may prevent undertaking change that is too risky. However, if resistance is a barrier to effective collaboration or a much-needed innovation, then it is a concern (Wade, Welch, & Jensen, 1994).

Resistance most often occurs as a response to change that has a personal impact. Piersel (1985) said that resistance can occur for a number of reasons: The person may not know what to do or expect; the person may have different expectations about what should be occurring; or the person may have no intent or need to problem solve due to previous unsuccessful results, an inability to recognize alternatives, or a need to avoid failure or the appearance of being unsuccessful or incompetent. Another concern may arise when people are not accustomed to having others provide input as to how they do their job and see the collaboration and change as a threat to their autonomy (Fiedler, 2000). In consultation, resistance may result from defensiveness on the part of the consultee to a consultant's attitude of superiority (Fishbaugh, 1997). Finally, some people tend to prefer sameness rather than change (homeostasis; Friend & Cook, 2003).

Nine types of resistance have been identified by Karp (1984): the *block, rollover, stall, reverse, sidestep, projected threat, press, guilt trip,* and *tradition.* The general considerations in dealing with resistance presented by Karp include allowing it to come to the surface by asking people for their feelings, showing that the resistance is honored by making eye contact and restating points, openly exploring the resistance by identifying how people feel, and rechecking with the people involved to make sure the understanding is accurate. Karp also recommended asking "what" or "how" questions rather than "why" questions, because the latter type tends to put people on the defensive. Another suggestion was to use "I" statements rather than "you" statements, because these also tend to make people respond defensively. Examples and strategies for dealing with the nine types of resistance are illustrated in Table 4.3.

Sugai and Tindall (1993) refer to resistance as roadblocks to the goals of consultation. They use a functional analysis approach to determine the roadblock by first identifying who is involved in the roadblock condition, identifying the setting or context, conducting the functional analysis, and identifying and defining observable behaviors that indicate a roadblock. Possible factors contributing to the roadblock condition may be attributed to the consultant (e.g., lack of training, having too many responsibilities) or to the consultee (e.g., not understanding

Table 4.3
Karp's Strategies for Dealing with Resistance

Type of Resistance	Example	Explanation	Possible Response
THE BLOCK	"I don't want to" or "I'd rather not!"	Most obvious form of authentic resistance. Easiest to work with. The resister is clear about what the demander wants.	"What are some of your objections?"
THE ROLLOVER (passive resistance)	"Tell me exactly what you want me to do."	Least common and one of the most difficult to identify and work with. Frequently the resister does not know the role, what he/she is resisting. Expressed by minimal compliance with the letter of the demand and no compliance with the spirit of the demand.	"Are you clear about what is being asked of you?" "How do you think this will change your role?"
THE STALL	"I'll get on it first thing Thursday," or "I'll try to rearrange my schedule for that."	Difficult to distinguish between a stall and an honest response to present conditions. Knowledge of how a person usually responds to requests or demands will make the distinction.	"What things may prevent you from starting this tomorrow or in the near future?"
THE REVERSE	"Wow! What a great idea!"	A very subtle form of resistance and practically impossible to identify without knowing the resister well. Occurs as a statement of enthusiastic support when what you were expecting from this individual was a hard time. The resister tells you what you want to hear—and then immediately forgets about it.	"I'm pleased with your response. What aspects do you like best?"
THE SIDESTEP	"Let Sally try it first; then I'll try it."	Expressed as a counterdemand to get someone else to do the desired thing. The appeal is to your sense of fairness. "How come you didn't tell Pam she had to do this?" This then puts you on the defensive to justify your choice.	"I understand your concern; what can I expect from you?"

Source: From "Working with Resistance," by H. Karp, 1984, *Training and Development Journal, 38*(3), pp. 69–73. Adapted by permission.

Type of Resistance	Example	Explanation	Possible Response
THE PROJECTED THREAT	"The (teachers) won't like it."	The resistance expressed here is in terms of an implied threat that someone else with some power won't approve of your demand. The third-party's view may or may not be positive.	"I appreciate your concern and will check it with the others. In the meantime, what are your plans for . . . ?"
THE PRESS	"You owe me one."	An authentic resistance. The resister does not want to cooperate and is calling in an old debt to get off the hook. It is your decision whether this is an appropriate time to pay back a debt.	"I realize I may owe you one; however, what are you planning on doing to implement . . . ?"
THE GUILT TRIP	"See what you are making me do."	Guilt is a common tactic in shaping behavior. The resister's problem with what you want is his or her problem, not yours. It's good to work with the problem but not to shoulder it.	"I'm sorry this is a problem for you; however, what do you plan on doing . . . ?"
THE TRADITION	"But we've always done it this way."	The most time-honored/traditional approach. This approach really is an appeal to safety, not effectiveness. Most who rely on this approach are those who are unwilling to take risks and have a low opinion of their own creativity and resourcefulness.	"I agree that the old approach has merits, but what could we do to adapt it to this new approach?"

what is required, not knowing how to perform the task, not being properly reinforced for his efforts). Suggested solutions include skill training, more appropriate reinforcement, and listening to the teacher's concerns.

Final considerations in dealing with people who are resistant are concerned with the behaviors team members demonstrate in the situation. Individuals who want to help others cease being resistant must demonstrate a willingness and openness to accept a mutual commitment toward resolving the problem. This mutual commitment can be seen when team members are flexible and encourage individuals to express their ideas (Fuller, 1998); provide support for suggested strategies and communicate respect for others' expertise in order to build self-esteem (Aldinger, Warger, & Eavy, 1991); and model, shape, and reinforce problem solving and reduction of resistance (Brammer, 1988; Piersel, 1985). The importance of these strategies was reiterated by Fine et al. (1979) when they said, "If we are asking teachers to be nondefensive, to consider different facets of a situation, and to risk making choices without complete data, then our best ally may be the behavior we model for them" (p. 539).

Table 4.4
Contrasting Communication Strategies

Ineffective Communication	Desired Communication in Interactive Teaming
1. Psychologist to parent:	
"On the CAT your son was in the 10th percentile for his grade level. We think a placement in EMH class with an appropriate IEP would meet his needs. He has obvious reading and language deficits and his communication development is delayed. We suspect that he may also have BEH tendencies due to the frustration he has experienced in academic settings."	"I would like to explain the results of recent testing to you. Your son took a test in the areas of reading, language, and math. This chart illustrates how he did compared with others of his grade level. The types of questions he was responding to included (examples given). The results show that he has difficulty with reading comprehension, or understanding the meaning of what he has read. Have you noticed similar patterns as you read with him at home? Given this performance, what do you think would be the best plan for your child?"
2. Program administrator to special educator and parents:	
"The numbers in our programs for multi-disabled are low this coming year so we can't really justify having two classes at the elementary level.	"We are considering the best placements for our students with multiple disabilities for next year and wanted your input. One possibility is placing Jackie at a middle or high school level. This will enable her to have access to the computer lab and the classes on homemaking and work skills. What are your ideas on this?"
Therefore, we have decided to place the 15-year-old child at the high school level and move the other students into other classes. Jackie is verbal and does not need an augmentative communication system, so she does not need to be placed in the elementary nonverbal class. We want her to learn vocational and functional skills and continue to work on range of motion in PT. In addition, we do not think she needs APE any longer; instead we can have her work on computer literacy with the specialist and the OT."	

APPLICATION: Communication Strategies

Table 4.4 provides two illustrations of ineffective communication and desired communication in interactive teaming. In the first example, the psychologist is using several acronyms (e.g., CAT, EMH, BEH) with which the parent may not be familiar. In addition, several emotionally laden words such as "obvious reading and language deficits" are used but not explained. In the desired communication column, the psychologist tries to explain testing results and provides examples of questions. In addition, she asks for the parent's comments about a placement instead of presenting it as a decision that has been made without the parent's input.

In the second example, the program administrator presents a decision based on numbers rather than on what individual students need. In describing a program for Jackie, he does not state whether a high school placement is in the best interest of the child's overall development, nor does he request the parents' or special educator's input into the decision. Jargon such as "augmentative," "functional," and "APE" are used without explanation. In the desired communication column, the administrator presents a placement possibility, describes the potential benefits, and asks for ideas from the special educator and parents.

SUMMARY

An understanding of communication skills is an essential facilitating factor in interactive teaming. The areas encompassed in this understanding include the following:

- ◆ Awareness of a communication model that includes senders-receivers, messages, channels, feedback, noise, and setting.
- ◆ Sensitivity to characteristics of communication in interactive teaming.
- ◆ Consideration of personal, attitudinal, and experiential factors; backup support factors; and context or situational factors.
- ◆ Implementation of effective nonverbal, listening, and verbal skills.
- ◆ Knowledge of ways to manage conflicts in groups and strategies for dealing with resistant people.

The next chapter describes leadership skills for individuals on interactive teams. The strategies contained in Chapter 5 are vital to facilitate the teaming process.

ACTIVITIES

1. Observe an interaction between a professional and a parent. Describe behaviors that indicate respect and trust or those that indicate it is missing. How was rapport established and maintained? How did the professional indicate understanding and acceptance of cultural differences? Did verbal and nonverbal messages match?

2. Observe a team meeting among professionals. Was the situation proactive or reactive? What content-level sequences were used? Was jargon explained? Which verbal and listening skills were implemented? Were any judgmental statements or roadblocks evident? If so, what were the responses to them? If a conflict arose, how was it handled?

3. Conduct an informational interview with a parent or professional. Write your overall assessment of the interview. Also write an analysis of your use, and the interviewee's use, of effective communication strategies.

4. Design a checklist or rating scale of the behaviors you think are necessary for effective communication. Evaluate yourself on the behaviors. Observe a meeting and consider how the participants interact. If you think some people in the meeting are better at communicating than others, identify what behaviors or skills you think give them an advantage.

REFERENCES

Aldinger, L. E., Warger, C. L., & Eavy, P. W. (1991). *Strategies for teacher collaboration.* Ann Arbor, MI: Exceptional Innovations, Inc.

Arab, C. (1985, May). *Getting what you deserve: Assertive, aggressive, and non-assertive behavior.* Paper presented at the Florida Academy of School Leaders, Daytona Beach.

Bailey, D. B. (1987). Collaborative goal-setting with families: Resolving differences in values and priorities for services. *Topics in Early Childhood Special Education, 7*(2), 59–71.

Belton-Owens, J. (1999). Multicultural issues confronted by parents and families. In G. Boutte (Ed.), *Multicultural education: Raising consciousness* (pp. 232–260). Belmont, CA: Wadsworth Publishing.

Boyd, S. D. (2001). The human side of teaching: Effective listening. *Techniques: Connecting Education and Careers, 76*(7), 60–62.

Brammer, L. M. (1988). *The helping relationship: Process and skills* (4th ed.). Upper Saddle River, NJ: Merrill/Prentice Hall.

Brown, B., Pryzwansky, W. B., & Schulte, A. C. (1998). *Psychological consultation: Introduction to theory and practice* (4th ed.). Needham Heights, MA: Allyn & Bacon.

Bruneau-Balderrama, O. (1997). Inclusion: Making it work for teachers, too. *The Clearing House, 70*(6), 328–330.

Covey, S. R. (1989). *The 7 habits of highly effective people: Powerful lessons in personal change.* New York: Simon & Schuster.

Cramer, S. F. (1998). *Collaboration: A success strategy for special educators.* Needham Heights, MA: Allyn & Bacon.

Dettmer, P., Dyck, N., & Thurston, L. P. (2002). *Consultation, collaboration, and teamwork for students with special needs* (4th ed.). Boston: Allyn & Bacon.

Dieker, L. A., & Barnett, C. A. (1996). Effective co-teaching. *Teaching Exceptional Children, 29*(1), 5–7.

Egan, G. (1998). *The skilled helper* (6th ed.). Pacific Grove, CA: Brooks/Cole.

Egan, G. (2001). *The skilled helper: A problem-management and opportunity-development approach to helping.* Monterey, CA: Brooks/Cole.

Ehly, S. W., & Eliason, M. (1983). Communicating for understanding: Some problems in psychology and education. *Journal for Special Educators, 19*(3), v–ix.

Eisenhardt, C. (1972). *Applying linguistics to the teaching of reading and the language arts.* Columbus, OH: Merrill.

Fiedler, C. A. (2000). *Making a difference: Advocacy competencies for special education professionals.* Boston: Allyn & Bacon.

Filley, A. C. (1975). *Interpersonal conflict resolution.* Glenview, IL: Scott, Foresman.

Fine, M. J., Grantham, V. L., & Wright, J. G. (1979). Personal variables that facilitate or impede consultation. *Psychology in the Schools, 16,* 533–539.

Fishbaugh, M. S. E. (1997). *Models of collaboration.* Needham Heights, MA: Allyn & Bacon.

Fisher, R., Ury, W., & Patton, B. (1991). *Getting to yes: Negotiating agreement without giving in.* New York: Penguin Books.

Fong, M. (1986). *The levels of communication in personal relationships.* Unpublished manuscript, University of Florida, Department of Counselor Education, Gainesville.

Friend, M. (1984). Consultation skills for resource teachers. *Learning Disability Quarterly, 7,* 246–250.

Friend, M., & Cook, L. (2003). *Interactions: Collaboration skills for school professionals* (4th ed.). Boston: Allyn & Bacon.

Fuller, G. (1998). *Win/win management: Leading people in the new workplace.* Paramus, NJ: Prentice Hall Press.

Gladstein, G. A. (1983). Understanding empathy: Integrating counseling, developmental, and social psychology perspectives. *Journal of Counseling Psychology, 30,* 467–482.

Gordon, T. (1970). *Parent effectiveness training.* New York: Wyden.

Gordon, T. (1974). *Teacher effectiveness training.* New York: David McKay.

Grabe, M., & Grabe, C. (2000). *Integrating the Internet for meaningful learning.* Boston, MA: Houghton Mifflin.

Gray, J. (1992). *Men are from Mars, women are from Venus.* New York: HarperCollins.

Grieger, R. M. (1972). Teacher attitudes as a variable in behavior modification consultation. *Journal of School Psychology, 10,* 279–287.

Gutkin, T. B. (1996). Core elements of consultation service delivery for special service personnel: Rationale, practice, and some directions for the future. *Remedial and Special Education, 17*(6), 333–340.

Gutkin, T. B., & Curtis, M. J. (1982). School-based consultation: Theory and techniques. In C. R. Reynolds & T. B. Gutkin (Eds.), *The handbook of school psychology.* New York: Wiley.

Hallman, C. L., Bryant, W. W., Campbell, A., McGuire, J., & Bowman, K. (1983). *U.S. American value orientations* (Cultural Monograph No. 4). Gainesville: University of Florida, College of Education, Bilingual Multicultural Education Training Project.

Harris, K. C. (1996). Collaboration within a multicultural society: Issues for consideration. *Remedial and Special Education, 17*(6), 355–362, 376.

Heron, T. E., & Harris, K. C. (2001). *The educational consultant: Helping professionals, parents, and students in inclusive classrooms* (4th ed.). Austin, TX: Pro-Ed.

Hudson, P. (1987). *Proactive and reactive consultation: A model for preservice training.* Unpublished manuscript, University of Florida, Department of Special Education, Gainesville.

Hybels, S., & Weaver, R. L. (1997). *Communicating effectively* (5th ed.). New York: McGraw-Hill.

Idol, L., Paolucci-Whitcomb, P., & Nevin, A. (2000). *Collaborative consultation* (3rd ed.). Rockville, MD: Aspen.

Jackson, D. N., & Hughley-Hayes, D. (1993). Multicultural issues in consultation. *Journal of Counseling and Development, 72,* 144–147.

Karp, H. (1984). Working with resistance. *Training and Development Journal, 38*(3), 69–73.

Katzenbach, J. R., & Smith, D. K. (1999). *The wisdom of teams: Creating the high-performance organization.* New York: HarperCollins.

Kerlinger, F. N. (1986). *Foundations of behavioral research* (3rd ed.). New York: Holt, Rinehart & Winston.

Lang, D. C., Quick, A. F., & Johnson, J. A. (1981). *A partnership for the supervision of student teachers.* DeKalb, IL: Creative Educational Materials.

Lopez, E. C., Dalal, S. M., & Yoshida, R. K. (1993). An examination of professional cultures: Implications for the collaborative consultation model. *Journal of Educational and Psychological Consultation, 4,* 197–213.

Losen, S. M., & Losen, J. G. (1985). *The special education team.* Boston: Allyn & Bacon.

Lynch, E. W., & Hanson, M. J. (Eds.). (1992). *Developing cross-cultural competence: A guide for working with young children and their families.* Baltimore, MD: Paul H. Brookes.

Martin, J. N., & Nakayama, T. K. (2000). *Intercultural communication in contexts* (2nd ed.). Mountain View, CA: Mayfield Publishing Company.

McKenna, C. (1998). *Powerful communication skills: How to communicate with confidence.* Franklin Lakes, NJ: Career Press.

Miranda, A. H. (1993). Consultation with culturally diverse families. *Journal of Educational and Psychological Consultation, 4,* 89–93.

Overton, T. (2000). *Assessment in special education: An applied approach* (3rd ed.). Upper Saddle River, NJ: Merrill/Prentice Hall.

Owens, R. B. (1987). *Organizational behavior in education* (3rd ed.). Upper Saddle River, NJ: Prentice Hall.

Piersel, W. C. (1985). Behavioral consultation: An approach to problem solving in educational settings. In J. R. Bergan, *School psychology in contemporary society: An introduction.* Columbus, OH: Merrill.

Pruitt, P., Wandry, D., & Hollums, D. (1998). Listen to us! Parents speak out about their interactions with special educators. *Preventing School Failure, 42*(4), 161–166.

Pugach, M. C., & Johnson, L. J. (2002). *Collaborative practitioners, collaborative schools* (2nd ed.). Denver, CO: Love Publishing Company.

Ramirez, S. Z., Lepage, K. M., Kratchowill, T. R., & Duffy, J. L. (1998). Multicultural issues in school-based consultation: Conceptual and research considerations. *Journal of School Psychology, 36*(4), 479–509.

Rogers, C. R. (1961). *On becoming a person: A therapist's view of psychotherapy.* Boston: Houghton-Mifflin.

Sax, G. (1997). *Principles of educational and psychological measurement and evaluation* (4th ed.). Belmont, CA: Wadsworth Publishing.

Sonnenschien, P. (1984). Parents and professionals: An uneasy relationship. In M. L. Henniger & E. M. Nesselroad (Eds.), *Working with parents of handicapped children: A book of readings for school personnel.* Lanham, MD: University Press of America.

Spodek, B. (1982). What special educators need to know about regular classrooms. *Educational Forum, 46,* 295–307.

Sugai, G., & Tindall, G. (1993). *Effective school consultation.* Pacific Grove, CA: Brooks/Cole.

Tannen, D. (1990). *You just don't understand: Women and men in conversation.* New York: Ballantine Books.

Tawney, J. W., & Gast, D. L. (1984). *Single subject research in special education.* New York: Merrill/Macmillan.

Turnbull, A. P., & Turnbull, H. R. (1990). *Families, professionals, and exceptionality: A special partnership* (2nd ed.). Upper Saddle River, NJ: Merrill/Prentice Hall.

Turnbull, A. P., & Turnbull, H. R. (2001). *Families, professionals, and exceptionality: Collaborating for empowerment* (4th ed.). Upper Saddle River, NJ: Merrill/Prentice Hall.

Vargo, S. (1998). Consulting teacher-to-teacher. *Teaching Exceptional Children, 30*(3), 54–55.

Venn, J. (2000). *Assessment in special education: An applied approach* (3rd ed.). Upper Saddle River, NJ: Merrill/Prentice Hall.

Wade, S. E., Welch, M., & Jensen, J. B. (1994). Teacher receptivity to collaboration: Levels of interest, types of concern and school characteristics as variables contributing to successful implementation. *Journal of Educational and Psychological Consultation, 5,* 177–209.

Walker, M., & Harris, G. (1995). *Negotiations: Six steps to success.* Upper Saddle River, NJ: Prentice Hall.

Walther-Thomas, C. S., Korinek, L., & McLaughlin, V. K. (1992). *Managing conflict in team situations: RESOLVE.* Unpublished training materials. Williamsburg, VA: College of William and Mary.

Walther-Thomas, C. S., Korinek, L., McLaughlin, V. K., & Williams, B. T. (2000). *Collaboration for inclusive education: Developing successful programs.* Boston: Allyn & Bacon.

Weider-Hatfield, D. (1981). A unit in conflict management communication skills. *Communication Education, 30,* 265–273.

Weissenburger, J. W., Fine, M. J., & Poggio, J. P. (1982). The relationship of selected consultant/teacher characteristics to consultation outcomes. *Journal of School Psychology, 20*(4), 263–270.

West, J. F., & Cannon, G. S. (1988). Essential collaborative consultation competencies for regular and special educators. *Journal of Learning Disabilities, 21*(1), 28, 56–63.

Zirpoli, T. J., & Melloy, K. J. (2000). *Behavior management: Applications for teachers* (3rd ed.). Upper Saddle River, NJ: Merrill/Prentice Hall.

Developing Leadership and Service Coordination Skills

Topics in this chapter include:

◆ Discussion of essential skills for leadership of professionals.

◆ Description of the initial tasks of the team leader.

◆ Guidelines for procedures needed by subsequent team leaders who serve as service coordinators: coordinating services, delegating responsibility, providing follow-up, guiding paraprofessionals or volunteers, and working with special education advocates.

◆ Application of the interactive teaming model to a situation in which the service coordinator delegates to and provides follow-up with a paraprofessional.

At their first meeting, the team discussed the educational and social needs and placement options for Juan, an 11-year-old Hispanic boy with diabetes, who was having difficulties in reading achievement and social adjustment. The first meeting was attended by Juan's mother, his sixth-grade teacher, the special educator (a learning disabilities [LD] resource teacher), the speech-language therapist, and the school nurse; it was chaired by the school counselor. After hearing the parent's and teacher's descriptions of Juan's reading difficulties, the counselor noted that it was late and recommended gathering more information about Juan's diet, his classroom behavior, and his language abilities in English, his second language. When the team met again 2 weeks later, the special education teacher was the only person who had gathered additional information.

As the counselor attempted to initiate problem solving at the second meeting, he was puzzled by the group's reactions. He first noted that Juan's mother was not participating, even when she was asked to speak. Then he noted that the sixth-grade teacher responded with hostility to the report on classroom observations by the special education teacher, while the nurse and speech-language therapist completed unrelated paperwork. The second meeting ended as the first one had, with the counselor suggesting that the group still needed additional information. The parent walked quietly away, while several other participants muttered protests about wasted time.

This team had no goals and no operating procedures. The team suffered from a lack of direction because the counselor was viewed merely as a facilitator who convened the meeting and encouraged the discussion. Everybody was assumed to be working together but nobody was "in charge." The leader neither delegated responsibility nor conducted follow-up activities. The special educator, who took nondelegated initiative for conducting a classroom observation, was viewed by the classroom teacher as an intruder. Juan's mother, who did not feel it was her place to question the professionals about her child's educational needs, remained a passive participant. The school counselor, who did not understand the essential skills and procedures for team leadership, had apparently assumed that everyone on the team would just "collaborate."

In this chapter, the essential skills for team leaders are presented from the perspective that they involve the management of tasks rather than people. The initial tasks of the team leader are described, and the procedures used subsequently by the leader in service coordination and integration are discussed in detail. The term *service coordinator* is defined in IDEA 1997 as someone who coordinates all services across agency lines and serves as the single point of contact in helping parents to obtain the services and assistance they need. It is most often associated with early intervention services under Part C of IDEA. For purposes of this chapter, we will use the term *service coordinator* to describe the team leader for school teams working with all school-age students and their families. The activities of the service coordinators include:

1. Coordinating the performance of evaluations and assessments;
2. Facilitating and participating in the development, review, and evaluation of individualized family service plans [and individualized educational plans];

3. Assisting families in identifying available service providers;

4. Coordinating and monitoring the delivery of available services;

5. Informing families of the availability of advocacy services;

6. Coordinating with medical and health providers; and

7. Facilitating the development of a transition plan to preschool services [and post-high school services], if appropriate. (IDEA, 1997, Sec. 303.23)

Finally, the interactive teaming model is applied to the procedures for leadership in service coordination through an example of how a team leader can delegate to and provide follow-up on the paraprofessional's activities.

ESSENTIAL SKILLS FOR LEADERSHIP OF PROFESSIONALS

For an interactive team to function effectively, it needs a special kind of leadership. The management of professionals (such as those who make up the interactive team) is much more complex than the management of service workers. It is collegial rather than directive and needs to occur within an organization that is performance oriented rather than authority oriented (Kaplan & Owings, 2003; Peterson & Deal, 1998; Reinhartz & Beach, 2004; Simon & Newman, 2004).

In the interactive teaming model, the role of leader can be filled by any member of the team. The leader is selected by the program administrator, who delegates responsibility for coordination of services to this leader. The team leader is a service coordinator who maintains the continuity of the team over time and across meetings that focus on the special needs of individual students. For each individual student, the team also uses as its service coordinator the person with greatest knowledge of the services or content expertise about the case.

To be effective, the leader needs to be supportive of others as they carry out their tasks and must assume accountability for the overall effectiveness of the program. The team leader is aware of the different roles and perspectives of team members as described previously, and is able to select, from among the expertise presented by members of the team, the best person(s) to whom to delegate responsibility for coordinating a particular student's program. The leader needs to demonstrate all the skills, attributes, and behaviors of effective leaders in organizations. These skills, attributes, and behaviors are now summarized as a synthesis of the research on effective leadership.

Research on Leadership

Effective leaders can help professionals with different backgrounds and vocabularies to focus on a common set of future goals (Chenoweth & Everhart, 2002; Owings & Kaplan, 2003; Reinhartz & Beach, 2004; Simon & Newman, 2004). Research on leadership has been responsible for an evolution in understanding its components.

Early investigators observing leaders in diverse contexts have identified two broad dimensions of leadership. They determined that the effective leader needs to initiate *structure* and demonstrate *consideration*. To initiate structure is to establish patterns, methods, and procedures for accomplishing tasks. To demonstrate consideration is to develop trust, warmth, and respect with the staff.

Some early students of leadership described leaders as either task oriented or relationship oriented (McGregor, 1960), although Hersey and Blanchard (1974) were among those who questioned the dichotomous view. In their categorization of styles, Hersey and Blanchard suggested also that the effective leader had a range of styles, and that the ability to adapt style to the situation was an important dimension of effectiveness. Further expansion of the adaptation in leadership concept was proposed by Bennett and Anderson (2003) and Covey (1990).

The extension of Hersey and Blanchard's (1974) work into studies of effective school principals showed that these school leaders had a variety of styles, but all demonstrated that they were able to encourage staff collaboration and develop innovative practices (Dyer & Carothers, 2000; Simon & Newman, 2004). According to the research, the effective school leader develops positive relationships with colleagues and is capable of creating an open, supportive environment (Reinhartz & Beach, 2004). Covey (1990) emphasizes that caring and integrity must be genuine and integral to the leader's being, as opposed to superficially acquired techniques. For Lambert (2002), "The days of the principal as the lone instructional leader are over. We no longer believe that one administrator can serve as the instructional leader for an entire school without the substantial participation of other educators" (p. 37).

The concept of *power* was widely discussed as a leadership dimension in the early literature. Effective leaders are able to use power for organizational good, as opposed to personal gain (McClelland, 1975). The most productive exercise of power in the leadership of professionals comes through transformational leadership, which empowers others to become leaders within the school instead of followers (Bennett & Anderson, 2003). This concept is discussed further in Chapter 6. The team leader should keep in mind that the team's goal is continuous improvement. The critical steps in the continuous improvement cycle are (1) plan, (2) do, (3) check, and (4) act (Deming, 1986). This ongoing system evaluation enables team members to focus on a common goal, as well as identify and eliminate barriers to achieving this goal. A mind-set for long-range planning, with continuous improvement, is essential for the team leader, who can then encourage flexibility, risk taking, and innovation.

Bennett and Anderson (2003) summarize 14 different types of leadership, which are summarized in Table 5.1. Ultimately, an effective leader is someone who understands the complex challenges that schools face and matches the appropriate style of leadership to make improvements and influence change. Effective leaders have access to a repertoire of leadership approaches and will use them according to the problem's demands.

Table 5.1

Leadership Styles

Leadership Style	Description
Situational leadership	Leaders use a situation to negotiate power, build coalitions, and influence others.
Managerial leadership	Leaders focus on maintenance of the school's day-to-day business.
Instructional leadership	Leaders promote an effective instructional climate and help teachers with the curriculum.
Servant leadership	Leaders serve their constituents with little need for peer recognition or professional advancement.
White Knight and Black Hat leadership	Leaders come in to rescue or fix a problem as a white knight. If unpopular interventions are required they then wear the black hat.
Indirect leadership	Leaders lead by example by rolling up their sleeves and doing the work they want others to do.
Collaborative leadership	Leaders establish internal and external linkages for the school, fostering trust among the school faculty and partnerships in the community.
Ethical leadership	Leaders work from a strong value and belief system that includes the notions of caring, justice, and ethics.
Dialogical leadership	Leaders encourage recurrent interactions with school faculty and discussion of the issues facing the school and the community.
Transcultural leadership	Leaders are sensitive to, recognize, and accept different cultural values and beliefs.
Influencing leadership	Leaders are purposive in achieving organizational goals and enhancing productivity.
"Machiavellian" leadership	Leaders make strategic alliances with groups of teachers and allocate resources to the areas where change is most likely.
Transformational leadership	Leaders facilitate the development of leadership abilities within all staff, transforming them from followers to leaders.
Constructivist leadership	Leaders use a shared decision-making approach, often blurring the lines between followership and leadership.

Source: Adapted from *Rethinking Educational Leadership* (pp. 14–20), by N. Bennett and L. Anderson, 2003, Thousand Oaks, CA: Sage. Used by permission of Sage Publications, Ltd.

Overall, the characteristics and behaviors of empowered teacher-leaders, which are similar to those ascribed to effective leaders in general, are that they:

- Are hard working and creative;
- Collaborate with others to provide assistance;
- Empower team members;
- Take risks;
- Challenge the existing system;
- Communicate the shared vision;
- Engage in teamwork;
- Support and inspire others;
- Coach and encourage their teams; and
- Serve as role models and planners.

These teacher-leaders are more comparable to the team leaders described in this text. They do not seek full "leadership" roles as administrators; instead, they function as team leaders in collegial settings.

Recent studies have lent support to the earlier descriptions of the skills and characteristics of effective leaders, both in businesses and in school environments. For example, *Investor's Business Daily*, through an ongoing series based on extensive analysis of leaders, has identified 10 traits that characterize successful leaders. Their list begins with "How you think is everything: Always be positive. Think success, not failure. Beware of a negative environment." The final trait is "Be honest and dependable; take responsibility. Otherwise numbers 1–9 won't matter" (see, for example, Richman, 1999a, 1999b). The list goes on to highlight many of the qualities identified in earlier research: planning and implementing goals; being a continuous learner, hard worker, and innovator; analyzing feedback; and communicating effectively. Kelley (1991) indicates that a company's quality is heavily dependent on the quality of its "worklife" and that teamwork, which requires skills in both leadership and followership, is increasingly important.

Similarly, the leaders in effective schools are found to have skills and attributes that are characteristic of all effective leaders. Peterson and Deal (1998) stress the importance of the school leader in shaping the culture by communicating core values and traditions, speaking about mission, honoring the school "heroes," and celebrating their accomplishments. Jarvis and Chavez (1997) add a dimension they call "roles" (creator of context, seeker and initiator of communication, promoter of possibilities, and guardian of morale) to the traditional model of leader behaviors that focuses on responsibilities and relationships. The leader's style and value system are evident in almost every component of the school's personality or culture (Bennett & Anderson, 2003; Dyer & Carothers, 2000; Goldman, 1998).

The growing body of research on effective leaders and successful organizations, including schools, places an increasing emphasis on the importance of a positive culture and the leader's part in establishing that culture. Peterson and Deal (1998) define culture as ". . . the underground stream of norms, values, beliefs, traditions, and rituals that has built up over time as people work together, solve problems, and confront challenges" (p. 28). These authors define "toxic cultures" as those with negative values and disgruntled staff, where oppositional groups dominate, leading both faculty and students to a sense of hopelessness. Changing a toxic school culture into a positive and nourishing school culture is perhaps one of the greatest challenges facing school leaders (Barth, 2002).

Several authors have given examples of positive school cultures, with high levels of student and staff satisfaction and achievement. Schools with positive cultures have a shared sense of mission, with norms that emphasize collegiality, caring, and concern for student growth (Peterson & Deal, 1998; Reinhartz & Beach, 2004). Glasser (1997) has named these environments "quality schools," in which staff have demonstrated the power of showing care for students while giving them choices, as well as emphasizing the importance of seeking continuous improvement. Wasley, Hampel, and Clark (1997) also provide examples of high schools in which the staff has attempted to bring about whole-school change that emphasized a positive culture with student growth. They have identified seven interrelated clues to the success of schools in achieving this change, finding two critical considerations: civil discourse among participants, and rigorous analysis of inside and outside feedback. These descriptors are supportive of the earlier research on effective schools, adding emphasis on the variables that comprise interactive teaming.

Summary of Skills for Team Leaders

In summary, leadership has been defined as behavior that facilitates change. It has a dimension of power, which focuses on the strength necessary to accomplish goals that are believed to promote the common good. Effective leadership includes both an emphasis on fulfilling the organization's mission and on the development of trust and respect between the leader and group. From a synthesis of the behaviors, skills, and attributes found in the leaders and in the organizations that meet the criteria of excellence, six generic constructs that describe the effective leadership of professionals are proposed. Their definitions are presented in Figure 5.1.

As can be seen in Figure 5.1, the leader of professionals needs special skills to maintain the careful balance between directing the group's activities and allowing competent professionals the autonomy they require to function effectively. As indicated earlier, in reaching this balance, the leader must understand that his or her role is to manage tasks, rather than manage people. Finally, the team leader should expect complexity, conflict, and ambiguity. Bennis (1989) emphasizes that "sooner or later, each of us has to accept the fact that complexity is here to stay and that order begins in chaos" (p. 113).

Purpose: Support the instruction + integration of students w/ special needs

1. Initiating Structure. This is the leader's task-oriented behavior of stating the organization's purpose, establishing the mechanisms and procedures, and defining the roles of members, through which the organization may obtain its results (Bennis, 1997; Heskett & Schlesinger, 1996). It has a "power" dimension, focused on the use of power for corporate as opposed to personal uses (Covey, 1990), and for the educational leader, it includes a personal commitment to a cause that can benefit others (Reinhartz & Beach, 2004).

Goals: Support instruction. Reinforce instruction. Support/reinforce independence

2. Facilitating Goal Achievement. These are the leader's acts of implementation that enable the team members to collaborate in the fulfillment of their common purpose (Kaplan & Owings, 2003; Reinhartz & Beach, 2004). These acts include translating the organization's mission into specific goal statements, delegating tasks, and reinforcing excellence (Blanchard & Johnson, 1982; French, 2003).

3. Demonstrating Consideration. This is the leader's relationship-oriented behavior, which emphasizes the social and personal aspects of working with people in the organization and building positive, supportive relationships with team members (Reinhartz & Beach, 2004). It focuses heavily on providing the work group with support and demonstrating to them that they are respected, trusted, and valued (Covey, 1990; Glasser, 1997; Kaplan & Owings, 2003; Peterson & Deal, 1998).

Methods: Resource Room

4. Showing Adaptability. This is the leader's proactive and reactive behavior that may be classified as situational. It is based in part on Hersey and Blanchard's (1974) concept that leaders have not only a dominant style (task oriented or relationship oriented) but that effective leaders also have a range of supporting styles from which they can select, depending on the situation (Bennett & Anderson, 2003). It is dependent on skill 5.

5. Using Direct Feedback. This is the skill of listening and being available that shows the leader believes the organization's mission, its workers, and its constituents are important (Bennett & Anderson, 2003; Glasser, 1997). It includes the leader's assessment of the actions, needs, and viewpoints of patrons, faculty, and students, and the use of this insight in decision making (Covey, 1990; Deming, 1986; Reinhartz & Beach, 2004; Scholtes, 1988).

6. Encouraging Innovations. This is the behavior through which the leader builds in provisions for growth, change, and development, both for individuals and for the organization (Dyer & Carothers, 2000; Joyce & Showers, 1995). It includes support of risk taking to encourage the development of a better service or product (Covey, 1990; Fullan, 2003). For the leader of the interactive team, this service or product is related to the program developed for the student with special needs.

Figure 5.1
Summary of essential skills for leaders of professionals.

INITIAL TASKS OF THE TEAM LEADER

The team leader's initial tasks set the stage for effective collaboration. These activities include (1) setting up the team, (2) identifying resources, and (3) establishing operating procedures. Each of these tasks is described in the following paragraphs.

Setting up the Team

The interactive team is a new and flexible group that is not a part of the established administrative structure within the school or clinical program. Chapter 3's discussion of the administrator's role pointed out that the administrator has overall fiscal and legal responsibility for the unit's program. This administrator—the principal or program director—does not usually function as the team leader and therefore needs to *delegate* to the team leader the authority to plan, implement, and evaluate programs for students with special needs. This is how the administrator gives the team its legitimacy and autonomy, as described in Chapter 2. It is also another way of showing that the team leader has the administrator's "permission" to accomplish the team's tasks, which is an essential part of delegating responsibility described later in this chapter.

In building teams, school leaders must begin by providing the organizational structure and incentives for teachers, parents, and community members to get involved on teams, committees, and groups (Reinhartz & Beach, 2004). School leaders must assure that teachers are given the time and resources to conduct their team's work. The work of school teams can sometimes be informal, such as teachers socializing at lunch or at monthly potluck dinners to discuss and resolve school business. Other times more traditional or formal teams are necessary to guide school change. When building teams, school leaders should consider the size of the team, the cohesiveness of team members, and whether to appoint a group leader or allow a leader to naturally emerge. The task for the team should be clearly outlined, with timelines established from the beginning. School leaders should give the team the necessary power to get the work done by outlining the team's responsibilities and expectations.

Today's schools have implemented various team supports to assist in working with students who are at risk for academic or behavioral problems. It is important to emphasize that a formal team is not created immediately for every student about whom a teacher, parent, or other service provider has a concern. Formal assessment for the purpose of determining whether or not special education is required occurs only after the classroom teacher has attempted to make ongoing changes in an existing program to improve the academic performance and/or social behavior of a given student. If student performance does not improve as a result of applying the performance-enhancing strategies and procedures used routinely by all teachers, then the teacher may call for assistance, initially to a grade level or school-wide team that is designed to meet the school's mission of academic improvement for all students. This team might be called the *prereferral team, child study team,* or *teacher assistance team.* The teacher with a concern would request assistance from other team members, who would offer suggestions. In requesting assistance, the teacher might summarize the problem by using information collected during classroom observations, usually made by a supportive colleague. The observations would include:

◆ Academic skills or behaviors of the student that seemed to interfere with learning, such as a lower level of performance, motivation, or interactions.

◆ Academic skills or behaviors that seemed to enhance learning, such as special interests or talents, leadership skills, insight, and so on.

In addition, the concerned teacher would provide a review of work samples completed by the student of concern, indicating any aspects of the problem as well as documenting any special skills that might be considered strengths. The team, working as a problem-solving unit, would suggest strategies that might further assist the teacher who presented the concern. This teacher, usually with help from a colleague, would implement the strategies recommended, documenting their effect on the student. If paraprofessionals or students-in-training are part of the classroom, one of these individuals might assist in making the observations and participate in the problem-solving team meeting's follow-up. Frequently, these informal procedures—characteristic of the things good teachers do on a regular basis—may enable the student to succeed without need for further intervention. These procedures are consistent with the goals of the Individuals with Disabilities Education Act (IDEA) in the sense that they try to prevent students at risk from failure who would require special education services.

When prevention strategies do not solve the problem, a formal referral is made. The legal requirements for parental notification and permission are followed for procedures that include diagnosis, placement, implementation, and follow-up. The school administrator should keep IDEA requirements in mind when setting up the team and delegating responsibility to the team leader. The law requires that the team developing the student's Individual Education Program (IEP) must include those persons who conducted this student's diagnosis and made placement decisions.

The team includes the following members:

◆ A representative of the local education agency (LEA) who is qualified to provide, or to supervise, special education programs, in addition to being knowledgeable about the general curriculum and the availability of resources. This individual must be able to make commitments of resources on behalf of the LEA.

◆ The student's parents or guardian.

◆ A regular education teacher.

◆ A special educator.

◆ An individual who can provide instructional interpretation of the diagnostic evaluations.

◆ The child with the disability, when appropriate.

If the team is considering the services for a student with transition needs, representatives of the agencies likely to provide or pay for these services would also be team members. A behavior specialist, bilingual/ESOL educator, or adaptive technology specialist would be included if the student's needs were related to these areas of expertise. Other members may, of course, be added if needed in an individual case.

Identifying Resources

The initial team leader will want to take steps to identify the human and fiscal resources that are available for the team's use. These steps include analyzing the expertise of potential team members, identifying the available fiscal resources that might be used to support the team's efforts, and organizing information about community resources that are available.

As a first step, the team leader will find it useful to analyze and prepare a brief outline of the professional training and expertise of potential team members, such as that provided in Chapter 3. This analysis will help team members understand the types of knowledge and skills they and others can contribute to the solution of a given student's problems. It will also be useful in helping the team identify the person who should serve as *major service coordinator* for each student's program planning, implementation, and evaluation.

Second, the team leader should obtain from the organization's administrator an outline of the *fiscal resources* that have been budgeted for use by the team. This outline is useful for preventing misunderstandings, such as assuming the budget is unlimited or not knowing that funds are available for particular purposes.

Finally, the team leader should obtain a list of community, state, and national resources (advocacy groups, professional organizations, and service agencies) that might contribute their expertise to the cases addressed by the team. It is useful, during the initial stages of establishing the team's workscope, to compile a reference guide of these resources. This step is the leader's way of showing that people are viewed as major resources, and that the team is concerned with helping people do their jobs effectively.

The types of resources that might be available include general and specialized health care providers, child-care facilities, and welfare and social service agencies. Team members should outline a systematic procedure for identifying these resources, which are available in any community. For example, several resources are available within any community, including the following:

◆ Public interest law firms.
◆ Banks and financial institutions.
◆ Jaycees/Rotary/Chamber of Commerce school-business partners.
◆ Big Brother/Big Sister groups.
◆ Foster homes/group homes.

- Faith-based organizations.
- Special groups: ARC, Parent-to-Parent Networks, School Advisory Councils, Parent-Teacher Organizations.

Establishing Operating Procedures

The team will function more effectively if it has a set of operating procedures that is understood by all members. This involves outlining the legal requirements, establishing the mission, and conducting effective meetings.

Outlining Legal Requirements.   It is important for the team leader to coordinate the legal requirements for procedures as team members work through the decision points of prereferral, screening, services, instructional planning, and evaluation. The leader will find it particularly useful to provide each team member with a written summary of required legal procedures under which the team needs to operate. These requirements include, but are not limited to, information on *informed consent, due process,* and *access to the general education curriculum.* A document explaining these procedures, as required by the jurisdiction in which the organization operates, is always available from the organization's administrator. Documentation of the special education procedures should be provided in the families' native language.

Specific procedural guidelines are also required during the team meeting for planning the special student's instructional program. A checklist of these procedures may serve as a guide to essential procedures during the program-planning meeting. A brief version of this checklist is shown in Figure 5.2. These legal procedures must be followed in the event of official referral for placement in special education programs.

Establishing the Team Mission.   Every team has a mission. The mission of the team responsible for planning and monitoring the program for a student with special needs is predetermined and defined by law in the IDEA 1997 amendments. During its early meetings, the team leader should clarify its mission. For the team that considers the instructional needs of many students, or meets regularly to propose solutions for building-wide problems, a mission statement will have to be developed. The group mission, if stated as a focused and relatively narrow purpose, will help the team direct its actions and set reachable goals. The team leader assists the group in seeing its mission as a clear statement of a problem to be solved. The problem statement guides decisions about what the team wants to accomplish, the information it needs to collect, and the strategies it should select (Chenoweth & Everhart, 2002; Reinhartz & Beach, 2004).

In establishing the mission, the team might use interactive discussions designed to help groups reach consensus. Although many strategies are available, only one is outlined here for illustrative purposes.

The procedures focus first on a *brainstorming* technique, which includes a series of questions to help the group focus (Chenoweth & Everhart, 2002). In implementing this technique, the leader poses written questions, which alternate from positive to negative and back again; for example, "What is the ideal mission of our team? What

Check When Completed

_____ 1. Positive beginning, start with introductions.

_____ 2. Designate recorder.

_____ 3. Discuss purpose of meeting.

_____ 4. Ensure parental input.

_____ 5. Review educational, medical assessments.

_____ 6. Summarize present levels of performance.

_____ 7. Determine service delivery model (i.e., co-teaching, consultation, small group, etc.).

_____ 8. State related services needs/times.

_____ 9. Explain extent of nonparticipation in regular programs.

_____ 10. Formulate annual goals/objectives (short-term objectives may be formulated at this time or at a future meeting and need not be overly detailed).

_____ 11. State needed modifications in district assessments.

_____ 12. Give dates, duration of special education services.

_____ 13. Determine assessment criteria.

_____ 14. List needed modifications and note any special considerations needed (behavior interventions, technology, ELL, Braille, etc.).

_____ 15. Designate responsibilities of persons present.

_____ 16. Provide participants with copy of recorder's report.

_____ 17. Obtain necessary signatures.

_____ 18. Positive ending, invite group to have future interactions.

Figure 5.2
Procedures for use in team meeting to plan student's instructional program.

might prevent us from reaching this ideal? In what ways might we begin to solve the problems that confront us? What might prevent us from succeeding? What are our next steps?" The idea behind brainstorming is to allow the members to state, in a series of rapid responses, all possible ideas that might help them define their group mission before narrowing down their focus to the most realistic set of guidelines.

The second part of the initial procedures for consensus building uses a concept outlined by Powers and Powers (1983) to facilitate ownership by all team members. After obtaining information from the group during a brainstorming session, the leader summarizes the statements that were made, giving credit to the individuals who suggested them. The leader then returns this summary to the group for review and feedback on its accuracy. This material thus represents the group's thinking, rewritten in a way to facilitate consensus building. The team leader may find that when a group disagrees or is simply unsure about what course to take, the techniques of brainstorming and consensus building are instrumental in maintaining the focus on mission.

During the initial stages of operation, the leader will also want to guide the group in deciding how it will reach consensus in the event of disagreement (Chenoweth & Everhart, 2002). For example, will they vote and be guided by majority rule? Or will they defer to the opinion of the person with the highest degree of knowledge about the issue? On a team in which professionals have specific types of expertise, intensive training, and strong opinions, it is difficult to establish meaningful interactions. The team's leader, by establishing effective operating procedures, can enable this group to function as a unit. Figure 5.3 lists some suggested operating rules for teams.

Conducting Effective Team Meetings. Chenoweth and Everhart (2002) and Scholtes (1988) have listed guidelines to help teams conduct effective meetings. The modified components of selected guidelines that apply most directly to the interactive school-based team are summarized here.

1. *Premeeting preparation.* The preparation for a meeting begins when members collect information on the nature of the problem to be discussed. Those who plan to present data and organize it to support their description of the current situation must address these questions:
   ◆ When, how often, and under what conditions does the problem occur?
   ◆ How does the current situation compare with the goal, ideal situation, or problem solution?

2. *Presentation/discussion.* Each team member who has relevant information prepares a brief presentation, taking care to communicate in jargon-free language. The procedures for effective communication within teams have been presented in previous chapters.

3. *Agenda development.* It is important to try not to "wing" a meeting. Instead, a meeting agenda should be circulated in advance, including the topic, the time for each item, presenter, and item type (discussion item or announcement). A well-designed agenda can double as a record of the meeting, and be used later

---

The team for problem solving and special program planning at Prairie Marsh Elementary School developed the following operating rules for their team:

1. Meetings will start and end on time.
2. Members will arrive on time, with assignments completed, prepared to contribute, using researched information and data whenever possible.
3. Confidentiality will be honored.
4. Every member will listen attentively and question respectfully when clarification is needed. No side conversations.
5. Decisions will be made by consensus; that is, all group members will agree that they can "live with" the decision and will support it following the meeting.

Figure 5.3
Sample operating rules for teams.

as a presentation outline for the team to communicate with the organization's administrator, funding agency, and others. Ideally, the final agenda item involves drafting the next meeting's agenda.

4. *Assigning roles.*   Team members should select a facilitator, recorder, timekeeper, and group members. Roles for the recorder and timekeeper should be rotated periodically.

5. *Documentation procedures.*   When item follow-up is required, it should be documented so each member's responsibilities are clear. A standard form might be developed for recording progress, using the meeting's agenda as an outline. The minutes of the meeting should include a description of topics, each followed by a summary of main points, decisions/conclusions, and next steps.

6. *Evaluation procedures.*   The most effective meetings are those that are evaluated by participants. This procedure helps the team leader make continuous improvements in the meeting process.

Those who have served as team leaders in large-group settings offer additional suggestions for the conduct of effective meetings. Facilitation specialist Tyree (1997), for example, has suggested that successful facilitators understand and explain to the group the "triad" in each situation: (1) the context–task and people variables of the problem, (2) the content–task or goal being addressed, and (3) the process–method used to address the content. For those situations in which the context is complex, either because the task or the people present unusual difficulties, it may be useful to separate the roles of the leader into two parts, one to deal with the process (an outside, neutral facilitator) and the other to manage the content (an insider, with special knowledge of the problem). Tyree also suggests that the facilitator monitor the progress of the meeting by checking frequently for consensus, using "thumbs up/down" votes on particular options or flagging with stickers any written items that they feel will require additional discussion.

Irvine (1998), a former school board chair, has provided additional suggestions for the team leader who operates in the public eye. She suggests that, prior to the public meeting, the leader initiate and maintain working relationships with members of the press, as well as parent and professional organizations, agencies, and interest groups. Her tips for running meetings smoothly include having ground rules for limiting speakers to 2 minutes each, maintaining eye contact with board members to ensure their understanding of items on which they are voting, and conducting orientation meetings for new members.

SERVICE COORDINATION PROCEDURES FOR TEAM LEADERS

As mentioned in the beginning of this chapter, a service coordinator functions as a conduit for all services that students are receiving. The service coordinator fills a leadership role originally called *care manager* (Young, 1987) or *case manager.*

Case management is defined as "a set of logical steps and a process of interaction within a service network which assure that a client receives needed services in a supportive, effective, and cost effective manner" (Weil, Karls, & Associates, 1985, p. 2).

The service coordinator—who might be the special educator, school counselor, a parent, or someone else—is the member with the greatest expertise in working with a particular student and family, and therefore is the major facilitator of services.

The *service coordinator,* who works with a specific student, has four major responsibilities.

1. Coordinating the services needed by the student and family.
2. Delegating responsibility for providing those services to the individuals best able to provide them.
3. Providing follow-up to ensure that goals are being met.
4. Guiding the contributions of paraprofessionals and volunteers who assist on the case.

Each of these responsibilities will be discussed briefly.

Coordinating Needed Services

Each service coordinator needs to administer the special student's program by interacting with other team members and agencies. Because the team will be working with individuals and groups from agencies outside its own organization, it is important for the service coordinator to follow established guidelines for *interagency collaboration.* The service coordinator will need access to a database showing the agencies with which the team may need to interact to obtain necessary services.

The service coordinator will need to make certain the database includes all necessary information about the agency's services and its procedures for referral. This database should include the following information:

◆ The name, address, e-mail, and phone number of the contact person.
◆ Information about when new referrals are taken.
◆ Type of information required (birth certificate, test data, etc.).
◆ Type of release form the agency requires, and its confidentiality.
◆ Type of service responsibilities the agency has.
◆ The agency's available funding options and constraints.

Several online resources are usually available for teams to use, including state, local school district, public health, and human resources Websites. The team can compile a list of the major Websites and information for each agency they use.

In addition to coordinating the student's program through interagency collaboration, the service coordinator should maintain records of the decisions the team has made, the dates they were made, and the people responsible for their implementation. These records will enable the service coordinator to track the progress of the case and request additional assistance from one or several members of the team as necessary.

Two additional areas require consideration by the service coordinator: the increasing use of technology and the importance of time management.

The uses of technology for education are growing at a pace and in a manner unimaginable even a decade ago. Adaptive equipment that ranges from wheelchairs able to traverse rough terrain to affordable voice-operated computers now enables persons with special needs to participate more fully in every aspect of daily life. Through wireless networks and telephone and cable alliances, instant global communication is becoming a reality. The barriers that exist in educational uses of technology are largely related to the need for replacing computers every 5 to 6 years, as well as the ability of individuals to accept this rapid pace of change, and of institutions to provide the essential training for its use (Garcia, 1998; November, 2003; Reinhartz & Beach, 2004). Increasing numbers of new professionals, including administrators, are receiving training in the application of computer technology to their career fields—Web browsers to locate home pages, online learning communities, PowerPoint for group presentations, software for creation of home pages, and spreadsheets for surveys and data analysis (November, 2003; Sharp, 1998). However, large numbers of practicing professionals are in need of additional assistance with the educational applications of technology. The service coordinator who oversees a given student's special program would be well advised to seek the assistance of the educator responsible for the school's technology program or an area business person with technology expertise. The team may find that it can communicate efficiently and effectively, for example, through use of e-mail and password-protected Websites to track student progress on a regular basis without calling too many time-consuming meetings. Virtual teams are becoming more popular for conducting school business and professional development activities (Sarker & Sahay, 2003). In addition, teams that collaborate across distance barriers, such as those that include members from a school and a university or service agency, are able to talk face-to-face using cost-effective interactive videoconferencing equipment such as iChat.

The overload of tasks and information has caused many persons with roles such as team leader to seek better ways of managing time. At the school level, faculty members have found that they can manage time more effectively by scheduling common time blocks for committee meetings (Shanklin, 1997) and by consolidating the number of committees or teams on which they serve (Morsink, 1999). Team members who complete similar kinds of paperwork tasks across cases will find that common recording forms are useful, not only for saving time, but also for ensuring compliance with laws. In the business arena, consultants are often hired to serve as "productivity coaches" who teach others how to manage time; a monthly advisory letter entitled the "Organized Executive" provides ongoing assistance

(Palmer, 1997). Some of the consultants recommendations are applicable to the school environment, including skimming through large amounts of information in a short time, while controlling interruptions, long meetings, and e-mail overload. Learning to delegate and to say "no" are among the solutions to time management across settings. Time can be saved on teams by using the strategies for conducting meetings outlined earlier in this chapter. The chapter's Application provides an example of effective delegation.

Delegating Responsibility

Since no service coordinator has either the time or the expertise to personally implement all aspects of the student's program, he or she needs to be able to delegate responsibilities to others. The process of *delegating* is most productive when it is guided by the leader's knowledge of each team member's task strengths and preferences (Dyer & Carothers, 2000; Reinhartz & Beach, 2004). The service coordinator who is most effective in delegating understands the importance of providing resources, encouragement, and supportive feedback (Simon & Newman, 2004).

Delegating refers to the assignment of part of the duties to another person who will assist with this task. The following seven-step method for effective delegating is derived from French's (2003) suggestions for working with paraeducators or paraprofessionals. In delegating responsibility, the service coordinator should:

1. *Set clear objectives.* Be clear about the purpose of the task and make certain to point out the intended outcomes.

2. *Select the right individual.* Match the task with the person who is skillful in that particular area, choosing from the paraprofessionals, volunteers, peer tutors, peer coaches, or other team members.

3. *Train the individual to carry out the task.* Make a checklist of the task, review it with the person, and demonstrate the task. Make sure they understand all the components of the task. Plan time for training sessions for new tasks.

4. *Get input from the individual.* To gain commitment to the work, ask the individual what he or she thinks about the suggested approach. Welcome his or her contributions to doing the task and review the task one more time to make sure he or she understands.

5. *Set deadlines, time frames, and follow-up dates.* Be sure to set a time and place to meet after the task is completed to monitor the results. It is not adequate to say, "Let's get together sometime and talk about it some more."

6. *Specify the level of authority.* Multiple levels of authority may need to be established for various tasks, such as (a) give full authority to take action, (b) give full authority but require them to stay in touch, (c) require them to get approval before taking action, or (d) require them to do only what has been delegated.

7. *Guide and monitor the task.* Build time to meet with the individual to review the task results and provide constructive feedback.

Throughout these steps, the effective service coordinator—as team leader—is communicating clearly, showing high expectations for results, and expressing confidence in both the importance of the task and the ability of the person to whom it is delegated. In the vignette that introduced this chapter, the team leader made major errors in delegating responsibility. He neither stated expectations clearly nor clarified the results that were required. Not granting "permission" or authority to the special education teacher to conduct observations in the regular classroom was another major error, which resulted in the classroom teacher's feeling that the special educator was interfering. Moreover, he did not establish guidelines for follow-up, so team members did not know they were expected to do more than just talk about the problem.

In explaining the importance of stating the task clearly, French (2003) indicates that an unclear task statement may cause the team member to spend a large amount of time and effort, only to be told that "this is not what was expected." It is easy to see how such misunderstanding can foster frustration, and even resentment, among the team members. French also elaborates on the importance of clarifying the expected outcomes, as opposed to specifying the exact procedures to be used. When the leader clarifies results, the person to whom the task is delegated feels free to apply professional knowledge and skill in determining how to achieve these results. Conversely, when the leader prescribes the details by which the task is to be accomplished, there is no respect shown for the person to whom the task is delegated. This type of delegating is a "put down" likely to be met with the (usually unspoken) response, "Well, if you know so much about my job, why don't you do it yourself?"

Providing Follow-Up

We have emphasized throughout the chapter that the service coordinator who assumes the leadership position is not an authoritarian. He or she develops the goals and objectives the team wishes the student to meet in collaboration with other team members. It is the service coordinator, however, who delegates specific responsibilities and then follows up by monitoring the progress of these assignments. The service coordinator gives both positive and corrective feedback during follow-up to the people to whom responsibility has been delegated.

While providing follow-up, the service coordinator needs to use the key principles that have been shown to motivate staff to improve their performance: enhancing self-esteem, expressing empathy, and asking for help (French, 2003). Using a calendar with timelines for follow-up, the service coordinator initiates contact with other team members. It is important for this leader to provide *supportive feedback* to all members of the group (Gersten, Carnine, & Greene, 1982). Supportive feedback is based on guidelines that enhance future interactions, and it includes the expression of willingness to help the team member who encounters difficulty in completing delegated tasks. The guidelines that seem most appropriate for the service coordinator's provision of feedback are adapted from the work of Developmental Dimensions (1981) and incorporate some of the strategies suggested by Blanchard and Johnson (1982). They include the following:

1. *Describe the problem clearly.* This is done by the team member who has experienced the problem. The team member who has made a direct observation that includes data-based input should use the data to describe the problem.
2. *Ask for the person's help in solving the problem.*
3. *Talk about causes of the problem.* The service coordinator should initiate this part of the discussion as an expression of empathy for the team member. The service coordinator should take care, however, not to let the discussion of causes become a dead-end explanation of why nothing can be done to solve the problem. The discussion should be kept short, then shifted to solutions.
4. *Brainstorm possible solutions.* The service coordinator requests possible solutions, saying, "Let's list some solutions we might try." The service coordinator writes them down, using phrases to describe each idea. When three or four potential solutions have been written, the service coordinator and team member look at them again and pick the one that has the best chance of initial success.
5. *Agree on the action and a follow-up discussion time.*   Decide what role each person will play in the implementation of this solution. For example, the service coordinator might say, "OK, then, you're going to . . . and I'm going to help you by. . . . Let's meet again Friday at 2 o'clock to talk about how well this solution is working."

Positive Feedback.   When providing feedback to the person to whom a task has been delegated, the service coordinator hopes to be able to acknowledge the job's success, thank the person, and praise his or her efforts. Praise is easier to provide than corrective feedback, although adults sometimes find it difficult to praise other adults in a sincere, helpful manner. It is easier to provide praise when the team has an established pattern in which the person to whom the coordinator has delegated a task expects feedback on performance (French, 2003). *Positive feedback* is most effective when it is delivered immediately, or as soon after task completion as feasible. It should be brief and highly specific, specifying the results that were accomplished (French, 2003). The service coordinator should also thank the person for helping and encourage the continuation of efforts on behalf of the team (Developmental Dimensions, 1981). An illustration of effective praise between professionals follows:

The school psychologist, as service coordinator, has delegated to the classroom teacher the task of implementing a behavioral support program for a boy named Tracy, who has been engaging in disruptive, off-task conversations during academic instruction. The psychologist, coming in to observe the effects of the program, notices great improvement in the boy's behavior because of the teacher's implementation of the plan. The psychologist says,

"You really kept Tracy on task during math class today! When he started talking about his favorite TV show, you just ignored him and called on Barbara. Preventing him from going off on a tangent increased the accuracy of the whole group on their math facts. Thanks for sticking with me on this. I know it's hard to ignore off-task behavior, but it pays off!"

This kind of specific feedback relates the teacher's contribution to the team's results, thereby showing the new program's effect. It heightens the feeling that the person being praised has accomplished something of importance and lessens the possibility that the praise will sound phony or exaggerated, as it would if the service coordinator simply had said, "You're doing just great!"

Corrective Feedback.   It is less pleasant for the service coordinator to give *corrective feedback* to a person whose work has not supported the team's efforts. However, without corrective feedback tasks lack clarity, and positive feedback eventually loses its meaning. Corrective feedback should be specific, including descriptions of both the behavior and its negative effect on the situation (French, 2003). Beyond this, the service coordinator should show a desire to be helpful, rather than appear punitive or vengeful. The service coordinator can demonstrate helpfulness by asking for reasons for the lack of effective contributions and by listening to the reasons with empathy, but without accepting them as excuses for continued ineffectiveness. The service coordinator can focus on problem solving by saying, "What can we do to prevent this problem from recurring?" The service coordinator and team member engage in some collaborative problem solving; they then agree on a follow-up to determine whether the proposed solution is working. Finally, and most important of all, the service coordinator expresses confidence in the person's ability to contribute increasingly to the team's efforts.

The emphasis in corrective feedback is on task completion that enables the team to reach its goal, rather than on the personal performance of the team member. The service coordinator's role is to work collaboratively with the person in need of assistance to design the solution to a shared problem. Although the leader is a collaborator, he or she is also the person in charge, the one who will follow-up on the strategy and retain ultimate responsibility for its effectiveness. It is important in this role to maintain a careful balance between being too directive and too "friendly." The overly directive service coordinator allows the team member to avoid assuming ownership or responsibility for the problem; the overly friendly leader appears too weak to provide the follow-up necessary for task completion.

Guiding Paraprofessionals and Volunteers

The team member who functions as service coordinator may also have the task of coordinating the work of *paraprofessionals, preservice students,* and *volunteers* who assist the team members in their roles as service providers or collaborators. In a number of school districts and clinical programs, paraprofessionals, who have some training but less than full certification in their field, are employed as assistants for the professionals in special programs. In many other programs, people with expertise in their own fields volunteer their time to help school or health-related personnel.

The team member's role in recruiting, training, and coordinating the work of these people is becoming increasingly important.

Paraprofessionals.   The role of the paraprofessional or paraeducator is to supplement the instructional or other support services provided to the student with special needs, under the supervision of the teacher or other professional responsible for those services (Giangreco & Doyle, 2002; Rosenberg, Robinson, & Fryer, 2002; Wallace, 2003). For the purpose of this discussion, the preservice student, who may be a student teacher or health professions-related intern, is considered a paraprofessional, because this person is not yet certified to conduct the duties of a professional. According to French (2003), the paraprofessional in the classroom most often engages in activities such as the following:

- Provides follow-up tutoring.
- Circulates throughout the room to check students' progress.
- Provides students with drills and reviews.
- Prepares instructional materials and games.
- Reads stories to students.
- Conducts small-group noninstructional and instructional activities.
- Corrects homework and workbook assignments.
- Arranges learning centers, demonstrations, and bulletin boards.

In a classroom for students with physical disabilities, the paraprofessional also assists students with functional skills such as dressing and eating, assists with the use of braces and other prosthetic devices, and helps with lifting and transferring, as from a wheelchair to a toilet. The paraprofessional may also help other team members, such as the computer specialist and the physical or occupational therapist.

French (2003) suggests seven general functions of paraeducator supervision.

1. Orienting paraeducators to the program, school, and students
2. Planning for paraeducators
3. Scheduling for paraeducators
4. Delegating tasks to paraeducators
5. On-the-job training and coaching of paraeducators
6. Monitoring and feedback regarding paraeducator task performance
7. Managing the workplace (communication, problem solving, conflict management). (p. 43)

French stresses the importance of working with paraprofessionals in a team relationship, in which the professional is the leader. The teacher, related professional, or service coordinator assumes the role of helping the paraprofessional develop additional skills. Through observation, supervision, and specific feedback, the professional with good communication skills can promote positive growth in the paraprofessional, ensuring that this individual will be a more effective member of the interactive team.

Volunteers.   Volunteers have assisted in schools on an organized basis since the National School Volunteer Program began in 1950. In 1981, business and industry leaders joined the efforts to provide assistance to school programs through the creation of the Advisory Council on Private Sector Initiatives (National Association of Partners in Education [NAPE], 1988). NAPE, now only functioning at a state level, reports that PARTNERS IN EDUCATION and its diverse membership represent over 7 million volunteers involved in more than 400,000 partnerships nationwide (NAPE, 2004).

School volunteers may be specialists in their own fields—writers, researchers, vice presidents, designers, marketing personnel, physicians, attorneys, photographers—some of whom are actively involved in their professions, and some of whom are retired. Several schools have used volunteers to assist with programs in literacy, dropout prevention, and drug abuse prevention. These volunteer partners represent a rich resource of knowledge and support for the interactive team. Volunteers may engage in activities such as the following:

◆ Tutoring students with special needs.
◆ Serving as mentors for students who lack adult role models.
◆ Sponsoring training, demonstrations, and tours for students.
◆ Assisting with projects or judging contests.
◆ Providing work internships and scholarships for students.
◆ Donating equipment and materials.

It is important for team members to work within their organization's overall system to identify and coordinate the efforts of volunteers, as well as assist in the design of a training program that will enable volunteers to work effectively with students who have special needs. These volunteers will appreciate guidance about the rules of the organization, as well as the instructional and management techniques that are effective with the type of special students to whom they are assigned. They will also appreciate both positive and constructive feedback when it is delivered sensitively, although the team leader is not in the position of serving as a "supervisor" of their efforts.

Several successful volunteer programs have been developed in schools. Volunteers in Education programs recruit members of local businesses, parents, and civic clubs to spend volunteer hours in school. Many focus on tutoring in reading and math activities. Other schools have Adopt-a-School partnerships which provide classrooms volunteers as well as scholarships for students to pursue postsecondary education. Developing and using community volunteers can become a source of pride for those individuals, schools, and businesses (Reinhartz & Beach, 2004). Both paraprofessionals and volunteers should be provided with guidance that recognizes their contributions and allows them to become respected members of the interactive team. The service coordinator is the team member in the best position to ensure that this occurs.

WORKING WITH A SPECIAL EDUCATION ADVOCATE

Today's schools increasingly require interactive team members to work with special education advocates. This work can often be adversarial and requires strong team leadership, communication, and group facilitation skills. Pittman (2003) outlines factors that are important in working with advocates. Team members interacting with special education advocates should have a positive frame of mind, recognizing that the ultimate outcome is to benefit children and their families. They should understand the law and their school district's procedures and practices regarding mediation and due process. Often parents bring team members to school because they are uncertain that the school is serving their child's best interest. Team members are often more knowledgeable about the student than the advocate. Therefore, it is important for team members to maintain a high level of accountability for the student's educational program and progress. Service coordinators and individual team members should approach the job of working with special education advocates in a calm and professional manner, with a strong understanding of the student's educational needs. "There is common ground [between school personnel and advocates]: meeting the student's leaning needs" (Pittman, p. 174).

APPLICATION

The following application illustrates the correct way for the team leader or service coordinator to delegate a task to a paraprofessional and to provide effective feedback while monitoring the task's completion. The task is presented as a series of examples, with comments on their appropriateness.

The service coordinator is a classroom teacher. The task is to conduct a follow-up review for a special needs student on a lesson the teacher has taught in reading.

Step 1: Set clear objectives.

Clear	Unclear
The teacher would like the paraprofessional to tutor Sonya, a 13-year-old with mild disabilities, on science vocabulary words. The eight words are part of an anatomy unit for science and the students will be tested next week.	The teacher would like someone to practice science vocabulary words with Sonya.

In the unclear example, the task is unclear and unfocused; in addition, the rationale or importance for teaching this task is not described.

Step 2: Select the right individual.

Clear	Unclear
The teacher approaches both the paraprofessionals about the task. She asks Rose to teach the science vocabulary task. The teacher explains that Rose has been working closely with Sonya and would establish rapport more quickly.	The teacher approaches both paraprofessionals and asks them to decide who would be best to tutor Sonya.

In the unclear example, the teacher is leaving it up to the paraprofessionals to decide who will tutor Sonya. This can put the paraprofessionals in an awkward position for deciding; in addition, it is not certain that both the paraprofessionals are familiar with the science unit and the vocabulary-drilling procedures.

Step 3: Train the individual to carry out the task.

Clear	Unclear
The teacher gives Rose a handout describing the vocabulary procedures for the eight science words. She reviews the task with Rose, showing her how to present the cards, how to wait for a response, how to prompt Sonya, and how to praise her for correct responding. The teacher also shows Rose how to keep data on Sonya's performance with the cards.	The teacher approaches Rose with the eight science vocabulary words on index cards and asks her to teach the words to Sonya.

In the unclear example, Rose receives no training or instruction on what is expected from the student during the vocabulary tutoring activity. It is up to Rose to decide the instructional strategies for the student.

Step 4: Get input from the individual.

Clear	Unclear
The teacher asks Rose to demonstrate the activity and review the procedures she will implement with Sonya.	The teacher asks Rose if she has any questions.

continues

Clear (continued)

The teacher then asks Rose if she has any questions. Rose suggests that after the completion of the science vocabulary drill, she take Sonya to the library to check out a book on the science topic. The teacher agrees.

In the unclear example, the teacher will not know whether the task is understood, because it is unlikely that the paraprofessional will ask any questions.

Step 5: Set deadlines, time frames, and follow-up dates.

Clear

The teacher asks Rose to begin the lesson at 10:30 A.M. and spend 20 minutes tutoring Sonya on the vocabulary words and 10 minutes going to the library to check out a book. The teacher would like Rose and Sonya back in the classroom promptly at 11:00 A.M. The teacher asks Rose to meet with her at 3:45 P.M. that same afternoon to review the results of the tutoring activity.

Unclear

The teacher asks Rose to touch base with her later in the week about the lesson.

In the unclear example, the plan for monitoring effectiveness is so open that nothing further will happen. The teacher will not know how Sonya did on her vocabulary activity.

Step 6: Specify the level of authority.

Clear

The teacher tells Rose that she has talked to Sonya about the science vocabulary activity and that Sonya understands that she will be responsible for doing a good job on the activity. If Sonya has any questions, Rose will handle the questions.

Unclear

The teacher tells Rose she has her permission to work with Sonya and to interrupt her at the math table if Sonya has any questions.

In the unclear example, the word *permission* may be demeaning to Rose, and having Rose interrupt the teacher (should Sonya have questions) implies that Rose cannot handle the authority to conduct the lesson.

Step 7: Guide and monitor the task.

Clear	Unclear
The teacher meets with Rose at 3:45 p.m. to discuss the results of the tutoring activity. If Rose has been successful in implementing the activity, the teacher provides specific praise. If Rose has been unsuccessful in completing the task, the teacher would provide corrective feedback and problem-solve strategies for improving the lesson.	At the end of the week, the teacher asks Rose to add eight more vocabulary words to the activity for the following week.

In the unclear example, the teacher does not know how well the activity is going with Sonya. She is adding more vocabulary words without checking if the tutoring is effective.

The effective leader gives both positive and corrective feedback during the monitoring of delegated activities. The specific substeps for conducting follow-up to encourage improved performance were outlined earlier in the chapter. In this application, only the most important of the substeps—describing the problem, discussing possible causes, listing alternative solutions, and agreeing on next steps—are illustrated.

The paraprofessional (PP) who has worked with Sonya describes a problem during the scheduled follow-up conference with the service coordinator, the teacher/ leader (TL):

PP: Sonya mastered six of the eight words I taught her, but she is still having trouble reading the other two words.

TL: What do you think caused this problem?

PP: I'm not sure. It could be that the two words were so similar that they were confusing to her. The words were *tibia* and *fibula.*

TL: Yes, those words do look and sound alike. That's a good observation. Do you have any other ideas?

PP: It was close to the end of the 20 minutes when I presented those words. She might have been more tired then. She seemed to be looking around at the other kids instead of concentrating.

TL: That's certainly consistent with what we know about Sonya's behavior and attention span. Let's list a few ideas about how we might modify the task next time you work with her to make it more effective.

The paraprofessional and the teacher/leader list four possible alternatives for task modification:

1. Reduce practice time from 20 minutes to 10 minutes at a time; repeat practice twice a day.
2. Remove Sonya from her desk during science vocabulary tutoring; place her in a quiet corner away from distractions.

3. Use practice alternatives that are more motivating, such as word games or computer-assisted instruction on the troublesome words.

4. Highlight the differences between the words *tibia* and *fibula*, either by printing the contrasting letter in red or pairing each word with a picture illustrating its meaning, to help Sonya develop her own device for learning the differences between the two words.

TL: Which of these alternative ways of changing the task do you think would be most effective the next time you work with Sonya?

PP: I'd like to try the last one—helping her develop some kind of trick for learning the differences in the two words.

TL: That sounds as if it might help her—not just for the next practice time, but over the long term—to develop a strategy for telling the difference between words that look and sound alike. Why don't you design a set of materials that highlight the differences in these words and their meanings? Then try it with her tomorrow and see whether she masters all eight words, including *tibia* and *fibula*. Let's get together again after school at this time tomorrow to see how well our new plan worked.

In this example of follow-up, the teacher serving as service coordinator provided an opportunity for the paraprofessional to function as an important part of the interactive team. The emphasis in follow-up was on the task, rather than on the performance of the paraprofessional. It was possible for the two team members to function well together because they focused on solving the problem—designing a task that was more effective in helping their shared student learn the target words. Moreover, although the professional was clearly "in charge" of the conference, the paraprofessional's observations, ideas, and contributions were important. This is how the team leader can obtain maximum efforts from all members of the interactive team.

SUMMARY

There are two types of team leaders. The person who calls and conducts meetings, collects and distributes information on resources, and maintains records is the official, designated, ongoing team leader. The temporary leader, called the service coordinator, changes with each case; this leadership role is given to the person with the greatest knowledge about the specific case being considered by the team. Both types of team leaders need special skills in the leadership of professionals:

◆ Skills that are similar to the skills, attributes, and behaviors of effective leaders in other organizations, including business and industry.

◆ Skills that focus on the management of tasks, rather than of individuals.

The ongoing, designated team leader has three tasks that set the stage for the effective functioning of the team in the future.

♦ Set up the team within the context of the organization.
♦ Identify resources for use by the team.
♦ Establish operating procedures.

Each designated leader, called a service coordinator, is responsible for overall coordination of a case that involves a specific student with special needs. The service coordinator is responsible for:

♦ Coordinating the services provided to the student or client.
♦ Delegating responsibility to other team members.
♦ Providing follow-up on the effectiveness of delegated tasks.
♦ Guiding the activities of paraprofessionals and volunteers who assist the team.

In this chapter, the work of the team leader has been outlined. The chapter's emphasis has been on the use of the leader as a collaborator who can encourage the full participation of each team member to reach the team's goal: the best possible program for a given student.

In the next chapter, the dimension of leadership as a facilitating factor will be explored further. The discussion will focus on ways in which professional development can be used to empower team members in their efforts to bring about long-term systematic change, which enhances the effectiveness of programs for students with special needs.

ACTIVITIES

1. Using the six steps presented in the chapter, write or act out the conversation you would use to delegate a teaching task to a practicum student in your classroom or clinical program. (Use any task of your choice.)

2. Explain the difference between listening with empathy to the reasons for a paraprofessional's problem in completing a task and accepting those reasons as excuses for failure to complete the task.

3. Using the guidelines presented in the chapter, write or act out the conversation you would use in giving your paraprofessional corrective feedback during follow-up on a task you had delegated. (Use any situation of your choice.)

4. Using the guidelines presented in this chapter, delegate a task to a paraprofessional or practicum student in your program, observe that

person completing the task, and provide feedback on the task performance during a follow-up conference.

5. Use directories, interviews, and other sources of information to develop a card file of community resources that might be used by an interactive team in your area.

REFERENCES

Barth, R. (2002). The culture builder. *Educational Leadership, 50,* 6–11.

Bennett, N., & Anderson, L. (2003). *Rethinking educational leadership.* Thousand Oaks, CA: Sage.

Bennis, W. (1989). *Why leaders can't lead: The unconscious conspiracy continues.* San Francisco: Jossey-Bass.

Bennis, W. (1997). 21st century leadership: Do you have what it takes? (E. Wakin, Ed.). *Beyond Computing, 6*(4), 38–43.

Blanchard, K., & Johnson, S. (1982). *The one minute manager.* New York: William Morrow.

Chenoweth, T., & Everhart, R. (2002). *Navigating comprehensive school change: A guide for the perplexed.* Larchmont, NY: Eye on Education.

Covey, S. (1990). *The 7 habits of highly effective people.* New York: Simon & Schuster.

Deming, W. E. (1986). *Out of the crisis.* Boston: MIT Center for Advanced Engineering Studies.

Developmental Dimensions. (1981). *Interaction management system.* Pittsburgh: Author.

Dyer, K., & Carothers, J. (2000). *The intuitive principal: A guide to leadership.* Thousand Oaks, CA: Corwin.

French, N. (2003). *Managing paraeducators in your school: How to hire, train, and supervise non-certified staff.* Thousand Oaks, CA: Orwin Press.

Fullan, M. (2003). Implementing change at the building level. In W. Owings & L. Kaplan (Eds.), *Best practices, best thinking, and emerging school issues in school leadership* (pp. 31–37). Thousand Oaks, CA: Corwin Press.

Garcia, R. (1998). Hang-ups of introducing computer technology. *THE Journal, 26*(2), 65–66.

Gersten, R., Carnine, D., & Green, S. (1982, March). *Administrative supervisory support functions for the implementation of effective educational programs for low income students.* Paper presented at the annual meeting of the American Educational Research Association, New York.

Giangreco, M., & Doyle, M. B. (2002). Students with disabilities and paraprofessional supports: Benefits, balance, and band-aids. *Focus on Exceptional Children, 34,* 1–12.

Glasser, W. (1997). A new look at school failure and school success. *Phi Delta Kappan, 78,* 596–603.

Goldman, E. (1998). The significance of leadership style. *Educational Leadership, 55*(7), 20–22.

Hersey, P., & Blanchard, K. (1974). So you want to know your leadership style? *Training and Development Journal, 28*(2), 22–36.

Heskett, J., & Schlesinger, L. (1996). Leaders who shape and keep performance-oriented cultures. In F. Hesselbein, M. Goldsmith, & R. Beckhard (Eds.), *The leader of the future.* San Francisco: Jossey-Bass.

Individuals with Disabilities Education Act (IDEA) Amendments of 1997, PL 105–17, 20 U.S.C. §§ 1400 et seq.

Irvine, J. (1998). My life as a chair. *The American School Board Journal, 185*(10), 45–46, 55.

Jarvis, M., & Chavez, C. (1997). Leadership and the triangle of success. *Phi Kappa Phi Journal, 77*(1), 35–37.

Joyce, B., & Showers, B. (1995, May). Learning experiences in staff development. *The Developer, 3.*

Kaplan, L., & Owings, W. (2003). Epilogue. In W. Owings & L. Kaplan (Eds.), *Best practices, best thinking, and emerging school issues in school leadership* (pp. 263–271). Thousand Oaks, CA: Corwin Press.

Kelley, R. (1991). *The power of followership.* New York: Doubleday.

Lambert, I. (2002). A framework for shared leadership. *Educational Leadership, 50,* 37–40.

McClelland, D. (1975). *Power: The inner experience.* New York: Irvington.

McGregor, D. (1960). *The human side of enterprise.* New York: McGraw-Hill.

Morsink, C. (1999). *21st century teachers for a better future. (Final Report to Howard Heinz Endowment).* Slippery Rock, PA: SRU College of Education.

National Association of Partners in Education. (1988). *1988 annual report.* Alexandria, VA: Author.

National Association of Partners in Education. (2004). *Mission.* Retrieved February 5, 2004, at http://www.napehq.org/

November, A. (2003). Using technology to change school learning culture. In W. Owings & L. Kaplan (Eds.), *Best practices, best thinking, and emerging school issues in school leadership* (pp. 95–102). Thousand Oaks, CA: Corwin Press.

Owings, W., & Kaplan, L. (Eds.) (2003). *Best practices, best thinking, and emerging school issues in school leadership.* Thousand Oaks, CA: Corwin Press.

Palmer, D. (1997, June). How America's most successful executives accomplish so much in so little time. *Executive Focus,* 23–24.

Peterson, K., & Deal, T. (1998). How leaders influence the culture of schools. *Educational Leadership, 56*(1), 28–30.

Pittman, M. (2003). Working with special education advocates. In W. Owings & L. Kaplan (Eds.), *Best practices, best thinking, and emerging school issues in school leadership* (pp. 171–176). Thousand Oaks, CA: Corwin Press.

Powers, D., & Powers, M. (1983). *Making participatory management work.* San Francisco: Jossey-Bass.

Reinhartz, J., & Beach, D. (2004). *Educational leadership: Changing schools, changing roles.* Boston: Pearson.

Richman, M. (1999a, February 16). IBD's 10 secrets to success. *Investor's Business Daily,* A8.

Richman, M. (1999b, August 30). IBD's 10 secrets to success. *Investor's Business Daily,* A4.

Rosenberg, S., Robinson, C., & Fryer, G. (2002). Evaluation of paraprofessional home visiting services for children with special needs and their families. *Topics in Early Childhood Special Education, 22,* 158–168.

Sarker, S., & Sahay, S. (2003). Understanding virtual team development: An interpretive study. *Journal of the Association for Information Systems, 4,* 1–38.

Scholtes, P. (1988). *The team handbook.* Madison, WI: Joiner Associates.

Shanklin, N. (1997). A run-away horse: Reining in committee work. In R. Benton (Ed.), *Partnerships for learning: Real issues and real solutions* (TECSCU Monograph Series, Vol. II, pp. 160–163). Oshkosh, WI: Poesch Printing.

Sharp, W. (1998). School administrators need technology too. *THE Journal, 26*(2), 75–76.

Simon, R., & Newman, J. (2004). *Making time to lead: How principals can stay on top of it all.* Thousand Oaks, CA: Orwin.

Tyree, R. (1997, May). *Introductory facilitation training.* Presentation to Department Chairs, College of Education, Slippery Rock University of Pennsylvania.

Wallace, T. (2003). *Paraprofessionals* (COPSSE Document No. IB-3). Gainesville, FL: University of Florida, Center on Personnel Studies in Special Education. Retrieved January 31, 2004, from http://www.copsse.org.

Wasley, P., Hampel, R., & Clark, R. (1997). The puzzle of whole-school change. *Phi Delta Kappan, 78,* 690–697.

Weil, M., Karls, J., & Associates. (1985). *Case management in human service practice.* San Francisco: Jossey-Bass.

Young, T. (1987). Therapeutic case advocacy: A summary. *Focal Point, 1*(3) 1–5.

Empowering Team Members
Through School Change
and Professional Development

6

Topics in this chapter include:

- Discussion of the terms *power* and *empowerment* as they relate to professional development and the process of school change.

- Description of the scientifically based approach to professional development.

- Description of the different levels of professional development for teams: awareness, initial implementation of new skill, and adapting and refining new practices.

- Guidelines and examples of several strategies for implementing professional development with educators and paraprofessionals.

- An application, showing how the level of a team's development might be viewed from the perspective of the leader's style.

The school-wide team that had met to evaluate and place students with special needs into inclusive classrooms at Manatee Elementary School was having difficulty implementing the inclusive program. The students they had identified and placed were functioning well, but three of the five general education teachers were feeling overwhelmed and ineffective in promoting student progress. Those general education teachers wondered if the team had made a wise decision in moving toward inclusionary practices. Although special education teachers had been assigned to support the general education teachers by helping with small group instruction and adapting materials, the general education and special education teachers rarely talked when they were in the classroom, and never met outside of the classroom activities. In these classrooms the special education teacher would drop by once a day for 1 hour to conduct instructional activities for only the students with special needs. The school psychologist tried to suggest collaborative team meetings and consultation, but her suggestions and services as a consultant to the three teachers were not welcomed. The other two classroom teachers were making better adjustments to their inclusive classrooms and were collaborating with the special education teachers, but their colleagues remained resistant to continuing the inclusive program.

Together, the special education teacher, the school psychologist, and the classroom teachers approached the school principal, who was new in the district and eager to establish her school as a model program for inclusion. The team agreed to support the principal's efforts in professional development by using consultants from the local university to help present information on inclusive practices to all the teachers and serve as coaches to individual teachers. With the support of the school principal, team members were provided release time through paraprofessional substitutes in order to meet at least twice a week during the lunch period. They also conducted a needs assessment to determine the types of problems the teachers were having with their students with special needs and the areas in which they felt least effective in assisting these students. They learned that the teachers were most concerned about managing the behavior of students with special needs during large-group instruction and providing students with academic instruction that would enable them to master the basic skills. With this information in hand, the team members began to design a plan for professional development to assist all five of the teachers in working more effectively with students with special needs in an inclusive classroom. University consultants presented a series of workshops and began observing and coaching teachers in the inclusive classroom.

An advisory group of teachers from another elementary school and parents from the PTA was asked by the principal to design a formal evaluation of the professional development program's effectiveness and to conduct this evaluation 1 year after its implementation. The evaluation plan was to focus on the effects of professional development on the whole school's sense of "mission" and teachers' and parents' satisfaction with the inclusion program. The evaluation would also include an analysis of the program's effect on the average student's academic achievement, as well as individual learning and behavior changes in students with special needs.

R ead between the lines of this case to see why an attempted change first faltered, then flourished. Experienced leaders seeking change understand that school improvement occurs best when it is based on empowerment and shared decision making, rather than on rule enforcement. In this chapter, the guidelines for use of professional development as a facilitating factor are outlined. Power is defined, and the distinction is drawn between power and empowerment. The best practices for empowering team members through professional development are outlined, and the relevant research on professional development is summarized. Levels of professional development that match the professionals' needs are described. Applications of each level are given, and the use of professional development as a facilitating factor in interactive teaming is explained.

POWER, CHANGE, AND EMPOWERMENT

Team members who recognize the need for a change in the behavior of others or in the culture of the organization in which they work often wish they had the power to implement this change. Professional development is one of the most effective ways to bring about change. Such development has the greatest effect when it is implemented by people who understand how it relates to the change process by empowering people rather than by imposing power on them.

As described in Chapter 5, effective leaders manage conflict creatively, encourage innovation, and create change while respecting divergent points of view. Today's school leaders are faced with increasing challenges in hiring highly qualified teachers. Because of the critical teacher shortages, many school administrators are hiring teachers who are not fully qualified. In order to build capacity, school leaders are turning to comprehensive programs of support and professional development. Transforming a school into a community of learners is a goal for today's school leaders. Yet, school teams must first understand the importance of power and how to use it effectively in school reform. A leader's power is based on the group's respect for his or her credibility and genuineness, as opposed to the leader's ability to act out superficial behaviors that give the appearance of power (Covey, 1990). A transformational leader not only inspires and is charismatic, but he or she helps others to be problem solvers and change followers (Reinhartz & Beach, 2004).

Responsible and Effective Use of Power

The term *power,* in this context, means the ability to accomplish team goals in providing the best possible program for all students, especially students with special needs. The use of power is discussed along two dimensions: (1) understanding the positive aspects of power and (2) recognizing and using established power. Each of these dimensions is discussed briefly.

Understanding the Positive Aspects of Power. It should be emphasized that power is equated with strength or effectiveness, but is not used as a synonym for autocratic leadership. As shown in Chapter 5, power is essential in the exercise of leadership that facilitates change.

Several types of power are available to the team member who wishes to be a leader for change: coercive, reward, legitimate, and expert power.

◆ *Coercive power,* which involves the use of threat or punishment, is used least often by leaders who wish to obtain cooperation; likewise, *reward power* is of only temporary value in facilitating behavioral or organizational change. Glasser (1997) has shown that coercive and reward power, in fact, have a negative effect on school climate and may interfere with change.

◆ *Legitimate power,* which is based on the group's acceptance of a common purpose, requires that the leader conform to this purpose and fit the group's concept of how their leader should behave. The use of legitimate power is the most desirable within the interactive team, although this is not the only type of power available to the team leader.

◆ *Expert power* is based on the group's perception that the leader has knowledge, insight, and vision. For the interactive team, expert power can also be appropriately used to initiate the changes necessary to implement a student's program. The expert is viewed as the one who can solve the problem or make something happen. The person who demonstrates expert power in a group is the one who comes prepared with facts and information. The data collected may take the form of charts and graphs, showing the student's responses to various types of programs; historical information, including test scores and work samples; or a summary of the research on a particular program that has been found effective. The team member with data is the individual most likely to be perceived by others as having the necessary expert power to bring about desired change.

Recognizing and Using Established Power. The team member who wishes to bring about positive change does not always have the power—either legitimate or expert—to do so. In this case, it is important for the person who wishes to facilitate change to recognize and use *established power* within the organization. Tucker (1972) has developed a well-established approach to planning change based on an understanding of power. The approach is presented as a flowchart, which follows a series of questions. Tucker's key for planning change has been adapted for use by the interactive team member and is presented in Figure 6.1. In Question 1, team members who wish to initiate change are asked to determine whether they have power. If they answer "yes," they have no obstacle and can go all the way through the flowchart, even skipping steps to accomplish their change. (There may be later consequences to skipping steps, because they may not have "institutionalized" the changes.)

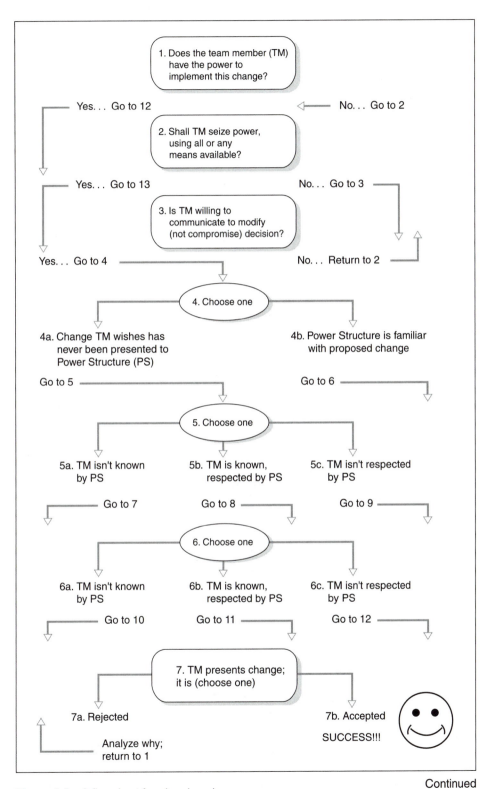

Figure 6.1 A flowchart for planning change.

Source: From *A Plan to Achieve Change,* by J. Tucker, 1972, Chattanooga: University of Tennessee at Chattanooga, College of Education and Applied Professional Studies. Adapted by permission.

Continued

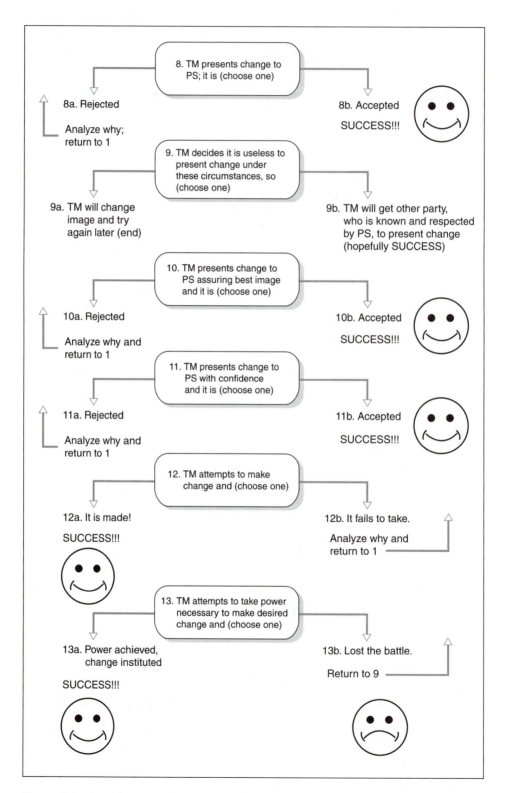

Figure 6.1 Continued.

If the team members have no power, they must decide whether to behave as revolutionaries or to "communicate the importance of that change to persons in power" (Tucker, 1972, p. 2). In most instances, team members do not have power and must propose their change through a third party who is known and respected by the organization's power structure. Tucker pointed out that this sharing of power involves both risk and compromise, but he suggested that it is the most effective strategy for the powerless beginner.

The "change" presented in the flowchart is the new program, which the interactive team wishes to implement to improve the services offered to students with special needs or their families. The team members responsible for implementing this program work within the organization's *power structure* to be sure the changes required by this program will be accepted by the organization's members.

In the flowchart, the team member asks a series of questions, in which the key issues are the following:

◆ Does the member have the power to bring about the desired change? If not, shall power be seized, or should the team member "give" the change idea to another person who may be more successful?

◆ Is the member willing to discuss the change with others, knowing that the proposal will be modified in the process of discussion?

◆ Is the team member known and respected by the power structure? If not, should the team member try to gain respect or, alternatively, "give" the change to a known and respected person for implementation?

As shown in Figure 6.1, the team member who is established within or respected by the power structure of the organization will be able to get necessary program changes accepted more readily than a person who is rejected by the power structure or is new to the organization. This strategy is particularly important for first-year teachers or new team members. In the latter instance, the team member will find that the most effective way to implement changes is by *giving ideas away to an established person who is respected and accepted by the power structure.* This concept is key to the understanding of how to use power by sharing it; this is called *empowerment.* Empowerment is a multidimensional social process that helps people gain control over their own lives (Page & Czuba, 1999). For people to be empowered, power must be able to change, be shared, and be expanded. For school teams, it is a process that fosters power in its members, for use in their jobs, by acting on issues that they define as important. Empowerment is essential in the process of change and will be discussed later in this chapter.

Bringing About Change

One might assume that when there is a compelling need for change, it would be easy to implement this change. Those who study the change process caution that this is not so (Chenoweth & Everhart, 2002; Fullan, 2000, 2003; Hall & Hord, 2001;

McLeskey & Waldron, 2002; Reinhartz & Beach, 2004). The difficulties in implementing change are shown in the following vignette.

Similarly to the faculty at Manatee Elementary, the faculty at Woodside Middle School had worked for 5 years to develop its mission and strategies for enabling all students to succeed. Woodside Middle School was considered a low-performing school and had a population of 90% of students on reduced or free lunch. After extensive discussions, involving the entire faculty and representatives from the community and local university, the school created a learning community with a model for inclusion of all students, particularly students with special needs and English language learners. Students worked together to solve problems, while teachers adapted instruction to the special needs and learning styles of every student and used authentic assessments such as projects and portfolios to document student success. Although the school became known for its effectiveness in using innovative strategies, there remained a disquieting skepticism on the part of the district's central administrators who were concerned about the lack of improvement in high-stakes test scores and annual yearly progress. Then the principal, who had been the instructional leader, left. The district selected a new principal who believed in the traditional model, emphasizing basic academic skills, with effectiveness measured by standardized tests. The whole-school changes that had been in effect for the past several years began to disappear.

From both successful and unsuccessful attempts at change, one can understand the importance of a supportive climate created by an internal team and endorsed by the organizational power structure. The prospective *leaders for change* need to understand that successful change can occur only when both internal and external people or groups directly responsible for problems are involved in the design and implementation of the *change strategy*. The preceding vignette shows a change that flourished, then faltered.

The Change Process.   Extensive studies have been conducted of change in educational organizations, including individual classroom changes, school-wide changes, and even district-wide reform. Most researchers agree that change is a process rather than a single event, and that change takes place slowly. Several of these researchers provide guidance on the way to manage successful change, often describing the lessons they have learned while implementing change. One of the most predominant school changes occurring in today's schools involves inclusion of students with special needs into general education classrooms. McLeskey and Waldron (2002) outline 10 lessons they learned when assisting a school in adopting inclusion.

◆ *Lesson 1. Change must be supported from both the top and the bottom.* Even though change can be initiated by anyone in the school, including parents, it must be supported by school administrators. Likewise, change initiated by administrators must be supported by teachers.
◆ *Lesson 2. Schools must be empowered to manage their own change.* Creating change requires that the people in charge of the change be given the power to manage the process.

◆ *Lesson 3. To develop a successful inclusive school requires major changes in the entire school.* Change is systemic and requires a comprehensive shift of thinking from all team members. Change in an inclusive school is not only about the special education program but requires all school personnel to commit to the changes in scheduling, curriculum modifications, attitudes, and values.

◆ *Lesson 4. Substantive change should transform current school practices and be not simply an "add-on."* Students with special needs included in a general education classroom should "fit in" to the total classroom system and not be seen as a separate group, with separate instructional supports within the classroom.

◆ *Lesson 5. Change should seek to make differences ordinary in the general education classroom.* The inclusion of students with special needs should be seen as a natural part of an ever-growing, diverse classroom. Differences among diverse students should be honored.

◆ *Lesson 6. Change has a ripple effect. It is systemic.* Any level of change in one aspect of a school will have an impact on other units throughout the school. If you include students with special needs in a third-grade class, it will influence the fourth-grade teacher receiving those children the following year. The change process can reverberate to other students, teachers, parents, school administrators, and school board members.

◆ *Lesson 7. Change must be tailored to each school.* There is no model. Inclusion in schools must be implemented on a school-by-school basis, taking into account the differences in personnel, resources, and school culture.

◆ *Lesson 8. Professional development must be provided as needed.* Several approaches to professional development are recommended, including visiting other programs that successfully include students with special needs and using situation-specific sessions to encourage problem solving among the team.

◆ *Lesson 9. Resistance should be expected.* The resistance often associated with change can be complex and come from multiple perspectives. Accepting the resistance as a normal consequence to change is much more beneficial than allowing it to become adversarial.

◆ *Lesson 10. The work of developing an inclusive school is never done.* Change is dynamic and requires ongoing attention and evaluation.

Other researchers (Chenoweth & Everhart, 2002; Fullan, 2000, 2003; Patterson, 2003; Reinhartz & Beach, 2004) provide guidance on facilitating change, as summarized in Table 6.1.

The goal of improving schools and educational outcomes for children is in the forefront of today's school reform movements. One of the most promising approaches to redefining schools is the transformation of schools as *collaborative learning communities,* environments in which individuals assist one another to make learning happen for all participants. Each member of the interactive team is part of

Table 6.1
Principles in Facilitating the Change Process

Conflict and resistance	Conflict and resistance are essential components of change, and must be managed productively.
Common vision	The role of vision is critical in the sense that all participants need to have the same vision in order to effect the change.
Redefining culture	The change process requires restructuring, beginning with an emphasis on redefining the culture of the school.
Professional development	Professional development approaches to team training, peer coaching, mentoring, and the use of action research are among the strategies recommended for facilitating school improvement.
Changes in personnel	School change may be jeopardized by changes in personnel. The discrepancy in knowledge or commitment between long-term team members and persons who are new to the organization can become a barrier in the process of change.
Mentoring newcomers	Mentoring programs are essential both for school leaders and for other personnel in order to prevent newcomers from ignoring the shared mission and allowing the culture to revert to old patterns.
Stages of concern	Team members go through stages of concern about change that first include basic awareness of how the innovation will affect them, and then move to concern for collaboration and how the innovation might be used to modify the whole system.
Evaluation and celebration	The team specifies milestones to measure its progress, and promotes public celebrations of success in the specific change project.

the learning community. The acceptance of collaborative learning communities as the framework for the school culture has also transformed our definition of an effective leader from "strong leader" to "facilitator." This emphasis is on power sharing, with a team approach to problem solving. Today, successful school leaders create this type of learning community (Du Four, 1998; Reinhartz & Beach, 2004). The leader is encouraged to lead "from the center" by helping staff create a shared mission, engage in collective inquiry with an experimental mind-set, and develop a results orientation that emphasizes continuous improvement. Leading for change presents a number of conflicts for today's leaders, as many may find it easier to continue their traditional practices. To keep people from reverting to the old ways, the transformational leaders persuade individuals that this change is better for them and for the organization. A collaborative learning community shifts our thinking from teaching to learning, from individuals to teams, and from a charismatic powerful leader to a community of learners.

Implementing Change Strategies.   Understanding the complexities of the change process can be challenging to interactive teams. However, many researchers provide excellent guidelines on actually implementing a classroom, school, or district reform program. Prior to implementing any given change, team members should (1) select the focus of change, (2) determine who to involve, and (3) decide how to intervene.

    1.   *Select the focus for change.*   The first guideline for the developers[1] is to determine the *focus for change.* Exactly what needs to be modified or developed? Tucker (1984) suggested that in selecting the change to be implemented it is important to consider the following:

- Change will occur more easily when it is *timely* and appropriate.
- The developers should determine whether the innovation has a *reasonable chance* of success.
- The developers should select the *least drastic* solution as the answer to the problem.
- Plans for change are more effective when they are designed with built-in *responses to the personal needs* of those affected by the change.
- In addition to communicating with those affected by the change, the developers must also remember to *communicate with those within the system who must approve the change.*
- The developers should remain *sensitive to the values* of those for whom the change is implemented.

    2.   *Determine who to involve.*   It is useful to *determine who to involve* in the design of the change strategy. Every group has influential people who must be involved if change is to occur. Even if the developer does not conduct a systematic study of the "real power" people, the developer can identify some people who need to be involved as key stakeholders in any change strategy (Chenoweth & Everhart, 2002; Tucker, 1984). Certainly, the developers must include the individuals with administrative titles who have responsibility for the program to be changed. Those who make decisions about the spending of funds will need to be consulted when money is involved. Elected or appointed representatives of particular constituencies need to be included, as do individuals in the system with knowledge about the particular topic (e.g., the school nurse when the education of children with AIDS is the issue; the facilities director when the change involves designing classrooms that are free of architectural barriers). Additionally,

---

[1] We are using the term *developers* to mean one or more team members who are initiating a change strategy in their school or community. Developers can be teachers, related service personnel, paraprofessionals, parents, and/or administrators. Another term for developers is *change agents*.

the diversity of the staff, students, and community should be represented. It is important to remember that anyone who will be affected by the change should be involved in some way in its design.

In trying to select specific individuals to involve in a planning group for change, the developers should consider the characteristics of the people themselves. Successful improvement teams place importance on shared respect and support among team members. Effective team members value consensus-based decisions on shared goals. They are also nurturing and enthusiastic about each other's contributions to the group effort. The team is more effective, then, when each member is empowered, and when the team itself has developed as a mature, supportive unit. People do not become involved in activities over which they have no influence. Lastly, the group should include people who may oppose the change so a sense of ownership can be developed among diverse constituencies. Once the team is functioning as a unit, there is a sense of pride among group members in their belonging to a winning team.

3. *How to intervene.*   After deciding on a focus and the people who will be involved, the developers decide *how to intervene* to facilitate the change. Often, a strategic plan or action plan must be developed outlining the sequence of steps to be taken in facilitating the change. No single model of implementing change is recommended. Individualizing the approaches to change depends on the nature of the change, the persons involved, and the resources available. Today schools and school districts are making changes in multiple aspects of educational reform including but not limited to:

♦ Using new technologies for instructional and administrative needs for technology;
♦ New literacy and reading programs;
♦ Implementing school-wide positive behavioral support systems;
♦ Implementing school-wide programs for improving standardized test scores;
♦ Supporting parent involvement through culturally responsive programs; and
♦ Redesigning paraprofessional's roles and responsibilities.

In summary, although change strategies should be individualized based on the type of change, several researchers recommend general guidelines for implementing change (Chenowerth & Everhart, 2002; Fullan, 2000, 2003; Tucker, 1984).

1. *Identify real and potential supporters.*   These may be friends or colleagues who share the belief in a need for change. Or they might be people who, with additional information, could become supporters. For example, if the change is to implement a school-wide positive behavioral support program, it might be beneficial to engage university faculty in special education as allies. Furthermore, the local Kiwanis club might be a good ally for funding the program.

2. *Test the waters.*   The developers might visit someone else's classroom or office and say, "I have an idea that I think might improve the program. I don't even

know whether it's feasible, but this is what it is. . . . What do you think about it? What are the chances we might be able to do that? Who else might be interested in this idea? Who would be against it? What problems might we face if we really wanted to do it?" In this manner, the developer talks informally with as many people as possible, modifying the plan as others make important suggestions. The individual who skips this step and presents the entire, new idea to the group will frequently find that the idea is rejected (Tucker, 1984). Individual contacts enable the developer to count the votes and incorporate the ideas of many persons who subsequently develop ownership in the plan.

3.   *Translate the change into language that others can understand.*   For advocates, the language of change is based on values, such as "equal opportunity" and "student rights." For policy makers, the language of change is directly related to accountability, in addition to dollars and cents. Successful change leaders may convince even a conservative administration that inclusion of students with special needs in general education classrooms rather than separate special education classrooms makes sense in terms of cost effectiveness, because gains in *all* students' academic achievement and social behavior improve in those settings and the consultative teacher role provides more support to multiple general education teachers.

4.   *Identify additional sources of support that may be used to supplement the regular budget.*   Both governmental agencies and charitable foundations often fund special projects through grants. Service clubs, which exist in every community, are always looking for worthy projects. Lions Clubs give glasses to needy children, while Shriners help build hospitals. Locate some other sources of funding that may help to get the project "off the ground."

5.   *Ask for technical assistance.*   If the proposal for change is technical or complex, ask for help from experts. On a public health issue, help may be available from the public health department or the public information office of the local hospital. When proposing a change that involves technology use, involve business personnel who are prominent in computer technology. Be sure that these people and their organizations are recognized for their contributions—through media exposure and letters of appreciation to their supervisors—so they will share ownership of the new idea. Failing to ask for help may be a serious error, because those who could be your strongest allies may become opponents if they think they are being bypassed or that the change agent is setting up a program that is competitive with theirs.

6.   *Share information on success.*   When students in a new reading program improve their achievement scores or work-study students receive excellent reports from their employers, let the media know. Pictures of successful students and human interest stories can enhance the public relations of the organization. Again, the "power people" (school principal or program director) should share in the good press so they can develop an even stronger sense of commitment to continue the innovative program.

Team members who attempt to bring about change will encounter false starts, resistance, and the need to go "back to the drawing board" many times before real progress can be made. The task requires patience and perseverance, as well as an understanding of the theories and strategies for facilitating change. The individual who follows these guidelines, however, may be able to minimize the discouragement and negative personal consequences of repeated failure.

APPLICATION

Two examples of initial strategies to facilitate change—one successful and one not successful—are given as follows.

Team A: School Truancy

Eager to minimize the problem of student absences from class and armed with funds from a small grant, the school improvement team decided to take a proactive stance, changing from former punitive responses to truancy to a system including positive reinforcement for students with perfect attendance. The team decided to notify parents when students had perfect attendance, then enter the names of students with perfect attendance in a drawing through which some would win gift certificates. The proposed change made the headlines of the local paper, with a negative report that students were being paid for attendance and a promise from the school board to punish those teachers who had suggested this illegal use of public money.

Team B: Inclusion

A new special education teacher, whose resource room served students with multiple and severe disabilities, was eager to promote the inclusion of her students into school-wide activities. She volunteered to sponsor the student council and the cheerleading club, as well as attend numerous school social and athletic activities. As she became known to the faculty and students as a whole-school supporter and participant, she provided information about the nature of various special abilities and disabilities. She also provided the school administrator with positive information about inclusion to share with the local paper. Gradually, with administrative and parental permission, she encouraged several student leaders to sign up for a "buddy" in her classroom. The student leaders visited her classroom and, by the end of the year, had begun to accompany their new buddies to school-wide activities.

ACTIVITY

Using the guidelines previously described, consider how Team A and Team B handled their change strategies. What were the steps of the change process that were ineffective in Team A's approach to change? What were the steps of the change process that were effective in Team B's approach to change? What did the implementation teams do correctly?

Empowering Others

This chapter's discussion of empowerment is focused on providing team members with both *legitimate power* through decision sharing and *expert power* through information sharing. Both types of empowerment are based on professional development, and their purpose is to enable team members to accomplish changes that benefit students with special needs.

Empowerment as Power Sharing.   Empowerment is illustrated in the way the team leader—a person with power—shares this power with others who can help to implement the necessary change (Du Four, 1998; Futrell, 2000; McLaughlin & Schwartz, 1998). Leading for change requires a ground-up approach, giving teachers, parents, and staff the ownership and power to implement change. Effective leaders are not dictatorial, wheeling power from the top and shouting ideas downward for others to implement (Reinhartz & Beach, 2004). They nurture learning communities composed of collaborative teams that work on the core principles of trust, cooperation, research, and technology. Leadership includes the use of consultation (in a process that emphasizes information exchange), coalition building, task orientation, conflict resolution, and flexibility. Many of these techniques have been presented earlier in the discussions on consultation and communication skills. Although the shared decision-making structure operates more slowly, it is no less decisive; the leader who is effective within this framework sets clear goals that have a greater chance for successful implementation because they are based on group consensus. Those who wish to establish their leadership on behalf of educational teams will be interested in developing shared power that is more descriptive of democratic than autocratic management.

Empowerment also takes on a dimension of personal development within the context of group growth. Covey (1990) emphasizes the importance of each individual's attention to his or her own personal energy needs, and suggests replenishment, inspiration, and stress reduction as forms of personal empowerment. Some of this inspiration and stress reduction that facilitate personal empowerment can result from the provision of a supportive work environment and of respect and recognition for each member's contributions to the team effort (Chenoweth & Everhart, 2002; Kaplan & Owings, 2003).

Empowerment as Knowledge Sharing.   Empowerment also involves the development of expert power or knowledge among staff members. In the interactive team, knowledge acquisition begins with information sharing among team members. Individuals engage in a type of professional development by sharing their specialized knowledge and skills with other team members. Such information sharing has been illustrated in the Chapter 3 Application showing an informational interview between a special educator and a speech-language therapist.

Ends and Page (1984) emphasized that the process of organizational team building begins with the development of skills in individual team members. They indicated that the process must be nonthreatening and that the change needs to be consistent with the individual's self-image. If these conditions are met, the team member goes through a four-stage process of change in learning the new behavior: recognizing the need to change, knowing what to change, desiring to learn, and practicing until the new behavior is acquired. The strongest teams are those in which individual members possess knowledge, skills, and positive dispositions.

The acquisition of knowledge, skills, and dispositions that results in empowerment is referred to as *professional development.* The educational organizations that are most effective in implementing needed changes are those in which a large number of individuals have been involved and have developed a sense of ownership for the new program (Reinhartz & Beach, 2004; Wang, 1998). These organizations are characterized by a sense of shared understanding about the changes that are necessary (Chenoweth & Everhart, 2002; Du Four, 1998). School effectiveness research has shown that the best schools are those in which the entire staff and the community share a sense of ownership and a belief in the ability to improve the outcomes of *all* students, including students with special needs (Cawelti, 2003; Owings & Kaplan, 2003). This sense of shared purpose originates in the development of knowledge, skills, and dispositions through professional development.

An example of professional development for a new teacher is found in the following application.

APPLICATION

Several parents in the district approached the director of special education to express their concern about a first-year teacher who was having difficulty in the classroom. One of the parents complained that her son, who had been suspended for hitting and kicking his teacher, had never done things like that before. The parent indicated that the new teacher seemed unable to control the classroom and that, when there was a problem, she went straight to the principal. Others stated that the children had responded much more positively to last year's teacher, and wondered what could be done. The director talked with the teacher and learned that this child was running out of the room. She tried to restrain him, but felt that she was unable to manage his behavior. The director invited the teacher to attend the forthcoming weekend institute on functional behavior assessment and positive behavioral supports (PBS), sponsored by the district and local college of education. The director also asked the school's behavior specialist to make follow-up observations and provide PBS assistance in the classroom. The director was pleased to hear that both the teacher and the children had been helped by this assistance.

BEST PRACTICES IN PROFESSIONAL DEVELOPMENT

The process of professional development in educational organizations was originally summarized by the National Inservice Network (NIN), a governmental agency active in the 1970s (Hutson, 1979). More current summaries of effective practices and their relationship to school improvement have been completed by Darling-Hammond and Sykes (2001), Lang and Fox (2003), Rhoton and Bowers (2001), Showers and Joyce (1996), and Wang, Haertel, and Walberg (1997).

Current research on professional development supports the newer models of inquiry grounded in concrete problems of practice. Teaching teams, study groups, school-based coaching, and action research projects within schools were found to be particularly effective (Darling-Hammond & Sykes, 2001). Several features of professional development have been identified, including:

◆ *Experiential.* Engaging teachers in concrete tasks of teaching, assessment, and observation that illuminate the process of learning and development, grounded in participants' questions, inquiry, and experimentation as well as profession-wide research.

◆ *Collaborative.* Involving a sharing of knowledge among educators, connected to teachers' work with their students as well as to exploration of the subject matter and teaching models.

◆ *Sustained and intensive.* Supported by modeling, coaching, and problem solving around specific problems of practice, connected to other aspects of school change. (Darling-Hammond, 2003, p. 82)

Other research on professional development highlights the importance of teacher input into decisions about professional development, including visits to other sites with successful programs and subsequent development of plans for application of these practices at their own sites (Lang & Fox, 2003). Many districts have increased the available time for professional development through extended school years, summer institutes, and block scheduling, which free up time for teacher teams to plan and learn together. Previously promoted best practices that have been supported by newer research include provision of released time or building in time during the school day, reimbursement for expenses, and the collaborative development of goals and strategies by teams of teachers and administrators; common current topics for professional development include inclusion practices, assistive technology, literacy and math skills, second-language instruction, and positive behavioral supports. Teacher-to-teacher networking (Pennell & Firestone, 1998) and new teacher induction programs were found to be particularly helpful (Du Four, 1998; Griffin, Winn, Otis-Wilborn, & Kilgore, 2003), while the creation of a community of learners has proven especially challenging at the high school level (Keifer-Barone & Ware, 2002; Wineburg & Grosman, 1998). In addition, the previously described models of support can be given on either an individual level (e.g., including a mentor teacher) or group level (e.g., led by professionals with teaming and group facilitation skills).

The explosion of technology leads both to an intensified need for staff development in the use of technology and an expanded opportunity for its use in the delivery of new information. Rapid advances in technology are creating a dynamic environment for tomorrow's students. November (2003) explains that to prepare students for the emerging information economies and societies, school leaders must change the schools' learning culture and use technology to create an environment in which to teach critical thinking and problem solving. In addition, she cites current practices that will require enhanced professional development and school improvement in the area of technology, including:

◆ Every teacher should have a Website that supports curriculum and assessment resources for students and families.

◆ Every student should take at least one online course in order to graduate, which will require every teacher to learn Web programming and new software for course development.

◆ Every student and teacher must become Internet-information literate.

◆ Every student and teacher should have access to learning through the Web 24/7.

◆ Every parent should have access to the Web (e.g., school-loan programs for handheld devices and laptops) and instructional support on how to use it to enhance their children's learning. (November, p. 99–100)

Hobbs, Day, and Russo (2002) describe an exciting interface between real professional development and technology. Virtual teams of beginning special education teachers and mentors used existing telecommunications technology to collaborate. The "Conference Room" site was developed as a highly confidential, online forum where small groups of collaborating special educators could present problem situations for analysis and recommendations by their peers.

Statewide networks, such as the Kansas Inservice Training System (KITS), have developed a Website for state-wide technical assistance for professionals working with preschool children with special needs. The KITS Website (www.kits.org) provides educators access to a technical assistance calendar, needs assessment protocols, individual technical assistance action plans, and downloadable training modules (Kansas Inservice Training System, 2004). Clearly, the role of technology in staff development cannot be overemphasized.

The traditional "drive-by" workshops and didactic dissemination of information as an approach to professional development is no longer supported by the research (Darling-Hammond, 2003; Lang & Fox, 2003; Little & Houston, 2003). Adult learning theory supports an approach to professional development that involves teachers studying, doing, and reflecting in collaboration with other team members. Transmitting information through PowerPoint lectures and handouts does not take into account individual participant needs. Instead, professional development that includes a combination of theory, demonstration, practice, feedback, and coaching has a powerful impact on teacher implementation of practices and student achievement (Joyce & Showers, 1995).

The content presented in a professional-development program is focused directly on teacher behavior and indirectly on student behavior. The best kind of professional development will affect student behavior because it results in the enhancement of teacher competency. Wang et al. (1997) and Joyce and Showers (1995) have shown evidence that professional-development programs for several models of teaching result in higher student achievement. The developer should know that these models have proved their effectiveness with students and would, therefore, be appropriate for use in whole-school professional development programs. The decision about content for professional development should also take into consideration the need of participants to obtain a basic level of knowledge about a program before they are able to "buy into" it (Showers , Joyce, & Bennett, 1987). School-wide needs assessment surveys can be disseminated in order to identify areas of professional development for groups of teachers.

There are three other special considerations for professional developers who wish to implement best practices. First, activities that are effective with one group may not be appropriate for others. That is, it may be important to design programs that are responsive to differences in the language and culture of various groups, such as providing evening sessions with supper and child care (Boone, 1990) or assisting participants with online sessions from their home (Hobbs, Day, & Russo, 2002), rather than requiring them to attend meetings at school. Second, developers should conceptualize the total plan for professional development, rather than view it as a single event in which all participants assemble to be lectured for an hour and then go back to their classrooms where nothing will change. The positive effects of continued support after the idea's initial presentation have been impressive (Glatthorn, 1987; Showers et al., 1987) and the applications of a new team model for "coaching" have been especially strong (Showers & Joyce, 1996). These will be discussed in greater detail later in the chapter. Finally, developers should be aware that certain individual traits or characteristics may influence the effectiveness of professional development programs. These include the probability of more positive responses by those who exhibit flexibility in thinking, as well as the effect of what the teacher believes about teaching and the way he or she teaches (Showers et al., 1987). Developers who wish to bring about change through team-member empowerment will be aware of these and other findings identified earlier as "best practices."

STRATEGIES FOR PROFESSIONAL DEVELOPMENT

Three of the most widely used types of professional development for teams are (1) knowledge sharing, (2) skill development through coaching/reflection, and (3) team development.

Today, *school-based staff developers* are increasingly being hired by school districts to work with teachers and staff (Richard, 2003). Their job titles include staff development teachers, academic coaches, lead teachers, instructional coordinators, mentor teachers, or content specialists. Some staff developers are assigned full-time development responsibilities, while others might split their time between their own teaching load and training. They are often responsible for guiding and working with both novice and veteran teachers on instructional strategies. Others may be assigned to managing school testing, analyzing and reporting on school performance data, overseeing the school's reaccreditation process, or leading committees to re-design or realign curriculum around state and local standards (Richard, p. 7). School-based staff developers serve a tremendous role in helping school improvement and reform efforts. Their effectiveness must be carefully evaluated in order to maintain their role on interactive teams.

One way to empower team members is to provide them with new knowledge or skills through formal, scheduled learning activities such as workshops or reading study groups. This is usually done through professional-development activities in which team members share knowledge that enhances their colleagues' understanding. Skill development can be accomplished through a combination of peer coaching and individual reflection during which team members observe each other and incorporate new learning into their existing structure of knowledge and skills. Finally, professional development can become an ongoing activity through which the team itself matures as a unit capable of functioning effectively. In the following discussion, strategies for professional development through formal knowledge sharing and coaching with reflection will be presented along with a summary of the extended teams operating in professional-development schools. The chapter's Application on page 243 will provide an activity for identifying the team's maturity level and need for professional development as a unit.

Sharing Knowledge

Two aspects of knowledge sharing will be discussed: (1) the importance of determining the knowledge or content to be shared through a needs assessment, and (2) the guidelines for presentation. This discussion is directed at the formal sharing of knowledge through professional development activities. Informal knowledge sharing, which occurs more frequently, has been described in the informational interview discussion in Chapter 3, and in the Chapter 4 description of communication skills.

Needs Assessment.   Researchers summarizing best practices suggest that content should be based on a needs assessment (Kampwirth, 2003; Lang & Fox, 2003; Little & Houston, 2003). That is, the content is selected on the basis of a survey of the staff members who will receive the new information. In a survey, they should be asked what they need to know in order to improve student achievement, state their major problems, and suggest needs for further training. Through this needs assessment, those who share their knowledge determine the information that should be presented. The needs assessment should not only be determined by teachers but by using:

◆ Administrators
◆ Clerical and operational support staff
◆ Counselors, psychologists, and social workers
◆ Parents

- School volunteers
- Health services workers
- District office officials
- Mentors and partners
- Neighborhood businesses
- Students

For example, North Central Regional Laboratories (Hassel, 1999) suggests enhancing professional-development needs assessments by involving parents in town meetings and brainstorming sessions, and by using students throughout the day in leadership teams. The whole community is brought in to focus on what it needs to do to have positive outcomes for students in its schools. Needs assessments can be done in various formats such as survey instruments, questionnaires, checklists, focus groups, or individual interviews. Teachers can also rank order priorities for training from a list of topics.

An example of a needs assessment instrument, developed by the Irving Independent School District in Irving, Texas, is presented in Figure 6.2. This needs assessment can be used to plan the content for a professional-development program in which the team members participate. More detailed assessment may be needed to narrow down the specific subtopics to cover within each topic area.

Guidelines for Presentation. The effective presenter of the professional-development program establishes expert power by demonstrating knowledge and speaking with confidence. This person uses visual aids to help focus information on the topic, establishes eye contact with other members of the group, and sits or stands in a position that is higher than others while presenting information. When the presenter is a newcomer or is younger than others in the group, it is particularly important for him or her to acquire the knowledge necessary for establishing the impression of expert power and to use effective presentation skills to enhance this image. A person who is highly respected by the group might help establish the newcomer's credibility by indicating that this person is an expert in the field and by showing some relationship between the experience of the presenter and that of the participants.

Information presenters should communicate clearly through correct use of media and an understanding of the most effective ways of presenting information. Effective use of media involves both its selection and its use. The first tendency of planners may be to overuse media, thinking that more is always better, as was shown tongue-in-cheek in a particular installment of the comic strip *Beetle Bailey*. In the strip, General Halftrack was shown conducting an inservice for his troops. He began by giving a progress report, saying "Enlistments are down," as he pushed a button and a big foot clamped down on the floor, "while discharges are up." The general shot off a rocket. "The picture looks cloudy," he said as smoke poured out of the chart. "Original estimates have been shot full of holes." You can picture his demonstration of a shower of bullets. "There is nothing to do but pick up the pieces

TOPICS: Please mark each item to rank order training topics that will benefit you in your current assignment. (5 = most preferred and 1 = least preferred)

Content—subject specific	5	4	3	2	1
Effective teaching practices	5	4	3	2	1
Discipline management	5	4	3	2	1
Assessment	5	4	3	2	1
Technology training	5	4	3	2	1
Parent communication/conferencing	5	4	3	2	1
Working with diverse populations	5	4	3	2	1
Group dynamics—working in teams	5	4	3	2	1
Leadership development	5	4	3	2	1
Curriculum integration	5	4	3	2	1
Conflict resolution	5	4	3	2	1
Classroom strategies/activities	5	4	3	2	1

DELIVERY FORMAT: Please mark each item to rank order your preferences of **delivery format**. (5 = most preferred and 1 = least preferred)

Instructor led	5	4	3	2	1
Active hands-on participation	5	4	3	2	1
Book study groups	5	4	3	2	1
Independent action research	5	4	3	2	1
Interactive distance learning (via satellite, cable, Internet)	5	4	3	2	1
Computer-based training	5	4	3	2	1
Videotaped instruction	5	4	3	2	1
Job embedded (on-the-job training)	5	4	3	2	1

TIME: Please mark each item to rank order your preferred **time** for professional development delivery. (5 = most preferred and 1 = least preferred)

School calendar days (before first day for students)	5	4	3	2	1
School calendar days (scheduled during the school year)	5	4	3	2	1
Saturdays	5	4	3	2	1
Summer	5	4	3	2	1
After contract hours	5	4	3	2	1
Spring break	5	4	3	2	1
Contract time for non-teaching staff	5	4	3	2	1
On-the-job training/job-embedded	5	4	3	2	1

Figure 6.2

Needs assessment for professional development.

Source: Adapted from *Professional Development Needs Assessment,* Irving Independent School District, Irving, TX. Retrieved January 29, 2004, from http://www.irvingisd.net/assessment. Adapted by permission.

LOCATION: Please mark each item to rank order your preferred **location** for professional development delivery. (5 = most preferred and 1 = least preferred)

Central administration building	5	4	3	2	1
Professional development center	5	4	3	2	1
Local university site	5	4	3	2	1
At your work site	5	4	3	2	1
Off-site within district	5	4	3	2	1
Out of district	5	4	3	2	1
Distance learning	5	4	3	2	1

PRESENTER: Mark each item to rank order **who** should deliver professional development. (5 = most preferred and 1 = least preferred)

Teachers/coworkers	5	4	3	2	1
Coordinators	5	4	3	2	1
Administrators/supervisors	5	4	3	2	1
School district training specialists	5	4	3	2	1
Outside consultants/university faculty	5	4	3	2	1

and start over," he said as little bits of paper were tossed into the room by a small catapult. The result was that people left the meeting whispering, "I could do without some of the visual aids." The point, of course, is for the presenter to consider whether visual aids will enhance or distract the audience from the message.

Visual aids are important because they help the presenter to focus the audience's attention, enhancing the presenter's image as one with expert power. PowerPoint slides are the most frequently used types of visual aids. To be effective, the slides should focus on key words, while the presenter elaborates on each point. If the presenter wishes to provide the audience with details on the information being presented, he or she can use PowerPoint handouts with notes attached. An attempt to provide these factual details without handouts would result in an overload of verbal information, thus increasing the chances for misunderstanding.

Effective presenters also employ other ways to enhance knowledge sharing in professional development programs. The following presentation guidelines have been modified from the work of LeRoux (1984)[2]:

1. Establish credibility through demonstration of knowledge.
2. Use notes (PowerPoint notes format), rather than read from a script.

---

[2] From *Selling to a Group*, by P. LeRoux, 1984, New York: Harper & Row. Adapted by permission of Harper & Row, Inc.

3. Face the audience directly, keeping your weight distributed equally on both feet and standing without your hands in your pockets.

4. Use gestures to enhance the presentation.

5. To use eye contact effectively, focus for about 3 seconds on each person.

6. Practice the art of asking questions.

7. Answer questions appropriately.

8. Build rapport with the audience by giving equal recognition to all participants.

LeRoux (1984) elaborates on the correct ways to ask and answer questions, because these are among the most difficult parts of any presentation. He suggests that the presenter begin by giving the audience permission to interrupt with questions and by mentioning that there will be a question-and-answer time at the end of the presentation. When finished, the presenter should say, "Now it's time for questions." The speaker can "warm up" the audience by saying, "First I want to ask you a question." The presenter should ask a simple question that participants can answer by raising their hands. The presenter might also prime the audience for questions by saying, "The question most frequently asked is. . . . Now, what are your questions?"

Finally, the correct way to field a question is to use the following three-step process:

1. Indicate whose question you are answering: Point to the person.

2. Give eye contact to the person asking the question.

3. When the person has finished, repeat the question so the entire group can hear it.

LeRoux (1984) also suggests that the presenter try to neutralize negative questions so they do not build-up resistance from the audience. For instance, after a presentation on inclusion, a classroom teacher in the audience might ask, "How am I going to have time to work with students with disabilities in my classroom when I have 35 other children?" The presenter could rephrase the question in a neutral way, such as "You're wondering whether you can deal with the increasing demands on your time in the classroom. Let me answer that by giving you some examples of how other teachers who are concerned about all of their students have dealt with this issue. . . ." The presenter is then in a position to give some useful suggestions, rather than being forced into a defensive posture. The answer should be brief, and the presenter should move on quickly to the next question.

Application of Knowledge Sharing. Suppose a new student with hearing impairments is enrolled in a local elementary school. Most of the teachers and staff are unaware of how to make accommodations to meet the student's needs. The itinerant teacher for students with hearing impairments agrees to conduct an in-service presentation for the teachers and staff at the school. She designs a 1-hour presentation aimed at attitude change and knowledge sharing for the whole staff. After a brief introduction and overview that establish her credibility and relate the presentation to the needs identified by the group, she presents:

1. An opening simulation, during which she plays a CD of conversations as heard by people with different types of hearing impairments.

2. A group discussion of the feelings and insights experienced by participants as they listened to the CD, followed by the development of a group-generated list of the types of difficulties that might be experienced by students with hearing impairments in the classroom.

3. A brief overview of information on hearing impairment, which includes the use of summative PowerPoint slides to illustrate how we hear, as well as presenting information about the three major types of hearing impairments.

4. An illustration of one method teachers can use to help students with hearing impairments in the classroom. This part of the presentation incorporates photographs or video clips within PowerPoint slides that illustrate the techniques.

5. A small-group activity, during which participants work together to develop a set of lesson materials for use with students with hearing impairments in their classes (these materials would be equally appropriate for use with all of their students). Participants work with others at their grade level to design a set of summative PowerPoint slides with an accompanying auditory script for a lesson they might teach in math, science, or social studies. The presenter circulates to give assistance while the participants work, and then collects the materials at the end of the session.

6. The presenter hands out a list of other suggestions that teachers might use to increase their effectiveness with students who have hearing impairments. She indicates that the lesson materials developed by each group will be typed and that the PowerPoint slides will be redesigned by students in the school's art class; these materials will be burned on CD-ROM and distributed to all members of the group for use in their classes.

7. The presenter obtains the participants' opinions about the effectiveness of the professional-development program, including (a) how much they enjoyed the presentation, (b) the degree to which they learned how to work more effectively with students with hearing impairments, and (c) whether they planned to use any of the knowledge they had acquired during the session.

This example of a professional-development program aimed at knowledge sharing has shown how the presenter can transmit relevant information to a diverse group of individuals. It has also shown how to use professional-development activities not only to increase the knowledge of participants, but also to establish a sense of teaming among staff members. The provision of follow-up materials, designed by participants, will further enhance the opportunities for continued interaction and cooperation among those who collaborated in their design.

Developing Skills

Team members can empower each other by engaging in activities that enhance their skills. The most effective means are based on knowledge about adults as learners. These include skill development through peer observation and coaching, as well as opportunities for the learner to reflect on what is learned and to incorporate new learning into one's own existing knowledge structure.

Several strategies can be used for developing skills in teachers and related service personnel. Lang and Fox (2003) encourage professional-development activities that match the teachers' needs. Different levels of understanding and skill development are needed and trainers should provide the appropriate strategy for each level. For example, some teachers just need basic information and awareness of a topic. In those cases, a workshop, short training sessions, or multisession conferences would be appropriate. Teachers who are at the initial implementation level of new practices might benefit from mentoring, coaching, case discussions, study groups, or action research projects to meet their professional-development needs. Teachers who have integrated new practices into their daily routine and are ready to refine those practices may benefit from professional-development strategies such as study groups, university or agency partnerships, curriculum development, and learning networks outside of the school system. For example, in Connecticut, middle school teachers needed an upgrade in their technology skills (Saylor & Kehrhahn, 2003). Technology Change Facilitators (TCF) were hired to assist with individual and group training activities and provide orientation sessions at the beginning of school. Yearlong professional-development activities included guided practice, individual goal management, learning teams, coaching, and technical assistance.

Assessment of professional development activities is critical. Teachers can document the impact of professional development through:

◆ Portfolios that include a collection of artifacts and evidence of teaching practices on student outcomes, and

◆ Journaling and reflection logs that summarize thoughts of what has been learned from the training and implementation experiences (Lang & Fox, 2003).

Developing Skills Through Coaching.   One of the most effective strategies for professional development has been *coaching*. In coaching, "teachers engage in open dialogue about teaching with the goal of continuous improvement of practice. A coach is a critical listener and observer who asks questions, makes observations, and facilitates reflection to help colleagues group. Unlike mentoring which is an experienced teacher assisting a novice, coaching provides a mechanism for the continuous growth and improvement of professionals at all levels" (Lang & Fox, p. 23). Coaching can be used with a wide variety of personnel, including school administrators and executives. Lubinsky (2002) reports on an effective coaching strategy used with school superintendents to enhance their leadership and problem-solving skills. In fact, a good way for professionals to find coaches is through the International Coach Federation (www.coachfederation.org).

In coaching, team members engage in frequent, ongoing observations of each other's performance, followed by conferences that focus on constructive feedback (O'Shea, 1987). Coaching provides team members with an increased amount and quality of supervised practice, as well as assistance in the transfer of newly developed skills (Neufeld & Roper, 2003). Coaching has been used effectively at both the preservice and inservice levels (Veenman & Denessen, 2001). In one interesting program, special education seniors were coached by teams of mentors that included special educators, general educators, and university faculty members (Duarte, 1992–93). In preservice education, coaching has been shown to improve the learner's ability to transfer new learning (Kurtts & Levin, 2000; Peterson & Hudson, 1989).

Coaching also increases desirable teaching behaviors and decreases undesirable ones (Peterson & Hudson, 1989; Veenman & Denessen, 2001). Coached teachers also seem to retain information longer and have a greater effect on the learning improvement of pupils in their classrooms (Showers, 1984). Most significant for team members, coaching improves collegiality because it reduces teachers' isolation and provides them with peer support (Wynn, 1987, 1988).

Evidence exists that coaching can produce the following outcomes, which are likely to improve instruction:

◆ Better targeted school-based professional development that addresses teachers' and principals' learning needs in light of students' needs;

◆ Teacher learning that carries over into classroom practice because the coach helps teachers implement what they have learned;

◆ A willingness among teachers to share their practice with one another, seek learning opportunities from their peers and their coaches, and willingly assume collective responsibility for all of their students' learning;

◆ High-quality principal leadership of instructional improvement; and

◆ School cultures in which instruction is the focus of much teacher and principal discussion, in which teachers and principals reflect on their practice and its impact on students, and use achievement data to drive instructional improvement. (Neufeld & Roper, 2003, pp. 26–27)

Coaching seems to be most effective when implemented by teacher groups who observe and assist each other as peers. Rogers (1987) has described one of these programs in detail, showing how teachers within the school worked together in teams of two or three to observe and videotape each other's teaching. Members of these teams ask their partners to help them identify a goal for improvement and then engage in observation of teaching performance. This nonjudgmental, supportive observation provides constructive feedback and thus facilitates the goal of self-improvement.

Showers and Joyce (1996), summarizing the literature on professional development that leads to student growth, have pointed out that simple exposure to new knowledge results in very low rates of teacher implementation, possibly as low as 10%. The addition of classroom follow-up, particularly through peer coaching, increases implementation of new practices significantly, in addition to motivating teachers to collaborate with one another. These authors now promote staff development that involves the entire staff of a school site, encouraging developers to work intensively with the staff to plan and organize the procedures. Showers and Joyce caution that peer coaching should not be used as an evaluation procedure. They caution further that when observers deliver verbal feedback, they tend to act as evaluators. Therefore, they have developed new role reversal procedures in which the observer is the team member being coached, while the one observed is the coach. Stating that learning occurs during collaborative planning, materials development, and reflection, Showers and Joyce have designed their staff-development programs to model these procedures. The recommendation for building in time for collaboration is high on their agenda. They also recommend that peer coaching teams be formed on the first day of training during which time developers provide opportunities for these teams to work through a sequence for planning long-term activities, monitoring their implementation, and measuring their impact on students.

Sahakian and Stockton (1996) provide an example of the collaborative model of peer observation. These authors argue that the older expectation of the clinical model, that an observer will see all steps followed during a single lesson, is unrealistic. Their observation model attempts to end the isolation of teachers by forming triads or teams that agree to observe one another regularly, biweekly, for a 4-week period every semester. Both peers and administrators are involved in observations. Team meetings led by the administrator focus on questions that enable teachers to analyze the instructional strategies they have observed. The triads develop their own issues for discussion, engaging in thoughtful reflection that leads them to common understandings of curriculum issues, as well as enhancing collegiality.

Developing Skills Through Reflection.   During the process of coaching, the team member is confronted with new information in the form of self-assessment, peer feedback, new research, and data on the performance of students. To increase the effectiveness of existing practices and to make new decisions, the team member needs to be able to synthesize this new information, reflect on its meaning, and incorporate it into his or her current cognitive framework. Because interactive teaming, like teaching, is an involved task that requires problem solving within circumstances lacking certainty, effective team members need to become deliberate and reflective decision makers (Patricia & Lamb, 1990).

Reflective logs or journaling has been a common approach to documenting teacher learning and growth. Teachers can respond to questions such as: "What am I learning about teaching and learning?" and "How can I be more effective?" (Lang & Fox, 2003, p. 23). Other forms of reflection can involve study groups, case discussions, and action research. Routman (2002) describes a "teacher-talk" program that resulted in 90% of the school staff attending weekly meetings on professional issues and topics. The professional conversations and reflection time resulted in teachers sharing more information and brought staff closer together. Routman suggests the following for creating time for weekly professional meetings:

◆ Establish before-school support groups.

◆ Start school late or dismiss students early one day each week.

◆ Devote faculty meetings to issues of the profession.

◆ Create common planning times.

◆ Hire roving substitutes.

◆ Add paid days to the school calendar.

◆ Add more time to the school day. (p. 33)

Teachers who participate in critical reflection on their personal performance and on student data will enhance their decision-making and problem-solving skills. It is suggested, then, that the team member can develop and retain new professional skills most effectively when encouraged to reflect on the observations made by a peer during coaching. The use of data-based problem solving has long been advocated in special education programs. Professional development is facilitated both through coaching and by opportunities to develop decision-making skills through reflection on personal performance and student achievement data (Neufeld & Roper, 2003; Peterson & Hudson, 1989; Showers, 1984; Showers & Joyce, 1996).

The federal No Child Left Behind law and budget concerns in many districts are requiring that schools be accountable for high-cost professional-development programs. The professional staff developers will need to determine the critical factors that make such programs successful, solve other pressing problems in schools that impact on staff developers' work, identify best-practice models, and reshape the on-site staff development programs around "what works" (Richard, 2003, p. 5).

Developing the Team

The final type of professional development to be discussed is the development of the team itself as a mature, supportive, effective functional unit. Schools can provide opportunities for teachers to develop interactive teaming skills through direct instruction on "team building." Teachers have opportunities to take courses and workshop sessions on "how to team." This explicit approach to providing teachers the skills required for teaming involves topics such as: how to analyze team personality profiles, how to conduct effective meetings, how to brainstorm ideas, and how to make decisions that are implemented (Keifer-Barone & Ware, 2002). One of the strongest new initiatives in team building takes place through university teacher preparation programs in models known generically as professional-development schools (Holmes Group, 1990). Many groups have recommended closer connections between theory and practice, as well as campus and field, in the preparation of teachers (Book, 1996; Buck, Morsink, Griffin, Hines, & Lenk, 1992; Darling-Hammond, 2001; Pugach & Johnson, 2002; Rice, 2002). Professional-development schools with campus-field collaboration have been implemented nationwide, providing preservice teachers with opportunities to develop skills in collaboration and simultaneous professional-development for current educators. This is particularly important in challenging teaching environments such as inner-city schools (Darling-Hammond, 2001; Howey, 1997; Ilmer, Snyder, Erbaugh, & Kurz, 1997; Pugach & Johnson, 2002; Teitel, 2000). In fact, the National Council for the Accreditation of Teacher Education (NCATE; 2001) has established standards in order to strengthen and support PDS development, assess progress within the PDS, and assure accountability.

Partnerships between universities and schools enable the partners to combine the theoretical and practical dimensions of research into best practices and provide the mechanisms for developing networks that can involve others (Fullan, 2000, 2003; Levin & Rock, 2003; Little & Houston, 2003). In some programs, teachers combine professional development opportunities with the acquisition of advanced degrees (Boyer, 1997), while in others preparation represents a dramatic departure from tradition by replacing all on-campus education classes with intensive field-based experiences in schools (Wilmore, 1996).

The efforts at collaboration between university and school district personnel add a new dimension of complexity to team building. Universally, the barriers cited include differences in vocabulary and environmental "cultures" between campus and school sites, as well as the need for extensive personal time investment (Morsink, 1999). Initial data on the effectiveness of collaborative experiences for preservice elementary and special education teachers suggests that field-based problem-solving interactions can enhance students' understanding of both the necessity and the complexity of the teaming process, and that individuals with differing perspectives can learn from one another in joint efforts to assist children (Levin & Rock, 2003; O'Shea, Williams, & Sattler, 1999). Among the most promising practices is the involvement of teacher educators as on-site teachers or university-school liaisons in public school classrooms as a way to enhance their understanding of instructional realities and incorporate them into their preservice programs (Brown, 1997; Little & Houston, 2003; Williams, 1999; Winograd, 1998).

Professional Development for Paraprofessionals

Professional development for paraprofessionals is a crucial component of educational improvement. Although all the previously discussed strategies apply when

TA TRAINING

training paraprofessionals, unique professional-development activ[...] required. According to reports, 10% of paraprofessionals' time is spen[...] the following activities:

- Providing instructional support;
- Providing one-on-one instruction;
- Modifying materials;
- Implementing behavior management plans;
- Monitoring hallway/study hall/other;
- Meeting with teachers;
- Collecting student data; and
- Providing personal care assistance. (Wallace, 2003, p. 13)

Clearly, paraprofessionals are spending more and more time on instruction, and that often means special training and preparation activities. Both IDEA and NCLB require that paraprofessionals have higher levels of training. Unfortunately, training for paraprofessionals remains minimal (Wallace, 2003). The areas of training needed are broad and can include:

- Communication and problem-solving skills;
- Positive behavioral supports;
- Specifics about disabilities;
- Transition-related information and job coaching;
- Special education law and confidentiality;
- Observation and data collection strategies;
- Use of computers and accommodations; and
- Health and safety.

Many of the same professional-development strategies used for training teachers are necessary, including on-the-job demonstration and skill implementation, mentoring and coaching, and individualized and long-term professional-development plans. Paraprofessionals are a key component to the interactive team; they benefit greatly from being empowered to provide higher-quality instructional programs to all students.

The team's development is the focus of this entire book, and its importance is highlighted in the basic principles of shared decision making and continuous improvement. Although it is not our intention to review these principles at this point, we have selected a summative activity through which the reader may consider data and reflect on information about the hypothetical team's need for professional development, as well as the leadership style most effective for teams at varying developmental or maturity levels.

APPLICATION

This activity is based on the early work of Hersey and Blanchard (1974) related to the leadership styles needed for effective management of groups. As indicated in Chapter 5, these authors have described the leader's behavior as either task oriented or relationship oriented. They have further indicated that the maturity of the group determines the degrees of directiveness and personal relationship that are appropriate for leadership of the group. It is important to specify that *maturity,* as used here, refers to the group's maturity as a team, a functional unit (not to the age level or the personality variables that may be synonyms for maturity in other contexts). Classifying leadership into four quadrants, Hersey and Blanchard indicate that the immature group needs the highest level of task direction and the lowest level of personal relationship. Conversely, the most mature group requires neither task direction nor relationship development. The four categories are as follows:

1. Below-average maturity group—high task/low relationship.
2. Average maturity group—high task/high relationship.
3. Average maturity group—low task/high relationship.
4. Above-average maturity group—low task/low relationship.

Using the application shown in Figure 6.3, read each of the 10 situations describing the team's behavior and make a decision about the team's maturity level as a functional group based on this information. Then select one of the four alternative actions, each of which indicates a particular level of the leader's style in task and relationship response.

When you finish, compare your selected actions with those of the designers, using the style-range answer chart shown in Figure 6.4. The answers A, B, C, and D are listed in rows reading across from the situation number. All answers that indicate the response for a particular "style" are found in the columns, reading down. That is:

1. Responses (high task/low relationship) for below-average maturity group
2. Responses (high task/high relationship) OR
3. Responses (high relationship/low task) for average maturity group
4. Responses (low task/low relationship) for above-average maturity group.

Absolute "right" and "wrong" responses are not given, both because we have taken some liberty with the original authors' ideas, and because we think your reflection on these decisions will lead to a lively discussion. From this activity, you should be able to make decisions about the types of behaviors that characterize mature and immature teams, and formulate some suggestions about the types of professional-development activities that might be appropriate for groups that exhibit these behaviors.

"You are the group leader . . . "

SITUATION

1. Your team members are not responding lately to your friendly conversation and low-key directions. They haven't followed through on IEP assignments.

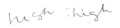

ALTERNATIVE ACTIONS

A. Insist on uniform procedures and task accomplishment.
B. Make yourself available for discussion but don't push.
C. Talk with team members, then set goals.
D. Do not intervene.

SITUATION

2. The effectiveness of your team is increasing. You have been making sure that all members are aware of their roles and performance expectations.

ALTERNATIVE ACTIONS

A. Be friendly, but continue to make sure that all members are aware of their roles and tasks.
B. Take no definite action.
C. Do what you can to make the members feel important and involved.
D. Emphasize the importance of timelines and tasks.

SITUATION

3. Members of your team are unable to solve a problem. You have previously left them alone. Group performance and interpersonal relations have been good. *high* *low*

ALTERNATIVE ACTIONS

A. Get involved with the group and work with the members in problem solving.
B. Let the group work it out.
C. Intervene quickly to correct and redirect.
D. Encourage group work on the problem and be available for discussion.

SITUATION

4. You are considering a major change in referral procedures. Your subordinates have a fine record of accomplishment. They respect the need for change.

low, low

ALTERNATIVE ACTIONS

A. Allow group involvement in developing the change, but don't push.
B. Announce changes and then implement with close supervision.
C. Let the group formulate its own direction.
D. Incorporate group recommendations, but design change yourself.

SITUATION

5. The achievement of your group has dropped during the last few months. Members have been unconcerned with meeting objectives, and have continually needed reminding to have their tasks done on time. Redefining roles has helped in the past.

ALTERNATIVE ACTIONS

A. Allow the group to determine its own direction.
B. Incorporate group recommendations, but see that objectives are met.
C. Redefine goals and supervise carefully.
D. Allow group involvement in setting goals, but don't push.

Continued

Figure 6.3

What is your leadership style?

Source: Reprinted from the *Training and Development Journal.* Copyright (February 1974), the American Society for Training and Development. Reprinted with permission. All rights reserved.

SITUATION	ALTERNATIVE ACTIONS
6. You are considering major changes in your team's structure. Members of the group have made suggestions about needed changes. The group has demonstrated flexibility in its day-to-day operations. *low / low*	A. Define the change and supervise carefully. B. Acquire the group's approval on the change and allow members to decide on implementation. C. Be willing to make changes as recommended, but maintain control of implementation. D. Avoid confrontations; leave things alone.
SITUATION	ALTERNATIVE ACTIONS
7. Group performance and interactions are good. You feel somewhat unsure about your lack of direction of the group. *low low*	A. Leave the group alone. B. Discuss the situation with the group and then initiate necessary changes. C. Take steps to direct team members toward working in a well-defined manner. D. Be careful of hurting leader-subordinate relations by being too direct.
SITUATION	ALTERNATIVE ACTIONS
8. Your superior has appointed you to head a task force that is far overdue in making requested recommendations for change. The group is not clear on its goals. Attendance at sessions has been poor. Their meetings have turned into social gatherings. The group has the necessary talent. *high / low*	A. Let the group work it out. B. Incorporate group recommendations, but see that objectives are met. C. Redefine goals and supervise carefully. D. Allow group involvement in setting goals, and don't push.
SITUATION	ALTERNATIVE ACTIONS
9. Your team members, usually able to take responsibility, are not responding to your recent redefining of standards. *high / low*	A. Allow group involvement in redefining standards, but don't push. B. Redefine standards and supervise carefully. C. Avoid confrontation by not applying pressure. D. Incorporate group recommendations, but see that new standards are met.
SITUATION	ALTERNATIVE ACTIONS
10. Recent information indicates some internal difficulties among team members. The group has a remarkable record of accomplishment. Members have effectively maintained long-range goals. They have worked in harmony for the past year. All are well qualified for the task. *low / high*	A. Try out your solution with subordinates and examine the need for new practices. B. Allow group members to work it out themselves. C. Act quickly and firmly to correct and redirect. D. Make yourself available for discussion, but be careful of hurting leader-member relationships.

Figure 6.3
Continued.

236

		(1)	(2)	(3)	(4)
1		A	(C)	B	D
2		D	A	(C)	B
3		C	(A)	D	B
4		B	(D)	A	C
5		(C)	B	D	A
6		A	C	(B)	D
7		C	B	D	(A)
8		C	(B)	D	A
9		B	D	(A)	C
10		C	A	(D)	B
		(1)	(2)	(3)	(4)
		HT/LR	HT/HR	HR/LT	LT/LR

Figure 6.4
Style range.

Source: Reprinted from the *Training and Development Journal.* Copyright (February 1974), the American Society for Training and Development. Reprinted with permission. All rights reserved.

SUMMARY

Members of the interactive team are interested in obtaining *power,* defined as the ability to facilitate change that improves programs for students with special needs. Power is obtained through empowerment—the provision of knowledge, skill, and change strategies to persons within the organization who serve these students or clients. The empowerment of individuals is accomplished through professional development, designed in accordance with information about the best practices for its use.

Three types of professional-development programs, increasing in complexity and effectiveness, are available to members of the interactive team:

- ◆ Sharing knowledge.
- ◆ Developing skills.
- ◆ Developing the team.

Professional development requires an understanding of the process of change and an ability by the developer to design a change strategy that will affect the entire organization in which students with special needs are served.

> Professional development can often best be sustained when teachers have opportunities to be part of *collegial networks* or cohesive professional communities of practice. In collegial networks that develop mutual goals and share information about their successes and failures, teachers have opportunities to feel supported and energized in meeting the needs of all students. (Mariage & Garmon, 2003, p. 216)

Effective professional development increases the team's power by empowering its members with knowledge and skills that assist them in implementing needed changes. The empowerment of family members, which enables them to function as full members of the interactive team, is described in the next chapter.

ACTIVITIES

1. Compare and contrast the following pairs of terms:
   - ◆ Power structure; change agent
   - ◆ Inservice training; professional development
   - ◆ Power; empowerment
   - ◆ Legitimate power; expert power
2. Through observation and discussion, identify one or two professionals in your program who demonstrate excellent skills that might be used by others. Plan a professional-development program that includes modeling, demonstration, and follow-up coaching by these exemplary professionals.

3. Conduct or design a needs assessment that might be used in planning a professional-development program for your organization.

4. Observe a meeting of a team that is planning a program for professional development. Explain how the leader involves (or does not involve) others in the decision-making process.

5. Design a knowledge-sharing professional-development program that meets the following criteria for oral presentation. Present it to members of your group and obtain their evaluation of its effectiveness.
   a. Brief overview/theoretical base presented.
   b. Interesting opener/closing.
   c. Appropriate media and handouts used.
      ◆ Designed to match purpose.
      ◆ Audiovisual combinations are summative.
      ◆ Momentum maintained during handout distribution.
   d. Effective activities.
      ◆ Designed to match objective(s).
      ◆ Designed to involve audience.
   e. Effective presentation.
      ◆ Demonstrated professionalism.
      ◆ Demonstrated knowledge.
      ◆ Used notes appropriately.
      ◆ Used nonverbals effectively (eyes, stance, gestures).
      ◆ Used verbals effectively (volume, inflections).
      ◆ Used questions appropriately (eliciting, responding, answering).
      ◆ Managed audience (developing rapport, managing disruptions).
      ◆ Used humor and/or examples.
      ◆ Avoided information overload.

REFERENCES

Book, C. (1996). Professional development schools. In J. Sikula, T. Buttery, & E. Guyton (Eds.), *Handbook of research on teacher education* (2nd ed.). New York: Macmillan.

Boone, R. (1990). The development, implementation, and evaluation of a preconference training strategy for enhancing parental participation in and satisfaction with the individual transition conference (Doctoral dissertation, University of Florida, 1989). *Dissertation Abstracts International, 51*(3), 816A.

Boyer, M. (1997). Staff development: Master teachers. *The American School Board Journal, 184*(7), 34–35.

Brown, B. (1997). *University faculty member exchanges places with third grade teacher.* Unpublished manuscript. Slippery Rock, PA: SRU College of Education.

Buck, G., Morsink, C., Griffin, C., Hines, T., & Lenk, L. (1992). Preservice training: The role of field-based experiences in the preparation of effective educators. *Teacher Education and Special Education, 15*(2), 108–123.

Cawelti, G. (2003). The new effective schools. In W. Owings & L. Kaplan, (Eds.), *Best practices, best thinking, and emerging school issues in school leadership* (pp. 45–52). Thousand Oaks, CA: Corwin Press.

Chenoweth, T., & Everhart, R. (2002). *Navigating comprehensive school change: A guide for the perplexed.* Larchmont, NY: Eye on Education.

Covey, S. (1990). *The 7 habits of highly effective people.* New York: Simon & Schuster.

Darling-Hammond, L. (2001). The challenge of staffing our schools. *Educational Leadership, 58,* 12–17.

Darling-Hammond, L. (2003). Enhancing teaching. In W. Owings & L. Kaplan (Eds.), *Best practices, best thinking, and emerging school issues in school leadership* (pp. 75–88), Thousand Oaks, CA: Corwin Press.

Darling-Hammond, L., & Sykes, G. (2001). *Teaching as the learning profession: A handbook on policy and practice.* San Francisco: Jossey-Bass.

Du Four, R. (1998). *The principal series, facilitator's guide for tapes 1–3: Creating a collaborative learning community.* Alexandria, VA: Association for Supervision and Curriculum Development.

Duarte, P. (1992–93). A mentorship program for special education seniors. *National Forum of Applied Educational Research Journal, 6*(1), 54–67.

Ends, E., & Page, C. (1984). *Organizational team building.* Lanham, MD: University Press of America.

Fullan, M. (2000). *Leading in a culture of change.* San Francisco: Jossey-Bass.

Fullan, M. (2003). Implementing change at the building level. In W. Owings & L. Kaplan (Eds.), *Best practices, best thinking, and emerging school issues in school leadership* (pp. 31–37). Thousand Oaks, CA: Corwin Press.

Futrell, M. H. (2000). Empowering teachers as learners and leaders. In *Readings on leadership in education: From the archives of Phi Delta Kappa International* (pp. 125–144). Bloomington, IN: Phi Delta Kappa Foundation.

Glasser, W. (1997). A new look at school failure and school success. *Phi Delta Kappan, 78,* 596–603.

Glatthorn, A. (1987). Cooperative professional development: Peer-centered options for teacher growth. *Educational Leadership, 45,* 31–35.

Griffin, C. C., Winn, J. A., Otis-Wilborn, A., & Kilgore, K. L. (2003). *New teacher induction in special education* (COPSSE Document Number RS-5).

Gainesville, FL: University of Florida, Center on Personnel Studies in Special Education.

Hall, G., & Hord, S. (2001) *Implementing change: Patterns, principles, and potholes.* Boston: Allyn & Bacon.

Hassel, E. (1999). Professional development: Learning from the best. Oak Brook, IL: North Central Regional Educational Laboratory.

Hersey, P., & Blanchard, K. (1974). So you want to know your leadership style? *Training and Development Journal, 28*(2), 22–36.

Hobbs, T., Day, S., & Russo, A. (2002). The virtual conference room: Online problem solving for first year special educators. *Teacher Education and Special Education, 25,* 352–361.

Holmes Group (1990). *Tomorrow's schools: Principles for the design of professional development schools: A report.* East Lansing, MI: Author.

Howey, K. (1997, November–December). School-focused teacher education: Issues to address. *Action in Teacher Education, XIX,* 4–5.

Hutson, H. (1979). *Inservice best practices: The learnings of general education.* Bloomington, IN: National Inservice Network.

Ilmer, S., Snyder, J., Erbaugh, S., & Kurz, K. (1997). Urban educators' perceptions of successful teaching. *Journal of Teacher Education, 48*(5), 379–384.

Joyce, B., & Showers, B. (1995). *Student achievement through staff development.* White Plains, NY: Longman Publishers.

Kampwith, T. J. (2003). *Collaborative consultation in the schools: Effective practices for students with learning and behavior problems* (2nd ed.). Upper Saddle River, NJ: Merrill/Prentice-Hall.

Kansas Inservice Training Systems (KITS). (2004). *Inservice training for early childhood professionals and families.* Parsons, KS: Kansas University Center on Developmental Disabilities. Retrieved January 2, 2004, from http://kskits.org/index.shtml

Kaplan, L., & Owings, W. (2003). Epilogue. In W. Owings & L. Kaplan (Eds.), *Best practices, best thinking, and emerging school issues in school leadership* (pp. 263–271). Thousand Oaks, CA: Corwin Press.

Keifer-Barone, S., & Ware, K. (2002). Organize teams of teachers. *Journal of Staff Development, 23*(3), 31–34.

Kurtts, S., & Levin, B. (2000). Using peer coaching with preservice teachers to develop reflective practice and collegial support. *Teaching Education, 11*(3), 297–310.

Lang, M., & Fox, L. (2003). Breaking with tradition: Providing effective professional development for instructional personnel supporting students with severe disabilities. *Teacher Education and Special Education, 26,* 17–26.

LeRoux, P. (1984). *Selling to a group.* New York: Harper & Row.

Levin, B., & Rock, T. (2003). The effects of collaborative action research on preservice and experienced teacher partners in professional development schools. *Journal of Teacher Education, 54,* 135–149.

Little, M. E., & Houston, D. (2003). Research into practice through professional development. *Remedial and Special Education, 24,* 75–87.

Lubinsky, L. (2002). Coaching our game. *Administrator, 59*(5), 42.

Mariage, T., & Garmon, A. (2003). A case of educational change improving student achievement through a school-university partnership. *Remedial and Special Education, 24,* 215–234.

McLaughlin, M., & Schwartz, R. (1998). *Strategies for fixing failing public schools.* Cambridge, MA: Harvard Graduate School, Pew Forum.

McLeskey, J., & Waldron, N. (2002). Professional development and inclusive schools: Reflections on effective practice. *Teacher Educator, 37*(3), 159–172.

Morsink, C. (1999). *21st century teachers for a better future* (Final Report to Howard Heinz Endowment). Slippery Rock, PA: SRU College of Education.

National Council for the Accreditation of Teacher Education. (2001). *Standards for professional development schools.* Washington, DC: Author.

Neufeld, B., & Roper, D. (2003). *Coaching: A strategy for developing instructional capacity.* Cambridge, MA: Education Matters, Inc. North Central Regional Laboratories. Retrived January 29, 2004, from http://www.ncrel.org/pd/vactrans.htm

November, A. (2003). Using technology to change school learning culture. In W. Owings & L. Kaplan (Eds.), *Best practices, best thinking, and emerging school issues in school leadership* (pp. 95–102). Thousand Oaks, CA: Corwin Press.

O'Shea, D., Williams, L., & Sattler, R. (1999). Collaboration preparation across special education and general education: Preservice level teachers' views. *Journal of Teacher Education, 50*(2), 147–158.

O'Shea, L. (1987). The supervision throughput model: Interpersonal communication skills and problem-solving procedures for effective intern supervision. *Teacher Education and Special Education, 10,* 71–80.

Owings, W., & Kaplan, L. (2003). *Best practices, best thinking, and emerging school issues in school leadership.* Thousand Oaks, CA: Corwin Press.

Page, N., & Czuba, C. (1999). Empowerment: What is it? *Journal of Extension, 37*(5). Retrieved January 13, 2004, from http://www.joe.org/joe/1999october/comm1.html

Patricia, L., & Lamb, M. (1990). Preparing secondary special education teachers to be collaborative decision makers and reflective practitioners: A promising practicum model. *Teacher Education and Special Education, 13*(3–4), 228–232.

Patterson, W. (2003). Challenges to leading and sustaining school change. In W. Owings & L. Kaplan (Eds.), *Best practices, best thinking, and emerging school issues in school leadership* (pp. 37–44). Thousand Oaks, CA: Corwin Press.

Pennell, J., & Firestone, W. (1998). Teacher-to-teacher professional development. *Phi Delta Kappan, 80,* 354–357.

Peterson, S., & Hudson, P. (1989). Coaching: A strategy to enhance preservice teacher behaviors. *Teacher Education and Special Education, 12,* 56–60.

Pugach, M., & Johnson, L. (2002). *Collaborative practitioners, collaborative schools.* Denver, CO: Love.

Reinhartz, J., & Beach, D. (2004). *Educational leadership: Changing schools, changing roles.* Boston: Pearson.

Rhoton, J., & Bowers, P. (Eds.). (2001). *Professional development leadership and the diverse learner.* Arlington, VA: NSTA Press.

Rice, E. H. (2002). Collaborative process in professional development schools: Results of a meta-ethnography, 1990–1998. *Educational Administration Abstracts, 37*(3), 279–412.

Richard, A. (2003). *The emergence of school-based staff developers in America's public schools.* New York, NY: Edna McConnell Clark Foundation. Retrieved January 31, 2004, from http://www.emcf.org/programs/student/student pub.htm

Rogers, S. (1987). If I can see myself, I can change. *Educational Leadership, 45,* 64–67.

Routman, R. (2002). Teacher talk (redesigning professional development). *Educational Leadership, 59,* 32–34.

Sahakian, P., & Stockton, J. (1996). Opening doors: Teacher-guided observations. *Educational Leadership, 53*(7), 50–53.

Saylor, P., & Kehrhahn, M. (2003). Teacher skills get an upgrade. *Journal of Staff Development, 24,* 48–53.

Showers, B. (1984). *Peer coaching: A strategy for facilitating transfer of training* (Report to the U.S. Department of Education). Eugene, OR: University of Oregon, Center for Educational Policy and Management. (ERIC Document Reproduction Service No. ED271849)

Showers, B., & Joyce, B. (1996). The evolution of peer coaching. *Educational Leadership, 53*(7), 12–16.

Showers, B., Joyce, B., & Bennett, B. (1987). Synthesis of research on staff development: A framework for future study and a state-of-the-art analysis. *Educational Leadership, 45,* 77–87.

Teitel, L. (2000). *How professional development schools make a difference: A review of research.* Washington, DC: National Council for the Accreditation of Teacher Education.

Tucker, A. (1984). *Chairing the academic department: Leadership among peers* (2nd ed.). New York: American Council on Education-Macmillan.

Tucker, J. (1972). *A plan to achieve change.* Austin: University of Texas, Department of Special Education.

Veenman, S., & Denessen. E. (2001). The coaching of teachers: Results of five training studies. *Educational Research and Evaluation, 7*(4), 385–417.

Wallace, T. (2003). *Paraprofessionals* (COPSSE Document No. IB-3). Gainesville, FL: University of Florida, Center on Personnel Studies in Special Education. Retrieved January 31, 2004, from http://www.copsse.org.

Wang, M. (1998, June 24). Comprehensive school reform can debunk myths about change. *Education Week, XVIII,* 39, 52.

Wang, M., Haertel, G., & Walberg, H. (1997). *What do we know: Widely implemented school improvement programs.* Philadelphia, PA: Mid-Atlantic Regional Educational Lab at Temple University.

Williams, A. L. (1999). *Participant responses to a rural university and urban elementary school collaboration around a preservice field-based seminar.* Slippery Rock, PA: SRU College of Education.

Wilmore, E. (1996). Brave new world: Field-based teacher preparation. *Educational Leadership, 53*(7), 59–63.

Wineburg, S., & Grosman, P. (1998). Creating a community of learners among high school teachers. *Phi Delta Kappan, 80,* 350–353.

Winograd, K. (1998). Rethinking theory after practice: Education professor as elementary teacher. *Journal of Teacher Education, 49*(4), 296–305.

Wynn, M. (1987). Student teacher transfer of training to the classroom: Effects of an experimental model (Doctoral dissertation, University of Florida, 1986). *Dissertation Abstracts International, 47,* 3008A.

Wynn, M. (1988, April). *Transfer of training to the classroom by student teachers: Effects of an experimental model.* Paper presented at the annual meeting of the American Educational Research Association, New Orleans, LA. (ERIC Document Reproduction Service No. ED239830)

Enabling and Supporting Families

7

Topics in this chapter include:

◆ The changing profiles of the American family.

◆ Research-based evidence on families of children with special needs.

◆ The various roles of professionals supporting families.

◆ The unique roles of family members collaborating with professionals.

◆ Strategies for collaborating effectively with families.

◆ An application for involving families in special education.

Linda is the single mother of a 6-year-old child with special needs, Miriam, and a 4-year-old child, Carlos. Linda lives in Miami with her mother, a native Cuban, who speaks Spanish. Linda has fought many battles in the past 6 years. Physicians told her that Miriam would not live to see her first birthday; ophthalmologists reported that the girl was totally blind; and physical therapists said she would never walk.

In spite of the gloomy prognosis, Linda was committed to making Miriam's life the best that it could be. Linda searched for early intervention services when Miriam was 18 months old. They attended early intervention programs, where Linda spoke with other parents of infants with special needs. Linda placed Miriam in public school programs for toddlers with special needs. She and Miriam attended summer camps for children with visual impairments and their families, where Linda learned physical therapy techniques needed to help Miriam with motor control and eating.

If there is a typical story of a parent of a child with special needs, this may be one. But Linda brings a new twist to the story. Linda is currently running her own advocacy consultation business. She collaborates with professionals and parents in school districts around Florida in an effort to meet the needs of children with visual and multiple disabilities. She serves as an advocate in due process hearings, and makes presentations at legislative hearings and many special education national conferences. Linda continues her battles for appropriate services for her daughter, and also fights for better services for other children with special needs. She is a distinct kind of parent, well versed in legal and educational issues, articulate in presenting her opinion, and an equal partner on the special education team.

Across the country in Boise, another mother, Susan, worries about whether her daughter will receive a quality educational program at their local public school. In this school, parents are required to sign a contract to volunteer in the school for 100 hours a year. Children whose parents volunteer can participate in a special program that includes field trips, school plays, guest speakers, and carnivals. Susan, a single mother of a 13-year-old boy with severe reading disabilities, works two jobs to make ends meet. Since her son was diagnosed with learning disabilities 7 years ago, she has been committed to helping her son. However, she is unable to volunteer in school. She reports that his teachers rarely call her about school activities or homework assignments and are "resentful" when she asks to schedule her son's IEP meetings early in the mornings before classes begin. Parent-school collaboration varies from family to family on a continuum of parent involvement levels.

During the past three decades, knowledge and research about families of students with special needs has grown. The passage of Public Law 94-142 in 1975, and subsequent reauthorization of the Individuals with Disabilities Education Act (IDEA) in 1997, recognized the role of the family as an integral part of the special education process. Special education personnel became aware of the need to develop skills in supporting and involving families. Although families were encouraged to participate in the development of their children's educational programs, the attempts to achieve such involvement yielded mixed results.

Parental involvement usually was limited to attending IEP or Individualized Family Service Plan (IFSP) conferences and approving program and placement decisions made by special education personnel (Summers, Gavin, & Purnell-Hall, 2003). Parents were merely consumers of services and typically were passive participants in the educational process. Furthermore, school administrators discouraged the involvement of parents in school functions (Turnbull & Turnbull, 2001) for fear that agitated and unsatisfied parents would instigate due process hearings and lawsuits. If school personnel did encourage *family-centered involvement*, it usually was regarded as more of a kindhearted or paternalistic gesture.

However, much has changed. Today, families are being asked to be collaborators and partners with schools. Additionally, the members of the partnership are not only the parents but all members of the family, including extended family members and non-blood relatives. Grandparents, brothers, sisters, godparents, and even close family friends are recognized as vital sources of support for the family (Turnbull & Turnbull, 2001). They often can influence the outcomes of students with special needs and should be included in any discussion of home-school collaboration. Today, families are respected as experts on their children and are valued for their equal and full partnership in the educational process.

The purpose of this chapter is to present the factors that influenced the changing attitudes of professionals about involving families in home-school collaboration and understanding families of children with special needs. A contemporary view of the role of the professional and family in a collaborative partnership is also described in this chapter. A discussion of the importance of understanding families from culturally and linguistically diverse backgrounds is given and strategies for involving the families of these types of students are discussed.

CHANGES IN THE FAMILY STRUCTURE AND PARENTAL INVOLVEMENT

American families have changed dramatically during the last few decades. The sociocultural conditions that currently influence the American family have implications for professionals working with families today (Hanson & Lynch, 2004; Harry, 2002; National Parent-Teacher Association, 1998). Although the majority of families in the United States still form the typical two-parent, middle-class household, atypical family structures and diverse economic and educational conditions in U.S. families are becoming more common. Reports from the U.S. Census (Fields, 2003) on the diverse structures and demographic profiles of today's families indicate the following:

◆ Seventy-two million children (defined as the population under 18) resided in the United States, up from 64 million in 1990.

◆ Between 1990 and 2020, the population ages 65 to 74 was projected to grow 74%.

- Sixty-nine percent of children lived with two parents, 23% lived with only their mother, 5% lived with only their father, and another 3% lived in households with neither parent present.
- Forty-four percent of children who lived with neither parent present were living in their grandparent's household.
- Thirty percent of all children under 18 living with a grandparent were living below the poverty line.
- Eleven percent of children living with a single mother lived in a household with their mother and her unmarried partner.
- Thirty-three percent of children who lived with a single father shared the household with his unmarried partner.
- Eighty-eight percent of all children under 18 were covered by health insurance.
- Ninety-seven percent of children living in households that received public assistance were covered by health insurance (probably because public assistance programs often provide a health insurance safety net for children in low-income families).

Additionally, other U.S. Census reports (Fields & Casper, 2003) indicate the changing demographics of the family unit in the United States.

- Of the 2000 population, an estimated 77.1% were White, 12.9% were Black or African American; 4.5% were Asians and Pacific Islanders; and about 1.5% were of the American Indian and Alaska Native population. Thirteen percent were of Hispanic origin.
- The Latino or Hispanic population rose nearly 57.9% between the 1990 and 2000 censuses.
- In 2000 one-half of Hispanics lived in California and Texas.

The Children's Defense Fund (2002) summarizes some very alarming facts on children and families.

- States spend on average three times more per prisoner than per public school pupil.
- Not a single state has shown a majority of the fourth graders reading and doing math proficiently.
- Nationally, there was a record number of children in foster care in 1999. Children adopted from foster care increased by 78%.
- One in seven youths is a high school dropout and one in eight is unemployed.
- More than 1.7 million youths were arrested in 2000. Almost one in five of the youths incarcerated were in adult facilities.

◆ In 1999, 3,365 children and teens, or nine a day, were killed by firearms. Three out of five were victims of homicide, while one-third were suicides.

◆ One in six babies is born to a mother who did not receive early prenatal care. One in four Black and Hispanic babies is born to a mother who did not receive early prenatal care.

◆ About one in four 2-year-olds are not fully immunized against preventable diseases.

◆ Two in five preschoolers eligible for Head Start do not participate in the program.

◆ Three in five preschoolers have mothers in the labor force.

◆ Many children and families still do not receive help paying for child care. Currently only one in seven children eligible for assistance through the Child Care and Developmental Block Grant (CCDBG) receives it.

Lastly, the National Coalition for the Homeless (2001) reported that families with children accounted for 36% of the homeless population, and those numbers are expected to continue to rise. The health and emotional outcomes for children without a home are devastating, with homeless children suffering higher rates of asthma, ear infections, stomach problems, speech problems, anxiety, and depression.

Today, the challenges facing school personnel are striking. Schools are being called on to serve an increasingly diverse and at-risk student and family population. The patterns of change in family structure and sociocultural influences indicate that the current needs of families are indeed diverse, requiring heightened sensitivity to effective ways to interact and engage families in a collaborative relationship. Researchers are clear that parent and family involvement is a wise investment for schools truly concerned about student outcomes. It is critical to understand that families represent the most powerful and pervasive influence that a child will ever experience and families who devote attention to the child may contribute more to the child's development than any extrafamilial factor (Fox, Dunlap, & Philbrick, 1997; Martin & Hagan-Burke, 2002; Summers et al., 2003). The research on parent involvement during the past 30 years documents the profound benefits for students, families, and schools when family members become participants in their children's education and their lives (National Parent-Teacher Association, 1998).

UNDERSTANDING FAMILIES OF CHILDREN WITH SPECIAL NEEDS

In recent years, the idea that families of children with special needs function normally and that the child exerts positive influences on family members has been stated definitively (Ferguson, 2002; Lambie, 2000; Snow, 2001; Turnbull & Turnbull, 2001). The role of the family and their involvement with school personnel have improved significantly, possibly due to changes in the areas of legislation, theory development, and improved research on family adjustment.

Legislative Factors

The passage of P.L. 99-457 in 1986 considerably influenced the roles and responsibilities of the parent and the professional in meeting the educational needs of children with special needs. Families receiving services under Part C early intervention programs are required under this legislation to have an IFSP. The intent of the service plan is similar to that of a child's IEP. However, the IFSP is designed to focus on generating individualized goals and services for meeting the needs of the families and young children with special needs being served in early intervention programs. Those needs may include parent support, counseling services, or parent education. Although Part C mandates services for families of young children with special needs, the implications of the IFSP will ultimately be for older children with special needs and their families.

IDEA 1997 emphasized the parents' role in working with schools. In particular, it requires that parents be provided a copy of their child's IEP. In addition, a parent has the right to ask for revisions of the child's IEP or to invoke due process procedures if he or she feels the child is not making adequate progress toward meeting the goals and objectives outlined in the document. Furthermore, states are required to offer mediation to parents as a voluntary option for resolving disputes. Mediation, however, cannot be used to delay or deny a parent's right to due process.

Furthermore, legislation under IDEA 1997 provided continued support for Parent Training and Information centers (PTIs) across the states and territories. Parent centers in each state provide training and information to parents of infants, toddlers, school-age children, and young adults with special needs as well as the professionals who work with their families. This assistance helps parents participate more effectively with professionals in meeting the educational needs of children and youth with special needs. To reach the parent center in your state, contact the Technical Assistance Alliance for Parent Centers at http://www.taalliance.org/. One national center (Minneapolis, Minnesota) and six regional Technical Assistance centers exist in the northeast (Newark, New Jersey), central east (Davidson, North Carolina); south (Clearwater, Florida); northern plains (Marion, Ohio); midwest (Colorado Springs, Colorado), and west (Navato, California).

Theoretical Factors

Various theoretical points of view related to families of children with special needs have been presented in recent literature. One of the most applicable is the *family systems theory* (Lambie, 2000; Turnbull & Turnbull, 2001). Theorists maintain that the underlying structure of the family can be conceptualized into four *family subsystems: marital, sibling, parental,* and *extrafamilial.*

The family's ability to function effectively depends on how clearly the boundaries and rules of the family are defined and how cohesive and flexible the family is during life-cycle changes. The underlying premise is that life events, such as the birth of a child with special needs, will affect not only the parents but also the siblings, grandparents, and friends. The implications of this theoretical framework are that interventionists are a part of the extrafamilial subsystem and therefore affect each member of the family, even though they may be involved directly with only one member, usually the mother. The traditional view of parent involvement and training with only mothers of children with special needs must be broadened to include fathers, siblings, grandparents, same-sex partners, and others who share in the care of these children.

Literature on theoretical approaches for understanding families provides professionals with a wealth of information. Lambie (2000) provides a review of family systems perspectives for understanding diverse families and families of children with special needs. Various approaches to understanding families give professionals many more tools to assess family functioning and adaptation to children with special needs.

Research Factors

The idea that families have a difficult time adjusting to the presence of a child with special needs has been a major concern of professionals working in special education. Ferguson (2002) stated that the traditional view of families of children with special needs was based on a deficit model in which much attention was placed on the pathology of families. In the traditional view, the goal of the professional was to remediate the deficits by helping families come to grips with the problems of having a child with special needs. Families were viewed as overly emotional, with family members rejecting or struggling with the acceptance of the child with special needs. These families were viewed as dysfunctional in contributing to their child's general welfare and educational program. Traditionally, the image of the family with a child with special needs was one of chronic sorrow, severe depression, and emotional turmoil.

No longer is the family viewed as pathological and unhealthy. Instead, the family is portrayed positively. During the past few years, researchers have reported on studies supporting the notion that families are not necessarily adversely affected by the presence of a child with special needs (Ferguson, 2002; Gallimore, Weisner, Bernheimer, & Guthrie, 1993; Singer, 2002; Turnbull & Turnbull, 2001; Ulrich & Bauer, 2003). In fact, some researchers found that families of children with special needs are as well adjusted as families with nondisabled children (Baxter, Cummins, & Polak, 1995; Cho, Singer, & Brenner, 2001; Krauss, 1993). The availability of *multifaceted family assessment* procedures—including survey instruments, rating forms, natural observation, and interviews—has yielded more sensitive data on families of children with special needs (Bailey & Simeonsson, 1988).

Some studies, however, report increased amounts of *family stress* when family members are coping with children with special needs who require high levels of supervision, require extensive long-term medical care, or have significant behavioral problems (Singer, 2002). How families cope with this stress influences their interaction with professionals in special education and other related fields. For example, intervention studies that focus on stress management, parent-to-parent help, behavioral training, journal writing, and respite care have been found effective in assisting parents (Singer, 2002). Thus, the goal of family intervention is to help families expand internal and external resources to meet the challenges and take advantage of the opportunities of family life. Providing families with interventions that help them adjust to caring for a child with special needs should be one goal of general and special education professionals.

Through support networking and advocacy efforts, parents are educated to be equal partners with educators. Many families have become sophisticated in working with school personnel by taking on a more active role in the educational process. Clearly, the relationship of the family and the professional has changed from coexistence to collaboration. In the next sections, the roles and responsibilities of professionals and parents within the collaborative partnership are delineated.

ROLE OF THE PROFESSIONAL

School personnel are responsible for initiating and maintaining a positive, interactive, and facilitative relationship with families of children with special needs. In this regard, the professional's role is multifaceted. Many school personnel feel comfortable with the more traditional responsibilities of providing information on student progress, results of diagnostic evaluations, inclusive educational placement strategies, and schedules of upcoming school events.

However, the role of the professional has expanded to include parent education and advocacy, medical report interpretation, active listening, and working with culturally diverse students and their families. The family's needs can range from information about due process hearings to help obtaining transportation, welfare payments, and food stamps. School personnel may take on the shared roles of social worker, attorney, physician, therapist, psychologist, clergy, and friend. Summers et al. (2003) review different partnership types based on Epstein's work of the 1990s. Table 7.1 outlines the types of partnerships and examples of what schools can do to encourage partnerships. The professional should not assume all these jobs without assistance or training, however.

Collaboration, role sharing, and role release are required for special educators and other team members to be successful in their expanded job responsibilities. Although many professionals may be willing to expand their roles in encouraging family involvement, few are trained to assume the added responsibilities. The various roles and responsibilities of the special education team members as collaborators are discussed next.

Providing Basic Information

The traditional role of the professional working with families has been as information provider. Teachers of students with mild disabilities, for example, usually provide the family with information on academic and emotional/social progress. The teachers and therapists of students with severe disabilities provide information

Table 7.1
What Can Schools Do About Parent Involvement?

Types of Parent Involvement	What Can Schools Do?
Building parenting skills	Conduct workshops, home visits, family support programs, and information exchange to help families understand their children's basic health, education, and welfare (e.g., material lending library on child development)
Communication between home and school	Provide communication with families through telephone contacts, school newsletters, report card exchanges, etc. (e.g., home-school journals)
Volunteering	Promote parent volunteering in classroom activities and other school-related events (e.g., attend field trips)
Extending learning in home	Involve parents in their child's learning through homework and school-related tasks (e.g., parent-child literacy programs)
Decision making	Encourage participation of parents in school decision-making processes (e.g., school advisory councils)
Collaborating with the community	Support parent representation in community and school partnerships (e.g., school scholarship programs through the local Kiwanis Club)

Source: From "Family and School partnerships: Building Bridges in General and Special Education," by J. A. Summers, K. Gavin, and T. Purnell-Hall, 2003, *Advances in Special Education, 15,* pp. 417–444. Used by permission from Elsevier.

on developmental progress, self-care skills, communication, and progress on related therapies such as occupational, physical, and speech therapy. As educators and families move toward more inclusive settings for students with special needs, the educator will need to provide information on students' integration into general education classrooms. Both general and special educators will need to be involved in information dissemination.

Information has been provided to families in many ways. Formal staffing and IFSP or IEP meetings are the most common arenas for professionals and families to interact. In some cases, special educators contact family members by phone, share daily logs with parents, or send notes home informing the family of the child's program.

How to Get Ready
____ 1. Make a list of questions and concerns.
____ 2. Ask your child if he/she has questions for the teacher.
____ 3. Arrange for a babysitter for small children.

Questions You May Want to Ask
____ 1. In which subjects does my child do well? Is my child having any trouble?
____ 2. Does my child get along with other children?
____ 3. Does my child obey the teacher?
____ 4. How can I help at home?

Questions the Teacher May Ask You
____ 1. What does your child like the best about school?
____ 2. What does your child do after school? (What are his/her interests?)
____ 3. Does your child have time and space set aside for homework?
____ 4. How is your child's health?
____ 5. Are there any problems that may affect your child's learning?
____ 6. What type of discipline works well at home?

At the Conference
____ 1. Arrive on time.
____ 2. Discuss your questions and concerns.
____ 3. Share information that will help the teacher know your child better.
____ 4. Take notes if you wish.

After the Conference
____ 1. If you have more questions or you ran out of time, make another appointment.
____ 2. Tell your child about the conference.
____ 3. Plan to keep in touch with the teacher.
____ 4. If you were satisfied with the conference, write a note to the teacher.

Figure 7.1
Parent checklist for IEP meetings.

Source: From *Strategies for Communicating with Parents of Exceptional Children: Improving Parent-Teacher Relationships* (pp. 283–284), by R. L. Kroth and D. Edge, 1997, Denver, CO: Love Publishing Company. Reprinted by permission.

Generally, it is helpful for professionals to provide parents with a checklist to help them prepare for the IEP conference. Figure 7.1 is an example of such a checklist. For more detailed information on preparing for the IFSP/IEP conference, see Turnbull and Turnbull (2001). Informal meetings provide professionals with time to share information with parents related to early developmental intervention, academic changes, behavioral problems, and therapy prescriptions.

Reporting Evaluation Results

The role of the team has been to interpret results of diagnostic evaluations to families. Providing diagnostic feedback is frequently the responsibility of a school psychologist or special education teacher. Informing family members about their child's educational or physical disabilities can be extremely sensitive and requires skills typically associated with problem solving, collaborating, and counseling. The professional who reports evaluation results in a sensitive way may still have families who are discouraged and, at times, shocked by the results of the evaluation.

Guidelines for providing families with test results have been stated in various sources (Teglasi, 1985; Turnbull & Turnbull, 2001). Additionally, Whitaker and Fiore (2001) and Kosmoski and Pollack (2000) provide educators with strategies for interacting with angry parents, including active listening, empathizing, establishing trust, and systematic problem-solving techniques. Team members should adhere to the following when providing diagnostic feedback:

- Provide feedback in a private, safe, comfortable environment.
- Keep the number of professionals to a minimum.
- Begin by asking parents their feelings about the child's strengths as well as weaknesses.
- Provide the evaluation results in a *jargon-free* manner, using examples of test items and behavioral observations throughout.
- Provide parents results from a variety of assessment activities, including standardized tests, criterion-referenced tests, direct behavioral observations, play-based or community-based assessment, and judgment-based approaches.
- Be sensitive to viewing the child as an individual and a "whole" child when reporting various evaluation results.
- Allow the parent time to digest the results before educational planning begins.
- Be sensitive to linguistically different families and the use of interpreters.
- Prepare for the session with other team members, clarifying any possible conflicts before the meeting.
- Use conflict resolution strategies to clarify any possible conflicts with families.

Understanding and Gathering Family Information

The role of the professional working with students with special needs has expanded significantly in the area of assessment instruments and analysis. No longer are team members asked to assess only the student's needs; they are now being asked to assess the family's concerns, priorities, and resources as well. Educational teams must understand the complex family system and know how to match intervention with the service needs of individual families. As mentioned earlier, the linear view of the child with special needs and the parent (most typically the mother) has been replaced with a systemic view of *family subsystems* (parental, marital, sibling, and extrafamilial; Turnbull & Turnbull, 2001). Bailey and Simeonsson (1988) stated that conducting family assessments does the following:

♦ Helps the professional understand the child as part of a family system.
♦ Identifies the family's service needs.
♦ Specifies the family's strengths and adaptations.
♦ Expands the efficacy of services and intervention.

Some of the most commonly used instruments and checklists for assessing family functioning, needs, and supports include the Family Needs Survey (Bailey & Simeonsson, 1990), Parent Needs Survey (Seligman & Darling, 1989), Parenting Stress Index (Abidin, 1986), and the Family Support Scales (Dunst, Trivette, & Jenkins, 1988). Mapping family history is often done using genograms or a drawing of a family tree (Lambie, 2000). Additionally, professionals can use informal procedures for gathering information on the family support network by using the ECOMAP (Hartman, 1978), a one-page visual representation of the family's relationships. Lines and circles are drawn to represent relationships with extended family and kin, friends and neighbors, church and coworkers, and schools and professional services represented by individuals or organizations. In addition to the existence of such relationships, participants describe the nature, strength, and reciprocity of their relationships indicated via various coding conventions. Figure 7.2 illustrates an ECOMAP for a single Puerto Rican mother with a child who has Down syndrome. It shows a concise and convenient mapping of the current relationships and interactions maintained by the family.

Although these instruments and procedures have been recommended by experts in the field, professionals must keep several cautions in mind when using the instruments. Many assessment tools involve personal questions, which some families might consider overly intrusive. The responsibility for administering such instruments may fall on a psychologist or social worker, neither of whom usually has the time to conduct such assessments. Special education teachers may find the instruments too detailed for use in the school setting. Furthermore, professionals may not have received training in administering many of the assessment tools and shaping their results into concrete family plans (Bailey & Simeonsson, 1988).

Research by Garshelis and McConnell (1993) found that individual professionals on interdisciplinary teams did not do well in matching the family's needs with the mothers' perceptions of family needs. The collaborative teaming process helped professionals come to consensus and more closely match the parents' perceived needs. The researchers concluded that professionals should allow parents to provide the team with perceived family needs, and should use those needs to guide the interventions developed with the family. Professionally directed assessments of family needs may not be accurate.

Professionals must be cautious when using family surveys with families of children with special needs. Some of the instruments lack validity and reliability and have small norming populations (L'Abate & Bagarozzi, 1993; Lambie, 2000;

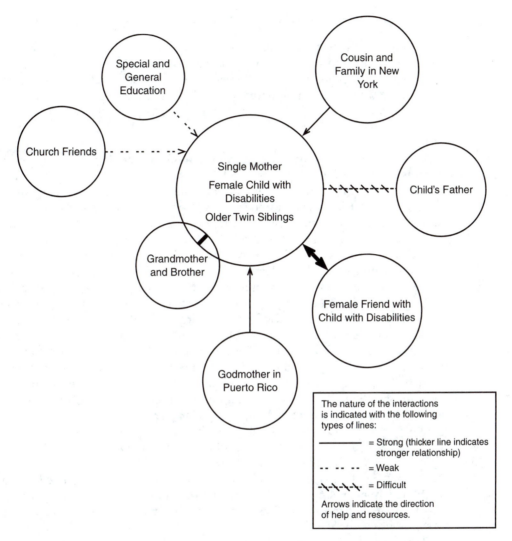

Figure 7.2
An ECOMAP.

McGrew, Gilman, & Johnson, 1992). Furthermore, professionals should be cautious when using the surveys with families from culturally and linguistically diverse backgrounds (Behar, Correa, & Beverly, 1993; Harry, 2002; Kalyanpur, Harry, & Skrtic, 2000). Few family instruments have been normed on culturally or linguistically diverse families, and the families' cultural values and beliefs might not be taken into consideration when interpreting the results. Professionals should keep in mind that each family of a child with a special need has unique characteristics and should be evaluated on an individual basis.

Providing Instruction to Families

Professionals in special programs frequently are involved in educating parents to implement educational programs at home. The educational objectives can vary from teaching parents specific strategies such as learning strategies for increasing word recognition to teaching parents time-out procedures for decreasing tantrum behavior. An abundance of research is available that supports the efficacy of educating parents in skills related to teaching students with special needs (Turnbull & Turnbull, 2001).

However, more recent trends in family literature indicate that the concept of parents as teachers and of professionals as parent trainers is questionable. Professionals must understand that although parents are effective in teaching and reinforcing behavior in their children, their role as teachers can be an added burden and source of stress for the family. Turnbull and Turnbull (2001) pointed out that families often do not have the time outside of their work and household responsibilities to "teach" their children. In many families the stress of daily intervention with their children can have detrimental effects on family members' interactions. Professionals must not assume that when teachers show parents how to implement a particular strategy or prescribed curriculum, that the parents, in turn, will be able to effectively teach the child the targeted skill (Parette & Petch-Hogan, 2000). Parents are often uncomfortable with the intervention and get frustrated if the child does not show progress. A more family-centered approach to teaching families specific interventions is often required, where parents can chose which activities they are most comfortable with. Professionals must know how to balance prescriptive interventions with naturally occurring opportunities that exist at home (Ketelaar, Vermeer, Helders, & Hart, 1998). Dunst, Leet, and Trivette (1988) found that adequacy of family resources and personal well-being affected the family's ability to adhere to prescribed interventions for the child. They concluded that some families did not follow through on prescribed interventions because they had to invest time and energy in meeting other family needs. Families with inadequate resources and social support did not carry out child treatments. To presume these families are resistant, uncooperative, or noncompliant is a grave error in professional judgment.

The following vignette illustrates these issues:

Mr. Fox has a 13-year-old son, Jason, with learning disabilities. At a recent IEP meeting, the general and special education professionals recommended that Mr. Fox follow-up with reading and math interventions at home. The techniques prescribed involve 30 to 40 minutes a day of oral reading, answering comprehension questions, and solving math equations. The IEP team also reports that Jason has been off-task during the school day and when they try to redirect him he often snaps back at them. The behavioral specialist also asked Mr. Fox to document incidences of noncompliance and aggressive outbursts in a weekly log. Mr. Fox leaves the meeting with pages of reading passages and comprehension questions, a workbook of math questions, and a behavioral recording sheet. On a follow-up visit to the school, Mr. Fox is asked to report on the progress of all the programs. He is embarrassed and says he has been unable to conduct the homework interventions at home. In fact, Jason has become increasingly frustrated with his father; he has begun to complain about his homework and has been defiant at home.

The professionals involved with Mr. Fox have good intentions for Jason's educational program, but they have not made a thorough assessment of the family's needs. Before recommending family intervention programs, professionals should have asked about other family members, working responsibilities of both parents, and daily routines and schedules of the family. The family systems approach acknowledges the right of Mr. Fox and other family members to identify their own priorities for Jason. The IEP team members could have suggested homework activities that reinforced reading and math but that were real-life assignments, like reading the newspaper or mail and figuring out the ingredients to make different food recipes. One of the teachers could have made a few initial home visits to assist with the homework assignments, demonstrating to Mr. Fox and Jason how to organize his homework time and offering simple rewards for completion of the assignment. Professionals must consider individualizing their approach to providing families with information about intervention strategies, resources, and advocacy (Turnbull & Turnbull, 2001). Specific suggestions for providing parents with information are discussed in the last section of this chapter, "Strategies for Supporting Families." Providing information is especially difficult when families are culturally and linguistically different from dominant-culture school professionals.

Understanding Culturally Diverse Families

Statisticians indicate that by 2050 about 53% of the U.S. population will be non-Hispanic White, 15% Black, more than 24% Hispanic, almost 9% Asian and Pacific Islander, and just over 1% American Indian, Eskimo, and Aleut (U.S. Census Bureau, 1998). It is projected that by 2050 the Black population will nearly double its present size; the Asian and Pacific Islander population will increase 3.5 times its 1995 level; and the Hispanic-origin population will increase by 3.5 times its 1995 level. The Hispanic-origin population will show the largest numeric increases of any other race or ethnic group. Additionally, 1 in 10 people in the United States is foreign born, with Mexico being the largest country of birth of the foreign-born population.

Because of the increased numbers of culturally and linguistically diverse populations in many school districts, educators are required to work with students and families from diverse cultural groups. Although most studies of families of children with special needs have been directed toward Anglo-American families in the dominant culture, an increasing number of studies have described families from culturally and linguistically diverse groups (Bailey, Skinner, Correa, et al., 1999; Bailey, Skinner, Rodriguez, et al., 1999; Blanes, Correa, & Bailey, 1999; Hanline & Daley, 1992; Heller, Markwardt, Rowitz, & Farber, 1994; Parette & Huer, 2002; Rao, 2000; Skinner, Bailey, Correa, & Rodriguez, 1999; Wathum-Ocama & Rose, 2002). The culturally diverse family—that is, the family from a cultural background other than Anglo-American—may not understand the special education needs of their child. Often because of language barriers, the family may not understand the nature of the child's disability, the educational services available for the child, or the expectations of professionals working with the child and family (Barrera & Corso, 2003; Harry, 2002; Kalyanpur et al., 2000). Nevertheless, the professional must view the culturally diverse family as having different values and beliefs that are positive (Barrera & Corso, 2003; Chrispeels & Rivero, 2001; Trotman, 2001). The belief system held by the family may actually be a strength for coping with and caring for the child with a disability.

The role of the professional working with the culturally diverse family is multifaceted. Professionals must first assess their own biases toward different ethnic groups. Second, they must make an effort to understand the family. At the same time, the culturally and linguistically diverse family must be helped to understand and participate in the traditional culture of schools. Acculturation into school life is a two-way process in which professionals and families collaborate. "Professionals who are hoping to make a difference for children must be willing to take the initiative in building a bridge between the cultures of diverse families and the culture of schools" (Harry, Kalyanpur, & Day, 1999, p. 7). Harry and colleagues outline four steps that are essential in building cultural reciprocity among families and school personnel. The four steps involve the following:

1. Identifying the cultural values that are embedded in our interpretation of a student's difficulties or in the recommendations for services, such as independence and individuality.
2. Recognizing whether the family being served understands and values the interpretations we as service providers place on the student's difficulties and, if not, having the family share why their values differ from ours.
3. Respecting the differences identified between the family and the school.
4. Determining the most effective way of adapting the professional's interpretation or recommendation to the value system of the family.

Guidelines for how professionals can encourage parent involvement (Chrispeels & Rivero, 2001; Ford, 1995; Hanson & Lynch, 2004; Trotman, 2001; Unger, Jones, Park, & Tressell, 2001; Wagner, Spiker, & Linn, 2002) are useful in working with families. Some additional strategies for professionals working with culturally diverse families include the following:

♦ Empowering families with skills for adapting and coping with a school system that may be very different from what they are accustomed to.
♦ Enabling families to reinforce educational programs at home in natural and functional ways.
♦ Assisting families through the transition from their native culture to the mainstream school culture, understanding that the native culture can be heterogeneous within groups such as Hispanics and Asians.

- Serving as *culture brokers* by providing a link between the majority and minority cultures.
- Linking with community leaders from the ethnic or racial group to help enhance the collaborative home-school relationship.
- Serving as mediators and advocates for the ethnic and racial group.
- Removing barriers such as cultural differences and linguistic and communication differences to enhance interaction between professionals and families.
- Assessing the family in terms of their experiences in their native country; the role of extended family members and siblings; the amount of community support available; religious, spiritual, and/or cultural beliefs; and parenting practices (e.g., discipline, independence).
- Providing information, written and oral, in ways that enable families to comprehend. Language and communication can be one of the biggest barriers to providing services to families from linguistically diverse groups.

Interpreting Information

For many families of children with special needs, the information given to them about their child's disability can be overwhelming. In particular, medical information can be difficult to understand and interpret. Professionals in special programs are typically the only people families can turn to when deciphering medical, psychological, and insurance reports. Interpreting information in terminology that a family understands is an appropriate role for the professional. Special educators and other school-based professionals may be more available than physicians to families seeking information.

Special educators, particularly school counselors and teachers of students with severe disabilities, can be greatly helped when team members, such as school nurses and public health officials, provide relevant medical information. Additionally, teachers of students with severe disabilities should have access to reference guides (e.g., *Merck Manual; Physicians' Desk Reference;* medical dictionaries; ophthalmology, ontology, anatomy, and physiology textbooks) that may help in the interpretation of medical reports.

The following vignette illustrates the role of the special education professional in translating information and the difficulty that may arise from that role:

Ms. Long, the early intervention teacher, and Mr. Franks, the physical therapist, make a home visit to inform Ms. Hupp, the single parent of Tina, a child with motor disabilities, of a new form of spinal surgery, "selective dorsal root rhizotomy." The PT explains the procedure to Tina's mother in clear terms. The procedure, although still in experimental stages, has significantly reduced hypertonicity in some young children with cerebral palsy. A rhizotomy involves cutting of selected spinal nerves that control the tone of certain muscles in the body. Mr. Franks uses pictures of the spinal area to help illustrate the procedure. Ms. Hupp is grateful for the information but confused about whether to pursue the surgical evaluation. She finally asks the teacher, Ms. Long, what she thinks of the procedure. Ms. Long says she herself is uncomfortable advising the mother on the surgery but refers her to a local physical therapist who has worked with children who have had the rhizotomy surgery. Ms. Long comforts the mother and says she understands how difficult it is for parents to have to make decisions about experimental surgery such as rhizotomy. She asks the mother if there are family members who can help her make the decision and suggests that she speak with the surgeon at length about the procedure's advantages and disadvantages. The mother says she will talk to her sister, call the surgeon, and get back in touch with the PT.

Parents often ask teachers to help them make decisions regarding medical, financial, or personal family matters. Parents who are young, inexperienced, less educated, or from diverse ethnic cultures often turn to school personnel for such help. Although this situation indicates that the parent trusts the professional, professionals may be uncomfortable with advising the parent on decisions involving an issue that is outside of their expertise. Professionals should provide as much information as possible and allow the parents to share their feelings. However, professionals must make it clear that the final decision lies with the family.

Furthermore, professionals are frequently put in the role of interpreting special education information for families who do not speak English or who cannot read. Using interpreters for non-English-speaking families can be a major help. Unfortunately, many interpreters used in the schools are not knowledgeable about special education terminology.

Providing parents with information and support may appear basic to school professionals. However, the task becomes a challenge when families lack basic information on special education, legal, medical, financial, and psychological issues.

Communicating Effectively

As illustrated in the previous section, the importance of being sensitive to the language and culture of parents is a prerequisite to effective communication with families of children with special needs. Other prerequisites exist for developing positive communication between families and professionals. Turnbull and Turnbull (2001) outlined three major skills needed.

1. Professionals must understand themselves and appreciate the personalities and behaviors of others.

2. Professionals and families must have mutual respect for and trust in each other.

3. Both families and professionals must view their relationship as a partnership and work collaboratively.

In their effort to communicate openly with parents, professionals must use good interpersonal communication skills. A comprehensive discussion of interpersonal communication including both verbal and nonverbal skills has been outlined in Chapter 4. When working with families, the professional's most important communication attributes are empathy, genuineness, and unconditional positive regard.

As professionals expand their roles and responsibility in family involvement, they will most likely come across difficult parents, who for various reasons may be angry, resistant, pushy, adversarial, or noncaring. Whitaker and Fiore (2001) warn that professionals may label parents inaccurately based on the parents' behaviors. Parents may be accurate in their feelings and perceptions of certain situations and factors that affect their children. Professionals must not yield to the temptation to blame, compete with, or undermine parents of children with special needs. Those who react to "difficult" parents by becoming defensive and fighting back will soon find that the foundation for developing a partnership will be weak. As mentioned earlier, Whitaker and Fiore, and Kosmoski and Pollack (2000) provide strategies for interacting with angry parents and resolving conflicts.

Communicating with families from diverse cultural and linguistic backgrounds can also be challenging to professionals. Several guidelines have been provided specifically to aid interpersonal communication with diverse families (Barrera & Corso, 2003; Hanson & Lynch, 2004; Kalyanpur & Harry, 1999). In particular, professionals should be sensitive to issues of nonverbal communication (e.g., eye contact, facial expressions, gestures, proximity, touching) among diverse cultural groups.

Professionals must understand that most families have strengths and that many parents are emotionally stronger as a result of having a child with special needs in the family (Barrera & Corso, 2003; Ferguson, 2002; Skinner et al., 1999; Turnbull & Turnbull, 2001). It is critical for professionals to refrain from viewing parents of children with special needs as dysfunctional and to respect their involvement on the educational team. The roles and responsibilities of professionals in creating a positive partnership with families are extensive. Nonetheless, it is not a one-sided association. The next section relates to the family's role in the establishment of the education team.

ROLE OF THE FAMILY

As the term implies, a partnership involves families becoming equal and active in the association with educators. For most families, the role of a collaborative partner is foreign and uncomfortable. Therefore, the responsibility for initiating the partnership may fall on the professional. However, for the relationship to be maintained, the parent must commit to helping professionals meet the unique needs of their children by sharing information, reinforcing school programs at home, asserting and advocating for quality services, and understanding the professionals' role.

Sharing Information

For professionals in special programs to understand their students' educational, medical, and emotional needs, comprehensive information is often required.

The family is usually in the best position to provide teachers and other professionals with such information. First, parents should feel comfortable releasing consent to the schools to obtain medical information on their children, especially in the areas of vision, hearing, and neurological status. If such information takes some time to be received by the professionals, the parent should try to keep the teacher and related service staff informed of any medical information that may indirectly or directly affect the child's physical and educational needs. The following vignette illustrates how one set of parents designed a practical way of informing teachers and other school personnel about the medical and educational history of their child with emotional disabilities:

In September, Mr. and Mrs. Bell, the parents of Michael, a 7-year-old boy with autism, came to school to visit with the special education teacher. Mrs. Bell brought a three-ring notebook with comprehensive information on Michael's disability, divided into five sections: medical, psychiatric, educational, financial, and resources. In addition, the Bells had included yearly pictures of Michael and samples of his drawings and preacademic work. During the conference, the Bells shared information on Michael's last school placement and on current psychiatric reports. The teacher appreciated the information, because she was still waiting for Michael's school folders to be transferred. She was unaware that Michael had been diagnosed with pervasive developmental disorder at the age of 3 and was currently on a strict gluten free/casein free (GFCF) diet. Mr. and Mrs. Bell signed consent for release of information forms for the teacher and left the teacher with copies of the most relevant reports.

In this case, Michael's parents were able to provide professionals with a comprehensive compilation of information on his medical and educational history. To help organize the numerous documents gathered over the years, the Bells assembled a notebook. For parents of children with medical needs and severe disabilities, keeping track of medical and educational information is critical. However, professionals must respect the fact that family history or social work reports may be too sensitive to release. If parents do not provide the teacher with important information, the teacher may become frustrated when trying to obtain the information from physicians, therapists, and other professionals.

Furthermore, families should provide education personnel with their beliefs and values related to child-rearing practices and discipline. Particularly for families from diverse cultural backgrounds, the values they hold about child development, behavior problems, and discipline techniques may be extremely important as educators match services with family concerns, priorities, and needs.

For Mrs. Kim, requiring her child to use an electronic speech communication system was difficult. The educational team had suggested that she encourage her 10-year-old daughter to use the system at home. Mrs. Kim said it was difficult to use the device because she was not fluent in English and the device had been programmed in English only. She also reported that she enjoyed using natural gestures and physical interactions when communicating with her daughter. After consulting with other families from Laos, the teachers realized that independence was not necessarily valued in children under the age of 10. The team adapted the communication program by programming the electronic device to speak in both Hmong and English. Over time, Mrs. Kim saw her daughter's communication skills improve and began to increase the use of the assistive device at home.

Other information parents can provide to teachers involves family activities that may affect the child's behavior or assist in supplementing educational programs. For example, families can tell teachers about vacations; relatives or friends the child cares about; and favorite restaurants, TV shows, or games the family enjoys. Teachers can relate the child's home experiences to educational activities at school. In particular, parents should keep professionals informed of any changes in the health of the child or family situations that may affect emotional behavior.

Reinforcing the School Program at Home

Many families are under added pressures with both parents regularly working outside of the home or single parents needing to work full time. Professionals must understand that parents often have to take care of family priorities before they can attend to school responsibilities. All children need unstructured time with their parents for fun, play, and sharing. It is easy for school personnel to so burden families with "ought to's" that parents feel guilty about taking time to simply play with their children. The parent must be viewed as a parent, not as another teacher.

Professionals can provide parents with intervention programs that can be easily integrated into normal family routines without making the family feel guilty for not being able to spend more time "teaching" their child. If math is an area that teachers think should be reinforced at home, they can ask parents to have their children add items at the grocery store or check the bill at a fast-food restaurant. For children with more severe disabilities, parents and siblings can usually help in activities such as teaching table setting, recognizing photographs of familiar objects, and even stimulating vision or hearing. Only if the family is willing should teachers provide families with sophisticated educational lessons requiring data collection or lengthy practice. Home programs often will not be effective if they are time-consuming or complex.

If possible, parents should try to attend school events involving their child's program. It may be helpful for them to meet and talk with other families. The school can often provide helpful information on various topics. Parents do not attend school meetings for many reasons: they are often scheduled at a time that interrupts work (e.g., 3 P.M.) or during mealtimes, and they take place in school buildings that may be far from home in unfamiliar surroundings. For families from diverse backgrounds, schools may be threatening places: school desks are uncomfortable, no drinks are offered, and babysitting services are not provided. Topics may be of no interest, or they may be subjects that some families consider inappropriate. Speakers may use jargon or present complicated concepts. Professionals and middle-class, Anglo parents may dominate discussions.

Culturally diverse parents who do not attend meetings may actually use their time more effectively at home with their children. Effective programs can be developed by asking a sample of parents from different groups within the school population what topics they want information about, when to schedule meetings, and where to have the meetings. To accomplish this, interpreters may be needed in some locations.

Advocating for Quality Services

As mentioned earlier, the professional who is competent in collaborating with others on the educational team must develop skills in assertive communication. This holds true for parents as well. The traditional role of parents involved in their child's educational program has been either passive, submissive behavior or aggressive, hostile behavior. These behaviors are exhibited in reaction to what families perceive as intimidation and control by school professionals. In turn, submissive or aggressive parental behaviors fail to earn respect from school professionals. Parents as well as professionals need to learn how to communicate effectively, showing respect for others while stating facts and opinions based on evidence in such a way that listeners do not become defensive. Developing skills in advocacy and assertiveness are important for parents and other family members. The responsibility for this preparation can fall on either the school or national parent organizations such as Parent to Parent and Parent Training and Information Centers. The following narrative illustrates why it is important for parents to communicate their expectations and goals assertively to professionals working with their children:

Mrs. Avila, a native Puerto Rican mother of an 18-year-old daughter with mild disabilities, attended an IEP meeting at which her daughter's transition program was discussed. Mrs. Avila was asked if she would consent to her daughter attending a community-based, supported employment work site at a local garden center. Mrs. Avila's first reaction was to ask the professionals if those were realistic expectations for her daughter's future. The transition specialist said it was an excellent opportunity for the daughter and presented retainment statistics and success stories on the work site. Mrs. Avila was intimidated by the professionals and consented to the work transition program without further discussion. During the following 6 months, her daughter became more social and independent at school and at home. She wanted to go out with her friends at the garden center. Mrs. Avila became distressed by her daughters "adult" behavior, concerned that something would happen to her daughter as she gained her independence. She wanted to protect her daughter from any harm, and became angry about the school's decision to place her daughter in the community-based work site. Mrs. Avila did not know how to work with the professionals on changing the transition program, and felt a loss of power and control over her daughter's supported employment program.

Mrs. Avila's situation clearly exemplifies what many families experience when working with professionals. Mrs. Avila believed that it was important to respect educational experts and not question their knowledge or authority. Turnbull and

Turnbull (2001) explained that parents' diminished sense of status and power in decision making is common. Families are usually outnumbered by professionals and made to feel less important in the educational process.

Families should not settle for second best. They should understand the limitations of the school system, but still push for quality programming. Families with skills in assertive communication and knowledge of the IFSP/IEP process are able to represent their child's interest in securing the best possible educational services (Turnbull & Turnbull, 2001). While their child is receiving services, families should remain involved and assertive. They should provide professionals in special programs with regular feedback on the educational program. Telling teachers what their goals, priorities, and expectations are for their child is important. If a problem arises, the parent should respect the chain of command and begin by speaking directly with the professional responsible for the child. If the problem cannot be resolved at that level, the parent should contact the teacher's supervisor, principal, and finally the superintendent for action. Most problems, however, can be resolved when an open, honest relationship exists between families and professionals at the school level.

Understanding the Professional's Perspective

If a collaborative partnership is to be maintained, families must understand the professional's perspective and the limitations the system places on their ability to act. With some insight into school policies such as teacher accountability, teachers' contracts, and teachers' unions, families can begin to understand the conditions under which the teacher functions. Employers, on one hand, expect the teacher to advocate on behalf of the school district. Families, on the other hand, need the teacher to advocate for better services for their children. If there is a conflict in providing the services, the teacher is often caught in between. External mediators serve a critical role in solving conflicts between families and schools.

Schools today are under extreme pressure from state education departments, and many face lawsuits from parents regarding appropriate services for students with special needs. Moreover, state and local communities are under pressure to provide better services with diminishing funds and personnel. Teachers are now under the microscope for ensuring that students pass state standards examinations and are being held accountable for the scores of the children in their classrooms. Families must understand the complexities of school systems and put themselves in the professional's shoes. Many authors provide useful information for both professionals and parents who want to advocate for quality services for children in the areas of due process, conflict resolution, advocacy, and parent involvement (Levin, Villegas, & Wrigley, 1999).

Epstein (1995) has suggested that schools create partnership action teams that focus specifically on family participation and school improvement. She suggests action teams develop 3-year plans that identify the school's strengths, needed areas for change, expectations, and links to student goals.

Parents need to see professionals as people who may become extremely emotionally attached to a child, typically acting as if they were the child's prime experts. Parents must remember that professionals can become protective of students and sometimes may not behave objectively. Professionals with special programs have a vested interest in their students' programs and are committed to getting the best possible services for their students. However, it is sometimes difficult for special education team members to remain completely objective about students. For this reason, both parents and professionals need to balance caring and objectivity.

A professional may wear a cloak of objectivity to hide feelings. But objectivity without caring is not desirable. It is not an error or a weakness to *care* or show authentic feelings; however, it is an error to allow feelings to overcome objectivity. Team members can help each other maintain this delicate balance, rather than scorning the member who errs in either direction. Together parents and professionals can foster an excellent relationship if they remember that the partnership's goal is to improve services to children with special needs.

STRATEGIES FOR SUPPORTING FAMILIES

The major roles and responsibilities of professionals and families have now been outlined. How professionals establish collaborative relationships with families is a concern that education professionals will have for years to come. There are no simple guidelines for involving families in the educational program of their children with special needs. However, Patrikakou, Weissberg, Hancock, Rubenstein, and Zeisz (1997) recommend four essential ingredients to building healthy communication between school and home. These ingredients are the four P's.

1. *Positive.* Remember to communicate praise and encouragement, not just concerns and problems.
2. *Personalized.* Parents will appreciate a personal note jotted on a school memo. Correspondence sent to parents can also be decorated by the student.
3. *Proactive.* Keep parents informed of upcoming events, class rules, school policies, and expectations; also, let them know immediately if there is a problem before it gets more severe.
4. *Partnership.* Encourage parents to respond to school notes by leaving space for comments or having them respond to a few quick questions.

Establishing effective interactions between families and professionals takes a commitment of time, energy, financial resources, and sensitivity from school administrators, direct service providers, and related service personnel. In Figure 7.3, practical strategies to meet the needs of families in special education programs are presented.

1. *Establish an advisory committee with parents and professionals to outline and monitor the "family-professional" goals of the school.* Have the committee follow a systematic plan for implementing parent training, advocacy, and information exchange (Epstein, 1995).

2. *Gather extensive information on the families' concerns, priorities, strengths, and needs.* Use a variety of informal and formal assessment instruments to gather information. Emphasize information gathered through family interviews. For special education teachers, formal psychosocial instruments may be too detailed. Use personal future-planning techniques such as the Making Action Plans (MAPs) to better understand the students' and families' priorities and needs (Falvey, Forest, Pearpoint, & Rosenberg, 1994).

3. *Identify family needs and preferences for school involvement.* The Family Information Preference Inventory (Turnbull & Turnbull, 2001) can be adapted to provide school personnel with information on the needs of parents in the areas of teaching the child at home, advocacy and working with professionals, planning for the future, coping with family stress, and using resources.

4. *Develop school manuals on school policies and procedures, curriculum, and transition.* Manuals for parents are available from many parent organizations such as PACER centers (http://www.pacer.org). However, individualizing manuals for each school district is advantageous because policies and procedures may be different across states, and curriculum, transition, and resource information may be specific to a school district.

5. *Provide parents with videotapes, films, and slide-tape presentations that provide instruction and support to families.* A resource center for such materials has been established by the Young Adult Institute/National Institute for People with Disabilities, 460 West 34th Street, New York, NY 10001. A variety of Internet sites (Early Childhood and Parenting Collaborative Information Technology Group [ECAP/ITG], http://ecap.crc.uiuc.edu/info/; National Information Center for Children and Youth with Disabilities, http://www.nichcy.org/; and National Parent Network on Disabilities, http://www.npnd.org/) provide valuable information for families on educating children with special needs. In addition, establish a materials lending library for families and a toy-lending library for parents of young children.

6. *Involve parents in individual classroom projects.* This may include publishing family recipe calendars in which each family has a favorite recipe printed, or a classroom newsletter in which current activities and news on each student or family can be distributed among the families. Design home-school diaries for the purpose of sharing individual information with families daily or weekly. Include photographs and charts that illustrate examples of the children's progress. Provide a system for distributing feedback on the child's behavior and progress using "happy-grams," a classroom Web page, e-mail, phone calls, or videotape.

7. *Develop a survival vocabulary list in the native language(s) of your families for use with parents and school personnel.* Include basic special education terminology, greetings, body parts, action words, calendar words, and so on. Silberman and Correa (1989) have published a Spanish survival vocabulary list for use with children with physical disabilities and their families.

Continued

Figure 7.3
Strategies for involving families.

269

8. *Provide parents with a current listing of respite care and babysitting services for children with special needs.* Keep a list of other resources on a bulletin board near the entrance of the classroom, such as announcements on family group meetings, weekend workshops, state or national conferences, television programs pertaining to special education, and handouts on preparation for IFSP or IEP meetings.

9. *Include parents* in transition planning; discussing the expectations of the next environment; and issues of inclusion, materials, or equipment necessary for the next environment. Have parents visit potential receiving classrooms, and provide team meetings with both exiting and receiving classroom personnel and families.

10. *Make extra efforts to include hard-to-reach families.* Provide single parents, fathers, and parents who live at a far distance from the school an opportunity to share in their child's learning by organizing activities that do not require them to come to the school building (Unger et al., 2001). Develop school activities that encourage parents to drop by, such as a monthly Donuts for Dad Day when fathers can drop by for breakfast and a visit with their children's teachers, or host a Family Dinner catered by a local restaurant at the school building. Include a Saturday Fall Carnival or have a Parents' Classroom at the school where parents can drop by and check out books and educational materials to take home.

11. *Organize a telephone tree for families in the classroom.* Use the telephone tree to remind parents of upcoming events including classroom learning units, field trips, holiday celebrations, and open-house meetings (Patrikakou et al., 1997).

12. *Communicate personally with the family.* Contact parents at least once a month through e-mail, a phone call, or quick "home note" that suggests ideas for home learning activities (Patrikakou et al., 1997). Provide the parent a place to respond to encourage two-way communication. Periodically, ask parents what the most effective form of communication would be for them.

13. *Encourage school administrators* to design full-service schools (Walker & Hackmann, 1999) that offer wrap-around services for the whole family, including on-site offices for social services, community college courses, child care, and health services.

Figure 7.3
Continued.

APPLICATION

An Individualized Family Service Plan (IFSP) was developed for the family of Rachel, a 2-year-old with special needs. Rachel was premature and evidenced retinopathy of prematurity (retinal damage that left her with very limited vision), motor impairment, and cognitive delays. The development of this plan involved all the skills described in interactive teaming. The parent, Janet Howe, a single mother with two children, was asked to provide the team with goals and needs relevant to her own family.

The parent, early intervention teacher, psychologist, school counselor, and physical therapist attended the initial planning meeting, which took place at the local community child-care center where the early intervention program is located. Ms. Howe began the meeting by stating her perceptions of Rachel's educational needs as well as the family's needs. Table 7.2 is an example of the goals developed based on Ms. Howe's family concerns, priorities, and needs. Ms. Howe and all the team members will meet every 6 months to discuss the IFSP's progress.

Table 7.2
Sample of an Individualized Family Support Plan

Area of Need	Suggested Goals
1. Ms. Howe needs babysitting once a week to attend the infant program's parent support group.	1. The local high school has developed a respite care program for parents in the community who need babysitting or homecare. The group will be contacted to provide Ms. Howe with volunteer babysitting services every week. The early interventionist will consult with the high school volunteer, orienting her to Rachel's special physical and cognitive needs.
2. Ms. Howe wants help in interpreting and understanding the ophthalmologist's reports.	2. The local itinerant vision teacher will be contacted to help Ms. Howe understand the effects of visual impairment on Rachel's overall development. Additionally, the vision teacher will sit down with Ms. Howe and review tape-recorded sessions of Ms. Howe's ophthalmologist visits. The ophthalmologist has agreed to be available to school personnel for added explanation of Rachel's condition on a consultative basis.
3. Ms. Howe is concerned about Rachel's language development. In particular, Rachel is using echolalia when engaged in communication.	3. The early interventionist and physical therapist will consult with the local university speech clinic/laboratory in an effort to improve their skills in early language development. The speech-and-language therapist will conduct a staff development workshop for all the personnel at the early intervention program on how to stimulate language in young children. If necessary, a formal referral will be made to the speech clinic.
4. Ms. Howe reports that her other child, Ricky, age 10, is exhibiting resentment toward Rachel by not helping around the house and refusing to watch Rachel while mother is cooking dinner. Ms. Howe would like some suggestions as to what to do.	4. The school counselor has arranged a sibling support group for brothers and sisters of children with special needs attending the early intervention program. A family therapist, Mr. Dodd, himself a sibling of an adult with special needs, conducts the groups once a month at the child-care center.

SUMMARY

This chapter has presented the issues related to establishing a partnership among professionals and families of children with special needs. Developing a collaborative relationship is not simple.

Professionals and parents must understand their roles and responsibilities in the partnership. The association involves a two-way commitment.

Many families are unable to find the time or energy to get actively involved with the school program. Families may feel powerless and insignificant in their child's education. They may be timid and nonassertive about their feelings, especially if they come from a diverse cultural background.

Professionals must not mistake a family's lack of involvement or shyness as not caring. Instead, they should find creative ways to keep parents informed and make families feel as though the "door is always open" to involvement.

Education professionals clearly serve a role in empathizing with families who are coping with and adjusting to having a child with a disability. They must identify the strengths the family brings to the collaborative relationship.

Providing families with the tools (support services) to cope with the care of a child with special needs becomes the major role of professionals. Support can come from many parts of the family subsystem, but for professionals it includes providing them with information and resources or services for their children.

The professional must view the family as the child's best expert. Families frequently report that professionals make them feel as if they do not understand their own child's problems, although they know and understand their children better than any professional can. Likewise, professionals working with children with special needs have expertise in specialized areas that parents may not realize. The mutual knowledge and expertise of both parents and professionals can be shared, and the result is quality services for children with special needs. Professionals must view the parents as equal and valued team members.

Clearly, professionals today see the value of involving families in the educational process. However, professionals may lack the skills needed to establish the parent-professional relationship. This chapter has attempted to provide education personnel with insight into the skills that are needed for the partnership.

ACTIVITIES

1. Generate a list of informational interview questions to ask families of children with special needs. Make sure the questions are stated in a manner that shows respect for the families. Practice asking the questions in a simulated role-play situation.

2. Make a home visit with someone at the local school (e.g., spe[...] teacher, psychologist, social worker, counselor). Observe how [...] is conducted. Be prepared to ask some general information q[...] the child. For example, ask family members (e.g., parent, sibl[...] family member) to describe things the child likes to do at ho[...]

3. Attend a local community family support group. Observe the group interactions. Write a brief reaction to the meeting, listing the activities that were most effective and those that were least effective during the meeting.

4. Analyze published videotapes on families' reactions to having a child with special needs. Discuss how the videotapes depict the strengths and the needs of the families of children with special needs.

5. Review selected articles from the journal *Exceptional Parent*. Create abstracts for the articles selected for their portrayal of the family experiences associated with caring for a child with special needs.

6. Generate a family-friendly survey for parents to complete prior to an IEP meeting to obtain more information on the parents' perspective.

REFERENCES

Abidin, R. R. (1986). *Parenting stress index* (2nd ed.). Charlottesville, VA: Pediatric Psychology Press.

Bailey, D., Skinner, D., Correa, V., Arcia, E., Reyes-Blanes, M., Rodriguez, P., Vázquez-Montilla, E., & Skinner, M. (1999). Needs and supports reported by Latino families of young children with developmental disabilities. *American Journal on Mental Retardation, 104,* 437–451.

Bailey, D., Skinner, D., Rodriguez, P., Gut, D., & Correa, V. (1999). Awareness, use, and satisfaction with services for Latino parents of young children with disabilities. *Exceptional Children, 65,* 367–381.

Bailey, D. B., Jr., & Simeonsson, R. J. (1988). Assessing the needs of families with handicapped infants. *Journal of Special Education, 22,* 117–127.

Bailey, D. B., Jr., & Simeonsson, R. J. (1990). *Family needs survey.* Chapel Hill: University of North Carolina, Frank Porter Graham Child Development Center, FAMILIES Project.

Barrera, I., & Corso, R. (2003). *Skilled dialogue: Strategies for responding to cultural diversity in early childhood.* Baltimore: Paul H. Brookes.

Baxter, C., Cummins, R. A., & Polak, S. (1995). A longitudinal study of parental stress and support: From diagnosis of disability to leaving school. *International Journal of Disability: Development and Education, 42,* 125–136.

Behar, L., Correa, V. I., & Beverly, C. (1993). *Family functioning analysis of Hispanic families of young children with disabilities: Implications for P. L. 99–457 and personnel preparation.* Manuscript submitted for publication.

Children's Defense Fund. (2002). *The state of children in America's union: A 2002 action guide to leave no child behind.* Washington, DC: Author.

Cho, S., Singer, G. H., & Brenner, M. (2001). Adaptation and accommodation to young children with disabilities: A comparison of Korean and Korean-American families. *Topics in Early Childhood Special Education, 20,* 236–249.

Chrispeels, J., & Rivero, E. (2001). Engaging Latino families for student success: How parent education can reshape parents' sense of place in the education of their children. *Peabody Journal of Education, 76,* 119–169.

Dunst, C. J., Leet, H. E., & Trivette, C. M. (1988). Family resources, personal well-being, and early intervention. *Journal of Special Education, 22*, 108–116.

Dunst, C. J., Trivette, C. M., & Jenkins, B. (1988). Family support scales. In C. Dunst, C. Trivette, & A. Deal (Eds.), *Enabling and empowering families* (pp. 155–157). Cambridge, MA: Brookline Books.

Epstein, J. (1995). School/family/community partnerships: Caring for the children we share. *Phi Delta Kappan, 76*, 701–712.

Falvey, M. A., Forest, M., Pearpoint, J., & Rosenberg, R. (1994). Building connections. In J. S. Thousand, R. A. Villa, & A. L. Nevin (Eds.), *Creativity and collaboration learning: A practical guide to empowering students and teachers* (pp. 347–368). Baltimore: Paul H. Brookes.

Ferguson, P. M. (2002). A place in the family: An historical interpretation of research on parental reactions to having a child with a disability. *Journal of Special Education, 36*, 124–130.

Fields, J. (2003). *Children's living arrangements and characteristics: March 2002.* Current Population Reports, P20-547. Washington, DC: U.S. Census Bureau.

Fields, J., & Casper, L. (2003). *America's families and living arrangements and characteristics: March 2002.* Current Population Reports, P20-537. Washington, DC: U.S. Census Bureau.

Ford, B. A. (1995). African American community involvement processes and special education: Essential networks for effective education. In B. A. Ford, F. Obiakor, & J. Patton (Eds.), *Effective education of African American exceptional learners: New perspectives* (pp. 235–272). Austin, TX: Pro-Ed.

Fox, L., Dunlap, G., & Philbrick, L. A. (1997). Providing individual supports to young children with autism and their families. *Journal of Early Intervention, 21*, 1–14.

Gallimore, R., Weisner, T., Bernheimer, L., & Guthrie, D. (1993). Family responses to young children with developmental delays: Accommodation activity in ecological and cultural context. *American Journal of Mental Retardation, 98*, 185–206.

Garshelis, J. A., & McConnell, S. R. (1993). Comparison of family needs assessed by mothers, individual professionals, and interdisciplinary teams. *Journal of Early Intervention, 17*, 36–49.

Hanson, M., & Lynch, E. (2004). *Understanding families: Approaches to diversity, disability, and risk.* Baltimore: Paul H. Brookes.

Harry, B. (2002). Trends and issues in serving culturally diverse families of children with disabilities. *Journal of Special Education, 36*, 131–138.

Harry, B., Kalyanpur, M., & Day, M. (1999). *Building cultural reciprocity with families: Case studies in special education.* Baltimore: Paul H. Brookes.

Hartman, A. (1978). Diagrammatic assessment of family relationships. *Social Casework, 59*, 465–476.

Heller, T., Markwardt, R., Rowitz, L., & Farber, B. (1994). Adaptations of Hispanic families to a member with mental retardation. *American Journal of Mental Retardation, 99*, 289–300.

Kalyanpur, M., & Harry, B. (1999). *Culture in special education: Building reciprocal family-professional relationships.* Baltimore: Paul H. Brookes.

Kalyanpur, M., Harry, B., & Skrtic, T. (2000). Equity and advocacy expectations of culturally diverse families' participation in special education. *International Journal of Disability, Development, and Education, 47*, 119–135.

Ketelaar, M., Vermeer, A., Helders, P., & Hart, H. (1998). Parental participation in intervention programs for children with cerebral palsy: A review of the research. *Topics in Early Childhood Special Education, 18*, 108–117.

Kosmoski, G., & Pollack, D. (2000). *Managing conversations with hostile adults: Strategies for teachers.* University Park, IL: Governors State University.

Krauss, M. (1993). Child related and parenting stress: Similarities and differences between mothers and fathers of children with disabilities. *American Journal of Mental Retardation, 97*, 393–404.

L'Abate, L., & Bagarozzi, D. A. (1993). *Sourcebook of marriage and family evaluation.* New York: Brunner/Mazel.

Lambie, R. (2000). *Family systems within educational contexts: Understanding at-risk and special-needs students* (2nd ed.). Denver: Love Publishing.

Levin, C., Villegas, A., & Wrigley, J. (1999). *Special education: A guide for parents and advocates* (4th ed.). Portland: Oregon Advocacy Center. Retrieved from http://www.oradvocacy.org/se_guide.htm

Martin, E. J., & Hagan-Burke, S. (2002). Establishing a home-school connection: Strengthening the partnership between families and schools. *Preventing School Failure, 46*, 62–65.

McGrew, K. S., Gilman, C. J., & Johnson, S. (1992). A review of scales to assess family needs. *Journal of Psychoeducational Assessment, 10*, 4–25.

National Coalition for the Homeless. (2001). *Homeless families with children.* Washington, DC: Author. Retrieved December 29, 2003, from http://www.nationalhomeless.org/families.html

National Parent-Teacher Association. (1998). *National standards for parent/family involvement programs* (pp. 7–9). Chicago: Author.

Parette, H., & Petch-Hogan, B. (2000). Approaching families: Facilitating culturally/linguistically diverse family involvement. *Teaching Exceptional Children, 33*, 4–10.

Parette, P., & Huer, M. B. (2002). Working with Asian American families whose children have augmentative and alternative communication needs. *Journal of Special Education Technology, 17*, 5–13.

Patrikakou, E., Weissberg, R., Hancock, M., Rubenstein, M., & Zeisz, J. (1997). *Positive communication between parents and teachers.* Philadelphia, PA: Laboratory for Student Success (LSS). Retrieved from http://www.temple.edu/LSS.

Rao, S. S. (2000). Perspectives of an African American mother on parent-professional relationships in special education. *Mental Retardation, 38*, 475–488.

Seligman, M., & Darling, R. B. (1989). Parent needs survey. In M. Seligman & R. Benjamin Darling (Eds.), *Ordinary families, special children: A systems approach to childhood disability.* New York: Guilford Press.

Silberman, R., & Correa, V. I. (1989). Spanish survival words and phrases for professionals who work with students who are bilingual and severely/multiple handicapped and their families. *Journal of the Division of Physically Handicapped, 10*, 57–88.

Singer, G. H. (2002). Suggestions for a pragmatic program of research on families and disability. *Journal of Special Education, 36*, 148–154.

Skinner, D., Bailey, D., Correa, V., & Rodriguez, P. (1999). Narrating self and disability: Latino mothers' construction of meanings vis-à-vis their child with special needs. *Exceptional Children, 65*, 481–495.

Snow, K. (2001). *Disability is normal.* Woodland Park, CO: Braveheart Press.

Summers, A., Gavin, K., & Purnell-Hall, T. (2003). Family and school partnerships: Building bridges in general and special education. *Advances in Special Education, 15*, 417–444.

Teglasi, H. (1985). Best practices in interpreting psychological assessment data to parents. In A. Thomas & J. Grimes (Eds.), *Best practices in school psychology* (pp. 415–430). Kent, OH: National Association of School Psychologists.

Trotman, M. F. (2001). Involving the African American parent: Recommendations to increase the level of parent involvement within African American families. *The Journal of Negro Education, 70*, 275–285.

Turnbull, A. P., & Turnbull, H. R. (2001). *Families, professionals, and exceptionality: Collaborating for empowerment* (4th ed.). Upper Saddle River, NJ: Merrill Prentice Hall.

U.S. Census Bureau. (1998). *1997 Population Profile of the United States.* Washington, DC: Author.

Unger, D., Jones, C. W., Park, E., & Tressell, P. (2001). Promoting involvement between low-income single caregivers and urban early intervention programs. *Topics in Early Childhood Special Education, 21*, 197–212.

Ulrich, M., & Bauer, A. (2003). Levels of awareness: A closer look at communication between parents and professionals. *Teaching Exceptional Children, 35,* 20–23.

Wagner, M., Spiker, D., & Linn, M. (2002). The effectiveness of the parents as teachers program with low-income parents and children. *Topics in Early Childhood Special Education, 22,* 67–81.

Walker, J. D., & Hackmann, D. G. (1999). Full-service schools: Forming alliances to meet the needs of students and families. *NASSP Bulletin, 83,* 28–37.

Wathum-Ocama, J., & Rose, S. (2002). Hmong immigrants views of the education of their deaf and hard of hearing children. *American Annals of the Deaf, 147,* 44–53.

Whitaker, T., & Fiore, D. (2001). *Dealing with difficult parents: And with parents in difficult situations.* Larchmont, NY: Eye on Education.

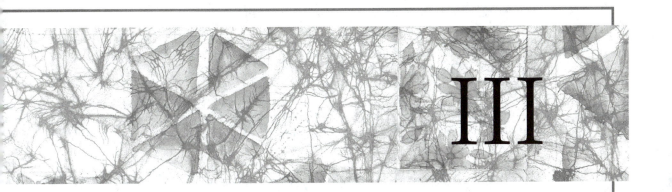

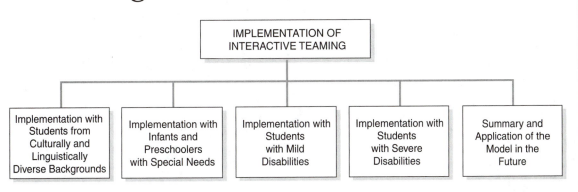

Implementation of Interactive Teaming

OVERVIEW

In Part II, the facilitating factors contributing to the effective implementation of interactive teaming were examined. All the factors described affect in various ways the implementation of services for students who are at risk or have one or multiple disabilities.

Regardless of the category or label of students, all interactive teams operate within a common framework of problem identification, intervention design and implementation, and evaluation of effectiveness. Other similarities include the necessity of collaboration among all members, role release in the sharing and use of the professional expertise of others, and the need for constant and clear communication among team members so that comprehensive and coordinated services can be provided to children and adolescents with special needs.

Some differences among the categories also exist. The roles of team members will vary in scope, levels of involvement, and the amounts and forms of direct (i.e., teaching) and indirect (i.e., consultation) services provided. In addition, there may be differences in the educational focus, such as academics versus self-care skills, and in the types of interventions that team members design and implement.

Chapter 8 examines implementation with culturally diverse students. Chapter 9 explains how interactive teaming can be implemented and delineates considerations and roles of service providers working with infants and preschoolers with special needs. Chapters 10 and 11 describe the implementation of interactive teaming with both students with mild and severe disabilities, respectively. Each chapter presents student characteristics, considerations for meeting educational needs, and a description of professional roles. The concluding chapter is comprised of a summary and extended case study illustrating the implementation of the interactive teaming model. Current trends and promising practices for the future also are included.

Implementation with Students from Culturally and Linguistically Diverse Backgrounds

Topics in this chapter include:

◆ The various educational needs of students from diverse backgrounds.

◆ Teaching strategies for working with students from diverse backgrounds.

◆ The unique roles of professionals working with students from diverse backgrounds.

◆ An application for team involvement in educational planning for students from diverse backgrounds.

Helena, a 10-year-old Salvadoran child, has become a problem for her fourth-grade teacher, Ms. Harris. She has been in the United States for 8 months and is receiving English instruction from Mrs. Garcia, the ESL (English as a second language) teacher. However, Ms. Harris reports that Helena is distracted during the day; she is not paying attention in class and cannot complete even the simplest first-grade worksheets. She has also observed the other children in her fourth-grade class teasing her and calling her names. She understands that Helena's parents are Spanish speakers and, because she does not speak Spanish, has not communicated directly with the family. Ms. Harris reports that she has adapted instruction to implement a token reward system for compliance, but Helena continues to fall behind in her academics and social interactions. She suspects Helena may have a learning disability that warrants special education services. Ms. Harris has told the school psychologist that she feels it would be best for Helena to be placed in a resource room for most of the day with ESL pull-out.

Frustrated with the situation, Ms. Harris has decided to let Helena work independently during the day and no longer requires her to participate in class lessons or student group projects. She has decided to wait until the prereferral and referral process is completed and does not seek any help from other professionals.

The education of students and families from linguistically and culturally differ-ent backgrounds in today's public schools is a critical and specialized area within general education and special education because of the dramatically chang-ing demographics of the United States. Large numbers of foreign-born and U.S.-born children from culturally diverse populations are entering public schools. Although this chapter focuses on students from ethnically or linguistically diverse backgrounds, it is important to note that today a broader definition of cultural di-versity must be understood. The word *culture* is used here in its broadest sense. It includes any group of people with a common set of values and a language. "Cul-ture represents the encompassing expression of a person's life . . . that subsumes racial and ethnic rituals, symbols, language, and general ways of behaving" (Dilworth-Anderson, Burton, & Johnson, 1993, p. 628). Culture provides the blueprint that de-termines who we are: how we think, feel, and behave (Gollnick & Chinn, 2001). Culture is also dynamic and ever changing as people learn to accommodate their environmental conditions. We often associate culture with surface characteristics such as food, behavior, dress, or language. However, to understand the true com-plexities of culture, we must see the deeper aspects of culture such as the group's worldviews, beliefs, and values (Barrera, Corson, & Macpherson, 2003).

Some might assume that any discussion about *cultural diversity* relates to His-panic, African American, Native American, or Asian groups (the groups most often given the term *minority*). However, for purposes of this chapter, cultural diversity can encompass groups such as the Amish, Mormons, Appalachians, armed forces, homosexuals, and the homeless. These groups often are underrepresented in dis-cussions of diversity. Although some of these groups may experience less economic or political subordination and may be more assimilated to the dominant culture (Gollnick & Chinn, 2001), they still possess distinct group identity and should be re-spected for their diversity. Overlooking the influences culture has on students and families who are not of color, have not immigrated to the United States, do not have an ethnic surname, or do not speak a native language other than English is an error in understanding cultural diversity.

Many students live in situations that may place them at risk for school discrimination or school failure. Some of these at-risk situations include the following:

◆ Students who are gay or lesbian.

◆ Students who come from migrant families.

◆ Students who live in poor inner city or rural areas.

◆ Students who have immigrated to the United States.

◆ Students who are homeless.

◆ Students who have HIV or AIDS.

◆ Students who are victims of child abuse or live in violent environments.

◆ Students who live with relatives, guardians, or foster parents.

◆ Students who are latchkey and unsupervised at home. (Salend, 2000)

The interactive team of professionals working with this special population must have a strong knowledge base in understanding differences (e.g., cultural, linguistic, religious, environmental, lifestyle) and in preparing these students for successful experiences in inclusive general education. Educators who do not understand the similarities and differences among and within groups can inadvertently marginalize students from diverse backgrounds from the dominant group, often resulting in lower expectations of students and poor educational outcomes for students. Professionals must develop cultural competence and culturally responsive practices when working with these students and their families.

The vignette about Helena is an example of what might happen if professionals are not sensitive to the special needs of students from diverse cultures and if collaboration with other professionals is not sought. Ms. Harris should have contacted other professionals for consultation on Helena's learning and behavioral problems. With the help of other professionals knowledgeable about Salvadoran students, an appropriate assessment of the situation and plan of action could have been implemented.

The purpose of this chapter is to highlight the specific needs of students from culturally and linguistically diverse backgrounds and to delineate the various roles of the professionals working with these students. First, a brief overview of cultural and linguistic differences will illustrate characteristics of students from culturally and linguistically diverse backgrounds. Some of these students are English language learners (ELLs), which may put them at risk for poor academic achievement or special education services. Second, a short discussion of the educational needs of students from culturally and linguistically diverse backgrounds is presented to suggest various service delivery options available for these students. Within the description of the educational needs of these students, assessment techniques and modified teaching strategies used for students from diverse backgrounds will be delineated. Third, the role of the professionals involved in the education of students from culturally and linguistically diverse backgrounds is presented. Cultural insensitivities can be found in all aspects of educating students from diverse backgrounds. The key to overcoming these insensitivities is to have a culturally competent interactive team available for instruction and collaboration.

UNDERSTANDING THE NEEDS OF STUDENTS FROM CULTURALLY AND LINGUISTICALLY DIVERSE BACKGROUNDS

Students from culturally diverse populations often experience academic under-achievement, high retention rates, high dropout rates, and are at risk for placement into special education due in part to their linguistic differences, their culturally determined behavioral characteristics, and their socioeconomic status (Artiles, Aguirre-Munoz, & Abedi, 1998; Artiles, Trent, & Palmer, 2004; Daugherty, 2001; Donavan & Cross, 2001; Gollnick & Chinn, 2001; Ortiz, 2000; Patton, 1998; Simon, 2001). If placed in special education, they are often not provided support in their native language, which can have an even greater effect on their linguistic and academic development (Barrera et al., 2003; Gersten & Baker, 2000; Ortiz, 2000). Students from cultural and linguistic backgrounds who receive special education services are more likely than White students to be removed from the general education classroom for all or part of their school day (Fierros & Conroy, 2002). Additionally, some students from culturally and linguistically diverse backgrounds are underrepresented in programs for gifted students (Daniels, 2001; Patton, 1997). Although the dilemma of disproportionality of students from culturally diverse backgrounds is complex and controversial, it is important to note that the interactive team plays a key role in reducing inappropriate placements in special education programs (Artiles & Ortiz, 2002; Donovan & Cross, 2001; Oswald & Coutinho, 2001). Errors in referrals to special education begin with the general education teacher and proceed to the prereferral and referral process. Bias in assessment and poor assessment procedures can place students from culturally diverse backgrounds or English language learners on a track to special education that may not be reversible.

The interactive team is responsible for distinguishing actual learning problems and giftedness from problems associated with learning English as a second language (ESL) or other linguistic differences; being in the process of acculturation to the dominant, middle-class Anglo school culture; or lacking educational experiences because of impoverished home environments. The following sections discuss characteristics that may be associated with students from diverse backgrounds. However, it is important to emphasize that the following descriptions of diverse students are not stereotypical of these students' overall personal characteristics. Regardless of the cultural background from which students come, each should be regarded as an individual possessing unique traits and strengths that must be considered if adequate educational services are to be provided.

Culture is a dynamic process that is full of changes. Students and their families from culturally and/or linguistically diverse backgrounds change as they come into contact with the dominant culture and their community's culture. Glenn (1989) warns that "we need an approach to education that takes seriously the *lived culture* of children and their families, not the fiestas and folklore that had meaning for their grandparents but are not part of the lives of families coming to terms with the losses and gains of immigration" (p. 779). Therefore, professionals must not assume that culture is an imprint that can be used with all individuals from that culture. To say that a child from Cuba lives the Cuban culture, thinks a certain way, and experiences a family structure particular to Cubans would be wrong. Given these cautions, the following sections outline characteristics that may place the student at risk for receiving appropriate educational services.

Language Characteristics

Many students from culturally diverse backgrounds have linguistic differences that affect their ability to succeed in an English-dominant school system. It is often critical to understand these linguistic differences so that professionals can accurately discriminate an actual language disorder from the natural progression of *second language acquisition* and acculturation. All aspects of language and speech development must be considered. These students often exhibit the usual problems associated with learning a second language, such as poor comprehension, limited vocabulary, grammatical and syntactical mistakes, and articulation difficulties (Bennett, 2003; Brice, 2002; Peregoy & Boyle, 2001).

There is evidence that many linguistically diverse students are identified as having a language disorder, usually related to articulation, when in fact they are exhibiting normal characteristics of second language acquisition (Brice, 2002; von Hapsburg & Pena, 2002). Table 8.1 outlines the stages of second language acquisition described by Clarke (1991) as cited in Winzer and Mazurek (1994). Therefore, it is critical for professionals working with students who are English language learners to know the differences between an actual language disorder and that of second language acquisition. A child who has a language disorder will evidence the problem in the native language as well. For example, a Hispanic child who has a problem with the omission of initial sounds will say "mida" for *comida* (food) or "anjo" for *banjo* (bathroom). Assessing students in their native language becomes a critical component of a culturally responsive educational process.

Furthermore, students learning a second language learn basic interpersonal communication skills (BICS) more easily than cognitive/academic language proficiency (CALPS; Cummins, 1994; Kader & Yawkey, 2002). Social language usually develops within 2 years; however, cognitive and academic language could take up to 5 to 7 years to learn, requiring extended instruction in the students' native language.

Additionally, students who speak with a *nonstandard dialect*, but are competent in English, frequently are discriminated against by professionals and peers (Delpit, 1995; Delpit & Dowdy, 2002; Gollnick & Chinn, 2001; Manning & Baruth, 2000; Salend, 2000). For example, it is estimated that between 80% and 90% of African Americans

Table 8.1

The Stages of Second Language Acquisition

Stage 1: Early Phase (Preproduction)

- May make contact with another child in the group.
- May show a silent period but use nonverbal gestures to indicate meaning, particularly needs, dislikes, and likes.
- Watches other children and may repeat words and phrases.
- May join others in a repetitive story or song.
- Responds to actions of songs.

Stage 2: Early Production, Emergence of Speech

- Starts to name other objects and other children; uses single verbs such as *come, look, go,* and adverbs such as *here* and *there.*
- Begins to put words together into phrases such as "Where find it?" or "Me put it."
- Enjoys sharing activities with children who speak a common language.
- May choose to speak only in the first language.
- Responds to stories, poems, and rhymes in English.

Stage 3: Familiarity with English

- Shows confidence in using English.
- Shows ability to move between the first and the second language.
- Can join conversations in English with peers.
- Shows confidence in taking part in small groups with staff and other children.
- Begins to sort out small details, such as *he* and *she* distinctions.
- More interested in communicating meaning than in grammatical correctness.
- Understands more English than he or she uses.
- Expands vocabulary for naming objects and events; begins to describe in more detail, such as by color, size, and quantity; uses simple adverbs.
- Shows confidence in initiating interaction.
- Continues to rely on support and friends.

Stage 4: Becoming Confident in English

- Shows great confidence in using English in most social situations; enjoys having fun with language.
- Has growing command of the grammatical system of English, including complex verbal meanings and more complex sentence structures.
- Uses pronunciation very like that of a native speaker.
- Has an extensive vocabulary.
- Continues to use own first language in groups.

Source: From *Special Education in Multicultural Contexts* (p. 360), by M. Winzer and K. Mazurek, 1994, Upper Saddle River, NJ: Merrill/Prentice Hall. Reprinted by permission.

in the United States use some form of Black English (Smitherman, 2000). Some researchers believe that African American Vernacular English (AAVE) or Ebonics is a valid language that is not inferior but simply linguistically different, like other dialects (Adger, Christian, & Taylor, 1999; Anokye, 1997; Craig, Thompson, Washington, & Potter, 2003; Smitherman, 2000). Latino, Native American, and African American students with nonstandard English dialects might be considered inferior by classmates and teachers. Teachers may have negative attitudes toward students and lowered expectations of these students' linguistic abilities. This comes at a time when the use of nonstandard English dialect among the youth culture is becoming more popular (Salend, 2000, Smitherman, 2000). Many may be referred to special education merely because the professionals believe that nonstandard English dialects convey an inability to function in a general education classroom. Professionals should respect these students and encourage bidialectal use of language, teaching students when to use standard English and when to use other dialects (Delpit & Dowdy, 2002; McWhorter, 2000; Salend, 2000; Smitherman, 2000).

Cultural Characteristics

Various learning and behavioral characteristics associated with students from culturally diverse populations are provided in this section. In general, professionals should avoid negative stereotypes or overgeneralizations when considering this information. There is, however, sufficient literature to support the differences in children's learning and behavioral styles, depending on their socioeconomic backgrounds and the individual child's cultural dominance.

Learning Styles.   Many authors have written about the diverse learning styles of students. Although no particular style fits a particular cultural group, it is important to know that students may need multiple approaches to learning. In particular, students from multicultural backgrounds may require special attention when matching the teaching style with their individual learning styles (Alder, 2000; Bennett, 2003).

According to Salend (2000), dimensions of learning styles instruction include the following:

◆ Environmental considerations such as background noise levels, lighting, temperature, and seating arrangements.
◆ Emotional considerations such as individual levels of motivation, persistence, conformity, responsibility, and need for structure.
◆ Grouping considerations such as learning alone or in groups, and with or without adults present.
◆ Physical considerations such as learning modality preferences, time of day, and need for food, drink, and mobility while learning.
◆ Psychological considerations such as approaching a task globally or analytically.

Salend (2000) described high-context cultures as those in which cooperation is encouraged, time schedules are flexible, and less authoritarian approaches are emphasized. In a low-context culture, competition, individualization, and strict adherence to time are the norm.

The current dominant middle-class culture of schools must be flexible enough to accommodate the diverse learning styles of all students, including students from diverse cultures. Alternative learning environments have been recommended for culturally diverse students (Bennett, 2003; Gollnick & Chinn, 2001; Ortiz, 2000; Salend, 2000). Classroom environments should include activities that are group negotiated, student-directed, noncompetitive, and cooperative. Activities that actively involve students in the learning process—such as field trips, art projects, and experience stories—would provide a better match for the needs of high-context learners. Educators should recognize that students must see themselves in the curriculum. Culturally and linguistically responsive instruction allows students to bring their life experiences, language, culture, norms and values, and physical attributes to the forefront of their school experiences (Blair, 2003; Gay, 2000; Taylor, 2000).

The learning styles of students also have been described as falling into two areas: (1) *field-dependent behavior* and (2) *field-independent behavior* (Bennett, 2003; Gollnick & Chinn, 2001). Field-dependent learners are concerned with the social environment. They react to support or doubt from others, prefer more personal relationships with teachers, and work cooperatively with others. Field-independent learners are task oriented, more independent of external judgment, prefer formal relationships with teachers, and work independently and for individual recognition.

For students who evidence field-dependent behaviors, teaching should more closely relate to a personalized and humanized curriculum that emphasizes the students' interests and experiences. Teachers should display physical and verbal expressions of approval and warmth together while providing lessons that encourage cooperation, informal class discussions, and the development of group feelings. A balance between both field-independent and field-dependent curricula should be maintained by professionals when working with students from diverse cultural and linguistic backgrounds. Educators must realize that no two students are alike and, therefore, teaching approaches must be based on individual student needs rather than on stereotyped learning styles.

Behavioral Styles.   Culturally and linguistically different students are often referred to special education because of certain behavioral characteristics that appear abnormal in U.S. classrooms (Hoover & Collier, 1985, 1991; Ishii-Jordan, 1997; McIntyre, 1999; Peterson & Ishii-Jordan, 1994). However, the behaviors exhibited by students from different cultures may be culturally appropriate in their native culture or may be normal reactions in the process of adjusting to culture shock or acquiring a second language.

Uri, a newly arrived 15-year-old Chechen student, has been referred to the school psychologist for counseling. His teacher describes Uri as severely withdrawn; he does not make eye contact or speak to her when she talks to him. She is concerned that Uri may be unable to survive in the general education classroom. The school psychologist contacts the social worker for the state Department of Human Resources. Uri was recently placed in foster care. Before his arrival in the United States, he had been living in a refugee camp with other Chechen orphan children. Although Uri's records did not clearly state his history, it was suspected that Uri had been traumatized by the war and was experiencing post-traumatic stress disorder. He arrived severely malnourished and with little if any educational experience.

An interactive team will need to collaborate with people who have recently immigrated from Chechnya to obtain information that might provide them with some insight into Uri's withdrawn behavior. Providing Uri with a school buddy and contacting a local college student who studied Russian and Chechen to volunteer to work with Uri a few hours a week might reduce Uri's anxiety and resistance to the school environment. Careful follow-up of Uri's classroom behavior and close interactions with Uri's foster parents should be carried out by all team members. If his behavior does not change after school counseling and tutoring intervention programs have been implemented in the general education classroom, a referral would be warranted.

Professionals working with culturally diverse students must obtain information about the conditions in which these students have lived. Many abnormal behaviors, including withdrawal, defensiveness, disorganization, and aggression, may be attributed to various sociocultural influences (Hoover & Collier, 1985; Ishii-Jordan, 1997; McIntyre, 1999). A report by the United Nations Children's Fund (UNICEF) estimated that 10 million children worldwide suffer psychological trauma from wars (cited in Sutton-Redner, 2002). Students adjusting to being refugees of war-torn countries and entering a new culture will most probably experience some degree of social trauma and emotional problems (Lynch & Hanson, 1998; Sutton-Redner, 2002), often described as post-traumatic stress disorders (Kinchin, 2001).

Working closely with family members, the team can begin to ameliorate the impact of culture shock often associated with immigration (Foner, 1997; Lynch & Hanson, 1998). Interactive teams also can carefully conduct functional behavioral analyses over time to separate the more subtle behaviors of second language acquisition and cultural adjustment from behaviors related to emotional problems (Ishii-Jordan, 1997; McIntyre, 1999; Ortiz & Yates, 2002).

Socioeconomic Characteristics

Some culturally and linguistically diverse students who have had extensive training in both public and private schools are from middle-class or upper-class families. A large percentage of culturally and linguistically diverse students come from poor homes and have had little preparation for school (Gay, 2000; Gollnick & Chinn, 2001; Salend, 2000; Winzer & Mazurek, 1994). Although the poverty rate had decreased by the end of the 1990s, the child poverty rate remained significantly higher than the rates for working-age adults and the elderly (U.S. Census Bureau, 2002). In 2001, 11.7 million children, or 16.3%, were poor. Children continue to represent a large share of the poor population (36%) even though they only make up about 26% of the total general population; there is also an increase of children who now fall under the "extreme poverty" line (i.e., living below half of the poverty line; Children's Defense Fund, 2001).

In 2001, approximately 11.7% of the U.S. population lived in poverty, while 21.4% of Hispanics and 22.7% of Blacks were poor. By comparison, 9.9% of Whites and 10.2% of Asians and Pacific Islanders were poor (U.S. Census Bureau, 2002). Table 8.2 illustrates the impact of child poverty on America.

Furthermore, it is estimated that more than 615,336 children are homeless and about 12% of the homeless students K–12 are not attending school (National Center for Homeless Education, 2003). "Half of the homeless are now families, and one-third of the residents of homeless shelters are children" (Gollnick & Chinn, 2001, p. 46). These students suffer from poor health, have no transportation to school, and do not retain important records and forms for school files. Many poor and culturally different students have been placed in special education or have dropped out of school (Gollnick & Chinn, 2001; Salend, 2000). Dropout rates for migrant students are estimated to be between 34% and 50% (Office of Migrant Education, 2002). It is estimated that the dropout rate for special education students is 50% higher than the average 25% rate for all students in the United States. According to the latest Pew Hispanic Center report, non-Hispanic Blacks and Hispanics are more likely to drop out of high school than are non-Hispanic Whites. In 2001, 7% of Whites ages 16 to 24 were not enrolled in school and had not completed high school, while 11% of non-Hispanic Blacks and 27% of Hispanics had dropped out. The high dropout rates for Hispanics is in part the result of the high proportion of immigrants in this age group who never attended school in the United States (Fry, 2003). In recent years, progress to combat dropout rates has been effective mostly with African Americans.

Some professionals view the lack of achievement by poor students as a problem inherent in the student, and they often assume that the families have failed to prepare their children for school and do not teach them the value of education (Gay, 2000; Manning & Baruth, 2000; Nieto, 2000). Teachers may fail to recognize that economic differences affect cognitive and learning styles of students, causing them to respond

Table 8.2

Impact of Poverty on America's Children

- Poor children's troubles include increased risk of stunted growth, anemia, repeated years of schooling, lower test scores, and less education, as well as lower wages and lower earnings in their adult years.
- Poverty is a greater risk to children's overall health status than is living in a single-parent family.
- A baby born poor is less likely to survive to its first birthday than a baby born to an unwed mother, a high school dropout, or a mother who smoked during pregnancy.
- Poverty puts children at a greater risk of falling behind in school than does living in a single-parent home or being born to teenage parents.
- Reasons for poor children's problems appear to include their families' inability to afford adequate housing, nutritious food, or adequate child care, as well as lead poisoning, limited learning opportunities at home, and severe emotional stress and family breakup caused by economic strains on the parents.

Source: From *Poverty Matters: The Cost of Child Poverty in America* (p. 1), by Arloc Sherman, Washington, DC: Children's Defense Fund, 1997. Reprinted by permission.

differently to instruction (Artiles & Ortiz, 2002; Gollnick & Chinn, 2001; Salend, 2000). Further, studies have shown that teachers pay more attention to students who are attractive, well dressed, and well behaved, whereas they may ignore or discriminate against students who may have unwashed and worn clothing or who are not so well groomed (Delpit, 1995; Delpit & Dowdy, 2002; Gay, 2000; Harry, 1992). Incidences of racism still exist in schools. Murray and Clark (1990) identified the following eight patterns of racism in school: hostile and insensitive acts toward others; bias in the use of punishment; bias in giving attention to students; bias in curriculum materials; inequality in the amount of instruction; bias in attitudes toward students; failure to employ educational professionals from various cultural backgrounds; and denial of racist acts. Obviously, the attitudes of educators must change if students from poor environments and from culturally and linguistically diverse backgrounds are to survive in school.

Several authors provide alternative ways to frame the problem of poor and at-risk students in schools today (Delpit, 1995; Delpit & Dowdy, 2002; Gay, 2000; Ladson-Billings, 1997, 2001; Nieto, 2000). They state that the reason students fail in school is that the school culture ignores and devalues the students' own cultural backgrounds and seldom adapts to students' individual differences. The need for reforming schools to accommodate the special needs of students from poor and culturally diverse populations is urgent. Around the nation many school leaders are recognizing the need for more family and community input, teacher-run schools, alternative schools, dropout prevention programs, and other innovative ways to adapt to the changing school population. Manning and Baruth (2000) and Bennett (2003) provide examples of promising practices in multicultural education, including suggestions for effective curriculum development, assessment alternatives, community and family programs, and instructional practices. Innovative programs are crucial to the success of culturally and linguistically diverse students in today's schools.

MEETING EDUCATIONAL NEEDS

A major function of the team serving students from culturally and linguistically diverse backgrounds is to prepare these students for acculturation to the dominant American culture without unwarranted stripping away of their linguistic and cultural characteristics. Many researchers believe that children should strive to develop bicultural competence by having the ability, the volition, and the capacity to negotiate comfortably two sets of cultural assumptions, patterns, beliefs, and behaviors (Delpit, 1995; Delpit & Dowdy, 2002; Gollnick & Chinn, 2001). Children who comfortably "code-switch" between the home dialect on the playground and standard English in the classroom are practicing bicultural competence. Each member of the interactive team must work cooperatively to assess and develop intervention programs that prepare students for their roles in their native community as well as the larger dominant communities. The educational needs of students from culturally and linguistically diverse backgrounds are complex in the areas of service delivery options, assessment, program design, and teacher competencies. The following section addresses these needs.

Service Delivery Options

Various service delivery models are being used with students from culturally and linguistically diverse backgrounds. Most schools are providing students who are English language learners with alternative programs such as bilingual education (use of native language and English) or *English as a second language* (use of English only). Although very controversial, bilingual education programs have been criticized as holding students back from learning English; some research indicates that students taught in an English-only immersion program perform better academically than students in a transitional program (Porter, 1997). Others report successful gains in English language and academic skills with bilingual programs (Baca & Cervantes, 1998; Genesee & Cloud, 1998; Thomas & Collier, 1998). However, if the English language learner evidences learning problems warranting special education, a combination of language and special education services must be provided. Preferably, ESL and special education services should be provided using a consultant teacher assistance model within an inclusive general education classroom.

Perhaps the most important issue is to find a set of program components that works well in a given unique community or school (August & Hakuta, 1997). Keeping a student in the general education classroom for the majority of his or her instruction is the goal for inclusion, and pull-out programs such as bilingual education, ESL, or special education should be kept to a minimum (Walther-Thomas, Korinek, McLaughlin, & Williams, 2000). It is the responsibility of the transdisciplinary team to work collaboratively to provide integrated service for students in the inclusive classroom. Methods for successful inclusion have been described by Salend (2000) and Baca and Cervantes (1998).

Assessment and Curricular Design

The most startling effect of cultural and linguistic differences on children occurs when professionals assume that students from culturally and linguistically diverse backgrounds appear to be developmentally delayed, learning disabled, emotionally disabled, or mentally disabled (Artiles & Ortiz, 2002; Artiles & Zamora-Duran, 1997; Harry, 1992, 1994; MacMillan & Reschly, 1998; Oswald & Coutinho, 2001; Salend, 2000). As mentioned previously, overrepresentation of culturally and linguistically diverse students in special education has been extensively reported. The issues are complex and specifically involve judgmental or biased decisions in the prereferral and referral process along with inappropriate assessment procedures (Figueroa, 2002; MacMillan & Reschly, 1998; Ortiz & Yates, 2002).

Students from diverse backgrounds taking standardized tests are hindered by their native language, their lack of familiarity with the tests' content and with test-taking skills, and possible bias of test administrators when attempting to understand the social and cultural factors associated with the assessment process (Salend, 2000). The school psychologist is in a particularly sensitive position when it comes to the use of standardized assessment instruments to place students from culturally and linguistically diverse backgrounds in special programs. This professional, more than any other team member, needs to take special care in assessing students using procedures for measuring first and second language proficiency, examining achievement and intelligence testing in students' primary languages, and documenting students' language use in natural environments (Rueda, 1997).

By not understanding the cultural values of students and their families, professionals may erroneously assess students' abilities, refer them to special education, and implement special programs ineffectively. Conversely, a professional who believes a student's learning difficulties are related only to the child's adjustment to the dominant culture may underestimate a true learning problem. Teachers in general, special, ESL, and bilingual education, together with speech and language professionals, and school psychologists must understand the cultural and linguistic context of the student's behavior and language when they observe the child to determine whether a true learning problem exists. Good observations of the child's behavior and native language in school and at home will help the professionals make these difficult decisions. Teamwork is critical in this process. Table 8.3 provides guidelines for team members when deciding whether the student's problems are related to lack of academic support, second language acquisition, cultural differences, or other student characteristics. Collaboration with families, communities, and related service professionals will be necessary for making an appropriate special education placement decision.

Many of the standardized tests are available in Spanish, but few are available in other languages, such as Haitian Creole, Russian, Vietnamese, Korean, Chinese, or Japanese. These languages are prevalent in schools with a high enrollment of culturally diverse students. However, caution should be taken in using translated tests. There is little empirical evidence that dual-language versions of tests are psychometrically valid (Figueroa & Hernandez, 2000; Olson & Goldstein, 1997). Readers are referred to recent publications (Figueroa, 2002; Hakuta & Beatty, 2000; Ortiz & Yates, 2002) for further guidance in selecting assessment and curriculum instruments.

Additionally, other forms of evaluation are necessary with this population. Informal assessment procedures—including authentic assessment, portfolio assessment, sampling language, direct observation, anecdotal records, videotapes, and writing samples—have been extremely effective in providing the interactive team with information on the culturally diverse students' abilities (Ortiz & Yates, 2002; Reschly, Tilly, & Grimes, 2000; Rueda, 1997). Procedures for collecting oral *language samples* usually involve tape-recording a sample of the student's conversations for 15 to 30 minutes on three occasions. A language sample provides the education

Table 8.3
Guidelines to Help the Team Rule Out Factors Other Than the Presence of a Disability
as the Source of Difficulties

- In addition to the general education teacher, have others (e.g., the ESL teacher, remedial program personnel, and parents) noted similar difficulties?
- Does the problem exist across contexts (e.g., in general education and ESL classes, at school, and at home)? For example, if the student acts out in class, do the parents report similar behavior at home?
- Are the problems evident in the student's first language? For example, do native speakers of the students' language have difficulty understanding him or her? Does the student have difficulty following instructions in the native language as well as in English? Has the student not learned to read in the native language, despite effective literacy instruction in that language?
- Is the student's progress in acquiring English significantly different from that of peers who started at about the same level of English language proficiency and have had comparable instruction?
- Is there evidence that difficulties can be explained by cross-cultural differences? For example, a lack of eye contact, which a teacher might interpret as defiance, could be considered appropriate behavior in the child's native culture, or a student's narrative patterns might reflect patterns typical of storytelling in the home culture.
- Are there other variables that could explain the difficulties? Such variables might include inconsistent school attendance or language variations typical of English language learners.
- Is there evidence of extreme test anxiety (as can occur when the child being tested has been in the country for only a short time)?
- Can problematic behaviors be explained by procedural mistakes in the assessment process (e.g., the child's age was calculated incorrectly)?
- Can problematic behaviors be explained by bias in operation before, during, or after the assessments? For example, bias is an issue when the student's teacher refers all English language learners in the classroom for special education, when the instruments used are not normed for English language learners or the adaptations used are inappropriate, and when the assessor's low expectations for student performance influence the administration and interpretation of results.
- Do data show that the student did not respond well to general education intervention? For example, were clinical teaching, support team interventions, and alternative programs unsuccessful in closing achievement gaps?
- Are the assessment results consistent with the concerns of the student's teacher and parents?

Source: From "Considerations in the Assessment of English Language Learners Referred to Special Education," by A. Ortiz and J. Yates, 2002, in A. Artiles and A. Ortiz (Eds.), *English Language Learners with Special Education Needs: Identification, Assessment, and Instruction* (pp. 80–82). McHenry, IL: Delta Systems.

professional with data on aspects of the student's language such as subject-verb agreement, past and future tenses, and vocabulary. It also samples the child's knowledge of various experiences within his or her own cultural and linguistic framework. Written language samples provide information about students' level of achievement in writing ability. Samples should be taken in both the students' own language and English. Analysis of the samples provides a basis both for assessment of students' skills and for planning instructional programs.

Instructional Strategies

A number of instructional strategies have been reported to be effective with students from culturally and linguistically diverse backgrounds (Baca & Cervantes, 1998; Banks, 1999; Banks & McGee Banks, 2004; Cloud, 2002; Gersten & Jiménez, 1998; Goldstein, 2002; Manning & Baruth, 2000; Putnam, 1998; Salend, 2000; Santamaría, Fletcher, & Bos, 2002). The basic components for teaching culturally diverse students are the same components used for teaching *all* students. Good instruction is good instruction, regardless of the recipient. Effective teaching strategies reflect the students' experiences and cultural perspectives. Often referred to as culturally responsive pedagogy, this approach recognizes the importance of including students' cultural references in all aspects of learning (Ladson-Billings, 2001); see Figure 8.1.

---

1. Allow students to develop ownership in learning by involving them in classroom management (Voltz & Damiano-Lantz, 1993).
2. Use cultural referents and student experiences during instruction (Salend, 2000).
3. Facilitate understanding of new words and phrases through use of rephrasing, pictorials, and pantomimes, and by writing keywords (Salend, 2000).
4. Use storytelling to encourage use of oral language skills (Maldonado-Colon, 1990).
5. Develop a reward system, using group or companion contingencies (Echevarria-Ratleff & Graff, 1988).
6. Present daily rehearsal of student expectations (Fradd & Tikunoff, 1987).
7. Offer a buddy or peer tutorial system (Salend, 2000).
8. Use an assortment of culturally appropriate teaching materials (Manning & Baruth, 2000).
9. Use children's literature that represents cultural diversity (e.g., ethnic groups, gender differences, diverse family structures, gay & lesbian families; Manning & Baruth, 2000).
10. Arrange a variety of high-context teaching activities (e.g., field trips, cooking activities, plays; Westby & Rouse, 1985).
11. Develop cultural reciprocity by involving families in educational programs and using community, family, and home cultural information to promote engagement in instructional tasks (Correa & Tulbert, 1991; Harry, Kalyanpur, & Day, 1999).
12. Use active learning techniques by which students can collaboratively share alliances (Adams & Hamm, 1991; Fradd & Bermudez, 1991).
13. Develop student's language competence through use of art forms, drama, simulations, role-plays, music, and games (Salend, 2000).

Figure 8.1
Classroom interventions successful with English language learner students in inclusive classrooms.

Another promising method of instruction for English language learners involves the Cognitive Academic Language Learning Approach (CALLA; Chamot & O'Malley, 1994). The CALLA integrates both content and language instruction by using higher-thinking skills and learning strategies (Gersten & Jiménez, 1998). Additionally, interventions with culturally and linguistically diverse students should do the following:

1. Use educational tools such as story maps, paragraph frames, and sentence starters to scaffold learning.
2. Promote language and literacy across the curriculum.
3. Provide an opportunity for the student to use native and English language skills.
4. Match the learning style of the student.
5. Connect the student's native heritage and culture as a context for instruction.
6. Promote confidence and elevate self-esteem in the student.
7. Encourage student-to-student interactions.
8. Involve collaborative learning communities.
9. Teach through conversation and promote complex thinking.
10. Provide the student with the tools necessary for inclusion into the majority school culture (Gersten & Jiménez, 1998; Santamaría et al., 2002; Tharp, Estrada, Dalton, & Yamauchi, 2000).

Additionally, strategies for teaching students with mild disabilities have potential application for students from culturally and linguistically diverse backgrounds. Some of these strategies will be discussed in Chapter 10, as they relate to working with students with mild disabilities.

ROLES OF PROFESSIONALS INVOLVED WITH STUDENTS FROM CULTURALLY AND LINGUISTICALLY DIVERSE BACKGROUNDS

Professionals involved with educating students from culturally diverse backgrounds must understand the complex aspects of cultural influences on the student and the family. Often interactive teaming revolves around the general education teacher and the bilingual education teacher. However, for English language learners the roles of the school psychologist and the speech-language therapist become critical, and if the student evidences any potential learning or behavioral problems, the special education professional must be involved.

The general roles of professionals were outlined in Chapter 3. Some specialized contributions of team members who work with students from culturally and linguistically diverse backgrounds are presented in Table 8.4.

Table 8.4

Roles of Professionals and Others Involved with Culturally and Linguistically Diverse Students

Personnel	Direct Service Provider	Team Member
Bilingual educator	• Assess language development in student's native language. • Provide academic instruction using native and English language, and native heritage/cultural context. • Communicate with family in native language or with interpreters.	• Serve as culture broker. • Conduct staff development on bilingualism/biculturalism. • Collaborate on bilingual techniques with other team members. • Integrate regular and special education curriculum into bilingual program.
Teacher of English as a second language (ESL)	• Instruct in English as a second language, minimizing the pull-out approach. • Communicate with family in their native language or with interpreters.	• Serve as culture broker. • Conduct staff development on factors affecting second language acquisition and language development. • Consult with team members on effective techniques for teaching students English.
General educator	• Conduct curriculum-based assessment to develop an appropriate academic program. • Provide peer tutoring or a buddy system for adjustment into the classroom. • Provide intervention that includes the student's cultural experiences. • Collect data and make referrals to bilingual education or special education when necessary.	• Integrate bilingual and/or special education techniques into general academic program. • Report on progress with inclusion in all areas including social/emotional adjustment. • Use native language aides, volunteers, and parents to assist in the classroom program. • Integrate a multicultural education program into the daily curriculum that promotes an understanding and respect for diversity and work closely with the librarian or media specialist to ensure a vast array of multicultural literature.
Special educator	• Conduct nondiscriminatory assessment in the areas of achievement and language. • Communicate cross-culturally with student and family. • Adapt teaching materials according to the needs of student. • Develop IEP in cooperation with general and bilingual educators. • Role release to general and bilingual educators effective teaching strategies including direct instruction, cooperative learning, learning strategies, and behavior management techniques.	• Serve as culture broker. • Accept shared responsibilities with bilingual/ESL/general educators. • Interpret assessment results. • Conduct staff development on special education and remediation techniques

Continued

Table 8.4
Continued.

Personnel	Direct Service Provider	Team Member
Title 1 teacher	• Instruct young children who qualify for Title 1 federal funds [low Socio-Economic Status (SES), English language learners].	• Share instruction techniques with special educator. • Prepare team for student's entry into general education. • Serve as culture broker.
Migrant teacher	• Provide instruction that prepares the child for inclusion in the general education curriculum. • Visit migrant camps or communities and communicate with the family.	• Provide team with information on migrant conditions of the family. • Maintain records with the Migrant Students Record Transfer System (MSRTS) • Encourage alternative methods of earning credits toward graduation. • Provide on-site tutoring programs. • Serve as culture broker.
School psychologist	• Conduct nondiscriminatory assessment in the areas of intelligence/achievement. • Maintain current cumulative records on students.	• Interpret test results. • Conduct staff development on working with culturally diverse families. • Explain all school procedures, policies, and legal mandates. • Participate in prereferral process.
Speech-language therapist	• Conduct assessment in both English and native language in the areas of language and speech development. • Conduct individual, group, or integrated therapy with students.	• Role release therapy techniques that can be integrated into all educational programs. • Interpret test results.
Guidance counselor/ social worker	• Assess student in the areas of adaptive behavior and vocational planning. • Provide individual or group therapy sessions to work on self-concept and self-esteem. • Communicate with families. • Establish families' concerns, needs, and priorities.	• Interpret results of testing and progress in counseling sessions. • Make home visits and report findings of family status. • Serve as liaison with other nonschool agencies.
Administrator	• Manage all aspects of school programs. • Assure that all programs are meeting the unique needs of LEP students. • Evaluate staff performance.	• Provide team with guidance on legal and district-wide policies and procedures. • Serve as meeting manager. • Support team in acquiring materials and resources necessary to deliver quality services.

Personnel	Direct Service Provider	Team Member
		• Be available to meet with families and parent groups. • Encourage a multicultural approach to all aspects of school life.
Parents/ family members	• Support school programs and assist in enhancing the child's development of English. • Support bicultural instruction.	• Provide team with information on language and cultural background. • Support parent organizations and parent education efforts by the school or community.

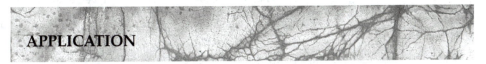

APPLICATION

In the vignette at the beginning of the chapter, Ms. Harris, Helena's teacher, had decided that the best way to cope with an English language learner was to not make many demands on her and instead refer her to special education. Unfortunately, for Helena to succeed in an inclusive educational environment, she will eventually need to attend to large-group instruction and stay on task. Providing her with individual worksheets will not prepare her for the next environment, fifth grade. The following solution to this problem exemplifies the interactive team approach.

Interactive Team Plan for Improving Helena's Attention to Task

The general education teacher, Ms. Harris, arranges a series of cooperative planning meetings. She asks each specialist to outline the concerns and needs for Helena's success in an inclusive classroom. Ms. Harris takes on the role of services coordinator by coordinating all information shared by the interactive team.

Mrs. Garcia, the ESL teacher, is invited to visit Ms. Harris's classroom and makes an anecdotal record of Helena's conduct. Both share their concern that Helena is having difficulty adjusting to the school environment and is behaving much like a child who does not understand the language and is in the initial stages of second language acquisition. They decide to use the prereferral team at the school, which includes the school psychologist, speech-language therapist, social worker, and the special education teacher for suggesting instructional and behavioral strategies to use in the fourth-grade classroom. Both Ms. Harris and Mrs. Garcia agree that Helena should be pulled out from the classroom only if necessary for ESL instruction. In addition, Mrs. Garcia will begin to visit Helena's classroom and integrate her instruction into Helena's daily classroom routine. Ms. Harris has also agreed to observe other English language learners, and to get ideas for classroom adaptations.

Ms. Harris contacts the school psychologist, the social worker, the special education teacher, and the speech-language therapist. These professionals also visit Helena's classroom and collect data on Helena's academic and behavioral performance. Each professional graphs those data and presents them at the prereferral meeting arranged by Ms. Harris. The speech-language therapist assesses Helena's ability to understand both Spanish and English.

During the prereferral meeting, all team members are present. Additionally, Helena's parents and an interpreter attend. The special education teacher provides the team with suggestions for instructional strategies to use with Helena and a positive behavioral support program that uses social praise as a reinforcer. All team members agree to participate in Helena's intervention programs to the degree appropriate. Everyone agrees that Helena would benefit from a buddy-system program with another student.

Each team member speaks empathetically with the parents about Helena. Her parents are made to feel comfortable and are asked throughout the meeting if they have any questions or suggestions. They help the team understand the experiences they had when they immigrated to the United States from El Salvador and explain Helena's previous school experiences. Helena's father says his daughter likes to listen to music and that music seems to bring her out socially. The father will bring a few of Helena's favorite CDs to school, so they can be shared with the other students and be available to Helena when she wants some time away from the classroom stresses.

Mrs. Garcia agrees to give Ms. Harris some strategies that can be integrated into the inclusive classroom. She will visit Helena in the classroom twice a week and facilitate the instructional strategies. The school psychologist is interested in Helena's adjustment to the "culture shock" of moving to the United States and offers to spend 15 minutes once a week with Helena, observing her adjustment to school. The family also agrees to participate in the plan and is given simple and functional ideas for home intervention.

The special education teacher will serve as a team consultant. If Helena is officially placed in special education, the teacher will take a more active role in intervention. Objectives are developed during the meeting, and various team members share responsibility for conducting the outlined interventions. The chart in Table 8.5 provides an overview of the various strategies that are implemented on behalf of Helena and her family. Team members agree to reconvene within 6 weeks to discuss Helena's progress. If progress is not seen within the 6 weeks, a formal referral to special education will be made.

SUMMARY

Culture often plays a significant role in educators' differential treatment of students and in students' interaction with peers and adults. Professional expectations for various groups or types of students, definitions of what constitutes "appropriate" and tolerable behaviors, and reactions to student behaviors are often based on cultural beliefs, values, and norms. When students' expressed values, attitudes, and behaviors are different from those of the profession in charge, these differences are often judged to be deficits, problems, or deviance rather than differences (Walther-Thomas et al., 2000).

Table 8.5

Interactive Team Problem-Solving Steps for Helena

Step 1. Ms. Harris, Mrs. Garcia, and the school psychologist will make home visits. They will gather information on Helena's educational history in El Salvador and understand the families' concerns, priorities, and needs for Helena's education. They will introduce the family to other Hispanic families in the community and involve the community outreach program to make sure that Helena and her family receive the support they need.

Step 2. Mrs. Garcia will administer an "interest inventory" to learn more about Helena's interests, likes, and dislikes, then share those results with Ms. Harris and the prereferral team to plan instruction and communication accordingly.

Step 3. Ms. Harris will work with the prereferral team to outline specific strategies for improving Helena's academic as well as behavioral outcomes. She will also increase opportunities to read aloud to the students, and have Helena participate in small-group speaking situations and choral speaking with audio-taped books and songs. She will reduce worksheet work and encourage cooperative learning activities.

Step 4. Mrs. Garcia, the ESL teacher, will work closely with Ms. Harris to assist in developing appropriate adaptations to Helena's instruction. Mrs. Garcia will meet weekly with Ms. Harris to integrate the teaching units into Helena's ESL instruction.

Step 5. Ms. Harris will begin to embed multicultural instruction into her daily teaching units. She will have a unit on families and talk to the children about differences related to language and the Hispanic culture. She will have students do book reports on Hispanics and other ethnic groups to teach them about cultural acceptance and friendships. Each student will conduct a home interview to understand his or her own cultural heritage. If Helena's family is comfortable with the idea, she will invite them to come to class to talk (with the use of an interpreter) about El Salvador.

Step 6. The principal at the school will provide inservice training (and other training in diversity) for teachers by Latino experts from the community who know Latinos' cultural backgrounds, strengths, and challenges. The speakers will address the similarities and differences found across Latino groups, including the diversity among Salvadorans.

The data on the prevalence of students from linguistically and culturally diverse backgrounds who are at risk for school failure indicate that school personnel must acquire the skills necessary to understand and work with this population. Interactive teaming is the most efficient way to meet these students' special needs.

By consulting and collaborating with others on the team, school personnel can design educational programs that are sensitive to the students' cultural backgrounds and specific learning styles. This chapter has provided an overview of what research shows are the best practices in working with students from diverse backgrounds. The major points discussed are as follows:

- Students from diverse backgrounds are a heterogeneous population, and negative stereotypes should be avoided when learning about cultural characteristics associated with their native cultures.
- Certain learning, behavioral, and socioeconomic characteristics related to students from diverse backgrounds place these students at risk for success in schools.

- A variety of service delivery options is available for students from diverse backgrounds. The goal, however, is to provide services that ensure inclusion into the general education program and protect the student from long-term placement in segregated programs.
- Comprehensive and nondiscriminatory assessment practices, involving both formal and informal procedures, will assist in deciding whether a student evidences a significant learning problem or evidences characteristics associated with second language acquisition and cultural acculturation.
- A variety of instructional strategies can be used in working with students from diverse backgrounds, including strategies developed for students with mild disabilities.
- The various roles of school personnel involved with students from diverse backgrounds are focused on enhancing students' use of English while supporting their native language and culture, providing a learning environment that promotes inclusion into the general education classroom, developing confidence and self-esteem in students, and providing family involvement in a manner that is sensitive to the native culture.

ACTIVITIES

1. Play a cultural simulation game such as *BaFá BaFá* (Shirts, 1977). Help the class acknowledge the diverse feeling of interacting with a different culture. Transcribe their feelings on transparencies as they are discussed.

2. Facilitate a cultural journey (Lynch & Hanson, 1998). Ask students to describe their own culture, beliefs, traditions, foods, and holidays. Have students describe family stories depicting their families' experiences in the United States. Ask students if they have ever experienced discrimination due to their cultural background.

3. Conduct an informational interview with a professional who is involved in the educational programs of students from diverse cultural backgrounds. Use the guidelines provided in Chapter 4.

4. Tour a school program serving English language learners. Observe the students' activities and schedules. Note if any special adaptations or curricula are being used. Observe any bilingual instruction occurring, and note the personnel who are proficient in two or more languages.

5. Volunteer in an after-school program for bilingual students, at-risk students, or immigrant adults. Note the characteristics of the students as related to their cultural backgrounds. Tutor non-English-speaking students in English. Find topics related to their culture to use as conversation warm-ups.

6. Obtain a language sample from a English language learner student. Consult with a speech-language therapist or a bilingual teacher regarding the

grammatical language structures used by the student. Evaluate the child's proficiency in English.

7. Compile a resource file of materials for your classroom that promotes multicultural education. Order catalogs that have multicultural educational materials such as books, dolls, crayons, and construction paper.

REFERENCES

Adams, D., & Hamm, M. (1991). Diversity gives schools infinite learning possibilities. *School Administrator, 48*(4), 20–22.

Adger, C., Christian, D., & Taylor, O. (1999). *Making the connection: Language and academic achievement among African American students.* McHenry, IL: Delta Systems.

Alder, N. (2000). Teaching diverse students. *Multicultural Perspectives, 2,* 28–31.

Anokye, A. D. (1997). A case of orality in the classroom. *The Clearing House, 70*(5), 229–231.

Artiles, A., & Ortiz, A. (2002). *English language learners with special education needs: Identification, assessment, and instruction.* Washington, DC: Center for Applied Linguistics and Delta Systems.

Artiles, A., Trent, S., & Palmer, J. (2004). Culturally diverse students in special education: Legacies and prospects. In J. Banks & C. McGee Banks (Eds.), *Handbook of Research on Multicultural Education* (2nd ed.). San Francisco: Jossey-Bass/A Wiley Company.

Artiles, A. J., Aguirre-Munoz, Z., & Abedi, J. (1998). Predicting placement in learning disabilities programs: Do predictors vary by ethnic group? *Exceptional Children, 64,* 543–559.

Artiles, A. J., & Zamora-Duran, G. (1997). Disproportionate representation: A contentious and unresolved predicament. In A. J. Artiles & G. Zamora-Duran (Eds.), *Reducing disproportionate representation of culturally diverse students in special and gifted education* (pp. 1–6). Reston, VA: The Council for Exceptional Children.

August, D., & Hakuta, K. (1997). *Improving schools for language-minority children: A research agenda.* Washington, DC: National Academy Press.

Retrieved from http://www.books.nap.edu/hal2/0309054974/gifmid/R1.gif.

Baca, L., & Cervantes, H. (1998). *The bilingual special education interface* (3rd ed.). Upper Saddle River, NJ: Merrill/Prentice Hall.

Banks, J. A. (1999). *An introduction to multicultural education* (2nd ed.). Boston: Allyn & Bacon.

Banks, J. A., & McGee Banks, S. (2004). *Multicultural education: Issues and perspectives* (5th ed.). New York: Wiley & Sons.

Barrera, I., Corson, R., & Macpherson, D. (2003). *Skilled dialogue: Strategies for responding to cultural diversity in early childhood.* Baltimore: Brookes Publishing.

Bennett, C. (2003). *Comprehensive multicultural education: Theory and practice* (5th ed.). Boston: Allyn & Bacon.

Blair, T. (2003). *New teacher's performance-based guide to culturally diverse classrooms.* Boston: Allyn & Bacon.

Boyden, J. (1993). *Families: Celebration and hope in a world of change.* London: Gaia Books Limited.

Brice, A. (2002). *The Hispanic child: Speech, language, culture, and education.* Boston: Allyn & Bacon.

Chamot, A. U., & O'Malley, J. M. (1994). *The CALLA handbook: Implementing the cognitive academic language learning approach.* Reading, MA: Addison-Wesley.

Children's Defense Fund. (2001). *The state of America's children yearbook 2001.* Washington, DC: Author.

Clarke, P. (1991, May). Does your programme support the development of English as a second language? *Resource Newsletter of the FKA Multicultural Resource Center,* 4–5.

Cloud, N. (2002). Culturally and linguistically responsive instructional planning. In A. J. Artiles & A. A. Ortiz (Eds.), *English language learners with special education needs: Identification, assessment, and instruction* (pp. 107–132). Washington, DC: Center for Applied Linguistics and Delta Systems.

Correa, V., & Tulbert, B. (1991). Teaching culturally diverse students. *Preventing School Failure, 35*(3), 20–25.

Craig, H., Thompson, C. A., Washington, J. A., & Potter, S. L. (2003). Phonological features of child African American English. *Journal of Speech, Language, and Hearing Research, 46,* 623–635.

Cummins, J. (1994). The acquisition for English as a second language. In K. Spangernberg-Urbachat & R. Pritchard (Eds.), *Kids come in all languages: Reading instruction for ESL students* (pp. 36–62). Newark, DE: International Reading Association.

Daniels, V. (2001). Responding to the learning needs of multicultural learners with gifts and talents. In C. Utley & F. Obiakor (Eds.), *Special education, multicultural education, and school reform: Components of quality education for learners with mild disabilities* (pp. 140–154). Springfield, IL: Charles C. Thomas.

Daugherty, D. (2001). *IDEA '97 and disproportionate placement.* Retrieved December 14, 2003, from http://www.naspcenter.org/teachers/IDEA disp.html

Delpit, L. (1995). *Other people's children: Cultural conflict in the classroom.* New York: The New Press.

Delpit, L., & Dowdy, J. K. (2002). *The skin that we speak: Thoughts on language and culture in the classroom.* New York: The New Press.

Dilworth-Anderson, P., Burton, L., & Johnson, B. (1993). Reframing theories for understanding race, ethnicity, and families. In P. G. Boss, W. J. Doherty, R. LaRoss, W. R. Schumm, & S. K. Steinmetz (Eds.), *Sourcebook of family theories and methods: A contextual approach* (pp. 627–649). New York: Plenum.

Donovan, M. S., & Cross, C. T. (Eds.). (2001). *Minority students in special and gifted education.* Washington, DC: National Academy Press.

Echevarria-Ratleff, J., & Graff, V. L. (1988). California bilingual special education model sites (1984–1986): Programs and research. In A. Ortiz & B. A. Ramirez (Eds.), *Schools and the culturally diverse exceptional student: Promising practices and future directions* (pp. 104–111). Reston, VA: Council for Exceptional Children.

Fierros, E., & Conroy, J. (2002). Double jeopardy: An exploration of restrictiveness and race in special education. In D. Losen & G. Orfield (Eds.), *Racial inequity in special education* (pp. 39–70). Cambridge, MA: Harvard Education Press.

Figueroa, R. (2002). Toward a new model of assessment. In A. Artiles & A. Ortiz (Eds.), *English language learners with special education needs: Identification, assessment, and instruction* (pp. 51–64). McHenry, IL: Delta Systems.

Figueroa, R., & Hernandez, S. (2000). *Our nation on the fault line: Hispanic American education. Testing Hispanic students in the United States: Technical and policy issues.* Washington, DC: President's Advisory Commission on Educational Excellence for Hispanic Americans.

Foner, N. (1997). The immigrant family: Cultural legacies and cultural changes. *International Migration Review, 31*(4), 961–974.

Fradd, S., & Tikunoff, W. (1987). *Bilingual education and bilingual special education: A guide for administrators.* Boston: College-Hill.

Fradd, S. H., & Bermudez, A. B. (1991). POWER: A process for meeting the instructional needs of handicapped language-minority students. *Teacher Education and Special Education, 14*(1), 19–24.

Fry, R. (2003). *Hispanic youth dropping out of U.S. schools: Measuring the challenge.* Pew Hispanic Center. Retrieved November 22, 2003, from http://www.pewhispanic.org/site/docs/pdf/high%20school%20dropout%20report-final.pdf

Gay, G. (2000). *Culturally responsive teaching: Theory, research, and practice.* New York: Teachers College Press.

Genesee, F., & Cloud, N. (1998). Multilingualism is basic. *Educational Leadership, 55,* 62–65.

Gersten, R., & Baker, S. (2000). What we know about effective instructional practices for English-language learners. *Exceptional Children, 66,* 454–470.

Gersten, R., & Jiménez, R. (Eds.) (1998). *Promoting learning for culturally and linguistically diverse students.* Belmont, CA: Wadsworth Pub.

Glenn, C. L. (1989). Just schools for minority children. *Phi Delta Kappan, 10*(70), 777–779.

Goldstein, B. S. (2002). Walking the talk: The joys and challenges of critical pedagogy. In A. J. Artiles & A. A. Ortiz (Eds.), *English language learners with special education needs: Identification, assessment, and instruction* (pp. 159–190). Washington, DC: Center for Applied Linguistics and Delta Systems.

Gollnick, D., & Chinn, P. (2001). *Multicultural education in a pluralistic society* (6th ed.). Columbus, OH: Merrill.

Hakuta, K., & Beatty, A. (2000). *Testing English-language learners in U.S. schools: Report and workshop summary.* Washington, DC: National Academy Press.

Harry, B. (1992). *Cultural diversity, families, and the special education system: Communication and empowerment.* New York: Teachers College Press.

Harry, B. (1994). *The disproportionate representation of minority students in special education: Theories and recommendations.* Alexandria, VA: National Association of State Directors of Special Education.

Harry, B., Kalyanpur, M., & Day, M. (1999). *Building cultural reciprocity with families: Case studies in special education.* Boston: Paul H. Brookes.

Hoover, J. J., & Collier, C. (1985). Referring culturally different children for special education: Sociocultural considerations. *Academic Therapy, 20,* 503–510.

Hoover, J. J., & Collier, C. (1991). Meeting the needs of culturally and linguistically diverse exceptional learners: Prereferral to mainstreaming. *Teacher Education and Special Education, 14*(1), 30–34.

Ishii-Jordan, S. R. (1997). When behavior differences are not disorders. In A. J. Artiles & G. Zamora-Duran (Eds.), *Reducing disproportionate representation of culturally diverse students in special and gifted education* (pp. 27–46). Reston, VA: The Council for Exceptional Children.

Kader, S., & Yawkey, T. (2002). Problems and recommendations: Enhancing communication with culturally and linguistically diverse students. *Reading Improvement, 39,* 43–51.

Kinchin, D. (2001). *Post traumatic stress disorder: The invisible injury, 2001 edition.* Oxfordshire, UK: Success Unlimited.

Ladson-Billings, G. (1997). *The dreamkeepers: Successful teachers of African American children.* San Francisco, CA: Jossey-Bass.

Ladson-Billings, G. (2001). *Crossing over to Canaan: The journey of new teachers in diverse classrooms.* San Francisco, CA: Jossey-Bass.

Lynch, E. W., & Hanson, M. J. (1998). *Developing cross-cultural competencies: A guide for working with children and their families* (2nd ed.). Baltimore: Paul H. Brookes.

MacMillan, D. L., & Reschly, D. J. (1998). Overrepresentation of minority students: The case of greater specificity or reconsideration of the variables examined. *Journal of Special Education, 32,* 15–24.

Maldonado-Colon, E. (1990). Development of second language learners' linguistic and cognitive abilities. *The Journal of Educational Issues of Language Minority Students, 9,* 37–48.

Manning, M. L., & Baruth, L. G. (2000). *Multicultural education of children and adolescents.* Needham Heights, MA: Allyn & Bacon.

McIntyre, T. (1999). *The culturally sensitive disciplinarian.* Retrieved December 14, 2003, from http://maxweber.hunter.cuny.edu/pub/eres/EDSPC715 MCINTYRE/C SenDiscip.html

McWhorter, J. (2000). *Spreading the word: Language and dialect in America.* Portsmouth, NH: Heinemann.

Murray, C. B., & Clark, R. M. (1990). Targets of racism. *The American School Board Journal, 177*(6), 22–24.

National Center for Homeless Education. (2003). *Data on homeless children and youth.* Retrieved November 22, 2003, from http://www.serve.org/nche/SEASdata.htm

Nieto, S. (2000). *Affirming diversity: The sociopolitical context of multicultural education* (3rd ed.). New York: Longman.

Office of Migrant Education. (2002). *Migrant education secondary student initiative*. Retrieved December 9, 2003, from http://www.ed.gov/admins/lead/account/secondarystudent.html?exp=0

Olson, J. F., & Goldstein, A. A. (1997). *The inclusion of students with disabilities and limited English proficiency in large-scale assessments: A summary of a recent progress*. Washington, DC: U.S. Department of Education.

Ortiz, A. (2000). Including students with special needs in standards-based reform: Issues associated with the alignment of standards, curriculum, and instruction. In *Conference proceedings of the 3rd mid-continent research for education and learning diversity roundtable* (pp. 41–64). (ERIC Document Reproduction Service No. ED449187)

Ortiz, A., & Yates, J. (2002). Considerations in the assessment of English language learners referred to special education. In A. Artiles & A. Ortiz (Eds.), *English language learners with special education needs: Identification, assessment, and instruction* (pp. 65–86). McHenry, IL: Delta Systems.

Oswald, D. P., & Coutinho, M. J. (2001). Trends in disproportionate representation: Implications for multicultural education. In C. Utley & F. Obiakor (Eds.), *Special education, multicultural education, and school reform: Components of quality education for learners with mild disabilities* (pp. 53–73). Springfield, IL: Charles C. Thomas.

Patton, J. M. (1997). Disproportionate representation in gifted programs: Best practices for meeting this challenge. In A. J. Artiles & G. Zamora-Duran (Eds.), *Reducing disproportionate representation of culturally diverse students in special and gifted education* (pp. 59–85). Reston, VA: The Council for Exceptional Children.

Patton, J. M. (1998). The disproportionate representation of African Americans in special education: Looking behind the curtain for understanding and solutions. *Journal of Special Education, 32*(1), 25–32.

Peregoy, S. F., & Boyle, O. F. (2001). *Reading, writing, & learning in ESL: A resource book, for K–12 teachers* (3rd ed.). New York: Longman Publishers.

Peterson, R. L., & Ishii-Jordan, S. (1994). *Multicultural issues in the education of students with behavioral disorders*. Cambridge, MA: Brookline Books.

Porter, R. O. (1997). The politics of bilingual education. *Society, 34*(6), 31–39.

Putnam, J. (1998). *Cooperative learning and strategies for inclusion: Celebrating diversity in the classroom*. Baltimore: Paul H. Brookes.

Reschly, D. J., Tilly, W. D., III, & Grimes, J. P. (2000). *Special education in transition: Functional assessment and noncategorical programming*. Longmont, CO: Sopris West.

Rueda, R. (1997). Changing the context of assessment: The move to portfolios and authentic assessment. In A. J. Artiles & G. Zamora-Duran (Eds.), *Reducing disproportionate representation of culturally diverse students in special and gifted education* (pp. 7–25). Reston, VA: The Council for Exceptional Children.

Salend, S. J. (2000). *Effective mainstreaming: Creating inclusive classrooms* (4th ed.). Upper Saddle River, NJ: Merrill/Prentice Hall.

Santamaría, L. J., Fletcher, T. V., & Bos, C. S. (2002). Effective pedagogy for English language learners in inclusive classrooms. In A. J. Artiles & A. A. Ortiz (Eds.), *English language learners with special education needs: Identification, assessment, and instruction* (pp. 133–158). Washington, DC: Center for Applied Linguistics and Delta Systems.

Shirts, G. (1977). *Bafá Bafá: A cross cultural simulation*. Del Mar, CA: Simille II.

Simon, M. (2001). Beyond broken promises: Reflections on eliminating barriers to the success of minority youth with disabilities. *JASH, 26*, 200–203.

Smitherman, G. (2000). *Talkin that talk: Language, culture and education in African America*. New York: Routledge.

Sutton-Redner, J. (2002). Children in a world of violence. *Children in Need Magazine*. Retrieved November 20, 2003, from http://childreninneed.com/magazine/violence.html

Taylor, S. V. (2000). Multicultural is who we are. *Teaching Exceptional Children, 32*, 24–29.

Tharp, R. G., Estrada, P., Dalton, S. S., & Yamauchi, L. A. (2000). *Teaching transformed: Achieving excellence, fairness, inclusion, and harmony.* Boulder, CO: Westview Press.

Thomas, W. P., & Collier, V. P. (1998). Two languages are better than one. *Educational Leadership, 55,* 66–78.

U.S. Census Bureau. (2002). *Poverty in the United States: 2001.* Washington, DC: Author.

Voltz, D. L., & Damiano-Lantz, M. (1993). Developing ownership in learning. *Teaching Exceptional Children, 25*(4), 18–23.

von Hapsburg, D., & Pena, E. (2002). Understanding bilingualism and its impact on speech audiometry. *Journal of Speech, Language, and Hearing Research, 45,* 202–213.

Walther-Thomas, C., Korinek, L., McLaughlin, V., & Williams, B. (2000). *Collaboration for inclusive education: Developing successful programs.* Boston: Allyn & Bacon.

Westby, C. E., & Rouse, G. R. (1985). Culture in education and the instruction of language learning-disabled students. *Topics in Language Disorders, 5,* 15–28.

Winzer, M., & Mazurek, K. (1994). *Special education in multicultural contexts.* Upper Saddle River, NJ: Merrill/Prentice Hall.

Implementation with Infants and Preschoolers with Special Needs

9

Topics in this chapter include:

◆ The characteristics associated with young children and their families.

◆ The various developmental and service delivery needs of young children and their families.

◆ The unique roles of professionals working with young children and their families.

Nicholas, a 4-year-old with cerebral palsy, attends a faith-based preschool in his local community. The public school program provides him with services from an itinerant early childhood special education (ECSE) teacher twice a week. The regular preschool and ECSE teachers work closely on (1) adapting the preschool environment for his motor needs, including positioning equipment, bathroom accommodations, and adaptive feeding utensils; (2) providing him with a computer and augmentative communication aids; (3) facilitating social interaction with same-age peers; (4) integrating his special language, cognitive, and physical therapy goals into a developmentally appropriate program; and (5) designing a data-collection system for monitoring his developmental progress.

All team members are briefed about Nicholas's family background. Although Nicholas's grandparents have legal custody of him, his mother, a single teenage mother living in another state, does take a role in his life when possible. Nicholas's speech and physical therapists and his service coordinator at the local children's medical center meet monthly with his grandparents and the early intervention teachers to discuss his progress, the family's needs, and preparations for Nicholas's transition to the kindergarten program in the local public school.

Interactive teaming may never be more important than when working with children like Nicholas and his family. With the passage of P.L. 99-457 in 1986 and the subsequent Part C services under the Individuals with Disabilities Education Act (IDEA) in 1997, early childhood personnel are realizing that skills in coordination of services, consultation with related personnel, and collaboration with families are critical. The services provided by these regulations should be multidisciplinary, coordinated, family-centered, and provided in settings where children without special needs are served (Correa & Jones, 2003; Dunst, 2002; Harbin, 1998; Hooper & Umansky, 2003).

Transdisciplinary teaming approaches are necessary in serving young children because of the large numbers of professionals involved in early intervention (Cook, Klein, & Tessier, 2004; McWilliam, 2000). Full-service programs in the natural environment for young children with special needs and their families involve professionals from health, education, and human services.

Programs under Part C of IDEA, Early Head Start, and Head Start programs mandate the expansion of interagency collaboration. States and local agencies serving infants and toddlers (birth to age 3) with special needs developed interagency collaboration councils (ICCs) as mechanisms for the coordination of services. Both Early Head Start and Head Start programs must delineate the services provided to children with special needs through interagency agreements (Wischnowski, Pfluke, & Twining, 2003). Although *collaboration* is the term used most often to describe interagency work, a more recent term, *service integration,* appears to capture a more intense, comprehensive, and unified state of collaboration (Summers, Steeples, & Peterson, 2001). Not surprisingly, states and local agencies vary tremendously in how they assemble the service integration system. Little is currently known about the extent to which these complex variations in the early intervention system affect positive outcomes for children and families (Spiker, Hebbeler, Wagner, Cameto, &

McKenna, 2000; Summers et al., 2001). Nonetheless, the role of the service coordinator is a critical piece to successful service integration and requires all the interactive teaming skills outlined in Part II of this book.

This chapter focuses on the specific components of early intervention that incorporate interactive teaming skills. First, a brief overview of the various conditions that make children eligible for early intervention services is provided to acquaint the reader with the increasing numbers of young children who are at risk. Second, a discussion of the intervention needs of young children with special needs suggests various service delivery options that are available for these children and their families. Within the description of the intervention needs of these children, assessment techniques and intervention strategies used for young children will be delineated. Third, the role of the professionals involved in intervention with young children and their families is presented. The key to providing a successful early intervention program requires that an interactive team be available for intervention, consultation, and collaboration.

CHARACTERISTICS OF YOUNG CHILDREN WITH SPECIAL NEEDS AND THEIR FAMILIES

Regulations under Part C of the IDEA provide eligibility criteria for three subgroups receiving early intervention: *established conditions, developmental delays,* and *at risk.* Some states serve all three subgroups of children while other states with large numbers of at-risk children have elected to use the criteria for established conditions and developmental delays.

The term *established conditions* refers to young children who have a genetic disorder, congenital malformation, or a neurological disorder that has a high probability of resulting in a developmental delay. The term *developmental delay* refers to young children who evidence a certain percentage of difference between their performance level and chronological age or a certain number of standard deviations below their chronological age based on quantitative and/or qualitative assessment. For a child to be eligible for services under the *at-risk* group, "children may currently demonstrate no abnormality, but have biological or environmental factors associated with their medical history or home context that increase the risk of delay in the future" (Brown, Thurman, & Pearl, 1993, p. 30).

The numbers of young children who could be eligible for early intervention services is increasing dramatically (Hooper & Umansky, 2004). Perhaps one of the most alarming statistics of risk factors facing American children today is that children living in poverty are more likely to have disabilities than their peers who live in middle- and upper-income families (Hooper & Umansky, 2003; Janko-Summers & Joseph, 1998). The factors that put poor children at risk include "neglected prenatal care, inadequate nutrition, lack of access to preventive health care, caregiver's mental and physical health problems and a host of other difficult life circumstances" (Janko-Summers & Joseph, p. 207).

Furthermore, increased numbers of infants suffering from fetal alcohol syndrome and fetal tobacco syndrome challenge early interventionists. These children may have lifelong disabilities caused by prenatal neurological damage resulting in cognitive and language delays as well as the presence of challenging behaviors (Habek, Habek, Ivanievic, & Djelmic, 2002; Jacobson & Jacobson, 2002). Similarly, children exposed to cocaine and other drugs pose a challenge to early intervention programs. Although the initial sensationalized problems of these children are not substantiated by current research, some research indicates that cocaine/polydrug-exposed children are significantly more likely to have mild cognitive delay (Klitsch, 2002; Laas, 2000). Intervention for these children often requires (1) a collaborative effort with medical, educational, and therapeutic programs; (2) treatment of the mothers' addiction; and (3) parental involvement, empowerment, and education.

Other groups of young children who are entering the early intervention arena include students exposed to lead poisoning. Ellis and Kane (2000) reported that 4.4% of preschool-age children in the United States had blood lead levels in the neurotoxic range, placing them at risk for impaired neurobehavioral functioning. Most of those children are inner-city African Americans living in poverty. Delays in development have been noted in these children including inattentiveness and mild learning disabilities.

Furthermore, a growing number of children are homeless or living in violent environments. Homeless young children may be at risk for developmental delays due to their transitory state and lack of access to basic resources such as food and medical care (Gollnick & Chinn, 2002; National Coalition for the Homeless, 2001; Salend, 2000). The effects of violence on young children also place the child at risk. Children who are abused can suffer significant emotional delays. However, current research indicates that children who witness violence and live in unsafe and stressful environments are also affected adversely, sometimes evidencing post-traumatic stress disorder symptoms such as emotional withdrawal, aggression, and inattentiveness (Sutton-Redner, 2002).

Finally, the number of children affected by medical conditions such as prematurity, cancer, medically fragile status, or human immunodeficiency virus (HIV; Hooper & Umansky, 2003) have needs that challenge early interventionists. Collaboration with medical personnel as well as social service personnel will be necessary. Personnel will need knowledge and understanding of the issues related to terminal illness, death, and dying. Collaboration with families whose young children are dying may be extremely difficult for early interventionists not prepared in these areas. Consulting with social workers, family therapists, and other mental health professionals may be an important first step for the interventionists.

A discussion of increasing numbers of at-risk children illustrates the changing causes of developmental delays today. By adding these at-risk children to the existing numbers of children with established conditions, one can better understand the enormous challenges that face early interventionists. Further complicating the challenges is the fact that families are no longer comprised of a working husband, a wife who stays at home, and siblings. Instead, today's family can include custodial grandparents, foster parents, same-sex partners, cohabitating couples, teen parents, parents with special needs, and single parents.

INTERVENTION NEEDS OF YOUNG CHILDREN WITH SPECIAL NEEDS

Young children with special needs have different needs than elementary- or secondary-age children. Early intervention programs serving children from birth to age 5 *should not* involve teaching a lower extension of the elementary education curriculum. Early intervention programs should be family centered; include coordinated service delivery options that promote inclusion; use transdisciplinary play-based assessment approaches; and provide the child with individually and developmentally appropriate intervention.

Family-Centered Approaches

Family-centered approaches require that the interactive team place the needs and desires of the family and the child with special needs at the center of the intervention process (Hooper & Umansky, 2003). Dunst (2002) characterized family centeredness as practices that

> treat families with dignity and respect; individualized, flexible and responsive practices; information sharing so that families can make informed decisions; family choice regarding any number of aspects of program practices and intervention options; parent-professional collaboration and partnerships as a context for family program relations; and the provision and mobilization of resources and supports necessary for families to care for and rear their children in ways that produce optimal child, parent, and family outcomes. (p. 139)

The major goal of this approach is to support families in their natural caregiving roles by building on unique individual and family strengths, and to enable and empower families to meet their own needs in ways that create self-competence (Hooper & Umansky, 2004; McWilliam et al., 1998; McWilliam, Maxwell, & Sloper, 1999). Early interventionists who use family-centered practices do the following:

1. Recognize the family as a constant in the child's life and intervention settings as temporary.
2. Facilitate parent/professional collaboration in the care of the child, in the child's program, and in intervention policy.
3. Share information about the child in an unbiased, supportive manner.
4. Implement comprehensive intervention programs that include emotional and financial services for families, as well as child-directed services.
5. Recognize the individuality of families, including their strengths and patterns of coping and adjusting.

6. Incorporate the unique developmental needs of young children into the service delivery system.

7. Encourage parent-to-parent support systems.

8. Design intervention systems that are flexible, accessible, and responsive to the unique needs of different families.

9. Recognize and respect cultural and linguistic differences (McGonigel, Kaufmann, & Johnson, 1991).

Mahoney and Bella (1998) warn that although the IFSP has included family needs, concerns, and priorities, service providers must be responsible for monitoring the impact of services on the family. Unless the impact of family-centered practices on specific child and family outcomes is monitored, "we may fail to meet the goals of family-centered services—enhancing the effectiveness of families in nurturing and caring for their children" (p. 92). Furthermore, the IFSP document should be written in language that is clear and simple, be positive in describing the child's strengths, contain nonjudgemental statements, provide specific and functional outcomes for everyday routines, provide for services in natural environments, and encourage professionals to work together (McWilliam et al., 1998). For further information on writing an IFSP, refer to Polmanteer and Turbiville (2000) and Bruder (2000).

Service Delivery Options

Meeting the complex needs of today's young children and families requires the involvement of multiple agencies and programs. Most children who have significant disabilities due to established conditions or developmental delays receive services from the state's lead agency for Part C of the IDEA. These services can involve various agencies, including primary physician/health clinics; the Special Supplemental Food Program for Women, Infants, and Children; educational and therapeutic services for the child; protective services; mental health services; and case management services. Young children who are at risk are served by other agencies such as Head Start, Medicaid, Maternal and Child Health Block Grants, Title 1 Programs, social services block grants, or state appropriations programs. The high number of agencies and programs available for young children with special needs or at-risk children necessitates interactive teaming efforts by all personnel and the family.

Perhaps one of the most impressive models of interactive teaming can be found in the establishment of local interagency collaborative councils (LICCs; Hayden, Frederick, Smith, & Broudy, 2001; Roberts, Akers, & Behl, 1999). LICCs were first mandated by P.L. 99-457 and are now operating in all communities serving young children with special needs or at-risk populations. The following vignette helps illustrate the function of an LICC:

The case of Ryan, a 2.5-year-old diagnosed with lead poisoning, is discussed at the February meeting of the Jones County LICC. In attendance are Ryan's mother and his health care provider, the service coordinator for Part C, the Part C early interventionists, the Early Head Start director, the school district's prekindergarten special education supervisor, the school psychologist, the Head Start director, the supervisor for the elementary education program, the director of the regional resources center, and the social services worker. The service coordinator introduces the mother to the team and provides some background on Ryan's intervention needs. The boy receives services from the Part C early interventionists, but has been tested by the school psychologist and found to be ineligible for special education services when he turns 3 years old. The service coordinator would like to make sure Ryan remains in an early intervention program until he is 4, when he can attend Head Start.

The mother and health care provider provide the team with information on how Ryan is progressing. Ryan's major IFSP goals are focused on increasing his attention and engagement with toys and adult-child interactions. He has been improving since he started receiving early intervention services at home. The mother wants to earn her GED and get off government assistance by working part time, but she fears the home visit program will be discontinued. The Early Head Start (EHS) director believes Ryan would qualify for EHS services when he turns 4. She asks the mother if she would be interested in placing Ryan in a center-based program on the days she is working. The mother says she would like to visit the program first but is interested in the option. The EHS parent liaison would provide support to the home-care provider and make home visits in the evenings when the mother comes home from work.

The Early Head Start director would like to work closely with the Part C early interventionist to transition the IFSP to the EHS program. Head Start is now alerted to Ryan's referral when he turns 4, and the school district will monitor his progress as he nears kindergarten. The service coordinator suggests scheduling an IFSP transition meeting for all interested. The resource materials director offers office space for the meeting and reminds the EHS director that she may check out any early childhood materials Ryan might need in the child-care program. The school's prekindergarten special education consultant offers to help the Early Head Start teachers at the EHS program on a short-term basis. The social services worker mentions that his agency can provide transportation for Ryan to the EHS program if necessary. They will continue to provide Ryan and his mother with transportation to his health care provider.

Interagency coordinating councils integrate services for young children and their families. Cooperation, collaboration, and a genuine desire to share information are requirements for successful councils. The LICC has the potential of providing seamless services to young children and their families. Swan and Morgan (1993) and Hayden et al. (2001) provide excellent guides for creating effective local interagency coordinating councils. Swan and Morgan outline some of the key components to effective LICC collaboration.

1. One agency alone cannot provide all the services needed for a young child with special needs or at high risk, along with his or her family.
2. With limited resources and categorical focus, agency programs must coordinate efforts to avoid waste, unnecessary duplication, and service gaps.

316 Part III Implementation of Interactive Teaming

3. There is nothing to be gained by competition. The agency that provides the service is not as important as the fact that the child and family are appropriately served.

4. The differences across agency programs represent a strength, not a weakness or problem to be eliminated.

5. The service delivery system must consist of a variety of options from which families may choose.

6. Agency programs are "equal" in importance.

7. Agencies must provide mutual support and assistance to one another. Favorable trade-offs exist.

8. A structured system of interagency collaboration must exist. (Swan & Morgan, p. 15)

Once an LICC is created, service delivery options can be expanded. For example, if the LICC had not been working cooperatively, Ryan may have gone without services for a year and his mother might have felt pressured to stay at home, opting to remain on government assistance and not earn her GED. The absence of early intervention between ages 3 and 4 may have placed Ryan at risk for further developmental delays and placement into special education.

Service delivery options vary depending on the age and special needs of the young child. For newborns and infants with significant disabilities, service delivery begins in a *hospital-based program*. An understanding of the complex residual medical complication of critically ill newborns in neonatal intensive care units (NICUs) is extremely important for early intervention professionals (McNab & Blackman, 1998). NICUs are graded by the level of care provided, with the Level 1 NICU providing the routine newborn care. The Level 2 NICUs provide care for newborns with a moderate degree of illness or newborns with illnesses that are complex or difficult to diagnose. Lastly, Level 3 NICUs provide the most significant treatment for infants with severe illness (Brown et al., 1993). NICU programs have expanded to encompass a range of professionals, including pediatricians; neonatologists; NICU nurses; social workers; physical, occupational, speech-language, and respiratory therapists; audiologists; and infant developmental specialists (i.e., early childhood special educators). Most NICU programs focus on family support, including programs that encourage social interactions between the infants and their caregivers. A family-centered approach is most critical in the NICU where the emotional and psychological needs of families are emphasized (March of Dimes, 2003; McNab & Blackman, 1998). Another goal of NICU-based programs is preparing families for the transition from hospital to home. IFSP plans can be designed with families and professionals during the infant's stay in the NICU and follow the child to the Part C community or home-based program once he or she is discharged.

Infants being discharged from NICU are often linked to *developmental follow-up programs*. The purposes of this service delivery option include (1) providing ongoing support for families, (2) smoothing the transition for the infant and families,

(3) directing the family toward appropriate community resources, and (4) providing ongoing secondary care of infants (Brown et al., 1993, p. 224). Professionals involved with developmental follow-up programs must be closely linked with community services and the LICC. Follow-up programs are important for infants with established conditions as well as infants who are at risk for developmental delays.

Because of the IDEA 1997 legislation, services for young children with special needs should be in natural environments (i.e., those in which typically developing children would participate). Several service delivery models are used in early intervention that supports this philosophy.

Home-based programs are most appropriate for infants and toddlers with special needs who are younger than 18 months. Home-based programs require that professionals be competent in working with families within their home environment. This model of service delivery reinforces family-centered versus child-centered intervention; however, intervention is provided less frequently. Related service personnel must be careful to coordinate services with the quality advisor or home visitor to ensure that families are not overwhelmed by home visits and intrusion into their private lives. Transdisciplinary models of teaming are critical in home-based programs, where the home visitor has knowledge of all aspects of the infant's intervention program. Paraprofessionals have been effective as home visitors in early intervention programs by supporting parents of children with special health care and developmental needs and helping them navigate the service system (Rosenberg, Robinson, & Fryer, 2002). Other team members serve as consultants to the home visitor.

For some toddlers and preschoolers ages 18 months to 3 years, *center-based programs* in inclusive community child-care settings can be beneficial. For younger toddlers, half-day center-based programs may be more appropriate. Although contact with families may be less frequent, professionals must continue providing a family-centered approach to center-based services. Evening or weekend parent support programs can be established to meet the needs of some families. There has been a steady increase in services provided by early interventionists occurring in community-based settings (e.g., child-care sites, family center, churches, other service agencies, libraries) (Hooper & Umansky, 2003; Odom, 2002). The shift from segregated settings to community and neighborhood settings is positive and implies the need for more collaborative relationships across service providers. Consulting and collaborating with child-care providers, faith-based program providers, and other community-based providers becomes one of the most important roles of early childhood special educators as community-based settings become an available option for service delivery.

Several inclusive service delivery models have been described by Odom et al. (1999) and Odom (2002), including the following:

1. *Itinerant-direct service model.* The specialized professionals work directly with the children with special needs and are responsible for delivering the individual services.

2. *Itinerant teaching-collaborative/consultative model.* This model differs from the direct service model in that the specialized professional's role is to work with the classroom teacher to establish activities and experiences in the program without support.

3. *Team teaching model.* An early childhood teacher and special education teacher both teach in the same classroom.

4. *Early childhood teacher model.* An early childhood teacher has the primary responsibility for planning, implementing, and monitoring classroom activities and has little contact with specialized professionals.

5. *Early childhood special education model.* A reverse mainstreaming model where a special education teacher serves as the lead teacher and usually works with an assistant teacher.

6. *Integrative inclusive activity model.* Children with special needs are enrolled in an early childhood special education class, and developing children are typically enrolled in an early childhood classroom. Both classes are located in the same building. For a part of the day, and for certain activities, the two classes merge for integrative-inclusive experiences.

While these six models have been reported as some of the most common examples for serving young children with special needs, other researchers have reported over 22 different classroom patterns for early intervention (Dunst, Bruder, Trivette, Raab, & McLean, 1998). No matter what model is employed, however, each requires some degree of collaboration and interactive teaming among professionals. For example, Sadler (2003) provides a list of skills that itinerant early childhood special education teachers should know and do to ensure quality programs. The itinerant teacher has two major roles: (1) providing direct services (usually once a week), and (2) offering collaboration-consultation services. In those roles, itinerant teachers need to do the following:

♦ Stay current on best practices in preacademic instruction and guide families to quality programs.

♦ Know when children need an annual goal for preacademic skills on their IEP.

♦ Know how to write preacademic objectives that are relevant to the child, family, and classroom.

♦ Know a continuum of techniques that could be used to teach these objectives in community settings. (Sadler, p. 9)

The transition from Part C to Part B usually occurs when the child reaches his or her third birthday. The IDEA regulations require that a transition plan be developed no later than 90 days prior to the child's third birthday. The plan should outline the process that will be incorporated in selecting and preparing the receiving program for enrollment of the child. Most communities offer Part B programs for 3- to 5-year-old children with special needs in local elementary schools. In those cases, family members are encouraged to visit the receiving program and coordinate the child's transition into the public school. This can often be a difficult transition for families who have become indoctrinated to a more personal, family-centered approach and now face a more child-centered and public school bureaucratic system. The child's IFSP can be used as the transition document; however, some school districts prefer to reevaluate the child and develop a new IEP. Because transition services occur across agencies and are sometimes extremely complex, collaboration is essential. To establish a community-wide transition system, professionals and families should seek technical assistance, and sample policies and procedures should be used to develop local transition models (Rosenkoetter, Whaley, Hains, & Pierce, 2001).

Assessment Techniques

An important component of early intervention programs involves assessment of young children and their families. The IFSP should address child needs and outcomes as well as family concerns, priorities, and needs requiring professionals to understand comprehensive ecological assessment techniques.

Arena assessments have become one of the most promising approaches to child assessment. These assessments require interactive teaming skills from each professional. Working together with the family, early intervention professionals provide a natural play environment in which to observe the infant interacting with toys, objects, adults, and peers. Linder (1997) describes a transdisciplinary play-based assessment technique that involves multiple professionals observing the abilities of young children through play. The play facilitator interacts with the child, providing opportunities for other team members to observe developmental skills in the language, cognition, motor, and social/emotional domains. Planning the play activities is an important initial step for the transdisciplinary assessment team. A parent facilitator is selected to work with the family member present during the play session and gather information on the family's needs and concerns. After the assessment, team members review the videotaped assessment and work together to interpret the results and plan the intervention. The arena model of assessment encourages collaboration and consultation from all team members.

McLean, Wolery, and Bailey (2004) provide an excellent overview of assessment strategies for young children with special needs. Most approaches require some degree of interactive teaming.

Intervention Strategies

Effective early intervention programs provide individualized and developmentally appropriate practices in natural settings to young children with special needs (Bredekamp & Copple, 1997; Bredekamp & Rosengrant, 1995; Carta, 1995; Cook et al., 2004; Sandall, McLean, & Smith, 2000). For some children, specialized instructional strategies may be required. Cook et al. (2004) and Hooper and Umansky (2003) highlight some recommended strategies for early intervention.

1. Structure the physical space to promote play, engagement, and learning.
2. Structure the social environment by using models, proximity, and responsive adults to promote engagement and learning.
3. Use children's preferences to promote learning.
4. Structure routines using violation of expectancy, naturalistic time delay, and transition-based teaching.
5. Use structured play activities.
6. Use differential reinforcement, response shaping, and correspondence training.
7. Use peer-mediated strategies to promote communication and social skills.
8. Use naturalistic or milieu teaching strategies to promote communication and social skills.
9. Use response-prompting procedures and stimulus modification.

Many of these instructional strategies will have to be understood by families, paraprofessionals, and general early childhood educators serving young children with special needs in their early childhood programs. Special education personnel will help educators integrate these strategies into an early childhood program that supports developmentally appropriate practices (DAP). The following guidelines characterize DAP:

1. Activities should be integrated across developmental domains.
2. Children's interests and progress should be identified through teacher observation.
3. Teachers should prepare the environment to facilitate children's active exploration and interaction.
4. Learning activities and materials should be concrete, real, and culturally relevant to young children's lives.
5. A wide range of interesting activities should be provided.
6. The complexity and challenge of activities should increase as children understand the skills involved (Bredekamp & Copple, 1997).

No single philosophical approach to early intervention meets the needs of the diverse population. A combination of individualized and adapted instructional strategies with a DAP approach is the ideal model for early intervention.

Much attention has been placed on early literacy development (Barone & Morrow, 2003; Hockenberger, Goldstein, & Haas, 1999; Neuman, Copple, & Bredekamp, 2000; Rush, 1999) and linguistic performance (Crain-Thoreson & Dale, 1999) in young children with special needs and children at risk for learning. Furthermore, we are learning much more about early literacy development for children whose first language is not English (Tabors, 1997). Early interventionists should focus a majority of their instructional programs on developing children's early literacy skills such as listening, speaking, reading, and writing. Literacy is an integral part of the learning process and requires a strong partnership with family members at home.

Essential features of effective early intervention services include family-centered approaches, coordinated service delivery options, transdisciplinary assessments, and individualized and developmentally appropriate practices of instruction. Professionals from many disciplines are involved in providing effective services to young children and their families. Their roles and responsibilities are critical to the success of early intervention programs. The next section addresses the various roles of early intervention professionals.

THE ROLE OF THE PROFESSIONALS

Part C of the IDEA specified 11 disciplines that were actively involved in early intervention services in every state. The general roles of professionals have been outlined in Chapter 3; specialized contributions of team members who work with infants, toddlers, and preschoolers with special needs are outlined here.

Delineating the roles of each of the team members within the educational and community setting is a first step in clarifying each group's function on the team. Table 9.1 outlines the various roles and responsibilities in both direct service and team involvement.

Although family members are not delineated as one of the 11 disciplines in the Part C legislation, they play one of the most important roles on the interactive team. Families can do the following: (1) reinforce developmental and therapeutic programs in the home and community setting, (2) inform team members of the results of health-related appointments and treatment recommendations, and (3) provide team members with information on medical, behavioral, and family issues. In addition, families should be respected if they choose not to be actively involved because of external or family stresses (e.g., work schedules, family crisis; Hanson & Lynch, 2004; Lambie, 2000).

Other team members that may participate in interactive teams are agency or school administrators and paraprofessionals. Administrators may (1) support inclusive early education programs by providing resources and materials for those programs, (2) provide professional development to team members, and (3) advocate for the program. Paraprofessionals and volunteers can (1) ensure that the environment is ready and safe for young children, (2) provide follow-up to instructional programs throughout the day, and (3) assist in all early intervention activities by valuing child-directed and child-initiated responses. It is important for the teacher to outline the job-task descriptions for the classroom assistant as well as to think carefully about his or her role relationship philosophy. Cook et al.

Table 9.1

Roles of Professionals and Others Involved with Infants, Toddlers, and Preschoolers with Disabilities and Their Families

Personnel	Direct Service Provider	Team Member
Paraprofessional	• Prepare the room by setting up centers and materials for daily activities • Greet the children and assist with classroom routines such as lunch, toileting, and dismissal • Supervise lunch and playground activities • Make educational games and materials for classroom activities • Storing and filing classroom materials and educational games • Assist children with adaptive technology	• Support team by following through on educational and behavioral programs designed for children • Work with team to involve parents by assisting in contacting parents • Support team by accepting role-release jobs such as positioning, transporting, and placing children in adaptive equipment • Teach specific lessons planned by team members • Attend IFSP/IEP meetings and share observations of child's developmental progress • Accompany team members on home visits
Audiologists	• Determine auditory function and characteristic of hearing losses • Assess and monitor middle ear infections • Determine the relationship of auditory function and communication development • Recommend appropriate amplification or assistive devices	• Interpret all auditory function reports to family and professionals • Provide team members with instruction on hearing loss and use of amplification or assistive devices
Early childhood special educators	• Conduct screening and child-find programs • Assess children's developmental competence • Develop an individualized IFSP or IEP for each child and family • Assess family needs and strengths • Implement family support services or parent education • Evaluate program effectiveness • Advocate for children and families	• Coordinate interdisciplinary services • Integrate and implement inter-disciplinary team recommendations • Coordinate services from multiple agencies • Provide consultation to other professionals, families, and other caregivers • Support inclusive early intervention by serving as itinerant/consultant to the early childhood educators
Early childhood general educators	• Develop learning environments and activities that promote DAP philosophy • Develop learning environments and activities that promote social	• Integrate interdisciplinary team recommendations • Collaborate with ECSE on instructional strategies and social integration for children with special needs

322

Personnel	Direct Service Provider	Team Member
	interactions of children with and without disabilities • Integrate multicultural education into all aspects of program • Provide families with information and support related to enhancing the development of the child • Evaluate program effectiveness • Advocate for children and families	• Provide consultation to other professionals, families, and other caregivers
Nutritionists	• Develop nutrition care plans through assessments of nutritional status, food intake, eating behavior, and feeding skills	• Coordinate nutrition services • Provide consultation and technical assistance to parents and team members • Provide preventive nutrition information, services, and guidance • Make referrals to community resources
Nurses	• Assess physiological, psychological, and developmental characteristics of the child and family • Plan and implement interventions to improve the child's health and developmental status • Develop medical plans to treat underlying causes of medical or developmental problems • Administer medications, treatments, and regimens prescribed by a licensed physician • Monitor complex medical procedures (tracheotomy suctioning, catheterization procedures, G-tube feeding, mechanical ventilation, etc.)	• Collaborate with caregivers and team members to meet basic health and daily care needs of the child • Assist in interpreting all medical information and reports • Make referrals to community resources
Occupational therapists	• Assess children's developmental levels, functional performance, sensory processing, and adaptive responses • Assess family-infant interactions • Recommend, select, design, and fabricate assistive seating and orthotic devices • Prevent secondary impairments	• Provide consultation to other professionals and families on the child's functioning and integrate therapy recommendations • Consult with caregivers and team members on adaptive or assistive devices

Continued

Table 9.1
Continued.

Personnel	Direct Service Provider	Team Member
Physicians	• Provide services to the child, including assessment, comprehensive medical care, diagnosis, treatment, and referral	• Provide consultation and instruction to parents and team members • Consult in community settings to provide diagnostic and treatment services
Psychologists	• Administer psychological and developmental tests and other assessment procedures • Plan a program of psychological services, including family counseling, parent training, and child development	• Integrate and interpret assessment information to parents and team members • Coordinate psychological services • Collaborate with team members on family needs and strengths
Physical therapists	• Assess for motor skills, neuromotor, neuromusculoskeletal, cardiopulmonary, oral motor, and feeding • Implement environmental modifications and recommend adaptive equipment and mobility devices	• Provide consultation to teach handling, positioning, and movement techniques to facilitate motor functioning and posture • Collaborate on methods for integrating therapy into the child's program
Social workers	• Make home visits to evaluate a child's living conditions and patterns of parent-child interaction • Assess psychosocial development of the child within the family context • Provide individual or group counseling for family members	• Build partnerships with the family • Consult with team members on family needs and strengths • Coordinate community services • Consult with team members on the impact of culture on the family, and how to provide culturally competent intervention
Speech-language pathologists	• Assess communication and oral-motor abilities • Plan and implement appropriate therapeutic programs • Design augmentative communication systems including manual sign language, computerized communication devices, or picture/symbol systems	• Provide consultation to caregivers and team members regarding communication and oral-motor therapy programs • Refer children to medical or other professional services as necessary
Vision specialist	• Conduct assessment of functional vision • Determine the relationship of development and visual loss	• Interpret visual functioning to caregivers and team members • Consult and refer children to medical or other professional services necessary

Source: Adapted from Bailey (1989). Case management in early intervention. *Journal of Early Intervention, 13,* 120–134.

Personnel	Direct Service Provider	Team Member
	• Provide early orientation and mobility programs • Recommend assistive or low-vision devices	• Collaborate on designing environments that accommodate the child's visual loss • Teach caregivers and team members sighted-guide techniques • Assist caregivers and team members with pre-Braille or low-vision instruction

(2004) outline a range of role; relationship philosophies that move from an authoritative style to one that involves coaching. The three philosophies range in assistance and supervision as follows:

◆ *The teacher is the authority who makes all decisions and issues directives.* Paraprofessionals given little or no freedom are dependent on the teacher to tell them what to do, when, and how, since only the teacher's way is "right."

◆ *The teacher asks for suggestions and discusses child-instructional issues.* Paraprofessionals have some involvement with the teacher in planning and moderate autonomy to perform tasks within the general guidelines.

◆ *The teacher serves in a counseling or support role when needed.* Paraprofessionals are assigned broad tasks and are trained and coached by the teacher to function independently in planning and carrying out activities consistent with educational philosophy.

These authors further describe methods for recruiting paraprofessional services, communicating expectations, providing constructive feedback, and evaluating paraprofessional services. Paraprofessionals and volunteers are often from the children's community culture and can serve as cultural mediators to the team.

The role of the *quality advisor* or *service coordinator* can vary with individual children and families. A paradigm of service coordination has emerged under Part C that emphasizes family-driven versus agency-driven practices (Cook et al., 2004; Dunst, 2002). Two levels of service coordination and integration have been defined in the literature (Summers et al., 2001). One level is coordination of community services and the other level is coordination of child and family services. The interagency coordinating councils are the primary vehicles for the community level of service coordination. The service coordinator's role is to organize comprehensive services and mobilize resources when necessary. It is important to note that family members can serve as their child's primary service coordinator under Part C regulations. At the family level, the service coordinator assists specific families in the ongoing process of coordinating and monitoring services across the various providers. The individual service coordinator helps the family identify short-term and long-term outcomes and support services needed, and also helps the family gain access to these services (Cook et al., 2004). If services do not exist, the service coordinator mobilizes resources and services required.

The role of each team member is critical to the success of providing coordinated and appropriate services to young children and their families. In previous chapters we have discussed the importance of developing interactive teams. Professionals and family members often do not possess the knowledge and skills necessary to collaborate and work effectively in teams. In early childhood, models of inservice that emphasize an interactive team approach to learning and implementing recommended practices have been effective (Olson, Murphy, & Olson, 1998; Palsha & Wesley, 1998). For example, in the Building Effective Successful Teams (BEST) inservice model, the team, not separate individuals, is responsible for completing and applying information from inservice training materials (Olson et al., 1998), thereby creating a stronger connectedness among the individuals in the team. Three self-study packages were developed for inservice training areas: (1) team building, (2) activity-based programming, and (3) building partnerships with families. Figure 9.1 describes one of the team-building exercises used for evaluating how well teams communicate.

The Ball of Yarn Game

Directions: You will all be sitting on the ground in a circle or around a table. Only the person holding the ball of yarn may speak. The person with the ball must keep it until someone signals nonverbally that he or she wishes to have it. The person who is passing the yarn holds on to an end of it so that a pattern starts to emerge as the yarn unwinds. The individual holding the ball may refuse to give it to a member who requests it. The discussion should last for 10 minutes, at the end of which time there will be an elaborate pattern of yarn on the ground between the participants from all the times the yarn was passed from hand to hand. Start your discussion by deciding what to discuss. [For this chapter's exercise, the participants should discuss a topic related to early intervention and early childhood special education.] The individual who starts this discussion can ask the questions, "O.K. What shall we discuss?" After completing the game, discuss what the yarn "interaction-o-gram" tells you. Then answer the following questions.

- What do the patterns you see tell you about your team?
- What does this tell you about active or silent members?
- What did it feel like to hold the ball or to want the ball when you couldn't have it?
- How does this game reflect the real communication patterns on your team?

Figure 9.1
Example exercise from the BEST inservice project.

Source: From Building Effective Successful Teams: An Interactive Teaming Model for Inservice Education, by J. Olson, C. L. Murphy, and P. D. Olson, 1998, *Journal of Early Intervention, 21*(3), p. 344. Copyright 1998 by the Division for Early Childhood. Adapted with permission.

Although interactive teaming is highly effective in working with young children and their families, it requires more than direct intervention from an array of experienced professionals. Developing effective early childhood interactive teams takes training, time, trust, and commitment. The efforts being done in early childhood special education toward this end are commendable. General educators and special educators of school-age children might benefit from adopting or adapting the unique features of early intervention collaboration outlined in this chapter.

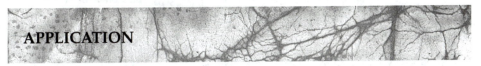

APPLICATION

In this section, we follow Anthony, a 5-year-old with developmental disabilities, through the various service agencies he and his parents have used during the past 5 years. Anthony's parents have worked with personnel from the local hospital, follow-up clinic, early intervention program, child-care center, and school district during the past 5 years as they have been transitioned from one service agency to another. They say the transitions have been smooth and the personnel supportive and collaborative. The following paragraphs describe the various steps and strategies that were used during each of the transitions. The *assess-plan-implement-evaluate* framework for transition planning was used by each sending and receiving program or agency (Rosenkoetter, Hains, & Fowler, 1994; Wesley & Buysse, 1996).

Hospital Transition

Anthony was born 3 months premature and weighed less than 4 pounds. He stayed in a Level 3 NICU for 3 months while physicians monitored bleeding in his head, respiratory problems, and severe jaundice. During that time, Anthony's parents connected with the NICU family support program. The program team consisted of a social worker who specialized in working with NICU families, a developmental psychologist, Anthony's primary physicians, a nurse, and a service coordinator from the hospital's neonatal follow-up program.

Team members met regularly to discuss Anthony's progress with the family, and extended family members were encouraged to participate in these sessions. The social worker invited the parents to attend an NICU parent support group, which met in the evenings once a week. Anthony showed much improvement during his stay in the NICU and was moved to a Level 1 NICU after 3 months.

The team began to prepare the family for the first transition: taking Anthony home. The nurse provided the family with instructions for Anthony's heart monitor, medication regimen, and dates for home visits. The service coordinator provided the family with information on the follow-up clinic and scheduled their first appointment, and the developmental psychologist reported her findings from neurobehavioral and developmental assessments. Anthony appeared to have some moderate developmental delays, and early stimulation and intervention strategies were discussed with the family. The social worker invited the parents to attend the 1-year reunion for families that had been part of the support group. A discharge conference was scheduled with the family and the team; thus, an IFSP was created. All the information on the transition activities, programs, and agencies, phone numbers, and scheduled appointments were given to the parents in the transition notebook.

Neonatal Follow-Up Transition

Anthony was home at 5 months and was being followed up by the nurse and service co-ordinator. The primary concerns and intervention program were focused on Anthony's medical stability and early development. After 3 months, the family and service coordinator met with the home-based teacher from the local Part C early intervention program. A new transition team was formed consisting of the home-based teacher, family therapists, and psychologist. They met for a few evenings to discuss the transition from follow-up clinic to the home visitation program.

Anthony had improved medically and was to be monitored by the follow-up clinic annually. The team discussed Anthony's continued delay in gross motor and cognitive skill development and his IFSP was updated. The family concerns and outcomes were focused on providing an early stimulation program and finding a support group for the mother, who was feeling isolated from other parents.

Home-Based and Center-Based Early Intervention Transition

The home-based teacher visited the family every week, providing them with activities for developmental stimulation. The early intervention program began providing monthly physical therapy and speech therapy services. The teacher and parents, however, were shown the therapeutic programs to integrate into Anthony's daily routines. His mother began attending a support group at the early intervention program.

When Anthony turned 15 months, the home-based teacher initiated the transition plan for him to enter a local child-care program serving children with and without disabilities in a natural environment. The parents and home-based teacher observed the classroom and evaluated what would be necessary for him to attend. The parents attended the IFSP transition meeting and three new members joined the team: the child-care classroom teacher, the nutritionist, and the occupational therapist. A plan was developed that included scheduling transportation, ordering positioning equipment and feeding utensils, and scheduling a phase-in period. Three months later Anthony began to attend the local child-care center. Anthony's parents linked up with the early intervention family support group. The parents and team met every 6 months to review the IFSP.

When Anthony turned 28 months old, another transition meeting was scheduled. This time the child-care center teacher and parents went to the local school district prekindergarten program. They evaluated the environment, and talked with the principal, teacher, and school psychologist. The school's early childhood teacher also visited Anthony at the child-care center. He was referred to the special education program and a psychological assessment was completed. The child-care center team (sending agency) and the school district team (receiving agency) met to plan for the transition to the prekindergarten program at the elementary school. The plan included (1) a sending and receiving agency communication plan, (2) a plan to expand the IFSP outcomes to IEP goals, and (3) a plan to evaluate Anthony's transition.

School District Transition

The receiving agency implemented the specified objectives in the transition plan and prepared the environment to meet his needs. When Anthony turned 3, the parents and team met once again and evaluated if the school district was ready to receive Anthony.

All documents were transferred to the early childhood teacher, including data collection and anecdotal progress notes. The parents were linked with the school's parent support group and were introduced to all school staff. The first day of school, Anthony's child-care center teacher stayed with him in the classroom. The transition was smooth, and Anthony adapted well to his new program.

Observations

In less than 3 years, Anthony's family dealt with more than 13 professionals. Each transition brought the parents stress and anxiety. However, the team members were sensitive to the needs of the family adjusting to an infant with special needs. The family-centered approach was evident throughout the process. Parents were included in all meetings when they were able to attend. No decisions were made without them. They were empowered to assess-plan-implement-evaluate each of the programs before the transitions. Each team member was treated with equal respect and openness. Documentation was provided for the family at each step of the way. For programs serving young children with special needs to be seamless in the delivery of services, professionals and parents must communicate, collaborate, and consult.

SUMMARY

Collaboration and teaming are integral components to serving young children with special needs and their families. Legislative backing for cooperation and integration of a system that has typically been fragmented has created a great opportunity to improve services to these individuals. The diverse characteristics of the young children receiving services in early intervention programs further justify the need for interactive teaming. More and more children live in environments or suffer from physiological conditions that put them at risk for developmental delays. Additionally, personnel must understand that the advantages of family-centered approaches far outweigh the agency-driven or child-centered approaches of yesterday's programs.

A continuum of service delivery options is necessary to meet the needs of infants, toddlers, and preschoolers with special needs and their families. However, those options and that array of services must be closely coordinated and monitored. Intervention strategies must be individualized and developmentally appropriate for all children, and transdisciplinary-arena assessments should be supported by the team. The family should be empowered to take an active role in deciding what they need and how they want those needs met. The roles of professionals on the early intervention team should be formed around the family, enabling the family to make informed decisions. As equal partners, each team member can offer valuable information and skill development to the team. Collaboration and consultation among early interventionists can result in high-quality services for young children and their families.

ACTIVITIES

1. Conduct an informational interview with a professional who is involved in early intervention programs for young children with special needs or at risk. Use the guidelines provided in Chapter 3.

2. Attend a local interagency coordinating council meeting. Observe the teaming and collaboration skills among the professionals.

3. Volunteer at a local child-care center, an early childhood prekindergarten program, an Early Head Start or Head Start classroom, or NICU "cuddle program." Use child-directed approaches to play and develop social interactions with children.

4. Invite family members of young children with special needs to participate in class lectures about family-centered intervention.

5. Invite neonatologists, nurses, or developmental psychologists to visit the class to talk about how parents are involved in the care of NICU infants and get information on how the hospital deals with drug-addicted or HIV-infected babies.

6. Attend tours of schools and community agencies serving young children with special needs or children at risk. Note the goal and mission of the various agencies as related to the quality of services provided to the children and their families.

7. Play the "Ball of Yarn Game" in class over an early childhood topic familiar to the small group of students in class.

REFERENCES

Bailey, D. B. (1989). Case management in early intervention. *Journal of Early Intervention, 13,* 120–134.

Barone, D., & Morrow, L. (2003). *Literacy and young children: Research-based practices.* Port Chester, NY: National Professional Resources.

Bredekamp, S., & Copple, C. (1997). *Developmentally appropriate practices in early childhood programs* (rev. ed.). Washington, DC: National Association for the Education of Young Children.

Bredekamp, S., & Rosengrant, T. (Eds.). (1995). *Reaching potentials: Transforming early childhood curriculum and assessment* (Vol. 2). Washington, DC: National Association for the Education of Young Children.

Brown, W., Thurman, S. K., & Pearl, L. E. (1993). *Family-centered early intervention with infants and toddlers: Innovative cross-disciplinary approaches.* Baltimore: Paul H. Brookes.

Bruder, M. B. (2000). *The individual family service plan (IFSP).* Arlington, VA: ERIC Clearinghouse on Disabilities and Gifted Education. Retrieved December 27, 2003, from http://ericec.org/digests/e605.html

Carta, J. (1995). Developmentally appropriate practice: A critical analysis as applied to young children with disabilities. *Focus on Exceptional Children, 27,* 1–14.

Cook, R. E., Klein, M. D., & Tessier, A. (2004). *Adapting early childhood curricula for children in inclusive settings* (6th ed.). Upper Saddle River, NJ: Merrill/Prentice Hall.

Correa, V. I., & Jones, H. A. (2003). Early childhood special education. In F. Obiakor, C. Utley, & A. Rotatori, *Advances in special education: Psychology of effective education for learners with exceptionalities* (pp. 351–372). Stamford, CT: JAI Press.

Crain-Thoreson, C., & Dale, P. (1999). Enhancing linguistic performance: Parents and teachers as book reading partners for children with language delays. *Topics in Early Childhood Special Education, 19,* 28–39.

Dunst, C. J. (2002). Family-centered practices: Birth through high school. *Journal of Special Education, 36,* 139–147.

Dunst, C. J., Bruder, M. B., Trivette, C., Raab, M., & McLean, M. (1998). *Increasing children's learning opportunities through families and communities.* Early Childhood Research Institute, Year 2 Progress Report, Submitted to the U.S. Department of Education, Office of Special Education Programs, Washington, DC.

Ellis, M., & Kane, K. (August, 2000). *Lightening the lead load in children.* American Family Physician. Retrieved December 31, 2003, from http://www.aafp.org/afp/20000801/545.html

Gollnick, D., & Chinn, P. (2002). *Multicultural education in a pluralistic society* (6th ed.). Upper Saddle River, NJ: Merrill/Prentice Hall.

Habek, D., Habek, J. E., Ivanievic, M., & Djelmic, J. (2002). Fetal tobacco syndrome and perinatal outcomes. *Fetal Diagnosis and Therapy, 17,* 367–371.

Hanson, M., & Lynch, E. (2004). *Understanding families: Approaches to diversity, disability, and risk.* Baltimore: Paul H. Brookes.

Harbin, G. (1998). Welfare reform and its effect on the system of early intervention. *Journal of Early Intervention, 21,* 211–215.

Hayden, P., Frederick, L., Smith, B., & Broudy, A. (2001). *Tasks, tips, and tools for promoting collaborative community teams.* Denver: Collaborative Planning Project, University of Colorado at Denver. Retrieved January 11, 2004, from http://www.nectac.org/inclusion/collab/natlcollab.asp

Hockenberger, E. H., Goldstein, H., & Haas, L. S. (1999). Effects of commenting during joint book reading by mothers with low SES. *Topics in Early Childhood Special Education, 19,* 15–27.

Hooper, S. R., & Umansky, W. (2003). *Young children with special needs* (4th ed.). Upper Saddle River, NJ: Prentice Hall.

Jacobson, J., & Jacobson, S. (2002). Effects of prenatal alcohol exposure on child development. *Alcohol Research and Health, 26*(4), 282–286.

Janko-Summers, S., & Joseph, G. (1998). Making sense of early intervention in the context of welfare to work. *Journal of Early Intervention, 21,* 207–210.

Klitsch, M. (2002). Children with prenatal cocaine exposure have elevated risk of cognitive impairments at least until age two. *Perspectives on Sexual and Reproductive Health, 34*(6). Retrieved December 31, 2003, from http://www.agi-usa.org/pubs/journals/3431702.html

Lambie, R. (2000). *Family systems within educational contexts: Understanding at-risk and special-needs students* (2nd ed.). Denver, CO: Love Publishing.

Lass, N. (2000). Understanding cocaine's effect on the developing brain: Implications for the classroom. *Lutheran Education, 136,* 103–115.

Linder, T. W. (1997). *Transdisciplinary play-based assessment: A functional approach to working with young children.* Baltimore: Paul H. Brookes.

Mahoney, G., & Bella, J. M. (1998). An examination of the effects of family-centered early intervention on child and family outcomes. *Topics in Early Childhood Special Education, 18,* 83–94.

March of Dimes. (2003). *Parenting in the NICU.* White Plain, NY: Author. Retrieved December 31, 2003, from http://www.marchofdimes.com/prematurity/5430.asp

McGonigel, M. J., Kaufmann, R. K., & Johnson, B. H. (Eds.). (1991). *Guidelines and recommended practices for the individualized family service plan.* Bethesda, MD: Association for the Care of Children's Health.

McLean, M., Wolery, M., & Bailey, D. (2004). *Assessing infants and preschoolers with special needs* (3rd ed.). Upper Saddle River, NJ: Merrill/Prentice Hall.

McNab, T. C., & Blackman, J. A. (1998). Medical complications of the critically ill newborn: A review for early intervention professionals. *Topics in Early Childhood Special Education, 18,* 197–205.

McWilliam, R. A. (2000). Recommended practices in interdisciplinary models. In S. Sandall, M. E. McLean, & B. J. Smith (Eds.), *DEC recommended practices in early intervention/early childhood special education* (pp. 47–54). Longmont, CO: Sopris West.

McWilliam, R. A., Ferguson, A., Harbin, G., Porter, P., Munn, D., & Vandiviere, P. (1998). The family-centeredness of individualized family service plans. *Topics in Early Childhood Special Education, 18,* 69–82.

McWilliam, R. A., Maxwell, K., & Sloper, K. (1999). Beyond "involvement": Are elementary schools ready to be family centered? *The School Psychology Review, 28,* 378–394.

National Coalition for the Homeless. (2001). *Homeless families with children.* Washington, DC: Author. Retrieved December 29, 2003, from http://www.nationalhomeless.org/families.html

Neuman, S., Copple, C., & Bredekamp, S. (2000). *Learning to read and write: Developmentally appropriate practices for young children.* Washington, DC: NAEYC.

Odom, S. (2002). *Widening the circle: Including children with disabilities in preschool programs.* New York: Teachers College Press.

Odom, S., Horn, E., Marquart, J., Hanson, M., Wolfberg, P., Beckman, P., Lieber, J., Li, S., Schwartz, I., Janko, S., & Sandall, S. (1999). On the forms of inclusion: Organizational context and individualized service models. *Journal of Early Intervention, 22,* 185–199.

Olson, J., Murphy, C. L., & Olson, P. D. (1998). Building effective successful teams: An interactive teaming model for inservice education. *Journal of Early Intervention, 21,* 339–349.

Palsha, S., & Wesley, P. W. (1998). Improving quality in early childhood environments through on-site consultation. *Topics in Early Childhood Special Education, 18,* 243–253.

Polmanteer, K., & Turbiville, V. (2000). Family-responsive individualized family service plans for speech-language pathologists. *Language, Speech, and Hearing Services in Schools, 31,* 4–14.

Roberts, R., Akers, A., & Behl, D. (1999). *Opening doors through state interagency coordinating councils: A guide for families, communities, and states.* Logan, UT: Early Intervention Research Institute at Utah State University.

Rosenberg, S. A., Robinson, C., & Fryer, E. (2002). Evaluation of paraprofessional home visiting services in children with special needs and their families. *Topics in Early Childhood Special Education, 22,* 158–168.

Rosenkoetter, R., Whaley, K., Hains, A., & Pierce, L. (2001). The evolution of transition policy for young children with special needs and their families: Past, present, and future. *Topics in Early Childhood Special Education, 21,* 3–15.

Rosenkoetter, S. E., Hains, A. H., & Fowler, S. (1994). *Bridging early services for children with special needs and their families.* Baltimore: Paul H. Brookes.

Rush, K. L. (1999). Caregiver-child interactions and early literacy development of preschool children from low-income environments. *Topics in Early Childhood Special Education, 19,* 3–14.

Sadler, F. (2003). The itinerant special education teacher in the early childhood classroom. *Teaching Exceptional Children, 35,* 8–15.

Salend, S. J. (2000). *Effective mainstreaming: Creating inclusive classrooms* (4th ed.). Upper Saddle River, NJ: Merrill/Prentice Hall.

Sandall, S., McLean, M., & Smith, B. (2000). *DEC recommended practices in early intervention/early childhood special education.* Longmont, CO: Sopris.

Spiker, D., Hebbeler, K., Wagner, M., Cameto, R., & McKenna P. (2000). A framework for describing variations in state early intervention systems. *Topics in Early Childhood Special Education, 20,* 195–207.

Summers, J., Steeples, T., & Peterson, C. (2001). Policy and management supports for effective services integration in early Head Start and Part C programs. *Topics in Early Childhood Special Education, 21,* 16–30.

Sutton-Redner, J. (2002). *Children in a world of violence. Children in Need Magazine.* Retrieved November 20, 2003, from http://childreninneed.com/magazine/violence.html

Swan, W. W., & Morgan, J. L. (1993). *Collaborating for comprehensive services for young children and their families: The local interagency coordinating council.* Baltimore: Paul H. Brookes.

Tabors, P. O. (1997). *One child, two languages: A guide for preschool educators of children learning English as a second language.* Baltimore: Paul H. Brookes.

Wesley, P. E., & Buysse, V. (1996). Supporting early childhood inclusion: Lessons learned through a statewide technical assistance project. *Topics in Early Childhood Special Education, 16,* 476–499.

Wischnowski, M., Pfluke, J., & Twining, D. (2003). Head Start and school district collaborations: Writing an interagency agreement. *Young Exceptional Children, 6,* 11–17.

Implementation with Students with Mild Disabilities

10

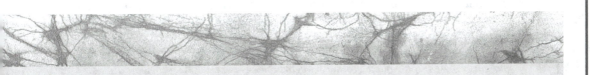

Topics in this chapter include:

- ◆ Characteristics of students with mild disabilities.

- ◆ Educational needs of students with mild disabilities.

- ◆ Service delivery options.

- ◆ Teacher competencies and selected teaching strategies.

- ◆ Description of roles of interactive team members.

- ◆ An application illustrating team members working together to meet the needs of a student with mild disabilities.

Andy, a personable 13-year-old, has become increasingly difficult to manage in Ms. Baker's eighth-grade math class. Although Andy repeated third grade, he is still behind in mathematics compared with his classmates. He is aware of the difficulties, and lately he has been acting out as a way of avoiding assignments. Rather than begin his seatwork when Ms. Baker gives an assignment, he gets up out of his seat to sharpen a just-broken pencil, or he turns to another child to talk. If he does get started on an assignment and has to erase a mistake, he angrily wads up the paper and begins again. Because of his poor math skills and the avoidance behaviors, he is falling further behind each day.

Ms. Rhodes, Andy's mother, is a single parent holding down two part-time jobs to support Andy and his older brother, Gregory. She is aware of his problems and is concerned, but when she has time to help him with his homework, he often demonstrates the same behaviors he does at school.

Andy was referred for testing in the middle of third grade, and by the end of the year, he was placed in a resource room for students with learning disabilities. In her summary of the psychological assessment, Dr. Eaddy noted Andy's low tolerance for frustration and his reluctance to attempt tasks because he did not want to fail.

Ms. Rodriquez, the resource teacher, has begun to work with Andy on his math and reading skills for 45 minutes each day. He seems to look forward to coming to the resource room because there are only six other students in the class, and he receives more individual attention. Even in this small setting, though, he glances around to see if other students are watching his struggles with math.

Ms. Rodriquez and Ms. Baker have asked the speech-language therapist for assistance in developing Andy's vocabulary and other types of language activities in which he can be successful. Mr. Morrow, the therapist, provided a number of activities that Andy seemed to enjoy initially, but he now appears to be growing wary of doing them because none of the other students are doing similar assignments.

Andy's strongest suit is his skill in sports. Lately he has become increasingly competitive because this is the only outlet in which he thinks he can do better than his peers. The emphasis on winning has alienated two of his friends, who have chosen to play with others because Andy seems so intent on winning rather than having fun or participating as a team player. The adapted physical education teacher, Ms. DiCicco, has suggested that during the PE period the teachers involve all the students in cooperative games so the interactions among the students will be more positive.

This vignette illustrates the complex array of problems that many students with mild disabilities or those considered "at risk" often face in school settings. This complexity presents real challenges to interactive team members in their roles as collaborators with other professionals and as direct service providers. In cases like Andy's, the interactive teaming model requires cooperation, commitment, and coordination of efforts among all the personnel involved to ensure continuity and comprehensive academic, social, and behavioral programming.

This chapter includes a discussion of the characteristics and needs of students with mild disabilities. Service delivery options, teacher competencies, and selected strategies also are presented. The last section of the chapter contains information on the roles of the professionals who may be involved in programming for children and adolescents with mild disabilities.

CHARACTERISTICS OF STUDENTS WITH MILD DISABILITIES

As discussed in Chapter 1, this country is experiencing a dramatic increase in the number of students considered at risk for school difficulties or failure. Many of these students will eventually be documented as having mild disabilities at some point in their school years; that is, they will be identified as having learning disabilities, mental retardation, or mild emotional/behavioral disorders. Currently, these students make up almost 90% of the school-age population identified as having disabilities, and they often have similar characteristics and needs (Mercer & Mercer, 2001; Morsink, Thomas, & Smith-Davis, 1987).

The term *mild disabilities* can also include students with sensory disabilities (e.g., vision and hearing), physical or health impairments (e.g., cerebral palsy or epilepsy), and communication disorders (e.g., speech and language problems). These students can be considered to have a mild disability if the severity of their disability and the extent of their educational needs are such that they are appropriately served in a general education classroom for at least part of the day. In addition, these students would be provided other types of services, such as speech-language therapy or remediation from a special educator, as needed.

Brief descriptions are provided to highlight characteristics of students in each area. Although this information will be familiar to special educators, school psychologists, and other personnel who received training on learners with exceptional needs as part of their programs, it is included here as reference material for interactive team members who may not have this knowledge or who need to update their information. The references cited in each area will be of further assistance to those who need more information. Additional material on pupils whose sensory, physical, or intellectual disabilities are more severe is provided in the next chapter.

Learning Disabilities

There has been longstanding concern by many authorities in the field regarding the definition of learning disabilities (Fuchs, Mock, Morgan, & Young, 2003). Mercer (1997) noted that the discrepancy between estimated ability and actual academic performance was the "common denominator" in defining this area of exceptionality. The most frequently used method for determining this discrepancy involves comparing the student's performance on an IQ test with performance on a standardized achievement test. This IQ-achievement discrepancy is fraught with problems and many experts agree that the assumptions underlying the IQ-achievement method are unsupported (Vaughn & Fuchs, 2003). A special issue of *Learning Disabilities Research and Practice* was recently published to address the concern and offer a solution through redefining learning disabilities as a response to instruction (Vaughn & Fuchs).

Specific academic difficulty areas typically include oral language, reading skills and comprehension, written expression, and mathematics calculation and reasoning. Other characteristics that may be present are visual and auditory perceptual disorders; lack of metacognitive strategies; social-emotional problems, including lack of motivation and hyperactivity; memory difficulties; motor disorders; and attention problems and hyperactivity (O'Shea, O'Shea, & Algozzine, 1998). Hallahan, Kauffman, and Lloyd (1999) observed that persons with learning disabilities also exhibit wide interindividual and intraindividual differences, and they often have other disabilities as well.

Emotional Disturbances/Behavior Disorders

Kauffman (1997) commented: "Defining an emotional or behavioral disorder is unavoidably subjective, at least in part" (p. 21). He noted that conceptual models, complexities of measurement systems for emotions and behaviors, the relationships among behavioral problems and other exceptionalities, and the transience of problems during developmental stages also compound the difficulty in determining accurate definitions. Another issue is the subjectivity of standards for determining a behavior disorder because expectations may vary by sex, age, subculture, community, and economic conditions (Cullinan & Epstein, 1994).

Identification procedures vary from state to state, but the most frequently cited characteristics are school learning problems (not due to mental retardation); difficulty in establishing and maintaining satisfactory interpersonal relationships; inappropriate feelings and manifestations of behaviors, unhappiness, or depression; and in some cases the existence of physical problems influenced by personal or school situations. Emotionally disturbed children frequently are impulsive, distractible, and hyperactive.

Attention-Deficit/Hyperactivity Disorder (AD/HD)

AD/HD is reported to affect between 3% to 5% of students in the United States (Tannock & Martinussen, 2001). The IDEA includes students with AD/HD under the category of other health impairments. The American Psychiatric Association (APA; 2000) describes the essential feature of AD/HD as "a persistent pattern of inattention and/or hyperactivity-impulsivity that is more frequently displayed and more severe than is typically observed in individuals at a comparable level of development" (p. 85). The three subtypes of AD/HD are (1) predominantly inattentive (IN), (2) predominantly hyperactive-impulsive, and (3) combined. Common characteristics across all three types include inattentiveness, disorganization, and poor motivation that interferes with academic performance as well as social and emotional development (Salend & Rohena, 2003).

Barkley (1998) describes students with AD/HD as displaying deficits in the four executive functions of behavioral inhibition (nonverbal working memory; internalization of speech; self-regulation of affect, motivation, and arousal; and reconstitution). As a result, they may experience cognitive, language, motor, and emotional problems.

Mental Retardation

The definition of mental retardation has evolved from one focusing primarily on significantly subaverage intelligence and associated adaptive behavior impairments to one that stresses interaction among the major dimensions of an individual's capabilities, the environments in which the person functions, and the need for varying levels of support (Beirne-Smith, Ittenbach, & Patton, 1998). The American Association on Mental Retardation (AAMR) revised the definition of mental retardation in 2002 as "a disability characterized by significant limitations both in intellectual functioning and in adaptive behavior as expressed in conceptual, social, and practical adaptive skills. This disability originates before age 18." (See Chapter 11 for more details.) The needed levels of support are based on four dimensions: (1) intellectual functioning and adaptive skills, (2) psychological/emotional considerations, (3) physical health/etiology considerations, and (4) environmental considerations. The four levels of needed support identified by the American Association on Mental Retardation (2002) are intermittent, limited, extensive, and pervasive.

Visual Impairments

Students with visual impairments exhibit a wide range of abilities. Some may have sight that is useful for some purposes, while others are blind or have such profound visual impairments that their vision is not usable as an educational medium. Because students with visual impairments have a limited ability to learn incidentally from their environment, they may experience difficulties in language, cognitive, motor, and social development (Heward, 2003; Turnbull, Turnbull, Shank, & Smith, 2004). They often need assistance with orientation, mobility (i.e., moving around in their environment), and daily living skills, in addition to other academic needs (Shea & Bauer, 1994).

Hallahan and Kauffman (2000) described educational definitions of blindness based on the method of reading instruction. They noted that individuals who have such severe impairments that they must use Braille or other aural methods such as audiotapes are considered blind, and those who can read print with or without magnifying devices have low vision.

Hearing Impairments

Although hearing loss exists on a continuum from mild to profound, hearing impairments are typically described in two groups: (1) *deaf* people, whose loss is so great that their hearing is not functional for everyday life; and (2) *hard-of-hearing* people, who have some degree of functional hearing with or without a hearing aid. The two predominant types of hearing impairments are *conductive*, which occurs in the outer or middle ear, and *sensorineural*, which occurs in the inner ear.

The effects of hearing loss influence language and communication development, as well as the social and emotional functioning of students. Children with hearing loss have difficulty with all areas of academic achievement, especially reading and mathematical concepts (ASHA, 2003). In addition to academics and social adjustment, students with hearing impairments may need help with listening skills and other forms of communication such as speech-reading, cued speech, and sign language (cf. Moores, 1996).

Physical Impairments

Physical impairments and special health care needs were defined in P.L. 94-142 and restated in amendments to the Individuals with Disabilities Education Act (IDEA). Three areas are included: (1) orthopedic impairments, (2) other health impairments, and (3) traumatic brain injury.

Orthopedic impairments include such congenital abnormalities as clubfoot, impairments caused by diseases such as poliomyelitis, and impairments resulting from other causes such as cerebral palsy. The impairments may range from mild to severe, and they *may or may not* be accompanied by other disabling conditions such as mental retardation or sensory deficits. Students with orthopedic impairments may need training in daily living and social skills, assistive technology devices to aid them in communication, and modifications for written assignments and tests. They also may require services to help them with physical flexibility and movement, or medication and special diets (Hill, 1999).

Other health impairments include chronic or acute problems such as asthma, hemophilia, epilepsy, AIDS, or diabetes that adversely affect educational performance. Traumatic brain injury is an acquired injury to the brain resulting in total or partial functional disability or psychosocial impairments. For students in both of these categories, modifications of instructional and service delivery options will be required and should be reviewed on a regular basis to ensure consistency with the child's or adolescent's current functioning level (Heward, 2003).

Communication Disorders

Communication disorders often overlap with other types of disabling conditions such as hearing impairments, mental retardation, cerebral palsy, or learning disabilities (Kirk, Gallagher, & Anastasiow, 1997; Wiig & Semel, 1984). Communication problems may take the form of a speech impairment, language impairment, or both. *Speech impairments* include articulation problems (e.g., substitutions or distortions of sounds), voice disorders (e.g., inappropriate quality or loudness), or fluency disorders (e.g., stuttering). Students with *language impairments* may experience difficulty with language comprehension and/or expression. Impairments may involve the form of language (phonology, morphology, syntax), the content of language (semantics), or the function of language in communication (pragmatics). In addition to remediation on the specific type of deficit, a student with a speech or language disorder may need help in an academic area such as reading, or with social interactions with peers including the possible use of an augmentative communication device (cf. Shames, Wiig, & Secord, 1998).

Considerations

Several considerations regarding students with mild disabilities are worthy of mention at this point. The first is that not all of the students within a category will exhibit all of the characteristics cited at any given time. Second, students may have combinations of conditions, such as behavior and speech disorders, that warrant a variety of services. Third, professionals should try to ensure that the difficulties or disorders being identified are not due to the cultural differences discussed in Chapter 8. Finally, labeling should be kept to a minimum because of the possible adverse reactions of parents or students. Instead, interactive team members should focus on students' strengths and specific needs, such as reading comprehension or interacting appropriately with peers, rather than on categorical labels.

MEETING EDUCATIONAL NEEDS

Based on the preceding description of characteristics of students who may be considered to have mild disabilities, the educational needs that emerge can be put into five major categories: (1) academic remediation, (2) social interactions, (3) self-concept and motivation, (4) behavior management, and (5) special education and support services (e.g., orientation and mobility, counseling, physical therapy, etc.). To consider ways of addressing these needs, four programmatic areas are discussed: (1) the process of identifying problems and designing interventions, (2) service delivery options, (3) teacher competencies, and (4) selected teaching strategies.

Although the emphasis in this section is on teachers and teaching strategies, many of the principles can be implemented by team members with other areas of expertise, such as psychology, adapted physical education, assistive technology, and speech-language therapy. These principles should be viewed as supplementary and complementary to existing literature on competencies and effective strategies in each individual field, not as replacements for them. Also, these competencies are in addition to those already discussed as necessary for functioning as a successful team member.

Problem Identification and Designing Interventions

The actual steps used in problem identification and intervention design should be based on the sequence described in Chapter 2. These steps ensure *understanding and clarity of the problem, discussion of previous interventions, identification of data collection procedures and data decision rules, consensus on interventions to be attempted,* and *procedures for evaluating effectiveness and making modifications as necessary.*

These procedures can be beneficial in programming for students with mild disabilities at various times or decision points. First, for at-risk students, the procedures can be viewed as preventive and prereferral measures. Second, if difficulties persist, team members may decide to proceed with a referral for screening, while they can continue to meet to discuss interventions and provide ideas and support to each other. Third, if the child is placed in a special program or is receiving other types of services, the team members should continue to consult and collaborate to ensure that the child's total program is cohesive. Fourth, since the majority of students with mild disabilities are placed in general education classrooms, teachers will need to collaborate with special education and related services personnel on identifying desired student behaviors and appropriate teaching or management strategies. Evaluation should be ongoing during all of these situations; that is, team members should be assessing the effectiveness of the interventions, as well as their consultation and collaboration skills, and assisting one another to make whatever modifications are deemed appropriate (Fishbaugh, 1997; Mostert, 1998). The focus should be development of school-based teams working toward comprehensive, integrated, and programmatic approaches to students' problems (Adelman & Taylor, 1998). Dettmer, Thurston, and Dyck (2002) have outlined procedures for evaluating the context, process, and content of the teamwork.

As illustrated in the vignette about Andy, a number of personnel may be involved in the interactive teaming situation and also in follow-up consultation with other team members. Role release will need to occur in all of these contexts, along with sensitivity to cultural differences, attention to the perspectives of others, expertise in communication, and effectiveness in leadership strategies.

Service Delivery Options

Students with mild disabilities receive services in several settings with IDEA requiring that each student be educated in the least restrictive environment (LRE). The LRE for each student will depend on the severity of the problem. The team involved in making placement decisions considers a range of services to determine the optimal placement for meeting the student's special education needs. Today, special education services are provided across a continuum from least restrictive (the general education classroom, the classroom with consultation, resource room) to most restrictive (separate schools, residential schools, hospitals). (A complete description of the continuum of educational services for students with special needs can be found in several sources including Heward, 2003.)

Most students with mild disabilities spend the majority of their day in a general education classroom. According to the 24th Annual Report to Congress (U.S. Department of Education, 2002), 75% of students receiving special education were in general education classrooms more than 40% of the time during the 1999–2000 school year. Some students will be fully included in the classroom (i.e., receive all instruction in the general education classroom). Other students will be assigned to the general education classroom but also spend a portion of the day in a resource program providing specialized instruction in small groups. A small percentage of students are educated in separate classrooms and schools (U.S. Department of Education, 2002).

Regardless of placement, the 1997 reauthorization of IDEA provides that students with special needs must have access to the general curriculum and participate in state- and district-wide assessments as a method of ensuring quality teaching, learning, and educational outcomes. Providing access to the general curriculum is best achieved through collaboration. Collaboration allows both general and special education teachers, related services personnel, parents, and others involved to draw on each other's expertise, interests, and strengths to ensure the success of all children (Turnbull et al., 2004).

Recent research supports the importance of collaboration to guarantee student success. When investigating teachers' perceptions of curricular and instructional changes needed to develop and implement inclusive school programs for children with mild disabilities, McLeskey and Waldron (2002) describe collaboration as a "cornerstone" to success. In their study of elementary and middle schools identified as achieving exemplary results for all students, Caron and McLaughlin (2002) describe these schools as having strong collaborative communities. Wallace, Anderson, and Bartholomay (2002) found that school-wide approaches and classroom factors associated with collaboration were important to the success of the four inclusive high schools they investigated.

An increasingly popular method of providing special education services for students assigned to general education classrooms is cooperative teaching or co-teaching. Cook and Friend (1995) defined co-teaching as occurring when "two or more professionals jointly deliver substantive instruction to a diverse, or blended, group of students in a single physical space" (p. 1). These authors offer a set of questions for teachers to consider in order to create a collaborative working relationship in a co-teaching model. These questions are included in Table 10.1.

Bauwens, Hourcade, and Friend (1989) described three cooperative teaching options: (1) complementary instruction, in which the regular educator maintains primary responsibility for teaching subject matter and the special educator focuses on the students' mastery of academic survival skills; (2) team teaching, in which the teachers jointly plan and deliver instruction; and (3) supportive learning activities developed by the special educator to supplement the content delivered by the regular educator. Expanding on their earlier work, Bauwens and Hourcade (1997) noted that the critical feature in cooperative teaching is that two educators possessing distinct sets of skills are working in a coordinated fashion to teach academically heterogeneous students in a general education classroom. Gable and Manning (1997) also described similar service delivery models, which they labeled *cooperative teaching options* and *collaborative instructional options*. These options are summarized in Table 10.2.

Co-planning and meeting on a regular basis have been identified as critical to effective co-teaching (Dettmer et al., 2002; Dieker, 2001; Hourcade & Bauwens,

Table 10.1
Questions for Creating a Collaborative Working Relationship in Co-Teaching

Topic	Questions
Instructional beliefs	• What are our overriding philosophies about the roles of teachers and teaching, and students and learning? • How do our instructional beliefs affect our instructional practice?
Planning	• When do we have at least 30 minutes of shared planning time? • How do we divide our responsibilities for planning and teaching? • How much joint planning time do we need? • What records can we keep to facilitate our planning?
Parity signals	• How will we convey to students and others (for example, teachers, parents) that we are equals in the classroom? • How can we ensure a sense of parity during instruction?
Confidentiality	• What information about our teaching do we want to share with others? • What information should not be shared? • Which information about students can be shared with others? • What information should not be shared?
Noise	• What noise level are we comfortable with in the classroom?
Classroom routines	• What are the *instructional* routines in the classroom? • What are the *organizational* routines for the classroom?
Discipline	• What is acceptable and unacceptable student behavior? • Who is to intervene at what point in the student's behavior? • What are the rewards and consequences used in the classroom?
Feedback	• What is the best way to give each other feedback? • How will you ensure that both positive and negative issues are raised?
Pet peeves	• What aspects of teaching and classroom life do each of us feel strongly about? • How can we identify our pet peeves so as to avoid them?

Source: From "Co-Teaching: Guidelines for Creating Effective Practices," by L. Cook and M. Friend, 1995, *Focus on Exceptional Children, 28*(3), pp. 1–16. Reprinted by permission of Love Publishing Company.

2001; Walther-Thomas, Korinek, McLaughlin, & Williams, 2000). Planning helps co-teachers define their individual roles and responsibilities in the co-teaching process (Walther-Thomas et al.), determine student academic and behavioral goals and outcomes (Dieker, 2001), develop instructional accommodations and materials, and develop an evaluation plan (Bauwens & Hourcade, 1997). As Salend and his colleagues (1997) noted, cooperative teaching brings academic instruction and supportive services to students in the environment where the need exists. Effective co-teaching will involve teachers addressing concerns such as respecting skill differences and recognizing the mutual strengths of all individuals involved, confronting differences, creating a sense of community, changing language, noting changes in students, and receiving administrative support (Salend et al.).

Table 10.2
Cooperative Teaching Options and Collaborative Instructional Options

Cooperative Teaching Options

- **Shadow Teaching**

General educator is primarily responsible for teaching specific subject matter, while the special educator works directly with one or two target students on academics and/or behavior.

- **One Teach/One Assist**

General educator is primarily responsible for teaching a specific subject, while the special educator circulates around the classroom and offers individual students assistance.

- **Station Teaching**

General educator is primarily responsible for teaching specific subject matter to subgroups of students, who rotate among the learning stations.

- **Complementary Teaching**

General educator is primarily responsible for teaching specific subject matter, while the special educator assumes responsibility for teaching associated academic skills (e.g., note taking, test taking) or school survival skills (e.g., sharing, self-control).

- **Parallel Teaching**

General educator and special educator divide the class into two smaller groups to provide more individualized instruction.

- **Supplementary Teaching Activities**

General educator is primarily responsible for teaching specific subject matter, while the special educator assumes responsibility for giving students content-specific assistance (e.g., reinforcing content through small-group activities or outside assignments).

- **Team Teaching**

General and special educator share equal responsibility for planning, carrying out, and evaluating the lesson.

- **Alternative Teaching**

General educator is responsible for teaching the majority of students, while the special education teacher assumes the responsibility for teaching a select group of students who require significant curricular accommodations.

Collaborative Instructional Options

- **Same**

Students with special needs participate in regular class instruction and pursue the same content objectives within the same instructional material. When teaching all students the same content, consider team teaching, station teaching, parallel teaching, or supplemental teaching.

- **Multilevel**

Students with special needs participate in regular class instruction, but pursue different content objectives, based on their individual needs.

Example: The majority of students will use a fourth-grade textbook for health instruction, while selected students with special needs follow along in second-grade level material, using study guides. During class discussion, special needs students are asked basic questions about the content and/or parallel textual material (e.g., health content from a second-grade book, IEP-related questions).

Continued

Source: From "The Role of Teacher Collaboration in School Reform," by R. A. Gable and M. L. Manning, 1997, *Childhood Education, 73*(4), pp. 219–223. Reprinted by permission of the authors and the Association for Childhood Education International.

Table 10.2
Continued.

- ***Curriculum Overlapping***
Students with special needs participate in the same large-group instruction, but pursue objectives from different academic and/or social areas.

Example: In a cooperative team learning activity, the majority of students have a content-specific assignment, while selected students with special needs serve as timekeepers (e.g., to work on telling time), or are paired with two students without special needs who model and reinforce attention-to-task, positive socialization, and/or responses to basic content objectives. When teaching different yet complementary content, consider complementary teaching, shadow teaching, or a parallel teaching arrangement.

- ***Alternative***
Students with special needs pursue different activities/content objectives from the rest of the class.

Example: While the majority of the class completes a writing assignment, students with special needs receive instruction in an unrelated area from another person (e.g., peer tutor or special education teacher). When teaching separate content, consider an alternative teaching arrangement.

Teams can conduct functional behavior assessments (FBAs) mandated by P.L. 105-17 to develop behavioral intervention plans (BIPs) for students with a history of inappropriate behavior or whose behavior is such that placement for services may change (Jolivette, Barton-Arwood, & Scott, 2001). Jolivette et al. have recommended methods for team collaboration during the FBA and BIP process while considering each team member's perspective of the student, level of expertise, commitment level working style, and role interpretation. Todd, Horner, Sugai, and Sprague (1999) described the use of teams to provide a systems approach to behavioral support services. They outlined four patterns of problems and intervention systems: school-wide, nonclassroom or specific settings, classroom settings, and individual students with chronic behavior problems. Increasingly, schools are moving to the use of school-wide systems to define, teach, and support the positive behavior of all children. In this method, all teachers and school staff participate in the planning and implementation of the program developed.

Crisis intervention and management is another important team function. Roberts, Lepkowski, and Davidson (1998) suggest that teaming approaches be implemented after crises such as student suicides. The focus of these teams is to create comprehensive postintervention plans to handle crises that impact groups of students or an entire school.

Another level of collaboration necessary for students with mild disabilities centers around the transition to postsecondary activities. While an increasing number of students with mild disabilities continue their education as college students (Janiga & Costenbader, 2002), they are less likely than their nondisabled peers to choose vocational or academic programs (Blackorby & Wagner, 1997). Providing appropriate transition services is essential to ensuring successful transition to postsecondary activities. Appropriate transition services include establishing collaborative relationships with other agencies that are involved with postsecondary programs for young adults with disabilities as well as working with the student and his or her family in determining their own goals.

Teacher Competencies

A sampling of research in the past 20 years in regular and special education on competencies for general and special education teachers reveals that the skills identified often are quite similar. Researchers such as Brophy (1979), Good (1979), and Stevens and Rosenshine (1981) stressed teacher behaviors that included a teacher-controlled approach, activities with an academic focus, sufficient time for instruction, an emphasis on classroom management, practice opportunities for student responses, material taught in small steps, and frequent testing of student learning with appropriate feedback.

Englert (1984) identified competencies in the areas of classroom organization; teaching and maintaining rules and procedures; allocated and engaged time; and lesson introduction, demonstration, practice, and evaluation. Morsink et al. (1987) suggested that four generic sets of competencies were suitable for teachers of students with mild disabilities: (1) teacher-directed instruction, (2) provision for students to engage in active academic responding with teacher feedback, (3) contingent reinforcement of appropriate student behaviors, and (4) adaptive instruction geared to individual needs for differences such as longer learning time, simplified language, or concrete materials. Wolery, Bailey, and Sugai (1988) listed the areas of child development, curriculum content, disabling conditions, principles of learning and behavioral procedures, and instructional monitoring and evaluation procedures as essential knowledge and skills for teachers.

In a research synthesis by the Northwest Regional Education Laboratory (1990), the following recommendations were developed based on effective teacher practices:

- Use a preplanned curriculum with learning goals and objectives sequenced to facilitate student learning.
- Form instructional groups based on student achievement levels and review and adjust group membership as skill levels change.
- Use classroom management strategies that minimize disruptive behaviors.
- Hold students accountable for appropriate behavior and achievement and give help immediately when they experience problems.
- Provide additional learning time on priority objectives.

Simmons and Kameenui (1991) described the importance of teachers using principles of instructional design, information analysis, and taxonomies of knowledge. Algozzine and Ysseldyke (1992) designed a conceptual model for effective instruction that included four components: (1) planning instruction (e.g., deciding what and how to teach), (2) managing instruction (e.g., preparation and establishing a positive environment), (3) delivering instruction (e.g., motivation, feedback, and active involvement), and (4) evaluating instruction (e.g., monitoring student understanding and making decisions about performance). Application examples of their model are provided in a special focus section on effective instruction in *Teaching Exceptional Children* (see Algozzine, Ysseldyke, & Campbell, 1994).

Based on their review and synthesis of the effectiveness research, Mercer and Mercer (2001) identified four sets of instructional variables related to student learning: (1) focus on time for learning, (2) ensure high rates of student success, (3) provide positive and supportive learning environments, and (4) plan and maintain a motivational environment.

As more students with special needs are served in general education classrooms, teacher competencies related to knowledge, skills, and dispositions necessary to implement inclusive practices have been identified. Hamill, Jantzen, & Bargerhuff (1999) surveyed teachers and administrators working in inclusive programs for their perceptions of important teacher competencies. Results indicated that in addition to competencies related to classroom practices and the ability to adapt instruction and knowledge of student learning, teachers cited communication, cooperation, and flexibility as the skills critical to implementing inclusive services (Hamill et al.). In writing about what matters most for 21st-century teachers, Darling-Hammond (1997) suggested that all teachers should be skilled in collaboration. She specifies that teachers should know how to collaborate with colleagues and parents and they should be able to facilitate collaboration between students (Darling-Hammond, 1998).

Finally, collaboration is the content of standard 10 of the Council for Exceptional Children (CEC) content standards for all beginning special education teachers. This standard recognizes the importance of effective collaboration for meeting the needs of students with special needs. (Refer to the CEC Website, http://www.cec.sped.org/ps/perf_based_stds/standards.html, for the complete list of standards.)

SELECTED TEACHING STRATEGIES

In terms of teaching techniques, the team members will need to consider the academic and behavioral problems presented by the student. Only a selected number of strategies will be cited to illustrate the range of possibilities that might be appropriate for students with mild disabilities. More detailed information on teaching methods for specific academic and behavioral problems is available in a number of textbooks, such as those by Bos and Vaughn (2002), Hallahan et al. (1999), Jensen and Kiley (2000), Mercer and Mercer (2001), Olson and Platt (2000), O'Shea et al. (1998), Vaughn, Bos, and Schumm (2003), and others. Additional information can be obtained on Websites such as www.ldonline.org, www.ldanatl.org, and www.cec.sped.org.

Most students with mild disabilities will need to be taught general strategies for *how* to learn (Deshler & Schumaker, 1986) as well as student-directed learning strategies that, in turn, provide the skills (Wehmeyer, Sands, Knowlton, & Kozleski, 2002). Students who are experiencing difficulties in mathematics need to acquire a cognitive strategy for solving different types of problems (cf. Montague & Bos, 1986), as well as self-monitoring strategies (Frank & Brown, 1992). Students with sensory impairments may need help developing residual hearing and listening skills, while students with physical disabilities or communication disorders may need help with alternative communication strategies.

Nevin and Thousand (1986) identified a number of promising practices that can be used in regular classroom settings: (1) curricular adaptations, (2) mastery learning, (3) individualized learning, (4) peer tutoring, (5) accelerated learning systems, and (6) applied behavior analysis. Henley, Ramsey, and Algozzine (1993) described several approaches and strategies that have received attention in recent years including integrated teaching, whole language, the Adaptive Learning Environment Model, skillstreaming, and direct instruction. Bos and Vaughn (2002) provided an overview of the use of cognitive behavior modification, modeling and demonstration strategies, reflective thinking, information processing and schema techniques, and microcomputers and multimedia systems. Other methods that have been shown to improve academic functioning, as well as social interactions, are cooperative learning strategies, such as the jigsaw technique (cf. Aronson, Blaney, Stephan, Sikes, & Snapp, 1978; Johnson, Johnson, Warring, & Maruyama, 1986; Lloyd, Crowley, Kohler, & Strain, 1988; Putnam, 1998). Learning styles instruction (Carbo, 1990) and teaching school survival skills to adolescents (Schaeffer, Zigmond, Kerr, & Farra, 1990) also can enhance achievement.

Schumm, Vaughn, and Harris (1997) advocated the use of a "Planning Pyramid" that considers the following aspects of instruction: teacher, topic, content, student, and instructional practices. Orkwis and McLane (1998) described universal design principles that apply to content, goals, methods, and manner of assessment. They defined universal design as "the design of instructional materials and activities that allows the learning goals to be achievable by individuals with differences" (p. 9). Lenz (2003) offers an instructional planning method for determining the critical ideas that students must know from a specific content being taught. Using a pie slice analogy, Lenz discusses determining content that all, most, and some students will know that supports the critical ideas.

Kling (1997) asked teachers to rate preferred strategies based on specific children's behaviors. Their ratings appear in Table 10.3. Burke, Hagan, and Grossen (1998) described the use of big ideas, conspicuous strategies, primed background knowledge, mediated scaffolding, judicious review, and strategic integration as ways to accommodate diverse learners. A summary of their work is included as Table 10.4, and additional information can be found at the following Website: http://idea.uoregon.edu/~ncite/. Swanson (1999) investigated the effectiveness of interventions such as sequencing, segmentation of information, modeling problem-solving steps, presenting cues to prompt strategies used, and directed response/questioning of students. His results indicated that a combined strategy

Table 10.3
Preferred Strategies Used with Specific Children's Behaviors

Behavior	Strategy Used	Rating
1. Hyperactivity/ distractibility	daily home reports	5
	individualized instruction	5
	timer	5
	sticker charts	5
	time recording on papers	5
	* organizational folders	4
	praise	4
	humor	4
	copy cards at desk	4
	opportunity for movement	4
	teacher/pupil conference	4
2. Disorganization	self-monitoring charts	3
	teacher monitoring work	3
	self-monitoring chart	5
	positive reinforcement	5
	** one paper at a time	5
	assignment pads	5
	parent signing homework	4
	folders for papers	3
3. Talkative	parent conferences	5
	teacher prompts/signals	4
	seating in front of room	4
	read story geared to problem	4
4. Disruptive behavior	daily home communication	5
	student explanation of behavior	5
	positive reinforcement	5
	nonverbal skills	4
5. Unmotivated	positive reinforcement	5
	parent signature of homework	5
6. Belligerent behavior	positive reinforcement	5
	provide leadership role	4
7. Socially immature	consistency	5
	firm expectations	3
8. Slow worker	modify amount of work	5
	clock to budget time	4
9. Academic problems	reinforcement and repetition	5
	one-to-one instruction	5
	concrete materials	5
	smaller quantities of work	5
	provide tests in segments	5

Note: Ratings indicate how 26 teachers rated each strategy's *usefulness,* after 1 year of trial, on a Likert scale from 1 to 5, with 1 being the least effective and 5 being the most effective.

Sample expansions of strategies:
* Organizational folders: File folders of different colors were provided for each student. Some teachers established a notebook for the folders so that papers would be in one place. Teachers provided students with reinforcers for papers so that torn papers would not fall out of the notebook.

** One paper at a time: Teachers used several methods, such as baskets in a designated place, where students could return a completed assignment and collect a new paper. The strategic placement of these baskets was important. Some students needed the opportunity for movement, but it was essential to place them in an

Source: From "Empowering Teachers to Use Successful Strategies," by B. Kling, 1997, *Teaching Exceptional Children, 30*(2), pp. 20–24. Reprinted by permission.

Behavior	Strategy Used	Rating	
	self-monitoring charts	5	area where they would not disturb
	visual aids to show directions	5	others. Some teachers found it was
	peer tutoring	5	effective to number assignments in
	study guides	5	order and place "work to do" in a
	home/school reinforcement	5	folder in students' desks to reduce
	change course requirements	4	clutter.
	oral or untimed tests	4	

and direct instruction model was the most effective intervention. Additional strategies to address academic difficulties are listed in Table 10.5.

Considerations

The decision-making process for determining which strategies to recommend and use may occur in a decision-making or problem-solving group (Pugach & Johnson, 2002). As Jolivette et al. (2000) noted, the characteristics, perspectives, expertise, commitment, and role interpretation will influence the team dynamics. For example, Martens, Peterson, Witt, and Cirone (1986) identified considerations for making suggestions to regular classroom teachers about behavior problems. They noted that teachers classify strategies in terms of effectiveness, ease of use, and frequency of use. They cautioned consultants to be aware of the extent to which the interventions they suggest are similar to those a teacher may already be using, and the degree to which a teacher's behavior will have to change in order to implement an intervention.

Guskey (1990) provided a framework for synthesizing diverse instructional strategies: (1) instructional strategies should share common goals, (2) strategies should complement each other, (3) time should be taken to experiment and adapt strategies to individuals and classrooms, and (4) educators should recognize that the combined beneficial effects of several strategies will surpass the effects of any single strategy. A final set of considerations is the procedural principles identified by Idol, Nevin, and Paolucci-Whitcomb (1994) designed to facilitate the performance of learners with special needs in inclusive classrooms:

1. Procedural principles designed to facilitate teaching and learning of difficult-to-teach learners must be easy to implement in inclusive classrooms.

2. Teaching and learning procedures should be designed for use with any student who is achieving poorly, rather than for a single learner with special needs.

Table 10.4
Ways to Accelerate Student Learning

The National Center to Improve the Tools of Educators (NCITE) has identified six features of instruction that effectively accommodate and accelerate student learning.

1. Big Ideas

Big ideas are concepts and principles that facilitate the most efficient and broadest acquisition of knowledge across a range of examples.

A social studies example of a big idea: Human rights problems are associated with the need to achieve religious freedom; freedom of speech; equal protection under the law; and equal rights for women, minorities, and different social classes.

2. Conspicuous Strategies

Conspicuous strategies are an approximation of the steps experts follow covertly to solve complex problems and difficult tasks.

For example, the steps in the strategy for science inquiry are (a) identify the variable to test, (b) create a condition that changes that variable, (c) keep the other variables the same, (d) gather data, and (e) interpret the outcome.

3. Primed Background Knowledge

Before understanding of new information can occur, necessary background knowledge must be taught or "primed." This requires teaching component steps and concepts that allow an in-depth understanding of a big idea or strategy.

For example, in writing instruction, if students are to write good narrative explanations, they should have some knowledge of words indicating chronology, such as *first, then, next, after,* and *finally.*

4. Mediated Scaffolding

Scaffolding refers to the guidance, assistance, and support that a teacher, peer, or task provides to a learner.

For example, in teaching reading comprehension, the teacher's frequent interspersed questions are a scaffold that can gradually be reduced as students become able to interact with text on their own.

5. Judicious Review

Judicious reviews should be (a) sufficient for initial learning to occur, (b) distributed over time, (c) varied for generalizability, and (d) cumulative.

An example of judicious review in math is incorporating a review of addition, subtraction, multiplication, and division facts even when introducing new knowledge, such as fractions.

6. Strategic Integration

Strategic integration is the process where prior learning is integrated into more complex concepts.

For example, in beginning reading instruction, teachers can provide decodable text as students are learning letter-sound relationships to figure out words.

Source: From "What Curricular Designs and Strategies Accommodate Diverse Learners?" by M. D. Burke, S. L. Hagan, and B. Grossen, 1998, *Teaching Exceptional Children, 31*(1), pp. 34–38. Reprinted by permission.

Table 10.5
Strategies to Help Students Achieve Basic Academic Skills

Strategies That Help	Strategies That Do Not Help
Mostly narrow teacher questions with a "right" answer	Mostly open-ended questions **or** Nonacademic conversation
Calling on nonvolunteers or using patterned turns to select students to answer questions	Selecting only volunteers when calling on students to answer questions
Immediate feedback (as to right or wrong) to students' answers	Not giving clear feedback to students' answers
"Staying with" a student until he or she answers a question	Quickly letting someone else answer; leaving a student with little or no feedback
Short and frequent—rather than long and occasional—paper-and-pencil activities	Games, artwork, many interest centers
Specific praise for good performance	Vague or general praise, or praise when it isn't especially deserved
Covering material thoroughly	Covering a lot of material quickly
Much time spent in teacher questioning, feedback, and supervised practice	Much class time spent in anything else
Time spent in structured learning activities led by the teacher	Time spent in unstructured or free time
Instruction broken down into small steps, short activities sequenced by the teacher	Long, unbroken periods of seatwork or independent work, with students' choice of activities or sequences
Plenty of practice (repetition) with frequent correction and praise	Little practice **or** Independent practice without prompt feedback
A lot of supervision and help, in whole-class or group settings	Individualized, self-paced instruction; independent work
Continuous teacher direction of student behavior and activity	Situations calling for much pupil self-control or self-direction
Materials or questions at a level of difficulty at which students have a high rate of success	Challenging materials or questions, or work in which students are not likely to know most of the answers
Many opportunities and much encouragement to answer teacher questions	Few opportunities or little encouragement to answer questions frequently

3. Teaching and learning procedures need to be based on the use of classroom curricula.

4. Teaching and learning procedures must include components that teach learners to generalize.

5. Teaching and learning procedures need to be useful for group instruction.

6. Learners must be directly taught the skill areas they are required to master.

Wolfe (1998) made an observation that is important for all interactive team members who are providing direct services and collaborating with other professionals to remember: "Teaching is decision making and the more we know about the science of teaching the better we can artistically apply that knowledge" (p. 64). Schamber (1999) commented that diversity in members of teaching teams is a major benefit since it provides multiple perspectives in dealing with students and other issues.

ROLES OF PROFESSIONALS INVOLVED WITH STUDENTS WITH MILD DISABILITIES

As described in Chapter 3, interactive team members involved in the education of students with mild disabilities can serve in two types of roles: collaborator/consultant and direct service provider. In both roles, the professionals will apply the knowledge from their own areas of specialization; participate actively in planning, decision making, implementation, and evaluation of interventions; and ensure that programming is provided in a comprehensive and coordinated way (Johnson, Pugach, & Devlin, 1990).

In the role of collaborator/consultant, team members should consider the types and degree of services required and determine which academic or behavioral management strategies are warranted based on the student's needs. Donaldson and Christiansen (1990) designed a *collaborative decision-making model* that can be used as a guide to select appropriate options for service delivery, instruction, and behavior management (see Figure 10.1). In this model, team members will need to consult/collaborate by identifying the problems presented, deciding on the appropriate placement in the continuum of services, and determining which instructional or behavior management strategies to implement. The final part of the cycle involves evaluating the success of the options or interventions, and deciding what procedures for follow-up or alternative placements are warranted. Additional examples of the types of contributions and activities interactive team members can participate in as direct service providers and collaborators/consultants are provided in Table 10.6.

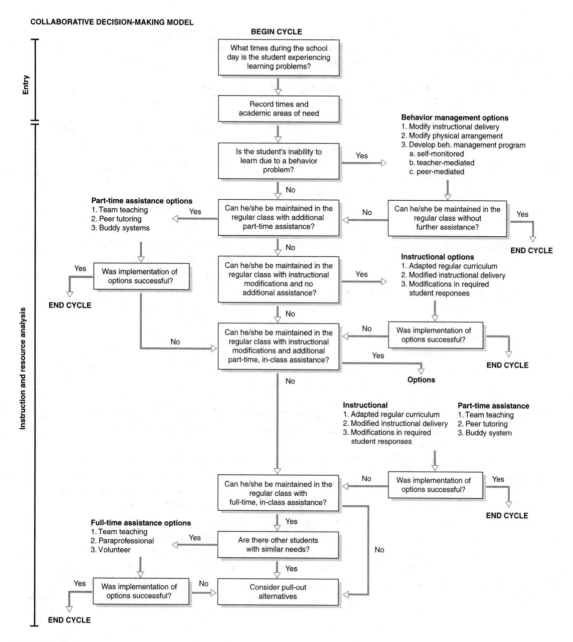

COLLABORATIVE DECISION-MAKING MODEL

BEGIN CYCLE

Entry

What times during the school day is the student experiencing learning problems?

Record times and academic areas of need

Is the student's inability to learn due to a behavior problem? — Yes →

Behavior management options
1. Modify instructional delivery
2. Modify physical arrangement
3. Develop beh. management program
   a. self-monitored
   b. teacher-mediated
   c. peer-mediated

No

Part-time assistance options
1. Team teaching
2. Peer tutoring
3. Buddy systems

← Yes — Can he/she be maintained in the regular class with additional part-time assistance? ← No — Can he/she be maintained in the regular class without further assistance? — Yes → **END CYCLE**

No

Yes → Was implementation of options successful?

END CYCLE

Can he/she be maintained in the regular class with instructional modifications and no additional assistance? — Yes →

Instructional options
1. Adapted regular curriculum
2. Modified instructional delivery
3. Modifications in required student responses

No

No — Was implementation of options successful? → **END CYCLE**

Instruction and resource analysis

Can he/she be maintained in the regular class with instructional modifications and additional part-time, in-class assistance? ← No

Yes

No

Options

Instructional
1. Adapted regular curriculum
2. Modified instructional delivery
3. Modifications in required student responses

Part-time assistance
1. Team teaching
2. Peer tutoring
3. Buddy system

Can he/she be maintained in the regular class with full-time, in-class assistance? — No — Was implementation of options successful? — Yes → **END CYCLE**

Yes

Full-time assistance options
1. Team teaching
2. Paraprofessional
3. Volunteer

← Yes — Are there other students with similar needs?

No

Yes

Yes → Was implementation of options successful? — No → Consider pull-out alternatives

END CYCLE

Figure 10.1
Collaborative decision-making model.

Source: From "Consultation and Collaboration: A Decision-Making Model," by R. Donaldson and J. Christiansen, 1990, *Teaching Exceptional Children, 22*(2), pp. 22–25. Reprinted by permission of the authors and the Council for Exceptional Children.

Table 10.6
Role of Professionals and Others Involved with Students with Mild Disabilities

Personnel	Direct Service Provider	Team Member
Special educator	• Assess educational achievement. • Design instructional program. • Implement academic/behavioral strategies. • Follow-up on skills taught by others.	• Serve as case manager. • Interpret assessments. • Observe in other settings. • Consult on individualizing instructional techniques.
General educator	• Implement academic/behavioral strategies. • Assist in social integration.	• Consult on curriculum. • Consult on group management techniques.
Parent	• Reinforce academic and behavioral programs at home.	• Provide background information. • Consult on possible interventions.
Administrator	• Reinforce appropriate behavior.	• Provide information on services available in school and community. • Assist with scheduling and class size.
Psychologist	• Assess psychological functioning.	• Interpret test results. • Collaborate in designing interventions and data-collection strategies.
Speech-language therapist	• Assess speech-language development. • Remediate speech-language disorders in individual or small-group sessions.	• Interpret test results. • Provide follow-up materials for other team members. Consult on strategies to use.
Counselor	• Provide counseling on self-concept, getting along with adults and peers, and so forth.	• Collaborate with others about emotional or behavioral situations.
Physical and occupational therapist	• Assess physical and occupational needs. • Provide physical therapy. • Provide occupational therapy.	• Interpret test results. • Collaborate with others on ways to enhance physical development or classroom modifications.
Hearing and vision specialists	• Assess hearing and vision. • Teach strategies such as auditory training, listening skills, orientation, and mobility.	• Interpret test results. • Teach others how to use special equipment or materials.
Adapted physical educator	• Assess psychomotor skills. • Remediate areas of physical fitness.	• Collaborate in designing cooperative games and motor development activities.

APPLICATION

The vignette about Andy at the beginning of this chapter contains descriptions of several behaviors that an interactive team could target for change. However, in a team meeting the professionals and Andy's mother agreed that the most problematic behavior in all settings (e.g., general education classroom, resource room, home, playground) was his unwillingness to begin tasks on time. Instead, Andy used a variety of avoidance tactics, including breaking pencils and arguing, to keep from starting his assignments.

The team members decided that a behavior management system using a contingency contract might help modify Andy's behavior. Because Andy enjoys sports, the adapted physical educator, Ms. DiCicco, agreed to allow him to be her "assistant" when she coached the soccer team if he met the conditions of the contract.

The regular classroom teacher, Ms. Baker, said she would like to focus on math seatwork for purposes of the contract. Ms. Rodriquez, the resource teacher, identified writing journal assignments as the area of concern in her classroom. Mr. Morrow, the speech-language therapist, cited oral language practice activities as a goal, and noted that this should be assessed in all settings because Andy received speech therapy only once a week. Andy's mother, Ms. Rhodes, said she wanted him to begin his homework assignments promptly. The objectives and personnel involved in Andy's program are listed in Table 10.7.

The team members discussed the level of performance that should be required for Andy to earn the privilege of being Ms. DiCicco's assistant with the soccer team and decided that a success rate of 60% (i.e., three out of five assignments) for three consecutive days would be a good starting point. They based this decision on a desire for Andy to experience success and receive the reinforcement early in the program so that he would be motivated. They agreed to gradually increase the percentage and the number of days as his behavior improved.

Ms. Rhodes said she would like to be the one to explain the program to her son, and everyone else supported this idea. Then the team members discussed a system for collecting and sharing their data with Ms. Baker, who would determine if the criteria had been met and notify Ms. DiCicco that Andy was eligible for the reward. The team members agreed to meet again in 2 weeks to evaluate the effectiveness of the program, and discuss any needed modifications.

Table 10.7
Interactive Team Plan for Andy

Objectives	GenEd	SpEd	Parent	APE
1. Andy will begin his math seatwork within 2 minutes of the assignments being given.	x			
2. Andy will request help within 5 minutes of the directions being provided instead of crumpling up his paper.	x	x	x	
3. Andy will begin his homework within 2 minutes of his mother's request to start.			x	
4. Andy will distribute equipment for the soccer team within 2 minutes of the request by the adapted physical educator or coach.				x

SUMMARY

The characteristics of students with mild disabilities often are similar. Their needs can be categorized into five areas:

◆ Academic remediation
◆ Social interactions
◆ Self-concept and motivation
◆ Behavior management
◆ Special education and support services

To meet these needs, interactive team members should implement a process for problem identification and design interventions, use appropriate service delivery options, demonstrate competencies, intervene with effective teaching strategies, and evaluate and adapt programs as necessary.

A number of personnel are involved in the education of students, both as direct service providers and as team members who serve as collaborators/consultants. It is essential that all of these people work together in a cohesive and coordinated manner, keeping students' needs as the focus of attention, in order to provide effective programs. Chapter 11 describes how professionals and parents serve as interactive team members for students with severe disabilities.

ACTIVITIES

1. Conduct informational interviews with a regular educator, resource teacher, and parent about the characteristics of a child with a mild disability. Compare their comments on the child's academic and behavioral needs.

2. Volunteer to tutor or provide a special activity for a child with a mild disability. Describe your observations of the child's behaviors and interests.

3. Observe a child in three different settings, such as regular and special education classrooms and speech-language therapy. What similarities and differences did you notice in the child's behavior and performance?

4. Attend a school-based committee or teacher-assistance team meeting. Based on your observations of the meeting, answer the following questions: Who attended the meeting, and did everyone participate? How was information presented? What characteristics and needs were mentioned? Which academic and behavior management strategies were discussed? How were decisions made?

REFERENCES

Adelman, H. S., & Taylor, L. (1998). Involving teachers in collaborative efforts to better address the barriers to student learning. *Preventing School Failure, 42*(2), 55–60.

Algozzine, B., & Ysseldyke, J. E. (1992). *Strategies and tactics for effective instruction.* Longmont, CO: Sopris West.

Algozzine, B., Ysseldyke, J. E., & Campbell, P. (1994). Strategies and tactics for effective instruction. *Teaching Exceptional Children, 26,* 34–36.

American Association on Mental Retardation. (2002). *Mental retardation: Definition, classification, and systems of supports* (10th ed.). Washington, DC: Author.

American Psychiatric Association (APA). (2000). *Diagnostic and Statistical Manual of Mental Disorders* (4th ed., rev.). Washington, DC: Author.

American Speech-Language-Hearing Association (ASHA). (2003). *Effects of hearing loss.* Retrieved November 1, 2003, from http://www.asha.org/public/hearing/disorders/effects.htm

Aronson, E., Blaney, N., Stephan, C., Sikes, J., & Snapp, M. (1978). *The jigsaw classroom.* Beverly Hills, CA: Sage Publications.

Barkley, R. A. (1998). *Attention-deficit/hyperactivity disorder: A handbook for diagnosis and treatment* (2nd ed.). New York: Guilford.

Bauwens, J., & Hourcade, J. J. (1997). Cooperative teaching: Pictures of possibilities. *Intervention in School and Clinic, 33*(2), 81–85, 89.

Bauwens, J., Hourcade, J. J., & Friend, M. (1989). Cooperative teaching: A model for general and special education integration. *Remedial and Special Education, 10*(2), 17–22.

Beirne-Smith, M., Ittenbach, R., & Patton, J. R. (1998). *Mental retardation* (5th ed.). Upper Saddle River, NJ: Merrill/Prentice Hall.

Blackorby, J., & Wagner, M. (1997). The employment outcomes for youth with learning disabilities: A review of the findings from the National Longitudinal Transition Study of special education students. In P. J. Gerber &

D. S. Brown (Eds.), *Learning disabilities and employment* (pp. 57–74). Austin, TX: Pro-Ed.

Bos, C. S., & Vaughn, S. (2002). *Strategies for teaching students with learning and behavior problems* (5th ed.). Needham Heights, MA: Allyn & Bacon.

Brophy, J. E. (1979). Teacher behavior and its effects. *Journal of Educational Psychology, 71,* 733–750.

Burke, M. D., Hagan, S. L., & Grossen, B. (1998). What curricular designs and strategies accommodate diverse learners? *Teaching Exceptional Children, 31*(1), 34–38.

Carbo, M. (1990). Igniting the literacy revolution through reading styles. *Educational Leadership, 48*(2), 89–92.

Caron, E. A., & McLaughlin, M. J. (2002). Indicators of Beacons of Excellence schools: What do they tell us about collaborative practices? *Journal of Educational and Psychological Consultation, 13*(4), 285–314.

Cook, L., & Friend, M. (1995). Co-teaching: Guidelines for creating effective practices. *Focus on Exceptional Children, 28*(3), 1–16.

Cullinan, D., & Epstein, M. H. (1994). Behavior disorders. In N. G. Haring, L. McCormick, & T. G. Haring (Eds.), *Exceptional children and youth* (6th ed.). New York: Merrill/Macmillan.

Darling-Hammond, L. (1997). What matters most: 21st-century teaching. *The Education Digest, 63,* 4–9.

Darling-Hammond, L. (1998). Teacher learning that supports student learning. *Educational Leadership, 55,* 6–11.

Deshler, D. D., & Schumaker, J. B. (1986). Learning strategies: An instructional alternative for low-achieving adolescents. *Exceptional Children, 52,* 583–590.

Dettmer, P., Thurston, L. P., & Dyck, N. (2002). *Consultation, collaboration, and teamwork for students with special needs.* Boston: Allyn & Bacon.

Dieker, L. A. (2001). What are the characteristics of effective middle and high school co-taught teams for students with disabilities? *Preventing School Failure, 46*(1), 14–23.

Donaldson, R., & Christiansen, J. (1990). Consultation and collaboration: A decision-making model. *Teaching Exceptional Children, 22*(2), 22–25.

Englert, C. S. (1984). Measuring teacher effectiveness from the teacher's point of view. *Focus on Exceptional Children, 17*(2), 1–14.

Fishbaugh, M. S. E. (1997). *Models of collaboration.* Needham Heights, MA: Allyn & Bacon.

Frank, A. R., & Brown, D. (1992). Self-monitoring strategies in arithmetic. *Teaching Exceptional Children, 24*(2), 52–54.

Fuchs, D., Mock, D., Morgan, P. L., & Young, C. L. (2003). Responsiveness-to-intervention: Definitions, evidence, and implications for the learning disabilities construct. *Learning Disabilities Research and Practice, 18*(3), 157–171.

Gable, R. A., & Manning, M. L. (1997). The role of teacher collaboration in school reform. *Childhood Education, 73*(4), 219–223.

Good, T. L. (1979). Teacher effectiveness in the elementary school. *Journal of Teacher Education, 30,* 52–64.

Guskey, T. R. (1990). Integrating innovations. *Educational Leadership, 47*(5), 11–15.

Hallahan, D. P., & Kauffman, J. M. (2000). *Exceptional learners: Introduction to special education* (8th ed.). Boston: Allyn & Bacon.

Hallahan, D. P., Kauffman, J. M., & Lloyd, J. W. (1999). *Introduction to learning disabilities* (2nd ed.). Boston: Allyn & Bacon.

Hamill, L. B., Jantzen, A. K., & Bargerhuff, M. E. (1999). Analysis of effective educator competencies in inclusive environments. *Action in Teacher Education, 21*(3), 21–37.

Henley, M., Ramsey, R. S., & Algozzine, R. (1993). *Characteristics of and strategies for teaching students with mild disabilities.* Boston: Allyn & Bacon.

Heward, W. L. (2003). *Exceptional children: An introduction to special education* (7th ed.). Upper Saddle River, NJ: Merrill/Prentice Hall.

Hill, J. L. (1999). *Meeting the needs of students with special physical and health care needs.* Upper Saddle River, NJ: Merrill/Prentice Hall.

Hourcade, J. J., & Bauwens, J. (2001). Cooperative teaching: The renewal of teachers. *Clearing House, 74*(5), 242–247.

Idol, L., Nevin, A., & Paolucci-Whitcomb, P. (1994). *Collaborative consultation* (2nd ed.). Austin, TX: Pro-Ed.

Janiga, S. J., & Costenbader V. (2002). The transition from high school to postsecondary education for students with learning disabilities: A survey of college service coordinators [Electronic version]. *Journal of Learning Disabilities, 35*(5), 462–468, 479.

Jensen, R. A., & Kiley, T. J. (2000). *Teaching, leading, and learning: Becoming caring professionals.* Boston: Houghton Mifflin.

Johnson, D. W., Johnson, R. T., Warring, D., & Maruyama, G. (1986). Different cooperative learning procedures and cross-handicap relationships. *Exceptional Children, 53,* 245–252.

Johnson, L. J., Pugach, M. C., & Devlin, S. (1990). Professional collaboration. *Teaching Exceptional Children, 22*(2), 9–11.

Jolivette, K., Barton-Arwood, S., & Scott, T. M. (2000). Functional behavioral assessment as a collaborative process among professionals. *Education and Treatment of Children, 23*(3), 298–304.

Kauffman, J. M. (1997). *Characteristics of emotional and behavioral disorders of children and youth* (6th ed.). Upper Saddle River, NJ: Merrill/Prentice Hall.

Kirk, S. A., Gallagher, J. J., & Anastasiow, N. J. (1997). *Educating exceptional children* (8th ed.). Boston: Houghton Mifflin Company.

Kling, B. (1997). Empowering teachers to use successful strategies. *Teaching Exceptional Children, 30*(2), 20–24.

Lenz, K. (2003). *Smarter planning: Considering curriculum in light of standards-based reform.* Retrieved November 11, 2003, from University of Kansas Center for Research on Learning Website at http://www.kucrl.org/archives/classroom/smarter.html

Lloyd, J. W., Crowley, E. P., Kohler, F. W., & Strain, P. S. (1988). Redefining the applied research agenda: Cooperative learning, prereferral, teacher consultation, and peer-mediated interventions. *Journal of Learning Disabilities, 21,* 43–52.

Martens, B. K., Peterson, R. L., Witt, J. C., & Cirone, S. (1986). Teacher perceptions of school-based interventions. *Exceptional Children, 53,* 213–223.

McLeskey, J., & Waldron, N. L. (2002). Inclusion and school change: Teacher perceptions regarding curricular and instructional adaptations. *Teacher Education and Special Education, 24*(1), 41–54.

Mercer, C. D. (1997). *Students with learning disabilities* (5th ed.). Upper Saddle River, NJ: Merrill/Prentice-Hall.

Mercer, C. D., & Mercer, A. R. (2001). *Teaching students with learning problems* (6th ed.). Upper Saddle River, NJ: Merrill/Prentice Hall.

Montague, M., & Bos, C. S. (1986). The effect of cognitive strategy training on verbal problem solving performance of learning disabled adolescents. *Journal of Learning Disabilities, 19*, 26–33.

Moores, D. (1996). *Educating the deaf: Psychology, principles, and practices* (4th ed.). Boston: Houghton Mifflin.

Morsink, C. V., Thomas, C. C., & Smith-Davis, J. (1987). Noncategorical special education programs: Process and outcomes. In M. C. Wang, M. C. Reynolds, & H. J. Walberg (Eds.), *Handbook of special education: Research and practice* (Vol. 1). New York: Pergamon Press.

Mostert, M. P. (1998). *Interprofessional collaboration in schools.* Needham Heights, MA: Allyn & Bacon.

Nevin, A., & Thousand, J. (1986). What the research says about limiting or avoiding referrals to special education. *Teacher Education and Special Education, 9*, 149–161.

Northwest Regional Educational Laboratory. (1990). *Effective schooling practices: A research synthesis 1990 update.* Portland, OR: Author.

Olson, J. L., & Platt, J. M. (2000). *Teaching children and adolescents with special needs* (3rd ed.). Upper Saddle River, NJ: Merrill/Prentice Hall.

Orkwis, R., & McLane, K. (1998). *A curriculum every student can use: Design principles for student access.* ERIC/OSEP Topical Brief. Reston, VA: The Council for Exceptional Children.

O'Shea, L. J., O'Shea, D. J., & Algozzine, R. (1998). *Learning disabilities: From theory toward practice.* Upper Saddle River, NJ: Merrill/Prentice Hall.

Pugach, M. C., & Johnson, L. J. (2002). *Collaborative practitioners, collaborative schools* (2nd ed.). Denver: Love Publishing.

Putnam, J. W. (1998). *Cooperative learning and strategies for inclusion: Celebrating diversity in the classroom* (2nd ed.). Baltimore: Paul H. Brookes.

Roberts, R. L., Lepkowski, W. J., & Davidson, K. K. (1998). After a student suicide, the TEAM approach. *Education Digest, 64*(2), 50–55.

Salend, S. J., Johansen, M., Mumper, J., Chase, A. S., Pike, K. M., & Dorney, J. A. (1997). Cooperative teaching: The voices of two teachers. *Remedial and Special Education, 18*(1), 3–11.

Salend, S. J., & Rohena, E. (2003). Students with attention deficit disorders: An overview. *Intervention in School and Clinic, 38*(5), 259–266.

Schaeffer, A. L., Zigmond, N., Kerr, M., & Farra, H. E. (1990). Helping teenagers develop school survival skills. *Teaching Exceptional Children, 23*(1), 6–9.

Schamber, S. (1999). Surviving team teaching's good intentions. *Education Digest, 64*(8), 18–24.

Schumm, J. S., Vaughn, S., & Harris, J. (1997). Pyramid power for collaborative planning. *Teaching Exceptional Children, 29*(6), 62–66.

Shames, G. H., Wiig, E. H., & Secord, W. A. (1998). *Human communication disorders* (5th ed.). Boston: Allyn & Bacon.

Shea, T. M., & Bauer, A. M. (1994). *Learners with disabilities: A social systems perspective of special education.* Madison, WI: Brown & Benchmark Publishers.

Simmons, D. C., & Kameenui, E. J. (1991). Knowing what you teach: A first step in instructional design. *LD Forum, 17*(1), 23–26.

Stevens, R., & Rosenshine, B. (1981). Advances on research in teaching. *Exceptional Education Quarterly, 2*(1), 1–9.

Swanson, H. L. (1999). Instructional components that predict treatment outcomes for students with learning disabilities: Support for a combined strategy and direct instruction model. *Learning Disabilities Research and Practice, 14*(3), 129–140.

Tannock, R., & Martinussen, R. (2001). Reconceptualizing ADHD. *Educational Leadership, 59*(3), 20–25.

Todd, A. W., Horner, R. H., Sugai, G., & Sprague, J. R. (1999). Effective behavior support: Strengthening school-wide systems through a team-based approach. *Effective School Practices,* *17*(4), 23–33.

Turnbull, R., Turnbull, A., Shank, M., & Smith, S. (2004). *Exceptional lives: Special education in today's schools* (4th ed.). Upper Saddle River, NJ: Merrill/Prentice Hall.

U.S. Department of Education. (2002). *24th annual report to Congress on the implementation of the Individuals with Disabilities Education Act.* Retrieved November 10, 2003, from Strategic and Annual Reports from http://www.ed.gov/about/reports/annual/osep/2002/index.html

Vaughn, S., Bos, C. S., & Schumm, J. S. (2003). *Teaching exceptional, diverse, and at-risk students in the general education classroom* (3rd ed.). Boston: Allyn & Bacon.

Vaughn, S., & Fuchs, L. S. (2003). Redefining learning disabilities as inadequate response to instruction: The promise and potential pitfalls. *Learning Disabilities Research & Practice, 18*(3), 137–145.

Wallace, T., Anderson, A. R., & Bartholomay, T. (2002). Collaboration: An element associated with the success of four inclusive high schools. *Journal of Educational and Psychological Consultation, 13*(4), 349–382.

Walther-Thomas, C., Korinek, L., McLaughlin, V. L., & Williams, B. T. (2000). *Collaboration for inclusive education: Developing successful programs.* Boston: Allyn & Bacon.

Wehmeyer, M. L., Sands, D. J., Knowlton, H. E., & Kozleski, E. B. (2002). *Teaching students with mental retardation: Providing access to the general curriculum.* Baltimore: Paul H. Brookes.

Wiig, E. H., & Semel, E. (1984). *Language assessment and intervention for the learning disabled* (2nd ed.). Columbus, OH: Merrill.

Wolery, M., Bailey, D. B., & Sugai, G. M. (1988). *Effective teaching: Principles and procedures of applied behavior analysis with exceptional students.* Boston: Allyn & Bacon.

Wolfe, P. (1998). Revisiting effective teaching. *Educational Leadership, 56*(3), 61–64.

Implementation with Students with Severe Disabilities

11

Topics in this chapter include:

◆ The characteristics associated with students who have severe disabilities.

◆ The various educational needs of students with severe disabilities.

◆ Selected teaching strategies for working with students who have severe disabilities.

◆ The unique roles of professionals involved with students who have severe disabilities.

◆ An application for team involvement in educational planning for students with severe disabilities.

Mr. and Mrs. Fredricks arrive at their daughter's elementary school for their annual IEP meeting. Sally, 7, has been diagnosed with severe neurological impairment due to spinal meningitis contracted at age 2. Sally is an attractive child who appears to react positively by smiling and using a variety of vocalizations to communicate with her family, teachers, and peers. She enjoys participating in group activities involving a touch screen on a computer, and she loves to swim in the local YWCA swimming pool twice a week. However, Sally evidences severe seizure disorders requiring anticonvulsant medication and is currently fed through a gastrointestinal tube (G-tube).

Additionally, Sally has been diagnosed with cortical blindness, although she is able to track a brightly colored object 2 feet from her eyes. Although she has no severe maladaptive behavior at this point, Sally has required behavioral management procedures to decrease eye poking, which frequently occurs during transition periods throughout the day. Sally has one older brother, who attends the same elementary school. She spends most of her day in an inclusive classroom with her first-grade peers.

As her parents enter the principal's conference room, Sally's first-grade teacher, the special education teacher, the school psychologist, the school counselor, and the principal greet them. At first glance it appears to be a typical reunion in a typical school setting. However, within the next 10 minutes the room slowly fills with the following team of professionals: a physical therapist, an occupational therapist, a school nurse, a pediatric neurologist, a speech/hearing clinician, an itinerant vision teacher, an orientation and mobility specialist, a representative from the Commission for the Blind, the behavioral specialist, and the school district's special education director. The Fredricks have also invited a parent advocate and their personal lawyer. Now, with 19 people in the room, the school counselor begins the meeting by asking all members of the team to introduce themselves. One and a half hours later, the meeting comes to a close with Mr. and Mrs. Fredricks expressing satisfaction with the decisions made on behalf of Sally's educational services.

Although this scenario does not happen frequently, scenes similar to it occur in many U.S. schools serving students with severe and multiple disabilities. Such service is perhaps idealistic, but it is warranted by the nature of the students for whom individual educational plans must be developed. The education of students with severe and multiple disabilities requires of professionals an extraordinary amount of cooperation, collaboration, and interaction. In fact, Rainforth and York-Barr (1997) have written a text devoted to the topic of collaboration and teaming for students with severe disabilities.

In the vignette, Sally has special educational as well as medical needs that must be met by the educational system. In her case interactive teaming is the *core* of her educational program. This chapter introduces the specific needs of students with severe and multiple disabilities and delineates the various roles of the professionals working with these students. Within the descriptions of the students and of the roles of the professionals working with these students, strategies and techniques used for students with severe or multiple disabilities are presented. More than any group of at-risk students, the group evidencing severe impairments requires a comprehensive interactive team approach.

Before discussing the role of the professionals involved in the education and treatment of students with severe disabilities, this chapter first describes the general characteristics and needs of these students. Brief descriptions are provided to highlight characteristics of students in each area. Although information on the characteristics of students with severe disabilities will be familiar to special educators, school psychologists, and other personnel who have received training about these students, it is included here as reference material for interactive team members who may not have this knowledge or who need to update their information. The references cited in each area will be of further assistance to those who need more information.

CHARACTERISTICS OF STUDENTS WITH SEVERE DISABILITIES

Although students with severe disabilities are a fairly heterogeneous group, they have some common characteristics and educational and medical needs. The abilities of this population are sometimes overlooked when a description of their special needs is presented. In fact, the definition of the population has shifted from a deficit approach to more valuing descriptions that affirm the growth potential and unique capacities of individuals with special needs (Rainforth & York-Barr, 1997). Although the term *students with severe disabilities* remains common in the literature, other terms used for this population include *students with significant disabilities* and *students with low incidence disabilities* (those that occur in fewer than 100,000 persons). The Association for Persons with Severe Handicaps (TASH; 1991) considers persons with severe disabilities as

> . . . individuals of all ages who require extensive ongoing support in more than one major life activity in order to participate in integrated community settings and to enjoy the quality of life that is available to citizens with fewer or no disabilities. Support may be required for life activities such as mobility, communication, self-care, and learning as necessary for independent living, employment, and self-sufficiency. (p. 30)

Similarly, the American Association on Mental Retardation (AAMR; 2002) has revised their definition of mental retardation as follows:

> Mental retardation refers to substantial limitations in present functioning. It is characterized by significantly subaverage intellectual functioning, existing concurrently with related limitations in two or more of the following applicable adaptive skills: communication, self-care, home living, social skills, community use, self-direction, health and safety, functional academics, leisure, and work. Mental retardation manifests before age 18.

The AAMR revised definition also describes the intensities of support, which range from intermittent, limited, and extensive, to pervasive (see Figure 11.1). Most individuals with severe disabilities require limited, extensive, or pervasive supports (Westling & Fox, 2004).

Intermittent

Support on an "as-needed basis." Characterized by episodic nature, person not always needing the support(s), or short-term supports needed during life-span transitions (e.g., job loss or an acute medical crisis). Intermittent supports may be high or low intensity when provided.

Limited

An intensity of supports characterized by consistency over time; time limited but not of an intermittent nature; may require fewer staff members and less cost than more intense levels of support (e.g., time-limited employment training or transitional supports during the school-to-adult provided period).

Extensive

Supports characterized by regular involvement (e.g., daily) in at least some environments (such as work or home) and not time limited (e.g., long-term support and long-term home living support).

Pervasive

Supports characterized by their constancy, high intensity; provided across environments; potential life-sustaining nature. Pervasive supports typically involve more staff members and intrusiveness than do extensive or time-limited supports.

Figure 11.1

AAMR definition of intensities of supports.

Source: From *Mental Retardation: Definition, Classification, and Systems of Supports* (9th ed.), by the American Association on Mental Retardation, 2002, Washington, DC: Author. Reprinted by permission.

Students with severe disabilities have much to offer society. The types of students considered as having severe disabilities vary from state to state. Students with severe disabilities have been described as having learning challenges, including (1) acquiring new skills rapidly, (2) retaining skills they have learned, (3) generalizing skills from one situation to another, (4) synthesizing skills learned separately into meaningful and functional routines, and (5) multiple and complex needs related to medical, health, orthopedic, sensory, and affective conditions (Rainforth & York-Barr, 1997). The following discussion provides additional descriptions of some of the characteristics found in this population. However, it is important to remember that all students are individuals with unique capabilities. Generalizations of these characteristics to all students with severe disabilities would be inaccurate. The information helps establish the need for medical, social, and educational collaboration when providing services to them.

Physical and Sensory Impairments

Students with severe disabilities frequently evidence orthopedic and sensory disabilities (Sacks & Silberman, 1998; Westling & Fox, 2004). In the United States, approximately one child in five with multiple disabilities appears to have hearing impairments, and about two in five appear to have vision impairments (Orelove & Sobsey, 1996, p. 414). The numbers of children with multiple and sensory impairments, however, could be increasing due to improved medical advances for the treatment of premature and/or low birth weight infants. Many of these students evidence severe motor impairments due to cerebral palsy. Students with both physical and sensory impairments have a number of needs. Appropriate intervention requires attention from medical personnel in the areas of physical and occupational therapy, as well as neurology, ophthalmology, and audiology.

Challenging Behavior

Students with severe disabilities often have associated *excessive behaviors* such as self-injury, stereotypy, aggression, or social isolation. Students need treatment in these areas if their behaviors appear to be interfering with school and community functioning. With the most severe behaviors, professionals will usually need to form a committee to assist in monitoring treatment and progress and to ensure that the individual's rights are respected.

A comprehensive and functional behavioral analysis (FBA) of what may be causing the behavior is important (Horner, Albin, Sprague, & Todd, 2000; O'Neill & Johnson, 2000; Reid & Nelson, 2002). Identifying positive behavioral supports through an assessment-based approach helps professionals and parents better identify the functions of specific behaviors. As part of the behavioral assessment, professionals must understand the communicative function of excessive behavior (Carr et al., 1999; Durand & Crimmins, 1992). In conducting an FBA an interactive team will collect data from multiple sources (e.g., permanent records, parent interviews, teacher interviews, and direct observations).

In some of the most severe situations, medical professionals are likely to be involved in the intervention if medication is required. It is estimated that 15% to 20% of those in special education classes are taking mental health (psychopharmacologic or psychotropic) medications (Carroll, 1998). Antipsychotics or neuroleptics medications such as Thorazine® (Chlorpromazine), Mellaril® (Thioridazine), Haldol® (Haloperidol), or Prolixin® (Fluphenazine) have been used for individuals with schizophrenia. However, newer medications are now available including Clozaril® (Clozapine), Respidal® (Risperidone), Zyprexa® (Olanzapine), Seroquel® (Quetiapine), Geodon® (Ziprasidone), and Abilify® (Aripiprazole). The new generation of antipsychotics have less incidence of side effects such as tremors, shuffling gate, difficulty sitting still, dry mouth, blurred vision, and constipation. These medications are now included in behavioral therapy with persons with developmental disabilities. Additionally, anticonvulsants such as Depakote® (Divalproex Sodium), Neurontin® (Gabapentin), and Topamax® (Topiramate) are being used by psychiatrists for aggressive/combative behavior and bipolar disorders. Unfortunately, there are significant side effects when anticonvulsants are used, such as nausea, diarrhea, liver toxicity, hair loss, dizziness, and stomach upset (A. L. Correa, personal communication, 2003). Additionally, some of these medications have not been extensively studied regarding their effects on young children. It is important for the educational team working with students with severe emotional disorders to be aware of the side effects of medications and collaborate with families and the appropriate medical personnel. For more information on the most commonly used anticonvulsants with an explanation of untoward reactions and side effects, see Carroll (1998), and Rutecki and Gidal (2002).

Medical Conditions

Students with the most severe disabilities often have associated medical problems such as the need for tracheostomy suctioning, gastrostomy feeding, oxygen supplementation, seizure monitoring, or clean intermittent *catheterization* (CIC; Bigge, Best, & Heller, 2001; Heller, Fredrick, Best, Dykes, & Cohen, 2000). The ability to administer routine medical and emergency procedures will be required of all professionals working directly with the student who has complicated medical needs. Additionally, the increased numbers of students with traumatic brain injuries, fetal alcohol syndrome, and prenatal exposure to polydrug use challenge medical, social, and school personnel.

Certification in procedures such as cardiopulmonary resuscitation (CPR) and first aid should be required of all professionals working with this population. Additionally, special education personnel should know about infection control procedures associated with communicable diseases such as infectious hepatitis, herpes, cytomegalovirus (CMV), and acquired immune deficiency syndrome (AIDS). Students with severe disabilities may also be taking anticonvulsant medication such as Depakote, Neurontin, Topamax, and Gabpentin to control seizure activity. Professionals must understand their side effects (e.g., drowsiness, lethargy, and impaired vision) and their influence on student performance (Rutecki & Gidal, 2002).

The characteristics associated with students with severe disabilities are numerous, complex, and often not consistent among the population. By assessing and analyzing these students' strengths and weaknesses, team members can develop appropriate instructional programs. The complex nature of these students' disabilities make program development a challenge.

MEETING EDUCATIONAL AND COMMUNITY NEEDS

A major function of the team serving students with severe disabilities is to help them reach their optimal potential for independence and community living with nondisabled people. Interactive teams in special education are being challenged by the continuing movement toward inclusive education (U.S. Department of Education, 2003), including inclusion of students with the most severe disabilities into general education (Janney & Snell, 2000; Sailor, Gee, & Karasoff, 2000; Westling & Fox, 2004). Early participation in inclusive classrooms can prepare students to function successfully in their home communities. Several studies have documented the specific strategies used by team members for successful inclusion (Dennis, Edelman, & Cloninger, 2001; Hunt, Doering, Hirose-Hatae, Maier, & Goetz, 2001; McDonnell, Mathot-Buckner, Thorson, & Fister, 2001; Snell & Janney, 2000; York-Barr & Kronberg, 2002). Hunt and her colleagues developed the Unified Plan of Support (UPS) process to guide collaborative teams in including students with significant disabilities into general education classrooms. The collaborative process includes four key elements:

1. Identifying the learning and social profile of each focal student.
2. Developing supports to increase the students' academic success and social participation in classroom activities.
3. Collaborative implementation of the plans of support.
4. A built-in accountability system. (p. 243)

The most effective school practices for serving the needs of students with severe disabilities are "(a) inclusion, (b) collaborative teams, (c) integrated therapy, (d) systematic, activity based instruction, (e) data-based decision making and (f) positive behavior supports" (Snell & Brown, 2000a, p. 116). If schools support these practices, three major student outcomes can be achieved. Billingsly, Gallucci, Peck, Schwartz, and Staub (1996) and Staub, Schwartz, Gallucci, and Peck (1994) outline the three desirable outcomes for students in inclusive settings as follows:

1. The *skills outcome* encompasses the abilities that an individual needs to acquire (e.g., functional academics and useful social, motor, and communication skills).
2. The *membership outcome* encompasses belonging to a group and being treated as a group member (e.g., developing peer affiliations and peer groups during and after school).
3. The *relationship outcome* includes ongoing, familiar, social interactions with others (e.g., play, companionship, friendship).

Meyer and Eichinger (1994) developed Program Quality Indicators (PQIs) to evaluate effectively the outcomes of inclusive programs and provide guidance in program development for students with severe disabilities. The PQI checklist contains 38 items in the areas of local agency district indicators, building indicators, educational and placement and related services indicators, and individual student and program indicators. Teams of school personnel can use this instrument to make decisions about educational programming and services.

The educational needs of students with severe disabilities are complex in the areas of support services, assessment, program design, and teacher competencies. The following section addresses these needs.

SUPPORT SERVICE OPTIONS FOR INCLUSION

The nature of support services provided to students with severe disabilities does *not* typically include general education academic curriculum, but instead focuses on an adapted academic curriculum and functional life routines necessary for community life (Browder, 2001; Snell & Brown, 2000a; Westling & Fox, 2004). The interactive team that promotes inclusive education comprises parents, members from related service professionals, general and special education personnel, and vocational and community personnel.

The continued push for inclusion (Sailor et al., 2000, Westling & Fox, 2004) has left many professionals in a quandary about how best to provide the full range of educational and therapeutic support services to students in their home schools and in the general education classroom. In a study by Strong and Sandoval (2000), several concerns surfaced from families, students, and general education teachers about including students with neuromuscular diseases into general education classrooms. For families, the concerns were related to communication with schools, talking about death, and the need to be empowered. For students, the concerns were related to a sense of belonging, learning about the disease, self-concept as the disease progressed, and ongoing loss of abilities. For general education teachers, the concerns were related to communicating with parents, fears and attending to medical needs of the student, support in the classroom/collaboration, setting appropriate expectations, and the need for flexibility and adaptability. Although the study focused on students with neuromuscular disease, the concerns about inclusion and solutions for better collaboration and communication are clear for many students with severe disabilities. York-Barr and Kronberg (2002) chronicle a team's 2-year experience in including students with severe disabilities into a middle school. They found that the essential ingredients for change involved constant administrative support; sufficient time for preplanning and team-building; support for teacher coverage for the first 2 weeks of implementation; relationships between general and special education teaching teams that were contributive, equitable, and empowering; ongoing external support from university faculty; and summer planning days.

A transdisciplinary team model is critical and allows the general and special educator the opportunity to integrate therapy techniques throughout the student's daily program. Figure 11.2 describes four different team support approaches for instructing students with severe disabilities in inclusive educational settings. Wolfe and Hall (2003) outline a collaborative team process for inclusion that identifies a cascade of integration options for students with severe disabilities, including unadapted participation in the general curriculum, adaptations to the general curriculum, embedded skills within the general curriculum, functional skills within the general education curriculum, and functional curriculum outside the general education classroom (p. 57). Additionally, several instructional strategies have proven to be effective in benefiting both students with severe disabilities and their peers without disabilities. Those strategies include multi-element curriculum structures (teaching different objectives in the same curriculum domain as their peers without special needs), accommodations (modifying instructional materials), and peer tutoring (students act as instructional helpers for one another) (McDonnell & Fister, 2001).

Ultimately, the optimal inclusive placement for a student would be in a chronological-age-appropriate school setting, with the natural proportion of students with special needs to students without special needs, and incorporating community-referenced programming that incorporates aspects of building

*Pinnacle
K-6*

- *General education teacher with team planning and consultation from special education.* The student with special needs is taught with peers using the same or adapted methods, but with no extra staff support.
- *Collaborative teaching (also called team teaching or co-teaching).* Two or more team members plan and teach the entire class (students with and without special needs) cooperatively, usually for part of the day.
- *Pull-in with collaborative teaming.* Special education teacher or another team member (e.g., related service staff) teaches or provides support to the student(s) with special needs in the context of a general education classroom or school activity. Classmates typically are involved in the same or similar activities as the students with special needs and may participate together in small or large groups.
- *Pull-out with collaborative teaming (also called alternative activities).* Support is provided by special education staff or other team members (e.g., related services staff, vocational teacher) to the student with special needs in a setting away from the general education classroom for a particular reason identified by the team (e.g., to give privacy, more space, access to materials not in the classroom). Other classmates may accompany the student who is removed from the general education setting. Any use of pull-out depends on team collaboration to be effective and needs to be regularly reevaluated.

Figure 11.2
Team support approaches.
Source: From "Development and Implementation of Educational Programs," by M. E. Snell and F. Brown, 2000, in M. E. Snell and F. Brown (Eds.), *Instruction of Students with Severe Disabilities* (5th ed., p. 132). Adapted by permission of Pearson Education, Inc. Upper Saddle River, NJ.

friendships and quality of life (Downing & Eichinger, 2003; Orelove & Sobsey, 1996; Snell & Brown, 2000b; Westling & Fox, 2004). Under the mandates of the reauthorization of the IDEA in 1997, creative placement options have also been proposed for young preschoolers with special needs and young adults with special needs under *transition* programs. For infants and preschoolers, service can be provided in home-based or center-based programs in the most natural environments. Placing early intervention programs in regular child care, Early Head Start, or Head Start settings is strongly supported by many school districts. A transition plan for moving the services from Part C (birth to 3 intervention) to Part B must be developed at least 90 days prior to the child's third birthday.

Similarly, secondary transition programs are being developed in many middle and high schools. The Individual Transition Plan (ITP) is written as part of the IEP as early as the student's 14th birthday, and a required statement of community agency responsibilities and goals must be written by the time the student is 16 years old. Close collaboration with families, educators, and adult services agencies such as state human service agencies (e.g., vocational rehabilitation, development disability) and private organizations (e.g., the ARC) is critical for a successful transition to postschool life (Brolin & Loyd, 2004; Moon & Inge, 2000; Sitlington, Clark, & Kolstoe, 2000; Westling & Fox, 2004).

Assessment and Program Design

Assessment and program development for students with severe disabilities are not simple processes. The interactive team must be prepared to provide *multifaceted assessment* of students in the areas of vision, hearing, sensorimotor development, functional/ecological inventories, and family functioning. Several researchers provide an excellent description of the assessment process and procedures recommended for developing an appropriate and functional IEP for students with severe disabilities (Brown & Snell, 2000; Rainforth & York-Barr, 1997; Westling & Fox, 2004). Furthermore, there is growing support for the use of authentic assessment approaches that include portfolios documenting what the student actually learns through various methods (e.g., videotapes, audiotapes, interviews, observational data, social validation, permanent products of student work, medical and physical evaluations, curriculum-based assessment, ecological inventories, and functional assessments; Siegel-Causey & Allinder, 1998).

The reauthorization of IDEA in 1997 also mandated the use of functional behavioral assessments and the development of behavioral intervention plans of support for students with behavior problems, such as self-injury, aggression, and property damage. The positive behavior support plan should include the following:

- A rationale for the comprehensive support plan.
- Operational definitions of the problem behaviors.
- Summary (hypothesis) statement from the functional assessment.
- An overview of the general approaches selected for intervention.
- Emergency or crisis procedures.
- A detailed implementation plan.
- An evaluation plan.

This approach to behavioral intervention should require team consensus and guide new support members who must learn and implement the comprehensive plan at later points in time (Horner et al., 2000).

The number of published assessments and curricula for students with severe disabilities is limited. Some of the most widely used materials for program development are the *Syracuse Community-Referenced Curriculum Guide* (Ford et al., 1989), *Choosing Options and Accommodations for Children (COACH*; Giangreco, Cloninger, & Iverson, 1998), and the *Activities Catalog* (Wilcox & Bellamy, 1987). The *Perkins Activity and Resource Guide* (Cushman, Heydt, Edwards, Clark, & Allon, 1992) and the van Dijk approach to assessment (Nelson, van Dijk, McDonnell, & Thompson, 2002) would also be beneficial for some students who have severe disabilities but are not sensory impaired (Cushman et al., 1992). Additionally, Brown and Lehr (1993) and Brown, Evans, Weed, and Owen (1987) have described an assessment-curriculum model for designing intervention programs for students. The *Component Model of Functional Life Routines* offers an assessment and curriculum model for generating skills that are functional, structured, and comprehensive in the domain areas of personal management, vocational school, leisure, and mobility. Additionally, Brown and Snell (2000) described the *ecological inventory*, which generates skills by breaking down the domains into environments, subenvironments, activities, and skill sequences. As outlined in Chapter 9, an abundance of assessment/curriculum models is available for use with young children with special needs. The most recent and promising materials for use with children birth to age 6 are the *Assessment Evaluation Programming System* (AEPS) and its curriculum guide (Bricker, 1993; Cripe, Slentz, & Bricker, 1993).

Several curriculum materials for transition planning that emphasize student involvement have been described by Rusch and Chadsey (1998) and Brolin and Loyd (2004), including *ChoiceMaker Self-Determination* (Martin & Marshall, 1995), *Whose Future Is It Anyway?* (Wehmeyer & Kelchner, 1995), *Next S.T.E.P.: Student Transition and Educational Planning* (Halpern et al., 1997), *Life Centered Career Education (LCCE) Mild/Moderate Curriculum* (Loyd & Brolin, 2002), and *TAKE CHARGE for the Future* (Powers, Sowers, Turner, Nesbitt, Knowles, & Ellison, 1996). Two programs that focus specifically on career planning are the MAPS (Falvey, Forest, Pearpoint, & Rosenberg, 1992) and the PATH (Pearpoint, O'Brien, & Forest, 1993). For example, in the PATH process a group facilitator takes the team (usually with the student involved) through an eight-step process that includes:

1. The dream.
2. Sensing the goal, positive and possible.
3. Grounding in the now.
4. Who do we enroll?
5. Recognizing ways to build strength.
6. Charting actions for the next 3 months.
7. Planning the next month's work.
8. Committing to the next steps.

The goals for many of these programs involve preparing the student for postschool goals, such as integration into the community, through *group-home* or supported-living arrangements, supported employment, and community-based vocational programs.

Since the passage of No Child Left Behind (2002), schools are accountable for student outcomes through the use of high-stakes standardized state assessments. All states must test children in language arts/reading and math, and by 2007, science. For students with significant disabilities who may not be on a standard diploma track or have a more functional curriculum, alternative assessments are necessary. Alternative assessments have been defined as alternative ways for assessing progress toward the same standards as all other students are working toward (Browder et al., 2003). The formats most often used for alternative assessments include observations, interview/surveys, record reviews, and portfolios. Although portfolio assessments are preferred, the process is time-consuming and does not necessarily lead to improved instruction for students or access to the general education curriculum (Browder et al., 2003). The majority of states use special scoring rubrics to score student performance on skills checklists. Interactive teams are being challenged to find better ways to use the data gathered by alternative assessments to improve students' instruction, enhance student expectations, evaluate programs, and link assessment to the general education curriculum. IEP teams should focus on developing standards-based IEPs that link IEP objectives to a standard from the general curriculum (Browder & Spooner, 2003). The team process of creating standards-based IEPs includes:

- Identifying the state's standards and extending them to real-life indicators for students with significant disabilities.
- Identifying the student's level of functioning with the standards in mind. Linking the students' annual goals to the standard.
- Reviewing IEP goals that were not linked to standards and trying to align them to current state standards.
- Reviewing standards that are not on the IEP and generating new ideas for annual goals. (Browder & Spooner, 2003)

Specialized Curriculum Components

A variety of domain areas have been proposed for students with severe disabilities. For younger students a developmental model has been used most frequently. For school-age and older students an ecological or functional model has been proposed. The following sections cover a few of the components included in the IEP for a student with severe disabilities.

Physical Management Component.   Although a large percentage of students with severe disabilities may have physical impairments, some of these students may not need specialized equipment or physical management. However, for those who have physical disabilities, specialized equipment (e.g., wheelchairs, walkers, positioning equipment, prone standers, and adapted bathroom seating) is often required for use in the classroom and at home.

The student with severe impairments often is unable to maintain proper body alignment and posture. Without a stable body, the student will be unable to perform even minimal tasks such as eating, bathing, brushing his or her teeth, or going to the bathroom. Teachers and parents need basic skills in relaxing the *hypertonic* (spastic/high muscle tone) student to dress the student or change diapers. Additionally, for students with *hypotonic* muscle tone, the physical therapist (PT) or the occupational therapist (OT) can instruct the special education staff and parents on how to alert the child's neurological and motor system to provide the child with appropriate stimulation.

The physical therapist develops a program of assessment and intervention after the physician has referred the student for these services. Assessment of the disability includes a determination of the strength and range of movement, and the relationship between the movement and the individual's ability to learn or perform learning-related functions. Because it is important to continue the physical therapy program regularly, the PT and OT often work collaboratively with special educators, classroom teachers, and parents, who are responsible for carrying out some of the programs in the therapist's absence. The nature and type of program designed for the student with movement disabilities may include the following:

◆ Neurodevelopmental treatment.

◆ Lifting, transferring, carrying, and positioning techniques.

◆ Adaptive equipment (e.g., rolls, wedges, standing boards, corner chairs, scooter boards, TumbleForm positioning aids, wheelchairs, and transport chairs) (Campbell, 2000).

Assistive technology has contributed significantly to students' ability to participate in typical environments. One of the most significant technologies available for some students with physical impairments is speech recognition systems such as IBM's ViaVoice and Dragon Systems' Naturally Speaking (Bowe, 2000). Educational teams need to be aware of available technology, and often an assistive technology expert can help the interactive team with its understanding of the hardware and software needs for individual students.

Sensory Enhancement Component.   Technology for students with sensory disabilities is also enhancing the access to educational information and increasing quality of life for many. With students who have visual or hearing impairments, sensory aids such as glasses, contact lenses, hearing aids, or FM systems may be necessary. For students with visual impairments, the advent of speech synthesis technology has made print media easily accessible (Bowe, 2000). Additionally, special *mobility aids* such as the traditional long cane, the Mowat Sensor, Pathsounder, or Sonicguide, prescribed by an *orientation and mobility specialist,* may be needed for students with multiple disabilities who are blind (Blasch, Wiener, & Welsh, 1997). Functional orientation and mobility techniques have also been developed for students with more significant disabilities (Perla & Ducret, 1999; Tolla, 2000).

In some cases, if the student is deaf-blind, a *communication system* such as the Tandom and/or manual signing system is essential. Interventions with aids such as the Tellatouch (Silberman, 1986) or vibrotactile devices (Niswander, 1987) have been valuable for deaf-blind students.

Finally, the use of functional vision (Langley, 1980, 1986) and auditory assessment will be a critical part of the initial evaluation of students with multiple disabilities. Additionally, interactive team members must strive to achieve an individualized set of environmental adaptations for each student including therapeutic positioning, lighting and contrast, and audition (Sobsey & Wolf-Schein, 1996; Utley, 1993;

Westling & Fox, 2004). Table 11.1 provides a checklist for team members to complete when working with students who are deaf-blind. The checklist can also help teams prepare environmental settings for many students with severe disabilities.

Table 11.1
Environmental Checklist

Environmental Checklist

Name of Student _____ Date _____

SECTION I—THERAPEUTIC POSITIONING

1. Overall Body Positioning (Sitting)

____ a. Student is upright, or reclined slightly, with hips, knees, and ankles at 90-degree angles, or other angle(s) recommended by a therapist.

____ b. Student's head is neutral and upright, with or without external support.

____ c. Student's arms are supported by the table top or wheelchair tray so the elbows are flexed between 90 and 120 degrees.

2. Overall Body Positioning (Sidelying)

____ a. Student is supported correctly (i.e., lower shoulder is forward; head is in alignment with the spine; hips, knees, and ankles are flexed; pillows are placed between and below bony prominences).

____ b. Student is lying on the side that results in the better eye (if known) being on the upper lateral half of the body. (**Note:** *Consultation with the team is recommended to determine whether sidelying on a particular lateral half of the body may be contraindicated.*)

3. Overall Body Positioning (Supported Supine)

____ a. Student is supported correctly (i.e., head in alignment; chin slightly flexed; shoulders rounded forward slightly; hips, knees, and ankles flexed).

____ b. Student's head is stable with or without external support.

4. Position of Peers, Adults, and Materials

____ a. Depending on the student's head control, materials are placed horizontally, vertically, or somewhere in-between those points.

____ b. Peers or adults position themselves at or near the student's eye level during interaction.

SECTION II—LIGHTING

1. Amount and Type of Light (indoors)

____ a. A combination of light sources (i.e., natural light plus incandescent light, etc.) is available.

____ b. The entire work surface is illuminated evenly (dependent upon specific task requirements).

____ c. Supplemental lighting is available (if necessary).

2. Position of Light

____ a. Student is positioned so that all sources of natural light (e.g., windows) are behind him rather than behind the instructional/social/communicative partners.

Source: From "Assessing the Instructional Environment to Meet the Needs of Learners with Multiple Disabilities Including Students Who Are Deaf-Blind," by B. L. Utley, 1993, *Deaf-Blind Perspectives, 1*(2), pp. 5–8. Reprinted by permission.

Environmental Checklist

_____ b. Supplemental light source originates from over the student's head so the shade directs the light on only the task materials (if necessary).

OR

_____ c. Supplemental light source originates from behind and over the shoulder of the student (e.g., over the left shoulder for those who use the right hand and vice versa).

OR

_____ d. Supplemental light source originates from behind and over the shoulder of the student on the lateral half of the head where the most functional eye is.

3. Glare

_____ a. Work surface is made of (or covered with) nonreflective material.

_____ b. Materials are made of nonreflective material (if possible).

_____ c. The amount of light emitted in the direction of the eye is limited or eliminated.

4. Contrast

_____ a. For tasks that rely on materials that are black or dark in color, the background surface is lighter to enhance contrast. Light-colored materials use a dark background surface.

_____ b. Select or purchase materials that contrast with the work surface (if possible).

Note: The items listed on the checklist are to be viewed as _preliminary only._ A more thorough assessment should be made by team members according to the knowledge base of their respective disciplines.

Medical Support Component.   The special education team can perform most of the techniques required by students with severe disabilities who are medically fragile. With close supervision from medical staff such as the school nurse, team members can administer complex medical procedures such as tube feeding, suctioning, colostomy care, and clean intermittent catheterization (CIC). However, administration of medication and heart or oxygen monitoring procedures may still be the main responsibility of the school nurse. Yet, reports by school nurses contribute significantly to the problems of service delivery. Some schools are using the states' Nurse Practice Act to delegate some of the specialized health procedures to nursing assistants, health technicians, or other unlicensed assistive personnel (Bigge et al., 2001; Heller et al., 2000), but caution must be taken with these policies. Clear school district policies and procedures must be outlined to protect students, teachers, and medical personnel from accidents.

In a study by Heller et al. (2000), teachers reported that for the most part they are responsible for implementing medical procedures on a daily basis. A list of the 10 most common health-related procedures needed in school settings is given in

Figure 11.3. Ault, Rues, Graff, and Holvoet (2000) describe each of the medical procedures and discuss their use in a classroom. They also outline a sample individualized health care plan that can be used by the interactive team serving children with health care needs.

Interestingly, Heller et al. (2000) reported that only 46% of the respondents lived in states that provided state guidelines outlining who is responsible for performing health care procedures. Nonetheless, most personnel responded that their schools had written procedures for emergency management, dispensing medication, and specialized health care procedures. When asked about training, the respondents reported that nurses provided most of the training, while the child's parent was the next highest source of training. Furthermore, the study reported that students infrequently performed their own specialized care procedures. Training students to partially participate or directly perform their own procedures should be encouraged by educational teams.

Teachers indicated that it would be beneficial if nurses could work in collaboration with the teachers and share the responsibilities of health-related procedures. Additionally, few teachers reported that their districts had written guidelines or procedures to meet the health-related needs of students with severe disabilities. In most schools, medical and educational services may be fragmented and students are still underserved when it comes to their health-related needs. The requirements for coordinated planning, particularly for early intervention services under Part C, are designed to help professionals work together more effectively in the treatment of students with severe or multiple disabilities. As more students who are medically fragile enter the public school system, services for these students will be more clearly defined (Bartel & Thurman, 1992; Bowe, 2000). Students with communicable diseases such as hepatitis, herpes, human immunodeficiency virus, and cytomegalovirus require special disease control procedures in classroom environments (Ault et al., 2000; Bowe, 2000). Many of these students require frequent hospitalizations and would benefit from a school-to-hospital transition plan to ensure continuity in educational services (Borgioli & Kennedy, 2003).

Figure 11.3

Ten most common health care procedures needed in the school setting.

Source: From "Specialized Health Care Procedures in the Schools: Training and Service Delivery," by K. W. Heller, L. D. Fredrick, S. Best, M. K. Dykes, and E. T. Cohen, 2000, *Exceptional Children, 66*(2), pp. 173–186. Copyright 2000 by the Council for Exceptional Children. Reprinted with permission.

1. Tube feeding
2. Colostomy/ileostomy care
3. Clean intermittent catheterization (CIC)
4. Suctioning
5. Tracheostomy care
6. Ventilator management
7. Inhaler/nebulizer administration
8. Oxygen delivery
9. Insulin injections
10. Blood glucose testing

Self-Care Component.   A major component of support services for students with severe disabilities is that of developing self-care skills, such as using the toilet, dressing, eating, and personal hygiene. Often, medical professionals and school nurses can provide information as to the readiness of the student for toilet training. Additionally, it is common for feeding programs to be designed for students who are dependent on adult intervention. Often, the OT will design or adapt a self-feeding device to help the student gain independence. Moreover, an OT or speech-language therapist might develop a program for the classroom staff to implement in the area of stimulating the development of *oral-motor skills* such as swallowing, sucking, and chewing.

School personnel will need to provide appropriate facilities for training students in self-care skills such as using the toilet, bathing, and dressing (Bigge et al., 2001; Campbell, 2000; Farlow & Snell, 2000; Westling & Fox, 2004). Family involvement is critical and instructional manuals, such as *Steps to Independence* (Baker & Brightman, 1996), can be used to assist families in this area of programming. Additionally, Farlow and Snell (2000) support the use of peers in assisting with certain self-care skills such as grooming and dressing.

Communication Component.   The student with severe or multiple disabilities may be able to communicate using alternative and augmentative communication systems. Students who are unable to use speech as their major communication mode may use gestures, manual signing, communication boards, or electronic devices such as Zygo's Macaw, Prentke Romich's Liberator, and the Dynavox System as an alternative to speech. Augmentative communication systems such as communication boards or electronic speech-output or scanning devices can be designed for individual students by the speech-language therapist and a team of service providers (Bowe, 2000; Downing, 1999). Speech-language therapists, occupational therapists, and special and general educators may all need to understand a simple electronic switch assembly for adapting toys and communication devices (Bowe, 2000; Burkhart, 1980, 1984; Glickman, Deitz, Anson, & Stewart, 1996).

For the student with severe or multiple disabilities, the team works on developing language production, concept development, and speech articulation (Langley & Lombardino, 1991). Treating a student who has no formal speech production (verbalizations) and may have a poor prognosis for speech involves developing pragmatic and prelinguistic communication behaviors, such as attending, requesting, rejecting, imitating, turn-taking, and naming (Langley & Lombardino, 1991; Orelove & Sobsey, 1996). Wetherby, Warren, and Reichle (1998) and Siegel and Wetherby (2000) provide guidelines on how to recognize, support, and teach nonsymbolic communicative interactions in the context of daily routines.

The team also may be involved in analyzing the communicative function of a student's excessive behavior, such as hand biting or aggression, and developing an intervention program that provides the student with an alternative means of communicating frustration, boredom, or attention by using gestures or signs (Durand, 1990; Durand & Crimmins, 1992). Whether language takes the form of facial reactions, signing, gesturing, pointing, or verbalizations, teaching students with severe disabilities functional language communication within a social context is a major educational goal.

Community-Based Functional Component.   For school-age students with severe disabilities, the sole use of developmental checklists describing the step-by-step sequence of infant and early childhood development for program implementation is no longer appropriate. As described earlier, a more functional approach to developing curriculum has become the major focus of special education programs. This requires administrative support and resources to develop intervention programs that integrate training in the areas of school, domestic, vocational, community, and leisure skill development (Brown & Snell, 2000; Snell & Brown, 2000a). Simulated school environments can no longer suffice for all-school training and intervention. School personnel must access natural community environments, which contain normal prompts and cues. Such environments benefit the student in learning how to wash clothes in a laundromat, shop for food at the grocery store, or ride the bus to a supported employment program every day.

Family and Friends Involvement Component.   Involvement of the family in teaming is critical to the success of educational and vocational intervention with students who have severe disabilities. Because of the nature of the student's disability, the family may have added pressures and stressors that will affect their life adjustment (Salisbury & Dunst, 1997; Turnbull & Turnbull, 2000). Families often have the medical information about their children that is needed for school programs. Conversely, school professionals can help families obtain and interpret medical information that is necessary for the student. The ultimate responsibility for care and future adjustment of the child with severe disabilities lies with the family members. Their involvement through training and advocacy will be critical once the public school program has ended.

The family also plays a critical role in the implementation of inclusive education programs. Families of students with severe disabilities are often reluctant to approve a general education setting for their children. Their concerns often relate to placing their children in general education classrooms that are already overburdened and unwelcoming to their children. Families fear that untrained teachers will be unable to accommodate their children's needs given their heavy work loads (Palmer, Fuller, Arora, & Nelson, 2001). However, some parents support their children's placement into general education because they believe that there will be higher expectations and more stimulating environments for their children. Parents also believe that their children will improve their social skills and develop friendships if placed in general education classrooms (Palmer et al., 2001). The important point to remember is that the decision of inclusion into general education settings must be based on effective collaboration and communication with parents. Team members must see that the decision on least restrictive environments should be a shared decision with parents and respect the family's concerns, beliefs, and values.

Friends and peers also are an important part of the lives of students with severe disabilities. Team members should focus on enhancing and facilitating social and friendship relationships among students with severe disabilities and students without disabilities (Strong & Sandoval, 2000). The students with severe disabilities and their friends should be included in many aspects of designing educational programs. Several person-centered planning models have been described in the literature; some are used in conjunction with transition planning described earlier in this chapter. An excellent method for doing a person-oriented plan is Personal Futures Planning (Mount & Zwernik, 1989). This method serves as a tool for fostering new ways of thinking about students with severe disabilities. When futures planning, a small group of people (e.g., family, peers, neighbors, community leaders, teachers, and administrators) agree to meet for mutual support, brainstorming, and strategizing. The goals for this team are to discuss the student's hopes, interests, skills, and life goals in order to develop an action plan for reaching those goals through home, school, and community supports. Within the context of person-centered planning, the team should focus on ways to develop self-determination in students with severe disabilities. Promoting self-determination requires students with special needs to exert control over their own lives through developing skills in choice making, self-advocacy, positive perceptions of control and efficacy, and self-knowledge and awareness (Brolin & Loyd, 2004; Martin et al., 2003; Wehmeyer, Agran, & Hughes, 1998, 2000; Wehmeyer & Palmer, 2003). Students with the most significant cognitive disabilities may depend on trusted allies (e.g., parents, siblings, friends, service providers) to collaborate with on decision making about quality of life enhancement (Turnbull & Turnbull, 2001).

Futures planning can complement the development of an IEP process. A similar approach to planning programs for students with severe disabilities is the McGill Action Planning System (Falvey et al., 1992; Vandercook, York, & Forest, 1989). MAPS uses support teams in a manner similar to that of Personal Futures Planning to brainstorm and develop goals for the student.

SELECTED TEACHING STRATEGIES

Several strategies are described in this chapter to illustrate the types of techniques that can be used for students with severe disabilities. More detailed explanations of the best practices for teaching these students are found in several textbooks, such as Browder (2001), Rainforth and York-Barr (1997), Ryndak and Alper (2003), Westling and Fox (2004), and Snell and Brown (2000b).

One frequently used teaching strategy involves applied behavior analysis. Within the general application of the approach, the teacher selects functional skills for the student and breaks each skill down into small, teachable tasks. Once the task sequence has been established, educators must provide a consistent application of prompting and reinforcement procedures. Team members must consider the following components of instructional procedures (Rainforth & York-Barr, 1997):

◆ Setting, grouping, positioning
◆ Equipment/materials

- Initial instruction and prompt
- Correct response
- Time delay and correction
- Reinforcement
- Frequency to teach
- Frequency of data
- Type of data
- Criterion for change

A number of *time delay* or *prompting sequences* have been shown to be effective with students with severe disabilities. The sequence of providing *least-to-most prompts* involves allowing wait-time for the student to perform the task step independently before providing help. For example, using the *increasing prompts strategy* for teaching a student to feed himself cereal with a spoon involves first providing the student with the natural cue of the cereal and the spoon. If the student does not respond, a verbal prompt ("Pick up your spoon") might be used. If, after a designated time period, the student does not begin the task, a gesture or model can be used, such as picking up the spoon and scooping up some cereal. Again, a wait-time occurs, and if the student has not responded, the teacher might provide the most intrusive prompt—taking the student's hand and guiding him through the task of scooping the cereal.

The other prompting strategy is that of *graduated guidance*. In this strategy the teacher begins with total physical assistance by taking the student's hands and moving him through the complete task of scooping up the cereal. After repeated trials, the teacher would begin to decrease her physical assistance when she judged that the student was becoming more independent. The teacher would decrease the prompts until she was merely shadowing the student's hand as the student ate the cereal.

Additionally, reinforcement procedures would be implemented when necessary. The most natural reinforcers, such as social praise, should be tried first, before more artificial reinforcers (e.g., toys, prizes, or edibles) are used.

Instruction of students with severe disabilities should occur in the environment most natural to the task. If a student is being taught to brush her hair, the teacher should provide the training in the natural environment (e.g., bathroom, dressing table). Often, instruction occurs in simulated settings due to a lack of available natural environments. Although they are not as effective for maintenance and generalization of skills to the natural environments, simulated settings may be necessary.

Furthermore, when teaching students with severe disabilities, use of functional and age-appropriate materials is critical. For example, in teaching a 16-year-old student to operate a tape recorder, the use of a child's toy machine would not be recommended. Instead, a regular tape recorder should be used. A variety of materials and experiences should also be used for training generalization across tasks. For example, if a student is learning to use bathroom facilities at school, she should eventually be instructed to use facilities in other settings, such as her home, fast-food restaurants, and the laundromat. In particular, the various settings may require different skills in flushing toilets, dispensing soap, and drying hands.

Instruction of students with severe disabilities requires ongoing data-based programs, using effective behavior analysis procedures (Ryndak & Alper, 2003; Snell & Brown, 2000a; Westling & Fox, 2004). Keeping detailed records of progress on skill sequences helps the teacher make program changes. Additionally, because students with severe disabilities may not progress as quickly as their peers without disabilities, measuring behavior and recording the progress are critical in instruction.

Students with severe disabilities may be limited by physical or sensory impairments; however, their limitations should not exclude them from participating in age-appropriate routines shared by their peers without special needs. Instruction should be given in inclusive settings with peers without special needs and involve adaptations when necessary. The *principle of partial participation* (Brown et al., 1979) affirms that students with severe disabilities can take part to some degree in age-appropriate activities. For example, excluding students from a school play production because they cannot speak clearly would be contrary to the principle of partial participation. Instead, the school play could be adapted so that students who are unable speak can use a tape recorder, sign with the use of an interpreter, or play parts that require no speaking.

Various teaching strategies have been discussed, showing that instruction for students with severe disabilities is challenging and complex. As students become more involved in inclusive settings, team members will need specific guidance in instructional procedures for general education classes. Stainback and Stainback (1996), Hunt and Goetz (1997), Giangreco (1996), and Westling and Fox (2004) provide excellent guides for developing instruction in inclusive settings. Repetition and systematic generalization of training are required.

Figure 11.4 outlines eight principles that characterize educational teamwork and influence how teams make decisions about teaching students with severe disabilities. If programs are not carefully designed and implemented, students, families, and teachers will experience failure and frustration. An interactive team can provide support and contribute creative teaching strategies that are sure to be effective with students. These specific roles and responsibilities are discussed in the next section.

ROLES OF THE PROFESSIONALS INVOLVED WITH STUDENTS WITH SEVERE DISABILITIES

Given the wide range of characteristics of students with severe disabilities, a number of professionals with varying areas of expertise may be needed to plan the students' programs. The professionals who serve these students need to coordinate their efforts. Effective leadership, good communication skills, and effective professional development procedures, all of which have been outlined in previous chapters, facilitate coordination. The general roles of professionals were discussed

---

Educational Programs Are Student Centered

Teams consider students' well-being as their core purpose by giving the student team input; using peer contributions; acknowledging family input; and focusing on a person-centered approach.

Educational Programs Are Team Generated

A cohesive team designs programs.

Educational Programs Are Both Practical and Valid

Teams select goals and objectives that are usable and efficient.

Educational Programs Are Socially Valid

The team asks the question "So what?" Is this change/idea/objective important to the student?

Educational Programs Reflect Functional Priorities

Functional skills are those skills that, if not performed by a student, must be completed for the student by someone else.

Educational Programs Require Active Participation

Student's participation may be partial or complete, but it is best when performance is meaningful and active rather than nonpurposeful and passive.

Educational Programs Foster Self-Determination

Acknowledges that students must make decisions about themselves, attain independence in useful routines, evaluate their own performance, and make adjustments to improve themselves.

Educational Programs Are Individualized

Teaching is tailored to the student's strengths, needs, and individual characteristics.

Figure 11.4

Guiding team principles.

Source: From "Development and Implementation of Educational Programs," by M. E. Snell and F. Brown, 2000, in M. E. Snell and F. Brown (Eds.), *Instruction of Students with Severe Disabilities* (5th ed., pp. 121–124). Adapted by permission of Pearson Education, Inc. Upper Saddle River, NJ.

in Chapter 3; specialized contributions of team members who work with students with severe disabilities are outlined in this chapter.

Delineating the roles of each of the team members within the educational and community setting is a first step in clarifying each group's function on the team. Table 11.2 outlines the various roles and responsibilities in both direct service and team involvement.

Serving students with severe disabilities carries with it unique challenges that involve collaboration with related service professionals and paraprofessionals. Although role release among related service professionals and educators is expected for interactive teaming to be successful, Utley and Rapport (2000) found that professionals are still reluctant to release certain aspects of their jobs to other team members. There was support among the teams to engage in collaborative problem solving. Yet, physical and occupational therapists were unwilling to share their expertise related to assessment, design, and implementation of therapeutic techniques

Table 11.2
Roles of Professionals and Others Involved with Students with Severe Disabilities

Personnel	Direct Service Provider	Team Member
Special educator	• Conduct multifaceted assessment in the areas of vision, hearing, sensorimotor development, functional/ecological inventories, family functioning. • Monitor under supervision any medical and behavioral procedures. • Implement computer and augmentative communication systems. • Provide physical management and proper positioning in equipment. • Conduct functional programming emphasizing independence in school and community integration.	• Serve as service coordinator. • Accept role-release responsibilities from related service personnel. • Interpret multifaceted assessments. • Consult on individualized instructional strategies with general educators serving students in inclusive settings. • Advocate for student and family needs.
Physical therapist	• Assess posture/motor development. • Conduct direct therapy for specific motor problems within an integrated classroom environment. • Order and prepare adaptive equipment. • Monitor use of braces and orthotic devices.	• Conduct staff development on therapy treatment. • Role release the least complex treatment procedures (e.g., range of motion). • Integrate motor goals into daily life routines. • Consult with other medical personnel (orthopedist, neurologist, nurse, etc.).
Occupational therapist	• Assess fine motor, oral motor, vocational, and leisure skills areas. • Order and modify special devices. • Design feeding programs. • Conduct eye-hand coordination and fine motor skills programs.	• Conduct staff development on therapy treatments. • Role release the least complex treatments (e.g., feeding procedures). • Integrate fine motor goals into daily life routines. • Consult with other medical personnel.
School nurse/ nutritionist	• Dispense medication. • Monitor complex medical procedures (tracheostomy suctioning, catheterization procedures, G-tube feeding, mechanical ventilation, etc.). • Conduct first aid and minor emergency safety procedures. • Prepare appropriate, well-balanced meal plans.	• Conduct staff development on health-related procedures. • Role release the least complex procedures (e.g., postural drainage, gastrostomy feeding, prosthesis care). • Consult with other medical personnel. • Implement and orient staff to emergency procedures involving life-threatening situations. • Contact family for ongoing status of medical/nutritional needs. • Consult staff on side effects of medications.

Continued

Table 11.2
Continued

Personnel	Direct Service Provider	Team Member
School psychologist	• Assess psychological and adaptive behavior functioning. • Conduct behavior management programs for severe maladaptive behavior.	• Conduct assessments jointly with other team members if special adaptations must be made (e.g., severe vision, motor, hearing impairments). • Interpret test results to team and family. • Conduct staff development on behavior management procedures.
Family	• Reinforce functional/behavioral programming. • Reinforce related services programs (e.g., PT, OT). • Attend all health-related appointments.	• Provide information on medical, behavioral, and family issues. • Accept role-release responsibilities for intervention programs (e.g., PT, OT). • Consult with staff on medication, personal care, physical management, and adaptive devices.
School counselor/ social worker	• Provide individual family assessment and counseling. • Provide social service resources. • Make home visits.	• Consult with staff on foster care or public assistance programs. • Provide information on family needs and adjustment. • Serve as liaison with related social service agencies.
Speech language therapist	• Assess and intervene on speech-language impairments. • Conduct functional assessments of hearing. • Design augmentative communication systems. • Intervene on prelinguistic communication behaviors.	• Interpret results of traditional and informal observations of student's speech-language functions. • Provide staff development on alternative speech communication programs, augmentative communication devices, and prelinguistic communication techniques. • Provide integrated therapy programs throughout the student's functional curriculum.
Para- professional	• Conduct health-related and personal hygiene procedures under supervision. • Prepare inclusive classroom for daily activities. • Prepare and assist at mealtimes. • Conduct small-group intervention programs.	• Provide information on the progress of assigned data-based programs. • Share ideas for effective classroom management. • Attend staff development programs (e.g., basic first aid, physical management).

Personnel	Direct Service Provider	Team Member
Para-professional (cont.)	• Assure that equipment and classrooms are safe and sterile. • Organize students' personal hygiene and clothing materials. • Assist in community-based programming. • Collect basic intervention data, under supervision. • Support students in inclusive settings.	
Administrator	• Reinforce behavioral management procedures. • Encourage involvement of families at whatever level they choose to participate.	• Support staff by providing staff development appropriate to their needs. • Support program by providing adaptive equipment and material. • Provide information on funding resources related to hiring of para-professionals and contracting with private agencies for PT or OT services. • Provide financial and transportation support to community-referenced programming. • Coordinate parent advisory councils. • Provide information on due process and legal action issues. • Arrange the school building to maximize interactions between students with and without special needs. • Arrange school schedule to allow for collaboration and formal staff meetings. • Arrange the school's schedule to avoid reliance on separate pull-out therapy programs.
General educators	• Include the student in large- and small-group instruction. • Use accommodations and adaptations for instruction. • Use appropriate assistive technology throughout the day. • Ensure opportunities for friendship networks and social skills development.	• Participate in the ecological assessment of students for the IEP. • Collaborate with special educators and paraprofessionals on instructional activities. • Assist in planning for functional life skills and community activities.

(e.g., passive range of motion, postural alignment). Likewise, special educators were unwilling to share applied behavioral strategies and curriculum design (e.g., discrete trial format, functional curriculum). The study highlights that the role-release process may be the most difficult step for team members to implement. Additionally, the job responsibilities delegated to paraprofessionals serving students with severe disabilities has become a topic of much attention. Unfortunately, paraprofessionals have been "underappreciated, undercompensated, and asked to undertake critical instructional responsibilities without sufficient role clarification, planning by qualified professionals, supervision, or training" (Giangreco, Edelman, & Broer, 2003, p. 63). Without appropriate supervision and support, paraprofessionals can have inadvertent detrimental effects on the inclusion of students with severe disabilities in the general education classroom. For example, the one-on-one model of paraprofessional support, where the student with significant disabilities is assigned to a paraprofessional for part or most of the day, can:

◆ Interfere with peer interactions.

◆ Make students with special needs dependent on adults.

◆ Separate classmates from students with special needs.

◆ Leave students with special needs at a loss for personal control.

◆ Limit access of students with special needs to quality instruction.

◆ Decrease teachers' interactions.

◆ Interfere with the general education teacher's ownership and shared responsibility of educating the students with disabilities (Giangreco, Broer, & Edelman, 2001).

The *Guide to Schoolwide Planning* developed by Giangreco and his colleagues (2003) can serve as a tool for designing effective paraprofessional service delivery models by school teams. The guide assists schools in hiring, training, and assigning roles and responsibilities to paraprofessionals so that there are positive outcomes for students, teachers, and paraprofessionals.

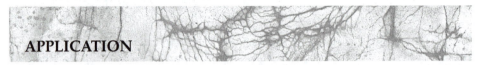

APPLICATION

The team members who serve students with severe disabilities are often confronted with the need for *role release* (Utley & Rapport, 2000), in which more than one person on the team performs the same function, such as implementation of a behavior management program. The professional development function, used for related services training, is also important in interactive teaming. At times this involves sharing information from one's own discipline with others so they can implement their component of the program effectively; at other times it requires the ability to respect and accept the consultation of parents and other professionals who are specialists in various aspects of the student's care program (Bailey, 1984; Bowe, 2000; Rainforth & York-Barr, 1997). The following vignette illustrates the application of the concept of interactive teaming to areas outside of the traditional role responsibilities of the team members.

Becky, a 15-year-old student who has traumatic brain injury from an automobile accident, is receiving services from an occupational therapist, a behavioral specialist, an itinerant vision teacher, a special education teacher, and a speech-language therapist. One of Becky's high school teachers, Ms. Stone, coordinates a conference that all four professionals and the family attend for purposes of professional development and role release. In the conference, the occupational therapist, Ms. Edwards, explains neurodevelopmental treatment (NDT) techniques (Bobath & Bobath, 1984; Campbell, 2000) for helping Becky to coordinate her arm and hand function and stabilize her trunk during mealtimes. Ms. Edwards demonstrates these techniques with Becky while she is eating lunch. Ms. Stone and the parent model the facilitation procedure in front of the occupational therapist and ask for feedback on their use of the technique.

Later, in Becky's classroom, the vision teacher shows Ms. Stone and the parent how to present Becky with computer switches in ways that stimulate eye-hand coordination, visual tracking, and information processing. Ms. Stone and the parent now practice both NDT techniques and vision integration activities, and both professionals give them feedback. Finally, the behavior specialists and special education teacher show Ms. Stone and the parent the best ways to help Becky maintain her attention on tasks and organize the tasks in an activity. The special educator incorporates the NDT procedure and the vision activity while modeling and prompting Becky to focus on a computer math game. Once again, Ms. Stone and the parents model all the techniques and ask for feedback.

Becky's mother (with Becky's assistance) shares with the team Becky's favorite hobbies, music preferences, television shows, and the foods she likes and dislikes. Her mother also updates the team on her medical status, her medication, and the reports from Becky's neurologist. By the end of the session, all four professionals and the parents have shared knowledge of their own disciplines and demonstrated the proper use of the techniques with Becky.

The professionals and parents leave the conference with added knowledge and skills for integrating the techniques into Becky's home, school, and community program. For purposes of checking appropriate use of the procedures and discussing Becky's progress, the team will arrange a monthly follow-up consultation. Within 6 months, the school's transition specialist will join the team on behalf of Becky's transition from school to work. The transition specialists will begin the process of acquiring new knowledge about the other disciplines involved with Becky's educational program and share her expertise through the transdisciplinary role transition process.

The role of the team leader becomes one of service coordinator for an integrated therapy program. Instead of providing Becky with an isolated therapy program in which the related service professional removes her from the inclusive classroom and provides treatment in a private therapy room, the therapist and special education teacher train the general teacher, the family, and paraprofessionals to perform educational, behavioral, and therapy techniques in the classroom, home, and community. Additionally, Becky's friends learn how to best interact with her and support her during activities in the inclusive classroom.

In the interactive team approach, the therapist and special education teacher still provide some direct services to the student on a weekly basis. Those services are often provided within the classroom setting, and when appropriate, they are used for demonstration and training of general education staff, families, and peers.

SUMMARY

The interactive team serving the needs of students with severe or multiple disabilities comprises a complex group of medical and educational professionals. The team serving students with severe disabilities is at risk for wars over turf. The range of differences in the terminology of the disciplines is enough to cause confusion among the group. The meetings conducted by this interactive team often overwhelm the core members of the team, the family. Yet, as much as any group of professionals, the family must work cooperatively for the good of the student. The nature of the student's condition can be so complex that if collaboration is not established, the student's educational as well as health-related needs will not be met.

Working closely with the families and the students' friends, professionals can orchestrate the delivery of services to students with severe disabilities, whether those services involve physical therapy, occupational therapy, speech therapy, medical interventions, or functional community-based programming.

ACTIVITIES

1. Conduct an informational interview with a professional who is involved in the educational programs of students with severe disabilities. Use the guidelines provided in Chapter 3.

2. Attend a group home or vocational program for individuals with severe disabilities. Observe for skills that will be needed by younger students to function in these future environments.

3. Volunteer to teach a functional skill to a student in a local school program. Offer to take the student into the community to learn this skill. Use a task analytical approach to breaking down the functional skill, and apply intervention strategies to implement the program.

4. Ask individuals from the community who have multiple disabilities such as cerebral palsy and blindness to speak to the class about their impairments, how they have adapted, problems they have encountered, and the community services available to them.

REFERENCES

American Association on Mental Retardation. (2002). *Mental retardation: Definition, classification, and systems of supports.* Washington, DC: Author. Retrieved December 14, 2003, from http://www.aamr.org/Policies/faq_mental_retardation.shtml

Ault, M. M., Rues, J. P., Graff, C., Holvoet, J. F. (2000). Special health care procedures. In M. E. Snell & F. Brown (Eds.), *Instruction of students with severe disabilities* (5th ed., pp. 245–290). Upper Saddle River, NJ: Prentice Hall.

Bailey, D. (1984). A triaxial model of the interdisciplinary team and group process. *Exceptional Children, 51,* 17–26.

Baker, B. L., & Brightman, A. J. (1996). *Steps to independence: Teaching everyday skills to children with special needs* (3rd ed.). Baltimore: Paul H. Brookes.

Bartel, N. R., & Thurman, S. K. (1992). Medical treatment and educational problems in children. *Phi Delta Kappan, 74,* 57–61.

Bigge, J. L., Best, S. J., & Heller, K. W. (2001). *Teaching individuals with physical or multiple disabilities* (4th ed.). Upper Saddle River, NJ: Merrill/Prentice-Hall.

Billingsly, F., Gallucci, C., Peck, C., Schwartz, I., & Staub, D. (1996). "But those kids can't even do math": An alternative conceptualization of outcomes for inclusive education. *The Special Education Leadership Review, 3,* 43–56.

Blasch, B., Wiener, W., & Welsh, R. (1997). *Foundations of orientation and mobility.* New York: American Foundation for the Blind.

Bobath, B., & Bobath, K. (1984). The neurodevelopmental treatment. In D. Stratton (Ed.), *Management of motor disorders of children with cerebral palsy.* Philadelphia: J. B. Lippincott.

Borgioli, J., & Kennedy, C. (2003). Transitions between school and hospital for students with multiple disabilities: A survey of causes, educational continuity, and parental perceptions. *Research & Practices for Persons with Severe Disabilities, 28,* 1–6.

Bowe, F. (2000). *Physical, sensory, and health disabilities: An introduction.* Upper Saddle River, NJ: Merrill/Prentice Hall.

Bricker, D. (1993). *AEPS measurement for birth to three years* (Vol. 1). Baltimore: Paul H. Brookes.

Brolin, D., & Loyd, R. (2004). *Career development and transition services: A functional life skills approach* (4th ed.). Upper Saddle River, NJ: Merrill/Prentice Hall.

Browder, D., & Spooner, F. (2003). Understanding the purpose and process of alternative assessment. In D. L. Ryndak & S. Alper (Eds.), *Curriculum and instruction for students with significant disabilities in inclusive settings* (2nd ed., pp. 51–69). Boston: Allyn & Bacon.

Browder, D., Spooner, F., Algozzine, R., Ahlgrim-Delzell, L., Flowers, C., & Karvonen, M. (2003). What we know and need to know about alternate assessment. *Exceptional Children, 70,* 45–61.

Browder, D. M. (2001). *Curriculum and assessment for students with moderate to severe disabilities.* New York: Guilford Press.

Brown, F., Evans, I., Weed, K., & Owen, V. (1987). Delineating functional competencies: A component model. *Journal of the Association for Persons with Severe Handicaps, 12*(2), 117–124.

Brown, F., & Lehr, D. (1993). Meaningful outcomes for students with severe disabilities. *Teaching Exceptional Children, 4,* 12–16.

Brown, F., & Snell, M. (2000). Meaningful assessment. In M. E. Snell & F. Brown (Eds.), *Instruction of students with severe disabilities* (5th ed., pp. 67–114). Upper Saddle River, NJ: Merrill/Prentice Hall.

Brown, L., Branston, M. B., Hamre-Nietupski, S., Pumpian, I., Certo, N., & Gruenewald, L. A. (1979). A strategy for developing chronological age appropriate and functional curricular content for severely handicapped adolescents and young adults. *Journal of Special Education, 13,* 81–90.

Burkhart, L. J. (1980). *Homemade battery-powered toys and educational devices for severely handicapped children.* 8503 Rhode Island Ave., College Park, MD 20740.

Burkhart, L. J. (1984). *More homemade battery devices for severely handicapped children—With suggested activities.* 8503 Rhode Island Ave., College Park, MD 20740.

Campbell, P. H. (2000). Promoting participation in natural environments by accommodating motor disabilities. In M. E. Snell & F. Brown (Eds.), *Instruction of students with severe disabilities* (5th ed., pp. 291–329). Upper Saddle River, NJ: Merrill/Prentice Hall.

Carr, E. G., Levin, L., McConnachie, G., Carlosn, J., Kemp, D., Smith, C., & McLaughlin, D. (1999). Comprehensive multisituational intervention for problem behavior in the community: Long-term maintenance and social validation. *Journal of Positive Behavior Intervention, 1,* 5–24.

Carroll, S. (1998). Medical management of behavior and emotional problems in children and adolescents: A primer for educators. Retrieved January 2, 2003, from the National Association of School Psychology Website at http://www.naspcenter.org/adol_meds.html

Cripe, J., Slentz, K., & Bricker, D. (1993). *AEPS curriculum for birth to three years* (Vol. 2). Baltimore: Paul H. Brookes.

Cushman, C., Heydt, K., Edwards, S., Clark, M. J., & Allon, M. (1992). *Perkins activity and resource guide: A handbook for teachers and parents of students with visual and multiple disabilities.* Boston: Perkins School for the Blind.

Dennis, R., Edelman, S., & Cloninger, C. (2001). The Vermont state I-Team then and now: Twenty-five years of technical assistance and training to support the education of students with severe disabilities. *Rural Special Education Quarterly, 20,* 30–39.

Downing, J. (1999). *Teaching communication skills to students with severe disabilities.* Baltimore: Paul H. Brookes.

Downing, J., & Eichinger, J. (2003). Creating learning opportunities for students with severe disabilities in inclusive classrooms. *Teaching Exceptional Children, 36,* 26–31.

Durand, V. M. (1990). *Severe behavior problems: A functional communication training approach.* New York: Guilford Press.

Durand, V. M., & Crimmins, D. B. (1992). *The motivation assessment scale (MAS) administration guide.* Topeka, KS: Monaco.

Falvey, M., Forest, M., Pearpoint, J., & Rosenberg, R. L. (1992). *All my life's a circle: Using the tools of circles, MAPS, and PATH.* Toronto, Canada: Inclusion Press.

Farlow, L. J., & Snell, M. E. (2000). Teaching basic self-care skills. In M. E. Snell & F. Brown (Eds.), *Instruction of students with severe disabilities* (5th ed., pp. 331–380). Upper Saddle River, NJ: Merrill/Prentice Hall.

Ford, A., Schnorr, R., Meyer, L., Davern, L., Black, J., & Dempsey, P. (Eds.). (1989). *The Syracuse community-referenced curriculum guide for students with moderate and severe disabilities.* Baltimore: Paul H. Brookes.

Giangreco, M., Broer, S., & Edelman, S. (2001). Teacher engagement with students with disabilities: Differences between paraprofessional service delivery models. *JASH, 26,* 75–86.

Giangreco, M., Edelman, S., & Broer, S. (2003). Schoolwide planning to improve paraeducator supports. *Exceptional Children, 70,* 63–79.

Giangreco, M. E. (1996). *Vermont interdependent services team approach. A guide to coordinating education support services.* Baltimore: Paul H. Brookes.

Giangreco, M. F., Cloninger, C. J., & Iverson, V. S. (1998). *C.O.A.C.H.: Choosing outcomes and accommodations for children* (2nd ed.). Baltimore: Paul H. Brookes.

Glickman, L., Deitz, J., Anson, D., & Stewart, K. (1996). The effect of switch control site on computer skills of infants and toddlers. *American Journal of Occupational Therapy, 50*(7), 545–553.

Halpern, A. S., Herr, C. M., Wolf, N. K., Lawson, J. D., Doren, B., & Johnston, M. D. (1997). *NEXT S.T.E.P.: Student transition and education planning. Teacher's manual.* Austin, TX: Pro-Ed.

Heller, K. W., Fredrick, L. D., Best, S., Dykes, M. K., & Cohen, E. T. (2000). Specialized health care procedures in the schools: Training and service delivery. *Exceptional Children, 66,* 173–186.

Horner, R. H., Albin, R. W., Sprague, J. R., & Todd, A. W. (2000). Positive behavior support. In M. E. Snell & F. Brown (Eds.), *Instruction of students with severe disabilities* (5th ed., pp. 207–243). Upper Saddle River, NJ: Merrill/Prentice Hall.

Hunt, P., Doering, K., Hirose-Hatae, A., Maier, J., & Goetz, L. (2001). Across-program collaboration to support students with and without disabilities in a general education classroom. *JASH, 26*, 240–256.

Hunt, P., & Goetz, L. (1997). Research on inclusive educational programs, practices, and outcomes for students with severe disabilities. *Journal of Special Education, 31*(1), 3–29.

Janney, R., & Snell, M. E. (2000). *Teachers' guide to inclusive practices: Modifying schoolwork.* Baltimore: Paul H. Brookes.

Langley, B. (1980). *Functional vision inventory for the multiple and severely handicapped.* Chicago: Stoelting.

Langley, M. B. (1986). Psychoeducational assessment of visually impaired students with additional handicaps. In D. Ellis (Ed.), *Sensory impairments in mentally handicapped people* (pp. 253–296). San Diego: College-Hill Press.

Langley, M. B., & Lombardino, L. J. (1991). *Neurodevelopmental strategies for managing communication disorders in children with severe motor dysfunction.* Austin, TX: Pro-Ed.

Loyd, R. J., & Brolin, D. E. (2002). *Life centered career education: Mild/Moderate curriculum training manual.* Arlington, VA: The Council for Exceptional Children.

Martin, J., Mithaug, D., Cox, P., Peterson, L., Van Dycke, J., & Cash, M. (2003). Increasing self-determination: Teaching students to plan, work, evaluate, and adjust. *Exceptional Children, 69*, 431–447.

Martin, J. E., & Marshall, L. H. (1995). Choice-Maker: A comprehensive self-determination transition program. *Intervention in School and Clinic, 30*, 147–156.

McDonnell, J., & Fister, S. (2001). Supporting the inclusion of students with moderate and severe disabilities in junior high school general education classes: The effects of classwide peer tutoring, multi-element curriculum, and accommodations. *Education and Treatment of Children, 24*, 141–160.

McDonnell, J., Mathot-Buckner, C., Thorson, N., & Fister, S. (2001). Supporting the inclusion of students with moderate and severe disabilities in junior high school general education classes: The effects of classwide peer tutoring, multi-element curriculum, and accommodations. *Education and Treatment of Children, 24*, 141–160.

Meyer, L. H., & Eichinger, J. (1994). *Program quality indicators (PQI): A checklist of most promising practices in educational programs for students with severe disabilities* (3rd ed.). Seattle, WA: The Association for Persons with Severe Handicaps.

Moon, M. S., & Inge, K. (2000). Vocational preparation and transition. In M. E. Snell & F. Brown (Eds.), *Instruction of students with severe disabilities* (5th ed., pp. 591–628). Upper Saddle River, NJ: Merrill/Prentice Hall.

Mount, B., & Zwernik, K. (1989). *It's never too early, it's never too late: A booklet about personal futures planning.* St. Paul, MN: Metropolitan Council.

Nelson, C., van Dijk, J., McDonnell, A., & Thompson, K. (2002). A framework for understanding young children with severe multiple disabilities: The van Dijk approach to assessment. *Research and Practice for Persons with Severe Disabilities, 27*, 97–111.

Niswander, P. S. (1987). Audiometric assessment and management. In L. Goetz, D. Guess, & K. Stremel-Campbell (Eds.), *Innovative program design for individuals with dual sensory impairments* (pp. 99–126). Baltimore: Paul H. Brookes.

No Child Left Behind Act of 2001. (2002). Pub. L. No. 107–110, 115 Stat. 1425.

O'Neill, R., & Johnson, J. (2000). A brief description of functional assessment procedures reported in JASH (1983–1999). *JASH, 25*, 197–200.

Orelove, F. P., & Sobsey, D. (1996). *Educating children with multiple disabilities: A transdisciplinary approach* (3rd ed.). Baltimore: Paul H. Brookes.

Palmer, D., Fuller, K., Arora, T., & Nelson, M. (2001). Taking sides: Parent views on inclusion for their children with severe disabilities. *Exceptional Children, 67*, 467–484.

Pearpoint, J., O'Brien, J., & Forest, M. (1993). *PATH: A workbook for planning positive possible futures: Planning alternative tomorrows with hope for school, organizations, businesses, families.* Toronto, Canada: Inclusion Press.

Perla, F., & Ducret, W. (1999). Guidelines for teaching orientation and mobility to children with multiple disabilities. *RE:view, 31*(3), 113–119.

Powers, L. E., Sowers, J., Turner, A., Nesbitt, M., Knowles, E., & Ellison, R. (1996). TAKE CHARGE: A model for promoting self-determination among adolescents with challenges. In L. E. Powers, G. H. S. Singer, & J. Sowers (Eds.), *On the road to autonomy: Promoting self-competence for children and youth with disabilities* (pp. 291–322). Baltimore: Paul H. Brookes.

Rainforth, B., & York-Barr, J. (1997). *Collaborative teams for students with severe disabilities* (2nd ed.). Baltimore: Paul H. Brookes.

Reid, R., & Nelson, J. R. (2002). The utility, acceptability, and practicality of functional behavior assessments for students with high incidence problem behavior. *Remedial and Special Education, 23*, 15–23.

Rusch, F. R., & Chadsey, J. G. (1998). *Beyond high school: Transition from school to work.* Belmont, CA: Wadsworth.

Rutecki, P., & Gidal, B. (2002). Antiepileptic drug treatment in the developmentally disabled: Treatment considerations with the newer antiepileptic drugs. *Epilepsy & Behavior, 3*, S24–S31.

Ryndak, D. L., & Alper, S. (2003). *Curriculum and instruction for student's with significant disabilities in inclusive settings* (2nd ed.). Boston: Allyn & Bacon.

Sacks, S., & Silberman, R. (1998). *Educating students who have visual impairments with other disabilities.* Baltimore: Paul H. Brookes.

Sailor, W., Gee, K., & Karasoff, P. (2000). Inclusion and school restructuring. In M. E. Snell & F. Brown (Eds.), *Instruction of students with severe disabilities* (5th ed., pp. 1–30). Upper Saddle River, NJ: Merrill/Prentice Hall.

Salisbury, C., & Dunst, C. J. (1997). Home, school, and community partnerships: Building inclusive teams. In B. Rainforth & J. York-Barr (Eds.), *Collaborative teams for students with severe disabilities* (2nd ed., pp. 57–88). Baltimore: Paul H. Brookes.

Siegel, E., & Wetherby, A. (2000). Nonsymbolic communication. In M. E. Snell & F. Brown (Eds.), *Instruction of students with severe disabilities* (5th ed., pp. 409–452). Upper Saddle River, NJ: Merrill/Prentice Hall.

Siegel-Causey, E., & Allinder, R. M. (1998). Using alternative assessment for students with severe disabilities. Alignment with best practices. *Education and Training in Mental Retardation and Developmental Disabilities, 33*, 168–178.

Silberman, R. K. (1986). Severe multiple handicaps. In G. T. Scholl (Ed.), *Foundations of education for blind and visually handicapped children and youth: Theory and practice* (pp. 145–164). New York: American Foundation for the Blind.

Sitlington, P., Clark, G., & Kolstoe, O. (2000). *Transition education and services for adolescents with disabilities* (3rd ed.). Needham, MA: Allyn & Bacon.

Snell, M. E., & Brown, F. (2000a). Development and implementation of educational programs. In M. E. Snell & F. Brown (Eds.), *Instruction of students with severe disabilities* (5th ed., pp. 115–172). Upper Saddle River, NJ: Merrill/Prentice Hall.

Snell, M. E., & Brown, F. (Eds.). (2000b). *Instruction of students with severe disabilities* (5th ed.). Upper Saddle River, NJ: Merrill/Prentice Hall.

Snell, M. E., & Janney, R. E. (2000). *Practices for inclusive schools: Collaborative teaming.* Baltimore: Paul H. Brookes.

Sobsey, D., & Wolf-Schein, E. (1996). Children with sensory impairments. In F. P. Orelove & D. Sobsey (Eds.), *Educating children with multiple disabilities: A transdisciplinary approach* (3rd ed., pp. 411–450). Baltimore: Paul H. Brookes.

Stainback, S., & Stainback, W. (1996). *Inclusion. A guide for educators.* Baltimore: Paul H. Brookes.

Staub, D., Schwartz, I. S., Gallucci, C., & Peck, C. A. (1994). Four portraits of friendship at an inclusive school. *Journal of the Association for Persons with Severe Handicaps, 19*, 314–325.

Strong, K., & Sandoval, J. (2000). Mainstreaming children with a neuromuscular disease: A map of concerns. *Exceptional Children, 65*, 353–366.

The Association of Persons with Severe Handicaps. (1991). Definition of the people TASH serves (Document 1:1). In L. H. Meyer, C. A. Peck, & L. Brown (Eds.), *Critical issues in the lives of people with severe disabilities* (p. 19). Baltimore: Paul H. Brookes.

Tolla, J. (2000). Follow that bear! *Teaching Exceptional Children, 32*, 72–77.

Turnbull, A., & Turnbull, H. R. (2000). Fostering family-professional partnerships. In M. E. Snell & F. Brown (Eds.), *Instruction of students with severe disabilities* (5th ed., pp. 31–66). Upper Saddle River, NJ: Merrill/Prentice Hall.

U.S. Department of Education. (2003). *Twenty-fourth annual report to Congress on the implementation of the Individuals with Disabilities Education Act.* Washington, DC: Author.

Utley, B. L. (1993). Assessing the instructional environment to meet the needs of learners with multiple disabilities including students who are deaf-blind. *Deaf-Blind Perspective, 1*(2), 5–8.

Utley, C., & Rapport, M. J. (2000). Exploring role release in the multidisciplinary team. *Physical Disabilities: Education and Related Services, 18*(2), 89–118.

Vandercook, T., York, J., & Forest, M. (1989). MAPS: A strategy for building vision. *Journal of the Association for Persons with Severe Handicaps, 14*(3), 205–215.

Wehmeyer, M. L., Agran, M., & Hughes, C. (1998). *Teaching self-determination to students with disabilities: Basic skills for successful transition.* Baltimore: Paul H. Brookes.

Wehmeyer, M. L., Agran, M., & Hughes, C. (2000). A national survey of teachers' promotion of self-determination and student-directed learning. *The Journal of Special Education, 34*(2), 58–68.

Wehmeyer, M. L., & Kelchner, K. (1995). *Whose future is it anyway? A student directed transition planning process.* Arlington, TX: The Arc National Headquarters.

Wehmeyer, M. L., & Palmer, S. (2003). Adult outcomes for students with cognitive disabilities three years after high school: The impact of self-determination. *Education and Training in Developmental Disabilities, 38,* 131–144.

Westling, D. L., & Fox, L. (2004). *Teaching students with severe disabilities* (3rd ed.). Upper Saddle River, NJ: Merrill/Prentice Hall.

Wetherby, A., Warren, S., & Reichle, J. (Eds.). (1998). *Communication and language intervention series: Vol. 7. Transitions in prelinguistic communication.* Baltimore: Paul H. Brookes.

Wilcox, B., & Bellamy, G. T. (1987). *The activities catalog: An alternative curriculum for youth and adults with severe disabilities.* Baltimore: Paul H. Brookes.

Wolfe, P., & Hall, T. (2003). Making inclusion a reality for students with severe disabilities. *Teaching Exceptional Children, 35,* 56–60.

York-Barr, J., & Kronberg, R. (2002). From isolation to collaboration: Learning from effective partnerships between general and special educators. In W. Sailor (Ed.), *Whole-school success and inclusive education: Building partnerships for learning, achievement, and accountability* (pp. 163–181). New York: Teachers College Press.

Summary and Application
of the Model in the Future

12

Topics in this chapter include:

◆ A summary of the major features of the interactive teaming model.

◆ An extended case study, showing how the whole model might be implemented.

◆ Application of the model in the future, with a summary of current trends and predictions for future implementation.

Teachers and related professionals, who once functioned in isolated class-rooms and clinical programs, are now encouraged to collaborate as members of an interactive service team. The factors that provide the context and rationale for this change include the following:

♦ Professionals in special programs face conflicting demands to produce students with high levels of achievement and to respond to those with special needs that range from learning and behavior problems to cultural and linguistic differences.

♦ Educators and related professionals are being increasingly pressured to collaborate in the solution of growing education-related problems, because in the future most of our students will have complex special needs. Current programs are ineffective in serving the increasing numbers of students with such needs; previously proposed solutions that do not take into account the body of knowledge about the process of change will also be ineffective.

♦ Those who have summarized the research on effective schools suggest that teachers in these schools are committed to a central mission: maximizing the educational opportunities for their students by working as a team to achieve this goal. Conversely, researchers who have studied the teachers' sense of efficacy have identified teachers' feelings of isolation as a major barrier to their believing that they are facilitating growth in their students.

♦ Public Law 94–142, amended in 1990, and again in 1997 as the Individuals with Disabilities Education Act, P.L. 101-476, requires that special education and *related services* be provided for students with special needs. This requirement suggests that people from many disciplines are potential members of the team. The more effective programs of the future will require collaboration among professionals and between professionals and parents.

♦ Currently, education, medical, and social services professionals are not being prepared as team members. Newly trained professionals in general education and in social services professions lack the ability to address these complex problems and to function as collaborative members of interactive teams.

FEATURES OF THE INTERACTIVE TEAMING MODEL

The model proposed in this book—interactive teaming—is a response to the nation's increasingly complex problems in special needs programs. It incorporates the features of high expectations, teacher empowerment, and parent-professional collaboration, which together characterize effective schools for students with special needs.

The interactive team is an educational and health-related group that functions at the highest professional level, using both consultation and collaboration in its efforts on behalf of students with special needs. Components of this model are used in programs that provide educational, medical, and social services to students with severe disabilities, and in "learning community" programs that are described in the school improvement literature.

This model for interactive teaming has been described in detail in this text. The three parts focused on context and foundations, facilitating factors, and implementation. The context and foundations section included the framework and rationale, the historical foundations of consultation and teaming, and the dimensions of the interactive team. The facilitating factors were identified as understanding the roles of team members, enhancing communication skills, developing service coordination skills, empowering team members through professional development, and enabling and supporting families. Four types of implementation contexts were presented, including implementation with culturally and linguistically diverse students, infants and preschoolers with special needs, students with mild disabilities, and students with severe disabilities.

An extended case study, drawing together multiple facets of the model, follows.

APPLICATION: Extended Case Study

Ethan, a minority-group 8-year-old, is both gifted and learning disabled. His mother, who is divorced, is a physician, and Ethan has already decided that he wants to be a lawyer. Born with cerebral palsy that has left him with motor disabilities but without speech impairment, Ethan has an overall measured IQ of 136, with a verbal score that is 40 points higher than his performance score. On the achievement tests measuring basic skills, Ethan scores at the ninth-grade level in reading and at the first-grade level in basic mathematical skills. He also has great difficulty in manuscript handwriting, and he resists his teacher's efforts to instruct him in cursive writing, although all his classmates are beginning to use it and his teacher requires it.

Sometimes Ethan annoys his teachers—the third-grade classroom teacher; the special education resource room teacher; and the music, art, and physical education teachers—because he likes to have them explain their reasons for everything they ask him to do. He is very logical and rule oriented, in addition to being quite good at verbal reasoning. Ethan argues with teachers when they ask him to do something he chooses not to do, and he is becoming disruptive in the classroom. Ethan realizes that each of his teachers has different expectations for classroom behavior and consequences when the rules are broken, and he has become quite effective at playing one adult against another.

Ethan is talkative and cheerful; he has many friends in his third-grade classroom who volunteer to push him around the school in his wheelchair. They also volunteer to help him with his math and handwriting assignments, which are difficult for him. Most recently, several other students in his classroom have begun to use his strategy of arguing with the teacher when they choose not to follow her instructions.

Ethan's classroom teacher, who has taught third grade in this district for 17 years, believes strongly that rules are rules, and that they apply equally to all students in the classroom. She has become frustrated with his behavior, particularly when he fails to turn in his assignments and when he encourages the other students to defy her authority. Ethan's art and PE teachers allow him to do pretty much as he pleases in their classes; they believe he "has physical disabilities and we shouldn't expect much from him in art or physical activities." His music teacher encourages him to express himself verbally whenever he chooses and has made him the master of ceremonies at the school's music programs. His special education teacher, who works with him for one hour a day on math skills, has a strict contingency management program, through which he can earn tokens that accumulate for free time.

Ethan's mother, who is nationally recognized as an authority in her field of medicine, is busy and travels a lot. She adores Ethan and gives him every cultural and material advantage—they go to concerts and lectures together, and she has bought him his own computer with a complete set of games. His mother also makes an effort to work with Ethan on his schoolwork at home, but she thinks the behavior problems he is having at school are the school's responsibility. Ethan's mother is pleasant and cooperative, and she has agreed to support the school's efforts by enforcing a consistent regimen for him at home. She believes, however, that the school personnel should design the school-based program.

The district superintendent is pleased that Ethan's mother does not object to his placement in this school, which contains a large number of low-income students. The superintendent is concerned about the school's attrition rate; it has a largely transient population, and students who enter in the fall rarely remain for the entire school year. He is also concerned about the low level of students' academic achievement and about problems with teacher morale as reported by the president of the professional association. The superintendent is considering making Ethan's school a "magnet," to which residents of the community could choose to send their children because of special programs offered. He is particularly interested in the development of science and computer labs for which he has obtained support from the local Chamber of Commerce in a school-business partnership.

The interactive team that meets to review Ethan's progress in his special program has more than his academic achievement to consider. His case is one in which all the issues of interactive teaming will need to be incorporated.

Step 1

The team meets to review Ethan's progress. Those present are the special educator, classroom teacher, psychologist, music teacher, school principal, and Ethan's mother.

The team follows the steps in program review, shown earlier in Figure 5.3. The special educator will be the team leader, or service coordinator. It is the group's consensus that Ethan should continue in the part-time special education program for help with math. Ethan's mother agrees to make his home use of computer games contingent on his conceptual understanding and mastery of the math facts for addition and subtraction for the numbers 0 through 20. Plans are made for additional testing of Ethan's fine motor skills by a physical therapist and for suggestions on the development of appropriate adaptive handwriting devices by an adaptive technology specialist. After this testing is completed, the special educator and classroom teacher agree that they will meet to plan a program related to his development of handwriting skills. Ethan's classroom teacher expresses a concern that his behavior problems are related, in part, to the fact that the adults in his life have conflicting standards for his behavior; his mother agrees. The principal, recognizing this statement as an opener for his agenda—establishing school-wide goals for students—suggests that he will follow-up on this problem with the entire school staff and with the PTA. Each team member leaves with a written record of the decisions made, the people responsible for implementing each, and the projected date for their next contacts.

Step 2

The physical therapist and the adaptive technology specialist conduct an assessment of Ethan's abilities and limitations in fine motor skills, then discuss their findings with his mother. All conclude that it is unrealistic to expect him to develop cursive handwriting skills at this time and agree that he might be encouraged to develop keyboard skills on the computer, provided it could be equipped with an adaptive device. They report this decision to the service coordinator and the special educator. Together, this subgroup laments that the school has no current resources for obtaining these specialized materials, although they have heard the rumor that the school may be receiving a computer lab.

Step 3

The classroom teacher teams with Ethan's mother to provide a program for at-home computer game use, contingent on mastery of math facts. Deprived of the free use of his computer, Ethan becomes furious and begins to throw tantrums at home and in school. Ethan's mother calls to relate her disappointment with the program. The classroom teacher relates her concern to the special educator, the team leader (or service coordinator), who takes two aspirins and goes to bed.

Step 4

The special educator and the classroom teacher meet the next day. The classroom teacher discusses her concern over Ethan's increased behavior problems, and together the two team members brainstorm possible solutions to their problem, using the problem-solving sequence suggested in Chapter 6. They decide to contact Ethan's mother to request an observation of his home computer setup and to enlist her help with the problem.

Step 5

The special educator, classroom teacher, and Ethan's mother meet briefly in Ethan's home, where he proudly shows his teachers his computer games. Ethan's mother, who has learned about the superintendent's proposed program for school computers, suggests that she might work with the Chamber of Commerce's committee to explore the extension of computers into the school's programs for exceptional students. The special education teacher asks the district's adaptive technology specialist to explore the use of adaptive equipment that might enable Ethan to develop computer skills as a substitute for cursive writing. The classroom teacher agrees to take data on Ethan's behavior in the classroom in an attempt to isolate the variables that intensify his outbursts and lack of compliance with class rules.

Step 6

The principal calls a meeting of the representatives of the school's professional organization to present the superintendent's request for development of a magnet school program in their building and to obtain their input on needs for professional development and the additional resources needed to make the school program a model. Ethan's teacher, who is a member of this committee, discusses her previous interactions with Ethan's mother about the possibility of creating a school-business partnership for the new computer lab.

This news is received with enthusiasm, and several teachers suggest that the school plan a professional development program to provide teachers with additional skills related to the effective use of computers. The music teacher cautions that although new skills in computer use might motivate students and enable teachers to better use technology, the acquisition of computers would not solve the school's basic problem: the increase in students' misbehavior. Ethan's classroom teacher agrees that computers are no panacea and again expresses her concern about the lack of consistency in school rules as a contributing factor to students' misbehavior.

The principal, after listing the teachers' ideas for professional development and school improvement, identifies the need for consistent rules as the group's highest priority. He repeats this process in his meeting with the school's PTA steering committee, and he learns that parents share the teachers' concerns about misbehavior. Then he contacts one of his former professors at a nearby university to help the staff and community develop a uniform set of standards for student behavior.

Step 7

Through a needs assessment, the professor determines that teachers and parents have two major concerns about student behavior.

1. *Poor social behavior.* Students lack the ability to get along together.

2. *Inappropriate academic behavior.* Students fail to raise hands, comply with teacher requests, and complete tasks.

In a school-wide staff meeting attended by representatives from the PTA, the principal shares the results of this needs assessment as the first step in identifying the school's common goals for student expectations. The professor, who serves as their consultant, organizes the teachers, parents, and other professionals into grade-level clusters. Their first task is to generate a list of positive student behaviors that enable students to get along with others; their second is to generate a list of positive student behaviors that enhance learning. The groups are then asked to rewrite these statements as rules for student behaviors. After grade-level consensus has been reached, the groups meet with those in the grades above and below their own to identify the commonalities in their rule statements. The result is a set of school rules for student behavior for which both teachers and parents have ownership.

Step 8

The building staff adopts the school-wide rules for students' behavior, and Ethan begins to encounter uniform expectations for his performance in all classes. After initial protests, he begins to comply with the rules. His classroom teacher is pleased with this change in his behavior and reports positively to the special educator and to Ethan's mother.

Step 9

The special educator, classroom teacher, and Ethan's mother meet. They discuss both his progress and their efforts in identifying adapted computer equipment that might be used with Ethan in developing his typing skills. The classroom teacher, who is able to see a positive change in Ethan's overall behavior, is now willing to modify her standards for his handwriting performance, and she agrees that the development of keyboard skills for use on the computer would be an acceptable substitute for his learning of cursive writing. Ethan's mother has obtained support from the Chamber of Commerce to include adaptive computer equipment in its plan for the whole-school computer lab. The special educator, with assistance from the adaptive technology specialist, has identified the necessary software.

Step 10

The Chamber of Commerce committee approaches the superintendent with a plan to provide the volunteer services of several computer specialists in implementing the lab. When the photographer from the local paper comes to cover the story, Ethan is shown using the new equipment, with assistance from his classroom teacher. The principal is quoted as saying this represents a school-wide effort to improve the quality of instruction for all students. The superintendent's comment reveals this small step as part of his master plan to make Ethan's school a magnet. Ethan's mother makes a positive statement about the need for professional parents to continue their support of the district's excellent public school program.

The special educator, the team leader (or service coordinator), is present in the background and smiling. This effective leader has empowered others to implement a program that benefits a specific student with special needs, while simultaneously contributing to school-wide improvement.

APPLICATION OF THE MODEL IN THE FUTURE

Futurists examine current trends as a knowledge base from which to predict the future. In making their predictions, futurists tend to be optimistic. The authors of this book are optimistic in their prediction that a collaborative model such as interactive teaming will be the major pattern for future service delivery to students with special needs. This optimistic prediction persists, despite acknowledgment of the history of failed past predictions, the barriers to teaming, and the need for continued research, simply because the need for this model is so compelling.

Current Trends That Affect Programs for Students with Special Needs

Although support for education programs has declined, the number of students at risk for school failure has risen dramatically, and public awareness of the need to collaborate in the solution of this problem has grown. The following discussion summarizes trends affecting schools and prompting the need for collaboration. First, trends occurring on the mega level of society along the dimensions of accountability, the economy, technology, medicine, and demographic shifts are presented, followed by trends at the macro level of school restructuring.

Mega Level: Society.   The following paragraphs summarize the need for collaboration at the mega level of society:

1. *Trends in accountability.* The current value system has shifted from an emphasis on human rights to a focus on excellence, as a way of ensuring this nation's economic supremacy. Excellence was initially defined in terms of more rigorous standards and a greater concern with college-bound students. Beginning in the mid-1990s, federal legislation, including the 1994 Improving America's Schools Act (IASA), the 1997 reauthorization of the Individuals with Disabilities Education Act (IDEA), and the 1998 Perkins Vocational-Technical Education Act, required student assessment on core academic standards to be conducted at least twice during elementary, middle, and high school levels of schooling (McDermott, 2003). The passage of the No Child Left Behind Act of 2001 (NCLB) has once again brought national attention to standards-based education reform. The goals of NCLB are ambitious and controversial. On the one hand, proponents of the law see it as a way to improve the educational opportunities for all students, narrow the achievement gap between ethnic groups, and provide options to parents when schools fail (Goertz & Duffy, 2003; Paige, 2002). Opponents argue that high-stakes testing results in a narrowed focus of curriculum and instruction, limited teacher flexibility, and increased grade retention and dropout rates (see Darling-Hammond, 2003; Linn, 2003).

   School improvement following accountability legislation must be a collaborative effort (Linn, 2003). Referring to Porter and Chester's discussion of "symmetric accountability" systems, Linn suggests that the responsibility for success must be shared among students, teachers, administrators, and policy makers.

   The national value system is also characterized by a growth in emphasis on the safety of "old ways." Evidence of this trend is found, for example, in increased censorship and in controversy over bilingual education, both of which emerged in the late 1980s (Gold, 1987; Mirga, 1987). This retreat to the old ways is not entirely negative, however, because it includes a renewed emphasis on the work ethic and on the concept of volunteerism, which have positive implications for the future of collaborative programs.

2. *Trends in social institutions.* One major trend in social institutions affecting the climate in which education is delivered is the changing structure of the traditional family. Seen by many as the "decline of the family" the topic is

debated by politicians, sociologists, and others (Bengtson, 2001). Results of the high divorce rate and single parenting can have negative effects on the psychological, social, and economic well-being of children. Families appear to be evolving into a variety of relationships termed the "postmodern family condition" (Stacey, 1996) that are more diverse and fluid. In addition, the population distribution across age groups has also changed and multigenerational relationships are becoming more important to family structures (Bengtson, 2001).

Other societal concerns may be influenced by the changes in family structure. Child abuse increased 55% between 1981 and 1985, with estimates ranging from 150,000 to 1.5 million cases a year (McClellan, 1987). In 2001, an estimated 903,000 children were found to be victims of child abuse or neglect and more than half were removed from their homes (U.S. Department of Health and Human Services, 2003b). The National Center for Educational Statistics (NCES; U.S. Department of Education, 2003) estimates that half of school-age children in kindergarten through eighth grade are in nonparental care after school, with 13% of children caring for themselves. These changes in families as a social institution indicated a need for public assistance that is too complicated to be delegated solely to the public schools. Congressional action on family leave was an indication that this need was being recognized.

Family, community, and school partnerships have always been a key to successful student outcomes. The previously described issues stress the increasing importance for school personnel to develop collaborative relationships with the families and communities of the students they serve.

3. *Trends in the economy.* The current economic recession has had enormous consequences for schools. The most recent fiscal survey of states (National Governors Association, 2003) indicates that while the economy appears to be improving, it may be several years before schools begin to recover. States also have had to pay for the mandates of NCLB to improve test scores. School finances are the worst they have been in 10 years (National Education Association, 2002).

Funding for special education programs has been a concern since the passage of P.L. 94-142, as it has never been fully funded. As a result, there is a backlog of referrals for the placement of students in special programs. These students were not being served effectively in general education programs, which were struggling with fewer teachers and more students, and attempting to respond to individual differences by dividing students into ability tracks (Oakes, 1986). The effect of actions such as these reached the workforce, and in the 1980s business leaders began to recognize that poorly supported education programs increased their costs for training (Iacocca, 1989). In addition, research has shown that money spent on preschool education programs (Hodgkinson, 1988; Reynolds, Temple, & Suh-Ruu Ou, 2003) and transition training for adolescents with special needs (Viadero, 1989) was particularly well spent in terms of cost-effectiveness.

Funding for school programs has been a consistent problem for most schools. Economic climates change, and making the best use of available resources is always beneficial. Collaborative teams using a systematic decision-making process are more likely to develop creative ways to use existing resources.

4. *Trends in technology.* The use of computers is a major trend in technology that affects the educational program. Computers are used extensively in school programs, although there is a need for professional development programs that enable teachers to use computers effectively (Garcia, 1998; McGroddy, 1997; Sharp, 1998). Interactive technology is emerging rapidly, as shown by support for e-commerce, wireless communication, multimedia learning, and the paperless office. There is continuing work with computers to develop artificial intelligence; meanwhile, microchips have been used to reactivate neurological responses in people whose limbs have been severed. Though computers promise improvements in education for the future, these innovations are still expensive and not widely available. Recognition of this need has prompted the computer and communications giants to initiate a series of education partnerships that have the potential for school improvement. The use of technology fosters collaboration with those who can help teachers learn to use it as a powerful teaching tool in the classroom and with other teachers as they share what they are learning.

5. *Trends in medicine.* A number of diseases—smallpox, TB, measles, and polio—seemed to be controlled in the 1980s and 1990s by advances in medicine, better health care, and widespread immunizations. New diseases, however, have become more prevalent, as witnessed by the transmission of ebola and the West Nile virus, which are probably related to worldwide travel patterns. The increased numbers of school-age children with AIDS became, as early as the 1980s, a growing health problem for schools (Carney & Cobia, 2003; Reed, 1988). Increased need for funding strained the health care system; new proposals for national insurance may compete with funding of education.

Mental health problems have increased significantly. It was estimated as early as the 1980s that between 12% and 19% of children were in need of some sort of mental health treatment, and that 70% to 80% of them were not receiving it (Flax, 1989; Tuma, 1989). Recent estimates by the U.S. Department of Health and Human Services (2003a) indicate that as many as 6 million youths may have emotional problems severe enough to disrupt their ability to interact effectively. The school-related problems of drug abuse have been documented in detail (Newcomb & Bentler, 1989). These conditions exist simultaneously with a dramatic increase in antisocial behavior among youth

(Patterson, DeBaryshe, & Ramsey, 1989), and the growth of violence is a major societal concern (American Psychological Association, 1993; Lawrence, Muire, & Stanley, 1999).

The encouraging aspect of this trend is that it precipitated a more general recognition of the problems of at-risk students as early as the 1980s (Brown, 1985). There is increased attention to adolescent sexuality, teen pregnancy, culture and identity, and the effects of the environment in its discussion of child development and their relation to social policy (Horowitz & O'Brien (1989). More recent discussion has focused on the resilience of children as an ordinary process of human development and adaptation. Furthermore, this point of view offers new direction for policies and practices that enhance the development of children growing up disadvantaged and in adverse environments (Masten, 2001).

6. *Demographic shifts.* One final trend occurring on a national level is the resegregation of schools. A recent report from the Civil Rights Project at Harvard University indicates that schools are 12 years into a process of resegregation, receding to levels not seen in three decades (Frankenberg, Lee, & Orfield, 2003). The project used data from the NCES Common Core of Data for 2000–2001 and previous school years to evaluate desegregation patterns. These researchers found that while the schools in the south are currently the most integrated, they are the most rapidly resegregating. Nationally, the largest school districts are vastly non-White. In addition, there appears to be an emergence of substantial groups of schools that are virtually non-White and are educating about one-sixth of the nation's Black students. These schools are most often associated with enormous poverty, limited resources, and social and health problems. The project also found that Latino students are the most segregated minority group—segregated by race, poverty, and language. This group also has the highest dropout rate. The group found two basic causes of resegregation: (1) changes in the racial composition of communities and school-age population, and (2) changes in the desegregation plan.

Segregation is also a problem for many of the recent immigrant students. As mentioned in Chapter 1, there has been a significant increase of students whose primary language is not English (Snyder & Freeman, 2003). These children also tend to live in poverty, attend schools where they are segregated linguistically, and have a high rate of high school dropout (Fix, Zimmerman, & Passel, 2001).

The concern for this trend is the potential loss of gains made by school desegregation. Previous research found that outcomes for students in integrated environments included enhanced learning, higher educational and occupational aspirations, and positive social interaction with diverse racial and ethnic backgrounds (Kurlaender & Yun, 2002). Indeed, solving the problem of resegregation demands a collaborative effort at many levels.

In his discussion of the need for visionary leadership, Nanus (1992) describes some of the forces that will influence the development of organizations in the 21st century. These include the following:

1. Explosive technological change caused by simultaneous and mutually reinforcing breakthroughs in materials, genetics, information sciences, space technology, automation, and instrumentation.

2. The dominance of postindustrial economies based on information, knowledge, education, and services.

3. The globalization of business, politics, culture, and environmental concerns.

4. The restructuring of national economies to accommodate intense international competition, and the gradual transition from military to economic dominance in global affairs.

5. The erosion of confidence in all institutions, including governments, families, and religions, and the resultant search for self-sufficiency and meaning in work and grass roots activism.

6. High economic stress resulting from heavy debt loads, global competition, vulnerable banking systems, and deferred costs of a decaying infrastructure and environmental cleanup.

7. Demographic and sociocultural shifts toward far more diversity and fragmentation of values, lifestyles, and tastes.

8. Relative affluence in material goods coupled with "new" scarcities (for example, job security and parental time for children) and increased personal risks from crime and environmental pollution.[1] (p. 174)

The observations of Nanus regarding forces that will influence the future are supportive of those made earlier by others, and suggestive of the need for increasing levels of collaboration between and among individuals and groups.

Macro Level: School Restructuring.   Restructuring of the public education system is one of the major trends with positive implications for the future of interactive teaming. In an extensive report on the status of restructuring in the early 1990s, writers at *Education Week* outlined seven areas in which change must occur if renewal is to succeed.

1. *The balance of power.* This requires a shift in power from administration to groups consisting of the principal, teachers, parents, staff, businesspeople, and students. In this team approach, constituents make decisions about

---

[1] From *Visionary Leadership*, by B. Nanus, 1992, San Francisco: Jossey-Bass. This material is used by permission of John Wiley & Sons, Inc.

issues as diverse as budget, personnel, and curriculum. Although it is difficult for a council that was chosen to represent diverse points of view to develop a shared vision, it is believed that success can be achieved if more team training is provided and results are not expected too soon (Bradley & Olson, 1993). These groups function as collaborative problem-solving teams to address the broad range of concerns evident in every school.

2. *Time and space.* This involves modification of the regular hours, straight rows, and standard way of teaching. Alternatives include the extended day or year, use of learning centers, and incorporation of work outside of school in community projects or real-world applications of learning. Although there are concerns about the cost and need for teacher time, there are also some promising innovations, which involve school/university/community partnerships. Again, the need for collaboration is apparent (Sommerfeld, 1993).

3. *The coherent curriculum.* The emphasis on critical thinking requires that teaching and learning become central to reform, using state frameworks for broad concepts rather than teaching specific lists of competencies. Although there are parental concerns that children will not acquire specific skills, teachers indicate that student interest and risk taking increase with teaching that is interdisciplinary, rather than fragmented into academic specialty areas (Viadero, 1993).

4. *Outcomes for student performance.* This involves a change from a time-based or credit-hours enrolled format to an emphasis on what students will know and be able to do as a result of their education program. This movement has been controversial in many states and there are questions about the measurement of outcomes, although several states have progressed in developing ways to deliver these programs effectively (Rothman, 1993).

5. *Professional development.* This involves the development of professional learning communities within schools; that is, reculturing to allow school professionals to engage in meaningful conversations to facilitate school improvement (Fullan, 2000). Implementation of learning communities helps overcome teacher isolation and link classrooms to outside, real-world experiences. Although the need for additional team training is noted, existing models incorporating professional academies and teacher centers have been successful in helping new teachers adapt to special learning needs of the new student population (Bradley, 1993).

6. *Dollars and sense.* This involves attempts to reduce disparities in school spending across rich and poor districts. Initiated by a series of school finance lawsuits against states, it has resulted in the development of creative proposals, including the establishment of baseline or supplementary support from state and federal governments (Harp, 1993).

7. *Signing up the public.* This requires development of public awareness of the serious educational problems and their effect on the economy and on global competitiveness. Both the dissemination of information in ways the public can appreciate and the ability of educators to listen to public concerns are suggested. The involvement of business and industry leaders, parents, and volunteers is suggested and examples of success cited (Walsh, 1993).

These trends were still in evidence at the end of the 20th century.

The need for education in interactive teaming skills, including collaboration, communication, and cultural sensitivity, is apparent in these proposed macro-level changes. The relationship of the macro level to the special program changes is seen in the support from the special education community for appropriate inclusion, when possible and appropriate, of special students as part of the range of services and improvement of the entire educational system (Council of Administrators of Special Education, 1990; Kovaleski, 1992; Turnbull & Cilley, 1999).

MAJOR TRENDS IN PROMISING PRACTICES: THE 1990S

Two major trends in promising practices were seen during the 1990s that relate to and predict success for the interactive teaming model in the future: (1) the emergence of collaboration as a defining characteristic for the Beacons of Excellence schools, and (2) the rapidly increasing number of efforts to restructure teacher education. Each is summarized briefly in the following sections.

Success of Beacons of Excellence Schools/ Learning Communities

While the Individuals with Disabilities Education Act (IDEA) fosters collaboration in several areas, the 1997 reauthorization further reinforced the notion by requiring increased coordination between general and special education teachers in developing and implementing a student's IEP. In 1997–1998, the Office of Special Education Programs funded seven Beacons of Excellence grants as part of a directed research priority. The purpose of these projects was to study schools and programs in which outcomes for students with special needs were achieved in the context of exemplary results for all students (Henderson, 2002). In a special 2002 issue of the *Journal of Educational and Psychological Consultation*, reports from three of these projects were highlighted for the collaborative practices and features that were common across all three.

Using a variety of methods to study schools in different contexts, these projects found that collaboration emerged as a defining characteristic for all schools, reinforcing the importance attributed to the process. The studies included elementary, middle, and high schools located in communities across the country in urban, suburban, and rural areas. Schools in these studies ranged in size and socioeconomic levels, and included diverse student populations. Collaboration in these schools took many forms, with co-teaching occurring most often, but even that took multiple forms. Other collaboration occurred in planning-related co-teaching and in periodic joint planning around curricular standards and student expectations (Caron & McLaughlin, 2002). One school formed collaborative structures with local government, industry, and colleges around transition to postsecondary settings (Wallace, Anderson, & Bartholomay, 2002). Informal communication was often cited by school staff as crucial to their success (Schulte, 2002).

In her commentary on the projects, Schulte (2002) suggests that the presence of a "collaborative ethic" is evident in the way that other forms of collaboration emerged across all studies. Teachers in these schools demonstrated a shared responsibility for student learning and supported each other in their efforts to achieve positive outcomes. In addition, administrative support was demonstrated through school structures that supported collaboration between general and special education. For example, one study reported the importance of school policy that gave teams decision-making power in curriculum, assessment, and instructional accommodations (Morocco & Aguilar, 2002).

The information provided by these projects adds to and supports what we already know about the role of collaboration in achieving successful outcomes for students with special needs. Since special education research has concentrated on intervention with individuals and small groups of children, this focus on the school level is also important. This level of research should help to understand the factors involved in adoption and sustained use of evidence-based practices as well as insights into school change (Schulte, 2002).

School change occurring in the late 1990s is reflected in a new paradigm that includes a view of the effective leader as a facilitator, capable of sharing power with members of a team (Keller, 1998). Within each classroom, the new paradigm has shifted from a focus on teaching to an emphasis on student learning (Lasley, 1998). The new paradigm, derived from the research on school effectiveness, includes a change in the school environment from a series of separate, individual classrooms to a collaborative learning community, in which participants share a common vision for maximizing the learning of all students (Du Four, 1998; Fullan, 2000; McLaughlin & Schwartz, 1998). Strategies for creation of these new learner-centered environments have attracted the attention of many groups, including the Society for College and University Planning (1998). This group has conceptualized the design of new learning "spaces," which are conducive to collaboration among learners and between learners and teachers at the higher education level. These trends are representative of the continuation of development in the new learning paradigm.

Restructuring Teacher Education

Public concern about the quality and accessibility of education extended to concern about teacher education. In the 1990s many university programs began to restructure their efforts in teacher education through initiatives including organized professional networks (American Association of Colleges for Teacher Education, 1990; Goodlad, 1992; Holmes Group, 1990).

These restructuring efforts were further encouraged by a major policy report in 1997, which summarized the importance of quality teacher preparation and support for the kinds of schools that had been identified in the effective schools research. The Report of the National Commission on Teaching and America's Future (Darling-Hammond, 1997) has outlined the conditions for ensuring teachers' professional competence as a "three-legged stool"—preparation program accreditation, (initial) teacher licensing, and (national board) certification.

The first two apply to preservice preparation programs, for which the commission recommends accreditation for the preparing institution. Accredited programs undergo rigorous review by trained colleagues, including an examination of their curriculum and structure, as well as a review of the criteria applied to selection of their faculty and students. Licensing provides the beginner with a permit to teach, after having met specific state and national standards for entrance into the profession. New teachers are expected to demonstrate their competence in knowledge of subject matter; understanding of teaching, learning, and development; and ability to assess students, plan curriculum, create a positive learning environment, and collaborate with parents and colleagues.

The provision of coordinated programs, such as those found in professional development schools, is highly recommended. These programs enable preservice students to apply what they have learned about teaching within the context of classrooms, under joint supervision of university and K–12 faculty members. Among the most interesting of these restructured teacher preparation programs are those able to create meaningful partnerships with K–12 schools (Kochan & Kunkel, 1998), particularly if they are able to incorporate action research that relates their teaching practices to the learning of their students (Keating, Diaz-Greenberg, Baldwin, & Thousand, 1998).

Additionally, the restructured programs promise to provide preservice teachers with more and better opportunities to understand students from differing cultural backgrounds. This essential feature enables teachers to comprehend the effects of race, ethnicity, social class, and gender on children's formation of knowledge (Sleeter & Grant, 1999). Moreover, teachers with a high degree of multicultural expertise will be able to interact effectively in diverse cultural situations (Liedel-Rice, 1998; Smith, 1992). While about 90% of all teachers are White and female, the number of students from differing backgrounds is increasing rapidly. Kunjufu (1993) emphasizes that the issue is not the race or gender of teachers, but rather the teachers' expectations for students: Too often, teachers believe that children from low-income, single-parent families have no potential. The disproportionate number of students of color who drop out of school or who are placed in low-ability groups or special education programs underscores the importance of preservice education that enables teachers to understand children's individual differences. Increasingly, restructured programs are providing preservice teachers with supervised, directed experiences that prepare them to become culturally responsive (Ford, 1992; Garibaldi, 1992; Klug, Pena, & Whitfield, 1992; Liedel-Rice, 1998; Nel & Sherritt, 1992).

Alternative Certification Programs

Traditional teacher education programs cannot meet the current and growing demands for special education teachers. During the 1990s, The United States Department of Education (USDOE) estimates indicated that 30,000 special education positions were filled by uncertified personnel each year (McLeskey, Tyler, & Flippin, 2003). This persistent shortage is a major contributing factor to the rapid growth of alternative methods for obtaining teaching credentials that have developed. In a recent review of the literature on alternative certification programs, Rosenberg and Sindelar (2003) described these programs as ranging from emergency certification survival training to sophisticated high-tech programs; however, all methods avoid college and university preparation programs. Alternative programs are usually shorter than traditional programs, and rely heavily on field experiences with less formal classroom instruction.

In reviewing the literature, Rosenberg and Sindelar (2003) found certain characteristics of individuals using an alternative route to certification. These individuals had a bachelor's degree in a noneducation field (i.e., math, science, and foreign language) and had experience in business, industry, or the military. When changing careers, participants tended to come more often from lower salaried jobs instead of professional positions. They also found that participants were older than 25, more often male, and included more racially and ethnically diverse groups.

Evaluation of the effectiveness of alternative certification programs suggests they were more successful when the content was substantive and had a programmatic focus, they were planned and delivered in collaboration with institutes of higher education, they employed higher education supervision and mentoring, and they were of adequate length and included a variety of learning activities. Finally, these authors expressed concern about a number of issues related to alternative routes to certification currently being used. First is the lack of a consistent definition for what constitutes an alternative certification program. Second, there are no professional standards specified for developing and implementing alternative certification programs. Without a set of standards for implementation, it is difficult to know the extent of the knowledge base of the graduates or how they were inducted into the classroom. Given the critical need for qualified teaching professionals, it is only likely that these programs will continue to grow. As Rosenberg and Sindelar (2003) suggest, well-conceptualized alternative certification programs may be one of the solutions to meeting the need for qualified special education teachers.

PROMISING SOLUTIONS: THE FUTURE MODEL

These trends support the prediction of a growing awareness of the need for professional collaboration and public support for special needs programs. At the same time that recognition of the need to collaborate has grown, professionals have acquired additional evidence that collaborative efforts result in improved education, both for students at risk and for schools in general. Examples of this evidence include the following:

◆ Heightened awareness of the special needs of children from the diverse subgroups within the African American, Latino, and American Indian communities, and increased understanding of how collaboration can lessen these children's sense of alienation from school (Altenbaugh, Engel, & Martin, 1995; Kunjufu, 1993; Reeves & McDonald, 1989; Snider, 1990; West, 1990).

◆ Understanding that the current increase in problems such as school dropout is not simple in origin. These difficulties have multiple causes and manifest medical problems such as teen pregnancy, school problems related to failure, and economic problems such as the need for adolescents to work (Altenbaugh et al., 1995; Gastright, 1989). Consequently, these problems require intervention by multiple agencies.

◆ Insight into the national commission's (Darling-Hammond, 1997) recommendations for school improvement through empowering school leadership and teacher preparation. Early reforms focused on university-school collaboration, staff development, and teacher empowerment can work in the nation's worst inner-city schools, including those in Chicago (Walberg, Bakalis, Bast, & Baer, 1989); Los Angeles (Sickler, 1988); New Haven, Connecticut (Comer, 1989); Miami (Olson, 1989); and Hammond, Indiana (Olson & Rodman, 1988; Schmoker & Wilson, 1993).

◆ Evidence of the effectiveness of collaboration from the synthesis of the knowledge on school-based management (David, 1989) and on professional development involving collaboration through peer coaching, both in general programs (Chrisco, 1989; Raney & Robbins, 1989; Showers & Joyce, 1996) and in special education programs (Ludlow, Faieta, & Wienke, 1989; Peterson & Hudson, 1989; Rush, Shelden, & Hanft, 2003).

◆ A trend for collaboration among community service agencies and a growing body of knowledge to provide assistance to those who establish medical/educational/social services family centers (California School Boards Association, 1992; Imel, 1992; National Center for Schools and Communities, 1998; O'Neil, 1997).

◆ Encouraging new studies about the resilience of children who, because of personal and environmental adversities, succeed in spite of predictions that they will fail; from these studies we can abstract the importance of effective nurturing of teachers, and also regain confidence in the human spirit (Backett-Milburn, Cunningham-Burley, & Davis, 2003; Cohen, 1993; Edelman, 1992; Wang, 1998).

◆ Accumulating data from education reform programs that show the effectiveness of strategies that emphasize the elements important in interactive teaming and in adaptive instruction (Henderson, 2002; Wang, Haertel, & Walberg, 1997). There is also growing evidence of the value of teaching special educators to collaborate as a way to increase their effectiveness (Bullough et al., 2003; O'Shea, Williams, & Sattler, 1999; Pugach & Allen-Meares, 1985; West & Idol, 1987) and their sense of efficacy (McDaniel & DiBella-McCarthy, 1989).

◆ Research on learning has improved our understanding of how the human brain functions (Wolfe & Brandt, 1998). Research in the areas of metacognition and cooperative learning has also sharpened our insight into the teaching-learning process, showing the similarity between effective programs for students with special needs and for all students (Brandt, 1992; Glenn, 1989; Sommerfeld, 1993). Techniques for using structure and advanced organizers, teaching self-questioning skills, and using mnemonics can help students learn and retain information (Deschler, 1998; Hock, Deshler, & Schumaker, 1999). Cooperative learning (Johnson & Johnson, 1975), the subject of a large amount of research, shows promise for enhancing the ability of all students to learn and help each other, and for increasing their social interactions (Box & Little, 2003; Villa & Thousand, 1988); it has been particularly effective in teaching high-order skills.

◆ Realization that the solution to better programs for students at risk lies in the understanding that these complex problems involve changes in both students and systems, and that these changes are best implemented by groups of individuals who work together to "make what is into what ought to be" (Cuban, 1989, p. 800) in their individual organizations.

APPLICATION

Now that you have completed this book, try to apply your understanding of interactive teaming to the observation of a team meeting, using the observation guide given in Figure 12.1. Watch for examples of effective and ineffective communication, power and empowerment, cultural sensitivity (or lack thereof), and effective or ineffective strategies for running a meeting. Summarize what you see and discuss your observations with others in your class.

Observation Guide to be completed as you watch a real or taped meeting of a professional team in action. As you observe, complete this Observation Guide, "Power/Authority in Teaming" (Dykes, 1987). A sample of this activity, completed by Naomi Miller (1989) follows.

Note: Read this entire description before you begin.

Observe the team for 10 minutes to get an idea of who has the most authority, the nature of the authority (G = group given, S = self-proclaimed, D = declared by third party, R = granted by rules or law). In a second 10-minute observation, complete the following table. Identify the team member with the most power or group control at the end of each 1-minute period. Time each observation separately; take data and record on the table. Then, begin the next 1-minute sample.

P = Power   S = Source

Minute	1	2	3	4	5	6	7	8	9	10
Team Members	P/S	P/S	P/S	P/S	P/S	P/S	P/S	P/S	P/S	P/S
1. Counselor	/S	/S	/S					/S		
2. Psychologist					/D	/D				
3. Sp. Ed. Teacher									/G	/G
4. Parent				/D			/D			
5.										
6.										
7.										

Source: G = Group
          S = Self-proclaimed
          D = Declared by role
          R = Rules/law

The chart is a record, showing team members who seemed to have the most power at the end of each 1-minute sample during a 10-minute observation.

Responses by Naomi Miller (1989) to form developed by Mary Kay Dykes (1987). Observation Guide for Power/Authority in Teaming (assignment for EEX 6786, Fall, 1989). (Unpublished manuscript). Gainesville, FL: University of Florida.

Figure 12.1

Observation of an interactive team.

Source: This exercise was designed by Mary K. Dykes of the University of Florida. She uses it to prepare future special education teachers to work effectively as team members and it is reprinted here with her permission.

418

Upon completion and evaluation of your grid on the previous page, answer the following questions:

     A.   Did one person stay in a more authoritative role than others? Why?

Answer:

> *The counselor in this IEP staffing attempted to exert more control than the other members. She appeared to be trying to prove her role in the team, as she is the newest permanent member of the group.*

     B.   Did the power figure change? If so, how did the new person gain power—usurp, demand, request, or another means?

Answer:

> *Power figures changed throughout the meeting. The main leader, the counselor, tended to usurp power that appeared to be resented by the other members of the group. The psychologist, an intern, requested control. She took her cue from the counselor but was received well. The special education teacher demanded control and she spoke from a strong knowledge base. Parent control was requested when the other members indicated a time for involvement.*

     C.   Did individuals use authority (power) to benefit the group or were relations strained within the group? How do you know? (verbal or nonverbal)

Answer:

> *Relations between the counselor and the group appeared strained. The other members were not comfortable with the amount of attempted authority. She exhibited an overexerted trunk—lean, louder voice, and tenser actions. The other members related well together; eye contact, posture, tone, and gestures all indicated good communication.*

     D.   Were attempts made to get all members to contribute? Were the efforts usually made by the same person(s)? Explain. How were the efforts made (vocal, nonvocal, pause/eye contact, etc.)? Were efforts successful?

Answer:

> *The group functioned collectively. The counselor distributed control between members. First, they went over introductions and then the counselor gave control to the psychologist to go over psychological reports. At certain points throughout the conference, parent participation was invited. Finally, the counselor directed involvement to the IEP formulation, and this is where the special education teacher took over. In the end, the special education representative tried to involve the parent through questions. Control was distributed from the counselor to the psychologist through verbal cues, whereas a gesture was made when the counselor directed the power to the special education teacher. Most other efforts were verbal.*

Continued

E. What, if any, relation did you observe between power and a team member's use of data? (If the individual brought actual assessment or observation data to conference, was he or she viewed as high or low power? Why?)

Answer:

The psychologist produced data from the psychological report. She gained a high power control base when presenting the data and this was viewed as her knowledge power base. The parent was in agreement with the results of the data.

F. List observed and personal and/or professional characteristics of those who had (1) the most power and (2) the least power.

Answer:

	Most	Least
Personal:	Empathetic, calm, sincere, and understanding, good eye contact.	Demanding in nonverbal indicators. Overwhelming.
Professional:	Task-oriented, directly involved, invited involvement. Worked from experience.	Pushy on signing of papers. Tried to accept personal responsibility for student improvement.

G. List procedures a high-power team member used to facilitate the team efforts.

Answer:

Positive: *The special education teacher was very confident with her position. She allowed the counselor and psychologist to take their positions also. She displayed verbal and non-verbal cues showing interest. She handled her "duties," explaining the program, IEP formulation, and getting signatures with ease. She explained her information in under-standable terms and made the parent feel comfortable.*

Negative: *There were moments when her involvement could have directed conversation and eased tension rather than the counselor taking control of the situation. She ended the meeting somewhat abruptly by saying that she had to go to another appointment. No opportunities for future interaction were indicated.*

H. Were some team members prepared but spoke only when specifically requested to do so? How could you handle such a situation?

Answer:

Yes, the psychologist took control when it was time to display the psychological reports. The situation will probably be resolved when she becomes more comfortable with the authoritative position she holds. It was her first IEP conference and she was just testing her abilities.

Figure 12.1
Continued.

I.   What, if any, role did age, sex, years of experience, or professional training (e.g., therapist, physician, educator, psychologist) have in determining who the team members perceived as the authority or power figure? Did you observe a professional or personal "pecking order?" Explain.

Answer:

As already mentioned, the special education teacher's experience at the position and in this location enabled her to be very confident in her role. The lack of professional training of the school psychologist stood in the way of her performance. Finally, the counselor's fight for power inhibited her effectiveness. The only person who was involved in a "pecking order" was the counselor; the others ignored the undercurrents.

J.   Identify the most effective team member. Identify the least effective team member.

Answer:

The most effective team member was the special education teacher. She was involved, prepared, and comfortable, which set the interaction at ease. She did not allow the meeting to stray from the topics, yet still allowed for parent and professional involvement.

The counselor was the least effective in this meeting. She was trying very hard, too hard it appeared. She was the one to greet the parent and pushed too hard to try to appear friendly. Her power-seeking behaviors undermined her effectiveness.

Observe each for 3 minutes—keep a running log of what each was doing (e.g., eye contact with, posture, attention, etc.). Contrast the two sets of behavior.

Answer:

Most effective: Attentive, eye contact maintained with person in control. She was in control after the first 8 minutes while formulating the IEP She had a relaxed, confident posture along with an authoritative voice and tone.

Least effective: Once she was out of her "director" role, she began to slouch and look at her watch. She was writing on some other papers that she was working on. Her attention was minimal.

SUMMARY

The failure to collaborate on problem solutions has intensified professionals' difficulties in providing universal, free, appropriate education through our public schools. Moreover, school failure has been accompanied by economic consequences to industry, and political consequences to the nation. It has, therefore, attracted the attention of leaders in business and industry who now wish to join in partnerships with educators and to assist in school improvement. An abundance of evidence shows that (1) collaboration is needed, (2) increased collaboration results in improved schools, and (3) the improvement of programs for students with special needs supports, rather than conflicts with, overall efforts to improve schools. The interactive teaming model presented in this book has shown how professionals who work in programs for students with special needs can collaborate and consult effectively.

ACTIVITIES

1. Imagine that the year is 2010. You dropped out of teaching during the last decade of the old century. Because you lived in another country and had no further interest in education in the United States, you did not obtain any information about trends and issues. Now in 2010, you return and seek a job as a special education teacher. *You are told that public school special education no longer exists.*

   Debate and discuss this scenario, using evidence gathered from your analysis of current issues and trends. What might have caused this to happen?
   - Could it be that the numbers of children with special needs became so large that all education programs were combined into a common, mediocre system?
   - Or are there no more public schools at all? Are some children now educated in private schools, while others receive instruction on home computers or do not receive any education?
   - Did special education programs collapse in failure under the pressure of a new generation of children damaged by poverty-induced malnutrition and psychological disorders?
   - Could it be that special educators, in whose classrooms students were taught only basic low-level skills, were viewed as incompetent teachers in the new century, and that special education, now outdated, was eliminated from the public schools?
   - Or were special educators so idealistic and so naive about the realities of power and politics that they were unable to work constructively within the system to bring about needed changes?
   - Did teacher's unions, under pressure from child advocates to place all students with severe and multiple disabilities in regular classrooms, lead a parent rebellion that resulted in the repeal of P.L. 94-142 and its antecedents, so that students with special needs were subsequently expelled from the public school system?
   - Could it be that the costs of national infrastructure repair, health care spending, and new prison construction, with a simultaneous increase in the number of older Americans, became so great that there were no tax dollars left for special education?

What else might have caused the decline of special education? Choose one of these hypotheses or create your own. Then, outline a series of strategies you could use to implement the reversal of these negative trends.

2. Read the chapter's case study on Ethan carefully. What do you think might have happened behind the scenes to enable things to happen at just the right times? Who could have been responsible for these covert activities? If you were a member of this team, would you engage in such activities? Why or why not?

3. Design a change strategy for the educational organization in which you work or plan to work. Incorporate the facilitating factors discussed in this book, and identify the barriers you will probably encounter. Then provide a step-by-step set of activities to implement this change. Discuss the strengths and weaknesses of your proposal with others in your class and make revisions based on their suggestions for improvement.

4. Debate this prediction for the future: The majority of programs for students with special needs will be delivered by teams, using models such as interactive teaming. Provide evidence, pro or con, to support your point of view.

REFERENCES

Altenbaugh, R., Engel, D., & Martin, D. (1995). *Caring for kids: A critical study of urban school leavers.* London: Falmer Press.

American Association of Colleges for Teacher Education. (1990). Clinical schools update. *AACTE Briefs, 11.* Washington, DC: Author.

American Psychological Association. (1993). *Violence and youth: Psychology's response* (Vol. I). Washington, DC: American Psychological Association Commission on Violence and Youth.

Backett-Milburn, K., Cunningham-Burley, S., & Davis, J. (2003). Contrasting lives, contrasting views? Understandings of health inequalities from *children* in differing social circumstances. *Social Science and Medicine, 57*(4), 613–623.

Bengtson, V. L. (2001). Beyond the nuclear family: The increasing importance of multigenerational bonds. *Journal of Marriage and the Family, 63*(1), 1–16.

Box, J. A., & Little, D. C. (2003). Cooperative small-group instruction combined with advanced organizers and their relationship to self-concept and social studies achievement of elementary school students. *Journal of Instructional Psychology, 30*(4), 285–287.

Bradley, A. (1993, March 24). Basic training. *Education Week, 12*(26), 13–18.

Bradley, A., & Olson, L. (1993, February 24). The balance of power. *Education Week, 12*(22), 9–14.

Brandt, R. (1992). On building learning communities: A conversation with Hank Levin. *Educational Leadership, 50*(1), 19–22.

Brown, R. (1985). *Reconnecting youth: The next stage of reform.* Denver, CO: Business Advisory Commission, Education Commission of the States.

Bullough, R. V., Jr., Young, J., Birrell, J. R., Clark, D. C., Egan, M. W., Erickson, L., Frankovich, M., Brunetti, J., & Welling, M. (2003). Teaching with a peer: A comparison of two models of student teaching. *Teaching and Teacher Education, 19*(3), 57–73.

California School Boards Association. (1992). *Cutting through the red tape: Meeting the needs of*

California's children. West Sacramento, CA: Author.

Carney, J. S., & Cobia D. C. (2003). The concerns of school counselors-in-training about working with children and adolescents with HIV disease: Training implications. *Counselor Education Supervision, 42*(4), 302–313.

Caron, E. A., & McLaughlin, M. J. (2002). Indicator of Beacons of Excellence schools: What do they tell us about collaborative practices? *Journal of Educational and Psychological Consultation, 13*(4), 285–313.

Chrisco, I. (1989). Peer assistance works. *Educational Leadership, 46*(6), 31–34.

Cohen, D. (1993, June 9). Schools beginning to glean lessons from children who "defy the odds." *Education Week, 12*(37), 1, 16–18.

Comer, J. (1989). Children can: An address on school improvement. In R. Webb & F. Parkay (Eds.), *Children can: An address on school improvement by Dr. James Comer with responses from Florida's educational community* (pp. 4–17). Gainesville, FL: University of Florida, College of Education Research & Development Center in collaboration with the Alachua County Mental Health Association.

Council of Administrators of Special Education. (1990, September 29). *Position paper on least restrictive environment.* Las Vegas: CASE Board of Directors.

Cuban, L. (1989). The "at-risk" label and the problem of urban school reform. *Phi Delta Kappan, 70,* 780–784.

Darling-Hammond, L. (1997). *Doing what matters most: Investing in quality teaching.* New York: National Commission on Teaching and America's Future.

Darling-Hammond, L. (2003). Standards and assessment: Where we are and what we need. *Teachers College Record,* Content ID = 11109. Retrieved January, 2004, from http://www.tcrecord.org

David, J. (1989). Synthesis of research on school-based management. *Educational Leadership, 46*(8), 45–53.

Deschler, D. D. (1998). Grounding intervention for students with learning disabilities in "powerful ideas." *Learning Disabilities, 13,* 29–34.

Du Four, R. (1998). *The principal series, facilitators guide for tapes 1–3: Creating a collaborative learning community.* Alexandria, VA: Association for Supervision and Curriculum Development.

Dykes, M. K. (1987). *Observation guide for power/authority in teaming.* Unpublished manuscript. Gainesville: University of Florida Department of Education.

Edelman, M. (1992). *The measure of our success: A letter to my children and yours.* Boston: Beacon Press.

Fix, M., Zimmerman, W., & Passel J. S. (2001). *The integration of immigrant families in the United States.* Washington, DC: The Urban Institute, 2001. Retrieved January, 2004, from the National Institute for Literacy Website at http://www.nifl.gov/

Flax, E. (1989). Serious gaps cited in services aiding child mental health. *Education Week, 8*(38), 1, 27.

Ford, B. (1992). Multicultural education training for special educators working with African American youth. *Exceptional Children, 59,* 107–114.

Frankenberg, E., Lee, C., & Orfield, G. (2003). *A multiracial society with segregated schools: Are we losing the dream?* Retrieved January, 2004, from http://www.civilrightsproject.harvard.edu

Fullan, M. (2000). The three stories of education reform. *Phi Delta Kappan, 81*(8), 581–584.

Garcia, R. (1998). Hang-ups of introducing computer technology. *The Journal, 26*(2), 65–66.

Garibaldi, A. (1992). Preparing teachers for culturally diverse classrooms. In M. Dilworth (Ed.), *Diversity in teacher education—New expectations.* San Francisco: Jossey-Bass.

Gastright, J. (1989, April). Don't base your dropout program on somebody else's problem. *Phi Delta Kappa Research Bulletin,* No. 8, 1–4.

Glenn, C. (1989). Just schools for minority children. *Phi Delta Kappan, 70,* 777–779.

Goertz, M., & Duffy, M. (2003). Mapping the landscape of high-stakes testing and accountability programs. *Theory into Practice, 42*(1), 4–11.

Gold, D. (1987, November 18). New Jersey relaxes bilingual education rules. *Education Week, 7*(11), 5.

Goodlad, J. (1992). On taking school reform seriously. *Phi Delta Kappan, 74,* 232–238.

Harp, L. (1993, March 31). Dollars and sense. *Education Week, 12*(27), 9–14.

Henderson, K. (2002). Collaboration to benefit children with disabilities: Incentives in IDEA. *Journal of Educational and Psychological Consultation, 13*(4), 383–391.

Hock, M. F., Deshler, D., & Schumaker, J. B. (1999). Tutoring programs for academically underprepared college students: A review of the literature. *Journal of College Reading and Learning, 29*(2), 101–121.

Hodgkinson, H. (1988). The right schools for the right kids. *Educational Leadership, 45,* 10–15.

Holmes Group. (1990). *Tomorrow's schools: Principles for the design of professional development schools.* East Lansing, MI: Michigan State University.

Horowitz, F., & O'Brien, M. (1989). Introduction to special issue. Children and their development: Knowledge base, research agenda, and social policy application [Special issue]. *American Psychologist, 44*(2), 95.

Iacocca, L. (1989, March 22). Remarks to the National Association of Manufacturers, Washington, DC.

Imel, S. (1992). *For the common good: A guide to developing local interagency linkage teams.* Columbus, OH: Center on Education and Training for Employment, Ohio State University.

Johnson, D., & Johnson, R. (1975). *Learning together and alone: Cooperation, competition, and individualization.* Upper Saddle River, NJ: Prentice Hall.

Keating, J., Diaz-Greenberg, R., Baldwin, M., & Thousand, J. (1998). A collaborative action research model for teacher preparation programs. *Journal for Teacher Education, 49*(5), 381–390.

Keller, B. (1998, November 11). Research: Principal matters. *Education Week, XVIII,* 25–27.

Klug, B., Pena, S., & Whitfield, P. (1992). From awareness to application: Creating multicultural reform despite political correctness, a case study. In C. Grant (Ed.), *Multicultural education for the twenty-first century.* Proceedings of the Second Annual Meeting of the National Association for Multicultural Education. New Jersey: Paramount Publications.

Kochan, F., & Kunkel, R. (1998). The learning coalition: Professional development schools in partnership. *Journal of Teacher Education, 49*(5), 325–333.

Kovaleski, J. (1992). *Developing effective instructional support systems in schools: Functions of the IST.* Harrisburgh, PA: Pennsylvania Department of Education.

Kunjufu, J. (1993, February 24). *Developing a positive self-image in Black children.* Address to University Community. Slippery Rock, PA: Slippery Rock University.

Kurlaender, M. & Yun, J. T. (2002). *The impact of racial and ethnic diversity on educational outcomes: Cambridge, MA school district.* Civil Rights Project, Harvard University. Retrieved January, 2004, from http://www.civilrightsproject.harvard.edu

Lasley, T. (1998). Paradigm shifts in the classroom. *Phi Delta Kappan, 80,* 84–86.

Lawrence, B., Muire, C., & Stanley, G. (1999). The public school as wasteland. *Contemporary Education, 70*(2), 18–24.

Liedel-Rice, A. (1998). *Program follow-up study of former urban student teachers in their second through sixth year of teaching.* Slippery Rock, PA: Slippery Rock University College of Education.

Linn, R. (2003). Accountability: Responsibility and reasonable expectations. *Educational Researcher, 32*(7), 3–13.

Ludlow, B., Faieta, J., & Wienke, W. (1989). Training teachers to supervise their peers. *Teacher Education and Special Education, 12,* 27–32.

Masten, A. S. (2001). Ordinary magic: Resilience processes in development. *American Psychologist, 56*(3), 227–238.

McClellan, M. (Ed.). (1987). *Child abuse* [Hot Topics Series]. Bloomington, IN: Phi Delta Kappa.

McDaniel, E., & DiBella-McCarthy, H. (1989). Enhancing teacher efficacy in special education. *Teaching Exceptional Children, 21*(4), 34–39.

McDermott, K. A. (2003). What causes variation in state's accountability policies? *Peabody Journal of Education, 79*(4), 153–176.

McGroddy, J. (1997, October). *Transforming the future through technology.* Address to Teacher Education Assembly, annual meeting of PAC-TE, Grantville, PA.

McLaughlin, M., & Schwartz, R. (1998). *Strategies for fixing failing public schools.* Cambridge, MA: Harvard Graduate School, Pew Forum.

McLeskey, J., Tyler, N., & Flippin, S. (2003). *The supply of and demand for special education teachers: A review of research regarding the nature of the chronic shortage in special education* (COPPSE Document Number RS-1E). Gainesville, FL: University of Florida, Center on Personnel Studies in Special Education. Retrieved January, 2004, from http://www.coe.ufl.edu/copsse/index.php

Miller, N. (1989). Sample responses to Dykes' *Power/authority in teaming.* Unpublished manuscript. Gainesville FL: University of Florida Department of Special Education.

Mirga, T. (1987, September 9). Textbooks do not imperil Christians' beliefs, 2 courts rule. *Education Week, 7*(1), 10, 23.

Morocco, C. C., & Aguilar, M. C. (2002). Coteaching for content understanding: A schoolwide model. *Journal of Educational and Psychological Consultation, 13*(4), 315–347.

Nanus, B. (1992). *Visionary leadership.* San Francisco: Jossey-Bass.

National Center for Schools and Communities. (1998). Community schools in the making. In *Conversations: Supporting children and families in the public schools.* New York: Fordham University Center.

National Education Association (NEA). (2002). Taxing times for public education. *NEA Today.* Retrieved January, 2004, from http://www.nea.org/neatoday

National Governors Association and the National Association of State Budget Officers. (2003). *The fiscal survey of states.* Washington, DC: Author.

Nel, J., & Sherritt, C. (1992). Bridge building and student resistance: Increasing teacher commitment to multicultural education. In C. Grant (Ed.), *Multicultural education for the twenty-first century.* Proceedings of the Second Annual Meeting of the National Association for Multicultural Education. New Jersey: Paramount Publications.

Newcomb, M., & Bentler, P. (1989). Substance use and abuse among children and teenagers. Children and their development: Knowledge base, research agenda, and social policy application [Special issue]. *American Psychologist, 44*(2), 242–248.

Oakes, J. (1986). Keeping track, part 1: The policy and practice of curriculum inequality. *Phi Delta Kappan, 68,* 12–17.

Olson, L. (1989, June 7). Dade County will solicit ideas nationwide for design, structuring of 49 new schools. *Education Week, 8*(37), 1, 21.

Olson, L., & Rodman, B. (1988, June 22). The unfinished agenda, part II. *Education Week, 7,* 17–33.

O'Neil, J. (1997). Building schools as communities: A conversation with James Comer. *Educational Leadership, 54*(8), 6–19.

O'Shea, D., Williams, L., & Sattler, R. (1999). Collaboration preparation across special education and general education: Preservice level teachers' views. *Journal of Teacher Education, 50*(2), 147–158.

Patterson, G., DeBaryshe, B., & Ramsey, E. (1989). A developmental perspective on antisocial behavior. Children and their development: Knowledge base, research agenda, and social policy application [Special issue]. *American Psychologist, 44*(2), 329–335.

Paige, R. (2002). An overview of America's agenda. *Phi Delta Kappan, 83*(9), 708–713.

Peterson, S., & Hudson, P. (1989). Coaching: A strategy to enhance preservice teacher behaviors. *Teacher Education and Special Education, 12,* 56–60.

Pugach, M., & Allen-Meares, P. (1985). Collaboration at the preservice level: Instructional and evaluation activities. *Teacher Education and Special Education, 8*(1), 3–11.

Raney, P., & Robbins, P. (1989). Professional growth and support through peer coaching. *Educational Leadership, 46*(8), 35–37.

Reed, S. (1988). Children with AIDS: How schools are handling the crisis [Special report]. *Phi Delta Kappan, 69,* K1–K12.

Reeves, M. S., & McDonald, D. (1989, August 2). Stuck in the horizon: A special report on the education of Native Americans. *Education Week, 8,* 1–16.

Reynolds, A. J., Temple, J. A., & Suh-Ruu Ou. (2003). School-based early intervention and child well-being in the Chicago longitudinal study. *Child Welfare, 82*(5), 633–656.

Rosenberg, M. S., & Sindelar, P. T. (2003). *The proliferation of alternative routes to certification in special education: A critical review of the literature* (COPPSE Document Number RS-10E). Gainesville, FL: University of Florida, Center on Personnel Preparation in Special Education. Retrieved December, 2003, from http://www.coe.ufl.edu/copsse/index.php

Rush, D. D., Shelden, M. L., & Hanft, B. E. (2003). Coaching families and colleagues: A process for collaboration in natural settings. *Infants and Young Children, 16*(1), 33–47.

Schmoker, M., & Wilson, R. (1993). Transforming schools through total quality education. *Phi Delta Kappan, 74,* 389–395.

Schulte, A. C, (2002). Commentary: Moving from abstract to concrete descriptions of good schools for children with disabilities. *Journal of Educational and Psychological Consultation, 13*(4) 393–402.

Sharp, W. (1998). School administrators need technology too. *The journal, 26*(2), 75–76.

Showers, B., & Joyce, B. (1996). The evolution of peer coaching. *Educational Leadership, 53*(7), 12–16.

Sickler, J. (1988). Teachers in charge: Empowering the professionals. *Phi Delta Kappan, 69,* 354–356.

Sleeter, C., & Grant, C. (1999). *Making choices for multicultural education* (3rd ed.). Columbus, OH: Merrill/Prentice Hall.

Smith, G. (1992). Multicultural education: Implications for the culturally responsive teaching of all our children. In C. Grant (Ed.), *Multicultural education for the twenty-first century.* Proceedings of the Second Annual Meeting of the National Association for Multicultural Education. New Jersey: Paramount Publications.

Snider, W. (1990, March 7). Children's Defense Fund joins call to improve education of Hispanics. *Education Week, 9*(24), 4.

Snyder, T. D., & Freeman, C. E. (2003). Trends in education. *Principal, 83*(1), 50–52.

Society for College and University Planning. (1998). *Creating tomorrow's learner-centered environments today!* PBS Adult Learning Service Satellite downlink, October 22, 1998.

Sommerfeld, M. (1993, March 3). Time and space: From risk to renewal. *Education Week, 12*(23), 13–19.

Stacey, J. (1996). *In the name of the family: Rethinking family values in the postmodern age.* Boston: Beacon Press.

Tuma, J. (1989). Mental health services for children. Children and their development: Knowledge base, research agenda, and social policy application [Special issue]. *American Psychologist, 44*(2), 188–199.

Turnbull, R., & Cilley, M. (1999). *Explanations and implications of the 1997 amendments to IDEA.* Upper Saddle River, NJ: Merrill/Prentice Hall.

U.S. Department of Education, National Center for Education Statistics. (2003). *The condition of education 2003,* NCES 2003–067. Washington, DC: U.S. Government Printing Office.

U.S. Department of Health and Human Services. (2003a). *Child and adolescent mental health.* Retrieved December, 2003, from http://www.mentalhealth.samhsa.gov/publications

U.S. Department of Health and Human Services. (2003b). *Child maltreatment 2001.* Retrieved December, 2003, from the Administration for Children and Families Website at http://nccanch.acf.hhs.gov/topics/overview/facts.cfm

Viadero, D. (1989, May 3). "7 of 10 handicapped graduates found 'productive.'" *Education Week, 8*(23), 6.

Viadero, D. (1993, March 10). The coherent curriculum. *Education Week, 7*(24), 10–15.

Villa, R., & Thousand, J. (1988). Enhancing success in heterogeneous classrooms and schools: The powers of partnership. *Teacher Education and Special Education, 11,* 144–154.

Walberg, H., Bakalis, M., Bast, J., & Baer, S. (1989). Reconstructing the nation's worst schools. *Phi Delta Kappan, 70,* 802–805.

Wallace, T., Anderson, A. R., & Bartholomay, T. (2002). Collaboration: An element associated with the success of four inclusive high schools. *Journal of Educational and Psychological Consultation, 13*(4), 349–381.

Walsh, M. (1993, April 7). Signing up the public. *Education Week, 12*(28), 9–14.

Wang, M. (1998). Resilience across contexts: Family, work, culture and community. *CEIC Review, 7*(1), 1, 26.

Wang, M., Haertel, G., & Walberg, H. (1997). *What do we know: Widely implemented school improvement programs.* Philadelphia, PA: Mid-Atlantic Regional Educational Lab at Temple University.

West, F., & Idol, L. (1987). School consultation: Part 1. An interdisciplinary perspective on theory, models, and research. *Journal of Learning Disabilities, 20,* 388–408.

West, P. (1990, February 21). Interior Department sets 4 objectives for Indian education. *Education Week, 9*(22), 1, 24.

Wolfe, P., & Brandt, R. (1998). What do we know from brain research? *Educational Leadership, 56*(3), 8–13.

Name Index

Subject Index